Enlightenment and Revolution

PASCHALIS M. KITROMILIDES

Enlightenment
and Revolution

THE MAKING OF MODERN GREECE

HARVARD UNIVERSITY PRESS   Cambridge, Massachusetts, and London, England
2013

An earlier version of this work was originally published in Greek as *Neoellinikos Diaphotismos. Oi politikes kai koinonikes idees* by the Cultural Foundation of the National Bank of Greece, copyright © 1996

Library of Congress Cataloging-in-Publication Data
Kitromilides, Paschalis.
  [Neoellinikos diaphotismos. English.]
  Enlightenment and revolution : the making of modern Greece / Paschalis M. Kitromilides.
     pages cm
  "An earlier version of this work was originally published in Greek as Neoellinikos Diaphotismos. Oi politikes kai koinonikes idees"—Title page verso.
  Includes bibliographical references and index.
  ISBN 978-0-674-72505-8
  1. Enlightenment—Greece.   2. Greece—Intellectual life—18th century.
3. Greece—Intellectual life—19th century.   4. Greece—Politics and government—18th century.   5. Greece—Politics and government—19th century.   6. Political science—Greece—Philosophy—History—18th century.   7. Political science—Greece—Philosophy—History—19th century.   8. Social sciences—Greece—Philosophy—History—18th century.   9. Social sciences—Greece—Philosophy—History—19th century.   I. Title.
  B3511.E54K47 2013
  949.507—dc23   2013002891

In memoriam

Mikis I. Kitromilides (1914–1961)

Magda M. Kitromilidou (1919–2004)

Contents

Preface

While the manuscript of this book was being prepared for publication in the spring and early summer of 2012, Greece was in the throes of a deep political crisis. The focal points of the crisis were the two electoral contests of 6 May and 17 June 2012, which unleashed in full force a politics of unreason in Greek public life. The world watched, bewildered, as Greece's political class engaged in the electoral contests, unable to bring themselves to agree on a way out of the crisis, which since 2009 had been threatening the economy of the country with collapse and was ruining the prosperity and cohesion of Greek society. The politics of unreason escalated during the preelection campaigns with its edge in arguments contesting Greece's membership in the European Union and the monetary union, blaming as usual everybody else except the Greeks themselves for the country's problems and voicing the most extreme varieties of populist rhetoric of an erstwhile Third-World style. The hardship generated by the economic crisis made public opinion quite receptive to this rhetoric. The consequence, as registered in the results of the two elections, was the collapse of the two-party system that had dominated Greek politics since the restoration of democratic government in 1974. Not only was the two-party system replaced by a fragmented multiparty chorus, but the extremes of the political spectrum emerged considerably strengthened: the main party of the Left, which rode the wave of social discontent engaging in rhetorical populism, emerged as the main opposition force, while at the extreme Right political forces espousing chauvinistic, xenophobic, and racist positions were returned to parliament with nonnegligible shares of the vote. A coalition government managed eventually to be formed, on a pledge to honor Greece's obligations under the bailout agreements, thus keeping the country in the European Union and setting it on the road of reform in the institutions of governance and in the structure of the economy to make it again viable. For the time, in the summer months of 2012, the catastrophe seemed to have been averted. The politics of unreason still survives, however, not only at the extremes of the political spectrum but in the populist discourse of the main opposition party on the Left, which appeals with attractive if questionable promises to a significant part of public opinion. At the moment of writing these lines, all this leaves the prospects of the country uncertain and the much-needed reeducation of public opinion in the values of citizenship and political and social responsibility a still-elusive necessity. The political developments, nevertheless, revealed that the economic crisis, in which the country had been plunged since 2009, was in fact the symptom of a deeper and endemic pathology in the country's political life.

The economic crisis was felt in Greece in 2009, in the wake of the 2008 international banking crisis. Its origins went back to public policies in the 1980s, with huge spending and skyrocketing expenses of the public sector. Consequently, huge foreign borrowing was needed to finance domestic spending. The cost of the 2004 Olympics absorbed a part of this spending and borrowing, but in this case expenses only compounded the already serious problems of foreign debt incurred in the 1980s and the 1990s. In fact, as was revealed by the economic crisis that escalated in 2010, Greece's foreign borrowing was of such enormous proportions that a possible Greek default could affect the stability of the world economy.

To cope with the crisis, Greece had to sign two bailout agreements in 2010 and 2012 with its creditors, the European Union, the European Central Bank, and the IMF, and had to submit to an international control mechanism, which imposed serious austerity measures. As a consequence of austerity and enormously increased taxation, serious hardship and social dislocation have been set in motion, with uncertain results for the future of the country.

There can be little doubt that these catastrophic developments have been the result of the irresponsibility of the country's political class. The political leadership, which after 1981 had promoted, with grandiloquent egalitarian slogans, the policy of uncontrolled public spending and engaged in huge foreign borrowing to cover costs, had done so in order to serve narrowly calculated party interests, to distribute favors to party followers and political clients mostly through appointments and salary increases in the public sector and in local government, and to avert political costs to themselves. This approach to politics proved an extremely successful recipe for winning power under "socialist" populism in the 1980s, and on account of this success it was adopted invariably by all who followed in power since then, whether "modernizers" or conservative liberals. It was this logic of public policy that eventually led the country to the brink of economic collapse and brought about the harsh austerity of the present. To put the whole question on a more theoretical level, the Greek political class, by conducting the affairs of the country in this way, failed dismally the test of statesmanship, by looking, to remember John Rawls, to the next election rather than to the interests of the next generation.

What makes this judgment more serious is the inescapable conclusion that it is impossible to find any excuses or alleviating circumstances in Greece's history since 1974 to absolve the country's political class of this story of irresponsibility and mismanagement. Following the restoration of democratic government in 1974, the country was given by its Western allies plenty of opportunities to compose and set itself on a course of modernization and development. Thanks to the determination of a great statesman, Constantine Karamanlis, who led the country after 1974, Greece was admitted to the European Economic Community in 1981 and became one of the original members of the European Union. In 2002 it also joined the European monetary union. These memberships brought to the country enormous amounts of structural funds, meant to be spent on major public works, on the modernization of state structures, and on the development and diversification of the economy. The inflow of funding raised prosperity in Greek society to levels approximating those of Western Europe. An unseen aspect of this process of social change, nevertheless, was the deepening of inequalities below the surface of prosperity, with new wealth being concentrated in the hands of an economic oligarchy, which furthermore throve on tax evasion. This became obvious with the coming of the economic crisis and austerity later on.

It is the argument of this book that to understand the present crisis one has to look at the origins of Greek political culture and the ideological traditions that shaped the Greek political community in the nineteenth century. After thinking about the character of Greek political life for a long time I am convinced that the answer to questions about contemporary problems goes back to what in this book is called the failure of liberalism.

In terms of public morality, that failure fundamentally involved an inability to distinguish the public from the private. This was expressed in a generalized public hypocrisy about individualism and its values, which were considered morally objectionable. By extension, the basis of arguments about rights, privacy, and difference remained anemic and suspect from the vantage point of the prevailing corporatist moral culture. The blurring of the distinction between the public and the private and the failure to recognize the moral autonomy of each sphere were disguised behind a monolithic culture of nationalism that required consensus on what was considered national interest. This bred intolerance, which precluded dissent as a legitimate form of public discourse. That intolerant nationalist culture was reinforced after the Greek Civil War of the late 1940s and by the political climate of the Cold War, which dominated Greek politics until the mid-1960s. This political culture and the nationalist values that lent it moral legitimacy were discredited by association with the military dictatorship of 1967–1974. In turn this made possible, despite the efforts of some political leaders to restore a liberal democratic political culture in the country in the late 1970s, the replacement of the discredited culture of national values by a new authoritarianism, deriving from leftist ideology. This became dominant after 1981 and delivered the country to the defeated of the Civil War with the argument of rectifying the injustices perpetrated against them by the Cold War state. This created a new political class and a vociferous "progressive" intelligentsia that have dominated and plundered the state and the institutions of public life (including the universities) ever since and led the country to the present catastrophe, indifferent and even censorious toward "bourgeois" notions and values such as the public interest, respect for law and rules of conduct, and ideas of probity, rectitude, and honesty. All was legitimate in the name of the "people" and of the "progressive"

transformation of Greece. The mass media abetted in the most unscrupu-
lous way this attitude and vulgarized its messages, making them the dominant ideology in the country. To the historian of political ideas this recalls,
of course, the rhetoric of the nineteenth century in the name of the "nation"
and the fulfillment of its preordained mission in history, which would tolerate no dissent or deviation.

This book has been inspired by the wish to understand why this has been
so. The reader will judge whether the hints at answers put forward in the
following pages are convincing or not.

Note on Transliteration

The only standard system for the transliteration of the Greek alphabet into languages written in Latin characters is that used for the transliteration of classical Greek. The transliteration of ancient Greek, however, is quite inappropriate for rendering the spelling and especially the phonetics of modern Greek. Accordingly, the following modifications have been introduced to make it conform more to the modern morphology and sound of the language. Diphthongs have generally been retained, except in those cases where the modern pronunciation of Greek requires a consonant to be adequately rendered (e.g., 'aftou', not 'autou'). The Greek vowels 'η' and 'ι' have been uniformly rendered with 'i', and similarly 'o' and 'ω' have been rendered with 'o'. The Greek 'υ' has been rendered with 'y', except when it forms part of a diphthong; then it is rendered by 'u' (e.g., 'tou'). The rough breathing has been dropped.

Consonants have generally been rendered phonetically. Thus the Greek 'β' has been rendered by the Latin 'v' rather than 'b'. The Greek consonant 'φ' is rendered by 'ph' in all words with an ancient Greek root. Conversely,

Greek names with Latin roots (e.g., Constantinos) have been transliterated as closely as possible to their original form.

The names of modern Greek authors appear in the form used by the authors themselves if they have published work in a foreign language. Inevitably some inconsistencies will remain, but I hope the reader will find this understandable in a book of this nature. Place names have been used in their standard forms in the English language; otherwise they have been transliterated following the general rules adopted in this book.

Enlightenment and Revolution

Introduction to the
American Edition

BOOKS, LIKE ALL other products of cultural expression, tell stories, but they have their own individual histories as well. This book is no exception. The history of each book supplies intimate knowledge which can help decipher the inner logic and the deeper motivations that went into its writing and also can help chart its course in the life cycle of the culture of which it forms a part. It might be useful, therefore, to begin this attempt to introduce the American reincarnation of this book to its prospective English-reading audience with a few words about its history.

The American edition of this book is an intellectual homecoming for me. It makes available the mature version of a work which many years ago and in a considerably different form was presented as a doctoral dissertation at Harvard University. That project involved an attempt to write the history of modern Greek political thought at the time of the Enlightenment. The motivation of the project was both intellectual and political. On the intellectual level, the purpose of the research I undertook was to draw scholarly attention to a rich range of sources written in modern Greek, which formed an important stage in the long tradition of Greek political thought but had been disregarded by scholarship in Western languages. The intellectual interest and significance of this corpus of sources consisted in the fact that it recorded the encounter of the oldest European tradition of political reflection with the challenge of modernity and at the same time represented perhaps the earliest instance of the transmission of the philosophical, political, and moral ideas of Western modernity into a context beyond that of their original inception, thus essentially inaugurating, at the period of the turn from the eighteenth to the nineteenth century, the worldwide process of the globalization of Western ideas and values.

It was this double encounter that made the phenomenon of the modern Greek Enlightenment an inviting object of scholarly attention. This had just been recognized and pointed out by Elie Kedourie, the initiator of the contemporary critical study of nationalism. Kedourie had pointed to the significance of the inception of Greek nationalism, meaning the emergence of modern secular, political, and cultural reflection in the Greek language as a precocious instance of the universalization of modern Western thought. In a meeting in London in 1974, Elie Kedourie urged me to engage in the study of the Greek Enlightenment in order to make accessible to scholarship the source material and the content of reflection expressed in Greek that illustrated this process of intellectual change.[1]

On a political level, the motivation of the work derived from the profound anguish and soul searching that had gripped the younger generations of Greeks, especially those studying in universities in Western Europe and North America, over the origins and causes of authoritarianism in Greek society, which had led to the military dictatorship that ruled Greece from 1967 to 1974 with such catastrophic results, especially for my own native island of Cyprus. The work I eventually produced belonged to a group of doctoral dissertations produced in Europe and America probing this question. Whereas most other works sharing this motivation looked at the structural or institutional factors that could explain the rise of authoritarianism in Greek society, my work, which was probably the last one in that frame of mind, looked at the domain of ideas and at the role of ideological factors in the formation of the Greek political community. What primarily excited my interest was the discovery, which came so unexpectedly in reading the eighteenth- and early nineteenth-century material, that Greek thought at that early stage of its encounter with secular modernity was very different from what we had conventionally understood to be its defining orientation and dominant content. Upon reading the source material, it was discovered to be much more open and critical and full of alternative possibilities than what became conventional wisdom afterward. What made up the literature of the Enlightenment in the Greek language appeared as a record of liberal democratic political thought with a strong dimension of social criticism that gave it a radical character, unlike anything observable in the discourse that dominated Greek political culture in the nineteenth and twentieth centuries. The excitement of that discovery determined the character of my project. I decided to do two things: first to "politicize" the study of the source material, that is, to take it out of the philological approach in which it had been treated by Greek literary scholarship until then, and secondly to internationalize it, not just by bringing it to the attention of international scholarship but trying to show its relevance for a broader and more nuanced understanding of the complex phenomenon of the European Enlightenment itself.

To "politicize" the study of the Greek Enlightenment meant to treat it methodologically through an approach drawn from the history of political thought. At the time I became engaged in this project, in the mid-1970s, the full impact of the Cambridge school of the history of political thought had not yet been felt. Political theory in America, to the extent it was taken seriously in a discipline dominated by behavioral political science, was limited to analytical approaches and had not yet witnessed the regeneration brought about by the publication in 1971 of John Rawls's *Theory of Justice*. The only place in America to study the history of political thought was Harvard, where a tradition of great scholarship, comprising the work of Charles Howard McIlwain, Carl Friedrich, and Louis Hartz, and running through the entire twentieth century, had established the subject as a legitimate academic field in the Department of Government. I was fortunate to be admitted to Harvard in 1972 and to be exposed to this tradition of scholarship. I was taught by people who carried on this earlier tradition of the history of political ideas and supplied models of scholarship, which guided and inspired the work that eventually went into the making of this book. From Judith Shklar I learned the depth and also the antinomies of the continental tradition of political thought. Her erudition and critical temper strengthened me in my faith in skeptical liberalism as an ideological option that could supply viable responses to the dilemmas of modern politics. Michael Walzer's teaching revealed the inescapable truth that liberty without equality is not possible and that a democratic vision supplies the most effective framework for a critical understanding of the flow of political ideas in history. But it was his strong sense of the historicity of political ideas and of normative theoretical constructs that primarily influenced my work. Finally, Stanley Hoffmann's lectures on political doctrines in French society supplied a model of how to deal with the interplay of ideas, society, and politics in a long-term historical perspective and helped solve many methodological dilemmas in trying to develop an approach to Greek ideological traditions.

A year in Europe, primarily in Greece and Italy, on a Frederick Sheldon traveling fellowship from Harvard in 1975–1976, not only allowed me to expand and complete my research in the corpus of primary sources, but also brought me in touch with Franco Venturi's monumental work on the Italian Enlightenment. This work provided inspiration and models of narrative for the treatment of parallel cultural phenomena across the Adriatic and Ionian Seas in the Greek peninsula. What especially impressed me was Venturi's success in presenting the polycentrism of Enlightenment culture in Italy from Milan via Venice and Florence to Naples and also the extended time frame that integrated the Enlightenment into the broader flow of cultural and political change. At about the time I began writing, another major model of the new history of political thought became available—John Pocock's *Machiavellian Moment*. His narrative on the transfer and adaptation of ideas across time and geographical space provided further methodological models on how to develop arguments concerning processes of cultural transfers and evolution of ideas in Greek political thought.

This is how the present work was originally conceived and produced. The book did not appear in print until much later in a considerably revised and updated Greek translation. The Greek edition appeared in 1996 and has gone through a number of reprints since then.[2] It has also been translated into Romanian by Olga Cicanci in 2005 and into Russian by Mikhail Gratsianski in 2007.[3] Although a number of other books on the same subject and under the same title have appeared in Greek before and after the publication of this work, it remains to this day the only general synthesis, whereas all other books on the subject are collections of papers and articles, marked in many cases by the inevitable repetitiveness that characterizes such publications.

Writing in English on the Greek Enlightenment has been sparse, and the subject has generally remained rather marginal in scholarly literature. The

significance of the subject from the point of view of the history of philosophy was recognized long ago by Professor Raphael Demos of Harvard University. He published two articles on the subject in the 1950s, but that early
initiative had no follow-up. Subsequently the study of the subject received
authoritative if rather concise treatment by G. P. Henderson in his survey
of the revival of secular philosophy in Greek thought, but this initiative too
did not provoke further interest in the subject. A doctoral dissertation by
Loukis Theocharides at the University of Pittsburgh in 1971 on the basics
of the movement remained unpublished. An anthology of primary sources
by Richard Clogg has remained the only contribution that could serve as a
substantive introduction to the subject.[4] This relative paucity of specialized
literature on the Greek Enlightenment in English can probably explain the
absence of the subject from mainstream scholarship and the indifference
shown by general treatments of the Enlightenment to its Greek components. More recently, a notable exception in this regard has been the work
of Jonathan Israel, to which I will return.

The American edition of the present work is intended as a modest step
toward the rectification of this lacuna. In preparing the American edition
I have made no attempt to change the structure or theoretical framework
of the work that appeared in Greek in 1996. I have made the bibliographical updating I judged necessary, selecting from recent work what I found
essential contributions to the subject matter of the book. No attempt to be
exhaustive in this updating has been made. I have also synchronized, to the
extent possible, references already appearing in the annotation, which have
now been included in newer publications. Out of respect for the historicity
of historical scholarship, I judged that the theoretical framework, of the
work should not be tampered with. In originally developing this framework
my dialogue had been with the classic works of Paul Hazard, Ernst Cassirer,
and Peter Gay. I did not attempt to change this fundamentally because I am
a believer in the value of the classics of scholarship, and I am convinced that
they have more to tell us than the latest fashions. Scholarship, nevertheless,
is always in motion, with the production of new works of synthesis and
new classics. The major milestone in Enlightenment scholarship in the last
decade has been the imposing trilogy by Jonathan Israel, which I have tried
to draw into the discussion to the extent possible.

I am well aware that the model of American liberalism I set up in elaborating the theoretical and comparative framework of my analysis, based

as it is primarily on the work of Louis Hartz, could provoke objections from scholars who have either contested from a perspective of the history of republican ideas the predominance of liberalism in the American political tradition or have pointed to the multiple traditions, some of them authoritarian and antiegalitarian, which have contributed and shaped modern American political culture.[5] Such criticisms I would be glad to concede in recognizing that the American political tradition is much more complex than the application of a unilinear liberal logic in its interpretation might allow. Yet it should also be recognized that when juxtaposed to the political traditions of continental Europe, of which the Greek ideological tradition is one, the American tradition still comes across as what Tocqueville, and the Enlightenment before him, diagnosed it to be, a model of liberty in practice. It was this contrast that I sought to bring forward in outlining the American liberal model as a prism of comparison, which might make the discontinuities and failures of Greek liberalism more clearly discernible.

It is time to raise the critical question as to what this work has to say to contemporary concerns and debates in Enlightenment scholarship. I should perhaps begin with a few words about how I see the subject today after being engaged with it for so long. I admit that despite this long engagement my interest in the subject has remained as lively as ever. Although other periods of the history of political thought, such as classical antiquity and the Renaissance, have more recently attracted my interest, the Enlightenment and its study still remain for me the critical road to self-knowledge and self-understanding for us in the modern age. In a more specialized sense this holds true for modern Greece as well: understanding the reception and fate of the Enlightenment in Greek culture and politics holds the key to the understanding of contemporary Greece and its prospects. Yet thinking and researching on these matters over the years, especially examining the context of the Enlightenment's reception and the comparative aspects of the process from the point of view of the other Balkan traditions, has allowed me to appreciate the historical fact that the Enlightenment indeed represented a break and renovation in the Greek cultural tradition, but it also drew strength and vitality from it.[6] In what concerns the Enlightenment's relation with the Orthodox Church, as I had occasion to remark in a number of recent studies, the interplay, up until the 1790s, appears more complex than a simple dialectical opposition between two incompatible systems of values.[7] It is from this perspective that the evidence of this book, which surveys the sources in considerable detail, can be read as a pointer to a more nuanced understanding of the relation between religion and politics and religion and cultural change.

With these remarks we have moved into the territory of the multiple contexts with which the European Enlightenment can be connected and within which it should be understood. The hints about the peculiarities in the relation between politics, culture, and religion in the Orthodox world point to the significance of contextual preconditions and factors in understanding the local and regional expressions of the Enlightenment. Yet when the "national context" approach was introduced into Enlightenment studies exactly three decades ago the Greek world was totally ignored.[8] The evidence presented in the following pages could be read as a corrective of this omission but also as a set of pointers to a rectification of the limitations of the "national context" approach. It is true that this approach brought considerable pluralism into research on the Enlightenment and opened possibilities of comparative analysis. Yet the logic of "national context" involved an in-built anachronism in the very definition of what exactly was meant by the idea of the "national." The way the approach was put to practice in the 1981 collection under that title compounded the anachronism in that it projected twentieth-century state boundaries onto the geographical delineation of eighteenth-century intellectual phenomena. My criticisms of the national context approach have been recorded elsewhere, and there is no point in repeating them here. I should only repeat the suggestion that it would make more sense historically to replace the term "national" with the terms "regional" or "linguistic" to approximate a more accurate description of eighteenth-century conditions. On the basis of the evidence discussed in this work one could even try the idea of a "culture area" defined primarily by language in attempting to contextualize the regional expressions of the Enlightenment. What the following pages make clear is that the ideas of the Enlightenment were received and developed in Greek-speaking communities dispersed over a vast geographical space in Central, Eastern, and Southeastern Europe, Italy, and Asia Minor. The area that much later became the Greek state covered only a small fraction of that geographical space. It would thus make limited historical sense to attempt to contextualize the Greek Enlightenment by reference to the Greek national state that eventually inherited its intellectual legacy. On the contrary, it makes obvious historical sense to use language as the criterion of contextualization because this criterion ascribes unity to a complex and protracted movement of intellectual change, marked by considerable diversity. There is no doubt that the national factor features prominently into this process, and its articulation constitutes an essential component of change itself. In the following pages this aspect of the Enlightenment movement in the Greek culture area receives particular attention. The national factor, however, as a rule appeared as an outcome rather than as the moving force of the process of intellectual change, which involved to a considerable degree and as one of its decisive components the elaboration of new collective identities and the clarification of national definitions.

Another area of contemporary Enlightenment research to which the evidence presented by this book could be related is the question of cultural transfers.[9] The Enlightenment became a European-wide movement aspiring at human emancipation through the transfer of ideas across cultural traditions and languages. The Greek Enlightenment could be interpreted as a complex phenomenon of multiple transfers of ideas. All the mechanisms through which cultural transfers were transacted—geographical mobility, correspondence, and especially translation—form in fact the infrastructure of the Greek Enlightenment. Travel for commercial or educational purposes provided the outlet away from the inertia of immemorial time in traditional society, in isolated communities, and in repressive environments. Those who engaged in this form of mobility became, as a rule, though not always, bearers of modern ideas and secular values, men of the Enlightenment. Letters from those of them who stayed abroad transmitted such ideas and values back home. The Greek Enlightenment possesses an inestimable resource for the understanding of cultural transfers in the correspondence of Adamantios Korais, a corpus of letters that ranges from 1774 to 1833. This material is extensively discussed in the following pages.

The main agency of cultural transfer in the Greek Enlightenment was provided by translations. The literature of the Enlightenment in the Greek language was made up to a significant degree by translations and adaptations of works from Western languages such as French, Italian, and German. The translators of course intervened actively in the texts they rendered in Greek in order to serve the cause of cultural, social, and political change more effectively. Thus they enriched Greek culture with important writings in philosophy, literature, history, science, and religion. The craft of translation poses important theoretical problems for comparative literature and the history of ideas, which can be extensively illustrated by the evidence of the Greek Enlightenment.[10] Translation, therefore, as a channel of the Enlightenment forms a significant focus of the narrative of cultural history unfolding in this book.

On another level of analysis in recent Enlightenment research, the center-periphery nexus, the study of the Greek Enlightenment can provide insights that might contribute in recasting both the question and its conceptualization.[11] Viewing the issue of center and periphery from Southeastern Europe, we might pose the question, what exactly is meant by the notions of center and periphery? It is clear that the center of the Enlightenment as a whole was and remained in Northwestern Europe, in the classic triangle of London-Paris-Amsterdam. Beyond this conventional truth, however, which takes us back to Paul Hazard, there is room for many other refinements and specifications. The study of the Greek Enlightenment provides many relevant illustrations. The culture area defined by the Italian language from many points of view formed a periphery of the Enlightenment. Yet at the same time, the focal points of the Enlightenment in Italy were centers of transmission of Enlightenment ideas to the Greek world. Either through the channel of the "Adriatic Enlightenment" southward to its Septinsular component, or overland from Dalmatia to the Danubian principalities, Italian Enlightenment culture radiated ideas and lifestyles of modernity to the Balkan and Greek worlds.[12] Furthermore, the special ties of the Greek Enlightenment with Russia created a web of social, intellectual, and political relations and interactions, which in fact turned that easternmost periphery of the Enlightenment world into an important center of cultural reference for Greek thought and sensibility.[13]

Within the Greek culture area itself the prism of a geographical perspective can reveal a remarkable parallelism with the polycentrism that marked the Italian geography of the Enlightenment. The narrative of the transmission and the reception of the Enlightenment in the Greek world in the following pages illustrates the multiplicity of centers that formed the geography of the Greek Enlightenment, from the Danubian principalities to the cities of Western Macedonia and Ioannina, the Ionian Islands, Constantinople, and the cities of Western Asia Minor. All these hearths of the Enlightenment in the Greek world functioned as centers for the transmission of the Enlightenment into the Balkan hinterland, in the interior of Asia Minor as far as the Caucasus, and further east in the Mediterranean world to the threshold of the Near East. What is a center and what is a periphery then become rather relative notions, a point of encounter between cultural history and geography that invites reflection about conventional wisdom. The focal points of the Greek Enlightenment, themselves on the periphery of the broader world of the Enlightenment, functioned as centers that radiated the Enlightenment toward other cultural traditions and geographical regions. It is on this level of analysis that the continuities that provided a shared cultural substratum between the Enlightenment and the Orthodox tradition can be more clearly perceived.

The discussion of context, transfers, and centers-peripheries points forcefully to the diversity and multiplicity that marks the cultural map of the Enlightenment. This in turn raises the most thorny and controversial question in recent interpretative debates, the issue of the unity or plurality of the Enlightenment. The argument for plurality in response to the question of one or many Enlightenments has behind it the weight of one of the most authoritative voices in the historiography of ideas, John Pocock, who has said in no uncertain terms: "we can no longer write satisfactorily of 'the Enlightenment' as a unified and universal intellectual movement."[14]

But is it so? Pocock's thesis is appealing primarily to all those who are motivated by the wish to "deconstruct" the Enlightenment in order to undo its moral theory and its political values. This of course does not make it a sustainable position. The case for the Enlightenment in criticism of Pocock's thesis has been made by John Robertson, and there is very little I have to add to it.[15] In fact, I could suggest that the study proposed here of the Enlightenment in the culture area defined by the Greek language could be adduced as another case next to Robertson's comparative study of the Enlightenment in two outlying areas of Europe, Scotland and Naples, in order to illustrate the overall argument in support of at least a modicum of shared concepts and values focusing on the amelioration of the human condition, which supplied a core unity to the Enlightenment. In my judgment, to reduce the Enlightenment to a plurality of independent and unconnected regional or local movements of cultural or religious criticism in fact abolishes the very idea of Enlightenment itself. Why call these diverse movements Enlightenment and not something else?

Furthermore, it has to be asked what is gained in terms of historical understanding if we abandon the idea and the name of Enlightenment altogether. Upon serious reflection it would appear that the answer is not much indeed. Another quarrel over the name of Enlightenment, in the good old scholastic tradition of quarrels over names, could possibly supply satisfaction to the vanity of intellectuals participating in it, but would not contribute much to the advancement of knowledge.

The issue of the unity or plurality of the Enlightenment has been laid to rest by Jonathan Israel. In his imposing trilogy he has proposed a framework for understanding the Enlightenment as an evolving phenomenon "committed to the notion of bettering humanity" and "discarding traditions of the past either wholly or partially" all across Europe and in the Atlantic world. Israel dismisses the concept of distinct "national Enlightenments" as "altogether invalid" and argues, drawing on an enormous erudition, that despite regional and local variations, the Enlightenment could be understood as an interplay of moderate and radical streams within a single narrative of change and transformation.[16] All this culminated in a "democratic Enlightenment" motivated by the impulse toward a revolutionary transformation of the human condition.

Israel's *opera magna* were published many years after the writing of the original English-language version of the present work. Yet the evidence discussed in the following pages could be readily related to his conceptual framework. What is presented below is the story of moderate Enlightenment's repeated attempts over a long period of time, spanning the eighteenth century down to the 1780s, to promote the amelioration of Greek society and culture and to prepare the Greek people for liberation. This protracted preparation culminated in an articulate movement of democratic Enlightenment in the three decades between the French and Greek Revolutions, a democratic Enlightenment that aspired and attempted to bring about the "fundamental transformation" of Greek society. The stream of radical Enlightenment in Israel's sense of the term, that is, the fundamental critique of religion from the vantage point of the needs of society and morality,[17] is also present in the narrative of the Greek Enlightenment, although this radical stream emerges rather late and remains for the most part hidden behind anonymity, with the sole exception of the brave and tragic case of Christodoulos Pamblekis, in whose writings in the 1790s we have a clear echo of Spinoza's ideas.

Within the broad-ranging and all-encompassing narrative of the stages of the Enlightenment's evolution as the agency of modernity, Israel never loses sight of its local and regional expressions. This perspective brings into his narrative the evidence of the Greek case as well as a presence in the world of the Enlightenment. We have thus a first but important step towards the incorporation of the Greek evidence into the canon of Enlightenment research. This is a unique feature of Israel's work, and it marks a considerable advance over earlier classics from Paul Hazard to Peter Gay, which remained focused on the Northwestern European core of the Enlightenment.

Even the minimal incorporation of the witness of the Greek Enlightenment into a major and authoritative synthesis, such as Israel's, represents a vindication of one of the most serious motivations of the research incorporated into the following pages. That motivation derived from a research strategy that aspired to contribute, to the degree allowed by the limited abilities of the author, to an expansion of the canon of the history of political thought. Research on the Greek Enlightenment, as the following pages show, reveals a range of sources, which could be profitably added to the canon of the history of political ideas, not only to expand its basis of comparative judgment, but also for the substantive interest these sources present from the point of view of cultural and social criticism or the theoretical treatment of complex real world situations as happens for instance with the "multicultural"—*avant le mot* to be sure—proposal of Rhigas Velestinlis.

These introductory remarks could perhaps be drawn to a close by briefly pointing to a final level of analysis on which the evidence presented in this work might prove of relevance to the clarification of issues of theoretical debate. This is the domain of theories of nationalism. It is not of course possible to resume here with any adequacy the theoretical debate that has grown to huge proportions since the momentous changes of 1989–1990 and the subsequent worldwide upsurge of nationalism. This book, nevertheless, can perhaps make two small contributions to the contest of theories of nationalism, one substantive, the other methodological. Substantively the witness of the Greek intellectual experience recorded below illustrates the transition of a population defined by recognizable ethnic characteristics, primarily by religion and secondarily and rather conditionally by language, with rather fluid boundaries and possibilities of multiple memberships, to a modern national community, primarily defined by language and rigidly delineated by its attachment to a modern nation-state. The evidence of the Greek case can be used to control, adjust, and correct "modernist" theories of nationalism, to bring them in fact to a closer dialogue with historical evidence in order to test their hypotheses. It could also provide telling evidence on the more unrealistic and exceedingly ahistorical claims of "primordial-ist" theories by showing how a very old cultural tradition, marked by an impressive phenomenon of linguistic continuity over the course of three millennia, was redefined and adjusted to the requirements of nationhood by the power of the modern state.[18] The methodological contribution of this work could be seen as a reminder to scholars coming to the study of nationalism from the social sciences concerning how much can be gained by an intellectual history approach that makes it possible for the sources themselves to inform interpretation and judgment. These last two objectives have in fact been the major inspiration of the research effort codified in the following pages.

Prologue

The Political Meaning of the Enlightenment

THE PHILOSOPHY OF the Enlightenment in its mature formulation in the thought of the eighteenth century represented the final emancipation of the European mind from the fetters of the medieval worldview. By negating the philosophical presuppositions of medieval thought, and substituting an alternative set of cognitive and axiological premises, the philosophy of the Enlightenment claimed the eventual victory of modernity after long intellectual and political struggles in European cultural history.[1]

The Enlightenment signified the deliverance of human thought from the darkness of error, ignorance, and prejudice. Its sources were the Cartesian radical doubt toward all established authority and traditional opinion and the relentless war against the "infamous" superstitions of conventional religion initiated by Hobbes and Spinoza. The road to Enlightenment was opened with the clear comprehension of the nature, sources, and limits of knowledge, which were systematically explored by John Locke in his *Essay Concerning Human Understanding*. By determining the cognitive possibilities of the human mind and by thus destroying the foundations of error, Locke emerged as the true father of the Enlightenment. He stood at the point of departure of the arduous journey of the Enlightenment, which reached its culmination with the formulation of its most characteristic claim in Kant's invitation *"sapere aude."* The rise of modern science, the appeal to reason, empiricist epistemology, and the deism of freethinkers provided the philosophical presuppositions of the Enlightenment. Its intellectual temper was set by a spirit of opposition to all types of dogmatism, which turned the Enlightenment into a determined form of criticism. The critical spirit inherited from Pierre Bayle became the Enlightenment's foremost attitude.

The rejection of authority, the recognition of the empirical basis of the cognitive powers of the human mind, and the universal invitation to knowledge had clear political implications. The new epistemology had an obvious leveling thrust. Human beings emerged as independent monads with potentially equal cognitive capabilities and equally sound judgment that could be cultivated and improved by appropriate education. Consequently, all persons could theoretically claim equal political rights and equal abilities of criticism. Thus, liberalism, which sanctioned the autonomy and the rights of the individual, became the foremost political expression of the new philosophy. The liberalism of the Enlightenment was fortified by the secularized theory of natural law, which enshrined the principle of inalienable human rights as the essential content of the idea of human liberty.[2]

Practically, the Enlightenment represented an affirmation of all the political consequences of the emancipation of the human mind from the tutelage of authority: it proclaimed the rights of the individual; it fought resolutely against despotism, fanaticism, intolerance, and social injustice; it clamored for the ideals of liberty, equality, and fraternity in which it found a new religion of humanity.[3]

In terms of the conventional milestones of intellectual history, the maturity of the Enlightenment may be located in the period enclosed by the appearance of Montesquieu's *Persian Letters* in 1721 and the posthumous publication of Condorcet's *Sketch of a Historical Picture of the Progress of the Human Mind* in 1795. The moral temper of the movement was set by the promise of liberation from the darkness of superstition and traditional religion and by the will to question and dispute all conventional principles, opinions, and kinds of authority. Based on empiricist epistemology, the Enlightenment derived its greatest inspiration from modern science and deified Newton as the foremost representative of its achievements. A universal faith in education as the instrument for the propagation of the lights of the new science found its characteristic expression in encyclopedism and in the popularization of basic scientific knowledge. The fascination with and faith in the new science was expressed with equal intensity in the quarrel between Ancients and Moderns. Not only scholastic Aristotelianism and its intellectual progeny were rejected and ostracized from philosophy, but more generally the achievements of modern science appeared to dwarf the civilization of the Ancients. Despite the vocal objections of those who carried on the older tradition of Renaissance humanism, the civilization of modern Europe seemed superior to that of classical antiquity, and thus the Moderns eventually won the quarrel against the Ancients.

Besides the vindication of modernity, the cultural outlook of the Enlightenment was marked by a heightened consciousness of space and time, reflected in the discovery of a secular historical past and an expanded awareness of a wider world of infinite geographic and cultural variety. Largely the product of increased geographical mobility and intensified social communications, the awakened consciousness of space was vividly reflected in an enormous travel literature that influenced profoundly the political thought of the Enlightenment. The eclipse and gradual abandonment of the cosmology of traditional religion was a parallel process to the rise of the secular notions of time and space.

The rise of the Enlightenment was an embattled process. The vanguard of the struggle was occupied by the new enlightened intelligentsia. For the first time in the history of European civilization, a sharply self-conscious and committed intelligentsia, with an intense awareness of its social and intellectual role, developed across cultures and state boundaries acting as the evangelists of a cosmopolitan outlook of shared human values.[4] The cosmopolitan intelligentsia of the Enlightenment was held together by this shared outlook on the nature of things and by the common practice of social criticism and systematic resistance to the established Church and to official censorship. Their criticism was directed against entrenched prejudices and aspired to social change and political renovation, which for some time they were prepared to accept from the policies of monarchs who wanted to appear enlightened. Voltaire and Diderot were perhaps the most important representatives of this attitude. The basis and standard of their criticism was the idea of utility against which they judged the social relevance of institutions and values. A telling indication of the ideological change that had been achieved since the Middle Ages was the reduction of metaphysics to a term of abuse applied to the opponents of the Enlightenment. There could be no more characteristic indication of the change wrought since medieval times. The concept of utility also supplied the main ideological weapon in the battle against the madness of feudal privileges and rights that was at the forefront of Enlightenment social criticism.

The indictment of despotism and the quest for the rule of law that became the Enlightenment's foremost political preoccupation was expressed with greatest power and profundity in Montesquieu's *Persian Letters* and *Spirit of the Laws.* Against the depravity of despotism, the search for legitimate government initiated a problematic of freedom that led well beyond the Enlightenment's original liberalism. Inspired by Montesquieu's critical science of politics, Rousseau resumed Machiavelli's exploration of the conditions of civic order to arrive at a vision of the ethical community of morally reconstructed citizens who would realize their freedom and find their fulfillment in enacting and obeying the law that expressed the general will. In his own quest for a morally acceptable social order whose legitimacy would be beyond dispute, Mably arrived at a socialist utopia that he endowed with Spartan symbolism. The radical republicanism of Rousseau and Mably represented the Enlightenment's political alternative to the decay of despotism and the moral vacuousness of selfish individualism. It was inspired by concrete social criticism derived from a sense of moral outrage over the collective predicament of the popular masses at the basis of society whose condition remained beyond the theoretical purview of liberalism. The egalitarian aspirations of republican radicalism voiced the deep yearnings of the people and pointed at a wider political reality that hinged on the lower social orders whose needs went beyond the liberal claims that met the requirements of the ascending bourgeoisie.[5]

The intensity with which the philosophes identified with the cause of the Enlightenment as a personal destiny suggests that political choices can be explained as responses to a conception of the human predicament. An existential choice in the form of a passionate commitment to a public cause, typified so characteristically in the experience of the philosophes, derived from the psychology of modern men, who had just achieved their emancipation from corporate structures and traditional mentalities and found an alternative source of meaning in the effort to generalize the blessings of their own experience in enlightenment. It was this psychology that transformed the philosophes into evangelists of criticism and change and made the age of the Enlightenment a period of cultural strain that set European collective consciousness on its course of transition to modernity.

The movements of ideas that culminated in the Enlightenment emerged and matured in the societies of Northwestern Europe, which since the seventeenth century had assumed the leadership of the world economy and experienced the concomitant social and cultural changes that led to the emergence of modern Western society. From its natal region, the Enlightenment was transmitted in the course of the eighteenth century to other geographical and social contexts on the periphery of the European center of economic and political gravity. These fragments of the Enlightenment were sent to the West across the Atlantic and to the south and east of the European continent. In the New World, the fragment of the Enlightenment was received into a fledgling immigrant society that had detached itself from the societies of the old continent in the previous century and possessed a heritage of values and traditions greatly congenial to the absorption, incorporation, and eventual flowering of the new ideas.[6] Other fragments of the Enlightenment, however, were transmitted to the south of Europe into the Mediterranean world, where they collided with deeply entrenched traditional social structures and mentalities and systems of power that were inimical to the values and implications of the new philosophy.[7]

The diverse societies of Mediterranean Europe, despite the vast differences in their historical development in the late Middle Ages and in the early modern period, had since the sixteenth century been drawn together and formed a human and economic unit held together by transnational forces of commerce, demography, and culture.[8] From then on, the collective destinies of Mediterranean societies were shaped by their common multidimensional dependence on their northwestern neighbors. The major consequence of this dependence, which stamped the historical experience of all Southern European societies in the modern period, was reflected in the general delay, weakness, or absence of the processes that secularized European culture elsewhere and prepared the ground for the appearance of the Enlightenment.[9] The social and economic dimensions of this problem constitute the decisive explanatory variables, and they will be repeatedly alluded to in the following pages, but they are beyond the scope of the present attempt to follow a process of intellectual change generated by the reception of the Enlightenment into a particular cultural context.

In considering the propagation of the ideas of the Enlightenment, this monograph will be concerned with their fate in a society of the European periphery where the established Church and traditional culture had remained immune to the challenges of Protestantism and secularization, and the foundations of existing social structures were not seriously undermined by forces of social change. The survival of the traditional order, virtually intact through the eighteenth and into the nineteenth centuries, did not, however, prevent the emergence of intellectual movements inspired by the Enlightenment in the societies of Mediterranean Europe.[10] In fact the emergence of articulate local and regional Enlightenments in the outlying areas of Europe to the south and southeast could be considered as expressions of the richness and diversity of Enlightenment culture but also as indications of the deeper intellectual and moral unity that held together the far-ranging movement of cultural change.

Despite their socioeconomic backwardness and political decay in the eighteenth century, these societies had not been divested of their intellectual traditions, which had deep and ancient roots in the heritage of their respective historical pasts. Certain segments of the local intelligentsia, who happened to develop some contacts with innovative European culture, proved receptive to the new intellectual orientations, absorbed the new values, and gradually came to perceive the problems of their own societies in the terms formulated by the Enlightenment. This created cleavages in the ranks of the intelligentsia and inevitably generated ideological strife.

The Enlightenment could be perceived as a threat to the entrenched social order and its values. Its claims for cultural innovation and the practical implications of its philosophical ideas were often interpreted by its rivals as amounting to a rejection of the existing order of things. This turned the Enlightenment into a fundamentally political movement focused on the highest of stakes: the basic values and institutions of society; the shape of the body politic; the definition of an acceptable collective destiny; and the legitimate direction of the affairs of society. The mutual determination of the proponents and adversaries of the Enlightenment, in their increasingly rigidified positions after 1789 and the intensity of the conflict that ensued, derived from their acute awareness of the significance of what was at stake. The outcomes of these political and intellectual struggles shaped the future political traditions of the societies that experienced movements

of Enlightenment. The Enlightenment, therefore, was not only a central issue in eighteenth-century politics, but its fate has been intimately connected with the nature of modern political systems. This essay attempts to examine some of these political implications of the Enlightenment as an ideology of social and cultural change by looking at the concrete experience of modern Greek society. This perspective on the Neohellenic political tradition will hopefully illuminate in addition some recurring problems of Greek politics by pointing to their historical origins and wider cultural and ideological context.

CHAPTER ONE

The Long Road
to Enlightenment

THIS ESSAY ATTEMPTS to reconstruct a process of intellectual change and to identify the political problems that emerged from it by looking at the reception and fate of the ideas of the Enlightenment in the Greek cultural tradition. A number of important methodological issues, concerning the study of the history of ideas, arise from this project.[1] The primary focus of interest is on the effects produced by new ideas on the prevailing modes of thought in the culture that received them. The analysis proceeds by tracing the transmission of influences across cultures and the impact and manifestation of ideas in the collective thought of human groups as registered in the works of representative writers. These writers were not always original and most of their ideas were derivative. Much of their work consisted of translations or the popularization of ideas current in the great centers of learning of this period. Their work is, nevertheless, important because it expresses the aspirations, beliefs, and prevailing mentalities of a culture. Translations of foreign works, once made, published, and read, became integral possessions of the culture into which they were received. Finally, the works left behind by these literary representatives of the community may be important not simply as registers of collective mentalities, but in their own right as reflections on fundamental problems or as influential texts that shaped the cultural outlooks of certain groups and contributed to the process of intellectual and social change. As such they are important sources of insights into the period and into the cultural vision within which its problems were perceived.[2] Such is primarily the nature of the evidence on which the study of collective consciousness will have to be based.

Locating the *terminus a quo,* with which the explorations in the content of collective consciousness should begin, requires another methodological choice. The study of intellectual change requires a starting point in the crystallization of a certain mode of thought against and away from which subsequent evolution, caused by mutations in the intellectual presuppositions of social consciousness, will be traced. The end point will have to be a new pattern or configuration of ideas that will represent the transcendence of the original theory. Since this is a study of the influence and integration of the ideas of the Enlightenment into a culture other than those in which they originated, an acquaintance with the intellectual legacy of that culture and of its prevailing modes of thought and consciousness forms a necessary point of departure.

THE PHILOSOPHICAL HERITAGE OF THE GREEK EAST

In the Greek East, as in the Latin West, Aristotelianism had been the officially sanctioned philosophical doctrine inherited from the Middle Ages. Aristotle's philosophical categories had been absorbed into Byzantine philosophy so effectively that they became an integral part of the Christian thinking and spiritual tradition in the Greek East.[3] The prevailing Aristotelianism of Byzantine philosophy had been challenged in the eleventh century by Michael Psellos, who attempted to reinterpret Plato as a spiritual ancestor of Christian theology.[4] The Aristotelian legacy was reinforced in the Byzantine East in the fourteenth century, however, as a result of renovating intellectual contacts with the West, which for the first time brought Byzantine philosophy into contact with the great synthesis of Christian thought and Aristotelianism in the philosophy of Thomas Aquinas. These contacts produced the first translation of Aquinas's philosophy into Greek, by Dimitrios Kydonis in about 1354. The most serious challenge, however, came in the early fifteenth century, at precisely the time the Byzantine Empire was caught in its death throes, in the teaching of the Neoplatonist George Gemistos Plethon, who argued for a revival of Platonism, both as a spiritual and as a political doctrine, as the only hope for the dying empire's salvation. Plethon, who during his stay in Italy on the occasion of the Council of Florence in 1438–1439 had contributed decisively to the orientation of Renaissance humanism toward Platonism, insisted that only a spiritual regeneration of Byzantine thought and society, through a recovery of Platonic mysticism and a radical political reform of the decaying empire to turn it into a Hellenic republic on the model projected in Plato's *Laws,* could avert the impending final disaster.[5]

Plethon's political theory was based on a quite novel conception that emerged in late Byzantine thought as a direct consequence of the contraction of the empire and the concomitant decline of the imperial idea of a universal Christian state. Under the impact of these new political experiences, some Byzantine intellectuals, especially in the Greek states that sprang from the breakup of the empire after the Latin conquest of Constantinople in 1204, discovered a new ethnic identity for themselves and for the Greek-speaking Christian people who had survived as the core of the multiethnic society of Byzantium. This new identity was defined in terms of the Greek language and the intellectual parentage these late Byzantines felt with classical Greek civilization. The Byzantine Christians felt that these cultural characteristics distinguished them not only from the heathen barbarians to the north and east of the empire, but also from the Christian barbarians of the Latin West and most notably from the non-Greek ethnic elements in Byzantine society. Thus in the rump Byzantine states like the empire of Nicea in Northwest Asia Minor and the despotate of Mistra in the Peloponnese, ethnic homogeneity and the spirit of resistance against the pressures of foreign enemies fostered the emergence of the first incipient signs of a new collective consciousness that might eventually have evolved into a Neohellenic national consciousness on a pattern similar to that of the nations of Western Europe.[6] It was precisely at this time, out of the collapse of the medieval Christian commonwealth, that the trend toward distinct nationhood emerged in the societies that were to develop into the first dynastic European states (England, France, and Spain). Plethon's movement was the bravest indication of similar tendencies that appeared under comparable conditions in the Greek lands. Significantly, Plethon had insisted that the inhabitants of the late Byzantine territories that survived in the ancient Greek heartlands were "Greeks by birth" as testified by their language and national culture.[7]

Such manifestations of the sense of a new identity among Greek-speaking Christians, which have been characterized as a modern Greek "proto-nationalism,"[8] were submerged and dissipated by the Ottoman conquest of Constantinople in 1453 and the fall of the remaining free Greek states to the Ottomans in 1460 (Mistra) and 1461 (Trebizond). Besides its crucial political, social, and intellectual consequences, which proved the decisive determinants for the development of Greek society and culture in subsequent centuries, the Ottoman conquest, by decisively sealing off the Greek East from the fledgling Renaissance in the West, marked the triumph of a traditionalist outlook in the ideological controversies raging in Byzantium on the eve of the Fall. The movement of philosophical and political renewal inspired by Neoplatonism and the incipient articulation of a Neohellenic identity were obliterated.

Significantly, Plethon's writings were ceremoniously burnt in Constantinople by his philosophic opponent George Scholarios, who was elevated to the patriarchal throne after the Fall. A champion of Aristotelianism and a determined enemy of the heretical West, Scholarios, renamed Gennadios II upon his consecration as patriarch in 1454, presided over the reconstruction of Byzantine ideology that was to provide the context of Greek thought in the centuries of Ottoman rule.[9] Christian Aristotelianism triumphed in formal learning, and the East Roman ideals of universal monarchy and hierarchical society prevailed in political theory. The mantle of universalism was taken from the fallen empire by another supranational institution, the Orthodox Church, under the leadership of the Patriarchate of Constantinople. The Ottoman conquerors invested the Orthodox Church with important political functions by relegating to the patriarch and his bishops civil responsibility in the governance of the subject Christian Orthodox communities. The Church became the mediating institution between the Ottoman Sultan and his Christian subjects. In this way, the Greek-speaking and other Orthodox nationalities of the Balkans, represented by the ecclesiastical hierarchy of the Ecumenical Patriarchate, were integrated into the Ottoman social system of religious communities (millets) according to the stipulations of Islamic sacred law.[10] The manner in which the Church accommodated its ideology to the new political reality is of great interest for the history of political ideas. After the fall of the Christian Empire and the disappearance of the Orthodox emperor, the Church reconciled itself to coexistence with the non-Christian wielder of imperial authority, recognizing his sovereignty with complete loyalty and according him the appropriate honors, though it omitted the terms "holy," "Orthodox," and "pious," used formerly of the East Roman emperor as an element in the very existence and practice of the Church. After the conquest, the "king" continued to be a divinely ordained element of the natural order of things, of which the Church was part, though he ceased henceforth to be a vehicle of holiness and sanctity, or to participate in the internal life and worship of the Church.[11]

The new Ottoman imperial authorities that replaced the defunct Christian Empire assured to the Orthodox Church their protection against the intrusions of Catholicism from without. The anti-Latin attitude, which prevailed in the Orthodox Church following the Great Schism and was solidified after the Fall with the triumph of the antiunion party in Constantinople, coincided with the suspicion and hostility of the Ottomans toward the European powers that might check their further expansion or even attempt to organize a Crusade in the East against them. This coincidence of political interests between the Church and the Sublime Porte resulted in a common front against the West. The protection that this alliance assured to the Church, both from Catholic religious propaganda and from the ideological pressure of new European currents of thought, combined with the official toleration that Islamic law accorded to the "religions of the book" (Judaism and Christianity), provided substantive arguments for the policy of loyalty that the Orthodox Church followed toward the Ottoman state.[12] This political tradition, inaugurated by Patriarch Gennadios Scholarios immediately after the Fall,[13] was reiterated with vigor by the ecclesiastical leadership three centuries later in its battle against the Enlightenment. This was not simply a policy of expediency, but it could be justified on the strength of scriptural authority. By assuming this policy, the Church rendered unto Caesar what was Caesar's while pursuing its own spiritual purposes. By submitting to the powers that be, the Church could not only claim that it had secured their toleration in preserving the faith unadulterated, but also that it had turned the tribulations of captivity into a collective spiritual exercise and martyrdom on earth that might open the gates of heaven. From its vantage point, therefore, the Orthodox

Church was theologically in the right. The contradictions inherent in this position, especially regarding the alienation that temporal involvement of the ecclesiastical leadership of the subject Christian people meant for the inner spiritual and mystical life of the Church, could not of course cross the mind of or worry those critics of the Church who were later on to accuse it of collaboration with an alien despotic oppressor.

This was the formal ideological and institutional context of political and intellectual life in the traditional society of the "Orthodox East" under Ottoman rule. Despite the triumph of Christian Aristotelianism after the Fall of Constantinople, the devastating cultural consequences of the Ottoman conquest, of which the migration of the most distinguished Greek intellectuals to the West[14] was only the most dramatic and best-known symptom, essentially resulted in an eclipse of learning and philosophy in the Greek East for a century and a half after 1453. The absence of manuscripts of philosophical works copied in this period[15] offers unmistakable evidence for the decline of learning in the East at precisely the time that the West was experiencing the ferment of the Renaissance. Philosophy returned to the Greek East only when intellectual ties with the West were resumed in the seventeenth century. The main geographical channel through which these ties were resumed were the Greek territories possessed by Venice and the Greek colonies established in Italian cities, notably in Venice, since the end of the Middle Ages. In the absence of institutions of higher learning in the East after the Fall, Greek students from Latin-held territories (Chios, Crete, Cyprus, and the Ionian Islands) and gradually from elsewhere in the Greek world, gravitated toward the official university of the Venetian Republic, the University of Padua. Padua, immune from the pressures and intervention of the Inquisition and of the court of Rome, had become from the fifteenth through the seventeenth century a major intellectual center distinguished by a revival of classical studies and flourishing scientific research. In philosophy, the University of Padua had become the center of a flourishing Neoaristotelianism whose advent was due to the rediscovery of the original Greek texts of Aristotle brought to Italy by Greek scholars taking refuge from the Ottoman onslaught.[16] The effect of this rereading of Aristotle was the abandonment of the medieval tradition of Christian Aristotelianism, which had its original sources in the Aristotelianism of Averroes, and its replacement by a concentration of interest on Aristotle's texts on physics, which led to a naturalistic interpretation of Aristotelian philosophy. The Neoaristotelians of Padua attempted to remove the context of religious doctrine from natural philosophy and explained the natural world and its phenomena in terms of a strict causality.[17] It was this philosophy that was transmitted to the Greek East by the Greek students of Padua.

The most important of the Greek scholars who introduced Neoaristotelianism in the East was the Athenian Theophilos Corydaleus (1570–1646). At Padua, he had been a disciple of Cesare Cremonini, who had given an empiricist and naturalistic turn to Neoaristotelianism and had become known for his disputes with the Jesuits regarding freedom of scientific investigation.[18] When he returned to Greece, Corydaleus was summoned by the Patriarch Cyril I Loukaris in 1624 to reorganize the Patriarchal Academy of Constantinople as a central institution of higher learning for the whole of the Greek East. Cyril's initiative in the early part of the seventeenth century represented the first conscious program of cultural reconstruction undertaken by the leadership of Greek Orthodox society since the Fall of Constantinople. The patriarch's motivation derived partly from a desire to arrest the inroads of Roman Catholic propaganda into the world of Orthodoxy, and for this purpose he entered into extensive contacts with Protestant churches and governments, especially those of Britain and the Netherlands.[19] Cyril's policies came to a tragic end with his own execution by the Ottomans in 1638, but his program of cultural reconstruction had one lasting consequence: the introduction of Neoaristotelian philosophy in Greek learning. This was the achievement of Corydaleus's effective teaching at the Patriarchal Academy. He emancipated philosophy from theology and made Neoaristotelian studies, with emphasis on logic, physics, and the study of generation and corruption, the basis of higher education.

Corydaleus was a severe critic of medieval scholasticism, and in matters of religion he appears to have been a freethinker whose orthodoxy was held in question even by his closest disciples.[20] In the conflict between *fides* and *ratio,* Corydaleus seems, according to all available evidence, to have inclined toward the latter; and therefore he has been correctly characterized by his most authoritative biographer as the first "revolutionary thinker" in the Greek East and the initiator of free thought in Southeastern Europe.[21] In his own lifetime Corydaleus suffered from these orientations of his thought. He was chased from the Patriarchal Academy after Cyril's death, and to allay the suspicions of his orthodoxy, he accepted being consecrated archbishop of Nafpaktos and Arta in 1641 for one year only and subsequently returned to his birthplace, Athens, where he founded a school and taught philosophy until his death in 1646.

Nevertheless, it was not the nonconformist and revolutionary elements of Corydaleus's thought that survived in his intellectual legacy, which shaped educational life in the Greek East for a century and a half after his tenure at Constantinople. The model of higher learning he introduced there was imitated in the establishment of new academic institutions in Jassy and Bucharest, on Athos, Patmos, Chios, and elsewhere. His students at Constantinople inaugurated a tradition of Greek Neoaristotelianism, which through these schools was transmitted from generation to generation until, later in the eighteenth century, it collided with the Enlightenment. In the context of this system of higher education, Corydaleus's own commentaries on Aristotle became the exclusive textbooks of philosophical instruction, supplemented only by other commentaries composed by his disciples. In successive editions or in manuscript copies, these texts of Corydalist Aristotelianism circulated widely in Greek schools and became the mold of acceptable secular wisdom that supplemented traditional religious learning, thus strictly defining the parameters of Greek higher education. Deprived of its original renovating and nonconformist impulse, the Neoaristotelian tradition that developed out of Corydaleus's philosophic system became a severely constraining factor that in a few generations ossified Greek education. Corydaleus's Neoaristotelian successors developed into relentless enemies of modern philosophy and of scientific learning and opposed, some of them with fanaticism, any ideas of innovation of Greek culture in such directions. It was ironic that Corydalism, the legacy of the man who has been considered the first "freethinker" in Greek culture, should appear to later generations as primarily responsible for the sterility and ultimate bankruptcy of traditional Greek education. In it the Enlightenment found one of its primary targets.

Corydalist Aristotelianism provided the philosophical foundation for the elaboration of a synthesis of traditional political ideas. This synthesis represented a crystallization of ancient conceptions and notions about political order inherited from the Byzantine and Hellenistic traditions, recast in the language of a social morality and political theory relevant to the aspirations of a new lay leadership that emerged in Greek society toward the end of the seventeenth century. It was the first time that a secular group had risen to social eminence alongside the ecclesiastical hierarchy since 1453. This new social formation was the Phanariot aristocracy, a social group that rose to prominence through successful economic activity in the period of social change in Ottoman society toward the end of the seventeenth century. From economic success the Phanariots—named after their neighborhood of Phanari (Lantern) in Constantinople, where the Ecumenical Patriarchate also had its see since 1599—moved on to careers in scholarship and studies in the West that allowed them to assume the leadership of Greek education and to rise to prominence in the patriarchal court. Their knowledge of foreign languages and of the ways of the world made their services necessary to the Sublime Porte at a time when the Ottoman Empire, defeated in war and with its expanding vigor dissipated, had to enter into serious diplomatic dealings with major European powers. The Phanariots were thus co-opted into the Ottoman diplomatic service and became the Sublime Porte's chief negotiators in their capacity as Grand Dragomans—literally interpreters— of the Porte, a high office carrying the duties of a minister of foreign affairs, which was habitually reserved to a member of this group.[22]

The first Greek Grand Dragoman was Panayiotis Nikousios (1613– 1673), who held the office between 1661 and 1673 and was succeeded by Alexandros Mavrokordatos (1641–1709), founder of the greatest Phanariot dynasty. He had studied philosophy and medicine at Padua and received a doctorate from Bologna before assuming the duties of director at the Patriarchal Academy (1666), eventually entering the service of the Sultan. His great diplomatic achievement was the negotiation of the Treaty of Carlowitz in 1699.[23] Besides a number of textbooks, he left a body of political writings that represent the first articulation of Phanariot social thought. Certain dimensions of this outlook have to be identified in order to define the nature of the political consciousness of this early generation of Phanariot political and intellectual leadership, as the *terminus a quo* for the subsequent explorations in ideological change that eventually brought a transition to a radically different political consciousness among Westernized Greeks.

Alexandros Mavrokordatos is one of the most important among those figures in Greek political and intellectual history during the period of Ottoman rule who combined tradition and renewal in their wide experience and in the formation of their thought. While a medical student at Padua, two generations after Corydaleus, Mavrokordatos came into contact with the new theories of modern science, which were subverting Neoaristotelian orthodoxy at this university. His doctoral dissertation, which he defended in 1664 at the University of Bologna, was a critical study of the function of the heart in the circulation of the blood and was guided by a modern scientific approach: he distanced himself from the authority of antiquity and declared his faith in human judgment as the decisive criterion in the study of nature. Mavrokordatos adopted William Harvey's theory on the circulation of the blood, which had been formulated as early as 1619 but still encountered strong resistance from Neoaristotelian medicine in continental Europe, but he did not hesitate to differ from it, asserting that the lungs, and not the heart, were the primary cause of circulation.[24]

After he returned to the Greek East and began teaching courses in philosophy at the Patriarchal Academy (1665–1672), Alexandros Mavrokordatos, now the "Great Orator" of the Ecumenical Patriarchate, had no hesitation in teaching modern scientific views alongside the traditional curriculum of grammar, rhetoric, and Corydaleus's commentaries on Aristotle. He even added his own note to Corydaleus's commentary, *On Generation and Corruption*. Soon, however, his interests as a writer were, characteristically, adapted to the prevailing intellectual conventions of the Greek East. His familiarity with modern scientific knowledge cannot be detected in his main works, which fell within the canon of Corydalism's literary concerns: *Grammar Concerning Syntax, Synopsis of the Art of Rhetoric*. The most important component of his philosophy, however, his interest in issues of political morality, which permitted elements of modern European political thought to be grafted onto the body of Neoaristotelianism, remained unknown and inaccessible to his contemporaries.[25]

As a Western-educated Neoaristotelian, Alexandros Mavrokordatos possessed a keen awareness of the Greek past, but when he turned to the study of history, "the associate of wisdom, the fellow-traveler of truth, [. . .] the teacher of prudence,"[26] he decided to offer to his readers a profile of the "holy and venerable head" of the corpus of world history, the sacred history of the Jewish people. Such a survey of Jewish history since the time of Creation would be particularly edifying to the pious.[27] The past to which Mavrokordatos turned was not a distinct ethnic history but a common biblical past shared by all Christian peoples. History began with the Creation and with the destinies of the ancient Hebrews on the pattern of traditional Christian chronicles.

When it came to the present, Mavrokordatos outlined his views of politics and life in society in the *Reflections* he composed for the instruction of his sons, a text that remained unpublished in the family for more than a century.[28] The major values that dominated Mavrokordatos's political reflections were prudence and realism. His emphasis on them betrays the instinct for survival that a social group rising under the aegis of despotism felt necessary to cultivate. Mature realism and not disembodied idealism ought to be the standard of political comportment.[29] The appearance rather than the substance of virtue is the important thing in human relations.[30] A certain inspiration from Machiavelli and La Rochefoucauld[31] could be detected here. As far as service to one's masters was concerned, Mavrokordatos counseled unwavering loyalty: those privy to the secrets of power by virtue of their public office "should be blind when entering and deaf when exiting."[32] This counsel of blind loyalty to the powers that be reflected the Phanariot identification with the Ottoman state. The Grand Dragoman, who had handled the foreign relations of the Sublime Porte with a skill that fascinated and amazed his contemporaries, could not visualize any other political context or any alternative shape of public life. Although he felt a warm affection and a clear sense of attachment to his native island of Chios, which he described as "an unadulterated remnant of Hellas,"[33] as a public persona, Mavrokordatos could not conceive of his identity in terms differentiating him from his Ottoman masters. Thus the political consciousness of the dominant Greek intellectual elite at the threshold of the century of ideological change could be defined in terms of a double identification: on the dimension of the past, the Greeks identified with the one universal Christian people, the new chosen people of the Lord; on the dimension of the present, the Christian subjects were absorbed into a sense of Ottoman identity. Finally, in the domain of political action, the imperative of loyalty and submission dictated by a prudent instinct of survival precluded any form of politics as collective and purposeful activity for goals other than individual self-preservation and excluded entirely any conception of political change.

These themes were worked into a systematic political theory by the greatest of all Phanariots, Alexandros's son Nikolaos Mavrokordatos (1680–1730).[34] A profoundly learned and cultured man, he was the first Greek to be appointed hospodar (prince) in the Danubian principalities of Moldavia and Wallachia under the sovereignty of the Ottoman Sultan. Nikolaos Mavrokordatos occupied successively the thrones of both principalities (1709–1730), and he inaugurated the century of Phanariot rule that brought significant social changes and reforms in those feudal regions and set the context for remarkable cultural and intellectual development that turned the principalities into one of the major centers of the Enlightenment in Southeastern Europe. Nikolaos Mavrokordatos composed a series of political works that gave mature expression to early Phanariot political theory. In a set of private counsels he composed for his descendants, he exemplified the same concern with prudence and realism that had characterized his father's similar text.[35] Nikolaos's outlook, however, was that of the representative of a social group that had arrived and felt secure in its prominence. Prudence remained the primary virtue against the vicissitudes of fortune, but the anxiety of self-preservation was tamed by success. This allowed him to broaden his political perspective from a preoccupation with the tactics of survival to a consideration of social morality and of the nature of the virtuous political regime. In his treatise *De Officiis,* the influence of classical moral philosophy is evident. The author followed both Cicero and Aristotle in depicting a prototype of virtuous conduct and social justice. His aspiration was to endow the classical Aristotelian gentleman with Christian virtues. It was not an attempt to expand traditional Christian ethics by the incorporation of classical values in it, but rather to Christianize classical morality to suit the requirements of accepted moral codes. The treatise put primary emphasis on reason as the foremost human trait. The central and longest chapter in the book was dedicated to a discussion of man as a rational, social, and political creature.[36] Personal valor, prudence, and justice (the highest of virtues), probity, and liberality were extolled, but the argument's main weight fell on the Christian virtues of piety, penitence, humility, fear of God, and reverence for the Church.[37] Such were the moral duties of a rational being living in political society. They also constituted the ethical matrix of a virtuous ruler.

Nikolaos Mavrokordatos expressed his views on rulership in his selection of a text to be translated into Greek on the subject. He chose Ambrogio Marliani's *Theatrum Politicum.* The purposes of the translation were clearly stated in the translator's prefatory note: the book taught all the virtues of a perfect prince.[38] Justice, uprightness, and prudence were the virtues of kingship. The virtuous prince ought to know how to select the best ministers; he should be moderate in his demands from his subjects and faithful in his observance of the laws. His own civil legislation ought to be entirely subjected to Divine Law. In matters of religion and piety, the prince ought to be an example for all to follow. He should cultivate his mind and encourage the promotion of learning and letters. He ought to avoid flattery and be careful in selecting his friends, whose test would be their loyalty in difficult circumstances. Above all, the virtuous prince ought to be concerned with the salvation of his soul by avoiding arrogance and impudence in his happiness and by showing perseverance in the face of adversity, by fearing God, and by honoring His ministers.[39]

This conception of the virtuous prince essentially involved a Christianization of the ancient political theory of Hellenistic monarchy that had been transmitted through the Byzantine and the Western Middle Ages in the tradition of mirrors of princes. The theory was premised on a cosmic hierarchy within which it located the moral paternalism of kingship. The Phanariot princes, by choosing to claim the legacy of this tradition, essentially sought and found an ideology for their new political role. To consolidate their leadership at the top of their society, they needed the legitimacy of a moral tradition which they could only find by looking to the Christian past. In this sense they were the final exponents and interpreters of Byzantine political theory, under the conditions of the Ottoman conquest of the Orthodox peoples of Southeastern Europe.[40] Acceptance of and identification with the Ottoman present offered still another support to their dominance in that specific political context. This can explain the fully developed Ottoman consciousness of Nikolaos Mavrokordatos. His defense of Ottoman society, against what he considered as the misconceptions of European observers, clearly shows where his loyalty belonged.[41]

Nikolaos Mavrokordatos's theoretical position represented the final crystallization of Greek thought in the context of Ottoman society. His political theory occupied the middle point between the Byzantine *Weltanschauung,* which defined the ideology of the Greek-speaking Christians at the opening of the Ottoman period, and the revolutionary Neohellenic consciousness, which under the impact of the Enlightenment would bring a new self-definition of the Greeks. Early Phanariot thought sought its legitimacy in the tradition of Christian kingship, but its primary preoccupation was with the present, which was enclosed by Ottoman reality and the cosmopolitanism of European social and intellectual elites in the wider world beyond the confines of the Ottoman state. Both Alexandros and Nikolaos Mavrokordatos were keenly aware of and involved with this wider world. Their Ottoman consciousness was supplemented by a cosmopolitan

European consciousness. This becomes apparent from the private literary endeavors of Nikolaos Mavrokordatos and the wide range of his correspondence, which secured him a prominent position in the European "republic of letters" in the early eighteenth century. His copious correspondence with Jean Leclerc, publisher of the famous early-Enlightenment periodical *Nouvelles de la république des lettres,* and the admiration in which he was held by the German literary historian Johannes Fabricius are clear testimony to the place he won for himself in the cosmopolitan cultural and intellectual world of the early Enlightenment. His correspondence with Leclerc, in particular, has also preserved a very important piece of evidence for Nikolaos Mavrokordatos's political interests at the beginning of the 1720s: the expression of his wish to acquire John Locke's *Essay on Government.*[42] This is the earliest surviving testimony concerning John Locke's presence in the Greek political and intellectual tradition. Of the leading figures of Southeastern Europe, the only one who had an international reputation comparable with that of Nikolaos Mavrokordatos was his contemporary Dimitrie Cantemir, Nikolaos's predecessor on the throne of Moldavia.

The clearest evidence of Nikolaos Mavrokordatos's cosmopolitanism is provided by his novel *Philotheou Parerga,* which depicted an international group of cultured gentlemen promenading in an exquisite garden and discussing psychology, society, and culture from a vantage point of shared social and moral values. The framework of discourse and taste were the same for all interlocutors, and this identity of values was underlined by the invocation of another cosmopolitan age by the Hellenistic setting of the novel. It is remarkable to note the trans-European cosmopolitanism of which these cultured Ottoman Greeks partook long before they possessed a distinct historical consciousness and a sense of national identity. This was another salient dimension of Phanariot culture that was to survive even after the original theoretical synthesis of the Mavrokordatoi was transcended by later generations of Phanariots.

In light of this cultural background, it should not appear surprising that the first signs of intellectual change, suggesting openness and receptivity to the philosophical stirrings of the early Enlightenment, can be encountered in the thought of Nikolaos Mavrokordatos. Scattered in *Philotheou Parerga* one can identify several of the threads of the philosophy of the Enlightenment. The point of departure was the articulation of some reservations toward Aristotelianism. It was the first time in Greek thought that such criticisms were voiced. The initiative was all the more striking given the prevalence of Aristotelianism in Nikolaos's intellectual milieu (both his father and his tutor Iakovos Manos were known as prominent Neoaristotelians). Yet Nikolaos expressed openly his admiration for Aristotle's severest critic, Francis Bacon,[43] and asserted that the empiricist natural philosophy of the Moderns was much more reliable than Aristotelian physics.[44] If Aristotle himself had been alive in modern times, he would have been an eager pupil of the Moderns.[45] With this remark, Nikolaos Mavrokordatos took sides in the quarrel of Ancients and Moderns. The criticism of Aristotle was supplemented by Mavrokordatos's praise of Plato.[46] Mavrokordatos's admiration for Plato was a conspicuous feature of his philosophical makeup, and was shrewdly noted by his contemporary Dimitrios Prokopiou, a keen observer of contemporary Greek intellectual life. The source of Mavrokordatos's Platonism may be traced to the Renaissance Platonism of Marcilius Ficino and Pico della Mirandola, both of whom make an appearance in *Philotheou Parerga*.[47] Coming as it did at the threshold of the age of Enlightenment, Mavrokordatos's Platonism was an eloquent indication of the will at an emancipation of thought from the inflexible rigor assumed by Neoaristotelianism. Significantly, however, these predilections were not openly expressed. The work in which Nikolaos Mavrokordatos voiced his reservations toward Aristotelianism and his preference for the Moderns remained unpublished until 1800. Making such philosophic views public would not have been consonant with the queen of Phanariot virtues—prudence.

INCIPIENT STIRRINGS OF INTELLECTUAL CHANGE

The signs of intellectual change that first appeared in the Phanariot milieu did not remain isolated only in those circles. The gropings of a new outlook became manifest in Greek culture in the opening decades of the eighteenth century, indicating that the intellectual presuppositions of a new state of consciousness were in the making. The affirmation of the new philosophical presuppositions progressed throughout the first half of the eighteenth century in the form of scientific criticism of Aristotelianism, the expression of a preference for modern science and rational philosophy against traditional learning. Coming at a time that Aristotelianism was still the official philosophy and the patriarchate maintained a conservative attitude toward modern philosophy, natural science, and mathematics, any indications of alternative philosophic preference were bound to produce some dramatic cases of liberty of conscience.

The protagonist in the earliest documented such case was Methodios Anthrakitis (1660–ca. 1749), a clergyman and teacher of philosophy at Ioannina and Kastoria. Methodios was one of the last representatives of the tradition of religious humanism embodied in the pastoral and educational policies of the Church in the previous century. This tradition was represented by a remarkable series of distinguished prelates in the seventeenth century who played a leading role in the promotion of Greek education and used the popular language in their sermons in order to be understood by the people. Besides the Christian virtues, they preached the values of education and social solidarity in the cultivation of the morals of the people.[48]

Anthrakitis shared this attitude, which inspired his first book, *Christian Theories*. As stated in the preface, it was not a book of difficult discourse, but of simple and easily comprehensible reflections, accessible to all and aspiring to promote evangelical truth.[49] In the name of evangelical truth, Methodios pleaded for a humanization and rectification of ecclesiastical politics. He urged for a more faithful discharge of the hierarchy's pastoral duties.[50] He spoke up against exploitation and corruption in the ranks of the clergy and advocated more humanity and less severity in meting out ecclesiastical punishments, especially the pronouncement of excommunications for quite inconsequential reasons. "Alas what mercilessness and brutality, what inhumanity on the part of the good shepherd to trade excommunications for sordid gain."[51] For this reason, Methodios points out, "the natural laws are crying out against these careless and speechless prelates. Because . . . they break their spiritual promise and use their pastoral income for the plentiful enjoyment of their desires."

These observations by Anthrakitis are daring but not particularly original: they may be associated with earlier traditions of criticism of the higher echelons of the clergy, one important exponent of which was the seventeenth-century prelate Damaskinos Stouditis, author of a collection of sermons called the *Thisavros* that was popular throughout Southeastern Europe, as well as of a *Dialogue* against the obtuseness of the hierarchy.[52] Anthrakitis's writing, however, sets the traditional Christian sense of moral outrage at the wrongdoings of bad priests in the context of a still-distant wave of social criticism that was to be voiced decades later by the

Enlightenment. It is remarkable to note that Anthrakitis stated his social criticism in terms of an appeal to natural law. This dimension of his argument points to the fact that there was a transition in his thought from the tradition of religious humanism to a different tradition, one that appealed to standards immanent in the nature of things rather than to supernatural values. The transition was obvious in Anthrakitis's teaching. In his lectures at the school of higher education in Kastoria, he taught modern mathematics (geometry, algebra, and trigonometry) and philosophy following Descartes and Malebranche.[53] Although his mathematical writings survived and were later on published by Balanos Vasilopoulos,[54] one of his successors in the school of Ioannina, the sources are not very clear as to the philosophical content of his teaching. Did he espouse and attempt to propagate the metaphysical doctrines of Descartes or the religious philosophy of Malebranche? It is not certain, but it seems quite possible that Malebranche's heroic attempt to reconcile the antagonism of reason and faith through an "essay towards a liberal Christian philosophy"[55] might well have appealed to Anthrakitis's mathematical sense and his enquiring mind. In any case, he provoked the wrath of the Peripatetics, who could not tolerate any deviations from strict Aristotelian doctrine and accused him of heresy.[56] Faced by the terrible prospect of ostracism and persecution, Anthrakitis was forced to submit a confession of Orthodox faith,[57] but this did not save him from excommunication. In 1723, he was condemned and anathematized by the Synod of the Ecumenical Patriarchate as a follower of the heresy of Miguel de Molinos.[58] Two years later his excommunication was rescinded, but he was allowed to return to teaching only on condition that he would not deviate from Peripatetic wisdom.

The most important document that has survived from this episode clearly suggests what the main issue at stake in Anthrakitis's drama was. In a letter he addressed to the municipal authorities of Ioannina from Constantinople, where he went to face the charges of the Synod, he noted:

> Consider whether they are moved by zeal of faith and whether they are inspired by the Holy Spirit, those who collect books of logic and physics and Euclid and other mathematical treatises and they set up fires in churchyards [. . .] and threw them in [. . .] as if they were Arius's heresies [. . .] these books which are studied by all the world and have nothing at all to do with the faith.

[. . .] After this they composed a confession for me to sign [. . .] and I retired
to reflect about it and knowing it to be against my conscience [. . .] I went
into hiding [. . .] Now they contemplate sending word throughout continental Greece to excommunicate and expel all teachers everywhere.[59]

Hence, Anthrakitis appealed to the lay notables of Ioannina to submit a
stern petition to the Synod declaring that, as far as the teacher of their
community was concerned, they would be satisfied if he was not a heretic
in matters of faith and if he was upright in his morals, but they did not care
whether he was a follower of Platonic or Aristotelian doctrine, whether a
student of ancient or modern philosophy.[60]

With this appeal, Anthrakitis formulated the claim of freedom of conscience and of intellectual inquiry for the first time in modern Greek cultural history. The issue arose in connection with the problem of educational
renewal, which was among the earliest manifestations of the will to Enlightenment. It was remarkable that Anthrakitis, in his struggle for intellectual
freedom and renewal, could turn for support to the lay communal leadership
of the two commercial cities where he had taught, Ioannina and Kastoria.[61]
The willingness of these local secular leaders to stand by him in his contest
with the Aristotelian conservatives over the control of local education, and
in his confrontation with the highest Church authorities, indicated the new
social alignments that were to fight the battle of the Enlightenment.

It seems that the battle was already on its way in the third decade of
the eighteenth century. Anthrakitis may have been forced to recant and,
on the evidence of a surviving manuscript of a text on logic he composed,
he seems to have gone back to conventional philosophical teaching,[62] but
with his follower Pachomios, things turned out otherwise. Pachomios, also
a monk, had studied with Anthrakitis, and he emerged as a militant critic
of Aristotelianism and a follower of Malebranche.[63] The sources refer to
him as an "extreme slanderer of Aristotle."[64] It appears, however, that in the
early 1720s, at about the time that Anthrakitis's own drama was acted out,
Pachomios had attracted a following in the major urban center and port
of the Balkans, Thessaloniki. These followers of the new critic of official
philosophy asked for a school to be created for him to teach in, alongside
the existing schools where Corydalist philosophy was taught. This episode
also points at incipient social and cultural cleavages in the making in Greek
society over the issue of intellectual change. The patriarchate once again

intervened, but Pachomios refused to capitulate. As a consequence, he was exiled by the Church authorities to Mount Athos.

Nevertheless, in the face of the disapproval of the traditional leadership and despite the occasional outburst of hostility on the part of intellectual conservatives, the signs of ideological change kept multiplying in the Greek world. The geography of the Enlightenment was gradually taking shape. Besides the triangle of the commercial cities of Northern Greece (Ioannina-Thessaloniki-Kastoria, with a northwestern outpost in Moschopolis), where the first drama of the Enlightenment versus the "powers of darkness" was acted out in the adventures of Anthrakitis and his followers, and the Danubian principalities where the transient introduction of Platonic teaching was suggestive of an intellectual reorientation that was later on to turn that area into the major center of the Neohellenic Enlightenment, a third region where the indications of intellectual change were unmistakable was the Ionian archipelago.

Spared the tribulations of Turkish conquest by a protracted Venetian occupation, the seven islands off the western coast of Greece had an immediate access to European learning through their effective integration into the social and cultural life of Italy. Having escaped Ottoman captivity, the Ionian Islands were the only part of the Greek world with an integrally Western culture, as is immediately apparent from local traditions of art, literature, and music. Despite the repressive character of Venetian rule, it was natural that some of the stirrings of cultural innovation should be felt in the islands of the Ionian Sea. A British visitor to the islands in the middle of the eighteenth century, Alexander Drummond, was fascinated to find that modern mathematics and experimental physics attracted great interest among educated men and that Locke, Clarke, and Gravesande were well known and admired in learned circles on Zakynthos.[65] This outlook dominated the circle around the chief priest of Zakynthos, Antonios Katiphoros (1685–1763). Katiphoros had been educated in Italy and taught at the Greek College in Venice (the Flanginian School). His education in philosophy was broadened by his travels, which gave him the opportunity to meet some important figures of his period, among them Frederick II of Prussia. In Amsterdam, where he lived for a time, he probably became acquainted with the ideas of John Locke. He finally settled in his native island and acquired renown as a teacher of philosophy. His most famous putative student, Evgenios Voulgaris, had special praise for him in his survey of the state of contemporary Greek philosophy: he was exceptionally distinguished by the fullness of his erudition in all forms of discourse.[66]

Katiphoros stated his own views on Greek reeducation in the dedicatory epistle that prefaced his *Most Exact Greek Grammar*. That address to the leader of the Greek community of Venice conveyed a sense of the logic of Greek cultural revival already fledgling in Katiphoros's perception in the fourth decade of the eighteenth century. The leader of the Greek community of Venice, characteristically a merchant from Ioannina, was hailed as a pioneer in the Greek effort at cultural revival, of which the most constructive manifestations were the new schools recently endowed by the mercantile diaspora. Katiphoros's ambition for his new grammar, which consciously departed from the tradition of the medieval grammars of Laskaris and Gazis, was to see it introduced as a textbook in the new schools established under the aegis of the Greek commercial notables of Venice. They were seen as the leaders of the current of social and cultural change that the Greek communities abroad transmitted to Ottoman Greece. Katiphoros vividly sensed in his own day a rekindling of interest in the sciences, which had for a long time been exiled from Greece by the misfortunes of the nation. And he knew that it was a forward-looking and renovating spirit that animated the new movement of things. His own approach to grammar was consciously innovative, contrary to the prevailing conventions. This he did not feel to be in the least improper or out of place since he thought that it would make learning more effective.[67] "Because, although in matters of faith every innovation or mutation would be dangerous and soul-destroying, precisely the opposite was the case in the sciences."[68] The separation of learning from religion and the affirmation of the pursuit of novelty in science were decisive components of the will to intellectual change. The road to the Enlightenment was now open.

Katiphoros was not the only exponent of the new outlook in the Ionian Islands. In the neighboring island of Cephalonia, Vikentios Damodos (1700–1752), a pupil of Katiphoros at the Flanginian School (1716–1719) and doctor of law at the University of Padua (1721), had, after a brief period practicing law at Argostoli, retired to his native village, Havriata, and founded a school (1721) where for two generations he taught the principles of philosophy and composed a complete corpus of philosophical works. In the externals of his philosophy, Damodos did not depart from the forms and methodology of Corydalist Aristotelianism. But in nuances of emphasis and especially in his adoption of the vernacular language as the medium of his philosophy, his will to change became transparent. In this he was probably influenced by the climate of the Flanginian School and by Katiphoros. In the corpus of his work (most of which remained unpublished), a shift in emphasis from the Corydalists' insistence on logic and physics to ethics is perceptible. As against their overzealous reliance on the authority of Aristotle, in Damodos's work one finds a recurring, almost ever-present appeal to natural right reason. He defined it as that "light of knowledge which we received from nature"[69] that constitutes the fundamental difference between metaphysics and religion, which is based on revelation. Although his appeal to right reason and his discussion of natural law, especially in his *Synopsis of Moral Philosophy,* is not always distinguishable from that of more rigid Scholasticism, Damodos felt that he ought to differentiate his philosophical position from that of the Peripatetics. Although he proposed to expound logic following Aristotle, he was not of the opinion that he should feel constrained by Peripatetic views and proclaim them to the world as unconditionally true. His intention was to outline with due brevity only those rules that were sufficient for the logical conduct of the mind.[70]

These timid indications of a distancing from Aristotelianism, however, are not what give Damodos the stamp of the innovator. Over and above the shifts of emphasis in his published work, it is the unequivocal testimony of his unpublished writings that place him in the ranks of the pioneers of philosophical renewal. Recent research has restored this unpublished work and has established Damodos's identification with the philosophy of the Moderns and his orientation toward Cartesian rationalism.[71] If he taught these texts to his pupils at Havriata on Caphalonia, using the vernacular as his medium of instruction, moreover, this teaching was certainly one of his pioneering contributions to the creation of the appropriate philosophical framework for liberal thought in Neohellenic education and culture. This section of his work remained unknown, while, in contrast, those writings that were closer to the subject, methods, and spirit of Aristotelianism were chosen for publication shortly after his death—a clear indication of the processes of social control that determined the course followed by intellectual renewal.

There is a sense of social utility underlying Damodos's conception of the philosophical vocation. His quest for right reason, his striving to distill from the erudition of Aristotelianism only those rules that would be adequate for logical reasoning, derived from his desire to be useful to "all sorts of men" in his nation. This line of reasoning led him to select the "ordinary language" as the linguistic tool for his philosophy.[72] The liberal motivation reflected in these views was substantive as well as formal. In the *Moral Philosophy,* which was only published almost two centuries after his death, Damodos argued explicitly against despotic authority both in the household and in the community. The husband's authority in the family could not be arbitrary, but had to conform to certain norms of justice; likewise, the authority of the patriarch and the bishops was bound by the rules of civil society, and if a bishop issued an unjust command, the people had the right to resist.[73] This perspective on social relations, both in the private world of the family and in public life, which, for the Greek subjects of the Ottoman Empire, was mainly the sphere of the Church, might echo philosophical opinions that Damodos had heard during his education in Italy and that he adapted to the circumstances of Greek society. A strand of moral opinion with decisively political import was thus transmitted into Greek thought with the first gropings for intellectual emancipation from conventional intellectual authority.

Damodos's teaching was confined to a limited circle of students. Isolated as he was in his insular village, he remained almost unnoticed by his contemporaries, though after his death his work became widely disseminated, judging by the large number of manuscripts by which it has been transmitted.[74] Evgenios Voulgaris, however, writing a few years after Damodos's death, made no mention of his fellow Ionian Islander in his survey of modern Greek philosophy.[75] Voulgaris's silence probably reflects his disapproval of Damodos's views on the language question. In any event, Damodos's isolation in a rural community on the island was symptomatic of the conditions under which the syndrome of cultural change was set in motion. The three regions, where the origins of intellectual change in the Greek world could be traced early in the eighteenth century, experienced the first stirrings of Enlightenment quite independently of each other, as the result of concrete local conditions that provided a relevant context to the intellectual activity of men with a European education and a predilection for modern philosophy. At that early stage, which could be characterized as a pioneering phase of the Greek Enlightenment, the signs of intellectual change were limited to a few hearths in which the light of the new philosophy was lit, but which did not develop into overlapping circles that might provide the dynamic of a movement of cultural transformation. The potential for such development did not appear until the second, more determined generation of the Neohellenic Enlightenment emerged, for whom the cultural transformation of Greek society became a conscious objective and concrete program.

ENLIGHTENMENT PRESENCES

The most important representative of this new generation, and one of the towering figures of the Neohellenic Enlightenment as a whole, was still another native of the Ionian Islands, Evgenios Voulgaris (1716–1806). Born in Corfu, Voulgaris was, according to one testimony, a student of Anthrakitis in Ioannina before 1736,[76] and he possibly met Damodos on Cephalonia, which he visited in 1738.[77] Thus, even in his career as a student, Voulgaris provided those links that were needed in order to break the isolation of the various centers of the Enlightenment from each other. This characteristic was much more typical of his career as a teacher, which turned Voulgaris into the first articulate leader of the Enlightenment in Southeastern Europe.[78] His brilliance and erudition, his linguistic prodigy and competence in a wide range of disciplines, combined with his piety, which had led him at an early age into the celibate clergy impressed sufficiently the rich merchants from Ioannina who were settled in Venice to endow a modern school in their native city to which Voulgaris was appointed director sometime in the years 1742 or 1743. Thus, Voulgaris became a successor to Anthrakitis in the city, which by virtue of commercial and cultural ties with Venice, was developing into the cultural capital of Greece in the eighteenth century. At the new Maroutsaia School, Voulgaris taught modern science and rationalist philosophy. His teaching provoked the opposition of conservative elements entrenched in the educational establishment of the city, and Voulgaris was forced to move to Kozani in Western Macedonia, another area whose expanding overland trade with Central Europe brought tangible benefits to the cultural life of its cities. The intervention of the supporters of the Maroutsaia School led to Voulgaris's return to Ioannina from 1748 and 1752, when he was summoned by Patriarch Cyril V to assume the direction of the new academy founded on Mount Athos in 1749, on the initiative of the brotherhood of Vatopedi monastery. He taught there from

1753 to 1759 and had among his students several of the leading exponents of the Enlightenment in subsequent generations as well as some of their bitterest opponents.

Voulgaris's collision with the conservatives in the school and on the Holy Mountain[79] drove him to Constantinople, where the protection of the former prince of Moldavia, Gregory Ghikas, and of the pro-Russian Patriarch Seraphim II, enabled him to teach in the Patriarchal Academy from 1759 to 1762. His ideas encountered strong opposition there as well, and the accession of a new patriarch, Samuel I Chantzereis, who was suspicious of modern philosophy and a proponent of Aristotelianism, drove Voulgaris away in 1763. He left for the Danubian principalities and thence for Prussia, never to return to Greece.

In his twenty years of teaching in the Greek world, Voulgaris had brought the message of modern philosophy and science to the major centers of Greek learning and had presented a conception of the Enlightenment as the paradigm that should inform Greek reeducation. His own dynamism and the influence he acquired through his reputation, and through the propagation of his ideas by his students in the network of Greek schools in the Balkans and in Asia Minor, made the Enlightenment and its social and political implications appear as a credible option, relevant to the changing needs of Greek society under Ottoman rule in the eighteenth century. The Enlightenment, as a form of social consciousness and as an appropriate solution to the problems of Greek society and culture, owed to Evgenios Voulgaris its integration into the concerns of Greek intellectual life.

Voulgaris's specifically political solutions to the Greek problem were not articulated until later in the context of his mature political experiences at the court of Catherine II of Russia.[80] His philosophy of the Enlightenment, however, which had animated his teaching career and ideological controversies in Greece, was embodied in the works he published during his stay in Leipzig after his departure from Greece in the 1760s. In preparation of his publication projects, he apparently deepened his acquaintance with German rationalism, which constituted the major philosophical influence on his thought. Voulgaris's philosophy was informed by three fundamental principles of the Enlightenment: freedom of thought, rationalism, and faith in modern science. Although he always considered his work an integral part of a genuine tradition of Greek philosophy that comprised the philosophical heritage of classical Hellas, Christian patristic thought, and Byzantine philosophy, the foremost sources of his inspiration were the philosophical systems of the Moderns, notably Descartes, Locke, Leibniz, and Christian Wolff.[81] He used his immense erudition in ancient philosophy and Christian thought, which dominated the voluminous scholarly apparatus of his philosophical works, to support his novel arguments with an appeal to the legitimacy of traditional learning and accepted wisdom. His major philosophical work, the *Logic* he published in Leipzig in 1766, was an embodiment of this intellectual attitude. It seems that at the time he put the final touches to the text that had formed the basis of his earlier teaching and was already in wide circulation in manuscript copies, Voulgaris's attitude had evolved considerably. Having lived in two major centers of German rationalism, Leipzig and Halle, he appears to have absorbed to a considerable degree the secular values of the Enlightenment. In a letter describing his spiritual attitude at the time, he confessed that it was only the contiguity of his room with the local Greek Orthodox chapel that made him attend services: "living next door to the chapel I am in danger of becoming a friend of rituals."[82]

Despite all the respect he professed for Aristotle, his *Logic* was in purpose and in fact an indictment of conventional Neoaristotelianism. In Voulgaris's judgment it was the grip of Peripatetic philosophy over Greek thought that had sapped it of all creativity and had reduced it to heavy hibernation. Although the exponents of philosophy in the Greek East considered themselves Peripatetic, in fact they abstained from all intellectual peregrinations, and this immobility kept them away from true philosophy. In contrast to this state of things in the East, the nations of modern Europe had progressed marvelously in philosophy. This was the consequence of the abandonment of the champions of Scholasticism to their petty brawls and quarrels over empty words and the reorientation of European philosophy toward that type of eclecticism, which alone was acceptable to the lovers of true knowledge because it followed the dictates of right reason.[83] It was the emancipation of European philosophy from scholastic Aristotelianism, and the affirmation of the freedom of intellectual judgment by Bacon, Peter Ramus, Campanella, and others that made possible the appearance of Gassendi and Descartes, Galileo and Newton, Leibniz and Wolff, and all those who "caused philosophy to flourish more than ever before and to progress from strength to strength, and to enrich human life with plenty of knowledge, inventions and arts ignored by all previous ages."[84]

Modern philosophy had achieved all this because it uncompromisingly sought the truth and had as its only guide the quest of the light of reason. Philosophers, lovers of wisdom, were those who genuinely pursued truth and remained indifferent to the labels of philosophical sects, be they Peripatetic or Platonic, Ancient or Modern. In the spirit of true eclecticism, they gleaned from every nation and epoch and philosophical sect everything that they judged in line with sound philosophy, while discarding without prejudice all that was contrary to truth. The genuine philosopher of the Enlightenment was "an exact tracer of truth, an impartial critic of all reflection, an unwavering judge of all notions, holding philosophizing to be nothing else but to search for right reason."[85] This task could not be accomplished except in complete liberty of his opinion and the unfettered determination of his thought. Intellectual coercion is a much greater misfortune to the philosopher than physical slavery, the captivity of the body. Freedom in philosophy could not be accomplished if any standard of judgment other than right reason was used. Those who thought and judged not according to their own well-considered reflection, but in order to please others, could not be considered genuine philosophers by anyone.[86] Voulgaris's debt to Christian Wolff's embattled appeal on behalf of freedom to philosophize is obvious.[87] Voulgaris's plea for intellectual freedom was particularly directed to those who cherished the teaching of Plato and Aristotle. He felt that they could not be true to the spirit of these philosophers if they did not partake of their zeal for freedom in philosophical reflection. This would simply mean that only that part of Platonic and Aristotelian philosophy was acceptable that was judged and found in agreement with right reason. Their true follower should honor truth no less than the great Greek philosophers themselves did.[88]

The repudiation of authority, the affirmation of reason as the only standard of truth, and the uncompromising insistence on freedom of thought posed for Voulgaris the problem of the relation of philosophy to religion. He stressed that nothing that ran counter to the divine doctrines of the faith could be a genuine principle of sound philosophy.[89] At this point the limits to Evgenios's acceptance of the Enlightenment can clearly be discerned. The dilemma between the Enlightenment and Orthodoxy was resolved by positing a complete epistemological separation between philosophy and theology. The supernatural mysteries of religious dogma, being beyond the power of human comprehension, could not be subjected to philosophical investigation. These matters fell outside the province of reason and became known through revelation. Any kind of "philosophotheology" was an inappropriate pursuit in that it mingled things incompatible by their nature.[90] This attitude, which by separating religious doctrine from rational philosophy attempted to be true to both, involved a potential inner tension of which Voulgaris, as a philosopher and at the same time a devout Orthodox clergyman, appears to have remained unaware. His inspiration from German rationalism appears to have fortified him in this philosophical attitude. His reading in Christian Wolff comforted him. Leibniz had also stressed that Enlightenment is willed by God as a means toward the perfection of His human creatures and the advancement of the general good.[91] So Voulgaris's Christian conscience could not be disturbed by his advocacy of the Enlightenment so long as he drew the epistemological distinction between philosophy and religion, reason and revelation. On this point he appears to have missed the import of the philosophical presuppositions of Leibniz's attitude as he appears to have missed the practical implications of his own adoption of significant parts of Lockean epistemology.[92] Significantly, of the *Essay* he remarked: "the essay of the Englishman Locke, on human understanding, is greatly admired and widely consulted as an excellent guide to the right conduct of the mind."[93]

Another source of inner tension in Voulgaris's thought was his attitude on the language question. The problem of the language of Greek reeducation was one of the most controversial issues confronting the movement of the Enlightenment. The origins of the language question could be traced in the *diglossia,* the double-language that had emerged in Byzantine culture. It represented a split between the official language of the state, the Church, and formal intellectual life, which after the empire's linguistic and ethnic hellenization remained attached to ancient Greek usage in contrast with the changing language of the people among whom the use of a modern Greek vernacular was generalized by the tenth century. The new vernacular was recorded mostly in folk epic poetry and in the popular literature of the late Byzantine period. The preference for Attic Greek, however, was one of the issues that cut across the fierce ideological cleavages on the eve of the Fall of Constantinople among Byzantine men of letters. Ancient Greek remained the official language of the Church after the Fall, and it provided the linguistic medium of Corydalist philosophy. The first Phanariots were confirmed archaists. Alexandros Mavrokordatos used ancient Greek in his writings and in his letters, and he urged his sons to perfect their mastery of the ancient tongue.[94] Nikolaos Mavrokordatos remained faithful to his father's example and cloaked in ancient language even his affirmation of modern thought in *Philotheou Parerga*.

The only exception in this generalized use of ancient Greek among intellectual and social elites was represented by a remarkable tradition of ecclesiastical rhetoric that employed a simplified language comprehensible to the people—largely in response to Latin propaganda which always employed the vernacular—in order to make pastoral teaching more effective. This was one of the most constructive aspects of religious humanism and counted among its exponents some of the most distinguished and learned Greek Orthodox prelates since the end of the sixteenth century, reaching its culmination in the graceful eloquence of Ilias Miniatis at the turn of the seventeenth and eighteenth centuries.[95] Voulgaris, who gave to the tradition of religious humanism its broadest possible definition and guided it to the reception of the Enlightenment, regressed in the language question. He felt that modern vernacular did not possess the cultivation necessary to provide a suitable linguistic medium to philosophy. Therefore, those "booklets which pretend to philosophize in the vulgar tongue should be whistled at."[96] In this attitude Voulgaris regressed from the daring linguistic views of Katiphoros and especially of Damodos. In adopting it he may have been influenced by the example set by Christian Wolff and many other European academic philosophers among his contemporaries who used Latin in the composition of their works.

Wolff's arguments for the need of precision in the language of philosophy, which made it pertinent to retain some of the terms and usages of ancient philosophy, may have also influenced Voulgaris in his choice of archaism.[97] But in finding this methodological reason for his archaism, Voulgaris missed Wolff's strong caveat that the only purpose of philosophical style was to make the philosopher's meanings clear to the minds of others.[98] In adopting his impossible and artificial linguistic archaism, Voulgaris failed to achieve precisely that clarity necessary to philosophical style. This linguistic attitude gave to Voulgaris's Enlightenment a peculiarly aristocratic character for which he was to be severely criticized later by several of his successors in the leadership of the Greek Enlightenment.

Despite such incongruities, Voulgaris's philosophy was an unequivocal affirmation of the will to Enlightenment in Greek thought. This theoretical position found its practical expression in his teaching of modern philosophy and science. Besides his monumental *Logic,* in which he presented the philosophical doctrine of the Moderns as equally valid molds of wisdom as those of the Ancients,[99] he translated and taught Genovesi's *Metaphysics* and Gravesande's *Introduction to Philosophy,* Segner's *Elements of Mathematics,* and Tacquet's *Geometry.* These texts, which he used as the basis of his lectures during his teaching career in Greece, had circulated widely in manuscript copies as basic textbooks in Greek schools of higher learning throughout the second half of the eighteenth century.[100] They were published only much later, on the eve of Voulgaris's death, at the beginning of the nineteenth century. This belated publication was an important piece of evidence concerning both Voulgaris's continuing influence on Greek education fifty years after he retired from active teaching and also of the little progress that had been achieved in the production of teaching manuals after his departure. The same was true of his *Logic,* which continued to be copied and circulated in manuscript many years after its authoritative text was published in 1766.

For teaching purposes, associated particularly with his courses in philosophy at the Athonite Academy, Voulgaris attempted the first modern Greek translation of Locke's *Essay Concerning Human Understanding,* with which he had probably become acquainted as a result of studying Genovesi's metaphysics during his stay in Italy.[101] His pioneering contributions to the liberalization of Greek thought included the first translation of Voltaire, to whose *Des mensonges imprimés* he made a very complimentary reference in the *Logic.*[102] At a time when Voltaire was still alive and active in his controversies with the Church, Voulgaris rendered his *Memnon ou la sagesse humaine* in Greek verse.[103]

Two years later, Voulgaris was inspired by Voltaire's concerns and argumentation to take a truly monumental step, whereby he introduced into the Greek intellectual universe the idea of toleration. The occasion for this was provided by the publication in 1767 of Voltaire's *Essai historique et critique sur les dissensions des églises de Pologne,* which Voulgaris translated the following year, accompanied by his own extensive notes and comments in order to document the aggressive policy pursued by Rome and the Catholic Church against the other Christian confessions in Poland. Voulgaris's commentary clearly reveals his adherence to the principles of Orthodoxy, particularly when he is condemning Rome's attempts to impose on the Orthodox

Christians the decisions of the Council of Florence relating to the unification of the churches. His remarks on the episode of Meletios Typaldos, who, as archbishop of Philadelphia in charge of the ecclesiastical life of the Greek Confraternity of Venice, had accepted the principles of the pope, are particularly interesting. In the commentary, Voulgaris's attachment to Russian policy also becomes apparent for the first time.[104] To his edition of Voltaire's *Essai historique et critique,* Voulgaris appended his own "Essay on Religious Toleration" which, he informs the reader, "it seemed reasonable and necessary to add, as a subject that is frequently referred to, and which is of direct concern to the entire work here published."[105]

In his "Essay," Voulgaris sets forth in detail the reasons why "the forbearance that the Latins in our time call *tolerantia,* and which we may not inappropriately call *anexithreskeia*" is the proper attitude for all "pious souls" toward those who "set aside matters of faith," whom the faith, however, never allows us to treat "tyrannically and savagely and inhumanly."[106] In this way, the idea of freedom of religious conscience is associated with Christian piety, making it easier for the ethics common to the Enlightenment to be assimilated by the conscience of a Christian community. Voulgaris writes precisely from the point of view of a Christian community, and one of his main aims is accordingly to correct some of the excesses of which Voltaire is in his view guilty in the polemic against the Church expressed in the Frenchman's own *Essay on Religious Toleration* (1764). Essentially, Voulgaris attempts in his "Essay" to salvage the idea of religious toleration from what he considers to be Voltaire's excesses and make it familiar to the consciousness of believers by revealing its Christian content. Voulgaris's edition makes a highly important contribution in marking the first use of the text "religious toleration" in the Greek language. Voulgaris's introduction in Greek of both the idea and the term represents an important step by Greek thought along the road of Enlightenment. Thanks to Voulgaris, Greek thought now progressed from Wolff's appeal for freedom to philosophize to Voltaire's critique of the "powers of darkness" and appeared ready to follow in his crusade for religious toleration and freedom of thought.

Voulgaris's example was followed by his younger compatriot Nikiphoros Theotokis (1731–1800), whose career closely paralleled that of the senior man. Theotokis received his early education in the same intellectual milieu in their native Corfu. From 1749–1754 he studied medicine, mathematics, and physics at Padua and Bologna. Following a path common to the majority of intellectuals who aspired to a teaching career, he joined the ranks of the celibate clergy at a very early age. He taught at Corfu and in Constantinople and held the position of Director of the princely Academy of Jassy in the mid-1760s and again around 1775. He did not remain long in any of these positions, on account of the opposition to his scientific teaching on the part of conservative scholars and educators.[107]

His most important work, which deservedly earns him a place alongside Voulgaris as a founding father of the Enlightenment in Greek culture, is the *Elements of Physics,* which was published in Leipzig in the same year as Voulgaris's *Logic.* Theotokis's intellectual approach to his subject matter was marked by the pronounced liberal predisposition of the Enlightenment. He repudiated *ipse dixit* as an intellectually acceptable manner of proof and stressed that the only sound method of procedure in scientific research was free reflection on the data accumulated by reason, experience, and scientific codification.[108] It was with the guidance of such methodological presuppositions that he intended to make his contribution to the reeducation of his compatriots in the sciences of the Enlightenment. The lively awareness of the pressing need of far-ranging reeducation of his compatriots also dictated the choice of a simpler stylistic and linguistic approach to the presentation of the subject matter: in this matter, Theotokis consciously followed the example laid down by "the modern Writers in the Sciences"; for them, clarity and effective communication were the imperatives in the presentation of scientific material, and to this end the commonly intelligible simple style and diction had to be used.[109] In the main body of his work the language is simpler and closer to that used in everyday speech than it is in the prefatory addresses, which were intended to be read by princes and accordingly had to preserve the conventions of the socially acceptable. In this regard, Theotokis took a step beyond Voulgaris on the language question by recognizing the practical need to widen the audience and readership of Enlightenment culture if the efforts at intellectual renewal were to be successful.

Nikiphoros Theotokis also took a step beyond Evgenios Voulgaris on another critical ideological issue, which in the debates of the period concerning the nature of the universe touched in practice upon the question of whether or not to embrace the essence of the Enlightenment. This was the issue of the movement of the earth and acceptance of the heliocentric theory of the universe, which in the middle of the eighteenth century was a highly contentious, ideologically difficult issue in Greek culture, on account of the Church's official subscription to the geocentric theory. This stance was another product of the amalgamation of Orthodox theology with Neoaristotelianism in the eighteenth century and prevented men of learning who were fully cognizant of modern scientific theories, such as Chrysanthos Notaras and Vikentios Damodos, from openly professing the views of Copernicus, Galileo, and Newton, because they believed that they contradicted the theory of creation formulated in the Old Testament. Evgenios Voulgaris himself, for all his broad learning in matters of modern philosophy and science, remained irresolute on this, and despite the intellectual difficulty he felt in continuing to accept the Ptolemaic view, did not venture to declare himself unreservedly in favor of the Copernican system, but sought refuge in the compromise theory propounded by Tycho Brahe.[110] Nikiphoros Theotokis, in contrast, though distancing himself in his phrasing, for reasons of self-protection, was courageous enough to assert publicly that in physics and cosmology he supported the Moderns "regarding the movement of the Earth as a bare hypothesis."[111] In his account of the various theories and arguments relating to this in the main body of his book, this "bare hypothesis" is virtually the only subject discussed, confirming the author's predilection for it. The *Elements of Physics* is essentially an account of Newtonian physics with detailed references to the theory of inertia and to the force of attraction between bodies, which includes references to and rejections of rival scientific theories—not, of course, those of the supporters of the Ptolemaic system, but those held by the Cartesians. It is indicative of Theotokis's views that the longest chapter in the book is the one "Concerning Gravity," which even includes an account of the experimental confirmation of the law of gravity by Galileo and Newton.[112]

Theotokis's boldness in teaching the heliocentric system and publishing a treatise on Newtonian physics can best be appreciated by contrasting his initiatives with the case of the modern philosopher Nikolaos Zerzoulis (1706–1772/3) who, along with Voulgaris and Theotokis, was assigned by a contemporary observer to the trinity of "the leading men of learning" of the Greek people, "all three [being] capable of writing and lecturing with accuracy on any science."[113] Zerzoulis had studied mathematics and philosophy in Italy and composed a treatise on Newtonian physics, adapting the work of the Dutch natural scientist Musschenbroek. He did not dare, however, or did not find the necessary support, to publish his physics, or any other of his works recording his disputes with the "peripatetic" philosophers of his day. This failure and the disappearance of Zerzoulis's manuscript mark the limits of the receptivity of Greek society to the intellectual pursuits of modernity.[114]

The place occupied by Nikiphoros Theotokis as a pioneering exponent of the scientific spirit of the Enlightenment in Greek culture possesses a complex symbolism. On the one hand, it was Theotokis, through his writings, who introduced into Greek education and culture, with considerable clarity, the identification of the bearer of the Enlightenment preeminently with the student of science, that is, with the professional natural scientist and mathematician, as a distinct intellectual presence shaped by the "scientific revolution" of the seventeenth century. In addition to the *Elements of Physics*, Theotokis also had to his credit other scientific writings, treatises on mathematics and geography, which he presumably wrote for the needs of his pupils and which were widely circulated in manuscript form before being published later on.[115] Alongside this scientific identity, however, by which he is mainly known to students of the Enlightenment, Theotokis consistently devoted himself throughout his entire life to another intellectual pursuit: the writing and publication of a series of theological works of a catechetic, parenetic, and apologetic character, and also to the editing of patristic texts. Remarkably, these two sides of his career as writer and editor run parallel and are not ascribable to distinct phases of his intellectual development. This suggests that in his conscience they formed a single intellectual entity, in which different factors in the human intellectual experience were interwoven. It was on this compound of diverse intellectual experiences that the Greek Enlightenment was based in its beginnings, before internal tensions became apparent in the form of dramatic moral dilemmas in the subsequent history of cultural change.

GEOGRAPHICAL AND CHRONOLOGICAL PERSPECTIVES

With Voulgaris and Theotokis the intellectual presuppositions of liberal thought were introduced into Greek culture. The earlier gropings of rationalism in Greek thought finally found their articulation in a theory of Enlightenment. This provided the matrix of cultural change for which the more dynamic and forward-looking segments of Greek society yearned. Certain structural parameters of the movement of Greek Enlightenment emerge from the foregoing examination of the initial manifestations of this process of reorientation of Greek culture and need only to be spelled out. A first salient dimension of the process of intellectual change was its geographical pattern in the Greek world. The areas where cultural renovation was initiated have already been identified: the Ionian Islands, the Danubian principalities, and the triangle formed by Ioannina, Thessaloniki, and the cities of Northwestern Macedonia, extending as far north as the city of Moschopolis in Northern Epirus, which flourished as a cultural center in the early and middle decades of the eighteenth century. Politically these regions were fundamentally different from each other. The Ionian Islands were a Venetian territory up to 1797 when, upon the dissolution of the Serenissima Republic of Saint Mark, they passed to a succession of other European powers, beginning with revolutionary France. The Danubian principalities of Moldavia and Wallachia were under Ottoman suzerainty, but their location as a borderland between three antagonistic empires (Ottoman, Hapsburg, and Russian) had secured them a special political status of local autonomy under the rule of princes (hospodars) appointed by the Sublime Porte. The position of hospodar, held by native Romanian aristocratic dynasties until 1709, passed in that year to Nikolaos Mavrokordatos and alternated for the next century (until 1821) among eight Phanariot Greek and one Romanian noble families. Under the rule of the Phanariot princes, the principalities developed into major centers of the Greek diaspora with compact Greek settlements in their cities and experienced remarkable cultural progress. Finally, the third region of cultural change in Epirus-Western Macedonia was politically in the heartland of the Ottoman domains in the Balkans. What these disparate political and geographical regions had in common was, first, their distance from the seat of Ottoman power and its institutional appendage, the see of the Ecumenical Patriarchate, which was the center of gravity in the traditional power structure of the Orthodox community. It was the distance from the centers of established authority in Constantinople that enabled the first stirrings of the Enlightenment to surface in these regions. Distance in space, however, was a necessary geographic condition of the survival, but not a sufficient condition for the emergence of the Enlightenment. This was provided by another geographical factor, the proximity or access these regions enjoyed to important areas of European civilization: the Ionian Islands and Ioannina to Northern Italy, especially Venice; the Danubian principalities to Austria and the German states; Western Macedonia to Central Europe through active overland trade. It was these ties, mostly economic, cultural, and social, and in the case of the Ionian Islands, the integral bonds of direct political rule by a European republic, that provided the channels through which the influences of European thought and the ideas of the Enlightenment were transmitted to the Greek world.

An extension of the geographical basis of the Greek Enlightenment comprised the centers of the Greek diaspora in the cities of Western and Central Europe. A Greek colony existed in Venice since the end of the Middle Ages, and its membership was repeatedly replenished by immigrants from Greek islands under Venetian or Genoese rule and by successive waves of refugees as these territories fell to the Turks (Chios in 1566, Cyprus in 1571, Crete in 1669). Venice, one of the capitals of European humanism, had been a center of Greek letters since the Renaissance, and this tradition was preserved by successive generations of Greek intellectuals who belonged to the local Greek colony. Through its close commercial and cultural ties with the Greek East, which with the contraction of Venetian power in the eighteenth century were centered primarily in the Ionian Islands and the neighboring Western coast of Greece, Venice provided the major link between the Greek world and modern Europe. Of particular significance for Greek culture was the establishment in 1662 of a Greek institution of higher learning, the Flanginian School, which became in the subsequent century and a half the major stepping stone for Greeks pursuing higher education. Thus, most of the major representatives of the Greek Enlightenment passed at one point or other through Venice and participated in the intellectual life of the Greek colony. Venice was in addition the major center of Greek printing in the entire period of Ottoman rule, when the operation of Greek presses within the Ottoman Empire was either prohibited or, when permitted, precarious and short lived. Between the seventeenth and the beginning of the nineteenth century, three Greek printing houses operated in Venice (established in 1670, 1685, and 1755 respectively), and most Greek books were printed there.[116]

Around the middle of the eighteenth century, Greek merchants established colonies in Vienna and Trieste. The new communities were soon chartered by the Hapsburg emperor. They both became major centers of Greek economic and cultural activity. Most of the intellectual production of the Greek Enlightenment in terms of publication of books took place in the triangle formed by Vienna and the two Adriatic cities. Further west, Greek commercial communities, which developed into centers of intellectual life as well, existed in Amsterdam, Marseilles, and Paris. In Central Europe, especially in the cities of Hungary, a veritable Balkan Orthodox microcosm using Greek as the medium of communication had been planted as the consequence of the mobility generated by the overland trade of Western Macedonia. A network of Greek schools and libraries was created to meet the intellectual needs of these new communities. Finally, further East, the Greek diaspora extended into the new lands opened by the Russian conquests of the eighteenth century on the northern coast of the Black Sea, and the city of Odessa became the seat of a major Greek colony. These communities, especially those of the West, brought Greek culture in direct contact with modern European civilization and the thought of the Enlightenment and became the primary channels of transmission of the new ideas and experiences into the Greek world.

The geographical pattern of the Greek Enlightenment points at its sociological dimension as well. The regions in which novel ideas and imported cultural outlooks could find a certain receptivity were those where new social groups had emerged as a result of incipient changes in relations of production and exchange in local society. The emergence of new social groups in the structure of traditional society with new needs and interests made it possible for the exponents of the new ideology to find local supports: first, in their initiatives at intellectual innovation and, next, in their confrontation with traditional learning and ideology. The cases of both Anthrakitis and Voulgaris are indicative of the coincidence of purposes and interests between the intellectual representatives of the Enlightenment and the new groups of reforming princes and magistrates, merchants, traders, and local urban notables that sprang from the mutations in the rigid lines of social structures in Ottoman society. This coincidence that strikes one's attention in the earlier phases of the Enlightenment did not obviously involve any kind of one-to-one mechanistic correspondence in all cases. The social nexus of such associations became much more complicated later on.

The delineation of the sociological dimension of the movement of Enlightenment inescapably touches on differentiations that were observable on a temporal scale. Tracing the chronological dimension of the process of cultural change to its origins in the first inchoate gropings of the rationalist outlook points to the fact that, contrary to what was commonly believed concerning the lethargy of modern Greek thought until the beginning of the nineteenth century, the protracted intellectual process that led to the Enlightenment was already in the making at the time, characterized by Paul Hazard as the period of crisis in European conscience. This reorientation was unmistakably manifest in Greek culture in the second and third decades of the eighteenth century. The period through the 1760s witnessed the gradual growth of the movement. From original timidity, inarticulate purposes, and local isolation, Greek innovative thinking converged on the elaboration of the philosophical presuppositions of liberal thought by the time the first fully articulate generation of the Greek Enlightenment had attained maturity and made its intellectual attitude felt in Greek culture. Thus, if the first gropings of innovation make Anthrakitis and Katiphoros, Damodos and Nikolaos Mavrokordatos the intellectual precursors of the Enlightenment, the clear articulation of the will to Enlightenment by Voulgaris, Theotokis, and Zerzoulis turned them into its first and by then fully self-conscious generation. Voulgaris was the central figure in the new tradition: in his capacity as a student, he was connected organically to the early generation of pioneers, and he was the undisputed teacher of the second generation.

The early 1770s marked the critical watershed in the development of the movement. Major international events (the Russo-Turkish wars of 1768–1774 and the Treaty of Kuchuk Kainardji) set a new context for the intensification of domestic social and cultural change, which was effectively abetted by the transnational forces of commerce and demographic movements.[117] In the next fifty years, two more generations of the Neohellenic Enlightenment emerged. The second generation was made up of students of Voulgaris: Iosipos Moisiodax and Christodoulos Pamplekis, who were joined by Dimitrios Katartzis, the most splendid representative of the Phanariot Enlightenment. The third generation that brought the movement to full maturity was diffused widely in the Greek world both within Ottoman Greece and in the diaspora, but the basic pattern of direct intellectual parentage with the previous generation persisted in the mainstream of the movement. Grigorios Constantas and Daniel Philippidis, Rhigas Velestinlis and Constantinos Stamatis could all be considered disciples of Moisiodax and Katartzis. They formed what could be described as the Danubian group of the third generation of the Greek Enlightenment since their ideas were formed in the intellectual milieu of the principalities. The Greek intelligentsia of Vienna was an extension of this group, to which two other circles have

Centers of traditional learning

Hearths of Enlightenment culture

MOLDAVIA

Jassy

WALLACHIA

Bucharest

SERBIA

Constantino

Moschopolis

Thessaloniki

Kastoria   Kozani

Siatista

Ambelakia

Athonite
Academy

Kydonies

Metsovo

Zagora

Corfu   Ioannina   Tirnavos

Milies

ASIA MIN

Agrapha

GREECE

Chios

Smyrna

AEGEAN SEA

Athens

Cefalonia/Havriata

Zante

Patmos

Dimitsana

Siphnos

IONIAN SEA

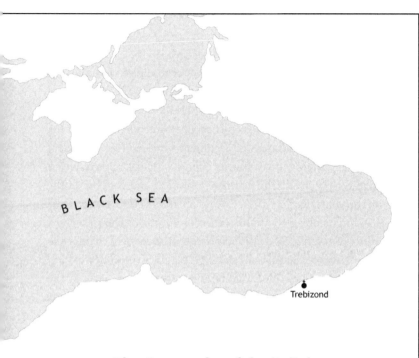

BLACK SEA

Trebizond

The Geography of the Enlightenment in Southeastern Europe

The emergence of schools of modern learning in the traditional educational centers of the Orthodox East delineates the geography of ideological conflict in the Greek world in the period 1800–1821

CYPRUS

Nicosia

Limassol

to be added in order to complete the survey of the Enlightenment's third generation: one centered on Paris around Adamantios Korais and the other centered on Ioannina around Athanasios Psalidas.

Out of these intellectual circles emerged younger disciples and followers of the Enlightenment who manned new schools and carried the message of the new ideas throughout the Greek world. It should be stressed that the crusade of the Enlightenment was not a cultural phenomenon limited to the Greek diaspora or to peripheral areas of Ottoman Greece. The movement was initiated in those outlying areas, but its effects were felt with intensity within the captive society itself. The ultimate ambition and purpose of the intelligentsia of the diaspora was the creation of intellectual centers and mechanisms that might bring the lights into the bosom of their enslaved homeland. In this they were to a considerable extent successful. Under the inspiration and guidance of the Parisian circle of Korais, a major new region was added to the geography of the Enlightenment in the very heart of the Ottoman Empire, centering on the triangle formed by the cities of Smyrna and Kydonies (Ayvalik) on the western coast of Asia Minor and the island of Chios. This was the most important although by no means the only case of the introduction of the Enlightenment in a hitherto closed area of Greek culture, which, on account of its close proximity to Constantinople, had been a bastion of traditional education and ecclesiastical learning until the early nineteenth century. The manifestations of intellectual and cultural change in this region, especially after the decline of the neighboring school on Patmos, which had earlier in the eighteenth century been a major center of Orthodox learning, may be regarded as the high point of the Enlightenment within the Greek-speaking geographical space. In the old Greek heartlands that also remained under the shadow of despotism, certain intellectuals of the diaspora managed to set up new model educational and cultural institutions for the intellectual reeducation of their native regions. Such initiatives were successfully undertaken in the flourishing villages of Mount Pilion and the area around Ambelakia in Thessaly, in Athens, and even in some towns and villages in the highlands of the central Peloponnese, among which Dimitsana was the most notable case.

As a consequence of the creation of the new schools, a reading public of the literature of the Enlightenment emerged within Greek society.[118] These readers of the literature of the Enlightenment, about whom we are rather well informed by subscriber lists in many books published between 1750 and 1820, were the most articulate and self-conscious segment of the new social strata produced by the long century of economic change that had been punctuated by a variety of novel commercial, manufacturing, and maritime activities. These developments had broken the isolation of traditional Greek society and led to increasing contacts with the dynamic and innovative societies and cultures of modern Europe. The changing needs, interests, and awareness of the new social groups provided the dynamic behind the movement that clamored for the transformation of Greek society. The intellectuals of the Enlightenment, especially of its later generations, emerged from the ranks of these new social groups for whom they acted, broadly speaking, as spokesmen. The emergence of the secular intelligentsia of the Enlightenment, who came from the mercantile classes and tended to supplant the earlier learned clergymen as the intellectual leaders of Greek society, is characteristic of the cultural changes that took place at the dawn of the nineteenth century.

The various groups and centers of the Enlightenment were far from isolated from each other. As true cosmopolites, the members of the third generation of the Greek Enlightenment moved continuously from one cultural center to another—except for Korais who, after settling in Paris in 1788, did not move from there for more than four decades. In addition to geographical mobility, the different groups were well aware of each other's ideas and intellectual activities through a variety of communication channels. Toward the close of the period, with the emergence of a lively periodical press, their channels of intellectual communication were regularized. In a very real sense, Greek culture acquired in this way its own "little flock of philosophes"[119] who were intensely conscious of themselves and of their mission and felt that they were an integral part of the cosmopolitan intelligentsia of the European Enlightenment.

There was a certain inner logic in this unfolding of the culture of the Enlightenment that is perceptible only retrospectively in a panoramic survey of the century of social and intellectual change in its entirety. The initial change in the philosophical presuppositions that had provided the context and parameters of thinking in the motionless centuries of certitude and faith had a direct implication for educational practice. New systems of instruction and a new philosophy of education were needed in order to transmit and put into practice the requirements of the new philosophy. Educational reform, by tampering with the established system of the transmission of

culture and the socialization of youth into the prevailing social consciousness, opened Pandora's Box. Change in the school meant cultural innovation in multiple contexts, and this had the most far-reaching implications
for society as a whole. These implications were naturally not lost on the
representatives of the established order, those who stood to lose if the state
of things was put to question. Obstacles were thus inevitably encountered
by cultural innovation, and this made its proponents, all those who did not
have any stakes in existing social and cultural structures, aware of the social
constraints confronting their effort. Consciousness of constraints precipitated social criticism, which was intensified as opposition became more
determined. The basic stakes in the conflict were thus gradually redefined
from an initial plea for educational reorientation to an eventual crusade in
the thirty years leading up to 1821 that put to question the basic structure
of society, the shape of the body politic, and the legitimate content of collective conscience. As the traditional order rigidified its stands toward the
claims of the Enlightenment, an alternative conception of things in the
shape of the moral revolution of republicanism marked the culmination
of the process of ideological change. That final stage could be regarded as
the Greek version of the "democratic Enlightenment" marking the closing
decades of the eighteenth century.[120] In the space of a century of change and
conflict, Greek consciousness, by reexamining itself and its social milieu
in the light of the secular ideas of the Enlightenment, achieved a transition from one stage to another. The following chapters trace this transition
by reconstructing the intellectual processes and the cultural dynamics that
contributed to it and charted its course.

CHAPTER TWO

The Formation of Modern Greek Historical Consciousness

THE "CONQUEST OF THE HISTORICAL WORLD" was an integral part of the intellectual experience of the Enlightenment. This intellectual achievement, however, presupposed the superseding of historical Pyrrhonism, which had undermined the earlier view of history during the initial phase of the Enlightenment, which coincided with the "crisis of the European conscience." The beginnings of historical criticism were associated with profound skepticism, with regard not only to Greek and Roman mythology, but also to the chronological accuracy of the Holy Scriptures, in consequence of which the traditional narratives of the past began to be perceived as frivolous tales. This assessment ultimately led to a different perception of time and a reexamination of the past from a new perspective. The reinterpretation of human actions and social phenomena occurred alongside the demythologization of natural phenomena by the new natural science. The intelligibility of the human past on the basis of logical criteria thus emerged as a specific component of the epistemological reconstruction achieved in the philosophy of the Enlightenment.[1]

The elimination of God secured independence to history, just as the "scientific revolution" of the seventeenth century had made natural science an autonomous intellectual sphere. Christian eschatology gave way to the teleology of reason. From the moment that the mythical account of the salvation of the world, as perceived by Bossuet, became lost in the labyrinth of events, the Enlightenment was able to develop its own approach to the study of the past. The new historiography was no longer concerned with the history of the Church and of the wars of empires. Hagiography, in both its religious and its secular guise, became irrelevant, and the history of great men was replaced by a new form of cultural and social history. This redefinition of the values of historical knowledge was largely the work of Voltaire and Montesquieu.

The new approach to the understanding of the past entailed an extension of the field of history. Enumeration of impressive events and prophetic and heroic narrative yielded to the analysis of culture and morals and was replaced by an attempt to understand the workings of societies and polities through a comprehension of their activating spirit.[2] The pursuit of this understanding was not disinterested. Historical knowledge was not an end in itself. Science had demonstrated that knowledge of the nature of things might have practical applications. The study of history might prove useful primarily by contributing to the creation of new forms of collective consciousness. It might teach how society works, but more importantly it might pinpoint the delusion, folly, and blind prejudices that were at the root of the decline of empires and the corruption of societies, as Gibbon was to demonstrate in exemplary fashion.

When, therefore, the investigation of the past uncovered evidence that called into question the conventional, long-accepted order of things, historical criticism became overtly subversive. In Italy, the writing of history in the hands of Giannone became a tool of social and religious criticism and, toward the end of the eighteenth century, historiography in Spain inaugurated the tradition of Spanish liberalism.[3] To these specific examples of the spirit of the new history could be added many examples from Greek historiography in the eighteenth century.

LEGACIES OF HISTORICAL CULTURE

The emergence of a secular historical consciousness among the modern Greeks followed a course shaped by the cultural heritage and the intellectual and political conditions prevailing in Greek society in the eighteenth century. The deeper logic of this process, however, was associated with the "dawn of the Hellenic day," as noted by Constantinos Koumas in the earliest review of Enlightenment historiography that we possess.[4] The whole movement of modern Greek historiography in the eighteenth century, reflecting the influences and stages that went into the making of the new history, adapted to the preconditions of a particular cultural context the cognitive aspirations of the historical theory of the Enlightenment and its implications for the redefinition of collective identity.

In attempting to trace this process of intellectual redefinition, the point of departure should be an examination of the ideas and content of traditional chronicles. These sources continued to be printed and widely read throughout the eighteenth and into the nineteenth century. They contained the elements that went into the making of the conventional attitude to the past, which was determined by religion, and shaped the traditional sense of time. They can therefore be studied as the registers of a certain consciousness of the past bequeathed by the tradition of centuries; they formed the background against which the process of secular historization had to develop.

The most broadly circulated of these chronicles was the so-called *Historical Book,* attributed pseudonymously to Dorotheos, nonexistent metropolitan of Monemvasia.[5] First published in 1631, it was reprinted at least twenty-four times by 1818. In the prefatory address, devout Orthodox Christian readers were instructed about the value of the study of the past as a source of moral direction. "History" was considered useful not only because it taught how to edify one's morals and how to govern one's household, but also because it showed how to command fortresses and rule the world in ways pleasing to the Lord. The purpose of this tradition of popular chronicles was to instill the "fear of God" in the masses of devout folk.[6] This objective was clearly reflected in the cast of the narrative in the vernacular, which could be readily understood by all even though they lacked training in classical Greek, which was the language of formal education and earlier historiography.

The main body of the book was taken up by biblical history. In the structuring of their content, the chronicles of the Ottoman period continued a much earlier Byzantine tradition. Narratives drawn from the Old Testament were followed up by the history of the ancient Hebrews down to their wars with other ancient Middle Eastern peoples and the history of Alexander's empire. In this way a piece of Greek history was interjected into the narrative of sacred history. It is noteworthy that Greek history did not appear until the Hellenistic period, which marked its intersection with ancient Hebraic history. Indeed, the focus of the narrative on Hellenistic history remained on such matters of concern to devout minds as the translation of the Scriptures and the condition of the Jews. The narrative continued with Roman history and the history of the Eastern Roman Empire from the foundation to the Fall of Constantinople and went on with the history of the Ottoman sultans and the expansion of their empire down to the time of the composition of the chronicle. Each new edition usually carried an updating of the narrative to the time of the reigning sultan. Ecclesiastical history received detailed attention throughout. Ancient Greece and her civilization remained beyond the chronicle's horizon, while the rule of the Christian Roman emperors and the Ottoman sultans in Constantinople was seen as one uninterrupted and natural sequence. The reigns of Christian kings and Ottoman sultans unfolded as a predictable unity, reflecting the order of the world and forming the temporal sequel to the biblical origins of history. The only occurrences that disturbed this almost halcyon sense of the past and precipitated some mild indignation or a critical comment were the scandals in the bosom of the Church that might upset the order of things.[7]

An outlook similar to that of the *Historical Book* was reflected in another chronicle first published in the seventeenth century and frequently reprinted throughout the eighteenth, *An Abridgement of Hierocosmic History,* written by Nektarios of Crete, the learned patriarch of Jerusalem (1602–1676).[8] The writing of history advanced two things, the reader was told in the preface. First, it preserved a memory of the deeds of the people of old; second, the knowledge of those deeds taught subsequent generations how to govern their transitory lives. In contrast to ancient pagan authors who had described the greatness of states and kingdoms and the wars of nations and kings, aiming at stimulating admiration for human virtue, the purpose of history had now been redefined: it was not concerned with the deeds of men, but with the miracles of divine providence and power through which one attained future beatitude.

The transcendental preoccupation obscured any sense of secular historical time. The outward dimension of political history was put forth without any questions concerning its logic or purpose. Politically, there was an essential identification with the Ottoman monarchy. Referring to the Ottoman conquest of the Middle East in the sixteenth century, the author, viewing developments from the vantage point of Jerusalem, rejoiced at the victories of the sultan that had finally returned those areas to the scepter of the Queen of the Cities. Thus, the confusion and turmoil of centuries had come to an end, and peace was restored in the region that comprised the holy places of the faith. Not for a moment did it occur to the pious author's mind that the Queen of the Cities, to whose sway Palestine and Arabia had resubmitted through the Ottoman conquest, was herself held captive by an alien non-Christian power. One finds here an expression of the identification of the leadership of Greek society with Ottoman rule, evident also in the Phanariots' attitude.

Greek history was conspicuously absent from the *Abridgement* as it had been from the *Historical Book*. A passing reference was made to Ptolemaic rule in Egypt, only because it fitted into the unfolding cosmological scheme that encompassed the Creation, biblical Hebraic history, the Hellenistic and Roman rulers of the ancient Hebrews, and the Christian Roman Empire. A sense of belonging to a collectivity denoted by "we Greeks" surfaced in the text, only in order to stress their religious distinction from the heretical Latin Christians.[9] An awareness of contemporary scientific observations, however, hinted that the distant effects of intellectual change had begun to penetrate into the fabric of this "hierocosmic" scheme of things. This awareness was reflected in references to the travels and explorations of the Portuguese around the African coast and by geographical observations on the floods of the Nile.[10]

During the course of the eighteenth century, a decisive contribution to the propagation of information about the past, which could be considered as the substratum to the emergence of a secular historical consciousness, came with the writings of the worldly monk Constantinos Kaisarios Dapontes (1713/14–1784). He was a prolific popularizer whose life was characterized by great mobility and whose main work consisted of long, versified, didactic narratives on an extensive range of religious and secular subjects. Dapontes's motivation was derived from a view of historical knowledge as "the most ancient, most necessary, sweetest, firmest, most honest, most glorious, most likeable, wisest thing" a man could possess. His aspiration was inherited from the seventeenth century: the moral edification of his readers through instruction based on relevant historical illustrations. The method consisted of using historical examples in order to project moral models worthy of imitation by one's audience. This approach to moral edification was seen as most effective because it was obviously pleasant and credible and thus easily communicable even to uneducated minds. A further advantage to be derived from moral familiarity with the past was the mutual acquaintance among peoples, since moral examples could be gleaned from any national history and be projected in all directions.[11]

Dapontes's best-known work in his own lifetime was the thick two-volume book *Mirror of Women*. Published in the same year and printed at the same press in Leipzig as Voulgaris's *Logic*, Dapontes's book represented a very different approach to the question of moral reform from that followed by Voulgaris.[12] In contrast with the aristocratic elitism of the *Logic*, which derived both from the difficulty of the subject and the archaic form of Greek used, Dapontes wrote in vernacular Greek, aiming to reach a wide audience. He hoped by doing so to spread his moral and pious message in a pleasant, attractive, yet at the same time instructive manner. The title evoked the Western literary genre of the "mirrors of princes," which, however, had deep Hellenistic and Byzantine roots. In Dapontes's hands the aristocratic and royal genre was adjusted to address the moral needs of a broader audience, in this case the whole female sex. Just as ordinary mirrors could be found in every home and helped people correct their appearance, Dapontes's *Mirror* would assist its female readers redress their moral defects, cultivate their virtue, and also please their hearts. In addition, it would inform them about "certain newly emerging political matters."[13] In this way the mirror, from being a handbook designed to educate rulers in the art of government, established by the long tradition of the "mirrors of princes," was transformed by Dapontes's stylistic choices into a tool for the reform of the general public. In purpose, content, and form, the book was typical of Greek eighteenth-century popular literature, and Dapontes was acclaimed as the great poet of the age.

An important dimension of Dapontes's account of the past was the interjection into the massive, scripturally based narrative of some passages drawn from classical history. The first signs of the articulation of an ethical message beyond Christian morality thus became visible. Leonidas's heroism at Thermopylae was extolled, while Achilles, Herakles, Theseus, and Alexander were placed on an equal footing with Samson in the pantheon of the brave men of history. Alexander in particular was praised as a model of exalted royal and human virtue. Alexander stood beside Herakles, David, and Constantine the Great, composing with them an integrated historical past of moral memories. This general ideological syncretism allowed Dapontes to draw close to the ethical vision of the Enlightenment. This is attested by a brief digression he devoted to Cynegirus's sublime heroism at Marathon. After extolling the civic symbolism of the hero's sacrifice, the poet concluded by pointing at its imperishable moral relevance through the centuries.[14]

Dapontes's approach to moral history enacted the initial steps toward the establishment of a tenuous connection between ancient and modern Hellenism in the consciousness of the broader public of his time. This connection eventually provided the fundamental ingredient to the making of a Neohellenic historical consciousness. Dapontes's intention did not extend beyond the popularization of past examples for purposes of moral didacticism. His long-term contribution, however, lay in the importance he attached to the imitation of nonreligious models, and in the propagation for the first time of nonreligious historical knowledge. This could be seen to amount to an initial step in a reorientation of historical thought. The classical memories and references punctuating his narratives reflected the first signs of a consciousness of Greek continuity. This as yet inarticulate consciousness, stimulated by Dapontes's contact with the millennarianism of the middle decades of the eighteenth century, germinated as well a vision of an eventual resurrection of a Christian Empire.[15]

In the massive body of his work, Dapontes showed a lively awareness of his contemporary world also. He was well informed about international relations and conflicts in Europe at the mid-eighteenth century. Furthermore, his writings about faraway places he had never in fact visited encompassed a fascination with the idea of a new world fledging in the richly endowed land of America. This was possibly the earliest reference to America in Greek literature. Nor was he ignorant of the almost mythical world of China or the neighboring principalities of the Tatars. Naturally he did not fail to reflect on the contemporary state of Greece. Politically, he shared the outlook and hopes of the Greek theory of enlightened despotism that prevailed in the courts of Wallachia and Moldavia, where he held office from 1731 to 1746. Fundamentally, however, he remained a popular versifier who registered the aspirations and responded to the intellectual needs of a public that extended far beyond the confines of political and intellectual elites.[16] The intellectual needs of this emerging, broader reading public were one of the signs of change that invited the popularized didacticism involved in secular historical knowledge. Besides Dapontes's writings, a number of popular biographies of Alexander[17] and Peter the Great responded to the same needs.

In the preface to the biography of Peter the Great, composed by Athanasios Skiadas, a Greek with Western culture, we encounter the projection of a new and articulate conception of history into the Greek intellectual universe. Acquaintance with the past and with the deeds of great men was worthwhile mainly on utilitarian grounds. Moral edification, though still clearly desirable, was only an incidental consequence. History was considered important primarily because it taught how to attain the aims of an individual or of a nation.[18] It was clear that a transition to a secular understanding of the past and of its uses was in the making among intellectuals in closest contact with the West. Dapontes, with all the breadth of his experience and awareness, never went so far. His thinking remained confined within the boundaries of the Orthodox mentality. However, both the articulation of the utilitarian view of history and the stimulation of historical curiosity by moral didacticism contributed to a more systematic exposure to secular historical time. The gradual intensification of this reorientation over the following decades registered the strides of the Enlightenment.

The new curiosity that was directed to the secular past involved a distancing from the religious frameworks of collective thought. Dapontes's moral didacticism retained an intermediate position between the traditional chronicles, which propagated the sacred conception of history, and the new historiography of the Enlightenment about to emerge at the time he was writing.

One of the earliest signs of new intellectual needs was Athanasios Skiadas's other project, which involved a translation of Fénelon's *Aventures de Télémaque* in 1742. Although Fénelon's political novel was pure fiction and was intended by its author as such, the Greeks read it as history and as an account of their ancestral civilization. Fénelon's account of Telemachus's wanderings in the Greek world in search of traces of his missing father expanded the horizon of the particular story by vividly depicting its geographical, cultural, and ethical setting. All this provided the more substantial and meaningful information that was required for a direct and intimate acquaintance with ancient culture, a need that could not be met by schematic narratives of outward events. Beyond meeting this requirement, the selection of Fénelon's work was a felicitous choice in another sense as well. In his circumscribed and respectful manner as the tutor and counselor to a future monarch, whom he hoped to instruct to be enlightened, Fénelon put forward some of the basic ideas of enlightened politics without being provocative. He did not challenge the principles of royal Divine Right, but he was uncompromising in his criticism of the vanity and egoism of monarchs (with the example of Louis XIV obviously in mind). His explicit affirmation of the moral primacy of the people and his defense of the rights of the subjects were put forward in order to stress that a ruler's only purpose and justification was to serve his people. If, succumbing to the temptations of kingship, a monarch abused his power and oppressed his people, he was surely inviting revolution. It was ideas like these that found their way into the new conception of politics and society, which was gradually maturing as the awareness of the modern Greeks' connection to classical Hellenism and their knowledge of ancient history expanded.[19]

ANCIENT HISTORY AS NATIONAL REEDUCATION

A major turning point in the development of a new historical outlook was marked by the publication at mid-century of a translation of Charles Rollin's *Histoire ancienne.* The publication of a sixteen-volume work on the history of ancient peoples, focusing primarily on the civilization of the ancient Greeks, was a clear sign of the new sense of time and the new understanding of history.[20] Such a far-ranging project, designed to increase familiarity with the classical past, can be taken as the clearest indication that a sense of a connection between ancient and modern Greeks was in the making.[21] This sense of continuity, stemming from an increased awareness of living in the same space and speaking a new form of the language of the Ancients, gradually became a critical dimension in the formation of the Neohellenic consciousness. Its specific content consisted essentially of a modern Greek claim of direct ancestry from the ancient Greeks. Concomitantly, this involved a self-conception of the modern Greeks as the natural heirs of classical civilization. These elements of the Neohellenic self-conception were put forward at varying levels of articulation in a wide range of sources over a long period of time and culminated in nineteenth-century historicism. The modern Greek Enlightenment spelled out the initial version of a historical doctrine that eventually provided the basis of national self-conception. The movement initially emerged as the expression of a general curiosity about the nonreligious component of the past, as a need for systematic knowledge later, and eventually as a plea for an intimate acquaintance with and revival of the civilization of the classical ancestors. In this final form, the original intellectual aspiration later on developed into a conscious national crusade.

Since its original publication in 1730, Rollin's *Ancient History,* explicitly composed according to advanced pedagogical principles, had become one of the major history textbooks in eighteenth-century Europe.[22] Montesquieu had counted Rollin, whom he characterized as the "bee of France," among the most admirable modern authors.[23] The Greek translation of Rollin became the primary historical reading and source of reference for educated Greeks for many decades. The theoretical exposition that introduced the first volume was a discourse on the utility of secular history. According to this opening programmatic statement, the purpose of historical study should be sought beyond the knowledge of past events. Its usefulness consisted in its lessons concerning the rise and decline of kingdoms: the causes of their glory, their true welfare, and their eventual demise. The author also pointed out the usefulness of the study of the moral cultures of different nations, especially of the opinions and virtues and even of the vices of rulers, who were responsible for the greatness and fall of nations.

An essential gain could, therefore, be derived from the knowledge of ancient history, according to Rollin. It taught the rules of politics and indicated the appropriate comportment and right opinions that were indispensable for a successful life in civil society. In addition, it helped cultivate one's mind by providing pleasing information on the development of arts and sciences. Beyond the recognition of these benefits of historical knowledge, it had also to be acknowledged that through the pages of secular history, no less than in the study of sacred history, one could follow the workings of providence and the unfolding of God's design for the salvation of mankind. Rollin's Jansenist sensibilities are echoed in these views. What really preoccupied the mind of the new age, however, and made secular historical knowledge appealing was its instructiveness about such human concerns as magnanimity and valor, foresight and experience in the art of government, civility and civic virtue, the equitable administration of justice, ingenuity of mind in the exact sciences, dexterity in the arts, and virtuosity in all things.[24] Thus, out of the pages of a textbook on ancient history emerged the moral and intellectual priorities of the Enlightenment, timid and circumscribed, to be sure, but nonetheless irresistible.

The ideas that transpired through the pages of Rollin's encyclopedic panorama of ancient civilization were visibly new and yet cast in a framework that made them congenial. They included an affirmation of the superior utility of secular history, recognition of the value of ancient cultures other than that sanctioned by biblical authority, a clear attack on superstition, and, politically, an espousal of the ideas and hopes of enlightened absolutism. All this, however, was carefully placed in a context of strict religious orthodoxy, and major attention was paid to the imperative of showing the close relevance of secular to sacred history. After all, Rollin was primarily known as a loyal disciple of Bossuet, and this connection normally ought to place the motives of his historical dissertations beyond suspicion.[25] Although this respectability kept him on the conservative side of the new historiography in the West, in the Greek context the selection of his work as the historical textbook of modern education assured a smooth opening to secular learning. The transition was initiated without a major ideological rupture that could provoke suspicions and reaction, undermining further progress. Rollin's history and Fénelon's political novel a few years earlier were relevant and credible choices for the specific context to which they had to be adapted. In a very real sense, their publication marked a watershed in the development of Greek historical thought.

Rollin's history became the most widely used history textbook in Greek schools during the fifty years following its publication.[26] As the eighteenth century wore on, formal education was increasingly oriented toward the pedagogical and curricular requirements of the Enlightenment. In connection with historical writing and its reading public, one has simply to point at a telling phenomenon: the frequent reprinting of the traditional chronicles throughout this time of intellectual change stood in lively contrast to the single edition of Rollin and in a very general way indicated the respective quantitative parameters of the two ideological viewpoints. The reason for not reprinting Rollin's history, however, was obviously not lack of interest or demand for the products of the new historiography. Copies of *Ancient History* remained in use and seem to have been rather easily available for several decades. On the other hand, the new historiography produced over the years newer works that made reprinting of the older source unnecessary.

This production increased as the Enlightenment moved toward its full flowering. Awareness of the utility of historical knowledge went hand in hand with a desire for a broader acquaintance with the culture of the ancient Greeks. The doctor-philosopher G. Sakellarios felt that of all the sciences that cultivated the human mind, history was the most useful. It connected the present with the past and projected before the human mind a mirror of human actions from which one could learn what was essential for rightful conduct and for a happy life among one's fellow human beings. In the civilized nations, not only those who were cultivated and educated, but practically every barely literate person, including children, possessed some historical knowledge. In the case of the Greeks, this was all the more regrettable because ignorance of history amounted to inadequate understanding of themselves since it meant ignorance about their own ancestors.[27]

This was to be remedied by the diligently composed, learned surveys of life and civilization in the classical Greek cities, by editions and commentaries on classical historians, and the publication of new textbooks on ancient history. One important variety of this literature was the so-called Archeologies, which surveyed the religion, political institutions, military organization, culture and learning, economic practices, and everyday private life of the ancient Athenians and Spartans. Although occasionally dry and wearisome, these overviews embodied the new conception of historical knowledge associated with the Enlightenment. Knowing the past now meant becoming familiar with a way of living and a mode of culture that was taken to characterize a distant phase of Greek history, which possessed an intrinsic merit of its own. This was a big step away from the didactic recitation of extraordinary happenings with metaphysical significance that was the stuff of the traditional chronicles. The understanding of the past as civilization channeled the political ideas and moral values of Enlightenment classicism into modern Greek thought. The study of classical civilization as an integral unity suggested that ancient Athens derived its political power and ethical and cultural greatness from its system of social and political institutions. Since it was a system based on the accountability of public officials to the body of the citizens, it was obvious that, so long as it worked, it secured Athenian greatness. Its neglect led to the city's decline and eventual submission to the yoke of the Romans.[28]

In this context, a rediscovery of Thucydides was eminently pertinent. In the European tradition, Thucydidean history had always been considered as an intensely political reading, and as Hobbes's example had hinted, it was particularly relevant at times of political ferment. This quality of the thought of the historian of the Peloponnesian War did not escape his new commentator, Manuel Tenedios, who, following Mably, described the text he was discoursing upon as a fitting reading for all those interested in the nature of politics, including of course reigning or aspiring rulers.[29]

Shortly after the beginning of the nineteenth century, the choice of Abbé Millot's *Elements of General History* as a new European historical work, selected for translation to replace Rollin's history, which was falling out of date, marked clearly the distance traveled by Greek historical thinking since the appearance of the first major source on ancient history. The sense of the inadequacy of the historical education of the modern Greeks in comparison to the enlightened nations of Europe continued to be pervasive and provided the primary motivation of the new initiative. In their prolegomena, the translators, Grigorios Constantas and Zisis Kavras, stated that what was sought was familiarity with the customs and spirit of the nations, with their political institutions, laws, and forms of government, a familiarity that would make possible an understanding of humanity. Of particular events, only those were deemed relevant that conveyed a sense of historical progress.[30] What was really important and useful was the capacity to exercise critical judgment in history.[31] Critical history stood in sharp contrast not simply to the traditional religious chronicles but also to Rollin. According to the translators of the new project, absence of critical judgment, inordinate length, and indulgence in pedantry were the obvious defects of the venerable work that deserved otherwise to be honored. History now became an invitation to critical thinking. The Abbé Millot himself was known to be a social critic who did not mince his words when it came to pointing out the abuses and vices of the ministers of both the altar and the state. In deciding to render Millot's work into their own language for the instruction of their compatriots, Constantas and Kavras were making a conscious choice of a comrade in arms.

According to the translators, the study of history provided the best training for the education of citizens. The Greeks and Romans were the moral models in practically everything that mattered in political and civic life. In studying their history, more emphasis had therefore to be given to the effects and achievements of their civic cultures and of their intellectual brilliance rather than to the chronology of their wars. Thus, the basic expectation of historical study might be realized: the attainment not of erudition, but of knowledge of humanity. This would be the cognitive basis of sound judgment and of wise action. From this vantage point, both the common errors of ancient historians and Bossuet's unreliability could be criticized. At the same time, skepticism, which was as pernicious as credulity, could be overcome. The optimistic possibilities of the new cognitive perspective could then be applied to the analysis of the moral and political lessons of the historical experience of the three great ancient polities, Athens, Sparta, and Rome.[32] The formulation of these concerns made it evident that the modern Greeks were searching for a new code by which to decipher the political thought and practice of their ancient forebears.

The forging of a secularized historical consciousness in modern Greek culture essentially meant the abandonment of the feeling of a biblical lineage, prevalent in the traditional mind, and its replacement by an active awareness of a distinct classical ancestry. Learning the history of the rediscovered world of ancient ancestors appeared as a practical necessity dictated by the new turn taken by the collective mind, a sensibility which now for the first time became so pressing among the Christian "Romans" of the Greek East. With it went a depreciation, obviously only among those who espoused and cultivated the new historical sense and cherished the new identity it nurtured, of the Christian history of the Greek people, that is, of that part of Greek history that connected the modern Greeks with a biblical rather than a classical genealogy. The transition from religious to secular time and the new sense of historical identity it fostered was obviously the product of influences from contemporary European classicism. Indeed, the zeal shown by foreigners in learning classical history even to the point of preferring it over the history of their own nations made the modern Greeks' ignorance of even the names of their illustrious forefathers increasingly embarrassing. For the more enlightened minds, there was a tragic dimension to this ignorance.[33] The feeling of lineage from the ancient Greeks, once discovered, posed the problem of historical continuity.[34] On what grounds could the modern Greeks claim continuity with a civilization more than two thousand years distant into the past? The answer was to be given more than half a century later in the mid-nineteenth century by Greek romantic historicism, but some of the intellectuals of the Enlightenment already tried to come to terms with the problem.

One dimension of continuity, on which the connection with the ancients could be based, was a newly discovered unity of the Greek intellectual tradition. The Greek language, which formed that tradition's medium of expression, appeared the most convincing type of external evidence attesting to the historical and cultural survival of the Greek people despite social upheavals and the occupation by insidious enemies of the space in which the ancient civilization had flourished. A biographical dictionary of Greek literature compiled by Anthimos Gazis bore testimony to this evolving theory of Greek history. In Gazis's scheme, the biographies of classical authors were followed in uninterrupted sequence by those of Greek writers of the Hellenistic and Roman periods through the Byzantine era up to the Fall of Constantinople. The last author whose biography was included was the chronicler of the Fall, Georgios Phrantzis. He had written "this chronicle and events that he saw with his own eyes and experienced, and, upon reading his work, who can contain the tears which are precipitated not so much by the captivity of the Nation, but by the stupidity of its rulers who goaded it right under the heavy yoke of tyranny?" was asked dramatically by the biographer.[35] Byzantium thus emerged as one of the major cognitive problems in elaborating a secular theory of Greek history. This, however, did not obscure the view of continuity of the Greek intellectual tradition. The Moderns, including the leading exponents of the Enlightenment, were mentioned by Gazis as continuators and heirs of Byzantine literature.[36]

Despite the Enlightenment's contempt for Byzantium, shared by several of its Greek representatives, the problem of establishing the modern Greeks' historical lineage made it impossible to ignore this phase of the history of the Greek East. For philosophical radicals, the problem was resolved by viewing the Byzantine heritage as an aberration in the development of Greek civilization. It represented the decadence of classical civilization, and its legacy was a fetter on Greek national revival. In short, the national revival was seen to be contingent on the eradication of all traces of Byzantinism (represented and nurtured by the Orthodox Church) from Greek life and thought. Although this was typical of the philosophic radicalism of the Enlightenment, it imposed serious strains on the incipient idea of historical continuity. In the face of such a wide gap of time, the connection with the ancient ancestors could not make full historical sense. One way out was to approach Byzantine history with the new cognitive criteria so as to clear away the veil of superstition that obscured it. This might make it possible identify in the Byzantine tradition the historical links connecting the Moderns to the Ancients. An edition of paraphrases of Byzantine historical texts published in 1767 had already broached in its preface the methodological problems of evidence and truth in historical writing. It thus provided an alternative to total rejection. The editor, Agapios Loverdos, cautioned in his proemium that not only the fragmentation of sources and the disagreements among historians, but also the play of imagination, subjective preferences, and prejudice distorted the available accounts of the past.[37] At the same time, awareness of the sources of distortion and misinterpretation made possible an approach that could distinguish between truth and falsehood. Thus even the study of Byzantine history could appear to be an acceptable preoccupation to an enlightened culture. The Enlightenment's greatest historical thinkers, Montesquieu and Gibbon, did not neglect this phase of the long history of the Roman Empire. The advantages of historical criticism were obvious for the new theory of Greek continuity: the new methods made it possible to shift the focus of investigation from the blatant picture of monkish obscurantism and the wretchedness of mass superstition to the discovery of the missing historical links that through the Middle Ages connected the Moderns with classical civilization.

The Byzantine embarrassment could thus be overcome without vindicating Byzantium itself or integrating it into the newly redefined national patrimony. The latter task was left to the romantic philosophy of history of the nineteenth century.[38] The strictures of foreign observers, however, who, inspired by the Enlightenment's historical theory of the corruption of the Romans, were accusing the modern Greeks of barbarism and degeneracy, could be answered. Not only the great contributions of classical antiquity to world civilization, but also Byzantium's achievement in preserving the Greek language and the tradition of the classics, and even those of the modern Greeks through the eighteenth century, could be marshaled in refutation of the arguments of "accusers of the Greek people," such as Cornelis de Pauw and J. L. S. Bartholdy.[39]

Their accusations, which concentrated on the moral and intellectual decline of the modern Greeks, struck at the Greek sense of national pride and dignity. The rights of the nation were defended in a *Historico-Critical Apology,* which projected before the forgetful conscience of the world the benefactions bestowed upon them by the Greeks. Greek self-confidence was nurtured by a consciousness of the great achievements of the ancients and their contribution to European civilization. "Greece has not only proceeded to brilliantly teach all the nations the virtues of civility and political order, but she will probably educate future generations as well through her virtue and wisdom." In addition, the author pointed out that the Greeks

contributed decisively to the triumph of Christianity: they safeguarded
Orthodox doctrine against heresy and spread the true faith. The cultural
achievements of the Greeks continued even during their captivity by the
barbarians down to the time of writing. In the face of the ignorance of
biased foreign critics, Greek cultural accomplishments were enumerated
century after century. Thus a pantheon of Greeks of outstanding wisdom
and virtue was depicted. The ancient philosophers and Byzantine men of
learning were listed along with the Greek scholars who flourished during
the period of Ottoman captivity. A clear sense of pride came across in the
encomia of the most distinguished of modern Greek scholars, with which
the survey reached its culmination. In this way, the author of the Apology
felt that he had succeeded in casting the history of Greek culture as an
unbroken continuum.[40]

A philosophy of history was implicit in such arguments. Toward the end
of the period of the Enlightenment, this philosophy was articulated in the
work of Grigorios Paliouritis, who depicted the broad logic of a sequence of
ancient cultural greatness, followed by the fall of Greece and her cultural
decline and the beginnings of a revival achieved by means of a universal
effort of all Greeks. The incipient revival was the product of a divine eros
that had gripped all Greeks both within Greece and in the diaspora.[41] The
enthusiasm that gripped the Greek world on the eve of the national uprising seemed to be inspired by the study of ancient history. The Greeks were
taught the virtues and achievements of their ancestors, and their zeal was
enhanced by the knowledge that those ancient ancestors lived under the
rule of laws and justice and enjoyed the fruits of liberty at a time that the
rest of humanity lived under tyranny. This made the contrast with the contemporary predicament of the Greeks even starker.[42]

The magnitude of the Greek problem was painfully illustrated by the
preference shown by the modern Greeks for the name Romans rather than
Hellenes in describing themselves. "When we hear the name Hellenes [. . .]
it displeases us. When we are called Romans we rejoice, acknowledging
thus unconsciously our shameful captivity by the people of Rome."[43]

The teaching of classical history was the only means through which
ancestral wisdom and virtue could be recovered. Paliouritis felt that an
up-to-date history text of greater accessibility than that of Rollin was necessary. The older work was long, discursive, and confusing. It mingled
Greek history with that of the Near Eastern peoples, thus interrupting its

continuity. A new, more sharply pointed and concise history would be more relevant to current needs by guiding the modern Greeks in the emulation of the virtues of their ancestors. Hence, parents were urged to put into the hands of their offspring the newly published books of Greek history in order to prevent them from indulging in the wasteful and morally harmful popular readings of the time. The immersion of Greek youth in readings about ancestral virtues and accomplishments would infuse them with courage and magnanimity.[44]

The theory of history that Paliouritis put forward in his history of ancient Greece was clearly inspired by the radical civic humanism of the Enlightenment. The ideas of civic humanism were amplified in another, slightly later work dealing with the civilization and culture of the Ancients, Paliouritis's *Hellenic Archeology,* issued as the third volume of his history. It was an intellectual history of classical Hellas, prefaced by a discussion of the social, cultural, and moral requirements of the Neohellenic revival. The account of classical civilization was cast in the framework of republican theory. It stressed the connection between the greatness of the Ancients and their public ethic and civic virtue. Historical change, the fall of the classical republics, and the loss of ancient liberty were explained in terms of the theory of moral disintegration and social corruption. This perspective on ancient civilization had obvious implications for modern politics: a moral culture emphasizing civic virtue and a system of republican institutions constituted the necessary concomitants of political liberty.[45]

Modern Greek interest in the political content of ancient literature, already evident in the rediscovery of Thucydides, could be put to radical uses in modern Greek education. This possibility comes across clearly in the inclusion of one of the most celebrated passages of Thucydides's history, Pericles's *Funeral Oration,* in one of the most radical books of Greek Enlightenment literature. This was Ioannis Vilaras's *The Romaic Language,* a brief book published in 1814 that put forward a proposal for a drastic reform of the grammar of the modern Greek vernacular. Vilaras not only called for the recognition of the spoken vernacular as the only language of intellectual life and literary production, but also advocated the abandonment of Greek historical orthography, which preserved in modern Greek the grammar and spelling of ancient Greek, and its replacement by a purely phonetic system of spelling. To demonstrate the workability of his proposal, Vilaras included in his book some very fine lyric poetry he had composed using the new orthographic system,[46] and two translations from classical Greek texts: Plato's *Crito* and Thucydides's *Funeral Oration*.[47] The choice of these two texts could be seen as an unequivocal statement of political preferences. Neither had been in the accepted canon of ancient learning that formed the core of the curriculum of conventional Greek education. That canon included selections from moralizing texts of the fourth century BC, from Hellenistic literature, and from Christian patristic thought.[48] Abandoning all this, Vilaras went back to two texts of the classical age that stand out for their powerful commitment to democratic patriotism. Both the *Crito* and the *Funeral Oration* extolled the unity of the individual with the civic order of the polis as the higher realization of the individual's moral freedom. The projection of the virtuous model of ancient democratic citizenship undoubtedly represented both a drastic break from the political ideology of Christian monarchy prevailing in traditional Greek thought and an eloquent indication of the subversive political implications of the rediscovery of the classics. The meaning of Vilaras's classical selections illustrated the essentially political content of linguistic reform projects and their radical purposes.

Eighteenth-century classicism was thus merely the threshold of political republicanism. The link with their ancient ancestors offered the modern Greeks not merely an awareness of their national past, on which they could base their collective historical identity, but also a standard against which to measure the political present and a framework in which to envision their future as a united national community.

CONTEMPORARY HISTORY

The discovery of the modern Greeks' ancient lineage and the construction of a distinct national past provided the basis of their sense of historical identity. A second dimension of the self-definition of the Greeks registered by the progress of eighteenth-century historical writing was the gradual sharpening of their awareness of contemporary power politcs. The number of accounts of contemporary events multiplied as the Greeks' curiosity was captured by the tumult of political history in the eighteenth century. The sources on contemporary history became avenues of political awareness that enabled the Greeks to conceive of themselves in the context of the international society of their time. The significance of this consisted in the comparison that it made possible between the Greeks' own condition and that of other nations. Immanent in such a comparison was a reinforcement of their sense of historical uniqueness as a nation with a distinct ethnic and political personality.

If the sense of the moral importance of history stimulated writing on ancient Hellas, the consciousness of the social utility of historical knowledge was reflected in accounts of contemporary events. Early in the eighteenth century (during the 1730s), the achievements of Peter the Great in regenerating his empire inspired a number of heroic biographies of the reforming emperor. Besides representing one of the earliest manifestations of Greek interest in international affairs at the time, these sources were politically significant as registers of the evolving Russian expectation—a hope that was to be fully articulated later on in the course of the century. As we shall see in greater detail in chapter 4, fostered by Russian propaganda, this hope visualized national redemption coming from the North.[49]

Shortly after mid-century something new emerged to stimulate the "historical curiosity" of the Greeks. According to the editor of the new publication, Georgios Constantinou, Greek historical literature was enriched with the initiation of a new series on world history, the like of which had not, up to then, seen the light. The aspiration of the series was to fill the gaps left by other historical books, which covered things old and past with partial accounts of only a few nations.[50]

Finally, the hour of contemporary world history had come. According to the general editor, it responded to an innate attribute of human curiosity that sought knowledge of the most distant parts of the world, of foreign nations and their civilizations. This was to be achieved through the examination of the geography, resources, cities, forms of government, laws, religion, customs, and culture of the several countries of the world. The new historical teleology culminated in a geography of human civilization, inspired by the contemplation of Europe, the most cultured part of the globe, but also seeking familiarity with the exotic civilizations of China and other distant lands.[51] The discovery of world history as the knowledge of distant places and civilizations was a clear sign of the expansion of historical space made possible by the secularization of historical knowledge: the world was no longer narrowly delimited by the geography of the true faith, but it grew wider and more diverse to encompass all the varieties of

human experience and to satisfy the wide array of new curiosities stimulated by the Enlightenment.[52]

International developments of immediate interest to the Greeks crowded
the second half of the eighteenth century, and stimulated the writing of
contemporary history. One such work, narrating the origins, outbreak,
and course of the second Russo-Turkish war of the eighteenth century, was
translated from the Italian and published by Deacon Spyridon Papadopoulos. The work was a Greek translation of a multivolume history of the Russo-
Turkish wars of 1768–1774, which had been published anonymously in
Venice by Domenico Caminer. The Greek version followed the very same
year.[53] As events became more and more pressing, with international wars
raging throughout Eastern Europe, and an intense need for information
was felt more directly, the difficulties of the task of writing contemporary
history were also perceived to be greater: events were unclear, the nature and
tendency of things was discernible only with greater uncertainty. Still, the
importance of a task such as the narration of the wars between Russia and
the Ottoman Porte and their repercussions throughout Eastern Europe was
felt to be compelling enough to sustain the translator in his effort to present
as complete an account as possible and to make it both appealing to his contemporaries and useful to later generations, whom it aimed to provide with
safe knowledge of the crucial events that marked his own time.[54]

In view of the importance of the task, the reliability of the knowledge
that was to be conveyed by the accounts of contemporary history became
a primary preoccupation. Obviously the problem was not simply epistemological. An account of the wars of the Hapsburg and Russian emperors
against the Ottomans had the utmost relevance to the emerging preoccupation with Greek freedom. It was by seizing opportunities arising out of
such configurations in international relations that Greek hopes for redemption might be fulfilled. Hence the task of contemporary history extended
beyond the curiosity of an awakening society and mere ethical edification
to deciphering political possibilities and providing the basis for a calculus of
national redemption.

An increasing awareness of the methodological problems involved in
such a crucial assignment became the basis of a distinction between ancient
and modern history. Knowledge of ancient history was undoubtedly useful due to its moral content. It was the foremost source of ethical lessons
that pointed to the rules of "Political Science."[55] However, although morally

sound, epistemologically this knowledge was suspect because of the subjective biases of ancient historians and the distance of the events they dis-
coursed upon—a distance that made critical scrutiny of their accounts
practically impossible. Consequently, contemporary history appeared to be
much more credible because

> we ourselves are witnesses and judges of events which we either watch or
> hear about while we are still alive and we thus can easily examine them with
> precision and distinguish truth from falsehood, without having to rely on
> the opinions of others.

These observations are taken from the prologue of yet another history of
contemporary events, compiled by the director of the Flangineion School
in Venice, Agapios Loverdos (1720–1794), in order to set out for his fellow
Greeks the circumstances of the beginning of the third Russo-Turkish war
of the century (1787–1792). Based on what he had gleaned from French and
Italian sources, especially the *Storia dell'anno,* an annual review of international events published in Venice, Loverdos's compilation sketched the
background to international relations during the years 1787 and 1788, in
order to account for the outbreak of "the present wars between the Aus-
tro-Russians and the Ottomans."[56]

Thus, reflection on the nature and possibilities of contemporary history
affirmed the primacy of individual judgment in the determination of truth.
This was the avenue for the spirit of the age of criticism to come into its
own. Another history of the Russo-Turkish wars pointed out that the study
of the past and the investigation of the present cultivated the faculties of
the human mind and gradually made men fit for life in civil society.[57] The
spirit of criticism appeared as a precondition to reflection on the collective
predicament. Contemporary history acquired thus a deeper meaning. This
attitude was reflected in the pages devoted to the Ottoman period with
which the archimandrite Kyprianos concluded his *Chronological History of
the Island of Cyprus.*[58] These pages could be considered as the most original piece in the entire historiographical production of the Greek Enlightenment, which consisted mostly of translations and adaptations. After a
survey of the history of Cyprus from the time of the Deluge to the Ottomans, based on selections and translations from various sources, Kyprianos
completed his edifice with his own picture of eighteenth-century Cypriot

society, encompassing its material and social life, its culture and spiritual traditions. Besides being an invaluable source of social history unsurpassed to the present day, this analysis developed into a reflection on the forces shaping the history of the Greeks in the Ottoman Empire, a register of the feeling of hardship, but also of the deeper yearnings of the subject people. The author was a man who as a peasant boy and a church official fully shared in the traditions of his native land, but also through his travels and studies in the West was aware of the lights of European culture.[59] His testimony, therefore, is uniquely valuable.

The author's objective was to instruct his compatriots about the illustrious past of their "famous native island" as a consolation amid their latest misfortunes. His declared intention was to do so by following the modern methods of historical criticism. His labors were primarily motivated by his dissatisfaction with the state of historical literature on Cyprus. He began with a critical examination of the sources from which he selected his materials. A clear indication of his application of historical criticism was the modernization of such technical components of the historical craft as chronology, geography, and cartography. In geography, he followed Buffon's theories.[60] The point of departure of his criticism was a rejection of the prejudices obfuscating the writing of the Latin chronographer of Cyprus, Etienne de Lusignan, though this author's "chorography" and history of Cyprus were Kyprianos's main source.[61] Lusignan's condescension and his religious intolerance toward the Cypriots were resented and criticized by Kyprianos as incompatible with the task of serious history writing. Fundamentally, the substance of his own critical method consisted in the rejection of the mythological narratives of ancient Greek and Latin poets as sources of historical evidence and in the exercise of his own judgment in assessing his sources against the evidence of his personal experience. His objective being to approach the truth as closely as possible, he rejected whatever did not square with his own direct perception of the facts, which as a native of the land he felt he possessed to a safer degree than foreign observers.[62]

Kyprianos warned the reader that religion was often put to political ends and became a cover for despotism. The union of authority and religion might secure the blind submission of the simple folk, who in their superstition and credulity believed that the divinity was the source of anything good or evil descending upon them. Such an irrational fear was always manipulated by the more cunning fellows as an effective instrument in establishing themselves as despots.[63] Not only did tyranny thrive on super-stition, but criminal adventurism and cruelty could find cover behind reli-gious pretexts. The prime example was the "achievements" of the Crusaders in the East, of which Cyprus had direct and bitter experiences.[64] The archi-mandrite of the Archdiocese of Cyprus had no hesitation in admitting, on the other hand, that popular beliefs and narratives about miracles tended to exaggeration and bordered on hyperbole.[65]

Reconstructing the past in a more critical spirit could also mean that the present might be faced without fatalism or resignation. Kyprianos tried to hearten his contemporaries to sustain the hardships of enslavement by pointing out that the past had been even more cruel than the present. Under the rule of Christian masters, such as the Frankish feudal lords and the Venetian mercantile oligarchy, exploitation and oppression had been worse than under the Turks.[66] So even though the inner logic of the history of their island might be considered as a sequence of disasters,[67] yet hope should not be abandoned. Indeed, by looking at the human stuff of Cyprus's history, one could not despair. There were many things to be proud of: a certain sense of greatness associated with the presence of so many illustrious men, saints, heroes, and scholars hinted that Cyprus was made for better things.[68]

Thus, from a discourse on the past, the work turned out to be a reflection on the collective predicament in the present. By dispelling various fatalis-tic, if comforting myths, Kyprianos's account in a way made clear that the calamities that appeared to pervade the history of Cyprus in the Chris-tian era were not an inexorable process. If earthquakes and the locust often descended upon Cyprus and made the recent past a period of natural disas-ters,[69] suffering and hardship were essentially the products of social causes. It was the social quakes of arbitrary and violent government, of economic oppression and exploitation, and the human locust of criminal and rapa-cious rulers that really made the effects of natural catastrophes unbearable. Still, if the basic causes of suffering were human, there were human ways of coping with them. The misery wrought by violent foreign conquest could be mitigated and overcome by the industriousness of the local people, and reconstruction could be achieved through the cultivation of the peaceful arts in which the Cypriots always excelled.[70] Social solidarity among the oppressed held the key to survival.[71]

Thus Kyprianos's account of Ottoman rule and its effects on Cyprus, although it underlined the bitter disappointment of the naive hope of the Cypriot peasantry who welcomed the Turks hoping for relief from Venetian oppression,[72] did not end in resignation. The history of adversity was accompanied by a pervasive sense of dignity. It derived from pride in the human qualities of a sociable, publicly minded, and law-abiding people,[73] from the feeling that life in Cyprus could be good,[74] from the lively consciousness of an illustrious cultural tradition and the legacy of great men. Hence, reflection on the predicament of the present could be transcended in a yearning for future redemption and a vision of recovery of a lost realm of freedom.[75]

SELF-AWARENESS OF A MODERN NATION

The process that led from the traditional perception of historical time, as recorded in the chronicles of sacred history, to the emergence of a distinct Greek historical consciousness, as reflected in eighteenth-century historiography, appears to have had three salient dimensions. One was the gradual consolidation of an ethnic link with the ancient Greeks who came to be thought of as the ancestors of the modern nation, which had survived the tribulations of the Ottoman conquest and was rediscovering its identity. The second dimension of the process was the awakening of a sense of the contemporary world, which gradually made the Greeks aware of the possibilities offered to them by the existing structure of international relations, so far as the prospects of their liberation were concerned. The third dimension emerged from the combined effects of the other two and consisted of an invitation to critical reflection on the social and political forces shaping the collective predicament of the Greeks under Ottoman rule.[76] Thus the transition to a secular sense of time and the infusion of the methods and orientations of Enlightenment historiography into Greek thought provided the modern Greeks with a sense of a distinct ethnic past as against the shared sacred past of all Christian peoples. It gave them an initial feeling of their separateness in modern international society and an intense awareness of their predicament under Ottoman rule, an awareness that stemmed from a double comparison: a devastating diachronic comparison with the greatness of their newly discovered classical ancestors and a synchronic comparison with the flourishing condition of the civilized nations of modern Europe. The second comparison was made very lively by the parallel emergence of an articulate geographical literature that was one of the major intellectual manifestations of the Greek Enlightenment.

These cultural developments constituted the formative elements that went into the making of a national consciousness. The subsequent evolution of the symbolic and moral content of this consciousness was shaped by the ethical classicism of the Enlightenment, which dominated the mature political thought of its Greek version and determined the explicit expression of the historical consciousness of modern Hellenism.

CHAPTER THREE

The Geography of Civilization

From Adulation to Revolution

THE INTELLECTUAL EXPERIENCE of the Enlightenment involved not only a discovery of secular time in the shape of social and cultural history, but also an expansion and secularization of the consciousness of space. This was largely the effect of the outpouring of travel literature that transformed the conception of space in eighteenth century thought. The pedagogical value of travel was generally recognized by successive generations of European thinkers from Fénelon to Rousseau. The unreliability of existing travel literature, composed by authors who carried their prejudices with them and traveled like courtiers rather than like explorers, did not obscure in Rousseau's estimation the value of travel as a means of overturning the empire of prejudice, as Montaigne had long before noted.[1] Indeed, travel as a quest for truth and for knowledge of mankind was reserved as the crowning stage in Émile's education. Thus, pedagogical travel, by liberating the mind from national and parochial prejudices and by expanding the knowledge of human nature and civilization, became an integral part of the experience of enlightenment.

In the literature of the Enlightenment, the philosopher was the man who traveled—the man of wide experience and clear perception of truth. With this preparation, he entered a society from without as a critic of the existing state of things and of traditional opinions dictated by prejudice. Thus, since the philosophical traveler was a social critic and open-minded, reflective traveling a means of enlightenment, the enormous proliferation of travel literature in the eighteenth century reflected the diffusion of the outlook of the Enlightenment.[2]

The awareness of a wider world undermined traditional notions of space. These notions were delimited by the immobility and parochialism of local culture and were extended beyond the horizon of the immediate locality only by a sense of the geography of faith that pointed toward Jerusalem as a cherished destination of pilgrimage. The impact of the Enlightenment substituted for the hope of pilgrimage a philosophical quest of knowledge and an experience of intellectual liberation. For the Enlightenment, consciousness of space, like consciousness of time, essentially amounted to a discovery of human civilization in all its richness and diversity. Thus, the geographical literature of the Enlightenment that embodied the new consciousness of space was essentially a social and cultural geography that responded to the requirements and curiosities of a cosmopolitan age.

FROM SACRED TO SECULAR GEOGRAPHY

Consciousness of space in traditional Greek thought was delimited by the geography of faith. Its content was largely furnished by descriptions of the Holy Land and the sacred mountains of Athos and Sinai.[3] These were the destinations of pilgrimages that every pious soul yearned to realize. For the great majority of the population such a pilgrimage represented the only form of geographical mobility that they might conceive of as a possible experience in their lifetime. The texts themselves talked of the holiest shrines in Christendom and the *loci* of miracles and described the tangible signs left behind by the passing of a holy presence in those sanctified places. In traditional consciousness, the geography of faith supplemented the accounts of sacred history by describing their physical settings.

This geography of faith greatly animated the religious imagination of the pious folk and thus formed an important part of popular culture. To the extent that formal learning was interested in theoretical knowledge of geography, it confined itself to the principles of Ptolemaic geography and persisted stubbornly for a very long time in the geocentric view of the universe.[4] This view continued to dominate the curriculum of Church-controlled schools even at the heyday of the Enlightenment. The strains and contradictions of the transition to a different mode of consciousness of space were represented in the publication of the astronomical treatise of Chrysanthos Notaras in the early eighteenth century. The author had learned astronomy from Cassini in Paris and attempted to introduce a scientific exposition of the principles of theoretical cosmography, but still insisted on the geocentric view.[5]

Already in the closing years of the seventeenth century, however, Western learning provided the stimulus to the appearance of an evolving geographical outlook that incorporated the concepts and orientations of contemporary European modes of knowledge. This development was reflected in the geographical treatise composed toward the end of the 1690s by Meletios Mitrou who, later in his career, became archbishop of Athens (1703–1714). Significantly, this change came with the assumption of a conscious cosmopolitan attitude and the adoption of a critical method based on the assessment of empirical evidence and drawing on modern geographical sources. The new method was owed to contemporary European sources, on which Meletios drew in order to supplement the evidence from ancient authors on which his work was largely based. Both the content and the title chosen by Meletios for his treatise, *Geography Old and New,* reflect his debt to the great seventeenth-century geographers Philippe Briet and Philippe Cluver; Meletios's obligation to the pioneers of modern cartography, Buondelmonti, Mercator, and Ortelius, is equally apparent.[6]

The greatest argument in favor of intimate acquaintance with the surrounding world was not the praises of ancient and modern sages that geography shared with history, nor its generally admitted practical utility. It was rather and most fundamentally its direct relevance to the purposes of the cosmopolitan human being. Geography acquainted the cosmopolite with the natural and social features of the world. Since the entire world was nothing but the great city of man, the greatest disgrace for its citizen would be the ignorance of the contours of the cosmos. The meaning of earthly life, transitory as it might be, came to be conceived in a new light. The main purpose of man as "cosmopolite" was, of course, to become an "ouranopolite" and gain the "future city" of heavenly life. Nonetheless, the discovery of the delights of the earthly world through the pages of geography led to a gradual reevaluation of what it meant to be a "cosmopolite." All this was premised on the acquisition of new kinds of knowledge that required a method of cognition different from that of traditional learning.[7]

The accounts of ancient geographers even when supplemented and corrected by modern geographical research were examined and fully utilized by Meletios, but they constituted nothing more than a starting point. The new geography was to be written on the basis of what direct observation could yield. The remnants of antiquity, inscriptions and ancient toponyms, were critically investigated by Meletios. For the first time, the critical assessment of available empirical evidence became a component of the method of learning and scholarly writing. On the basis of this method, Meletios surveyed the provinces and satrapies of the ancient and modern world, added accounts of great cities and kingdoms, and enriched his text with stories of the accomplishments of nations and great men.[8] Here one witnesses the transition from the geography of faith to a geography of human achievement.

The cosmopolitan outlook that made possible this approach to geographical knowledge nurtured also a feeling of genuine admiration for the achievements of European culture. The Europeans were seen as a collective cultural personality shining with virtue. They had distinguished themselves in refined mores, in the sciences, in arts, and in everything else useful to mankind. Although the author was aware of certain negative aspects of European society, like the despotism of the Roman Church and the Inquisition, his fascination with the great centers of European civilization formed the basic thrust of his narrative. The splendid city of Paris with its multitudes of civilized men, its academies and commerce, its magnificent buildings and political institutions filled the observer with enthusiasm. The civility and calm of the British, the greatness of London, and its commercial vigor also captured his admiration. In the Helvetian confederacy one met with a model of a free country that secured its freedom thanks to the fighting spirit and the bravery of its children. The Swiss, a nation by nature freedom-loving and surpassing all others in valor, had stemmed the German incursions on their liberty. Hence, they managed to consolidate a free and powerful community.[9]

This increased awareness of European models threw a different light on the condition of Greece. It was true that the remnants of ancient civilization reminded everyone of the great days of old. This, however, made awareness of the present all the more painful. Greece, whose name was great and much vaunted in ancient times, had become small and miserable.[10] The decline and fall of Greece was vividly stamped on the author's consciousness, and the cause of her sad state did not escape him: the Turks were the last in a long series of foreign conquerors who ruled over her. Meletios, like Montesquieu a little later, noted that the Turks brought misery and plunged the formerly splendid country into darkness and barbarism.[11] Wisdom, like the bird that leaves its nest, flew away from Greece and found refuge in modern Europe.

This was a remarkable text. Produced at the threshold of the Neohellenic Enlightenment, it introduced a pattern that ran through all the important geographical treatises of the eighteenth century and gradually shaped the conception of space that went into a new consciousness. Admiration for European civilization, awareness of the splendor of the Greek past, melancholy at the contemporary condition of Greek society became the basic components of the ideology that was registered in the new secular geography.

The themes first introduced by Meletios of Athens were amplified several decades later in two other geographical treatises that, although both written by clergymen, articulated the secular consciousness of space characteristic of the Enlightenment.

Gregorios Phatzeas, a native of the island of Kythera, priest of the Greek community in Venice, and later archbishop of Philadelphia in the same city (1762–1769), motivated by his zeal to be useful to his nation and the education of its youth, decided to do so by rendering into Greek Patrick Gordon's *Geographical Grammar,* which had already been through several English, French, and Italian editions. Phatzeas outlined his motives in an original introductory essay with which he prefaced his translation. His decision was prompted by his belief in the utility of geographical knowledge and its necessity to everyone desiring to entertain a clear idea of the world. The Greek translator was all the more proud of his gift to his nation because he believed that the new scientific methodology of the work was more appropriate to the nature of his subject matter. This new scientific methodology extended from a clearer and more effective manner of exposition to the use of visual aids such as maps, globes, and other illustrations for the popularization of the basic mathematical principles of theoretical geography. The preoccupation with the relevance of method was gradually becoming an overriding consideration. Not only was the method of the treatise incomparably superior to that followed by previous geographers, in the translator's opinion, more fundamentally it was a method that extended beyond the compilation of factual knowledge and the correction of the inaccuracies of the Ancients and provided the means through which the understanding could proceed on its own. The material presented in the treatise was selected not only on the principle of utility, but also in order to respond to the new concerns and curiosities stimulated by the Enlightenment. An important part of the description of each country was to be devoted to an account of its products and commerce, to reports on "remarkable, rare and curious things" encountered in it, to surveys of the state of secular and religious politics, the condition of letters and education, and the character of the people. In an incipient form, this orientation was first introduced in the pages of Meletios's work. But with Phatzeas it acquired more complexity and density, thus indicating not only the new interests that contemporary literature had to meet, but also the road traveled by the new cultural outlook. In the Greek context, this new information about the world and civilization beyond the confines of Ottoman Greece pointed at alternative models that could inform and guide the Greeks' efforts at social and cultural change—and it was at this point that the seeds of a revolutionary potentiality could be found.[12]

Russia offered an eloquent example of what cultural change and the progress of letters and enlightenment could bring. Motivated by the desire to transfer the Muses from the kingdoms of Europe to his own lands, Peter the Great managed to deliver his people from the inertia of idiocy and to inspire them with interest in education and learning. By freeing them from the darkness of ignorance, enlightenment also liberated them from debasing mores. The narrative described in detail the arduous task of Peter the Great: it involved first personal acquaintance with European civilization, which he acquired by travel and direct observation. As a consequence, he was able to adorn his kingdom with the sciences, the arts of war and navigation, and a high standard of civility among his subjects. He was so successful in implementing this goal that all of his subjects excelled in their particular vocations and in all the sciences, as well as in the arts of war and navigation. The eventual achievement consisted in the abandonment by the people of their pernicious habits and in the universalization of the mores of civility.[13] All this of course made enlightened despotism appear to possess a perfectly legitimate basis. This was a remarkable testimony to what could be achieved by following the examples set by European culture. Its clear implicit premise was the great desirability of cultural change that opened the road to progress.

If Russia represented what the effects of cultural change could be, the most inspiring models of European civilization were to be found in the West. France was the prime paradigm of modern civilization. The fertility of the land combined with the extraordinarily developed skills of the people made France the source of bounty. Material abundance formed the basis of the development of learning and the sciences in the highest degree possible. The French language was perfected to such a point that it became the language of wise and civilized men all over the world. In such a cultural environment, women no less than men elevated their mores to the height of honesty and virtue.[14]

Even more light was shining further north. In England, the national wealth produced by mercantilism, industrial development, and the export of industrial goods not only fostered the growth of splendid educational institutions, it also nurtured the ethic of free government. Being the product of a mixture of various nations of the North and South, the British achieved a remarkable moderation in their character. They had inventive, deft, and intelligent minds, and at the same time they were tolerant, stable, and apt in free thinking. Their magnanimity distinguished them always in both learning and war. Their bravery was renowned throughout Europe, and in the author's judgment they could rightly claim the first place among all those who excelled in science and wisdom. It was not difficult for such a people to achieve the best-ordered government in the world. Their monarchy combined all the advantages of both autocratic and democratic rule. A measure of their freedom and civilization was the widely respected rule of religious toleration that made it possible for everyone to profess and practice the doctrines of their own faith.[15] Thus, the geography of civilization was crowned by the projection of a prototype of liberty and a model of free government.

The comparison with the state of Greece was overwhelming. Here the translator expanded the original text with the insertion of his own commentaries on the condition of his homeland. The good government and greatness of antiquity and the glories Greece had experienced in the days of Alexander were gone. Catastrophe, alas, had befallen her. She declined and was divested of her previous splendor and glory. There were hardly any signs left

of her erstwhile greatness. Her people, the modern Greeks, were subjected
to the tyrannical yoke of the Turks. Most of her cities were in ruins, most of
the provinces deserted. The face of the country had been entirely deformed.
It was ruled by Turkish pashas who oppressed the land and the Christian
subjects without observing any law or principle of justice. They exercised
their authority by resorting to the methods of tyranny, injustice, and barbarism.[16] The Ottoman system of government was an absolute autocracy.
The life of the subjects was always exposed to the whims of their rulers.[17]
The Turks were impetuous and savage to the point that their mention alone
inspired the Christians with terror. There was no vice of which they did not
partake. Their sole good habit was that they kept their promises and were
dependable in their transactions. But this behavior was limited to foreigners
to whom the Ottomans appeared just and friendly. Finally, as far as their
religion was concerned, they were fanatic zealots.[18]

The effects of Ottoman rule in the Greek lands were devastating. Ever
since that catastrophic day of 29 May 1453, when the throne of the Roman
Empire—alas—collapsed and Constantinople became the metropolis of
the Turks,[19] the mores of the Greeks had constantly degenerated. In stark
contrast to the wisdom, virtue, and valor of the ancient Greeks, the modern Greeks had to fare as best they could under the barbarous tyranny of
the Turks. The perfected and eloquent dialect of ancient Athens had been
lost, education and learning declined under Turkish tyranny, and the land
in many regions of the empire, in Asia Minor, in Cyprus, and elsewhere,
though naturally rich and fertile, remained fallow and uncultivated.[20]

Yet all hope was not felt to be lost. The proximity of the monuments and
historic places of classical antiquity made the greatness of ancient Greek civilization a living memory and a familiar patrimony. Although some of the
most sacred of these monuments had been appropriated by the conquerors
and turned into shrines for their own worship, still the awareness of past
greatness was kindling some hope for the future.[21] This was sustained also
by some signs of a revival of learning. The geography of Greece thus turned
into a survey of the beginnings of the Enlightenment. Although colleges of
higher learning appropriately so called were lacking due to the adversities
of Turkish tyranny, still schools were to be found in which the Greek language was systematically taught. In addition there were even high schools in
which grammatical training was supplemented with the teaching of modern subjects. Such high schools that had enriched their curriculum with

the introduction of modern philosophy and mathematics were reported in Mount Athos, in Constantinople, and elsewhere.[22]

The secularized awareness of space and the novel preoccupations it reflected were thus gradually ingrained in the changing outlook of those segments of the Greek intelligentsia who were receptive to the influences of European culture. When, in the last quarter of the eighteenth century, the new geography was incorporated into school curricula,[23] the basic principles of mathematical geography and cosmography, supplemented with descriptions of the various countries and informed surveys of their political, social, economic, and cultural condition, were integrated into a new collective awareness of the world.

The primary intention of the new geography was fundamentally political. In his geographical treatise, another clergyman and later archbishop, Nikiphoros Theotokis, whom we have already encountered as the author of the first Newtonian treatise of physics in modern Greek and who almost succeeded Phratzeas on the throne of Philadelphcia in 1772, attempted a systematic comparative description of the forms of government prevailing in modern Europe. His classification scheme reflected the principles of Montesquieu's political Neoaristotelianism: the governments of Europe were divided into despotic, monarchical, aristocratic, democratic, or mixed forms.[24] In assessing these types, Theotokis, genuinely true to Montesquieu's spirit and purpose, concealed his preference but did not make secret his firm belief that despotic government, under which he had classified that of the Ottomans, was positively the worst variety.

Forms of government and institutional structures were seen to coincide with a distinct cultural ethic characterizing each European nation. The main thrust of Theotokis's geographical argument was a comparative assessment of the moral qualities composing the national character of European peoples. This was an applied moral sociology following Montesquieu's idea of the cultural spirit of political communities.[25] Thus, the Spaniards were noted for their seriousness, the Germans for their tolerance, high-mindedness, and industriousness, the Swiss for their gallantry and love for freedom. The French and the Italians were distinguished by their sharpness of spirit, their dexterity and vivacity, and their achievements in the arts. But the former, though enamored of both the Muses and Mars, were hollow and superficial while the latter were prone to vanity. The Dutch were tolerant and the most industrious of all European peoples. The British, whose monarch was limited by Parliament in matters of legislation and taxation,

were distinguished by their magnanimity, dexterity, seriousness, and apt-
ness in the advanced sciences. The Swedes were great freedom-lovers, while
the Russians, who had made great strides in the arts and sciences under
Peter the Great and Catherine II, were governed by an absolute monarchy
restrained by the laws. The Prussians cultivated all arts and sciences, but
excelled in the martial arts, while the Polish nobility, who cherished aristocratic freedom and honor, showed unmitigated cruelty to their peasants.[26]

The comparison of moral cultures was concluded by an analysis of the
reign of despotism in the Ottoman Empire. The Grand Seigneur or Sultan
of Turkey held absolute sway over the life and property of his subjects, who
were considered nothing but slaves. This double excess, excessive authority
and excessive subjugation, was the source of disorders and insurrections that
dramatized the cost of arbitrary government by showing that occasionally
it could involve no less than the ruler's life itself. The nature of the government could be shown once again to be interdependent with the character of
the people: the Turks tended to be generous and fascinated by commercial
deals, but fundamentally they were soft and lazy, superstitious, and hope-
lessly ignorant. Hence, the lands where the Muses used to have their exalted
abode could claim now nothing but the see of ignorance.[27]

GEOGRAPHY AS POLITICAL EDUCATION

The geography of civilization remained a central theme in the progress of the
Enlightenment. Geographical writing registered faithfully the new cultural
orientations. The self-consciousness of geographical literature as a channel
for the transmission of the Enlightenment found its manifesto in the *Theory
of Geography* published by Iosipos Moisiodax in 1781. Moisiodax began by
noting the want of geographical knowledge and by declaring as the substantive aspiration of his book the propagation of the modern theory and
empirical study of geography. His empiricism was combined with a utilitarian orientation. His purpose was to be useful to the widest possible audience, and for this reason he chose to write in the "common" style in order to
be understood by all. The empiricism of the new geography was quite daring, and its break with the past decisive. Moisiodax remarked that the Holy
Spirit might be an appropriate source of inspiration for theologians but not
for mathematicians. He also rejected both the Ptolemaic and the Cartesian
systems of astronomy and declared his allegiance to Newtonian physics. In

his view, modern science had superseded ancient learning fundamentally on account of the superiority of its empirical methods: direct observation, reliance on empirical data, and use of experiments.[28] Moisiodax's contribution in the *Theory of Geography* provided the foundation of a new intellectual approach to geographical writing. The change can be discerned by comparing the two most important Greek geographical books of the eighteenth century: Meletios's work at the beginning of the century, which still relied heavily on ancient sources; and the *Novel Geography* composed in 1791 by the hieromonach Daniel Philippidis (ca. 1755–1832) and the deacon Gregorios Constantas (1758–1844), both of them from Milies on Pelion, in the area of ancient Demetrias.[29] The two authors were Moisiodax's younger intellectual associates in the Danubian principalities during the last two decades of the eighteenth century and in their work followed the methodological approach he recommended: their discourse was the product of traveling, empirical observation, and sharp perception of contemporary problems. Moisiodax's method was applied in *Novel Geography* to the part of geography that he left out of his own treatise on mathematical geography: Philippidis and Constantas devoted their work to political and human geography, a subject that so much fascinated the mind of the Enlightenment.

In education and intellectual temper, the two were most representative of the type of learned *abbés* who sacrificed a career in the Church for the sake of enlightenment and as teachers and popularizers contributed so much to its progress on the continent of Europe. In the treatise of Philippidis and Constantas, the geography of civilization was carried one logical step further: the admiring survey of foreign cultures was used as the fitting context of self-criticism. The geography of human achievement and secular culture moved beyond the awe of the original discovery to stimulate reflection on the condition of Greek society and furnished the standards of its critical assessment.

The uncompromising commitment of the two authors to novelty and modern learning transpired throughout. The scientific spirit of the eighteenth century completely prevailed in the opening discourse on the elements of geography.[30] Even the standard courtesy to authority and respectability that required some reference to the arguments of ancient geographers was omitted. Furthermore Meletios, who opened the way to modern geographical writing, was criticized for relying too much on ancient sources. A convinced empiricism carried now the major weight in geographical methodology.[31]

The same irreverence to tradition and authority and the same sensitivity to living reality was reflected in the authors' attitudes toward religion and language. Their geography of world religions was just a factual account of religious preferences prevailing in different countries and continents, without any evaluative indications as to the truth of each religion: Christianity and its sects, Judaism, Islam, and even heathen paganism were described with equal detachment.[32] Linguistic and cultural prejudices, especially those betraying the cult of antiquity, were castigated. A good practical language like English was deemed preferable to the verbosity of atticizing Greek, and it was pointed out that revival of philosophy, as European historical experience had shown, was contingent on the use of a practical and living language. The assumption underlying these judgments was clearly stated: in a world pervaded by the single reality of change, utility was the measure of all things.[33]

A panorama of European civilization was painted in this spirit. Europe, the smallest of all continents, surpassed all others in the arts and sciences, in the rule of law and in orderly life, civilization, progress, and power,[34] but it was no longer the object of unquestioning adulation. A critical sense operated throughout with great sensitivity; a discerning eye was relentless in spotting the stigmas of European society. The two authors looked at Europe in much the same way as Montesquieu's Persian observers had done. Occasionally breathless in their admiration, finding everywhere models worthy of imitation in their homeland, they exposed and laid bare at the same time the various anomalies, defects, and vices that lay behind the glittering surface.[35]

Nature had bestowed on the countries of Europe all the blessings of temperate climate, fertile land, and bounty of resources that could assure the comfort and prosperity of their inhabitants. Italy was a case in point: she possessed in abundance not only what was necessary to life, but in addition all that could contribute to a happy life. Where this could not be achieved, the explanation could be found in prevailing social and political practices. Bad administration, the laziness of the inhabitants, and the insatiable greed of the rich were among the causes of human misery. Interference of the government in the economy was always followed by adverse consequences: its task ought to be to protect commerce, without becoming itself a trader, to prevent the emergence of monopolies, without taking them over itself.[36]

The festering sore from which most evils in Italian society emanated, however, was clerical corruption and the depraved moral condition of the Church. It was the greed of churchmen and their impositions on the peasants that brought famine to the people. The monks and nuns who filled the religious houses of Italy, escaping the responsibilities of civil society, lived off the labor and sweat of others promising in return a complete dedication to moral uprightness and prayers to God for the salvation of the world. Moral uprightness, however, was more frequent among laymen living in the world than among monks in their retreat. Indeed, the latter were more in need of the former's prayers for their own salvation. And this was known to be a universal, not a peculiarly Italian, phenomenon. Immorality, corruption, and exploitation had become integral parts of the vocation of the clergy. This appeared to result from the reduction of religious life in the Catholic Church to just a display of dramatic piety and hieratic superstition. Inner faith had been displaced by the external splendor of ceremonies that had turned the churches into some kind of theatre and a place for social intercourse, ostentation, and diversion.[37]

The decline of Italy, observable in the moral traits of her people, was the consequence of these practices. Political division, foreign domination, economic backwardness, and corrupt government in a country that had shown her great potentialities with her earlier magnificent contributions to civilization were symptomatic of this socially conditioned moral decline. In talking about the cultural greatness marking the Florentine past, the authors did not fail to pay tribute to Machiavelli, a "most profound" political thinker.[38] Observing the moral character of the Italians, one could not escape the conclusion that their ethical defects and failures were the products of an unfortunate political predicament and not the result of an inherent pernicious predisposition.[39]

That things could be otherwise was made clear by the experience of those regions which were blessed with enlightened government. Such had been the case under the administration of Grand Duke Leopold in Tuscany. Where formerly prevailed chaos, he brought order and progress. He instituted freedom of trade, curtailed clerical excesses and corruption, and fought against superstition. In Genoa also the discord and corruption that had undermined ancient republican liberty were contained, and a stable aristocratic regime was instituted through the intervention of Andrea Doria. This stability was the basis of the prosperity and power of the city.[40]

Since the character of government can be so decisive for the well-being and progress of society, the conditions of good government formed a central preoccupation in the analysis of the dynamics of civilization. One such condition that accounted not only for good and stable government but also for political greatness was found to be the civil religion of ancient Rome. The system of public religious practices, collective worship, and shared mythical beliefs made the ancient Romans conceive of their city and its glory as the product of their own strivings, the proper offspring of their efforts, sacrifices, and civic virtue. Coming to think of themselves as the fathers of their city, the Romans were infused with a patriotic zeal and enthusiasm that could only be compared to and understood as religious fervor. The constant war efforts in which Rome was engaged throughout her history kept this zeal and fervor unabated. It was such patriotic zeal that made the greatness of Rome possible.[41] Worldly achievements of such magnitude could justify the original seeds of religious belief and superstition from which Roman patriotic zeal derived. They also pointed to the potentialities of religion as a cohesive social spirit once it was freed from the plague of clerical corruption and deception. These views indicated clearly that the authors of *Novel Geography* espoused the theory of civil religion first expounded by Machiavelli and subsequently elaborated by Rousseau. This theoretical position was an important dimension of their social thought, which connected them with the Enlightenment's republican tradition, and as it will be shown below, it was not their only theoretical affinity with the heritage of civic humanism.

Another condition of good government was the virtue of the rulers. Moral paradigms from ancient and modern history indicated what could be achieved under the leadership of a virtuous prince. The actions and policies of such rulers ought to transcend considerations of private interest and to be motivated only by concern for the good of humanity. They should be equally concerned with the well-being of their own people as well as with that of their neighbors: this had been the case with Gelo of Syracuse, in whose humanism and virtue the Greek nation could take rightful pride. The examples of virtuous rule provided the only hope for the relief of mankind from the machinations of tyranny in which they were plunged by the relentless pursuit of selfish individual advantage. Such had been the origin of all kinds of pernicious behavior in modern society—an attitude that basically lost sight of the shared interest of humanity.[42]

The experience of greatness and decline marked also the social history of the other two Mediterranean societies surveyed by Philippidis and Constantas, Spain and Portugal. In their case too, tyrannical government, the corruption bred of idleness and luxury, and above all the plague of the priests and the Inquisition went a long way in accounting for the malaise of the two nations. Once again, on account of their past their potentialities were known to be such that hope for the future could not be ruled out. On the contrary, the recent experience and accomplishments of enlightened government in Spain had clearly shown that reform and improvement was possible once the relevant political conditions for it had prevailed. Indeed, a new golden age might have been dawning upon Spain.[43] Out of the survey of the human geography of Europe seemed to be emerging a conviction that political will and appropriately motivated leadership could guide a society out of the cycle of decline and corruption toward progress and enlightenment.

The problematic of political change thus became an integral part of geographical learning. When the geographers' attention turned to France, this problematic came forth at its greatest intensity: there was a profound awareness that this society, in which civilization had attained its most magnificent heights of accomplishment, was "undergoing a profound transformation."[44] The French people were among the foremost civilized nations of Europe, and their culture radiated throughout the continent. The rest of the European nations were reforming and shaping their ways on the models projected by the French, in much the same manner as the Greeks were imitated in antiquity—the Greeks of old, alas, who inspired admiration and fear, while in modern times they were either pitied or despised. Now the moment of the French had come: their tastes, their mores, their learning, and their language had become a shared patrimony of all those who aspired to partake of modern civilization. "Everywhere people strive to eat, drink, walk, socialize, dress, talk French."[45] The geography of France amounted essentially to an attempt at acquaintance with all those great hearths of civilization from where enlightenment radiated to less fortunate peoples. Its splendor was such that it dazzled the rest of Europe. Paris was seen as the heavenly city of enlightenment transposed on earth and made accessible to human aspirations.[46]

It was in this setting that the drama of political change was acted out. It almost seemed that revolution followed on the heels of enlightenment, that the full blossoming of civilization in all its manifestations set in motion the train of profound changes transforming French society. Observation and reflection on the nature and effects of civilization was in a way identified with contemplation of political change and revolution. The nature of change could be understood only on the basis of a familiarity with the institutions of the old regime: the system of absolute monarchical government, the aristocratic orders, and the *parlements* were described so as to indicate as effectively as possible the extent of the great change that was relentlessly altering everything. Its political effects involved a transfer of legislative power to the national assembly while the king was confined to the executive. Hereditary aristocracy and inherited privileges were abolished and peerage was to be used only as a reward of personal merit. Religious toleration was to be universally observed, and the numbers and powers of the clergy were severely limited. In short, "everything was changed and was still changing."[47] Change was not a sudden outburst. Its seeds went back at least fifty years and culminated in Necker's reforms. But his reform, for which he was so much praised by all wise Frenchmen, furnished the leaven of revolution.[48]

It was the first time that the vocabulary of political change was put into the language of the modern Greeks. The pristine innocence of a freshly awakened consciousness that sought to acquaint itself with the marvels of the world and the achievements of civilization opened the way for the exposure of the Greek mind to the theory of revolution: if an initial attempt at reform for the sake of efficiency and public welfare lay at the origins of the subsequent ferment, recalcitrant conservatism, narrow-mindedness, and the claims of irrational privilege only precipitated demagoguery, hardening of respective positions, and an eventual explosion and conflict out of all proportion to what was visualized by the original aspiration. This was the logic of revolution. Although the authors remained uncertain in their attitude toward it and concluded their analysis in suspended judgment, their anatomy of the French experience was an open invitation to Greek thought to reflect on the problem of political change and come up with the judgment they evaded.

GEOGRAPHY, CRITICISM, AND REVOLUTION

If they remained undecided before the French Revolution, the authors of *Novel Geography* were prepared and fortified by their itinerary in enlightened Europe for passing judgment on the condition of their own society. The human geography of Greece was prefaced by a brief survey of the historical destinies of the ancient nation inhabiting the southernmost regions of the Balkan Peninsula and the Aegean shores.[49] This was a story of the rise and fall of the nation that had emerged on the scene of history amid the drama of the Trojan War. It was a story of heroism and creativity, but also of conflict. Inevitably, corruption began producing its effects among the Greeks. The great victory against the Persian assault became a source of vanity, arrogance, and mutual envy, and this culminated in civil war, the destruction of civic liberty, and eventually the fall of classical Greece. Corruption subverted republican order in ancient Athens, where idleness, self-seeking, the pursuit of pleasure—to say nothing of the bribes of Philip of Macedon—displaced the ardent love of liberty and fatherland and obscured all conceptions of genuine glory.[50] Submission to the Macedonians opened the way to civil strife following the glorious interlude of Alexander's empire. The Roman conquest marked the final fall of Greece. True, a Christian Greek Empire centered on Byzantium emerged out of the Roman conquest of the East, but in a way this was only the prelude to further ravages and depredations in the hands of the Crusaders and the Ottoman Turks. The fatal year of 1453 marked the final disaster in the chain of political changes: the Greek Empire fell, and the shadow of debasing enslavement covered the whole of the Greek world. The dark ages of Greece began at about the time the West was emerging out of its own long lethargy.[51]

Deciphering the meaning of the past, in terms of the theory of history borrowed by the authors of the *Novel Geography* from the thought of radical civic humanism, was a prelude to criticism of the present. The journey through the Greek lands was an invitation to reflection upon the final social outcome of the degrading process of decline and corruption. It was a lively and purposeful peregrination, caught in the infinite fascination and curiosity accompanying the rediscovery of a space felt to be very close and intimate and yet very little known. The theoretical preference for concrete knowledge based on direct empirical observation, so often urged in the pages of the treatise, found its practical expression in the sharp sensitivity to the beauties and resources of nature, the constant awareness of the physical environment, and the full acknowledgment of the weight of natural forces, such as climate, on human affairs. It was known, however, that powerful as the impact of climate might be, still the decisive sources of social events were human and not natural. In dissecting these causes, too, the two authors followed Montesquieu closely.[52]

If there were so many social evils to be encountered in the Greek lands despite the temperate climate, despite the fertility of the soil, despite the bounty of nature, the cause was all too obvious: alien despotism. This was the mortifying legacy of the disaster of 1453. Despotism obstructed all progress. Its effects were to be seen everywhere: they extended to Turks as well as Greeks and the rest of the empire. Arbitrary, violent, and rapacious government fostered a sense of insecurity and desperation that drove the Christian subjects of the sultan to emigrate to neighboring countries where they could enjoy the benefits of the rule of law. Although this voluntary exile assured them the rights of life and property, amid their prosperity they sighed with nostalgia for the fair climes of their native lands.[53] Arbitrary government and rapacious exactions from the cultivators of the land led to neglect of agriculture, and it undermined all motivation for sustained economic activities. Hence poverty was widespread and famines frequent.[54] Rampant piracy at sea and banditry on land, bad and insecure roads, and a general reign of lawlessness prevented the real potential for commercial development from coming to fruition. Furthermore, the Greeks and other commercially inclined subject nations encountered serious obstruction of their economic activities on the part of the Turkish authorities. Hence, the massive flights of industrious and successful merchants abroad and the consequent serious damage to the local economy, which remained open to the plunder of European traders who made millions at the expense of the natives. All this profoundly pained an enlightened observer who knew very well what was in his land's best interest. But the rulers looked with contempt on these concerns, because they were so ignorant as to remain unaware of the damages that their administrative practices and neglect brought on their own domains. The king of Turkey, given the resources of his lands, could have had double the revenues of the king of France, but he hardly managed to collect an amount equivalent to one-third of them. "Those in command despise such concerns, but by perpetually despising them they had declined to such a contemptible state that they were despised by all."[55]

Such were the effects of despotic government. Every concerned enlightened person who could sense the causes of social evil was driven to despair at the sight of the state of the Ottoman Empire. And Turkey could have been a realm awesome externally, happy domestically, if only the law became sovereign. Good laws were the soul of societies, and in their absence human communities tended inescapably to perish. Good laws were those that protected one's life, property, honor, and freedom, and meted punishments to those who attempted to violate these rights. Such punishments ought to have been uniformly imposed regardless of who the violators were, because they were enemies and destroyers of civil society.[56]

Ottoman despotism, however, was not the sole source of the plight of Greek society. The modern Greeks themselves, corrupted to be sure by the effects of despotic government, were not innocent of responsibility for the condition of their society. The ancient curse of civil discord and dissension, which had planted the seeds of the corruption of classical greatness, vitiated all attempts of the moderns to lift themselves out of their debasement. Witness the experience of that quasi-republican community of unbending mountaineers at Mani: at the height of their power and conquering vigor, the Turks could not subjugate them, but managed to do so in their decay aided by the Maniots' disastrous domestic dissension and quarrels. Discord had also contributed to the decline and eventual destruction of Moschopolis, that great center of civic progress and culture in the eighteenth century.[57]

Discord was not alone in intensifying the depraving effects of despotism among the Greeks. Deeply ingrained prejudice was another symptom of corruption and a source of further moral debasement that found several manifestations. Religious intolerance was among its prime expressions. Greeks and Turks, cohabitants of the same lands, found it mutually impossible to tolerate each other's religious convictions. This was nothing but the effect of ignorance. One's religious convictions concerned exclusively one's relation with God. It was not a social concern. As far as human relations were concerned, men should love each other like brothers. Differences in religious beliefs should never become a source of social hostility. Such collective hostility should be solely directed against those who positively harmed civil society, while those who were misguided should be treated with pity and understanding. Hatred and violence only fortified people in their misguided beliefs, while love and reason helped them overcome their prejudices and give in to truth. Indeed, it appeared quite presumptuous for men to adopt the role of God's advocates as if the deity was incapable of defending its right. The ensuing pretentiousness and conflicts at the expense of sound human interests constituted in fact an insult to any religion. In religious matters, therefore, the authors felt toleration was the only attitude becoming to virtuous and enlightened men.[58] This eloquent argument for toleration was a quite appropriate practical implication drawn from the social analysis of religion attempted by Constantas and Philippidis.

Prejudice of a different kind lay at the source of the diverging opinions that found expression in the language question. The central problem here concerned the appropriate language of the Greek revival. What should the linguistic medium of reconstituted education and regenerated learning be among the modern Greeks? The end of the eighteenth century had witnessed the emergence of conflicting responses to this question, and the authors of *Novel Geography* registered their view on the problem in the context of that ongoing ideological debate.[59] The whole issue derived from a misguided linguistic prejudice entertained by some who thought that change in a language meant its corruption. This misconception so much blinded those who held it that they refused even to recognize that the modern Greeks possessed a language of their own. Prejudice had only hardened them in their ignorance. Arguing that the spoken language of the modern Greeks ought to be purified and cultivated, archaists thought that this could be achieved by moving the language away from its current spoken form and making it conform to the structure of ancient Greek. Constantas and Philippidis pointed out that the archaists failed to see that such a Procrustean exercise could only produce a linguistic monster, an artificial and unnatural mixture of assorted syntactical and lexical elements without a unified linguistic or dialectical basis. Thus, far from achieving the cultivation and intellectual perfection of the language, the archaists' efforts to make it conform to ancient Greek amounted in reality to its distortion and corruption, because it violated its natural structure and rhythm.

According to the two authors, this misguided contempt for the modern natural language of the Greek people was one of the sources of the prevailing ignorance and backwardness. For the wider masses of the people, education, conducted in a language they could not understand, remained inaccessible. Those who did manage to penetrate the sanctuaries of learning were bewildered by the hermeticism of the curriculum and of the language, and they wore themselves out in futile reading exercises based on ancient texts without learning anything of substance. In this way their reasoning and thinking capacities were gradually blunted. The stubborn effort to impose knowledge of a dead language was ultimately responsible for the prevailing ignorance. Indeed, contempt for the nation's natural language was not just the cause of cultural backwardness; in essence it amounted to a denial of the very humanity of those of its speakers who were ashamed to acknowledge it as their own—since language was the foremost characteristic of the human species, as the Enlightenment had so categorically insisted.

Contrary to the archaists' deeply entrenched prejudices, the education of the youth should begin with the study of their mother tongue, which is by nature the first step of learning. History and geography should be studied next, and afterwards, on these sound foundations, the children should embark on the study of foreign languages, the liberal arts, and sciences. Concerning the issue of cultivating and improving the language, it was clear that language was a natural growth with its own rules, and grammar was nothing but a description of the language, faithfully reflecting its natural logic and structure. Reversing the process and attempting to make the language conform its rules and passions to a preconceived grammatical and syntactical structure was nothing but distortion and an offense to nature. Resort to such practices ought rightfully to be the cause of shame. On the contrary, there was nothing to be embarrassed about in acknowledging the living version of Greek as the legitimate medium of the nation's expression.

Greek society was not alone in facing cultural problems of this nature. France, Germany, and Italy had experienced and resolved them in the past: everywhere the natural modern language had triumphed and marked the beginning of a revival of letters.[60] Implicit in this pointer was the authors' faith that their choice of the most radical among the alternatives debated on the Greek language problem would be eventually vindicated by a comparable revival.

Beyond the cultural problems that these debates dramatized, Greek society had to come to terms with another social evil, which the survey of European societies as well had repeatedly shown to be at the origin of national decline, corruption, and malaise. Although the authors themselves belonged to the religious orders, this evil, in their judgment, was nothing else but the social role of the clergy and especially of monasticism. Churches and religious houses were ever present in the Greek lands, and the most important among them were always noticed by the authors in their survey. But at the sight of the monastic republic on Mount Athos, their submerged contempt exploded.[61] Constantas and Philippidis wondered how it could be otherwise for any enlightened person who noticed the vast lands that supported the idleness of Athonite monks. Their fury was further compounded by familiarity with the social history of monasticism in the Greek Empire. Indeed, the expansion of monasticism, which was symbolized by the construction of religious houses on Mount Athos at the time of the Byzantine emperors, was responsible for the destruction of the empire and the degradation of Greece. The Christian emperors were misled by superstition to believe that they should encourage, honor, and support the religious orders—as if the monks rather than the soldiers would stem the assault of Arabs in the South, Turks in the East, Scythians in the North, and Latins in the West. At the time of the Christian emperors, Constantinople and the rest of Greece were full of monasteries, some of them very rich and populous. No decent human being would ever join those monasteries: this could be easily concluded from the fact that although the sincere monk should be supporting himself through his own exertion, even if he were the son of a king, those living in the monasteries were leading the good life at the expense of the rest of the population. In short, in the author's judgment, the monks had joined the monasteries to save their bodies rather than their souls.

Despite all this, the Christian kings were so blinded by superstition that they continued to increase the number of monasteries and to bestow privileges and donations on them, thus encouraging and rewarding laziness, hypocrisy, and dishonesty. The consequence of this was that even men of a better stamp were corrupted. Alas, this policy of suicidal folly undermined the foundations of civil society and spelled its disaster: precisely as the case might be with a hive bursting with drones. A political community, all of whose members were not equally active and diligent, tends sooner or later to perish. In such a society the idle consumer is the enemy of the hard-working producer. Violence, fraud, and hypocrisy is according to occasion used by the former at the expense of the latter. From such a society, patriotism and fairness, whose cultivation should be a king's first care and duty, tend to disappear. Following Montesquieu's explanation of the decline of the Christian Empire,[62] the authors of *Novel Geography* had managed to connect the syndrome of superstition and monastic idleness to the cycle of corruption that was responsible for the predicament of their society.

It was this state of affairs that so much agitated and distressed the two authors of *Novel Geography*. However, as was fit for enlightened thinkers well read in the great *Encyclopédie* and the works of the famed Montesquieu,[63] their distress was not translated into resignation and fatalism. Their itinerary did not simply heighten their awareness of the social problems plaguing the Greek lands. It also enabled them to glean the signs of hope

and to reflect on its possibilities. The major source of hope was increasingly to be found in the awareness of the Hellenic past. The remnants of
antiquity scattered throughout the Greek lands were the constant reminders
of a glorious national patrimony. Time and time again the two authors
would pause in their journey to observe and describe with affection and care
the broken marbles, mutilated statues, and crumbling temples that bore
witness confirming their highly prized sense of their ancient lineage. Even
where the tangible traces of antiquity had fallen prey to relentless time and
disappeared, ancient toponyms and historically relevant locations invited
accounts of past achievements and served as reminders of the glories of old.
Upon reaching Attica, at the sight of sacred Athens the intellectual journey
was transformed into a pilgrimage.[64] The authors' reflections on the political constitution, the civic culture, and intellectual achievements of ancient
Athens gave expression to their emotion. Here was a barren corner of land,
deprived of nature's great resources but which found its blessing in its natural poverty: this was what motivated its inhabitants to turn to the sea and
to commerce, to the crafts, the sciences, and the liberal arts. Such were the
origins of Athenian greatness. That barren corner of land was sanctified by
the flowering of the greatest civilization. Its moral dynamic was provided
by a religious respect of the public domain and ancestral values. This found
expression in the civil religion of the Athenian republic, whose public life
was governed by political rather than religious concerns.[65] The relevance of
the extensive treatment of Athens was taken to be self-evident, adequately
justified by the intrinsic importance of the subject that had inspired voluminous admiring accounts by so many foreigners. To the Greeks, such knowledge was a vitally relevant moral lesson and a pointer of hope to what might
have been.

     As the journey continued, the geography of hope was broadened. At Ioan-
nina, the revival of learning among the modern Greeks was proved to be a
practical possibility. The same was true of the experience of Moschopolis in
Epirus.[66] Although great men were but the creation of virtuous government,
the horizon of hope kept expanding: in Crete the survival of precious human
gifts in defiance of the degrading effects of despotism was proving that
the virtue of ancient Greeks had not altogether disappeared.[67] On certain
islands, notably Chios, a system of republican local government was practiced so successfully that it could be projected as a model for other regions
including the authors' own native community.[68] At Ambelakia in Thessaly,

the great strides of the spinning and dyeing industry and export trade and the concomitant social and educational progress of the community were proving the possibilities of organized cooperative ventures fostered by civic harmony.[69] What else could all this suggest but that the yoke of many centuries had not completely eradicated and stamped out that Hellenic spirit that inspired and motivated the ancient ancestors of the Greeks? Despite so many deprivations (of books, of schools, and of moral upbringing and culture in general), only a favorable wind was needed to blow to dispel the heavy fog and let that spirit shine again and radiate in the world.[70]

This deeply felt yearning for the reconstruction of Hellenism found its fullest expression in the sensitive sociology reserved for the analysis of the authors' native region, Magnesia in Thessaly.[71] A loving and vivid description of the natural surroundings conveyed an intense sense of beauty and bounty. The region was made up of twenty-four villages scattered on the slopes of Mount Pelion on the Aegean coast of Thessaly. Ottoman administration was somewhat better in this region, less high-handed and more fair-minded than was usually the case. Direct control by the capital prevented local Turkish potentates and adventurers from entering the region and resorting to their usual bestial barbarism. This administrative system of central protection and local autonomy could therefore have made the inhabitants happier than those who lived even under European governments. The authors lamented the fact that ignorance and its consequences, the vices and incompetence of local notables, made even this privileged region equally unhappy as the rest of the Ottoman Empire. Conflicts arose out of the strivings of some for primacy. This destroyed social harmony, led to tyrannical practices, and eventually impaired everyone's welfare. If they only followed the dictates of right reason, however, if they were guided by considerations of the common interest, which was in fact identical with each one's private interest, they could be the happiest men under the Ottomans. Nature had bestowed upon them plentifully her gifts, and fortune had graced them with a unique liberty that such happiness was easily within their reach, had it not been for the chaos of ignorance and its cursed children, the several social passions.[72] Even where fortune had not been so magnanimous, moral rectitude and practical spirit on the part of the primates, a greater degree of social solidarity among the inhabitants, and a collectively shared dedication to their homeland could have achieved extensive social benefits for their communities. Not only the material substratum but the moral infrastructure of civic progress was present: the mores of the people were polished and cultivated due to a network of Greek schools that extended to all villages. Hence, everywhere were to be found educated and respectable men. Superstition was generally absent. Contact with foreign lands through emigration had expanded the people's horizons, especially in certain communities. The climate was conducive to natural intelligence. In this milieu even the lower clergy were decent though they could have been much more competent in their spiritual duties, had the most reverend bishops of the area been more eager to meet their own obligations of pastoral guidance. Unfortunately, their graces were not interested in anything except their levies; under such leadership the Church, one could daresay, had become just a marketplace of sacraments.[73]

It was obvious that the potentialities of liberty, social reconstruction, and moral progress were immanent in the society of those small mountain republics. Once again the authors did not miss Montesquieu's message about the suitability of mountainous countries to liberty.[74] It appeared that for those potentialities to come to fruition it would only take a maturity of will, appropriate motivation, a shared desire to strive for their actualization. In turn, all this was dependent on a moral reconstruction of personalities, on training in enlightened social spirit. Such precisely was the target of the feverish exhortation of the authors to their compatriots. Pausing to reflect on the condition of their native community, agitated by an emotional outburst that was made all the more intense by their faith in the possibilities of enlightenment, they urged their fellow countrymen to transform themselves into citizens of a virtuous republic. Clearly, their inspiration was similar to that which guided Rousseau's interpretation of social life in rural Switzerland and his vision for Corsica. Like Rousseau, the two Greek geographers pleaded for a social character marked by equity, humanity, and good faith and for a pattern of social relations based on mutual benevolence and friendship.[75]

It was a plea against incompetent civic government and dissension, against indiscipline, envy, and mutual persecution. It was an invitation to strive for an improved public order and for general concord, deriving from an *eros* of the common good and disdain for self-seeking. Such *eros* of the public good was the cause of the prosperity of great kingdoms and countries, communities and individual families. Dissension and discord were the products of self-seeking and indifference toward the public interest.

Self-seeking was sheer folly because those who cared only for their private interests at the expense of the public were bound to eventually suffer if the community perished. The seeds of corruption of great realms and cities were laid as soon as their foremost citizens succumbed to the cursed lures of egoism. This was the result of ignorance, inexperience, and folly. Genuine and enlightened self-interest was primarily concerned with common and general welfare of which all particular interests partook. This was true virtue, the child of wisdom and prudence that taught the maxims of righteous human conduct. One could only wish that such enlightened self-interest should guide the motivations of all mankind![76]

The most telling advice pointing to such a course of action should come from the actual experience of the disastrous effects of dissension and self-seeking. Unwavering love of country and community should from then on become the driving motive. Such moral motivation would make possible a form of government that would oversee the common prosperity. This plea derived from the authors' sense of duty to draw from their learning in the Enlightenment useful lessons that might be of relevance to the common good of their native community.[77] This psychology, and the political theory that was connected with it, constituted a clear case of republican thought. The authors of *Novel Geography* combined the pertinent mental attitude with the characteristic perception of social and political problems that formed the essence of republican civic humanism. Yet this was not a utopian republicanism but a proposal of social and moral regeneration that remained conscious of the constraints and possibilities of a concrete social milieu.

The noble inspiration of the plea that concluded the geography of civilization carried a clear political message. Geographical literature had been from the very start a systematic projection before Greek consciousness of paradigms and models drawn from the experience of the enlightened nations of Europe. The civilization of the French, the liberty of the British, and the gallantry of the Swiss suggested what enlightenment could accomplish—everything that with its absence dramatized the depravity of Greek society. Indeed, the anatomy of Greek society within the framework set by the geography of human achievement exemplified very distinctly the two characteristic dimensions of the utopian outlook: a melancholy at the predicament of the present, morally debased and socially corrupt as it was, and a nostalgia for a lost golden past whose mutilated remnants survived as sad reminders.[78] This mental climate motivated the search for models that might guide an attempt at reconstruction. The weight of the present and of its mortifying problems was felt so constraining that the alternatives were not sought beyond living experience, in the realm of the ideal. Instead of visualizing an Atlantis or an Icaria as the basis of their criticism, the Greek geographers of hope limited their aspirations to the actual examples suggested by their acquaintance with European civilization. It was clear to them that improvement of education, reconstruction of social mores, and institutional reform in the direction of the European experience was the utmost that Greek society could hope to achieve. The social context within which the values of the Enlightenment were to be transferred was conducive only to careful and circumscribed reform, not to utopia.[79] This realistic conclusion nonetheless was profoundly revolutionary. Once acceptable alternatives could be visualized and realistically projected on the strength of their fruitfulness elsewhere, a theoretical revolution had been accomplished. This revolution in consciousness, based on the incontrovertible evidence of the geography of human achievement, carried with it clear practical implications. A program of social action was implicit in the geographical literature of the Enlightenment. Even gradual reform in the institutions and values of traditional Greek society on the European model would essentially amount to a social revolution. If the enlightened geographers did not articulate this implication of their vision, their conservative rivals sensed it from the outset and made it their battle cry.

The Greek observers' itinerary in enlightened Europe concluded in an existential experience much more profound and far-ranging than that depicted by Montesquieu in the *Persian Letters*. The Enlightenment of Montesquieu's Persian travelers, though genuine in its commentary on Persian mores, stopped at the confines of Persia. Within his own country, Uzbek remained a despot, and where his personal interests were at stake, he retained much of the cruelty and inhumanity of traditional practices. For the Greek geographers, the encounter with Europe and the experience of enlightenment nurtured an earnest yearning for change *within* their society. In this the Greek geographers shared Montesquieu's political attitude rather than that of his fictitious characters.[80] Montesquieu as the greatest political mind of the Enlightenment and the Greek authors as its genuine children appeared similarly concerned with the reform of their respective societies. The Greek learned *abbés* who had denounced the corruption of Church hierarchy and the depravity of monasticism had very little at stake in the existing order. This added psychological force to the subversive message of their passionate appeal for a transplantation of the models they found in the capitals of enlightenment into the soil of their own homeland. This was the revolutionary dynamic of the geography of civilization.[81]

CHAPTER FOUR

Enlightened Absolutism as a Path to Change

THE PARADIGMS OF civilization projected in the geography of human achievement were expected to be attained by means of the policies of change that might be followed by benevolent and enlightened princes. This expectation provided the psychological basis of the idea of an enlightened absolutism in the eighteenth century. Historical criticism has effectively pointed out the many ambiguities and inner contradictions in the nature of the concept as well as the limits of its applicability in describing actual historical experience and the political practice of eighteenth-century monarchs.[1] That the older popular term "enlightened despotism" is self-contradictory and hardly meaningful, as a description of even a modified phenomenon of modernization from above in the eighteenth century, is made plain by the fact that the words "despotic" and "despotism" were appropriated by European political thought in order to characterize and disparage the excesses of modern arbitrary autocracy and to denote resistance to it.[2] Despite the espousal of some of the Physiocrats' ideas and the consistent efforts of some eighteenth-century monarchs to create more efficient administration, and within the limits of their autocracies to introduce more humane government, absolutism even when it wanted to be enlightened was fundamentally incompatible with the principle of freedom and the rule of law enshrined in the political philosophy of the Enlightenment.[3] If subsequent historical appraisals have shown the severe limits of absolutism as a practical application of enlightened social principles,[4] the keenest political minds of the Enlightenment, Montesquieu and Rousseau, knew that from the very beginning. Montesquieu had insisted that despotism involved a pervasive silence and fear that turned political communities into deserts, and for Rousseau the concentration of power in the hands of one man meant the exile of politics and the destruction of freedom.[5] The Enlightenment was not and could never be a political theory of "enlightened despotism."

Montesquieu and Rousseau denied to absolutism even the benefit of doubt. Reflection on the actual political conditions of eighteenth-century Europe, however, and a consideration of the possibilities they felt immanent in certain initiatives and experiences of their time, led some other representatives of the Enlightenment to allow the benefit of doubt concerning a few cases of absolutism. Voltaire and Diderot both hated despotism and cherished a concept of liberty quite radical in its claims. Their preoccupation with social and cultural change, however, and their involvement in the practical politics of the Enlightenment as a movement of renewal, led them to pay serious attention to the intentions, policies, and achievements of some of the modernizing monarchs of their time. Voltaire knew, from his research on Russian history during the reign of Peter the Great, that absolutism possessed a unique dynamism, which, directed by a capable ruler, could bring about great achievements in renovating a backward society and opening its gates to the Enlightenment. Thus, in Peter he admired a hero of civilization, in contrast to Sweden's Charles XII, who was simply a hero of martial valor and conquest.[6]

Voltaire could, therefore, place some trust and hope in the intentions of Frederick of Prussia, who did not spare words in trying to flatter him and convince him of his sincere devotion to the Enlightenment. Disappointed upon direct contact with Frederick, Voltaire in his old age could still rediscover some hope in the policies of one of Peter's successors, Catherine II, who proved adept in deceiving him and nurturing his admiration.[7] From her distant empire, Catherine could as well capture the fascination of Diderot who, in his *Pages contre un tyran,* had torn apart the mythology about Frederick and dismissed him as a mediocre thinker, poor poet, and disappointing king.[8] His limited knowledge of the Russian situation colored his expectation from Catherine's policies with greater optimism, but he did not hesitate to voice his criticisms once he realized the way the empress twisted the ideas of the Enlightenment to serve her autocratic purposes.[9]

The fascination of the philosophes with enlightened absolutism indeed proved to be a mirage. They were disabused of their wishful thinking once they realized, upon closer examination of the nature of the phenomenon, that in adopting modern "enlightened" ideas and practices the chorus of so-called enlightened monarchs simply intended to make their autocracies more effective and enhance their power. The new outlook adopted by the disabused observers of enlightened absolutism was graphically expressed by the Abbé Raynal in one of the later editions of his *Histoire philosophique des deux Indes:* enlightened absolutism was acceptable only as a civilizing agent among uncivilized peoples and unenlightened societies.[10]

Yet this new posture, as well as the logic of Voltaire's and Diderot's flirtations with enlightened absolutism, revealed the substantive meaning of the idea as understood by the mind of the eighteenth century. It was seen as a potential agent of change and renovation. This is what made it provisionally appealing to the partisans of the Enlightenment who, encouraged by some initial achievements and the proclamation of good intentions, showed some willingness to give it a chance. In a sense this was a realistic calculation: absolutism was the predominant political reality of the eighteenth century, and the philosophes had to try to come to terms with it. Montesquieu, however, had warned that in fact all hope in absolutism was ill founded. Reform could not be achieved under the aegis of despotism because it tended to stifle the creative energies of a society. Absolutism could only exist in immobility and change in decay. The profession of good intentions by some of the modernizing monarchs obscured for a time Montesquieu's diagnosis and can explain the transient optimism of some of his philosophic brethren. The monarchs who wanted to appear enlightened were in fact good Machiavellians—their protestations to the contrary not withstanding—and knew how to gain the philosophes' approval through the art of appearances.[11]

If "enlightened absolutism" was meaningless as a political theory and devoid of substantial content as political practice, it represented the eloquent expression of a political psychology pregnant with expectations. The emergence of this political psychology, and its focus on absolutism's promise of change, was a powerful indication of the evolution of political consciousness in that age of Enlightenment. The static paternalism of traditional kingship had been replaced by the expectation of social change and cultural renewal embodied in the promises of "enlightened absolutism." Although this evolution occurred within the broad institutional parameters of a monarchical form of government, it represented a long itinerary toward a new level of political consciousness.

THE RISE AND FALL OF THE RUSSIAN EXPECTATION

In the Greek experience, a number of distinct but interlocking cultural and political currents provided the substratum for the elaboration of a theory of enlightened absolutism as the agent of cultural change and as the instrument of the moral and political regeneration of Greek society. One such current, entirely unrelated to the Enlightenment but springing deeply from Greek folk culture and popular hopes, was a universe of millenarian beliefs in a forthcoming day of redemption from captivity. These hopes were expressed in a body of folk legends and poetry that extended back to the traumas inflicted on popular psychology by the disintegration of the Byzantine Empire and the Fall of Constantinople.[12] The horrors of captivity in the hands of an infidel conqueror were expected eventually to come to an end with the resurrection of the lost empire of the Romans, once the sins that brought about captivity were expiated. Ottoman captivity was felt to be a collective earthly purgatory that held a certain, if dim and distant, promise of redemption.[13]

This substratum of folk millenarianism, pregnant as it always was with revolutionary potentialities,[14] provided the psychological basis for a political theory of national revival that gripped both the popular imagination and the political reasoning of Greek social and intellectual elites in the eighteenth century. Although some roots of the new theory could be traced in the heritage of models of Christian monarchy, the major stimulation for its emergence and development came from Greek perceptions of the possibilities of European international relations at the time and from the consequent reflections and calculations as to how these developments might influence the fate of the Ottoman Empire and the destinies of the subject peoples. The decisive development was the emergence of Orthodox Russia as a major power in the European state system at the threshold of the eighteenth century. Russia's ambitions and designs southward, which led her on an inevitable collision course with the Ottoman Empire, set the context for Greek calculations and hopes. The association of Russia with the Greek yearning for redemption displaced expectations, which at an earlier date had focused on the policies of other European powers, especially Austria and Venice, whose propaganda had done much to foster them.[15] The new power politics could derive an aura of legitimacy from the history of Muscovite-Byzantine relations in the medieval past and from the claims of Orthodox Russia to the mantle of leadership of the Orthodox world and her consequent obligations to intervene on behalf of the Orthodox peoples held in captivity by the Ottomans.[16]

In light of these developments, the traditional Greek hope of redemption was recast in a new political calculus in the reasoning of successive generations of Greek scholars and lay or ecclesiastical leaders. Redemption was expected to come through the intervention of the Third Rome where the might of an Orthodox empire had been transposed. This political calculation was endowed with the dynamic of broadly based popular appeal by forging a connection between the new reading of the possibilities of international life and the psychological force of the oracular tradition. The Russian expectation, which emerged out of these reorientations and became a dominant political force in Greek life throughout the eighteenth century, had already a distinguished history in the thought of such luminaries of Greek letters as the archbishop of Philadelphia, Gerasimos Vlachos, primate of the Greek Church in Venice and an eminent author and compiler of a major dictionary; Alexandros Mavrokordatos, the great master of Ottoman diplomacy at the turn of the seventeenth and the eighteenth centuries; Anastasios Michael from Naoussa, a member of the Royal Academy of Berlin and author of the *Vasilikon Theatron* [*A theater of kings*], which glorified the victories of Peter the Great over Charles XII of Sweden; and Kaisarios Dapontes, who was much admired as the greatest poet of the age. A figure of particular importance because of the response that he met, even though the arguments he adduced were rather eccentric, was Anastasios Gordios, who emphasized the importance of Russia as a bastion of the Orthodox faith, though at the same time ruling out the attainment of Greek political redemption through Russian intervention.[17]

The effective link between the Russian expectation and the tradition of popular millenarianism was worked out in the middle decades of the eighteenth century as the result of the activity of Theoklitos Polyeidis, an episcopal vicar who had left his ecclesiastical charge in Macedonia to travel in Central Europe in the 1720s and 1730s. The turn of military and diplomatic events in Eastern Europe at the time had created a climate conducive to a rethinking of the Greek problem. The defeats of the Ottoman Empire, which were sanctioned by the humiliating Treaties of Carlowitz and Passarovitz, and the first Russo-Turkish war of 1736–1739 induced for the first time some speculation on what advantages might be derived by the Greek nation out of these convulsions. Within this context, Polyeidis tried to promote the Greek cause by specifying the favorable international opportunities that might be seized by the Greeks. At the same time, by producing a new version of oracular literature, he attempted to mold a receptive popular psychology that could motivate the Greek masses to rally to the European rivals of the Ottomans in the event the powerful of the day heeded the Greek pleas.

Initially inspired by his travels in Germany and impressed by the rising power of Prussia, Polyeidis expected that the redemption of the Greeks might come through German intervention in the East. In the 1740s, while serving as Greek chaplain in Dresden, he had apparently placed some hopes in Frederick the Great. On the basis of some evidence of attempts to appeal to a wider public during his extensive journeys in several German cities, a tenuous connection has been suggested between his activities and the inception of the Germanic idea of the *"Drang nach Osten"* in the eighteenth century.[18] In any case, in the oracles that he finally composed, he reserved a preeminent role for the Germans in the affairs of the East. Ideally, his political objective was a united front of the two "blonde nations," Germans and Russians, against the Ottomans. This again represented a direct reflection of the diplomatic conjectures of the times as crystallized in the alliances during the war of 1736–1739.[19]

Despite this awareness of the facts of international life and his travels in the major centers of the German Enlightenment, Polyeidis persisted in a traditional ideology in trying to explain the misfortunes of his people. Talking about the political conditions of the East, he noted:

> Numerous nations—and among them we Greeks, except for those who are
> under the sway of Christian kings—are, alas, subjected for 282 years now

to the Turkish Empire; because in the year 1453, on the 29th of May, on a Tuesday, the brave hero Mohammed II ascended to the imperial throne of Constantinople, perhaps for the purpose of punishing those nations for their sins and moreover in order for all men to tread in the fear of God so that God would not deprive them of his mercy.[20]

It was thus the sins of the Christian people and not a certain political logic of history that could explain the collective predicament of the Greeks. National captivity was understood as the outcome of the unfolding of a providential purpose in human history—a meaning already spelled out in Byzantine cosmological eschatology. Polyeidis's explanation of the Fall of Constantinople and the reduction of the Christian Romans of the Eastern Empire to captivity was not different from that put forward by Byzantine intellectuals like Joseph Vryennios and Gennadios Scholarios who, three hundred years earlier, had witnessed the disintegration and fall of the empire.[21] Such was the ideological basis on which the new oracles were composed. Despite the new political objectives they were designed to foster, ideologically the new oracles belonged to a much older millenarian tradition.[22]

The new oracles were composed in the 1750s, but they had been in the making during a much longer period, stretching from the end of the reign of Peter the Great (1725) to the eve of the accession of Catherine II, whose advent to power is ignored in pertinent sources. The content of the oracles combined allusions to contemporary events, especially to the advent of Russian power, with a mystical religious symbolism derived from the *Revelation* of Saint John, in order to make cryptic and obscure forecasts about a future collapse of the Ottoman Empire amid great political convulsions and natural calamities. The redemption of the Greek people in a resurrected Christian empire would be the eventual outcome. With the text that he finally composed, Polyeidis gave shape to the rampant millenarianism and the outpouring of oracular literature that was stimulated by the impact of Russian power on the Balkans at about the mid-eighteenth century.[23] The center of the millenarian movement was that beacon of Orthodox faith and traditional culture, Mount Athos. Polyeidis absorbed these influences during his stay on Athos.[24] The composition of the oracles that he finally attempted reflected the hybrid of his experience. The eventual murky product registered in its obscurity and illogicality the fundamental contradiction between the two forces that Polyeidis tried to reconcile: the eschatological millenarianism of traditional culture and the chill spirit of contemporary *Realpolitik,* at a time when the classic idea of a balance of power was taking shape in European political thought.

Polyeidis was presumably aware of this tension, but the message of his oracles appealed widely to the emotions and the imagination of his compatriots. The oracles, which appeared under the fictitious name of "the blessed Agathangelos," circulated widely in manuscript throughout the Greek lands during the critical decades of the second half of the eighteenth century and nurtured Greek yearnings for redemption. According to a reliable testimony, no less a figure than the great exponent of Enlightenment, Evgenios Voulgaris, during his tenure in the post of director of the Athonite Academy, had some contact with Polyeidis and showed great interest in the millenarian movement, affirming that the oracular literature merited serious consideration.[25] This was a significant psychological preparation of the future turn in Voulgaris's political thought. It was not, however, until a relevant context was set by the circumstances of Catherine II's reign that a different ideology of the Russian expectation could bring together Voulgaris's enlightenment with his sensitivity to the psychological potentialities of millenarianism.

A distinct eighteenth-century influence, which built on the millenarianism of popular culture and elite political thought, was the great fascination with the achievements of Peter the Great in civilizing Russian society and raising his empire to the status of a great power. Peter was the foremost hero who captured the imagination of the eighteenth century. The subjection of the revered heroes of Israelite prophecy and Greek and Roman antiquity to the doubts of historical Pyrrhonism left the imagination of the eighteenth century open to the appeal of the contemporary champions of cultural change.[26] Peter of Russia was precisely such a hero, the first and greatest of the century. Later on he was to be joined in the imagination of the philosophes and of the enlightened public—at least for a time—by the benevolent and modernizing monarchs of Prussia and Austria and by one of his own successors, Catherine II.[27]

The fascination of enlightened European consciousness with Peter the Great and the accomplishments of cultural change in Russia found great

receptivity among the earlier generations of the Greek enlightened intelligentsia. Many Greek intellectuals were invited and warmly received in
Russia, and Russian propaganda did everything possible to incite the
admiration of the Greeks for the great achievements and the power of the
empire of a fellow Orthodox nation. These influences were reflected in the
proliferation and popularity of biographical writing on Peter the Great in
eighteenth-century Greek literature. In the 1730s, a biography of Peter was
published in Italian and Greek editions by the archpriest Antonios Katiphoros, who introduced modern European philosophy in the Ionian Islands.[28]
This source went through six editions between the 1730s and the 1790s. A
second biography of Peter, by Athanasios Skiadas, who had met the emperor,
was published in 1737. The wide appeal of that heroic literature, which
tended to modernize traditional hagiographical tastes among all strata of
society, was a good indicator of the broad consensus that prevailed in Greek
political thought at the early stages of the Enlightenment. The entire society looked in unanimity to Orthodox imperial Russia as the bastion of its
hopes. These Russian prospects were soon very effectively interwoven with
the rising tide of popular millenarianism. The Russian mirage was probably
the only part of eighteenth-century European thought that was met with the
receptivity of familiarity and intimacy in traditional Greek consciousness.
The combination of the intimacy of conventional beliefs with the intentions
of enlightened conscience provided the most fertile ground to Russian propaganda in the Greek lands in that period of southward Russian expansion
that generated three Russo-Turkish wars in the Balkans in the span of the
eighteenth century (1736–1739, 1768–1774, 1787–1792). From the outset,
Russian strategy placed a considerable premium on the friendly disposition
and active support for Russian objectives by the fellow Orthodox subjects
of the Ottoman Empire. Therefore, Russian propaganda among the Orthodox nationalities of the Balkans and their Greek lay and spiritual leaders
became an endemic component of Balkan politics. The major rationale and
basis of appeal of this propaganda was a promise of Russian protection and
eventually of active support for a liberation effort of the Christian nationalities under Ottoman yoke. Russian propaganda took many forms and
found willing adherents both in the ranks of traditional elites and among
enlightened intellectuals. The Russian expectation became an integral part
of a political outlook that remained unquestioned and generally shared for
many decades.[29]

One idiosyncratic manifestation of Russian propaganda was the activity of the charismatic evangelist Kosmas of Aitolia (1714–1779), who crisscrossed virtually the entire Balkans in the years 1761–1779, through his sermons exhorting the Christian population to resist conversion to Islam, which was apparently of considerable concern to the Church at this period. Father Kosmas accordingly operated systematically with the blessing of successive patriarchs of Constantinople, including Seraphim II (1757–1761), whose connections with Russian policy are well known. The broad response that his preaching met among the masses cannot be unrelated to the reawakening of millenarian visions about the middle of the century, but the wider range of the political program with which Kosmas's popular evangelism was associated can be discerned, albeit dimly, when account is taken of his relations with Evgenios Voulgaris and the circles of the Athonite Academy. Kosmas was appropriated later on by nationalist legend as a precocious exponent of nationalist ideals. As his teaching has been transmitted by oral tradition, it is almost impossible to verify its authenticity. These two factors make it methodologically very difficult to engage in serious study of this highly important manifestation of the dynamics of Greek politics in the eighteenth century.

It was on such a basis that the major representative of the earlier phases of the movement of Enlightenment, Evgenios Voulgaris, elaborated a theory of enlightened absolutism, consciously inspired by the Russian model, as the political expression of the will to cultural change. In his political theory of enlightened absolutism, the millenarian tradition found its rationalization.

Following the failure of his attempts to introduce the curriculum of Enlightenment in the major centers of training of Greek intellectual, political, and ecclesiastical elites, the academies of Athos and Constantinople, and after his travels in Germany where he published his major philosophical works, Voulgaris found refuge in the court of Catherine II. He had already earned renown as a scholar through the publication of his *Logic* and his translations of Voltaire. In Catherine's court, he found both an intellectual atmosphere congenial to his commitment to the Enlightenment and a political environment very much interested in the services he might render as a promoter of the Russian cause among the Greeks.[30] It was the time of Catherine's first war against the Ottoman Porte, and Voulgaris's authority as a distinguished intellectual and political figure in the movement of Greek revival could be quite useful in rendering the Russian cause and promises

credible in the eyes of his compatriots. This coincidence of purposes should
not be taken to suggest that Voulgaris, in elaborating his theory of enlightened absolutism, acted simply as a Russian agent. It is true that his increasing identification with Russian policy and his unwavering promotion of the
Russian expectation as the only workable solution of the Greek problem
created great personal and political stakes for him in the Russian cause—for
which, toward the end of his career, he was subjected to severe strictures and
open denunciations by younger partisans of the Enlightenment. Nevertheless, both in his espousal of the Russian expectation and in his articulation
of a theory of enlightened absolutism, Voulgaris worked out in good conscience and with complete intellectual sincerity the political implications
of the variety of moderate Enlightenment he had learned from German
philosophy, especially the thought of Leibniz and Wolff.

Appropriately, the most articulate statement of Voulgaris's political views
came with his rendering into Greek of Catherine's famous *Instruction* to
the *Zemstvo* of deputies who were charged with the composition of a new
code of laws for the Russian Empire.[31] The *Instruction* was a remarkable text
both for what it said and for the uses to which it put the social thought of
the Enlightenment in order to suit the requirements of absolutism. In its
structure and scope it was a treatise on government that appropriated Montesquieu's political sociology in order to appear enlightened, but remained
conservative in tone and purpose. Beyond the recognition of certain basic
human rights of the subjects, nothing was conceded by absolutism. The
treatise was prefaced by the philosophical reflection that to be in harmony
with nature, the laws should be relevant and congenial to the spirit of the
people for whom they were legislated.[32] Montesquieu would certainly have
been pleased with this approach to legislation as he would have approved
of the intention of the *Instruction* to create a government of laws in Russia,
to develop orderly procedures of administration, legislation, adjudication of
justice, and last but not least to regulate succession to the throne so as to
avoid the turmoil of civil wars. Public finance was also regulated according
to the standards of the economics of the Enlightenment.[33]

In a truly enlightened spirit, the new code of laws provided not only for
government and its institutions but for civil society and its moral and material well-being. It sought to encourage the increase of population, the liberal
arts and commerce, the growth of the cities, and the education of the citizens in the virtues of civility.[34] In all these measures, one could feel a desire

to foster the development of a middle class to balance off the nobility.[35] In this too, Catherine's purposes appeared informed by her reading of Montesquieu. The rule of law, however, which was expected to be thus instituted in the vast empire of all Russias, left one person beyond and above it: the monarch refused to abandon any of the prerogatives of the despotic patrimony. Despite the attempt to build up an edifice of universally applicable legal rules among the subjects, the system remained one of despotism. Although the very first chapter of the *Instruction* articulated the will to Enlightenment by proclaiming Russia to be a European state (thus distinguishing and lifting her above Asiatic despotism), in the immediately following chapter the real intentions of the new system became plain. Montesquieu's ideas on the connection between despotism and extensive states were twisted into an argument in support of autocracy in Russia.[36] Ignoring Montesquieu's defense of liberty and the separation of powers and his eloquent example of England as a case of an extensive state with the spirit and institutions of a modern republican polity, Catherine evoked the vast territorial expanse of her empire in order to justify her absolutism. She spoke of a government of laws only in the sense of regularized and predictable instrumentalities that could make absolutist administration more efficient. This autocratic purpose and Catherine's own despotic ways were transparent behind her intellectual predilection for the philosophy of the Enlightenment. Diderot understood all this very well. He recognized the real purposes of the *Instruction* and criticized them in his observations on Catherine's government, which, however, he left unpublished in his lifetime.[37]

Voulgaris expressed his political views in presenting the text of Catherine's *Instruction* to Greek readers. His argument opened with a substantive analysis of the political content and moral meaning of enlightened absolutism. It was a form of government marked by benevolent, if patronizing, care for the monarch's subjects, among whom it fostered fraternal feelings and mutual concern. Catherine's rule in particular was one of maternal providence reflected in her love and compassion for her subjects. These moral feelings lay at the root of her policies, which she put into practice by visiting her subjects throughout the empire, examining their local problems, and extending her benevolent assistance to all those who needed it. Her magnanimity extended across the border of her empire to neighboring nations, among whom she appeared as the champion of peace, order, and justice.[38]

In praising Catherine as an enlightened monarch whose concern for humanity, virtue, and wisdom were reflected in her draft of a new legislative code, which, in Voulgaris's mind, reckoned her among the great legislators of mankind, her Greek encomiast evoked in support of his arguments the authority of another enlightened monarch. Referring to the reception of her *Instruction* in Germany, he described the enthusiasm it inspired in Frederick the Great, "the hero and king of Prussia, the philosopher among kings."[39] The models of cultural and political reconstruction represented by the policies of these two enlightened monarchs were projected by Voulgaris as the matrices of change in Greek society.

Indeed, there was an additional reason why the Greeks should look to Russia. The victories of Catherine over the Turks at the time of Voulgaris's writing reinforced the traditional Greek expectation of freedom through Russian intervention. In Voulgaris's thought, the liberation of the Greeks from the Ottoman yoke was identified with an extension of Russian autocracy over the Orthodox nationalities of the Ottoman Empire. The might of the "Third Rome" would be the instrument of the resurrection of the empire of the Second Rome in a Greco-Russian condominium over the Balkans and the Greek East.[40] Regardless of his philosophical beliefs, Voulgaris in his capacity as an Orthodox clergyman capitalized on the possibilities of scriptural prophecy in order to make his advocacy of Russian-inspired enlightened absolutism more credible and appealing to the popular mind. This purpose was made clear by the incorporation into his analysis of the nature of enlightened absolutism of the scriptural passages recited at Catherine's coronation. His interpretations of the passages from Paul's *Epistle to the Romans* (16:1–2) and from Saint John's Gospel (10:16) read at the ceremony made plain the attempt of his argument to connect the advocacy of enlightened absolutism with scriptural authority and the millenarian tradition.[41] This thrust of his argument became explicit in his statement that, under the international circumstances of the time, the simple folk's minds were gripped by the oracles talking of the "blonde nation" as the agent of redemption. It was precisely on this popular psychology that Voulgaris wanted to superimpose the ideology of enlightened absolutism.

The logic of Voulgaris's political argument, therefore, involved fundamentally a rationalization of the traditional Russian expectation through an appeal to the model of enlightened absolutism. This model, as embodied in Catherine's policies, gave rational content to the mesmerism of the Third

Rome and responded to the groping for cultural and political change that animated enlightened Greek consciences. Voulgaris articulated the connection between the context of international relations and the content of political thought in his remark that the hopes of wretched Greece were heightened ever since Catherine's fleets sailed from the northern seas into the Aegean.[42]

The interaction between the analysis of international relations and political thought found its most fruitful expression in an essay entitled "Reflections on the Present Critical State of the Ottoman Empire,"[43] apparently motivated by the Russo-Turkish war of 1768–1774 and attributed to Voulgaris. The authenticity of the authorship can be accepted on the basis of the quality of its argument as well as on plausible internal evidence. The essay attempted to discuss in terms of the eighteenth-century theory of the balance of power the role of Turkey and Russia in the European state system. In a quite admirable manner, showing both great political realism and intimate knowledge of Ottoman society and government, the author refuted several misconceptions prevailing in contemporary European thought concerning the degeneracy and utter decay of Ottoman power. Despite their recent defeats, the author warned, the Turks were quick to learn from European civilization, and they could not delay for long in reconstituting their military might.[44] In that eventuality, they would be the greatest threat to the European balance of power. The rise of Russian power in the eighteenth century was an important example that had not been lost on the Turks. Russian power on the contrary, Voulgaris suggested, knew its limits and had no intention of disrupting the international balance of power, but it rendered great services to it by weakening the Ottomans and keeping them in check.[45]

Turning to an analysis of the Greek predicament in this context, Voulgaris referred bitterly to the repeated cruel disappointments experienced by the Greeks on account of the behavior of certain European powers that had remained indifferent to their plight or prevented their would-be liberators from coming to their aid. The essay concluded by suggesting that the partition of the European provinces of the Ottoman Empire and the creation of an independent Greek principality of moderate extent would be conducive to the preservation of the international balance of power.[46]

The connection between international relations and political thought as expressed in a rationalized Russian expectation continued to be the key to Voulgaris's reflections on the Greek problem. His focus remained on

Catherine's policies in the East, through which he hoped to see the double achievement of national liberation and cultural reform in his homeland. His hopes and reflections at each turn of Russian policy were recorded in the semipropagandist pamphlets that he published during the turbulent decade of the 1770s. During the second Russo-Turkish war of the century, the Greeks of the Peloponnese, stirred up by Russian agents and the appearance of a Russian fleet in the Aegean, had risen against the Turks in 1770. Abandoned by the Russians after a brief interlude of revolutionary fervor, they were subjected to savage reprisals by their Ottoman masters, who unleashed hordes of Albanian bandits to ravage the Peloponnese.[47] Amid the news of this tragedy, Voulgaris composed two appeals, one addressed to Catherine personally and another directed as a "supplication to all of Christian Europe." Both appeals entreated the Christian powers of Europe to come to the succor and rescue of the Greeks, whose lamentable fate under the yoke of the Ottomans and their latest disaster at the hands of the Albanian bandits were depicted in a shuddering account.[48] The war came to an end with the conclusion of the Treaty of Kuchuk Kainardji in 1774, which greatly enhanced Russian power in the Balkans and sanctioned Russian influence in the domestic affairs of the Ottoman Empire. In the same spirit that had inspired his earlier appeals, Voulgaris celebrated the Russian victory by composing a hymn to the trophies of peace and a triumphant song in ancient Greek meters.[49] Celebration of Russian triumphs was an integral part of the psychology of the Russian expectation that Voulgaris wanted to impart to his compatriots. A complete identification with the Russian cause required not only supplications and pious hopes, but also an ability of full empathy with the historical destinies of the great empire of a fellow Orthodox nation.

To the same end, Voulgaris translated into Greek two of Voltaire's narrative poems on the events of the war in the East. One of them, entitled "Voltaire's Epistle to the Empress of the Russians," epitomized in its verses the gist of Voulgaris's own political thought. The triumph that Catherine was expected to achieve was a double one: a victory over the tyrant residing in Byzantium, but also a conquest of the tyranny of superstition. The real triumph, however, would only follow the annihilation of Turkish tyranny with the resurrection of Greek civilization and virtue.[50] Characteristically, Voulgaris once again found in Voltaire the arguments and language he needed in order to convey his political message. Voltaire had supplied him with ammunition for his earlier campaign on behalf of philosophic and religious toleration. Now Voltaire's own expectations from Catherine's policies of enlightened absolutism proved useful to Voulgaris in his advocacy of his rationalized version of the Russian expectation. This position constituted the limit beyond which Voulgaris's political thought could not extend. In contrast to Voltaire, who was willing to give a chance to enlightened absolutism as represented by Catherine's policies and attempts at reform, but hated despotism as a form of government and had no faith in regimes that stifled liberty, Voulgaris could visualize no alternative political order. His hatred for despotism was consumed and exhausted in his loathing of Greece's Ottoman yoke. His circumspect and aristocratic enlightenment, which was rigidified with age and his rise to prominence in the Russian court, did not allow him to visualize any other dynamic of political and cultural change except reform introduced from above as a gift of benevolence from a magnanimous monarch.

It was natural, therefore, that Voulgaris would feel puzzled and estranged by the new problematic of liberty that visualized alternative and more effective patterns of change. As this problematic spread and was espoused even by his former students and admirers, Voulgaris followed a different path. He was engulfed by the tide of counterrevolutionary aversion that prevailed in the Russian court after 1789. Thus, in his old age, the dean of the Greek Enlightenment found himself in active opposition to those daring enough to follow the implications of his own original philosophic premises to their logical conclusions. To the end, Voulgaris remained true to his espousal of the cause of enlightenment. He never betrayed his original positions by accepting the arguments of militant Counterenlightenment. But he also refused to move further on the road he had inaugurated. His persistence in his earlier enlightened philosophical and scientific views, which he had valiantly tried to introduce into Greek thought, was made plain by his decision to publish in the last years of his life the textbooks he had written and used during his teaching career in the 1740s and the 1750s and had been circulating in manuscript copies in Greek schools ever since. His subsequent complaints about the attacks leveled against him by the younger partisans of the movement of intellectual renewal were, therefore, understandable and also symptomatic of the state of mind of a thinker whose graceful longevity dramatized the paradoxes involved in outliving one's own thought and ideological struggles. Voulgaris's attitude during the last years of his life, the years of his "conservative retraction," emerges vividly from his own words: "I dwell near the palace on the banks of the Neva. I spend most of my time indoors. I rarely venture forth. I enjoy the company of only a few. I converse mainly with the dead."[51]

DISAPPOINTMENTS

The strains of subsequent historical experiences and the elaboration of the intellectual preconditions of a more mature philosophical liberalism made Voulgaris's political solution to the Greek problem appear increasingly inadequate and irrelevant. In no other case was this political change expressed more characteristically than in the psychological and intellectual experience of the young philosopher Athanasios Psalidas (1767–1829). At the age of twenty-four, the young scholar from Ioannina had made his debut in Viennese intellectual circles with the publication of a learned bilingual discourse on *Vera Felicitas sive Fundamentum omnis Religionis* (1791), which he dedicated to "invictissimae ac religiosissimae Russorum Imperatrici Aecaterinae II." In the dedicatory epistle to Catherine, Psalidas outlined his views on enlightened absolutism. He declared that Catherine's rule had put into practice the Platonic apothegm that "the subjects prosper if a philosopher rules or if a ruler is given to philosophy." Catherine's practice of this maxim brought great welfare to her subjects. Her wisdom was reflected in her legislation, which was emulated by the enlightened monarchs of Europe. Her concern and providence for commerce, the arts, and the common good were so many temples to the Muses, to Mars, Minerva, Apollo, and Zeus. Her prudent judgment could sharply discern the relevant means to all ends. Where common human sense often led to impasse, her judgment triumphed. This high estimation of her wisdom was vindicated by her always felicitous choice of the best counselors, whom she employed in the public interest. The warm radiation of her wise policies was even felt in distant Greece, that glorious and prosperous land of old, which had been reduced to depravity by the yoke of the barbarians. Amid her present misfortunes, Hellas suppliantly extended her hands imploring the empress to come to her succor and redeem her from her yoke.[52]

Psalidas did not limit himself to this eloquent reaffirmation of the Russian expectation. During Catherine's second war against the Ottomans

(1787–1792), he attempted to provide the rekindled hopes of his compatriots with concrete content by recounting the great benefactions bestowed by Catherine on the Greek communities of southern Russia during a triumphant tour of that area on the eve of the war. Psalidas had just left his native Ioannina and was on a visit to his older brothers, who had relocated in southern Russia following the itineraries of commercial mobility at the time. He witnessed Catherine's benevolent disposition toward the Greek nation expressed practically in the many privileges she granted to the Greek settlers in the Crimea and in the newly acquired territories of New Russia on the northern shores of the Black Sea. He felt impelled to communicate all these hopeful omens to his compatriots in a pamphlet he composed when the war broke out. Catherine's great favors to the Greeks of Nezhin (Nizna) and Crimea were taken as indications of the secret designs she harbored for unfortunate Greece. These designs aimed to reintroduce the wisdom of Pallas Athena in Greece and to redeem the land from all traces of barbarism.[53]

Expectations once again rose high only to be bitterly disappointed. The declaration of the Russo-Turkish war in August 1787 created a notable stir in the Greek world, and Greek patriots rallied in support of the Russian cause. A Greek fleet, financed by the Greek community of Trieste, began operations in the Aegean under the command of Lambros Katsonis and caused considerable harassment to the Ottoman navy. A Greek memorandum was also presented to the Court of Saint Petersburg. It declared that the Greek nation was on the verge of rising against the Turks and expected the empress's grandson, the Grand Duke Constantine, to be proclaimed Emperor of Byzantium. All these hopes of the subjugated nation collided with the stark realities of international politics. The Treaty of Jassy in 1792 concluded the war and belied the hopes of the Greeks who were once again abandoned to their fate and to their own devices for the future.[54]

It was not the first time that the Russian expectation turned out to be only a passing mirage, the product of international conjunctures and wishful millenarian aspirations. Already in the 1770s Catherine's first war against the Ottoman Empire had stimulated such a high tide of hopes amid a millenarian delirium nurtured by her agents. The Greeks had risen in revolt against their masters. The revolt proved abortive, the Russian promises remained empty, and hopes vanished with the withdrawal of the Russian fleet from the Aegean. The rising of course took a very heavy toll in lives and material destruction—and also in desperation. A high Phanariot

magnate reflected upon the conclusion of the Treaty of Kuchuk Kainardji
between the empress and the Sublime Porte in 1774:

> If then, in the time appointed by the oracles, after so many and so great victo-
> ries of the Muscovites over the Ottomans, in such an opportune moment, we
> the *Romaioi,* have not been liberated, it is indeed difficult that the resurrec-
> tion of the Romaic Empire should occur in the future, seeing that no oracle
> of any other prophet remains concerning it; and not only difficult but almost
> impossible, on account of the persistence of our evil ways, our lack of mercy,
> our vengefulness toward one another and our customary invectiveness.

Similar views were expressed by that other prodigious propagandist of the
Russian expectation, Kaisarios Dapontes.[55]

The Russian expectation seemed to have its last chance in Catherine's
second war against the Turks. In the aftermath of that war, the original
doubts were transformed into final disillusionment. Twenty years after
Komninos-Ypsilantis had spelled out the terrible fear that the oracles
might have run their prophetic course and come to naught, Psalidas composed the epitaph to the Russian expectation. It was not a resigned elegy
to lost hopes, but a philosophical indictment of its false promises and of
those who still fostered them. Less than three years after expressing his
optimism in Catherine's secret design for Greece's redemption, the young
idealist critic of the Enlightenment made a dramatic transition from the
eloquent advocacy of the Russian expectation to a violent repudiation of
those who still persisted in it.

The obvious target was Voulgaris. He was the foremost exponent of the
Russian expectation, which he had lifted from the oracular maze of millenarianism, given it rational content, and translated into a comprehensible program of political action. Naturally the bankruptcy of this program
invited criticism of its major advocate. Voulgaris's authority and international influence as a scholar and national leader, however, made an attack
upon him by a young and unknown man almost inconceivable. Yet Psalidas
did dare to challenge the authority of the old man in a tract of 1795 entitled
Kalokinimata [Auspicious departures], which was presented as a critique of
Voulgaris's *Logic.*[56]

Essentially, this was a militant plea for a new ideological orientation of
Greek political thought. It registered the disillusionment with the older

faith in misguided hopes in foreign assistance and groped for a new beginning. The abandonment of the Greeks by the Russians and the consequent
disappointment of the Russian expectation naturally undermined the credibility of Voulgaris's political program to the benefit of a more militant
approach to the problem of enlightenment and national revival. Although
in his philosophical treatise of 1791 Psalidas emerged as an opponent of the
more radical trends of the Enlightenment, criticizing Spinoza and castigat-
ing Rousseau, Voltaire, and Helvetius, to whom he attributed materialist
tendencies,[57] there can be no doubt that the outburst of *Kalokinimata* bore
the stamp of the emotional soul-searching and uneasy expectancy precipitated in Greek thought by the French Revolution.

Psalidas's acerbity made what was intended as a philosophical and political critique appear as a personal libel against a venerable leader of the Greek
intellectual renaissance. To correct this impression, the younger man tried
to explain his motives by pointing out that in demythologizing Voulgaris
he did not intend to undermine or diminish his fame, but simply to open
up the eyes of his compatriots. His objective was to stimulate curiosity and
critical thinking, which would prevent them from succumbing to prejudices on the authority of *ipse dixit*. Their approach to learning should be
one of critical examination, research, and comparison on which to base
judgment of what was true and acceptable to reason and what was false,
which had therefore to be rejected. The criterion of judgment should not be
"who said it" but "how and why" one said something. Such critical spirit
was becoming to the genuine imitators and zealots of the modern Greeks'
famous ancient ancestors. Criticism alone could make the mind entirely
free of prejudice and authority—and this liberation was the hallmark of
true philosophy and right reason.[58]

The affirmation of the primacy of intellectual freedom was the precondition of the political criticism of Voulgaris. His attachment to Russia,
reflected both in his political program and in his choice of a life and career
in the Czarist court, in the final analysis amounted to a setback for Greek
revival. His insistence on living abroad minimized his contribution to the
enlightenment of his compatriots. His cosmopolitanism was misguided
because it betrayed inadequate patriotism and selfish motives. Voulgaris
appeared indifferent to the pressing needs of his homeland, made patriotism a secondary priority, and opted for the comforts and pleasures of life
in the Russian court. It was certainly sure, as he put it in the *Logic,* that

"the entire earth was the scholar's homeland and the world was his city"—
he indeed turned the entire globe into his homeland and Russia into his
city and made the bears his compatriots.[59] The tragedy of the Greek revival
was that his compatriots expected enlightenment and benefactions from
such a learned man! Psalidas wondered in his heart at the contrast between
this attitude and the moral message of the Greeks' illustrious ancestors.
The Ancients' patriotic sacrifices and dedication to their homeland spelled
out a lesson entirely different from that of Voulgaris's comportment—the
man whom only three years earlier Psalidas, in his youthful enthusiasm,
had characterized "the pride of the nation, the trophy of teachers, bishops,
and archbishops."[60]

If Voulgaris's program and attitude proved irrelevant to the Greek
revival, how else could the ancestral cultural glory be restored? At this point
Psalidas returned to a theme familiar to the psychology of Greek militants
of the Enlightenment. The cultural fetters of Greek society could be broken
only through imitation of the pattern set by the civilized nations of Europe.
The deadening teaching of the grammarians and scholastic logicians who
dominated Greek education had to be abandoned. Their contributions,
despite their presumption to serve the public good and to advance the cause
of philosophy, essentially amounted to mere name-dropping and a display
of verbosity. The Greeks had to look beyond this restricted education to
the curriculum of enlightenment proposed by Psalidas, which would comprise in addition to the traditional subjects of grammar, logic, rhetoric, and
metaphysics, modern experimental physics, ethics, natural law, world history, and geography.[61] With a view to implementing this program, Psalidas,
in the same year that he published *Kalokinimata,* abandoned the lights of
Europe and returned to his native town of Ioannina. An intellectual by conviction, he devoted his talents and his youthful vigor to the modernization
of education in his birthplace, thereby contributing to the development of
Ioannina into the most important center of the Enlightenment in mainland
Greece.[62] Psalidas undoubtedly believed that this was the appropriate practical response to Voulgaris's position. He may, however, have forgotten that
the Enlightenment in Ioannina owed its beginnings to Voulgaris teaching
at the Maroutsaia School, precisely fifty years before his own return to those
very battlements.

Voulgaris, aging but still vigorous, did not let Psalidas's repudiations
go unanswered. Obviously upset by the younger man's irreverence and

impudence, the patriarch of the Greek Enlightenment dismissed with bitter condescension what he felt to be the rage of an imposter. He insinuated that Psalidas's attack on the *Logic* might have been motivated by a cheap desire to undermine an older classic work in order to promote his own translation of Baumeister's treatise on the subject. Beyond personal invective, which he did not spare in his response, Voulgaris rebutted Psalidas's criticisms as irrelevant. He reminded his critic that the *Logic* had been composed according to "the moderns" and appealed to the authority of Bacon, Arnauld, and Genovesi in support of his argument.

Voulgaris had no doubt that, beyond cheap personal motives and envy, Psalidas's critique did not derive from a disinterested philosophical disagreement, but was essentially the product of political considerations, like the earlier complaints of that other relentless critic, Moisiodax. Voulgaris insisted that in their criticism of the difficulty of exposition and the impossibility of the *Logic's* archaic language, both Moisiodax and Psalidas refused to recognize that serious philosophical discourse could not be conducted in the vulgar vernacular of everyday life and remained blind to the simple fact that all men were not equally capable to engage in the trying task of the philosophical search for truth. As to Psalidas's specifically political criticisms, which questioned Voulgaris's patriotism and attachment to Russia, the old archbishop knew that they were designed to simply stain his good name and felt it beneath his dignity to reply. He reaffirmed, however, his faith in the wisdom and philhellenism of the Grand Empress Catherine II, the great benefactress and protectress of the Greek nation.[63]

In thus reaffirming his belief in aristocratic enlightenment and in the Russian expectation, Voulgaris made it clear that he could not bring himself to recognize the intellectual kinship between his own original position and Psalidas's attitude. He spoke in the 1790s with the voice of the 1740s and 1750s, and he naturally could not recognize that Psalidas's latest assault against him in reality represented a culmination of the crusade for renewal that Voulgaris himself had initiated half a century earlier. Psalidas appeared unconscious of the affinity too. In his impatience he failed to recognize that in his own revolt against *ipse dixit* he was resuming Voulgaris's original, if conditional, resistance to Corydalist Aristotelianism. In the same manner that Voulgaris had worked on behalf of the philosophy of the Moderns and had to sustain all the sacrifices and persecutions that this effort invited, Psalidas tried to subvert the establishment of a new authority represented by Voulgaris himself. Voulgaris in his old age and in his indignation at Psalidas's irreverence, perhaps understandably, could not perceive the affinity. Psalidas, however, was somehow unfair to the older man in overlooking the spiritual kinship between their respective programs of enlightenment. After all, his own more daring radicalism was possible only because Voulgaris's earlier efforts had taken firm root in spite of all adversities and constraints. Psalidas's assault on Voulgaris's authority in the name of freedom of thought and the independence of individual judgment symbolized dramatically the maturity reached by philosophical liberalism in Greek thought.

THE MATURE THEORY OF ENLIGHTENED ABSOLUTISM

The elaboration of a fully fledged theory of enlightened absolutism in Greek thought came as an outgrowth of the ancient tradition of mirrors of princes inherited from Hellenistic and Byzantine literature. Enlightened absolutism as an instrument of social and cultural change and a tribute to the rule of law represented a definitely new political theory, a new vantage point in the evolution of political ideas from the theory of virtuous kingship to a conception of the modern political community over which only law was sovereign. Yet coming as it did within the familiar framework of the symbolic language and literary style of traditional political discourse, the transition to a different level of political consciousness, which essentially marked the transcendence of the old theory, appeared as its culmination. Thus, the political arguments for enlightened absolutism came naturally to Greek thought and could be elaborated without eliciting suspicions and reactions. When originally presented by Iosipos Moisiodax and Dimitrios Katartzis in the 1770s and 1780s, such arguments were put forward to promote the cause of cultural change and political renewal. The congeniality of the theory of enlightened absolutism to Christian thought, however, was made plain three decades later when ideological conflict was at its prime. In that context, a conception of enlightened absolutism and controlled reform from above was championed by the opponents of Enlightenment as a way of arresting the tide of change.

The best example of the transition to a different level of political consciousness within the tradition of mirrors of princes was the modern Greek paraphrase of Isocrates's oration addressed to Nicocles, King of Salamis in

Cyprus, by Iosipos Moisiodax. A genuine representative of the Enlightenment, Moisiodax rendered the classic text of parenetic literature into simple
modern Greek in a quite free adaptation designed to stress certain political
lessons pertaining to the art of government. It was indicative of the intimate
bonds Moisiodax felt attached him to the cosmopolitan movement of the
Enlightenment that he translated his paraphrase of Isocrates into French
and published the volume under the title *Chapitres Politiques.*

The motto of the work was taken from Aristotle's definition of the just
ruler in the *Politics:* the true ruler is he who rules in the interest of the
subjects rather than in his own interest.[64] If these priorities were reversed,
Aristotle had cautioned, the ruler became a tyrant. This was clearly the message that Moisiodax wanted to convey in his *Chapitres Politiques.* The task
was quite delicate. How could one inspire the public virtues required by an
enlightened conscience and instruct against tyranny the Greek princes and
potentates who had to sustain the moral and social pressures of corruption
and despotism weighing on their captive society?

Moisiodax began by attacking precisely this point. His gift to the
prince was to be sobering advice on the good and evil intrinsic to rulership, designed to help him discharge his duties successfully and honorably.
In this Moisiodax drew a sharp distinction between his role as a political counselor and those who tried to ingratiate themselves to the prince
through flattery and materially precious gifts.[65] Moisiodax hastened to
warn the prince against the temptations and negligence that such cultivation of his vanity by parasites could bring, asserting that his primary care
should be the protection of the multitude of the common people against
the oppression of social potentates, court magnates, and state officials.
The peasants and lower popular orders of society, deprived of all voice
in matters of government, entertained as their only hope protection by
their prince against the excesses of forced labor, rapacious taxation, and
oppression emanating from his agents. The prince's duty and interest was
to avert and punish such excesses, because no monarchical or aristocratic
state could ever prosper so long as the lower orders remained dissatisfied
and seething with resentment.[66]

Such advice to the prince, despite the closing Machiavellian twist that
provided its inner rationale, was perfectly consonant with the paternalist
benevolence required of Christian monarchs and advocated by the theory
of traditional kingship. On this basis, however, Moisiodax could build

his plea for change, which constituted the core of his expectations from enlightened monarchy:

> Whenever the laws, usages and constitutions do not correspond to the public good or when they are positively defective, do not hesitate to either suppress or reform them. It is excessive reverence, indeed occasionally an affliction, to respect ancient traditions solely because they are ancient traditions.[67]

Beyond the definition of the purposes of enlightened absolutism, an integral part of any sound political counsel had to do with the instrumentalities of the art of government. How could the enlightened prince govern most effectively? In this connection Machiavelli's old maxims, despite the abuse that moralizing princes and their advisers had heaped on the great Florentine, seemed to have lost nothing of their relevance. In the conduct of government, in the dispensation of justice and in public ceremonies that brought him in direct contact with his subjects, the successful prince had to prove himself master of the art of appearances.[68]

The dignity that the reputation of justice assured to the prince was enhanced by a religious comportment distinguished by genuine piety, but free of ostentation and superstition. The enlightened prince should take the lead in the effort to arrest and reverse prevailing superstitious tendencies that consumed public and private wealth on lavish offerings to the Church and on other religious expenses, which oftentimes simply nurtured dissension and corruption in the ranks of the holy orders. Public philanthropies, the endowment of schools, and the promotion of learning would represent a much more becoming and dignified pursuit for princes. Such projects are more pleasing to God because they are consonant with the requirements of right reason and respond to the most widely felt needs of the community.[69]

Beyond the prince's personal conduct, another essential test that enlightened rulership had to meet arose out of the prince's choice of his staff and advisers. The prince's entourage, by mediating between him and the people and influencing and executing his policy, carried a decisive weight in the success or failure of his policy. His greatness and enlightenment would, therefore, transpire in his choice of friends and his selection of collaborators. The prince's genuine friends could not be those whose only preoccupation was to please him, but those whose wisdom, experience, and truthfulness could be useful in enhancing the prince's understanding and management of public issues. Veracity, dignified outspokenness, and dedication to truth should not embarrass or displease the prince. On the contrary, it should be actively solicited and honored in order to deject the swarm of sycophants and vile parasites who tended to gravitate around the throne—of which they constituted "the most abominable and detestable contagion." The flatterers and intriguers whose rise to prominence marked the transformation of rightful monarchy into tyranny should be turned away by selecting the prince's staff and public officials on the basis of merit.[70] Moisiodax knew from his reading of Montesquieu that fear was the principle of the social psychology of tyranny and was thus incompatible with a conception of enlightened government. By placing his confidence in the humanitarian optimism of the Enlightenment, he could conclude by diverging from Machiavelli's advice. Fear was not necessary to a successful prince whose rule was not an instrument of pleasure, but a source of obligation to supervise the happiness of the community.[71] The benevolent father and shepherd of the people had been transformed into the first servant of the commonwealth.

The effective integration of a program on enlightenment with a systematically formulated theory of enlightened absolutism came in the thought of Dimitrios Katartzis. A contemporary and an acquaintance of Moisiodax, Kartartzis shared with him the urgent sense of the need for cultural change in Greek society. The two of them were the foremost representatives of the second generation of the Greek Enlightenment. Katartzis was at the center of a circle of Greek intellectuals active in the Danubian principalities in the 1770s and 1780s who absorbed the influence of French Encyclopedism and were seriously preoccupied with the objectives and means of cultural renewal in Greek society. From the ranks of the disciples of Katartzis and Moisiodax emerged some of the bravest representatives of the Greek Enlightenment, Grigorios Constantas and Daniel Philippidis (authors of *Novel Geography*) and Rhigas Velestinlis. Among this newer generation, the preoccupation with cultural renewal was transformed into active interest in political change. This was only indicative of the effectiveness with which the seeds of Enlightenment were sown by Moisiodax and Katartzis in the consciousness of their disciples. Despite their shared intellectual concerns and orientations, socially and temperamentally Katartzis was quite different from Moisiodax, the rootless engaged intellectual with the tempestuous life and uncompromising thought.

Katartzis was the epitome of the enlightened Phanariot magnate. He held high judicial and administrative offices at the court of the Phanariot princes of Wallachia, and although he genuinely espoused the cause of the Enlightenment, he placed his faith in evolutionary renewal under the aegis of enlightened absolutism. His proximity to the source of power and the respect he enjoyed from those who exercised it seem to have fostered his belief that a unity of theory and practice of enlightenment could be achieved in the conduct of government by enlightened princes receptive to the counsel of philosophers like himself. This faith, bred by his social experience, prevented him from ever abandoning his moderation and his belief in evolutionary enlightenment. In contrast to Moisiodax, who later repudiated his faith in the possibility of enlightened absolutism, Katartzis never experienced a psychological revolution that could radicalize his thought. On the contrary, he compromised with the pressures and strains of the social environment and modified his program of cultural change, which finally remained unfulfilled. At the cost of this compromise, he retained both his psychological tranquility and his social and intellectual respectability. He was the least controversial among the major figures of the Greek Enlightenment during his lifetime, and he commanded almost universal respect and approval among all shades of Greek opinion, including the appreciation of some determined conservatives.[72]

Katartzis's program of cultural change involved primarily a far-ranging reform in education and language. Like all enlightened minds of his time, he felt that the system of Greek education was profoundly anachronistic and socially irrelevant. With its emphasis on dry scholastic learning and grammatical drilling in an incomprehensible language, it stifled creative energy in children's minds, inspired them with hatred of knowledge, and perpetuated ignorance and obscurantism in Greek society.[73] Although Katartzis felt intense dissatisfaction with this situation and pointed with urgency to the need for reform, he never concerned himself with the possible sociological reasons that could account for this state of affairs. If he did not inquire into the social causes of the problem, Katartzis was nevertheless quite explicit and daring in formulating his prescriptions for remedying the situation and meeting the challenge of the times.

Wholeheartedly given to the pursuit of the good of his homeland, Katartzis took it upon himself to emulate the ancient hero Protesilaos in leading the campaign against ignorance.[74] His program comprised three dimensions of cultural change. First and most urgently, a new pedagogical approach was required in the educational system. Reform in teaching practices and fundamental improvements in the manner of training the youth were essential to cultural progress and to the common prosperity of the nation and of each citizen in particular. To achieve this end, Katartzis outlined a new pedagogical theory derived directly from the educational ideas and the epistemology of the Enlightenment. He held Gassendi's cognitive principle "nihil est in intellectu quod non prius fuerit in sensu"[75] as a common maxim of truth. He believed, therefore, that the rearing and education of children should try to imitate the ways of nature and natural development by methodically impressing on their minds first simple and then more complex ideas. Their curiosity should be stimulated to make learning a lively and appealing pursuit. The nature of things and the meaning of words should be learned first as the essential basis on which formal learning, abstract knowledge, and complex combinations of ideas should proceed. The moral virtues, no less than knowledge, were the product of habit and had to be learned through exercise and familiarity. Underlying these views was the basic psychological theory of the Enlightenment that children, like adults, had passions and violent instincts, which should not be repressed but channeled by education and exercise into creative pursuits: "this would nurture the good habits, which were none other than the passions of the human soul transformed into virtues by reason."[76] The source of Katartzis's inspiration in advancing these arguments could be easily traced in the educational views of the *Encyclopedie,* especially as stated by D'Alembert, whom he admired, in the article "College." It has also been plausibly suggested that another source of Katartzis's pedagogical ideas was a treatise on education commissioned by Catherine II as part of her program of cultural change.[77]

The second dimension of Katartzis's program of cultural reform comprised a theory of drastic change in the language of teaching and writing. The incomprehensible language of the scholastic commentaries should be abandoned and replaced by the adoption of the modern Greek vernacular, what Katartzis called the "Romaic" language, the tongue spoken by the descendants of the Medieval Christian Romans of the Eastern Empire, that is, the modern Greeks. Katartzis's views on the language question constituted the most radical part of his theory of Enlightenment. In contrast and in conscious opposition to the venerable patriarch of the Neohellenic Enlightenment, Evgenios Voulgaris, who had insisted that only an archaic Greek tongue following the Attic style could adequately express the lofty notions of philosophy and therefore was the only language appropriate to the Enlightenment, Katartzis stressed the virtues and the perfectibility of the modern Greek vernacular. He emphasized that the spoken Greek vernacular was a perfectly adequate medium for the purposes of poetry, rhetoric, scholarship, and consequently for education and book writing. All that was needed was the systematization of the rules of its natural grammar and its cultivation by the learned men of the nation in order to bring it to a perfection equal to that of classical Greek and modern European languages. Indeed, Katartzis composed a *Grammar of the Romaic Language* as his contribution to this effort.[78] He was quite categorical concerning both the objectives of this linguistic reform and the wider obligations of men of letters to assist to its success:

> I passionately recommend this task to the learned and powerful men of my nation. If they put it to practice, they will witness the community benefit from the advantages that accrued to so many nations of Europe from the cultivation of their proper language and the study of the arts and sciences in their own tongue. I do not believe that there is anyone who does not cherish this aspiration for his own nation, but it is up to the learned and powerful to carry it out.[79]

The cultivation of the common language would become the effective avenue of cultural progress since it would liberate the creative energies stifled by scholastic education and its archaic tongue. Furthermore, the adoption of the vernacular would open up education and culture to the whole community and make the social advantages of Enlightenment accessible to all. This was precisely Katartzis's purpose: the language was not an end in itself; it was just a medium for the transmission and propagation of knowledge, useful and socially relevant knowledge. This attitude on the language question had a profoundly democratic meaning. It was precisely such meanings and intentions that made the language question an eminently political issue and a source of intensive controversy in subsequent Greek cultural history. At the very outset of the controversy, Katartzis gave the most daring and most radical response to the language question. His, of course, was the only reasonably possible response, but the political stakes in the controversy never quite allowed the issue to be settled the way he originally envisioned it. As a matter of fact, in the language he visualized and used in his writings, Katartzis went farther than any other advocate of the use of the common language among his contemporaries—including Moisiodax.

The selection of a linguistic medium was to find its fruition in what people would write and read in it and in the advantages that could be derived from such production. Next to the language question, Katartzis's most serious preoccupation was with the needs of Greek culture in useful books. To meet the needs of education in the Enlightenment and the requirements of cultural change, it was essential to produce new books and manuals. Katartzis knew that the composition of a book was not an easy task. A solution to this problem could be found in translations. His thoughts on this matter comprised the third dimension of his program of enlightenment. The basic needs of Greek culture in new books could be met by translating the most pertinent sources available in the languages of the civilized nations of Europe. Thus, the translation of European books became an integral part of Katartzis's program of cultural change. To guide prospective translators, he composed specific instructions on the method and technicalities of translation and urged all those who cared for their nation and cherished its improvement to undertake the translation of useful books.[80] His advice fell on fertile ground. Some of the most important works of the Enlightenment were translated in Greek by his associates and disciples. The first attempts to present Fontenelle, Montesquieu, Condillac, and Lalande to Greek readers were undertaken by members of the intellectual circle of Katartzis in the Danubian principalities.

Two paramount criteria guided Katartzis in the construction of his program of cultural change: utility and social moderation. The purpose of education and learning could be none other but social utility: a concrete contribution toward the solution of a social problem or a response to a specific need of the community. The cause of Enlightenment was meaningful because it could provide solutions to actual educational and cultural problems. Cultural change was desirable not for any doctrinaire ideological reasons, but for its intrinsic relevance to pressing needs of the nation. The specific needs of one's profession and of the nation as a whole and not some misguided pedantic fantasy should guide individual educational ventures. A utilitarian calculus based on a realistic appraisal of actual problems, possibilities, and needs was the only sensible approach to cultural change. Utilitarianism was dictated both by a prudent calculation of personal advantage and by a well-informed public-mindedness. Utility was indeed the measure of all things.[81]

The utilitarianism of cultural change was manifested in its contribution to social moderation. Reasoned changes and reforms to remedy generally recognizable abuses provided the most effective way to preempt unpleasant extremities. So long as the sterility of traditional education continued to tyrannize the Greek youth, it became more likely that the younger generations might reject their national heritage wholesale. The inadequacies of grammatical learning and of books in artificial ancient Greek made those interested in serious learning to turn increasingly to foreign sources and espouse foreign ideas and causes to an unbecoming degree. This immersion in foreign cultures might make the youth fall in love with foreign nations, hate their own, and forsake their religion. The inescapable consequence would be the disappearance of even an elementary knowledge of ancient Greek a generation later. To avoid such extremes, Katartzis felt there was only one way: an educational reform and the cultivation of the modern spoken language that would capture the interest and loyalty of the younger generation for their own culture. Once again the heavier duty fell on the learned men of the nation: they had to take the lead in the movement of cultural change by composing books in the Romaic language so as to meet the intellectual needs and zeal for learning of those groping for enlightenment. This was the only sound approach if cultural change was to be kept from getting out of hand. Katartzis knew and made it categorically clear that an attempt to arrest the pressures of cultural change by reinstituting in the East the Inquisition of the Roman Church was both unacceptable and doomed to failure.[82]

This conception of cultural change as a strategy against social extremism showed Katartzis to be a shrewd liberal tactician. The philosophical foundation of his political and social attitudes can be made clear by a consideration of his relation to the thought of the Enlightenment. Many of the exponents of the Enlightenment parade through Katartzis's pages, and the influence of the ideas of the major figures pervades his thought even if he does not always cite his sources or refers to them only by allusion. The influence of the Enlightenment remained strong even when Katartzis directly criticized some of its foremost representatives. Besides continually wrestling with the thought and arguments of major figures, Katartzis shaped many of his ideas by reading the works of some of the minor and now completely forgotten authors of the eighteenth century, such as Massuet and Réal de Curban. Those useful registries and codifiers of the currents of thought that pervaded the age are far from irrelevant to the history of ideas in that they recorded with immediacy and without the intervention of original thinking of their own the standardized views and outlook of the times. Katartzis paid so much attention to them precisely because he found in them the useful manuals that codified and made intelligible to average minds the basic ideas that he judged to be most needed and suitable to the practical purposes of his program of cultural change. Among the major figures dominating the pantheon of the Enlightenment, Katartzis referred only once to Montesquieu, whose theory of the spirit of the laws he considered indeed the source of sublime and profound ideas, but feared could be misleading to those who did not have a good grounding in the basic facts of jurisprudence.[83] Turning to Rousseau, Katartzis expressed some uneasiness regarding his discussion of society in terms of abstractions and his skepticism concerning the progress of civilization.[84] His reservations toward these more radical representatives of the Enlightenment culminated in his skepticism and occasional outbursts of hostility toward Voltaire. What made him uneasy was the spirit of Voltaire's criticism, which he saw as destructive of civil society and religion. "Voltaire with the pretext of talking against superstition, was in fact extremely superstitious in his impiety."[85] Yet despite these reservations, which could have been inspired by Katartzis's reading of Voltaire's critics, in many of its essentials his thought remained indebted to the ideas of the sage of Ferney.

Katartzis reserved his greatest enthusiasm for the monumental encyclopedic projects of the Enlightenment. His admiration for D'Alembert and Diderot and their great *Encyclopédie,* which codified and made immediately accessible the wisdom of the modern age, was boundless. His practical mind was gripped by infinite fascination with that treasure-house of modern scientific knowledge, which could provide the most effective instrument of social reform. The *Encyclopedie* was the epitome of an intellectual project whose social utility was unlimited in view of the practical uses it could have in the promotion of cultural change. In its volumes it had codified the latest advances of knowledge and discoveries of modern research, and it surveyed the panorama of human civilization from the vantage point of the philosophy of the Enlightenment. In addition to the *Encyclopédie* of Diderot and D'Alembert, Katartzis expressed great admiration for the *Encyclopédie Méthodique,* which began publication in 1782, precisely at the time he was composing his theoretical works. The systematization of knowledge represented in the conception and structure of the *Encyclopédie Méthodique* appealed enormously to Katartzis's methodical mind. Indeed, he considered the newer work as the "depository and synopsis of our human wisdom," the "most daring and inclusive" project undertaken by the human mind.[86] Katartzis was so fascinated with the intellectual and social utility of these great encyclopedic projects that in his analysis of the lacunae of Greek bibliography and the needs of Greek cultural reconstruction he discussed seriously the possibility of composing an encyclopedic compendium of knowledge in the Greek language and made specific suggestions on how to tackle the various problems that might emerge from such an undertaking.[87]

Philosophic encyclopedism was the essence of Katartzis's thought. In his most ambitious theoretical essay, entitled "A Discourse Urging 'Know Thyself',"[88] he discussed the meaning of ignorance and its dialectical opposite, wisdom, which he defined as self-awareness. His reflections on this most integral philosophic preoccupation of the Enlightenment were based on a theory of knowledge inspired by D'Alembert's system of human knowledge in the *Discours préliminaire.* Explicitly acknowledging Bacon and D'Alembert as his sources, Katartzis proposed a classification of human knowledge and cultural activity on the basis of the three faculties of the mind: memory, reason, and imagination.[89] By thus bringing out the cognitive dynamic of human knowledge, Katartzis expected to make it aware of itself, to open the road to wisdom through self-reflection. Such was the preeminent aspiration of the Enlightenment. This epistemological exploration had, of course, a practical objective in Katartzis's scheme. It sought to confront Greek culture with a mirror of its failures within the matrix of an enlightened epistemology. Appropriately, Katartzis's theory of knowledge was concluded with his survey of Greek bibliography and his suggestions on how to bring it up to date.[90]

This was the theoretical framework of Katartzis's political thought, which comprised two basic dimensions: a conception of the political community and a theory of its leadership. As a man of the Enlightenment, Katartzis had resolved the quarrel of Ancients and Moderns categorically in favor of the Europeans, who continued to progress in the sciences twenty centuries after the ancient Greeks had exhausted their excellence. In his consideration of political issues, however, he started with the formulations of Aristotle. His skepticism toward what he considered to be the extreme implications of the Enlightenment, and the importance he attached to the modern Greeks' classical and Christian heritage, prevented Katartzis from ever entirely shedding the Aristotelian influence from his thought. It will be remembered that his attack on traditional education was directed against scholastic commentaries on Aristotle and not on the philosopher's texts themselves. Katartzis never disputed that the Aristotelian corpus was a fountainhead of human wisdom. In addition, in Katartzis's eyes Aristotle's thought possessed an encyclopedic character that increased its utility over that of all ancient authors. In moral and political matters in particular, Aristotle's wisdom was unexcelled.[91]

The point of departure of Katartzis's political thought, therefore, were Aristotle's reflections on political community. It was true that the whole was prior to its parts, and thus the community enjoyed moral precedence over the family and the individual.[92] Therefore, the arguments put forward by Katartzis and the other partisans of Enlightenment for cultural change in the name of the good of the nation, even at the expense of sectional interests, were justified. But did the modern Greeks constitute an integral community, a nation? Katartzis argued that the modern Greeks constituted a political community bound together by commonly known and acknowledged civil laws and religious traditions. He rejected the vicious implication that on account of their captivity the political status of modern Greeks was equivalent to that of ancient helots, and they, therefore, did not meet the basic criteria of Aristotle's definition of citizenship. Against such arguments, Katartzis pointed out that if the Greeks did not entirely control the state under which they lived, they still participated in its administration. Their ecclesiastical leadership, civil mores, and religious traditions enjoyed the official recognition of their rulers and bound them to each other in one nation. In addition, many members of the nation rose to prominent positions in the administration of the state, and some even had personal access to the sovereign himself and participated in the responsibility of government. Finally, the nation was entitled to the rights of landed ownership, and in many parts of the empire, Greek communities enjoyed the privileges of liberty. By thus endowing Aristotle's definition of citizenship with concrete sociological content, Katartzis could set the criteria distinguishing a modern Greek nationality.[93]

Consciousness of belonging to a national community could be heightened by the pride of an illustrious historical ancestry that connected the modern Greeks with the heroes of classical Hellas and the champions of the faith in the Christian Roman Empire. By thus historicizing the meaning of the national community, Katartzis offered one of the earliest formulations of the theory of the historical continuity of the Greek nation that later on became the fundamental dogma of Greek nationalism. Nevertheless, his sociological understanding of the meaning of the national community led Katartzis to draw a distinction between ancient and modern Greeks. On the basis of the same logic that led him to accept a historical connection and filiation between classical Greek and the modern Romaic Greek vernacular, but to reject the grammatical identification of the two, he also rejected a completely shared identity between ancient and modern Greeks as social collectivities. Fundamental differences in their respective historical destinies, political condition, religion, mores, language, behavior, and even in such external indicators of social change as dress and housewares, pointed to the undeniable fact that although the modern Greeks were the historical offspring of the ancient Hellenes, still the two peoples formed quite distinct nations.[94] So defined, the national community was the source of feelings of dedication to collectively cherished ideals. In such sentiments, the Greeks, although they did not have a state of their own, were not different from any other nation. Indeed, the absence of an independent Greek polity meant that the Greeks cared about and loved their weakened and mutilated homeland more tenderly and zealously than those nations that knew that their countries enjoyed the blessings of autonomy and orderly national government. Consciousness of the bitter predicament of the present and of the glorious patrimony of history infused the sentiments of Greek patriotism with a unique intensity expressed in the attachment of the modern Greeks to the soil of their homeland and to the tombs of their fathers, in their perseverance under the yoke of slavery, and in the tears they shed upon reflection on the sacrifices of their ancestors. Far from being the asocial beasts, as implied in the sophistic distortion of Aristotle's words by their enemies, the modern Greeks were an intensely patriotic nation worthy of better things.[95]

It was this nation, which he felt to be his own, that Katartzis wanted to endow with the leadership it deserved. His program of enlightenment was designed with this end in mind. Among all the arts and sciences that the pursuit of enlightenment cultivated and perfected, the most exalted was the "art and science of ruling," which elevated those who assumed its responsibilities toward the eternal master of the universe. This onerous similitude could not be lived up to unless those carrying the burdens of rulership remained continuously vigilant and concerned with the condition, security, and happiness of the people entrusted to their care. If a ruler failed to benefit and edify his subjects, he transformed himself into a rebel against God, a rebel who usurped authority in order to satisfy his selfish passions, his vain glory, his greed, his flesh, and his belly.[96] The ideal of enlightened Christian rulership dominated Katartzis's conscience when he turned his attention to the problem of political leadership. The Christian philosopher, whom he visualized as the paradigm of enlightened virtue, could be the ideal ruler. He would be impartial and ever vigilant in looking after the prosperity of his people. He would enforce orderly government based on the permanence and stability of the laws. He would reward and rejoice in virtue, punish and grieve in vice, and in the same way he would strive to live up to the standards required by his divine prototype, he would require his subordinates to imitate his own virtuous conduct.[97] Such virtuous and enlightened rulers alone could shoulder the formidable task of guiding cultural change. As the history of modern European civilization had amply demonstrated, the test of greatness for a monarch came in the leadership he provided for the renovation and perfection of the arts and sciences and in the propagation of the lights of education among entire nations.[98]

Katartzis's expectations from enlightened absolutism were nurtured by the unity of the theory and practice of Enlightenment he perceived in the case of Frederick the Great—whose writings he had obviously read.[99] Frederick's example, as well as the impact and imitation of his policies by the rulers of the smaller German principalities, inspired Katartzis with the hope that a moderate enlightenment could indeed lead to cultural and social reform. The geographical proximity and the similarity in political conditions between the petty German states and the Danubian principalities seemed to have contributed significantly in shaping Katartzis's hopeful beliefs that the Phanariot princes, whom he served and advised, might successfully tread a comparable path. To instruct them in the tasks of enlightened rulership, Katartzis gleaned arguments from the venerable heritage of Byzantine mirrors of princes so familiar in the political tradition of Ottoman Greece. Among his sources in that tradition, the *Institutio Regia* of Theophylactus, archbishop of Bulgaria, was the most preeminent.[100] In addition, Katartzis chose to translate from the French one of the manuals of enlightened absolutism, Réal de Curban's *La science du gouvernement*. In his judgment, this was a useful and eminently practical work, which, besides emphasizing the crucial importance of instructing monarchs in their duties and in the science of politics, went on to offer an encyclopedic survey of the societies and political systems of the world as they existed both in antiquity and in modern times. Réal's work thus combined the elements of moral education with the basic empirical knowledge necessary to the tasks of government.[101] Katartzis therefore presented it confidently as a scientific source that could teach with certainty the duties of "good Christians, good men, good parents, good children and especially good rulers and good subjects." A Christian polity could survive and prosper only if these conditions were met. In the event of their corruption, the whole community was in peril.[102]

Although the selection of Réal de Curban's work for translation into Greek was not due entirely to Katartzis himself but was also an expression of the preferences of Prince Michael Soutsos, the ideological climate informing the work did not depart significantly from Katartzis's political thought. Réal de Curban, although little read by the 1780s and generally forgotten by later generations, was essentially a prophet of the social tensions and psychological stresses that culminated in the French Revolution. His argument for prudent conservatism and social harmony, based on an acceptance of things as they were, was dictated by fear of the cataclysmic consequences that might ensue if the social order was upset by minor changes based on the claims of reason and natural rights.[103] It was precisely such cataclysms and upheavals that Katartzis's social theory also wanted to avert. In Réal de Curban he found an ideological ally whose more explicit conservative argument clarified Katartzis's own position, which in the context of Greek society, by virtue of his sheer identification with French ideas, appeared more progressive than its social purposes actually were.

Moisiodax and Katartzis placed their hopes for enlightened absolutism in the Phanariot princes who in the eighteenth century ruled in the Danubian principalities of Moldavia and Wallachia under Ottoman suzerainty.[104] There was much in the Phanariot princes' record to justify these hopes. Under their regime important social changes had been introduced, most notably the legal abolition of serfdom by Constantinos Mavrokordatos in 1746–1749.[105] The cultural policies and the encouragement to learning shown by serious rulers such as Grigorios Ghikas and Alexandros Ypsilantis had opened the principalities to the Enlightenment.[106] The academies of the princely capitals, Bucharest and Jassy, became major centers of Enlightenment in Southeastern Europe. Moisiodax was associated with both academies, and Katartzis held high office in the court of Bucharest. So they both had a chance to observe enlightened absolutism at work from within. For a time it seemed that it could really put into practice the aspiration of cultural change. Moisiodax amply expressed this belief in his inaugural address, when he assumed the position of scholarch of the princely Academy at Jassy in 1765, and in the dedicatory addresses to the princes with which he repeatedly prefaced his books. Katartzis could sense the promise of enlightened absolutism in the respect and influence he enjoyed at the princely court and in the willingness of the princes to listen to his enlightened advice.

Yet it was this close association with the Greek practice of enlightened absolutism that made the two exponents of its theory conscious of its limits. Under the weight of a conservative turn in Phanariot circles after 1789, Katartzis was forced to abandon the most radical dimension of his theory of cultural change, his views on the language question. In a last, almost desperate, effort to save something of his program of enlightenment, he rendered the most important of his theoretical essays into a more purist language conforming to the conventions of grammar and diction acceptable in Phanariot society. Beyond that he kept silent and retained to the end of his days the respectability of high office and political moderation. In a sense, the political theory he elaborated in the 1780s came much too late. As became clear from the radical social and political protest articulated by the most promising of his disciples in the 1790s, the Greek Enlightenment was already groping for political expression in terms of a theory beyond the confines of enlightened absolutism. The vestiges of traditional thought and conservative practice that enlightened absolutism sought to preserve were unacceptable to radicalized enlightened consciences. As a consequence, Katartzis's work remained unpublished in its entirety during his lifetime and was not to be recovered until modern Greek consciousness attempted to reconstruct its own cultural history, almost two centuries later.

In the case of Moisiodax, the realization of the limits beyond which absolutism would not tolerate the aspirations of enlightened intellectuals committed to the cause of change provoked the outburst of a believer disabused of his ideological hopes. The adherents of cultural renewal had to compromise significantly their goals in order to satisfy the constraints imposed by the social establishment if they were to enjoy the support of the princes who would like to adorn their reign with the imprint of Enlightenment. The realization was painful, because it delineated the limits of Enlightenment under the aegis of absolutism. Besides the bitterness of disillusionment that this realization involved, it made Moisiodax conscious of the fundamental incompatibility between whatever pretensions so-called enlightened princes might have and the intellectuals' commitment to change. Out of this disappointment with the prospects of enlightened absolutism, Moisiodax groped for a formulation of a new conception of the intellectual as a revolted man, a revolutionary. The scholars who returned to the East from the academies of Europe, Moisiodax protested, were commonly considered to be unconventional and revolutionary, and he went on to ask:

> Is it a revolution if an educated man cannot suffer unjustifiable contempt heaped upon him? The multitude of hardships and dangers one had to endure on sea and on land, one's consciousness of one's ability, and finally the end for which one endured everything, namely one's reputation and good name—all these force one to refuse to tolerate dishonor.

Enlightened intellectuals could not put up with such treatment, Moisiodax insisted, because they were persons with a secular frame of mind and could not, therefore, display the patient endurance of apostles and martyrs. Modern secular intellectuals felt that they ought to enjoy a respect and station in society analogous to their worth and ability. This is what made possible the great strides of civilization in the nations of Europe. If the partisans of the Enlightenment in Greek society failed to receive a comparable treatment and witnessed instead worthless individuals enjoying social success, how could they not revolt? It was clear that Moisiodax alluded to the Phanariot courtiers who surrounded those in power and reaped the advantages attendant upon the ingratiation gained through sycophancy.[107] The eventual awareness of the workings of absolutism dispelled the mirage of its enlightenment. The philosopher was left with a revolted conscience, but this did not mark the end of his mental itinerary. The psychological revolt signified the transcendence of a state of consciousness and pointed toward the quest for a political alternative.

CHAPTER FIVE

Ancients and Moderns

Cultural Criticism and the Origins of Republicanism

THE QUARREL OF Ancients and Moderns as a dilemma of intellectual self-definition had already become noticeable in European culture during the Renaissance and went through a number of fluctuations and culminating points, particularly during the seventeenth century.[1] The advent of the Enlightenment, however, symbolized the final resolution of the dispute in favor of the Moderns. The nostalgia for classical antiquity that was associated with the revival of civic humanism gave expression to the radical current of the Enlightenment, and consequently belonged to the world of the Moderns.[2] Even the aspirations of the German Hellenists and Hegel's praise of the ancient Greek ideals of political morality represented not a rejection of the modern spirit, but rather a desire to perfect it ethically by invoking classical wisdom.[3] In this sense the appreciation of the early nineteenth century for the classics derived rather from the legacy of the Enlightenment than from any surviving attitudes of the supporters of the Ancients in the quarrel.

In modern Greek culture the Enlightenment provoked rather than resolved the dispute between Ancients and Moderns. Enlightenment rationalism and contact with modern science triggered an initially diffident challenge to the authority of Aristotle and his Neoaristotelian commentators, especially Corydaleus. This marked the appearance of the critical spirit that was responsible for the intellectual fermentation in Greek culture later in the eighteenth century. The confrontation between modern scientific attitudes and established Neoaristotelianism in Greek academic life reproduced the fundamental lines of the great European intellectual conflict of the previous century on the stage of Southeastern Europe during the century of Enlightenment.

The uniqueness of the Greek experience resided in the strong political overtones of the dispute. The Enlightenment called conventional Aristotelianism into question but at the same time encouraged in modern Greeks a new awareness of their national and cultural descent from classical Greece. This was the revolutionary discovery that shattered the old Christian cultural tradition, the self-definition of which had depended until then upon the shared spiritual heritage of all Christian peoples. The dispute between Ancients and Moderns did not, therefore, merely involve a choice between modern science and ancient authority. It also pointed to the need to reestablish a genuine link between the modern Greeks and their ancient ancestors as an essential precondition for their national revival. It was on the clarification of such dilemmas that the most crucial issue appeared to depend: the final recovery of national dignity and even, in the eyes of the most radical spirits, the political independence of enslaved Greece. The consequences of cultural choices for the collective destiny account for the political character of the late Balkan phase of the long European dispute. The importance of the quarrel was that it was one of the signs of the cultural changes that reestablished the missing links between the regional culture and the mainstream of European civilization, from which it had become severed as a consequence of the Ottoman conquest.

ENLIGHTENMENT AS A WAY OF LIFE

The dispute between Ancients and Moderns was consequently articulated around the issue of what were the appropriate relations between modern Hellenism and the two civilizations between which it placed itself: those of ancient Greece and modern Europe. The fundamental dilemma confronting Greek education and culture, and the recommended solution, were expressed with the greatest clarity by Iosipos Moisiodax (1730–1800), whose writings reflect one of the most perspicacious minds of the Neohellenic Enlightenment. Moisiodax, whom we have already encountered as an exponent of the theory of reforming monarchy in his early political thought, was heir to a tradition of critical thought that had made itself felt in Greek culture in the early eighteenth century. As we have seen, this tradition had emerged with the questioning of the authority of Aristotle by Methodios Anthrakitis and the introduction of modern philosophy by Evgenios Voulgaris. Voulgaris found it prudent to abandon the Greek world for the protection afforded by Russian enlightened absolutism, and it was left to the combative spirit of Moisiodax, pupil and admirer but also critic of the venerable old prelate, to carry the critical tradition to its climax.

For Moisiodax the Enlightenment was a mode of existence. The geographical, social, and cultural mobility marking his own experience was characteristic of a life shaped by the pursuit of enlightenment. A peasant boy from a village of "Moisiodacians," Cernavodă, on the south bank of the Danube in the Dobrudja region, he seized his only chance of education and social mobility by joining the ranks of the celibate Orthodox clergy. This brought him, as a young deacon, to the centers of Greek learning in the middle decades of the eighteenth century, at Thessaloniki, Smyrna, and finally to the Athonite Academy, where he studied under Voulgaris. He emerged entirely Hellenized from this educational experience, and he followed the itinerary of young Greeks seeking higher learning at the time. He went to Venice, where he served as a preacher at the Greek Church of Saint George during Lent 1759; he then studied at Padua and later conducted research work in Vienna. At Venice he published his first book in 1761–1762, a two-volume translation of Antonio Muratori's *Filosofia morale esposta e proposta ai giovani,* because he felt that moral knowledge was what his nation needed most. From the West he returned to the Danubian principalities to assume the duties of director of the academy of Jassy in 1765. In the prolegomena to *Moral Philosophy,* he outlined the method of enlightenment as he experienced it amid the toil, dangers, and myriad hardships that, as he put it, opened his own eyes.[4]

Moisiodax enlisted himself under the banner of the Enlightenment by joining the quarrel of Ancients and Moderns. His espousal of the cause of the Moderns was grounded on a reflection on Greek history and on a criticism of contemporary Greek society. He drew the familiar contrast between the glory of ancient Greece and the cultural depravity of modern Greek society, which he explained in terms of the republican theory of history. He thus placed the problem of decline and corruption in modern Greek society in broad perspective. Behind all misfortunes of the modern Greeks, he felt, lurked the specter of ignorance combined with discord mutually abetting and reinforcing each other. This was most painfully illustrated by the sorry condition of the leadership of Greek society—the ecclesiastical hierarchy, who ignored even the fundamentals of the faith; of the lay patriciate, Moisiodax commented: "And what benefit does the state expect from a politician who regards custom and legality indifferently as one and the same thing: who has neither learned, nor shows any desire to learn, what is law, or what is the polity?"[5]

In drawing this bleak picture of Greek society and in the anatomy of corruption that pervaded it, Moisiodax essentially formulated in negative terms his conception of the Greek problem. Ignorance was first and primary among the causes of social malaise. To the extent that ignorance could be conquered and eradicated, corruption could be tamed and social renovation achieved. On the basis of this understanding of the causation of social ills, Moisiodax's primary theoretical preoccupation revolved around the conditions of cultural renewal and the means of taming ignorance. His criticism was inspired by this pursuit, and it sought to expose the obstacles and constraints that had to be removed before ignorance could be conquered. Only after this initial phase of the task of criticism was accomplished could a positive program of cultural reconstruction be put to work.[6]

This feeling dispelled resignation and fatalistic acceptance of the irrevocability of national misfortunes. Striving for social improvement became a meaningful existential choice and criticism a pressing social vocation. Moisiodax was the characteristic representative of this outlook. With a discerning eye and incisive judgment, he directed his criticism at the most fundamental cultural contradiction of Greek society. This had to do with the place of ancient learning in modern culture. In considering this problem, Moisiodax fought a belated battle in the quarrel of Ancients and Moderns, long after the conflict had been resolved in European culture in favor of the Moderns. This was another indication of the odds that the Enlightenment had to face in the Greek context—odds of which Moisiodax was profoundly aware.

Modern Greek culture suffered from a double defect deriving from excessive esteem and at the same time from excessive neglect of antiquity, of ancient civilization. Excessive esteem had generated that thriving prejudice that insisted that everything invented or cultivated by the Ancients was beyond criticism and reproach. Excessive neglect of classical culture was essentially reflected in the scarcity, indeed, in the complete disappearance and unavailability among the modern Greeks of classical texts and writings of ancient authors. This was not all, however. Prejudicial esteem of the Ancients nurtured an irreconcilable hatred of the Moderns, while scarcity of classical texts had deprived the modern Greeks of the most basic knowledge about the Ancients. In short, ignorance was nurtured in both directions. Furthermore, he had no doubt that when the truth collided with prejudice or with arrogance, and especially when it ran counter to established interests, it was far from generally palatable. But gripped by his sense of vocation, he could not keep silent. He pointed out that the Ancients were indeed admirable for that part of learning that they had discovered and elaborated. They were even more admirable for being the first to break the ground in so many branches of learning and culture in such a difficult and remote time, without the help of modern means. Once all this was said and acknowledged, Moisiodax exclaimed with some impatience that even the Ancients were human, just human beings endowed with a finite and imperfect nature like the rest of humanity. In addition, they were vulnerable to the machinations of error, the brevity of life, the uncertainty of the times, and all the other constraints mankind is subject to. They had therefore to be critically appraised, taking all these factors into account. They had to be brought down to earth and demythologized. The lack of critical appreciation of the Ancients was the result of the total ignorance or hostile prejudice against modern learning. This, Moisiodax felt, was an entirely unwarranted attitude because it was based on uninformed and unsound judgment. Both elements of right judgment were absent from the Greek view of modern European learning. The Greek judgment was the product of prejudice, not of careful and exacting contemplation and of impartial comparison. No one went to such lengths. The Greeks passed judgment quite haphazardly so that a European observer was justified in charging that they had ordained ignorance and passion as critics of philosophy.

So much for the prejudicial esteem of antiquity. Turning to the problem of indifference and neglect of classical civilization, Moisiodax complained that it was dramatized by the absence of ancient authors from practically all existing libraries. Another bitter truth had to be recognized here: it was the indifference of the Greeks themselves that was responsible for this, and not the yoke of captivity, which was usually blamed for all failings and inadequacies of Greek culture. If modern Greek learning was plagued by all these inconsistencies and contradictions, the cause could be found at least partially in some practices of the Greeks themselves. Instead of endowing schools and contributing to education, they spent great sums on the erection and decoration of churches. Would it not be preferable to train the priests and spiritual leaders, to educate the youth, and to cultivate the flock's minds, rather than decorate the walls? These harmful practices should be exiled from Greece. If the modern Greeks really esteemed their ancestors, they ought to imitate the Ancients' willingness to learn from others, a zeal that even led them to travel abroad in search of knowledge and in pursuit of the paradigms of virtue. With this reminder to his compatriots, Moisiodax came full circle in his argument; the descendants of the ancient Hellenes should not be ashamed to learn from the nations of modern Europe.

This was another bitter truth that had to be recognized even though it might hurt national pride. Modern Europe, partly due to well-ordered administration and partly thanks to the love of local rulers for learning and culture, had surpassed in wisdom even ancient Greece. This was an unconventionally daring statement in the Greek context, although it came at a time when in Europe the Moderns were winning the battle against the Ancients. Moisiodax's opinion coming in 1761 preserved in the Greek context something of the freshness and militancy of Fontenelle's and Perrault's, and even Bacon's arguments of several decades earlier. The major difference now was that Moisiodax, despite his unequivocal preference for the Moderns, attempted to formulate a more balanced judgment of the Ancients and their achievements, knowing that this might lend to his arguments a greater claim to credibility. In essence, however, his elegy for the lost wisdom and virtue of Hellas was a lament on the predicament of modern Greece, whose interest and improvement was his primary preoccupation and consuming care.

Europe's experience and the models of European achievements held the answer to the problem of Greece's improvement. It was in Greece's interest to look up to Europe for inspiration and example; good sense made it imperative to look for one's interest everywhere and to pursue it wherever it could be found. Europe's example and Greece's interest dictated, first of all, a revolution in Greek education. The vigor of Greek youth should no longer be worn out in sterile grammatical exercises and scholastic commentaries. A conscious effort should instead be undertaken to imitate the Europeans in their efforts to make learning more appealing and effective. European education was open to free and unprejudiced thinking. European nations resembled a great beehive in freely borrowing from each other's culture and learning. In this they followed the example of bees that gathered everything useful wherever it could be found. Confronted with this exasperating contrast between the European experience and the Greek practice, Moisiodax returned to his initial plea. He appealed to his compatriots to overcome the contradiction between their blind esteem of antiquity, which stifled their own independent judgment on the one hand, and their neglect of ancient learning on the other, which deprived them of their own cherished patrimony. The only way to resolve the contradiction could be found in the imitation of Europe: "Greece does need Europe. Nowadays the one bursts with the lights of learning while the other lacks even the most essential of them."[7]

The lights of Europe would be enough to revive Greece's ancient splendor and might even lighten the burden of tyranny. By their own progress the Greeks might offer an example to their Ottoman masters to join the common efforts of civilized nations. Once again it appeared that the real root of Greece's tribulations was not captivity—itself only an effect, not a cause—but ignorance. The civilized Europeans pitied the Greeks more for their cultural backwardness than for their political captivity, which could be overcome once ignorance was stamped out. The foremost obligations of the modern Greeks, if they wanted to be true to their ancient patrimony and worthy of their ancestors who had become humanity's inspiring standard, was to raise their country from the degradation of ignorance. The great strides of all other European nations in civilization and progress, and the remarkable achievements of cultural change in Russia in the recent past, made the challenge facing the Greeks all the more urgent.[8]

In both his attitude toward modern European civilization and its achievements and in his hopes concerning the possible effects of its adoption by the Greeks upon their relations with their Ottoman masters, Moisiodax exemplified clearly the optimistic cosmopolitan faith of the Enlightenment. Profoundly self-conscious in his advocacy of the strategy of Enlightenment, Moisiodax admitted to the great liberties he took against conventions,

driven by his anxiety over the cause of change and the vision of a new society. He had only a simple but convincing excuse to offer: he spoke freely out
of a burning and genuine eros for the public good and out of great affection
for the Greek nation.[9]

PEDAGOGY AS CRITICISM OF SOCIAL INEQUALITY

The conception of the Greek problem as a question of cultural renewal was
strengthened by the experiences that awaited Moisiodax during his teaching career at Jassy and Bucharest. His original plea that cultural renovation
should begin from fundamental changes in the system of Greek education
developed into a fully fledged critique that began from a quite professional
examination of the technical problems of educational practice, but went
on to consider the social context and political implications of educational
choices. In his *Pedagogy*, published in 1779 in Venice, Moisiodax offered
a manual for the education of young gentlemen in moral and civic rectitude. His guiding principles continued to be informed with ever-greater
intensity by the aspirations of modernization and utility on the European
model. Thus, from the criticism of educational philosophies, structures, and
practices, he was inevitably led to a criticism of the social environment of
the educational system. This criticism was based on firsthand knowledge
of the society of Phanariot gentlemen thriving in the Danubian principalities under Ottoman suzerainty. His impatience and dissatisfaction with
that society, which belonged to the uppermost echelons of Greek social
structure, was obvious. After more than a decade, during which he tried to
instruct them and reform their moral character, his simmering resentment
at their obstructionism or indifference to his program of cultural renewal
was on the verge of explosion. Although the outburst did not come until
the publication of his *Apology* the following year, he was aware of the nonconformist turn of his thinking. He felt impelled to take some liberties in
talking about the social establishment, and he did so in full consciousness
of the unconventional meaning of his initiative.

The problem of education and its social implications, as Moisiodax perceived it, derived its urgency from the afflicting products of ignorance,
such as prejudice, vanity, mendacity, and groundless fears. The "Iliad of
evils" that haunted the face of the earth was the consequence of defective

upbringing and bad education. Nothing could be worse for a state than the union of ignorance and viciousness with power in the person of a ruler. In such unfortunate conjunctures, virtue and vice turn into their opposites as all moral notions are perverted and distorted. This danger, which Thucydides had seen as the extreme of social and ethical corruption reached only under the exceptional strain of civil war, Moisiodax felt to be permanently lurking in Greek society under Ottoman rule. It was a revealing measure of its corruption. The reason was simply that ignorance had developed into a most powerful force in Greek society, nurturing prejudices, superstitions, and irregularities that, because so pervasive, remained almost unnoticed. Such were the social dimensions of the problem that confronted Moisiodax. The sores of Greek society had developed into a poisonous gangrene, which could not be healed with the softening emollients of sycophants, but needed radical surgery and amputation. Moisiodax wished that a milder cure were possible—it would be more congenial to his own predilections. But he had concluded from bitter experience that only radical new departures could cure things and took it upon himself to break the new ground. This was not a gesture of vanity, or the impertinence of an imposter. Moisiodax knew that he was just another learned man among many others whose dignity he did not intend to affront. But his care for Greece's prosperity could not allow him to rest and keep silent.[10]

The concrete pedagogical program that Moisiodax put forward as the ground plan of the battle against ignorance was a direct free adaptation of Locke's *Some Thoughts Concerning Education*. Following Locke quite faithfully, Moisiodax based his pedagogical theory on the epistemological construct of human understanding as an original *tabula rasa* gradually inscribed with knowledge by experience. Little children resembled malleable wax, which can be easily reshaped on any given occasion. Hence the great dangers of corruption and distortion to which the character of children is exposed. To guard against such dangers, Moisiodax adapted Locke's advice on the domestic upbringing of children to suit the realities of the Greek situation. He warned against the dangerous role of ignorant, superstitious, and malicious servants as well as against the morally catastrophic impressions that could be stamped on children's tender souls by the improper behavior of their parents. As the children grew up into adolescence, particular care should be taken for their proper socialization into the ethic of moral and civil rectitude by exposing them to edifying domestic and public experiences. Turning from moral upbringing to the education of the mind, Moisiodax emphasized that learning alone was not adequate to regulate character and make man fit for living with others. Learning had to be combined with experience and acquaintance with human nature. The purpose of education was therefore twofold: it sought to combine sound and broad learning with moral rectitude.[11]

The remainder of the *Pedagogy* turned on a consideration of the problem arising out of the theory and practice of Greek education. With the incisive judgment of an experienced professional and the anxiety of a deeply concerned man, Moisiodax began with a criticism of traditional teaching methods. He recounted a grim personal recollection of his childhood teacher: "a man of a naturally sullen appearance with his wild beard," who inspired fear and mortified his students' desire to learn. Moisiodax felt that he had to spell out still another unpleasant truth: Greek teachers should alter their method and style of instruction; they should take a new course. The sullen look, the coarse voice, the severities of cudgeling could not work anymore. Experience and the triumph of ignorance had proved their bankruptcy. The failures of Greek education were compounded by its content. Dry grammatical drilling and sterile indulgence in scholastic logic, analytics, and metaphysics had proved utterly useless and irrelevant. They had nothing to contribute to the needs of life, and they consumed the youth's precious time and energy in superfluous pedantry.[12]

Against this mortifying educational system, Moisiodax proposed an alternative pedagogy that sought to make learning pleasant and attractive by appealing to the pupils' natural curiosity, by making plain to them the need and future utility of their training, by handling each student in an individualized manner, taking into account each one's personal traits, needs, and gifts. An approach to teaching that sought to level the personalities of individual students and required the same of all of them—a misfortune common throughout Greek education—was against nature and amounted essentially to tyranny. An individualized approach should also be employed in school discipline. Punishments should be moderate and restrained, well calculated as to their pedagogical effects lest they led to unintended traumatic experiences incapacitating the student's ability to learn. Corporal punishment was pointless if it did not impress on the student the just reasons of its imposition and should be used very rarely and with great restraint. The main purpose of this new pedagogy was to rectify the behavior and social mores of the students. In particular, it had to try to curb the arrogance and tendency to lie so common among the offspring of the gentry.[13]

The content of the new education should be based on a new curriculum that would require of its students reflection and judgment. Mechanistic learning and formal externalities should be dropped and replaced by substantive studies. The recitation and exegesis of patristic texts that distorted the Greek language and the thankless memorization of late Byzantine grammatical treatises should be replaced by a new curriculum in the classics. Ancient texts with an intrinsic interest and liveliness, such as Aesop's fables, might be used to stimulate children's interest, and the texts of ancient historians such as Herodotus, Arrian, and Xenophon would provide naturally appealing reading that would both sharpen the students' minds and cultivate their moral sense. The revised program of classical education should continue with Demosthenes and culminate with Thucydides. Both texts should be studied in their historical and cultural context in order to make plain their important political meanings that should appeal to and reinforce the readers' feeling of a shared identity. The preoccupations of the new pedagogy inevitably extended beyond the classics to embrace the branches of modern learning, the sciences made necessary by the flowering of Enlightenment: mathematics, physics, geography, history, ethics (for which Moisiodax had translated Muratori's two-volume textbook), and law, along with a systematic instruction in the modern Greek vernacular, in Turkish (the "language of the ruling race"), and in French and Italian (the "main languages of Europe") should form the core of the new curriculum. Education should encourage the creative skills of the students through the assignment of compositions designed to exercise their reflectiveness and abilities of expression—but care should be taken for the eradication of the temptation to relapse into the inflated and pompous "Asiatic" style.[14]

Such were the essential purposes of the curriculum of enlightenment. Moisiodax made no attempt to hide or disguise the real targets of his revised program. Its major objective was the emancipation of the human mind from traditional prejudices and superstitions. This was the foremost aspiration of the Enlightenment and, by making it the main objective of his new pedagogy, Moisiodax threw before modern Greek consciousness the challenge immanent in the invitation "écrasez l' infâme." The intensity with which he espoused this cause derived from his sense of the universality of superstition. It was ubiquitous in the monstrosity of error which was everywhere sanctioned by ignorance, simple-minded naiveté, and inherited custom. "Sorceries, vampires, witchcraft, ghosts, magic, enchantments, divination of dreams, omens of future catastrophes or epidemics derived from earthquakes, comets, eclipses"—all these and more formed a universe of "headless ideas" that could easily be imparted to tender minds and become the cause of paralyzing fears, idleness, and loss of good opportunities in daily life because of the false designation of certain days as inauspicious. The enlightening task of education should be to dispel such superstitions, erroneous beliefs, and misguided fears. The enlightened teacher should protect and disabuse his students from such follies by showing how they run naturally counter to right reason. In this, modern physics and natural history were the greatest help: they could most effectively repudiate headless ideas and chase away their mischiefs. Rhigas, the loyal disciple of Moisiodax, tried to do exactly this in his *Physics*. The eradication of groundless ideas could be secured only if religious instruction was simplified to the teaching of basic doctrines avoiding arguments contrary to reason.[15]

Moisiodax was aware that this was a quite unconventional program, formidable in its aspirations of change. It could be easily construed as pure libertinism by his critics and ideological adversaries. Inescapably, his contemplation of educational problems was broadened by a consideration of the constraints of the social environment. He knew that his call for educational reform amounted to a program of far-reaching political changes. He put forward a new and decisively modern conception of human behavior as purposive and planned activity, likened to a soundly built ship, manned by a well-trained crew and skillfully commanded by experienced and providential captains, navigating amid storms and tempests.[16] The prize of such experienced conduct, which combined personal exertion with civility, was the conquest of freedom.[17] This was clearly a conception that put to question the traditional structure of social relations marked by the morally sanctioned resignation to hierarchy. Escaping from one's prescribed station in life through Enlightenment and conscious activity and conquering one's freedom—precisely as Moisiodax did—would bring about a new form of community in which every man would be one among equal fellow citizens to whose common welfare a natural duty bound each to contribute according to his means. This was a universal human duty of which enlightened persons had a more immediate and intimate knowledge.[18]

Moisiodax had no doubt that this alternative conception of human relations, implicit in the educational reforms he advocated, was unacceptable and threatening to a society that he knew to be gripped by vanity, greed, and corruption. Such was the society of the Phanariot gentlemen in the Danubian principalities whom Moisiodax had tried to convert to the cause of Enlightenment. Their primary concerns were fashion and ostentatious dress, luxury and gambling, horse breeding and hunting. Furthermore, they tolerated a variety of sycophants, flatterers, and vile persons in their environment. These empty and vain sycophants thrived by flattering ignorance and nurturing prejudices against education—which, of course, might open their master's eyes to their corruption. Unfortunately, the parties of vile parasites always managed to appeal to the potentates. These gentlemen in their turn were rude, arrogant, self-centered, scornful, and entirely indifferent to the dignity of others. In addition, there were those preposterous hypocrites who pretended that the collective predicament of a captive nation could not afford the luxury of a reformed education. They forgot, of course, all those unnecessary religious expenses that alone could easily support a splendid academy.[19]

Moisiodax felt that his ideas and commitments had set him on an unavoidable collision course with this society. As a self-conscious enlightened intellectual, he felt free and detached from vested interests. Therefore he could claim that his judgment was informed by a sense of fairness that made it hard for him to tolerate hypocrisy and injustice. He had shed much sweat for the sake of the freedom of enlightenment, and he could not compromise it even at the cost of his life.[20] Agitated by the spectacle of his society, his sense of personal dignity and his sense of justice were in revolt.

MODERN PHILOSOPHY AND REPUBLICANISM

Moisiodax's protest was registered with unique intensity in the *Apology* he published in 1780. This was the outburst of a revolted man, but it was far from a simple compound of emotion. It represented one of the most mature, if militant, statements of the Greek Enlightenment. As a theoretical synthesis, it embraced all the dimensions of the enlightened outlook. It pleaded for enlightenment from the darkness of traditional authority and religious superstition. It argued vigorously the superiority of the Moderns over the

Ancients and deified Newton as the symbol of modern science. It ascribed an almost miraculous power to education and to the popularization of science as forces of change and progress and sanctified social utility as the measure of all things. Philosophically, the achievement of Moisiodax in the *Apology* was twofold: it combined the criticism of Aristotelianism and its cultural consequences with the positive elaboration and militant advocacy of the principles of the new philosophy. His consciousness of the magnitude of this task was clearly reflected in the tension that pervaded his thought, in the psychological anxiety registered on every page of the discourse.

The extensive essay that opened the *Apology,* as well as the two discourses on mathematics and philosophy, which were originally delivered, "according to the European custom," as inaugural lectures at the princely academy of Jassy when Moisiodax assumed its direction in 1765, outlined the philosophical premises of his mature thought.[21] His quarrel with the excessive esteem of antiquity of twenty years earlier was resumed in his systematic polemics against "the disgraceful tyranny of Aristotelianism," which fettered and obstructed all intellectual progress. Peripatetic logic had aged and decayed, while the principles of Aristotelian physics as well as Aristotelian astronomy had become the laughingstock of all free spirits. In short, Aristotelianism was refuted by reason, experience, and history. The purpose of this criticism, Moisiodax hastened to explain to his reader, was not to undermine the reputation of the great philosopher whose unsurpassed genius in ethics, dialectics, and poetics was readily acknowledged. But, being human, Aristotle philosophized like a man—and he went astray in physics and natural philosophy. Hence he had to be criticized and corrected—he could not be accepted as an unquestionable authority. The objective of Moisiodax was not to disparage and reduce the great philosopher into an object of contempt; it was just a plea for free and independent thinking.[22] By adopting this attitude toward ancient learning, Moisiodax came much closer to Montesquieu's mature consideration of the problem of Ancients and Moderns. This was another indication of his development since the time he had championed Fontenelle's combatively one-sided view[23]

Against Aristotelianism and the worship of antiquity, Moisiodax projected the astounding achievements of the Moderns, which sufficed to reduce to utter ridicule those who denigrated them as "blockheads." There was no art or science in which the Moderns did not improve and excel over the Ancients. Moisiodax was a passionate follower of modern "sound philosophy," which was based on mathematical reasoning, rationalist thought, and the discoveries of empirical science. "Healthy," as he called it, sound philosophy represented the emancipation of human thought from the wretched learning of scholastic logic and grammatical drilling that prevailed in Greek education. Brushing aside such outdated and decayed subjects, sound philosophy had made great strides in mathematics, in astronomy, in natural history, and in physiology, aided by the invention of new exact instruments of observation and experimentation. The triumph of modern science was the culmination of the progress of sound philosophy. Galileo, Descartes, and Leibniz joined the towering figure of Newton, the paramount hero of the Enlightenment, in Moisiodax's pantheon. As with his appraisal of the utility and merits of ancient learning, in the construction of his modern pantheon as well, Moisiodax proved an attentive reader of that manifesto of the Enlightenment, D'Alembert's *Discours préliminaire*.[24] The maturity with which Moisiodax integrated the principles of the new philosophy in his own thought and expressed them in his writing suggested his intellectual growth in the twenty years since his translation of Muratori.

Moisiodax advanced three substantive arguments on behalf of the superiority of modern philosophy. First, he emphasized that its empirical orientation helped effectively in stimulating curiosity that rekindled interest in learning, as witnessed in the experience of the civilized nations of Europe. Second, modern philosophy possessed an immediate relevance to the problems and needs of Greek society. The preference expressed by Moisiodax in this connection did not derive simply from epistemological criteria. His third argument was based on an appreciation of the social utility of a modernized, practically oriented, and widely accessible education. The utilitarian calculus that inspired Moisiodax was reflected in his admiration for the countless necessary and useful facilities that Europe enjoyed as a consequence of the practical applications of Newtonian science. Indeed, the practical utilitarian orientation constituted the decisive test of truth for modern philosophy. In studying the nature of things with the purpose of defining and enhancing human happiness, it sought whatever was useful and necessary, avoided all useless discourse, and considered instead the pressing needs of life. It was therefore of great social utility: it offered blueprints of right administrative practice to rulers, it guided the clergy in their pastoral duties, it taught the proper management of business and household, it provided appropriate training to the needs of youth and soothing consolation to the infirmities of aging.²⁵ It was these possibilities immanent in modern philosophy that made it eminently relevant to the realities of a society experiencing the first strains of change. Moisiodax's emphasis on the social relevance of modern philosophy and his appreciation of the practical utility of applied science amounted basically to a utilitarian outlook. Moisiodax shared these views with Katartzis. The two of them could be considered as the exponents of a Greek utilitarianism, which had its origin in the philosophic encyclopedism of the Enlightenment. Given the tensions within which the Greek Enlightenment developed, however, this utilitarianism did not form the basis of a unified liberal political theory in view of Moisiodax's eventual transition to a provisional republicanism and Katartzis's compromise with enlightened absolutism.

The further development of Moisiodax's argument was thrust on two levels: his reflections on the renovation of culture and educational reform, guided by the requirements of concrete practical needs, led him to a vision of a Hellenic renaissance. There was a logical connection between these two levels of change, derived from the pattern of cultural progress experienced by the European nations. Europe, "the happiest, loveliest, wisest region of the world," was conceived by Moisiodax since the time he composed the prolegomena to *Moral Philosophy* as the ideal that should guide Greek efforts. This attitude was the product of his espousal of the humanist cosmopolitanism of the Enlightenment: "I recommend generally modern philosophy for its capacity to familiarize the nations among themselves, making them mutually aware that all men are brethren and should love each other."²⁶ The choice of this philosophical position indicated that Moisiodax felt himself to belong integrally to the international flock of philosophes who strove for the propagation of the lights throughout Europe.

As a conscious enlightened intellectual, Moisiodax was motivated by a pressing zeal to work for the common good by promoting the cause of modern philosophy—to bring true enlightenment to his compatriots. He felt that only collective efforts on behalf of shared purposes could foster the cause of enlightenment and its benefits. Only if discord and dissension could be eradicated and all orders of society, especially those who enjoyed wealth and status, closed ranks and united their efforts, could the difficult task of educational change and cultural renewal be achieved. Such an effort would be in the common interest of the whole society because it would make available to all the great blessings of modern civilization. Such a turn of events might even mark the dawn of a new golden age in the Hellenic world. What the concrete political content of this golden future might be could be gathered from Moisiodax's admiration for the republican liberty and civic virtue flourishing in the Helvetian commonwealth:

> The private and public weal of the Swiss has always been famous among all European nations. Frugal and freedom-loving, they never desired to expand nor did they ever suffer to submit to monarchy, obeying always the authority of their laws which protect the weak from the tyranny of the strong. They all enjoy an equality unparalleled in the other republics of Europe.[27]

The projection of a republican model as a possible guide for Greek reconstruction indicated that in his political thought, Moisiodax had clearly progressed beyond his earlier views. As expressed in his *Paraphrase ad Nicoclem,* his views on the pertinence of enlightened absolutism for cultural and social change now belonged to the past, and Deacon Iosipos now sought new political routes that led toward republican models.

The vision of what might be achieved by cultural renewal agitated and irritated Moisiodax when he confronted the injustices and the obstacles with which the powers that be constrained and obstructed the course of change. The collision of vision and reality produced in his person the first revolted consciousness in the history of modern Greek and Balkan thought. He was the first to register militantly the will to personal emancipation from the corporate entities of traditional society. As a conscious individual, he struggled throughout his whole life to emancipate himself from tradition by asserting his independence from religious constraints in the pursuit of scientific truth and by breaking the bonds of conventional practices in his educational work. Stylistically, he expressed this will not only in the distinctly personal character of his emotionally charged prose, but more graphically in the frequent repetition of the first-person singular personal pronoun in his text. Morally, his individualism was expressed in his great concern with his reputation and good name, which grew into a real obsession as adversity and persecution obstructed his plans and ruined his life. He felt he was a "sensitive man" whose life had been disrupted by the Nemesis of a grim fate which had made him a "vagabond in foreign lands" and had caused him to age before reaching his prime.[28] It was obvious that for him the cause of Enlightenment represented an existential choice. In his dedication to cultural change for the common good, he found a mode of life that gave meaning to his newly discovered identity. The individual, who became conscious of himself by standing apart and turning against corporate structures and traditions, did not escape into the egoistic pursuit of personal commodious living, but discovered the meaning of his new life in the choice of a social cause and a public-minded ethic. This was what saved him from *anomie* and made him a revolutionary.[29] Moisiodax represents a typical and tragic case of the psychological predisposition that made the republican ethos of the Enlightenment possible. The cause of the community and public good was an existential choice that responded to and was expected to resolve the problems of the human predicament.

Moisiodax tried with all the energy of a modern man and the pugnacity of a committed intellectual to actualize the ideals that inspired his own life. He employed all his remarkable abilities and his impressively wide and profound learning to convert to his cause the political, spiritual, and intellectual leadership of his society. He knew that the common good could be effectively promoted only by collective efforts. In his writings and in his teaching in the most important Greek institutions of higher education of his time, he appealed to the new generations of his compatriots, the young gentlemen of Phanariot society and the rising intelligentsia of the Enlightenment. Naturally only the latter could understand and find his message relevant. From among his pupils emerged some of the bravest crusaders of the Enlightenment in Southeastern Europe: the authors of *Novel Geography* and Rhigas. However, the leadership of Greek society under Ottoman rule could not understand, let alone accept, the practical political and social consequences of Moisiodax's conception of the Greek problem as an issue of cultural renewal. With the exception of the reforming princes Grigorios Ghikas and Alexandros Ypsilantis, in Moldavia and Wallachia respectively, they rejected both his philosophy and his practical program and subjected him to remorseless persecution. He was accused of incompetence and scholarly inadequacy—his enemies insinuated that he did not want to teach ancient Greek grammar and scholastic logic because he did not understand them—and was forced to resign twice from the academy of Jassy.[30] When he refused to conform and keep silent and published the *Apology* as a reply to his slanderers and as a manifesto of his philosophy, a veritable conspiracy of silence suppressed both the book and its message for almost two centuries.

Moisiodax felt these persecutions to be a continuation of those to which his own teacher, Evgenios Voulgaris, was subjected during the brave early phase of his career. Although as a truly free spirit he had criticized the aristocratic elitism of Voulgaris's enlightenment and the philosophical shortcomings of his *Logic* and refused to acknowledge his elevation to the status of a new authority in Greek thought, Moisiodax did not hide his admiration for the older man.[31] His own experience of persecution inspired him with a more mature empathy with his teacher's fate. His elegy for the failure of Voulgaris's efforts in fact lamented his own bitter disappointment at the prospects of the Enlightenment in Greek culture:

> A grievous look on that much vaunted school on Athos whose failure and ruin, as it were, still exhales before our eyes, [should lead us to wonder]: Where is the renowned Evgenios [Voulgaris]? Where is that multitude of students who to the joy of all Hellas constituted a new Helicon, a new chorus of the Muses? He fled and they disappeared. The thunder of a Nemesis befell them and dispersed all those teaching and taught. That edifice which has caused so much admiring rustle in the Queen of the cities and in the rest of Greece, has now been reduced, alas, to a roost of ravens.[32]

CHAPTER SIX

The Revolution in France

The Glow and the Shadow

THE FRENCH REVOLUTION, as a great world historical drama with which a civilization reached its culmination and one historical epoch transcended itself into another, was felt in European consciousness as the realization of the Enlightenment. Hegel saw it as the triumph of absolute independence, which followed Enlightenment's battle with superstition.[1] Marx captured the way the Revolution was perceived in European conscience when he pointed out that it appeared as the actualization of the claims of "Practical Reason."[2] It was this perception of the French Revolution as the practical product of the Enlightenment that turned it into the great catalyst in the politics of the age. The mirage of a moderate enlightenment, which could be a useful ideology of reform and modernization ultimately expected to strengthen the existing order, was dispelled by the experience of what appeared to be the practical implications of the new religion of humanity. The French Revolution precipitated the delineation of ideological alignments throughout Europe and invited those interested in the public realm to take sides. To its enemies it signaled the apocalyptic destruction of the fabric of civilized society. To its partisans, it represented the triumph of reason and the vindication of humanity and projected a model of freedom over which to reflect in making their own political choices.[3]

It was precisely this dialectic that animated Greek political thought in the 1790s. The French Revolution had profound repercussions throughout Southeastern Europe, which were felt with particular intensity by those groups in the society of the Greek East receptive to the ideas of the Enlightenment.[4] The year 1789 inaugurated a tumultuous decade in Greek political and cultural history.[5] The conflicting options and rival visions of the future of the nation, presented to Greek conscience by the upheavals of European society, lay at the root of the painful soul-searching and the daring political imagination of the 1790s.

"AN EYEWITNESS OF AWESOME EVENTS"

Reflecting on the great political change that was transforming French society while they were composing their treatise, the authors of *Novel Geography* remained perplexed before what appeared like a glaring blaze and could not decide whether it was going to burn or illuminate humanity. Captivated and bewildered by the enigma, they left judgment to the wisdom of time.[6] Their faith in the religion of humanity, however, had prevented this uncertainty from influencing the attitude of other Greek observers of the drama of European politics. Among them the most articulate was Adamantios Korais, who had just completed his medical studies at the University of Montpellier. He had lived in major European cities long enough (as an unsuccessful merchant in Amsterdam in his youth, as a transient resident in Venice, as a student at Montpellier in his manhood), and he was thus disabused of the naive adulation evinced by some of his less sophisticated compatriots toward Europe. He knew very well that all the evils that one could encounter in his native East existed in full strength in enlightened Europe as well. The only difference was that in Europe these evils could be more effectively harnessed and brought under control by the prevailing culture and wisdom.[7] This did not diminish his excitement over the prospect of a visit to Paris, where he was invited in order to continue his research in the Royal Library. Aware that Paris had become the Athens of modern Europe, he expected that his research there would turn out useful and honorable to his nation.[8] In May 1788 he left Montpellier for Paris, where he was to spend the rest of his life. From the very first moment he felt intensely fascinated by the splendor of that most distinguished city. Larger and more populous than Constantinople, adorned by a multitude of academies and libraries, Paris was the abode of all arts and sciences. One could encounter everywhere learned and wise men and be informed about political and literary news from all over the world by obtaining newspapers available in every language. All this could surprise and impress anyone, Korais felt, but to a modern Greek this shining greatness brought melancholy along with admiration. The cultural achievements of the Moderns reminded one of maybe greater accomplishments reached by his own ancestors more than two thousand years earlier. This melancholy escalated into despair upon the reflection that Greece was now devoid of all these blessings. The rule of Solon's wise laws had been replaced by the reign of ignorance, violence, evil, swaggering, and shamelessness. The power once wielded by Miltiades and Themistocles had now passed, in Korais's judgment, into the hands of an ignorant and insolent rabble and barbarian monks—who in truth were even worse than the alien tyrants of the Greek people.[9]

An interplay of admiration and melancholy was the basic ingredient of the psychology of the Greek observers of Europe. Their despair exploded in indignation and protest when they encountered hostile attitudes, contempt, and lack of understanding on the part of modern Europeans for the Greek predicament. Korais was intensely aware of such attitudes. He felt gratitude for enlightened sages like Voltaire and Volney who advocated the overthrow of the Ottoman Empire as a stigma to European civilization and the liberation of Greece, but he resented deeply those who argued for the maintenance of the Ottomans as a useful power in Europe. It was an outrageous injustice to suggest that the debasement of the modern Greeks was such that no human force could lift them from it. No superhuman miracles were needed, but only freedom from the yoke of the Turks and from the arrogant lust for power of the monks, for the Greeks to emulate the Europeans' progress in culture and learning.[10] The Europeans had transposed ancient Greece to modern Europe, noted Korais, recalling the earlier observations of Moisiodax. Most admirable among them was the English nation, which had cultivated to the utmost perfection not just the sciences and learning but the sweetest of human gifts, freedom. Civil liberty reigned among them just like it did in ancient Athens. Its loss could account for the depravity and the misfortunes of modern Greek society. Having recently arrived in

Paris, the heart of European culture, Korais also hoped to visit one day the free nation across the English Channel in order to witness from nearby the practice of liberty.[11]

Having reached Paris full of such hopes, Korais soon found himself an eyewitness to the coming of the great Revolution. From the outset there was no doubt in his mind that he was witnessing a drama of world historical significance: "1789 is bound to be a memorable year in human history."[12] Hence Korais felt it incumbent upon him to record the events as the drama kept unfolding and to convey the remarkable news to his friends and compatriots. He was not a passive spectator. Intensely conscious of witnessing events of unique historical importance, he made a point of being always where the scenes of the great drama were acted out despite the risk this involved for his physical safety: "I was going out everyday in order to be an eyewitness of such awesome events, which for me, as for everyone else, were entirely new."[13] In relaying the news of the Revolution to his main correspondent at home, his friend and admirer Dimitrios Lotos, who had been for a time a chief church chanter in Smyrna, he urged him to communicate the news to other interested compatriots. Nor was there any doubt in these letters as to where Korais's loyalty lay; with all his soul, he was captivated by the cause of liberty and equality, as he observed the progress of the Revolution from its outbreak to its climax.

What follows is a reconstruction of Korais's impressions and reflections on the French Revolution, largely in his own words. By transcribing the narrative of his letters, with the occasional inaccuracies of his perception of the revolutionary events and the diverse psychological moods, from enthusiasm and deep emotion to anxiety, fear, and disenchantment, that he experienced as he followed the convulsions and changing fortunes of the Revolution, it might be possible to capture the interaction between Korais's evolving personal temper and the larger social context that forged his political thought.

As Korais saw it, the Revolution came as the unexpected, if inevitable, consequence of the economic malaise in which the excessive rush to interminable wars and the corruption of court potentates (to which he included the vanity of the queen and her entourage) had left the French monarchy. Unable to impose new levies on the already heavily taxed populace, the king convoked a general assembly of the nation for consultations on how to remedy the malady of the realm. In doing so he and his advisers could not suspect that the delegates of the third estate, who represented the masses of the people outside the privileged orders of clergy and nobility, would not satisfy themselves with just procuring new sources of revenue to save the solvency of the monarchy. It soon became clear that they would not confine their deliberations to this problem. They appeared instead determined from the outset to cure the causes of the festering economic sores of French society with the intention of preventing the recurrence of the epidemic. The only remedy was obvious to all: the extravagant court expenditures had to be curbed. More fundamentally, however, it was the causes of social inequality that had to be removed by abolishing the unfair privilege of tax exemption enjoyed by the two higher orders, the clergy and the nobility.

In Korais's judgment, it was clear that the health of the body politic could not be secured unless the basic stipulation of justice, which required all of its members to contribute to the common welfare according to their means, was put to practice. Narrow-minded egoism prevented the courtiers, nobles, and clergy from recognizing this simple truth and hardened them in their uncompromising defense of their anachronistic privileges. Their folly was such that not only did they ignore popular resentment, but they went to lengths of provoking it by rushing troops into Paris while the Assembly was still deliberating at Versailles. When these troops attacked innocent citizens, the indignation of the masses, kindled by inflated but not entirely unfounded rumors as to the intentions of the court and the privileged orders, exploded. Korais was present everywhere as the incidents were escalating into a revolutionary outbreak. He was at the Tuileries when the royal troops first attacked the populace without provocation. He witnessed the inflamed people of Paris arm themselves as the revolutionary fever took grip of their minds. On 14 July 1789 he watched breathlessly the hateful prison-fort at the Bastille stormed and taken by the people. He was awed by the bloodshed, but he did not question the justice of the people's rage.[14]

As the revolutionary fervor spread the tremors of political change from Paris to the rest of France, the representatives of the nation in the Assembly proceeded with the reconstruction of society. The privileges of the nobility, who appeared to Korais tyrannical and arrogant and struck him as aristocratic only in name but not in soul, were abolished. So were the privileges and immunities of the clerical lords. Those abodes of idleness, superstition, and corruption, the monasteries and nunneries, were closed down and the multifarious religious orders disbanded. Acting in true evangelical spirit, the Assembly divested the Church of most of its land and wealth. In doing so, the Assembly corrected a very old abuse, which thrived on the irrational superstition of misguided believers succumbing to the guile and deception of the monks. It was only just and natural for the inordinate wealth of the Church to be returned to its rightful possessor, the nation as a whole. As was recognized by a virtuous and enlightened prelate, the reverend bishop of Autun, the future Talleyrand, for whom Korais showed great admiration throughout his correspondence, the wealth of the Church was the rightful patrimony of the nation and not of the clergymen who reaped its fruits. It had, therefore, to be restored to the nation, liberating at the same time the Church of a burden unbecoming to the successors of the apostles. Indeed, the uses to which the material wealth of the Church had been put constituted an onus that simply had to be removed before the Church could be salvaged from its moral wreckage and recover the edifying simplicity and humility of evangelical Christianity.[15]

Such measures of social reform were followed by positive steps of constitutional change. The absolute powers of the French monarch—much to the chagrin of the court—were curtailed, and his authority was redefined on the model of that prototype of liberty, the constitution of England. With these social and constitutional reforms accomplished, the aspirations of enlightened humanity could be put to practice: the Assembly abolished aristocratic status and all legally sanctioned social distinctions, and legislated universal equality among all men. The natural fraternity of the progeny of Adam and Eve was thus triumphantly recognized.

This celebration of the spirit of humanity generated a new public ethic. Korais reported on the virtuous ladies of Paris who donated all their precious jewels to the National Assembly. Another example of the sense of freedom that had seized the people's minds came in the sermon of a preacher who, inspired by the popular cause, reinterpreted the meaning of the Scriptures as an argument for liberty. Beginning with Saint Paul's invocation of freedom as an invitation to reciprocal ministration, the preacher of liberty proclaimed that the crucifiers of Christ had been aristocrats (monks and nobles represented by the Pharisees) who did so because Jesus championed the people of the third estate and preached human equality and fraternity.[16]

Korais, who had abandoned his beloved native land for the sake of breathing the free air of the civilized nations, tried to capture the meaning of the new times and to relay it to his compatriots. Amid his rejoicing, however, he was aware of the conspiracies of the enemies of liberty—and this gave rise to anxiety in his mind. The Revolution might have accomplished the social and constitutional reforms required by the spirit of humanity, but those who had to lay down their privileges, power, and wealth, after an initial tactical retreat, were given to conspiracies against the Revolution. The king was a good-natured and decent man. Though reluctantly, because of his ancient dynastic habits and traditions, he seemed willing to abide by the new order. But being an uncunning and improvident man, he was an easy prey to bad influences and evil counsel. The queen and his two junior brothers were the main source of such influence. Their blindness was such that they could not perceive that the determination of the people to hold on to the accomplishments of the Revolution was such that an attempt by the king to resume the powers of absolutism and restore the old order was sure to lead to the horrors of bloodshed and civil war. The two brothers showed themselves such unrepentant believers in the bankrupt old order that they fled the country and joined the several emigré potentates of the high nobility and the clergy who had crossed into neighboring realms and had vowed to return and destroy the Revolution. And then there were the monks—the uncompromising and irreconcilable enemies of the social changes that had deprived them of their material wealth. Most of them refused to take the oath of allegiance to the new constitutional order and were causing many problems to the civil authorities. The ministers of the faith were adept masters of machination and deceit and could be found behind every plot and tumult against the Revolution. But their tricks could no longer deceive anyone. The Assembly, led by Mirabeau, whom Korais judged as the new Demosthenes in both eloquence and political shrewdness, proved superior to their schemes and scandals and managed to bring the Church in France, despite the pope's vehement opposition, under effective civilian control.

In every measure taken against the power and privileges of the clergy by the Revolution, Korais saw a lesson relevant to the most critical problem of his own society. It was true that the Orthodox Church in the East had a record of fewer abuses than the Roman Catholic Church in the West. Still, it was an equally plain truth that clerical corruption was the greatest plague of Greek society. So Korais missed no chance in stressing the relevance of the lessons of France for the purpose of curtailing the power and abuses of the corrupt Greek hierarchy and vile monastic orders whom he considered as positively worse despots than the Turks.[17]

Not only the National Assembly, but the masses of the French people, as well, could no longer be duped by the manipulation of superstition by the priests. The real effect of the Revolution had been that it opened people's eyes to the light of reason, and consequently they could not acquiesce any longer in the tyrannical rule of kings and priests.[18] The break with the superstitious past was so decisive that the pope's thunders and condemnation of the Revolution, which in ages past might have awakened the nightmares of hell in pious minds, Korais remarked sardonically, were received with mockery and derision, not only in Paris but in many provincial cities as well. Indeed, his holiness had become the laughing stock of France. Public scorn had undermined reverence for traditional religion so much that the papal encyclical condemning the oath of allegiance to the new constitution required of the French hierarchy, and threatening sanctions on earth and in heaven against Revolutionary France, was met with the burning of an effigy of the pope by a Parisian mob. Dressed in papal vestments and inscribed "Superstition" and "Civil War" on either side, the effigy was abandoned to the consumption of the flames, dramatizing in Korais's perception a prevailing belief among Frenchmen that Catholicism was among the most fatuous religions in the world.[19]

The Revolution had clearly penetrated the people's conscience. Not only was the senselessness of traditional religion with all its superstitious paraphernalia realized and overturned by the French revolutionaries, whose cause Korais espoused, but the new religion of reason seemed to be approaching its moment of triumph. In July 1791, before Korais's and other foreign observers' dazzled eyes, the citizens of revolutionary Paris in solemn, massive, and exalted procession transferred Voltaire's mortal remains, surrounded and adorned with all the symbols of the age of reason, for reinterment in the liberated city whose freedom he had prepared. His homeland, which in her freedom cherished his philosophic legacy, was now bestowing on him the rightful honors that tyranny had denied him. Partaking of the religion of humanity, witnessing the triumph of philosophy, and aware that his ancestral legacy was the distant source of that celebration of liberty, Korais shed bitter tears of desperation. He felt from the depth of his soul that under the barbaric tyranny of the Turks and the villainy of the monks, his own nation, Greece, the bountiful motherland of philosophers, had been reduced to sterility and barrenness.[20] The triumph of philosophy, which indicated that the end of the eighteenth century might bring the fall of despots and monks throughout Europe, could not console the deep sorrow in Korais's soul.[21] His mind was rejoicing in revolutionary Paris, but his heart was engrossed with the predicament of his homeland.

His exultation would not last for too long. A few months after he witnessed the triumph of philosophy, his restless perceptiveness was telling him that things were moving into a "labyrinth of evils."[22] The political catalyst for the new turn of events seemed to be the king's attempted flight in June 1791. That move of desperation showed conclusively to the king's enemies that he in fact had no intention to live up to his constitutional oath, nor did he harbor any loyalty to the new political order he was supposed to defend.[23] This misguided action unleashed the wave of social passions that had been excited by the fever of revolution. An inexorable logic of destruction was set in motion. It was already perceptible to Korais in the fanaticism that grew on all sides and the intensification of internal dissension into which the Revolution had begun to slip. Korais had already felt uneasy over the adverse effects that might follow the hardships (economic difficulties and food shortages) caused by the revolutionary upheaval in the daily life of the people. These everyday problems beneath the epic of the Revolution could easily complicate an impossible situation. It was already obvious to Korais that the heads of Frenchmen had become inordinately inflamed.[24] The same people whose wise comportment a few months earlier had shown them to be truly enlightened and moderate gradually came to behave with extreme imprudence and unwarranted insolence. In such a climate the "hypocrites of liberty" could thrive.[25] Liberty, like religion, Korais was sure, had its fanatics and sycophants, the opportunists who could dissimulate and show excessive zeal, thus making the most of changing situations. The monks, meanwhile, had kept busy inciting disloyalty and subversion against the Revolution (using even the confessional in spreading their poison in the hearts of naive believers) and secretly urging the king to refuse to sign legislation confiscating their properties.[26]

Under such conditions began that great political adventure that led from the triumph of Enlightenment to the reign of inhumanity and a new tyranny. The axis of the new drama was the gradual but unmistakable destruction of the authority of the king in the collective psychology of those who used to be his subjects. Korais's sharp political sense captured the dispelling of the royal mystique with unique clarity. When the turn of revolutionary events after the Fall of the Bastille forced the king to visit Paris, he was greeted by the dense crowds that flooded the streets of the city, not with the traditional cheer "Vive le Roi," but with the angry and ominous cheer "Vive la nation."[27] That new cheer signified that the tradition of centuries, the symbols of divine anointment, and the aura of thaumaturgical legends were dissipated by the Revolution that had gripped the minds of men. This subtle meaning of the psychological change, registered in the spontaneous and unconscious choice of popular slogans, was not lost on Korais's perceptiveness. From that moment on, he witnessed the steady erosion of royal authority as the tide of popular passions, rekindled, to be sure, by the "sycophants of liberty," kept rising. The beginning of the end was marked by the storming of the Tuileries in August 1792. It was evident that the mob was getting out of hand, and Korais's instinctive classicism could tell him that the Revolution was degenerating into that dreadful form of ochlocracy that horrified the greatest of ancient political philosophers. Amid the rising pressures of the mob, Korais feared that even the Convention's authority might break down, and in that eventuality, nothing could save the king and the remnants of the old order. Although Condorcet, one of the greatest orators in the Convention and, in Korais's judgment, the foremost living philosopher of France, whose antiroyal credentials were indisputable, tried to save the king by appealing to reason and humanity, he was not heard. Condorcet's failure appeared to Korais to indicate that, amid the rising tide of passion, the voice of reason was lost.

The official abolition of the monarchy only formalized in institutional terms what had already occurred irrevocably in the collective consciousness. The trial of the king that followed, not just for his own alleged crimes against the nation and the Revolution, but also on account of his dynastic ancestors' despotism, dramatized the strivings of the Revolution to affirm itself by destroying the legitimacy of the past. The urgency of this need was such that the timid appeals of humanity and compassion could not prevail. The French monarchy had to be demythologized for the Revolution to be safe. The king had to be the sacrificial victim in whose person the mystique of traditional authority was to be destroyed. On 21 January 1793, amid the crowds of revolutionary Paris, Korais witnessed the tragic dénouement of that agonizing and convulsive political drama. The "most illustrious, most powerful and most unfortunate" European monarch was delivered by his subjects to the hands of the executioner. Korais did not have any doubts about the political significance of the regicide he had witnessed. He knew that as a political act it had the same meaning as the execution of Charles I of England in the midst of another revolution more than a century earlier. The epilogue to the drama came with the destruction of the symbols of kingship: the royal crown and scepter were delivered to the state foundry to be melted and recast into coinage for public circulation. Thus the cycle of the destruction of the royal mystique was completed.[28]

Korais watched the drama acted out, agitated by the world historical significance he felt it possessed and appalled by the extremes to which inhumanity could escalate. He certainly felt compassion for Louis XVI as a human being and as the head of a defenseless family. He even admired the courage, dignity, and serenity with which the king had faced his tragic destiny. But these remained purely personal, private sentiments, through which one human being related to the fate of another. Korais was not prepared to pass judgment on the Revolution solely on the judicial merits of the regicide and the feelings of pity it provoked. He knew that revolutions had to be judged as integral historical unities and by their distant effects on the progress of society.[29] Nevertheless, although he did not presume to judge the fairness of the king's trial, he could not fail to state his wish that justice among men ought to be accompanied and complemented by forbearance and clemency.[30]

Korais reserved his judgment of the public justice of the trial, but he did not feel inhibited from evaluating the moral caliber of individuals as it was revealed in those tragic circumstances. He did not try to make secret his disgust at the treacherous conduct of the king's cousin, the Duke of Orléans, who out of "an excess of patriotic modesty" had assumed the presumptuous title of *"Égalité"* and voted repeatedly for the death of his royal cousin to prove his zeal for the revolutionary cause. Korais, however, predicted that the duke's design was simply to ride the wave of future politics by ingratiating himself with the republicans who dominated the scene at the time in order to eventually promote his own ambitions for the royal crown.[31] At this point too, the Greek classicist had shown himself to be a perceptive observer of extraordinary shrewdness and prescience. In the person of the Duke of Orléans, Korais could identify a prime representative of those "sycophants of liberty" whom he so much detested. In what heartening contrast did this despicable behavior stand with the conduct of the brave Malesherbes and a few other individuals who displayed courageous sympathy and compassion to Louis the man at his direst hour, thus vindicating some of the claims of the "enlightened age" that boasted the religion of humanity.[32]

With the proclamation of the Republic, the new mystique of the nation, which had succeeded the old mythology of kingship, found its institutional incarnation. France had revived the republican form of government as it was known in the political experience of ancient Greece and practiced in modern times in the republics of the Americans and the Swiss. Witnessing the enthusiasm with which the citizens of the French Republic rushed to the frontier to defend the nation and its Revolution against foreign enemies— and the fervor with which many French mothers volunteered the service of their only sons to the arms of the Republic—Korais felt that he understood exactly at last what the classical authors meant when describing the heroism of ancient Greeks at Marathon and Salamis. The ancient Greeks alone could pride themselves on comparable examples of courage and heroism.[33] Not only had foreign attacks against the French fatherland been repulsed by the brave armies of republican citizens, but a triumphant sweep of the Revolution seemed imminent throughout Europe. The tremors of revolution were felt everywhere, and the tyrants were trembling on their thrones.[34]

How could this phenomenon be explained? Once again classical wisdom appeared to Korais to hold the key to an answer. With their valor and prowess, the French had borne out an important observation of Hippocrates, Korais's intellectual mentor among the Ancients. That great master of medicine was an equally profound political thinker. In his admirable treatise *Of Airs, Waters, Places,* he had explained the superior martial valor and consequent victories of the Greeks as compared with their Asiatic enemies by reference to the social and moral effects of freedom. The explanatory comparison was between Greek freedom and Asiatic despotism. It was the psychological differentials of these diametrically opposed social and political contexts that could obviously explain the discrepancies in motivation and consequent prowess between Europeans and Asians, Greeks and Persians, free Frenchmen and the subjects of assorted European tyrants. Korais was aware that this social calculus of liberty and prowess, first formulated by Hippocrates, had formed the basis of the theory expounded by Montesquieu, the greatest political mind among the Moderns, in his book *De l'esprit des lois.*[35]

Amid the general enthusiasm, only one fear haunted Korais's mind as he observed the Revolution's progress: internal discord and its destructive

consequences, that ancient curse of freedom in republican polities.[36] Although
he felt and remained a sympathetic foreigner in Paris,[37] Korais cherished to
the utmost the accomplishments of the republican cause. He fully identified with the revolutionary side—using the first-person plural in his letters to describe the experiences and the perils of revolutionary France. That
is why he was so much grieved and agitated by what he perceived as the
moral dangers undermining domestically the Revolution. The main cause
of preoccupation remained the conceit and fanaticism of the sycophants of
liberty who continued to rekindle social passions for their own self-seeking
purposes. A telling instance of the extremity of their vanity was the assumption by some of such sonorous and presumptuous titles as "ambassadors
of mankind" and "orators of humanity."[38] As such shameless immodesty
became more uninhibited, Korais's apprehensions grew. He knew that liberty could not stand on its own and survive without virtue. On this count,
too, the Greek experience held the most relevant moral lessons. The Greek
triumphs at Thermopylae and Salamis were possible only on account of
the irreproachable public virtues of those who accomplished them. Once
these virtues were contaminated by corruption, Greek freedom declined,
and the Hellenes were subjugated first by Alexander's successors and next
by the Romans. Such was the supreme danger faced by the French Revolution as well. Despite the patriotic enthusiasm transpiring both in deeds of
real valor and in the revolutionary slogan "Freedom or Death," the ethical
condition prevailing around Korais kept him uneasy. Corruption, reflected
in the exploitation of public causes for the promotion of self-seeking private
ends, was so widespread that unless a decisive rectification of morals was
vigorously pursued, the cause of liberty seemed doomed.[39]

Korais's worst fears seemed to be coming true in the aftermath of the
drama of regicide. The destruction of the old mythology unleashed new
sinister forces of uninhibited passion and vindictiveness, which carried
through the unfolding political peripety from the destruction of the despotism of unreason to the emergence of the tyranny of terror. The sinister
face of the Revolution was represented by the sanguinary Marat, the former physician to the most reactionary of the king's brothers, the Count of
Artois. A member of the Convention that was disgraced by his presence,
he daily poisoned the minds of the Parisian public through his incendiary
newspaper *Ami du peuple*. It preached murder for the sake of public safety
and calculated that the consolidation of liberty required the execution of at

least one hundred and fifty thousand people.[40] Consternated by the excesses of the Terror, Korais, in an outburst of exaggeration, suggested that Marat's program was carried out by his kindred spirit Robespierre.

Morally overwhelmed, Korais had remained silent during the two years of the Reign of Terror, but he reserved a harsh epitaph to Robespierre in the aftermath of Thermidor. After sustaining the emotional tension of all those years of upheaval and revolution, Korais lapsed for a moment into melodrama: the tyranny of that "monster Robespierre" had inflicted profound wounds on France which only time and wisdom could heal. His rule was hateful to thousands of honest Frenchmen who resented, with Korais, the spectacle of the great Revolution degenerating in one stroke into barbarism and cannibalism, the century of Enlightenment overtaken by the assault of crime and ignorance audaciously rallying behind the banner of atheism, while the arts and sciences were reduced to lethargy by vandalism, and virtue and talent fell prey to the dagger of assassins.[41] This closing note in Korais's outraged lament on the hopes of the Revolution was an unmistakable elegy to Condorcet, whose enlightened conduct he so much had admired and whose tracts he forwarded to his compatriots to instruct them on the progress of the Revolution and of the human mind.[42]

Korais's interest in the fate of the Revolution was never diminished or discouraged by cynicism. He remained continuously in Paris, keenly watching the adventures of liberty. Even during an absence at Nemours in 1795–1796, forced on him by his failing health, he maintained a lively interest in revolutionary politics by closely following the press. He was among the first subscribers to *Précis de la Révolution,* he systematically pursued both the *Moniteur* and the *Feuille du Salut Public,* and he always seemed interested in exploring other "patriotic works" as well in order to stay well informed on the proceedings of both the Convention and the Jacobin club.[43] To the end of the revolutionary drama he remained an *"idolâtre de la liberté."* His passion for freedom was not diminished by the upheaval of the Terror. His sense of fairness simply revolted when he witnessed liberty divorced from justice. Like so many other European liberals, he was disenchanted with the excess to which the pursuit of liberty could lead. His veritable eros for liberty did not obscure in his eyes the truth that freedom without justice was not different from banditry. And in true Socratic spirit he declared that he could not tolerate injustice inflicted even on his enemies.[44]

Thus observing and reflecting on the epoch-making events of his time, the keenest political mind of the Greek Enlightenment reached philosophical and political maturity. Korais's reflections on the French Revolution formed the basis of his subsequent political thought, which brought the tenets of republican theory to bear on the Greek problem. For this reason, this early formative stage of his thinking had to be examined and reconstructed in some detail in order to spell out the liberal premises of his mature thought and of the republican synthesis that he proposed as a solution to the Greek problem. His liberalism was led to maturity by his observation of the political experience of revolutionary France. He gradually came to realize both the possibilities and the limits of republican liberty, but he never doubted its potential to transform and regenerate a corrupt society. His elegy for revolutionary France was in essence a moral lesson for subjugated Greece. Korais never wavered in this conviction. The extremities of the Revolution, however, which so much distressed his republican conscience, were readily seized by the enemies of Enlightenment in their battle against the rising tide of liberty.

FEAR AND REACTION

The original doubt that was posed by the authors of *Novel Geography* was soon resolved in the minds of the conservatives, who were already feeling uneasy with the strides of secular enlightenment in the society, and especially among the educated younger generations of their Orthodox community. The lines of a confrontation, between two fledgling rival outlooks viewing the problems and needs of Greek society in diametrically opposed ways, were already clearly discernible. The French Revolution, which seemed to give concrete political form to the philosophical and cultural aspirations of the Enlightenment, provided the catalyst for a confrontation. If the proponents of Enlightenment in France had championed a revolutionary upheaval, their admirers in the Greek world could not be expected to visualize anything less. The concessions that had to be made to the claims and requirements of the Enlightenment for the sake of a revival of Greek education and culture had proved subversive and treacherous. They could therefore be retracted, and the critics of traditional education and

traditional values could be exposed for what they were: the pernicious enemies of order, advocates of chaos, and adulterators of the genuine Christian
values of the Greek people. Gradually a systematically articulated theory
of Counterenlightenment matured out of this realignment of traditional
and conservative forces, but the initial polemics focused on the nature and
meaning of the events transpiring in France and their potential repercussions and implications for Greece's destiny.

The regicide, which dramatized the destruction of the old order, triggered the polemic. Korais's mature compassion was a far cry from the anxiety that the death of Louis XVI precipitated among Greek conservative
groups. A pamphlet translated from the Italian and printed in Venice early
in 1793 inaugurated the great lamentation for the innocent king who was
condemned by his own subjects. It was an irrational and most cruel act,
entirely groundless as far as the king's responsibilities were concerned. The
impertinent and vicious subjects had unjustly deprived their king of his
crown, but he was certain to receive a crown of righteousness in heaven.
The king proceeded to his end with heroism and serenity foreshadowing his
heavenly beatitude. His death was accompanied by the desperate laments of
his family blaming his unjust and ungrateful murderers. But it was greeted
by the malicious rejoicing of his ferocious and bloodthirsty subjects. To
pious souls, however, his martyrdom was reminiscent of the circumstances
of the death of Christ: his grave was guarded lest his body be stolen.[45]

Another epitaph recounting the events of the "illegitimate decapitation"
of the King of France was published in Vienna later in the same year.[46] The
forces of simmering reaction and fear were thus unleashed against the aspirations of the Enlightenment. The 1790s witnessed the initiation of a period
of factionalism and conflict in the broader community and in the Church,
which were interpreted quite perceptively by the chief chronographer of
the Ecumenical Patriarchate more than a century later as the direct consequences of the repercussions of the French Revolution in the East, and especially of the traumatic impressions created by the regicide.[47] In a way, the
traditionalist order in Ottoman Greece experienced certain tremors similar
to the outburst of despair and madness that followed the regicide of 1793
in France, so poignantly described by Albert Camus as the symptom of the
obliteration of an old ideology.[48]

The nervousness of the conservatives in the Greek context was expressed
in an all-out attack on the philosophy and the representatives of the

Enlightenment. Under the leadership of the patriarchate, this crusade found a multiplicity of targets and was channeled in a variety of directions at all levels of Greek society. Its manifestations included the violent polemic in 1793 against the teaching of Christodoulos Pamplekis, a Greek teacher of natural philosophy in Leipzig, who became the first intellectual since the time of Anthrakitis to be excommunicated and anathematized on account of his philosophical views.[49] The events in France, the teachings of the philosophes, notably Voltaire and Rousseau, that were felt to have paved the way to the Revolution, and their Greek sympathizers, were vehemently denounced in two important tracts also published in 1793. One was the *Dialogues of the Dead,* versified by the priest Polyzois Kontos.[50] In an exchange between Charon, Voltaire, and the mathematician Dupré on the way to Hades, the French Revolution and its values were stigmatized, and the pious were sternly warned against the soul-destroying effects of the new libertine morality. A second pamphlet, *The Misery of Conceited Sages,* pseudonymously attributed to Kelestinos of Rhodes, but composed by the foremost theoretician of the Counterenlightenment, the hieromonach Athanasios Parios, attempted for the first time a comprehensive refutation of the tenets of Enlightenment thinking and morality through a militant vindication of Orthodox dogma.[51]

These reactions to the French Revolution, which were crowded into the fatal year 1793, indicate the extent of conservative concern toward the inroads and potential effects of the maturing Enlightenment. The counterrevolutionary tracts were addressed mostly to the literate public. The wider masses of the faithful were, however, not neglected by the Church. In a series of pastoral encyclicals, the Holy Synod exhorted the inhabitants and clergy of those areas that were most exposed to the contagion of French ideas to protect the purity of their faith and to guard against the false promises and the contamination of the spreading wave of revolution. Such encyclicals were addressed to several dioceses in the Peloponnese and urged resistance to "the recently appeared pernicious mischief," to the citizens of Ioannina, Arta, and Parga in Epirus, to the inhabitants of several Aegean islands, to the clergy of Crete and of the cosmopolitan city of Smyrna in Asia Minor, and most notably to the people of the seven Ionian Islands that, upon the conquest of the Venetian Republic by Napoleon, passed under direct French rule.[52] The Ottoman government itself issued similar proclamations to the inhabitants of its Eastern provinces.[53]

Through such measures the Church, as the guardian of the traditional order, attempted to stem the effects of Enlightenment and to contain the influences of the French Revolution. In this the purposes of the Orthodox Church coincided with the interests of the Sublime Porte, which felt desperately pressured by the advances of the revolutionary French armies in Central Europe and in the Levant. Most of the anti-French activities of the Church in the 1790s, especially during the year 1798, were undertaken at the suggestion of the Porte, which could not tolerate any domestic unrest in the face of a virtual encirclement by a formidable external army. The Church, therefore, fortified in Christian doctrine and scriptural authority, could counsel resignation and submission to Ottoman rule as a divinely ordained power destined to protect the Christian people from heretical and godless snares against their genuine faith.[54]

These views were militantly expressed in the most notorious of counterrevolutionary pamphlets issued in the 1790s under the title *Paternal Instruction,* attributed to the patriarch Anthimos of Jerusalem, and printed at the newly reconstituted patriarchal press in Constantinople. The Ecumenical Patriarchate had not had a printing press since the reign of Cyril Loukaris in the early seventeenth century. The fact that a press under the direct control of the patriarchate could be reestablished at this time with the approval of the Ottoman authorities was indicative of the urgency felt by both the Church and the Porte to combat the currents of new ideas that were disseminated through the publications of the Greek printing houses of the diaspora, especially those of Venice and Vienna. The *Paternal Instruction* was a strong exhortation against the newly appearing "systems of Liberty," which the author considered a sure avenue to the loss of faithful souls—the latest of the contrivances through which the devil attempted to undermine the faith and lead the pious astray. As against the godless and corrupt talk of liberty, the author counseled submission to the powerful monarchy of the Ottomans which was God's gift to the Orthodox Christians whom it had protected from heresy. The Ottoman Empire was raised by God from naught at a time when the Christian Roman Empire began failing in matters of faith, in order to preserve Orthodoxy and the true faith from adulteration.

All true Orthodox Christians, therefore, should submit loyally and gratefully to their God-ordained masters and forget all idle talk about a deceptive liberty on this earth. The modern system of liberty that was imported at the time from the West into Orthodox lands stood in sharp contradiction to the Scriptures, and it involved nothing more than the pursuit of selfish interests and vile appetites. It was simply anarchy and disorder in which everyone tried to exploit everyone else for his own selfish gain. The Ottoman Empire was created by God and raised above all other monarchies in the world in order to serve as a bridle on Latin heresy and as an agent of salvation for the Orthodox.[55]

Such were the arguments of a foremost exponent of the Counterenlightenment, aptly characterized as "the Byzantine dogmatist of 1798."[56] These views, voiced at the time that the French had occupied the Ionian islands and had invaded Egypt, were an integral part of the Ottoman ideological counteroffensive and were bound to provoke a response from the partisans of the Enlightenment. The challenge was taken by Korais, who composed an anonymous polemic entitled *Fraternal Instruction*, published later in that year. The text of *Paternal Instruction* was reprinted in Korais's pamphlet, and its arguments were refuted in his own text. He began by disputing the authenticity of the authorship. No prelate of the Orthodox Church, let alone a patriarch, could in his right mind have composed such a treacherous argument. Therefore, Korais suggested, the aging patriarch's name was usurped by a traitor, an agent of Turkish tyranny, an enemy of the Greek nation, in order to lend credence to his outrageous arguments. By drawing this distinction, Korais showed himself a shrewd political tactician: aware of the influence and authority of the Church in Greek society and especially among the popular masses, he tried to avoid a direct confrontation by refusing to believe in the proposed authorship of *Paternal Instruction*. He could thus refute and discredit its arguments without engaging in a forthright attack on the Church, which he did not want to antagonize openly, and thus run the risk of making the cause of Enlightenment appear irreverent and antireligious. Since the main objectives of *Paternal Instruction* were to disguise Ottoman tyranny as a divine blessing and to vilify the idea of political liberty, Korais's main target in *Fraternal Instruction* was to unmask the evils of despotic captivity and to exalt the liberal ideal. In his indictment of Ottoman despotism, Korais lamented the cruelty and hardship it inflicted on the everyday life of its Greek subjects, and he pointed at the depravity, corruption, and superstition it wrought on the enslaved society and its spiritual leadership, whom it had transformed into so many corrupt Sardanapali and tyrants of the people. Against this sorry spectacle of captivity he unfolded the argument for liberty. He insisted that the Scriptures, no less than human reason, sanctioned obedience only to legitimate rulers. He exposed the sophistry that Ottoman tyranny was a divinely ordained shield of the purity of the faith by pointing to the example of the fellow great Orthodox nation of Russia that thrived under its own national government, preserving intact all articles of the true faith. He finally defined liberty as the ability of each citizen to do everything not prohibited by the laws that express the general will. The common voice of the people is truly the voice of God, and freedom is nothing other than the participation of the citizen in the social contract. Anyone who denied the reality of this freedom and its divine origin, Korais concluded, was an implacable enemy of the Greek nation and of the religion of Christ and a faithful slave of the Ottomans and all other tyrants, past, present, and future.[57]

This was the first time that an explicitly liberal political argument was articulated and projected before Greek consciousness. Korais's *Fraternal Instruction* was the first proclamation of the political liberalism of the Enlightenment as a matrix for the Greek future.[58] It was a fitting conclusion to the early phase of his political thought, and it marked the transition to the central preoccupation with the conditions and character of Greek freedom that were to dominate his later political theory. The politicization of the Enlightenment was the inescapable product of the controversies and the ideological ferment of the decade of the French Revolution whose waves were finally stirring the decaying despotism in the East.

To patriots like Korais the French advances in the Ionian Islands and in Egypt were the harbingers of the collapse of Ottoman despotism and were hailed as the prelude to Greek freedom. French republican liberty and the French designs on the East were presented to their compatriots as the best hopes for their collective future as a nation. Korais's *War Song* and his *Martial Trumpet-blast*, circulated anonymously at the dawn of the new century, conveyed the sense of a new expectation and articulated the hopes that activated a conscience deeply stamped by the French revolutionary experience. In them he urged his compatriots to rally to the French cause and support Napoleon's endeavors in the East.[59]

The transient hope that Greece's liberation and national rebirth might come by means of French intervention in the Ottoman Empire and reformation of Greek society on the model of revolutionary France dramatized not simply the appeal of French ideals among enlightened Greeks, but also a widespread disillusionment with the venerable tradition of the Russian expectation. The progress of Enlightenment had put to serious question the relevance of the hope of redemption from the North. Korais knew very well that the liberty he visualized was "incomparably different from Russian freedom."[60] Like many other cosmopolitan Greeks, he had followed with unfailing interest the recent war of Catherine the Great against the Ottomans, and he tried to pass the latest news as best as he could to his correspondents at home, correcting also the misinformation he occasionally detected in their perception of the events.[61] He knew, however, that Catherine the Great was among the enemies of the French Revolution, and thus he could not believe that she cared much about the freedom of the Greeks.[62] His firsthand experience of the contempt that some Europeans felt for the modern Greeks had taught him that the cause of Greek freedom could not expect much from outside supporters. To the extent that it did survive, the Russian expectation was reduced to a logic very different from that of the earlier millenarian dream. To an enlightened Greek, who conceived of himself as a citizen of the world and the kinsman of the partisans of humanity and justice, irrespective of national identity, Russia—despite the deprivation of freedom—held the attractiveness of the relentless enemy of his own despotic oppressor. Korais's consequent concern for Russian victories over the Ottomans derived from his estimation that under prevailing circumstances the Greeks could not achieve their liberty but gradually. The yoke of their despots had first to be shaken off by another despot, no matter who, so long as that new despot was less ferocious and slightly more enlightened than the Ottomans. Such a qualitative change in degrees of despotism was expected to open the way to Enlightenment by providing the means of instruction and cultivation similar to those available in the rest of Europe. Russian absolutism, since Peter the Great, had proved capable of achieving as much, and the Greeks were well aware of this. The Russian expectation could therefore be reinterpreted as no more than a condition of cultural change to be achieved not by benevolent Russian intervention on behalf of the Greeks, but as an unwilled contribution of a cultured despot pursuing his own imperialist designs.[63]

Even this minimal redefinition of the Russian expectation was on the wane. As a theoretical position and as a political program, it was completely discounted by Psalidas in his attack on Voulgaris, which has already been noted.[64] Another Greek patriot who enlisted himself in the effort to refute the Russian expectation was Constantinos Stamatis. A disciple of Katartzis in Wallachia before going to Paris, where he, too, keenly observed the great Revolution, Stamatis was a sympathizer and promoter of French policy in the East, and he eventually entered into the foreign service of revolutionary France. In a series of addresses to the Greek nation, composed in cooperation with the French agent Émile Gaudin, Stamatis sought actively to promote the new political orientation. Two of the addresses, circulated in 1798–1799 under the titles "To the Romans of Greece" and "Reflections of a Philhellene," explained the French presence in the Ionian Islands, countered the anti-French arguments of the patriarchal encyclicals, and urged the Greeks to rise against the Turks. The main target of the pro-French polemics, however, was Russian policy and its effects on the fate of the Greek nation since the treacherous behavior of Catherine II in the 1770s. In a third address to his fellow Ionian islanders after the transient French occupation of the Islands in 1797–1798, he urged them to strive for republican liberty and the national independence of their Hellenic motherland, against the disgrace of Ottoman tyranny and the deception of Russian promises.[65]

It was thus clear that by the end of the eighteenth century two diametrically opposed political views of the Greek problem had developed. The one was represented by the ecclesiastical leadership as the champion of the status quo and of the traditional order, and the other was espoused by the intelligentsia of the diaspora and by their ideological kinsmen in the centers of the Enlightenment within Greek society and visualized a new and radically different Greece on the model of the free republic of the French nation. The controversy between the authors of *Paternal* and *Fraternal Instruction,* respectively typical representatives of the social background and intellectual outlook of each viewpoint, dramatized very eloquently the ideological cleavage in pre-independence Greek politics.

A DECADE OF INTELLECTUAL FERMENT

The ferment generated in Greek society by the impact of the French Revolution was reflected not only in the political cleavages and ideological controversies of the 1790s, but also in the texture of cultural life in that decade. A few aspects of this cultural activity that carried with them direct political implications have to be identified in order to convey an impression of the

broader context within which the debate on the French Revolution was conducted. The density of cultural life was most graphically reflected in book
production. Between 1791 and 1799, Greek book production increased by
20.97 percent over the production of the entire eighteenth century. What
was significant in the rising indicators of book production was the absolute
and proportional increase of secular books: it has been estimated that of
the books published in the 1790s, 42.32 percent were of secular content.[66]
That more books of this character were published was an indicator of new
needs and curiosities that the traditional religious books or the popular
narratives that dominated the circulation of printed materials in previous
periods could no longer meet. The intellectual reorientation, hinted at by
these quantitative indicators, can be grasped through a consideration of the
content of some of the books printed in this decade. No better evidence can
be presented on this issue than a brief survey of the works selected for translation into Greek in order, as the translators felt, to cover some of the serious
lacunae in Greek learning that so much distressed all enlightened minds.

The strides of liberal consciousness were characteristically underlined
by the first Greek edition of Locke's *Essay*. The work, which had been
known to Greek thought for decades and in manuscript translations had
been included in the armory of the philosophical partisans of enlightened causes, was finally published in a Greek translation of John Wynne's
abridged version, based on the 1796 Italian edition by Francesco Soave.[67]
This abridgment, however, was a shortened but not a watered-down version.
It preserved precisely those passages and original formulations that articulated most eloquently the will to philosophical criticism and enlightenment.
Greek thought was systematically instructed on the nature and limits of
human knowledge, on the abilities of understanding, on the sources and
dynamics of deception and superstition. Innate ideas were shown to be
nonexistent, and experience and individual judgment were left as the only
sources of sound knowledge. In addition, Locke's critique of the scholastic
abuse of the language and of philosophical terminology provided the basis
of a plea for a clear, concise, and consistent use of the language and of words
as the medium of lucid reasoning. Thus the means of an intellectual reconstruction were made intelligible and were shown to be within human grasp.
Greek thought had finally acquired its manual of Enlightenment.

It was indicative of the intellectual quests of Greek consciousness during
the 1790s that the decade witnessed the translation of some of the most

important sources of European learning that had punctuated the unfolding of the Enlightenment. In 1794, Fontenelle's *Entretiens sur la pluralité des mondes* was translated.[68] The translator, Panyiotis Kodrikas, corrected in his commentaries many of the astronomical fallacies of the original, which had derived from Fontenelle's insistence on the application of the Cartesian theory of the heliocentric system.[69] Not only were Fontenelle's errors corrected, but the work was updated on the basis of the latest conclusions of astronomical research and observation. The purpose of this popularization of astronomical science was to dispel superstition, "the most monstrous distortion" of the human mind according to the translator. The real target was the destruction of superstitious ignorance that, at the end of the century of the Lights, attacked the Copernican theory of the universe on the argument that it ran counter to scriptural teachings. Such superstitious arguments, which supported the nonsense of the Ptolemaic system, tended to forget that the Bible, being a spiritual revelation of sacred truths, did not occupy itself with the scientific systems of astronomy. The purpose of the Scriptures was spiritual, not astronomical. The faithful, therefore, could perfectly revere the doctrines of the Bible and study the scientific discoveries of astronomy without any conflict in their conscience. It was superstition, prejudice, and fanaticism that created such conflicts by confusing the issues and by fighting with verbose arguments against the scientific truth of the heliocentric system that the great Newton had established on unshakable foundations.[70]

The translation of Fontenelle was followed in 1795 and 1796 by two different renderings of Montesquieu's *Considerations on the Causes of the Greatness and Decline of the Romans.*[71] A product of the awakening of a secular historical consciousness among the modern Greeks, the translation of Montesquieu's work became an effective medium for the transmission of republican ideas to Greek minds politicized by the new secular history. Presented to them by the translator, Georgios Emmanuel, as a contribution toward an increased acquaintance with the history of the Christian Roman Empire with which they identified their medieval past, Montesquieu's historical masterpiece offered an account of the historical developments leading through the decline and fall of the Roman Empire to the enslavement of the Romans of the East, and thus it constituted an explanation of Greece's captivity.[72] In essence this was an invitation to the Greeks to reflect on the conditions of their society in terms of the republican theory of corruption and decline. In this way it also set the framework for the elaboration of a problematic of freedom also in terms of republican thought.

The political purposes of this intensified interest in translations became evident with the publication of a Greek version of A. E. X. Poisson de La Chabeaussière's *Catéchisme républicain* in 1797.[73] Composed in the form of a dialogue on the model of customary religious catechisms used in French schools before the Revolution, the work, approved by the Convention for use in primary education in 1795, intended to introduce the ideas of the Enlightenment into the moral education of children. Not only were traditional religious ideas modified in conformity with the new ideological climate, but also the view of rigid social hierarchy was replaced by emphasis on the definition of democratic citizenship, its rights and duties. Although in France the publication of *Catéchisme républicain* represented a regression from the radicalism of the years 1792–1795 in the period after Thermidor, its translation into Greek—as well as its German, Dutch, and Italian versions—represented the spread of French revolutionary ideas that agitated European consciousness in the 1790s.[74]

CHAPTER SEVEN

The Enlightenment's Political Alternative

THE FERMENT CREATED by the French Revolution in Greek politics and Greek social thought in the last decade of the eighteenth century found its most dramatic expression in the intellectual and political activities of Rhigas Velestinlis (1757–1798). The seminal historical experiences that marked that decade, the bitter disappointment in Russian policies and promises following the conclusion of the Russo-Turkish war of 1787–1792, and the abandonment of the Greeks to their fate once again, as well as the excitement provoked by the French Revolution throughout Southeastern Europe, acted as catalysts for the emergence of a new style of politics that was conscious, purposeful, organized, and motivated by the quest for change. This new form of politics marked the culmination of a century of social change that had brought the liberal ideas of the Enlightenment, and the new moral and political aspirations they fostered, to maturity. Rhigas became the foremost representative of the new politics, which dramatized the bankruptcy of the hopes in enlightened absolutism as an agent of change that had been entertained by earlier generations of the Greek Enlightenment. As such, Rhigas emerged as the most articulate representative of a radical enlightenment that was actualized in the unity of theory and practice he achieved in revolutionary politics.

Rhigas's radicalism was the product of the concrete criticism of contemporary social realities that he experienced directly by growing up in Greek peasant society. His practical knowledge of the tribulations of peasant life at a time of social change preceded a career marked by considerable geographical, social, and intellectual mobility that acquainted him with all aspects of contemporary social structure. These experiences provided the existential basis of Rhigas's verdict on prevailing social and cultural conditions, and motivated him to proceed to the elaboration of an alternative conception of things. His alternative comprised a program of cultural change guided entirely by the philosophy of the Enlightenment and a radical restructuring of politics and society that involved a revolutionary overthrow of actual conditions and their replacement by a new republican order. This vision was the theoretical product of concrete experience and criticism, which typically arises in revolutionary situations, marking their most advanced and hence utopian political and ideological attainment. The content of Rhigas's eventual political position, which stressed the necessity to give socioeconomic substance to the political forms of republicanism, expressed precisely this revolutionary dialectic.[1]

A COMMITMENT TO THE PEOPLE'S ENLIGHTENMENT

Rhigas was born and raised in the village of Velestino in eastern Thessaly. His village was the traditional winter residence of the Vlach nomadic shepherds of the Pindus Mountains and this meant that he was probably bilingual. Following the typical social and geographical itinerary of the time, Rhigas pursued education and fortune in Constantinople and in the Danubian principality of Wallachia, where he came in touch with Phanariot society. His ideas matured under the impact of French philosophic encyclopedism, which dominated late Phanariot culture in the principalities. Rhigas apparently became a disciple of Moisiodax and moved in the remarkable intellectual milieu of Katartzis. In that context he associated with the articulate Greek intelligentsia who composed this circle: Constantas and Philippidis, authors of *Novel Geography;* Panayiotis Kodrikas, translator of Fontenelle; Neophytos Doukas; Constantinos Stamatis; Athanasios

Christopoulos—all of whom belonged to the third generation of the Greek Enlightenment. He seems to have developed close ties with the Phanariot administration of Nicholas Katartzas for a time in Wallachia, and with the Romanian dynasty of Brancoveanu. At the same time he developed close ties with local liberal French intellectuals and diplomats like the Count d'Hauterive and, later, Émile Gaudin. In this context, Rhigas conceived his program of enlightenment, which he attempted to carry out with his editorial projects. During at least two visits to Vienna in the 1790s, he produced a corpus of works that put the Enlightenment to practice by popularizing its intellectual and moral temper, and gave concrete expression to its political strivings in a program of radical republicanism.[2]

In the initial phase of this editorial program, during his first visit to Vienna in 1790, Rhigas published a *Florilegy of Physics for Sharp-minded and Knowledge-loving Greeks.* It was presented to the unfortunate descendants of the illustrious philosophers Plato and Aristotle by a "sensible patriot" who felt distressed observing them divested of all ideas of philosophy. The utmost of learning that some of them possessed was confined to the fruitless reading of a few books in ancient Greek over which they had bent thanklessly for long years. The echo of the pedagogical ideas of Moisiodax is clearly audible here. Being "by nature a lover of Hellas," Rhigas could not confine himself to lamentations. He knew that the national predicament could only be rectified through activism and Enlightenment. As far as his limited abilities were concerned, he felt that a relevant contribution might be a florilegy of what was essential in natural history. His contribution to the enlightenment of his compatriots could be made most effectively, he was sure, if the work was presented in a sound pedagogical manner that could reach the widest possible audience. To make the presentation of the material more lively and comprehensive, he composed the work in the form of a dialogue between a schoolmaster and a pupil. In this he followed Fontenelle's method. As the dialogue moved on, the enlightened teacher dispelled the misguided and impressionistic beliefs of his student about natural phenomena and gave him the basic facts of modern science. The avowed intention of this method was to open up the horizons of modern learning by stimulating interest, which would lead the youngster to immerse himself in the mathematical sciences through the pursuit of serious scientific works.[3] Still more essentially, Rhigas felt that he should spare his own readers the tribulations he experienced as a student when he was confronted with the linguistic riddles of a pretentious "Hellenism." Since his purpose was to be useful to his nation and not to display erudition or verbiage, he felt he should aim at clarity in his exposition so as to make the difficult ideas of physics plain and comprehensible to all. Hence, he chose to write in the common spoken language of his compatriots, following the teaching of Moisiodax in this matter too. The pedagogical inspiration of this attitude derived from his readings in Rousseau. To justify his choice philosophically, he quoted two passages from *Émile* on the detrimental effects of pedantic verbiage in the education of children, which sounded intimately relevant to the problems of traditional Greek education to anyone familiar with it.[4] Thus Rhigas, along with the authors of *Novel Geography,* achieved the transition of the third generation of the Greek philosophes to the cause of a democratic Enlightenment.

Criticism was the method *par excellence* of the new conception of Enlightenment. In the *Florilegy of Physics* Rhigas directed his criticism against traditional authority and superstitious beliefs. The authorities on natural history, sanctioned by the cultural traditions of the Greek East, Aristotle and Ptolemy, were subjected to critical refutation based on the scientific discoveries of the Moderns. On each subject of natural history various views and theories were outlined, and then their validity was assessed on the basis of modern, natural philosophers like Harvey, Fontenelle, and Buffon. Rhigas's main source of information was apparently the great French *Encyclopédie* of D'Alembert and Diderot, which he cites explicitly twice in his text. The decisive test for the acceptance or rejection of a natural theory was sought in the experiments and discoveries of modern scientists. The Moderns, however, did not simply replace the Ancients as a new fountainhead of authority beyond criticism. When those among them less astute in the natural sciences, like Voltaire, went astray in observations on natural phenomena, they did not escape a critical stricture, albeit with some embarrassment. After pointing out that Voltaire was wrong in suggesting that there were no tidal waves in the Mediterranean, Rhigas added, "I wondered how such a great mind could have made a mistake like that."[5]

The real target, nevertheless, was the superstition fostered by traditional beliefs among the simple folk. Rhigas remembered the irrational horrors provoked by the specter of vampires among his compatriots in his home town. He knew now the natural causes of the phenomenon that popular superstition took as vampires and stressed that it was entirely pointless to panic over the occasional optic phenomenon that was caused by the emission of fumes from the ground.[6] Not only could such blatant superstitions be dispelled by the knowledge of the simple facts of physics, but more mysterious and horrifying events like earthquakes and the drift of the continents could also be shown to be produced by natural causes.[7]

The real implications of the new science became transparent when the discussion reached the sensitive and controversial cosmological issue of the earth's motion around the sun, a matter of debate in learned Greek culture also. Rhigas knew that those who took the Old Testament literally as the law of their thinking believed in the geocentric view and held that the sun revolved around the earth. A wise Italian by the name of Galileo had proved the absurdity of this view and established the heliocentric view, but he was silenced by the Inquisition, and he barely escaped the fire on which heretics were burnt. The truth eventually triumphed, however, even though Galileo was silenced, because a Prussian, Copernicus, who was lucky to live beyond the grip of the Inquisition and the thunderbolts of papal excommunications, had already worked out the same ideas to their scientific conclusions. This great victory of science and truth, which had rectified the false beliefs and the ignorance of so many centuries, could only be achieved in a country where freedom reigned and where Haller's saying—"Whoever thinks freely, thinks well"—held sway.[8] This was the real message that Rhigas wanted to get across to his compatriots in presenting his *Florilegy of Physics* to their attention.

His vision of freedom was not limited to the emancipation of his compatriots' minds from the fetters of superstition and the authority of false traditions. He felt that liberation should be extended to people's sentiments and emotions as well. Enlightenment of thought and freedom of feeling were inseparable in his vision of human emancipation. This was reflected in another part of that first phase of his program of enlightenment, his adaptation for Greek readers of a selection of six short stories from Restif de la Bretonne's *Contemporaines melées*. Rhigas's book was published in 1790 under the title *A School for Delicate Lovers*. The content was quite daring for the morals of the time, so in his prefatory note to the readers, Rhigas anticipated prospective puritanical censures by pointing out that the love affairs he narrated all culminated in sacramentally blessed marriages.[9] His intention was to contribute toward a reconstruction of social morality on the model of the European experience by appealing to the sensibility of delicate youths of both sexes. The setting of the stories was Paris, which continued to exercise the fascination of the capital of lights on Greek minds.

The ideological significance of Rhigas's choice of Restif's work as the basis of his plea for the emancipation of sentiment can be fully appreciated only in the light of a consideration of Restif's relation to the Enlightenment. Restif's basic aspiration and claim was truthfulness to the contradictory reality of everyday life—a devotion that marks the advent of the ordinary individual in the history of literature. The conscious pursuit of this objective was made plain in the contrast Restif himself drew between his own focus on the ordinary person and Rousseau's depiction of the man of genius. This concentration on sociological reality betrayed a distinctly modern attitude, the concern for objectively ascertained empirical facts. With it went an explicit democratic aspiration articulated in Restif's radical social notions, which ranged from the prohibition of inheritance and the regulation of prostitution to a kind of communist exchange of labor and goods according to need and without money. Restif's desire to remold humanity and society, and his pride in his knowledge of the people and their cravings, enabled him to predict the coming of a revolution—but when the Revolution did come, he was disenchanted by its effects. His own revolution in social morality and literary style seemed to him the only genuine one.[10] It was of this revolution in social morality that Rhigas sought to make his compatriots aware.

Through his appeal to the emotions and to the passions of the heart, Rhigas expressed the new social ideals that agitated European consciousness at a time that the romantic impulse stirred new life into the liberal values of the Enlightenment. The main dramatic theme of each story was a love affair across social divisions. Restif de la Bretonne had declared that by dramatizing such affairs his purpose was to underline the fundamental fraternity that united all human beings beyond the artificial barriers of social prejudices and class distinctions. The sufferings and tribulations of the innocent and delicate protagonists of Rhigas's love stories constituted a moral protest against conventional interests and the hypocrisy of society—an appeal for moral and social liberation motivated by the yearnings of the human heart. Love was known to be the source of the greatest human happiness, and the moral claims of the delicate lovers were an appeal to their inalienable human rights based on the dictates of reason. Amid the anguish caused in their tender hearts by the obstacles that society put in the way of their love, the delicate lovers knew that all human beings were by nature equal, and their experiences had taught them that human freedom was the greatest good they could hope for. Inevitably, the protest of sentiment and the yearnings of the heart could only culminate in social criticism. Genuine nobility could be found only in the hearts of men, not in inherited privilege or in vain ancestral titles. Lest this reference to a titled nobility might obscure the real social target of the critique, Rhigas focused on the insensitivity of stubborn prominent families that clung to their social privileges and prejudices regardless of the human cost, even to their own offspring. Hence he could not hide his preference for the rising new social type of the useful and honorable merchant who stood in such lively contrast to the arrogant aristocrat. Eventually the call for the liberation of sentiments blossomed into an appeal to the source of the greatest emotion: patriotism. One's homeland was the source of the sweetest feelings, and people ought to work for its benefit. Love's greatest vindication was the noble prospect of procuring children to serve the motherland.[11]

Rhigas articulated the will to enlightenment of minds, but he also responded to the needs of a moral and emotional revolution that he felt was in the making in Greek society. He was joined in this by the young Cypriot Ioannis Karatzas (1767–1798), who was destined to share his martyrdom. While in Vienna, Karatzas published anonymously another collection of romances under the title *Results of Eros*—two years after Rhigas had brought out the *School of Delicate Lovers*. The new work moved the scene to the heart of Greek society at Constantinople and captured several revealing glimpses into Phanariot moral culture and lifestyle.[12] Once again the new morality of liberated sentiments was located within the constraints of the social structure. The new sensibility could be vindicated and the lovers' feelings could reach fulfillment only if they did not collide with the existing social norms, prejudices, and superstitions of a rigidly stratified society. If sentiments rose against such constraints, they could only end in tragedy. Thus, philosophical liberalism cultivated a clear sense of a new system of social relations that could provide the necessary context for the liberation of sentiment, the unencumbered expression of feelings, and the fruition of new sensitivities, until then suppressed by prejudice and superstition. The democratic Enlightenment found its unifying theme in this vision of a new human type, embodying the emotional yearnings and social aspirations fostered by the new philosophy.

The density of political experiences that awaited Rhigas upon his return from Vienna to Bucharest—especially his close contacts with spokesmen and supporters of revolutionary France and his involvement in local politics—amid the ferment generated by the news of the French Revolution that crowded the principalities at the time, provided the context of his transition from the vision of intellectual and emotional reconstruction to a militant patriotic ethic that would be eventually expressed in his revolutionary political theory. This was not a new commitment. The veiled references to freedom and the guarded patriotic invocations voiced in the works of the first phase of his program of enlightenment were made public under the pressure of political events and practical experience.[13] Another visit to Vienna in 1796–1797 marked the second phase of Rhigas's program. The political classicism of the Enlightenment provided him with the most effective and expressive medium for the propagation of the symbols and values of patriotism. The connections with the literary quests of the earlier phase were obvious in the collection of dramatic poetry that Rhigas chose to translate, this time under the title *Ethical Tripod*.

The book comprised versified adaptations of Marmontel's *La Bergère des Alpes* and Metastasio's *L'Olympiade*.[14] The selection of Marmontel's popular and moving work indicated clearly that Rhigas's preoccupation with the new sensibility of the liberation of sentiment, which motivated the composition of the *School of Delicate Lovers* in 1790, still persisted. In *La Bergère des Alpes* Marmontel gave currency to many of the sentiments and concerns that preoccupied Rousseau's literary writings as well in the same period. The sense of nature was no longer a contextual dimension, but it became part of the prevailing emotions. The anxieties of the soul and the fatal erotic passion that culminated in tragedy shattered the optimistic visions of easy human happiness.[15] Rhigas conveyed vividly all this pathos in his re-creation of the drama. These choices clearly indicate that in psychic predisposition and moral temper Rhigas stood very close to Rousseau's world. The primary motivation of the adaptation, however, became transparent in Rhigas's prefatory tribute to citizen Marmontel, the illustrious philosopher and member of the French Academy who, upon becoming a senator of the French Republic, extolled the sacred eros of the motherland that activated the ageless human heart.[16] In Metastasio's drama, the same emotions of tormented young lovers agitated the action, but the context of liberated sentiments was significantly shifted to the bosom of the Hellenic world. The emotional theme was underwritten by the symbols of Panhellenic bonds as expressed in the Olympic Games.[17] The valor and virtue of the protagonist, dramatized by his willing self-sacrifice in the name of a noble friendship, brought forth the heroic ethic of the ancient Hellenes whom their modern descendants longed to emulate. Thus Rhigas's literary pursuits, unified in their emotional content by the craving for the free expression of sentiments, were effectively integrated into a wider program of Hellenic patriotic revival.

The world of Hellenism was recovered in all its immediate intimacy and its cultural and ethical splendor in the Greek version of the Abbé Barthéle-my's *Voyage du jeune Anacharsis en Grèce*.[18] The translation of the multivol-ume work was an ambitious project sponsored by the Greek publishers of Vienna, the brothers Pouliou, who a few years earlier had inaugurated mod-ern Greek journalism with the publication in 1791–1797 of the first Greek news-journal, *Ephémeris*.[19] The journal carried mostly political and literary information and news on international affairs, responding to heightened political curiosities and concerns pressing on Greek consciousness during that tumultuous decade of war and revolution. The new publishing project undertaken in 1796–1797 came in the context of the upsurge of interest in classical civilization and the appeal of the Hellenic past that followed the discovery of the modern Greeks' historical and ethnic connections with ancient Hellenism through the new historiography of the Enlightenment. The translator, Georgios Sakellarios, had published a *Synoptic Archeology* of ancient Hellas the previous year.[20] In his preface to the first volume of *Voyage du jeune Anacharsis,* he stated the objectives of the Greek edition: it aspired to furnish the modern Greeks with a lively survey of the history and culture of their illustrious ancestors. According to the translator, the book in its original version had been known to Greeks for years, and many had moistened its pages with their tears reading about the achievements of their forefathers. Many more prospective Greek readers, motivated by concern with the future of the nation, longed for the rendering of the work into their own language. In this they joined several other cultured European nations that sought through close study of ancient Greek history to emulate the virtues of the ancient Hellenes.

In his public-minded project, the translator found the assistance of other Greeks who cared to work for the enlightenment of their nation and the revival of ancestral virtues among their compatriots.[21] One of them was Rhigas, who edited the fourth volume, which included his own translation of the chapters relating Anacharsis's itinerary in Thessaly, Rhigas's native region.[22]

The obvious reasons for Rhigas's choice threw into clear relief the psychological profile of an enlightened intellectual. His attachment to his native village from which he was forced away by Turkish tyranny—and to which he managed to refer even in a footnote in his *Florilegy of Physics*[23]—was the emotional leaven of his passionate patriotism. Besides this emotional commitment stood an intellectual preference. In choosing to invest his labor on a text dealing with a region with which he was intimately familiar, he could reasonably expect to render it and update it in a manner that would be empirically sound. In his translation he did precisely that. He added several observations and footnotes to Barthélemy's text that rectified oversights and inaccuracies in the original. With these corrections Rhigas attempted to indicate the continuity between the ancient and modern history of the surveyed region. Like his two fellow Thessalian geographers who had composed the *Novel Geography* a few years earlier, he showed great sensitivity to the natural beauty of his familiar landscapes as well as to the antiquities that reminded the modern observer of the classical heritage of the country. The *Novel Geography* was among his sources in his attempt to bring Barthélemy's text up to date and adapt it to the Greek context.[24] Following the example of his friends Constantas and Philippidis, he repeatedly touched on pressing modern problems. He noted that the ancient dances that Barthélemy mentioned were still danced in modern times, but their ancient Greek names were lost: "After having lost everything else, the names of the dances disappeared as well."[25] Amid this sense of loss and decline he paused for a moment to reflect on the condition of his native village, Velestino, which in more glorious and happier times was known as Pherae and had been Jason's kingdom. In Rhigas's own time it had become a place of sorrows where the frequent unjust loss of Christian lives, in the hands of the land's savage masters, would have driven them all away had not the natural beauty of the area consoled and heartened them to face adversity and persevere in the land of their ancestors.[26]

Thus the popular book of European classicism became in its Greek version a matrix of patriotism. The text itself, which celebrated Hellenic freedom, was printed in a manner that would make this message unmistakable. Whenever Anacharsis noted in his itinerary the ancient Hellenes' dedication to their motherland, their zeal for liberty, and their valor and unwavering strivings for the triumph of patriotic causes, bolder type was used in the Greek text to impress the emphasis more effectively on the readers' minds.[27] The identification of classicism with the cause of liberty was now complete. Hellas was inscribed on the banner of revolution, and the problematic of republican thinking emerged out of the venture into classical civilization. In the twelve cities of ancient Achaia, Anacharsis encountered the operation of a paradigmatic republican system of civil administration made possible by the exceptional natural circumstances of that area. The region was poor, without commerce or industry and the consequent dangers of luxury and corruption. Hence, the citizens could enjoy in peace the equality and freedom that was assured to them by wise legislation. As Polybius had suggested, social harmony and public peace were secured by the absence of turbulent spirits among the citizen body, by indifference to the ambition of foreign conquests, by the avoidance of contact with corrupt nations. The Achaians never resorted to lies or intrigues even against their enemies, and the institutional uniformity across all cities guaranteed the general harmony of the region that spread across all classes of citizens. The excellence of public life among the Achaians stood in lively contrast to the corruption reigning across the water in the Greek cities of southern Italy, which were ridden with discord and dissension.[28]

The symbols of Hellenic patriotism that Anacharsis's peregrination had impressed on the consciousness of the modern Greeks were charted out on Rhigas's monumental maps of Southeastern Europe. The editorial project of 1797 included a great map of Greece printed in twelve folios and depicting the whole area south of the Danube, the Aegean Islands, and the western part of Asia Minor.[29] This was an encyclopedic panorama of Hellenic greatness, recording both a conception of the Greek past and a vision of the Greek future. In the conception of the past, the emphasis was on the greatness of ancient Hellenism, depicting its widespread expansion in the "Greek East" and commemorating its victories against Asiatic barbarians, especially the epic of the Persian wars. Ancestral glory was projected throughout in lists of great men, in dates of heroic battles, in the reproduction of ancient epigrams and of 161 ancient Greek coins, which were scattered on the map to convey "a dim impression of archeology." Eight plans of famous ancient locations were inserted in the map to facilitate "comprehension of the journeys of young Anacharsis."[30] In addition, a plan of Constantinople and the Bosporus Strait was included on folio 1 of the *Chart*. This part had originally been printed separately in 1796 and then incorporated into the twelve-folio great map. The Greek past was thus graphically laid out in all its splendor and complexity before the consciousness of the modern Greeks.

The conception of the present sprang from a sad reminder occurring on the very first folio of the map, which depicted the ground plan of Constantinople and a panoramic modern view of the Queen of Cities. Next to a reproduction of the seal of Constantine Paleologos, the last Byzantine emperor, a simple phrase was inscribed: "and we were enslaved." The only comment that was added to the view of Constantinople was a simple epigram by Rhigas in Homeric Greek, lamenting the bitter fate of the pride of all cities, the queen of the world.[31] Yet this bitter destiny could not be accepted as the final conclusion of a glorious history. A more hopeful view of the future of Hellenism could be derived from two sources: first there was the inspiring sense of continuity with the ancient Greeks, displayed so characteristically in the recording of ancient and modern toponyms next to each other on the maps. Next there were the multiplying signs of an unmistakably new turn in the history of the Balkans, which pointed toward hopeful changes. These possibilities were obvious in the internal decay of the Ottoman Empire, dramatized by the emergence of defiant local potentates like Pasvanoglou of Vidin, with whom Rhigas was personally acquainted, who challenged the authority of the Sultan, as well as in the revolutionary efforts of popular Balkan heroes who undermined the despotic power of the empire. Last but not least, there was a sense of fraternity among the Balkan nations, a feeling that so deeply inspired Rhigas's efforts. In marking on the map a major shrine of Balkan orthodoxy, the monastery of Rila, he noted that it was the second most important monastic establishment of "our Serbian brothers."[32] This sense of pan-Balkan fraternity was surely ingrained in his soul by the example of his intellectual mentor Iosipos Moisiodax, a native of the Balkan heartlands who became by education and culture a Greek and was in sentiment one of the most committed spokesmen of the Neohellenic revival. Rhigas's admiration and affection for his teacher led him to note on his map the obscure village of Cernavodă just south of the Danube, of which the only claim to fame was that it had been the birthplace of Moisiodax.[33] Thus the name of the outspoken social critic was the only one of a modern intellectual to be recorded on the charter of Greek hopes.

The revolutionary purpose of the great map burst forward in the allegory that decorated its frontispiece. It depicted Hercules with his raised club chasing away an Amazon mounted on her horse. In his explanatory memoir on the symbols appearing on the map, Rhigas noted that the Herculian club signified Hellenic valor as against the Amazon's double axe, which represented Asiatic power.[34] The same appeal to the victory of Hellenism over Asiatic despotism was reflected in the engraving of Alexander the Great that Rhigas also printed in 1797. Alexander's portrait, surrounded by smaller portraits of his four major generals and four scenes from his great victories accompanied by laconic explanatory notes, combined Rhigas's message of Hellenic patriotism with the legendary traditions that had animated popular imagination for centuries.[35]

REVOLUTIONARY PLANS

Rhigas's publishing activity clearly had a practical purpose. It was designed to sow the seeds of a revolutionary effort that would overthrow Ottoman rule and achieve the liberation of the Greeks and the other Balkan nationalities. His editorial projects of 1796–1797 constituted the final stage in a program of enlightenment that aimed at the moral and psychological preparation of that supreme effort. He did not simply attempt to cultivate the ethic of Greek patriotism by propagating the classical symbols and ideals of a Hellenic revival that could appeal to the enlightened segments of Greek society, especially the enlightened intelligentsia, the educated youth and the political activists of the diaspora. He tried to reach beyond these social groups, who were the natural allies of his effort, by communicating the message of national redemption to the wider masses of Greek society in a language that was familiar to them and with symbols that they could understand. The picture of Alexander was such a medium of appeal to popular social psychology. In addition it seems that Rhigas tried to impart his message by issuing, probably during the first phase of his editorial program in 1790, the oracles of Agathangelos, which prophesied the imminent resurrection of the nation.[36] Originally composed, as already noted, by Theoklitos Polyeidis around the middle of the eighteenth century, the oracles constituted a quite popular text that had known wide circulation in manuscript copies since its appearance. The appeal of its millenarian themes among both the popular masses and the leadership groups in Greek society was a telling indication of the sense of discontent and the longings for a redemptive apocalypse that expressed the ferment generated by the disintegration of Ottoman power and the pressures of social and political change. In such situations in traditional society, millenarianism provides an outlet to the gropings of popular psychology, and correspondingly offers a means of effective communication between the masses and leadership groups, the latter consisting of either those traditional elements who want to lead the millenium or revolutionary intellectuals.

In publishing the oracles in the same year he published the *Florilegy of Physics* and the *School of Delicate Lovers,* Rhigas was not apparently relapsing into some kind of traditional millenarian ideology. On the contrary, the edition of Agathangelos attributed to him could be considered as telling evidence of his realistic appraisal of the practical possibilities and political parameters of any revolutionary attempt at national liberation. It was a clear sign of his awareness that the political aspirations of revolutionary Enlightenment could appeal to and mobilize the socially and ideologically modernized groups that represented only a very small if dynamic fraction of the society. These groups could provide leadership and visualize goals, but could not make a successful revolution by themselves. Hence Rhigas's urgency to reach out to the wider masses of the population by talking to them in their own symbolic language, which could move the yearnings and dreams that sprang from the depths of their own life and experience.

The problematic of revolution, which emerges from a consideration of the corpus of Rhigas's work, matured in his thought under the impact of the French revolutionary experience. Contemplation of this experience, and reflection on the possibilities it offered to the Greek nation, eventually led Rhigas to the final practical step contingent on every revolutionary calculus. The promotion of the cause of Enlightenment, the cultivation of the ethic of Hellenic patriotism, and the appeal to the masses culminated in practical attempts at organization aiming to rally the forces of a revolution. More than two centuries later, it is not entirely certain what Rhigas really organized.[37] The practical plans with which he was going to put his revolutionary program to action vanished in the tragedy that overtook the last phase of his activity and sealed his fate. Subsequent national mythology certainly magnified his program while his intentions were distorted to suit the requirements of conflicting ideological positions in Greek politics, as

Rhigas was claimed by both the nationalist right and the revolutionary left as a spiritual progenitor.[38]

The nature of Rhigas's political thought, however, and his solution to the Greek problem, can be adequately reconstructed strictly on the textual evidence of his surviving works. In addition, important documentary evidence, provided by the records of the interrogation to which he and his comrades were subjected by the Austrian authorities after their arrest in Trieste for subversive activities in December 1797, illuminates and confirms the conclusions of textual analysis.[39] His explicitly political treatise—his constitutional project for a Hellenic republic, outlined in his famous revolutionary pamphlet—represents the culmination of his political thought. The political context within which this constitutional project was conceived and spelled out was provided by Rhigas's organizational activities and plans for the liberation of Greece.

The oldest reliable testimony on Rhigas's plans for the liberation of Greece came from a prominent member of the Greek enlightened intelligentsia, Gregorios Constantas, coauthor of *Novel Geography*. He knew Rhigas in Bucharest, and they were both in Vienna in 1790 overseeing the publication of their books. According to Constantas, who lived to see the emergence of independent Greece, Rhigas was the first Greek patriot who thought of the revival of the nation in clearly political terms and visualized an independent Greek state. The source of his thinking, according to Constantas, were the papers of Alexandros Mavrokordatos, hospodar of Moldavia (1782–1786) who had harbored some plans for Greek independence and was forced to flee to Russian protection when the Turks were apprised of his designs.[40]

If such was the original source of Rhigas's plans, his program of enlightenment, shaped primarily by the influence of French philosophic encyclopedism, took an increasingly radical republican political orientation. After the final disappointment of all hopes of Russian assistance following the abandonment of the Greeks in 1792, he turned increasingly to the example of revolutionary France and gradually came to conceive the Greek political revival on the French model. Beyond this ideological inspiration, it seems that Rhigas saw a real opportunity for Greek freedom emerging out of the international ramifications of the French Revolution, especially following Napoleon Bonaparte's campaigns in Italy and the French occupation of the Ionian Islands after the disappearance of the Venetian Republic. The precise content of his conjectures in this direction have remained unclear due to very uncertain evidence as to his alleged plans or attempts at direct contact with Napoleon or even with French diplomatic agents in the Hapsburg domains.[41]

Such initiatives have apparently been magnified by subsequent legend. Nor is there evidence supporting with any certainty the existence of a secret revolutionary society led by Rhigas and working systematically for the liberation of Greece. Apparently the Austrian authorities, obsessed by the French menace, feared a huge plot behind Rhigas's activities, and the emperor himself took a keen personal interest in the matter. Moreover, as recently as 1796, the Hapsburg monarchy had suppressed in its Hungarian territories another Jacobin-inspired conspiracy, which had originated in the activities of Ignatius Martinovic, a professor of natural science. This was the immediate political context of Rhigas's arrest and eventual extradition to the Ottomans.[42] What does emerge clearly from the documentary record is that Rhigas, after completing his editorial program in 1797, left Vienna for an unknown destination in Ottoman Greece accompanied by a group of close collaborators. The group was held together not by the bonds of a secret society, but by a shared inspiration from the French revolutionary principles and a fervent dedication to Greek patriotism deriving from a veritable adoration of the classical Hellenic ideal.

So far as the Austrian interrogating officials could ascertain, Rhigas's plan was to start a revolt in Mani, the unsubjugated rugged peninsula of the southern Peloponnese, spread the revolt through cooperation with the mountain warriors of Souli in Epirus, proclaim the freedom of Greece, and introduce the French system of government in the liberated land. The ideological preparation of the revolt, the Austrian police were aware, included such literary projects as the translation of *Jeune Anacharsis* and the *Ethical Tripod,* the publication of the great map of Greece, the drafting of a revolutionary proclamation calling upon the Greek nation to rise for its freedom, and the composition of a popular revolutionary anthem modeled on the "Marseillaise." Finally, it was ascertained that a republican constitution had been drafted. The last three items (the proclamation, the anthem, and the constitution) were secretly printed in a subversive pamphlet that was to be distributed to the Greek subjects of the Sultan as part of the revolutionary effort. The indications that the interrogation could glean as to the content of that revolutionary manifesto suggested that its slogan was the French revolutionary maxim "liberty, equality, fraternity."

In its pages, in a very French manner, the monarchs of the world were insulted, the rights of man and the virtues of republican government were exalted, and freedom was celebrated.[43]

In his own testimony, Rhigas admitted that the motivation of his literary projects derived from his desire to enlighten his nation and to help his compatriots realize the sorry state of their subjugated homeland. He acknowledged a deep hatred against the barbarian Turkish race, and stated that next to the salvation of his soul his most earnest desire was to see the Turks expelled from Greece. He confessed that he had written to the French Consul in Trieste volunteering to serve as liaison between his Greek compatriots and the French high command in Italy. Concerning his constitutional projects, he admitted his interest in a translation of the French Constitution as a guide to Greek efforts, but he described as his intention the composition of an original constitution, following the French model but adapted to the spirit of the Greek nation.[44]

Rhigas's comrades were unanimous in their recognition of the need to reeducate and enlighten the Greek nation by making available good books of ancient Greek authors, as a prerequisite to the rising for national freedom. They also shared in the enthusiasm of the "Jacobins" of Central Europe for the French Constitution. A young man, Panayiotis Emmanuel from Kastoria, spoke favorably of French liberty and stressed that every Greek who knew something about the political systems of ancient Hellas could not but support the regime of revolutionary France, since it was mostly derived from Solonian legislation. This similarity that the Greek revolutionaries could discern between the republican French Constitution and those of ancient Greece dramatized even more the stark contrast between ancient Greek freedom and Turkish tyranny.[45] Another of Rhigas's comrades was occupied with a translation of Mably's essay *Observations sur l'histoire de la Grèce ou des causes de la prosperité et des malheurs des Grecs,* in order to instruct the modern Greeks about the virtues, gifts, and vices of their ancestors.[46]

The perception of a causal connection between Enlightenment and revolution—which a few years earlier was argued in relation to the French experience as well in the pages of *Novel Geography,* which Rhigas had obviously read—provided the theoretical foundation of the practical activity of Rhigas and his comrades. With their decision to transfer their efforts from the capitals of Enlightenment to the prospective ground of their revolution, they achieved a unity of theory and practice not always attained by

revolutionary intellectuals. Their organizational basis was certainly rudi-
mentary, if it existed at all beyond the bonds of a common ideological goal;
the details of their revolutionary plans were submerged by foreign persecution and later by national mythology; finally, their practical revolutionary
activities were preempted by martyrdom. Even the revolutionary manifesto
of their movement, Rhigas's pamphlet with the constitutional project of the
Hellenic republic, disappeared. All original copies of the pamphlet were
destroyed by the combined effects of persecution and fear. The discoveries
of the research of a whole century have produced only manuscript copies
and translations of the original pamphlet. On the basis of this evidence,
whose authenticity is firmly established, it is possible to reconstruct with
reasonable certainty the ideology that guided these revolutionary efforts
and to recover the precise shape of the political regeneration visualized by
the protomartyr of Greek freedom for his resurrected homeland. This vision
was embodied in Rhigas's revolutionary manifesto of 1797, *New Political
Constitution for the Inhabitants of Roumeli, Asia Minor, the Mediterranean
Islands and Wallachia-Moldavia.*[47] The pamphlet comprised a revolutionary
proclamation, a bill of human rights, and a constitutional project for the
Hellenic Republic and was concluded with a martial anthem.

JACOBIN POLITICAL THOUGHT IN SOUTHEASTERN EUROPE

The primary inspiration of Rhigas's political thought derived from Montesquieu's *De l'esprit des lois,* of which he had attempted a Greek translation
earlier in his career.[48] Montesquieu's indictment of absolutism had enabled
Rhigas to spell out in political terms his own intense hatred of despotism.
In his political radicalism, however, Rhigas went much beyond Montesquieu's original purposes. His revolutionary proclamation was a militant
paean against despotism and its degrading effects. Rhigas echoed a widely
accepted idea of the Enlightenment in claiming that despotism in the
Ottoman Empire had reached the utmost of debasement and corruption.
Tyranny had reduced even the most innocent and honorable citizens to
complete uncertainty and insecurity concerning their life, honor, and property. Driven to the extremes of indignation and despair by the injustice
and inhumanity of tyranny, the descendants of the ancient Hellenes, who
inhabited continental Greece, Asia Minor, the Mediterranean Islands, and

the principalities of Wallachia and Moldavia, united with their brethren who were forced by tyranny to flee to foreign realms, decided to appeal to heaven, seize the arms of vengeance, and rise against the tyrannical yoke of the most vicious and vile government. It was a rising in the sacred name of Law and Fatherland, inspired by the ideals of liberty, equality, and fraternity that prefaced the proclamation as the battle cry of the revolution. The descendants of the ancient Hellenes meant seriously their call to fraternity. They invited all other nationalities and ethnic groups, groaning under the unbearable yoke of Ottoman despotism, to join in the common crusade of liberty. Christians and Turks should put their religious differences aside and realize the common humanity that united all of God's creatures and the fraternity that, amid the shared vicissitudes of tyranny, brought together all human beings regardless of class and religion. Thus, all peoples yearning for their freedom discovered their fraternity in a common appeal to heaven, solemnly seeking to vindicate before the entire universe their sacred and irreproachable rights. For the Greeks it was a compelling invitation to recover the ancestral liberty. The political content of their free future, which was to be secured by the revolutionary effort, was suggested by the declaration of rights that preceded the main text of the constitution. The foundations of these rights were liberty, security, and the pursuit of happiness.[49]

Rhigas's charter of the rights of man followed faithfully the "Déclaration des droits de l'homme et du citoyen" that opened the French Constitution of 1793. It is noteworthy that of all the constitutional documents that attempted to put in concrete political and institutional terms the social ideals of the Enlightenment, which might have been accessible to Rhigas at the time (the American Constitution of 1787, the French Declaration of the Rights of Man and Citizen of 1789, and the French Constitutions of 1791, 1793, and 1795), he selected the most radical one. The constitution of year one of the Revolution, drafted by the Convention, which had for the first time been elected by universal male suffrage, was the eventual product of a constitutional process that was initiated by the formal abolition of the French monarchy and the proclamation of the Republic as soon as the Convention met in September 1792. The constitutional documents were finally approved by the Convention in June 1793, after a protracted political struggle between Girondinist liberalism and Montagnard social radicalism, expressed primarily in the controversy over the recognition of property as a natural right. The original liberal, if complicated, project drafted by

Condorcet was put aside, but Robespierre's refusal to include property among natural rights had also to be given up.[50] Although the primacy of liberal individualism was recognized, still the Constitution of 1793 retained a pronounced social orientation in the provisions for public assistance to needy citizens, in its recognition of the right to work, and in its emphasis on the necessity of general education (articles 21–22). Beyond the acknowledgment of these social rights in the Declaration, the specific institutional arrangements proposed in the main text of the constitution were dictated by a profoundly democratic inspiration. This came forth very clearly in the aspiration to make political participation as broad as possible by instituting universal male suffrage. The democratic tenor was underlined by the reservation of the first rank among fundamental rights to equality (article 2) and by the stress put on resistance to tyranny and on the right to revolt as the "most sacred and indispensable of duties" (article 35). The radical purposes of the Constitution of 1793 did not escape the attention of revolutionary democrats. Babeuf and Buonarroti extolled its virtues in 1796, and it remained the paradigm that inspired and guided the democratic tradition in French politics.[51]

It was precisely these radical democratic purposes that appealed to Rhigas and were stressed in his own adaptation of the Jacobin Constitution of 1793 for his Hellenic Republic. In the formulation of its principles, in its constitutional provisions and institutional arrangements, the Greek text follows closely its French model.[52] Rhigas's Declaration of the Rights of Man had 35 articles, and his constitution contains 124 provisions, precisely like the French originals. With the Greek version, the political and social ideals of the French Revolution were adopted as the guides of the Greek national rebirth. It was clear that, for Rhigas, alien despotism was only the immediate target and national redemption from the yoke of the barbarians simply a necessary condition for the initiation of far-ranging institutional, social, and cultural changes that would radically transform Greek society. National independence was a necessary condition for the realization of human and social freedom. This was the essence of Rhigas's revolutionary vision.

The social reconstruction that would follow the achievement of political independence was to be shaped by the recognition of the binding force of the liberal principles of the Enlightenment in the life of the new state. Individual liberty, defined as the power to do anything that does not harm the rights of others, was proclaimed a natural right. Concrete civil liberties—such as freedom of thought, speech, assembly, and religious faith, as well as liberty of the press—were affirmed as basic rights whose infringement amounted to tyranny and raised the specter of the overturned despotism. The code was equally affirmative on the regulation of penal justice, insisting on the principle of *habeas corpus* and stressing that penal laws could not be retroactive, that torture be absolutely prohibited, that all defendants were innocent until they were proven by due procedures to be guilty. In all of this, Rhigas clearly showed that he was familiar with Beccaria's arguments and the pertinent discussions of his times. Turning to the economic sphere, Rhigas affirmed all the principles of freedom in civil society, emphasizing that although wage labor should be unrestricted, slavery and serfdom should be prohibited and asserting that all types of professions, employment, and enterprise should be open to all who wanted to engage in them.[53]

The vindication of these general liberal principles, which could be taken for granted by all enlightened persons, represented profoundly revolutionary claims in Balkan society under Ottoman rule, because they projected an order of things at great odds with existing structures, familiar practices, and accepted values. Rhigas, however, went beyond mere liberal claims. The political and social system he visualized had a pronounced egalitarian character. Not only was equality proclaimed as the first and foremost natural right, but Rhigas insisted that in the Hellenic Republic no discrimination based on religion, language, race, or ethnic origin could be tolerated. All men were by nature equal, and consequently each and every citizen had an equal right to assist and participate in the making of the laws. Rhigas's egalitarian aspirations were not confined to these formal declarations. Their concrete social content was revealed in his insistence that the popular masses constituted the nation, and thus national representation should be based on them and not on the minority of the rich and social notables. Hence, it could be affirmed that before the law there were no rich and poor. An important step toward the recognition of the equality of women was taken with Rhigas's assertion of their duty to participate equally with men in national defense and to attend the system of compulsory public education.

Rhigas's hostility toward all forms of hierarchy transpired negatively in his total exclusion of the Church from the constitutional system of the

Hellenic Republic, and positively in his stipulation that military ranks could be in force only at times of war, while in peacetime no distinction between officers and soldiers was to be tolerated among men who recognized each other as equals and brothers. The will to social equality was expressed in specific provisions and policy directives that Rhigas formulated for the Hellenic Republic. First of all, all debts were to be abolished. The debts of cities, towns, regions, as well as those of private citizens, which had been incurred more than five years before the establishment of the republic and on which interest had been regularly paid, were to be abolished. The creditors had no right to exact any more payments of capital or interest from their debtors, since capital tended to double in five years at the then current rate of interest. Socially this was a remarkable provision that indicated Rhigas's sense of injustice at the widely spread practice of usury in his contemporary society. The gesture was also symbolically quite significant because it was modeled on Solon's *seisachtheia,* the suppression of all debts that the great ancient legislator decreed before introducing his legislation that reformed the institutions of ancient Athens. By inaugurating the new Hellenic Republic with such a measure of abolition of debts, Rhigas was appealing to the classical precedent set by the great founder of another Hellenic Republic.

Rhigas's social legislation did not stop at this symbolic measure that concluded the Declaration of Rights. The charter also acknowledged several important social rights. The recognition of everyone's right to work obliged the society to supply underprivileged citizens with the necessary means of production whose deprivation had forced them to remain idle and inactive. In addition, the state ought to assist those who were unable to work; it should care most particularly for the welfare of those who had been disabled in wars of national defense. Finally, Rhigas put a great premium on public education. The state should establish schools everywhere, even in the remotest of villages, for the education of all children of both sexes. Literacy was a public duty to which no exception could be tolerated. Education was the mother of progress, which made all free nations illustrious. Special care should be taken for the teaching of the Greek language and for the instruction and interpretation of the texts of ancient historians. This would assure the effective training of patriots. In the major cities, French and Italian, the tongues of the Enlightenment, should also be taught.[54]

It was within the framework of such egalitarian society that the radical democratic purposes of Rhigas's republic could be actualized. In the conception of both the basic principles of political life and of the institutional arrangements of the new republican order, Rhigas remained faithful to Rousseau's ideas, which had been the direct source of his Jacobin model. His democratic vision inspired his assertion that the people as a whole were the source of sovereignty. The sovereign people could make decisions on all issues without any limits to their authority. Popular sovereignty, which united all citizens on an equal basis, was to be exercised through universal suffrage and popular consent to the passage of legislation. Popular consent would be given through a system of primary assemblies and national representation. Government was to be opened up to all the people: every citizen was eligible to all public offices, which were to be distributed on the basis of merit and worth. Public office was just service to the community, nothing more. Its holders were responsible to their electors, and its exercise was temporary, for brief periods of time. Representatives to the National Assembly would be elected for one year only and were accountable to their constituents. The top executive Directory was to be composed of five members, whose duty was strictly to carry out the decisions and laws voted by the legislative power.[55]

Although Rhigas was well aware of and greatly admired Montesquieu's work, his radical democratic intentions did away with the liberal conception of the separation of powers. Not only was the executive organ strictly limited and subordinated to the legislative body, but the latter in its turn was entirely dependent on the popular will, not simply in terms of its accountability, but also through an institutional system of popular referenda that alone could ensure the ultimate ratification and legitimacy of any law. Rhigas's republic was far from a system based on representative government and parliamentary procedures. A great deal of initiative, especially over constitutional revision, was reserved directly to the people. Lest all these structural arrangements and institutions proved inadequate safeguards against the machinations of tyranny, the protection and defense of the constitutional system of the republic was entrusted to the vigilance of all virtuous and freedom-loving men who had sworn to wage eternal war against all tyrants. The right of revolution was the ultimate safeguard of freedom. If the government violated or usurped the rights of the people and remained contemptuous of their grievances, the people should unite and rise against their tyrants. The greater the tyranny, the more determined the people should be in their resistance and in their effort to revenge their rights. The most courageous and liberal patriots should get out on to the mountains and on the highways and lead their compatriots to rise and take arms, close their ranks, and set upon their tyrants to vindicate their liberties. The Lockean resonance of this final appeal indicates graphically the revolutionary impact that the prudent Englishman's ideas and language could have once integrated into the problematic of continental revolutionaries. Rhigas could conclude his project for the political reconstruction of Hellenism by insisting that revolution was the most sacred of all human rights and the most indispensable of the duties of the citizen.[56]

There was a final problem that Rhigas's constitutional project had to come to terms with. As a careful student of Montesquieu, Rhigas knew that simple imitation of foreign models and crude transplantation of institutions could not be expected to work. Forms of government and institutional structures had to be organically adapted to the specific conditions and to the social spirit of the lands for which a constitutional proposal was put forward. The problems of a particular society could not be resolved by appeals to abstract principles, or even worse, by Procrustean attempts to force upon all societies the same institutional forms. Montesquieu's great admirer and Rhigas's master, Rousseau, knew that he had to take into consideration every minute empirical detail pertinent to a particular country in order to make sound constitutional proposals for the real world. In drafting his projects for Corsica and Poland, he tried to do precisely that. The specific problem that Rhigas had to cope with might be considered twofold. It had to do with the territorial extent and the ethnic diversity of the new republic. How could radical republicanism, with all its stipulations for direct popular participation and initiative in the process of government, work over a territory stretching all over Southeastern Europe, the offshore islands of the Greek peninsula, and most of Asia Minor? All geographical indications in the constitutional projects, and more precisely the great map of Greece, clearly suggested that such would be the territorial basis of the Hellenic Republic. Rhigas had enough faith in the effectiveness of republican institutions and perhaps even more in the moral and psychological power of the ethic of patriotism and free citizenship that he did not worry much about this problem. Theoretically, he had no reason to worry, since neither Montesquieu nor Rousseau excluded the possibility of an extensive republic, although both of them stressed the difficulties and dangers that might jeopardize its survival. Montesquieu had felt that a solution to this problem might be a confederation of republican communities.[57] Rhigas, however, excluded this possibility for the Hellenic Republic, which had to be unitary and indivisible—clearly a comment on the state of anarchical disorganization and lawlessness to which the Ottoman Empire had been reduced by political decay and the consolidation of the power of local potentates at the end of the eighteenth century. Obviously, the precedent of the Jacobin constitution settled the problem on Rhigas's mind: France, for which the constitution of year one had been written, was territorially the most extensive country in Western Europe, roughly equal to the extent of the projected Hellenic Republic envisioned by Rhigas in the southeast. Rhigas can, therefore, be counted among those heirs of Rousseau who, immersed in the revolutionary fervor of the epoch, aspired to expand the scope of republican radicalism from small nations to large territorial states, hoping to attain their objective by cultivating civic virtue among the masses of the population. Thus this last generation of the great tradition of European radicalism, which descended from the civic humanism of the Renaissance, expected to transcend the severe limits imposed on projects for virtuous republics by the enormous difficulties inherent in their task.[58]

A thornier problem might be that posed by the ethnic diversity of the new republic—all the more so in view of the silence of Rhigas's sources on the implications of such an issue for republican government. How could the descendants of the ancient Hellenes, the modern Greeks, join with the multilingual Christian nationalities of the Balkans, the Serbs, Bulgarians, and Vlachs, as well as the Albanians, the Armenians, and the Jews, and even the Turks themselves in forming a viable political community? Maybe the desperate indignation to which the shared plight of despotism had driven all these nationalities could bring them together in their appeal to heaven, in the revolution that would overthrow tyranny. But how could they construct an integral and indivisible republic? This was the real challenge to Rhigas's political theory.

The first step toward the resolution of this problem took the form of Rhigas's emphasis on the artificial character of all distinctions based on language, religion, and race. Such external differences could not be allowed to obscure the fundamental truth of the natural equality and fraternity of all human beings. Hence, a community of diverse ethnic groups was in principle possible. Now the dilemma became what to do with all these artificial differences—should they be uprooted and stamped out or accommodated within the framework of the new community? Rhigas recognized the basic equality of all citizens as individuals regardless of ethnic affinities, but he also emphasized the equality of the nationalities that joined the social contract of the republic.[59] A variety of national identities was thus recognized as one of the dimensions of the political sociology of the new state. The constitution enshrined this principle of double equality by first acknowledging that the Hellenic Republic comprised diverse nationalities and religions and stating unequivocally that such diversity in faiths was not regarded with any hostility. Sovereignty in the state, however, was reserved *not* to these nationalities but to the people as a whole, comprising individuals regardless of corporate identities based on language, religion, or ethnic origin.[60] The sovereign people were one and indivisible. The institutions of the republic were framed in such a manner as to underline this unity. Political unity would become operative within the context of the spirit of patriotism expressed in the symbols of republican Hellenism and the ideals of revolutionary Enlightenment making their inroads into Balkan culture at the time. The political ideology of democratic Enlightenment was expected to provide a civic culture that would animate the new political institutions. Such would be the moral basis of the new republic. The values of a revived republican Hellenism would provide the ethical content of its political life.

By putting his faith in these moral components of his scheme, Rhigas framed his solution to the ethnic problems of his polity in the historical terms of his contemporary culture.[61] At the end of the eighteenth century, Greek was the *lingua franca* of the Balkans and the Levant, and the spread of Greek education and culture in the area was the gauge of the strides of enlightenment and national "awakening" throughout Southeastern Europe and the Eastern Mediterranean. Through the network of Greek schools and with the medium of the Greek language, the culture of the Enlightenment made itself felt in the collective consciousness of Southeastern European peoples. Greek intellectuals and Greek publications had been for decades the most conscious and outspoken exponents of the spirit of the new age in the area. Indeed, in the context of the backward and conservative society of the Balkans, the Greek-speaking intelligentsia, the Greek commercial bourgeoisie, and the middle-level public functionaries in the Phanariot administrations constituted the only conscious revolutionary element.[62] Rhigas had crosscutting ties with all these social groups to which he belonged in successive stages of his career. His own life experiences, his geographical and intellectual itinerary from the school of Zagora on Mount Pelion to the educational institutions of Constantinople, and to the great cultural centers of the Danubian principalities and the Greek diaspora in Central Europe, perhaps most decisively the example of his culturally Hellenized mentor Moisiodax, must have convinced him of the great potentialities of republican Hellenic culture as a unifying bond among enlightened individuals, liberated from traditional corporate attachments. He was, therefore, led to put too much faith in the progressive and unifying possibilities of the culture of the Enlightenment and to hope that the sheer moral force of republican patriotism would allay ethnic antagonisms, nurture interethnic solidarity, and cultivate loyalty to the unitary institutions of the new republic.

In taking this view of the ethnic problem in Balkan society, Rhigas obviously gave too much weight to an optimistic appraisal of the potentialities of practical experiences strictly delimited and determined by a particular configuration of historical and cultural circumstances. He thus did not really confront the tensions and contradictions that formed the heart of the ethnic problem. In particular, he failed to anticipate the force of the new collective identities bred by modern nationalism, which emerged from the very cosmopolitan culture of the Enlightenment and replaced, without wholly obliterating them, premodern corporate attachments. Indeed, part of the legacy of primordial sentiments and loyalties was absorbed into the new nationalisms, thus strengthening their appeal to the masses. Rhigas did not foresee that the impact of the Enlightenment and the example of the Greek national "awakening" itself were bound to generate parallel, if somewhat delayed, developments among the other Balkan nationalities as well. The pressures of these other nationalisms—which were to a considerable degree stimulated by resentment against the prolonged Greek supremacy in the region—would inevitably disrupt any attempts modeled on Rhigas's scheme for a multinational republic.[63] This historical criticism, however, is possible only with the benefit of hindsight, which of course Rhigas lacked. The tensions and strains in his approach to the ethnic problem should be appraised in the light of the fact that he was the first republican thinker who attempted to come to grips with an issue that proved so vexing both theoretically and politically to several subsequent generations.

Although Rhigas's scheme did not resolve the basic theoretical tensions posed by the question of nationalism, a final word of explanation is essential. His solution to the ethnic problem may appear, in the light of subsequent nationalist history and conflicts, as essentially amounting to an invitation to other Balkan nationalities and ethnic groups to selectively Hellenize themselves. His purpose, however, was by no means to undermine the integrity of these other peoples. His insistence on ethnic rights could be judged as an adequate pointer to his respect for the autonomy of different nationalities as a matter of principle. The assumption that potential political problems among different ethnic groups composing one unitary state might be preempted by the common espousal of a republican civic culture was not inspired by a chauvinistic preference, but by an optimistic faith in the possibilities of the Enlightenment to reconcile antagonisms, to promote common human purposes beyond sectional separatism, and thus assure a rational and progressive resolution of political problems. The logic of nationalism proved all this to be just a utopian aspiration, but the significance of Rhigas's vision should not be lightly dismissed. His faith in the primacy of basic human rights and democratic principles, over the claims of corporate identities and loyalties, and his belief that wider political and social purposes might reconcile ethnic and other forms of particularism was an important lesson that was not lost on later generations of democrat thinkers and his own successors in the tradition of Balkan cooperation. Seen in this perspective, Rhigas's scheme might appear as the most radical solution possible to an explosive problem, put forward even before that problem itself became fully apparent in all its complexity.

Rhigas's projects and visions represent the most eloquent expression of the ferment generated in Greek consciousness and more generally in Balkan society by the French Revolution.[64] His great achievement consisted in capturing a broader social feeling of excitement and expectancy and recasting it in the concrete intellectual and political terms that could best articulate it: such was the language of Hellenic republican patriotism. Theoretically, his accomplishment was remarkable in that he combined the aspiration of national redemption with the necessity of radical social transformation, profound moral reform, and ethical reconstruction of personalities. Republican freedom and national independence were conceived as interdependent. This dialectic was extended to the practical dimension of Rhigas's work. His systematically conceived program of enlightenment with all its intellectual radicalism and lofty idealism never lost sight of concrete practical purposes. This was what turned it into a call to revolution. The unity of theory and practice that Rhigas achieved in his work was best reflected in the receptivity that his revolutionary message found among those to whom it was primarily directed. Although his plans for a revolutionary effort in Greece itself were preempted by his martyrdom, Greek patriots everywhere were strengthened in their determination against tyranny by his sacrifice.

The intellectuals of the diaspora extolled Rhigas's work and sacrifice as the first contribution to the crusade of liberty. Both Korais in *Fraternal Instruction* and the anonymous patriot who composed *Hellenic Nomarchy* paid tribute to Rhigas's memory and urged the nation to follow his heroic example.[65] But even more important, Rhigas's message spread among the masses in subjugated Greece and especially among the forces of Greek resistance, the bands of *klephts,* the mountain warriors who in their social banditry and unbending defiance of the authority of Ottoman and Christian lords provided an outlet to social protest simmering among the subject people. It was to them that Rhigas alluded when he entrusted the defense of his constitution to "the vigilant protection of the virtuous and freedom-loving men who, refusing to submit to the yoke of tyranny, embraced the life of warriors and took up arms swearing eternal war against tyrants."[66] It was for them that he composed the patriotic hymn "Thourios," which closed the revolutionary pamphlet of 1797. This martial anthem, for which Rhigas had borrowed a title from the ancient Spartan poet Tyrtaeus, was addressed to those who had taken to the mountains and lived on the slopes and in caves like solitary lions on account of the bitter captivity of their homeland. They were urged to rise, inspired by the spirit of patriotism and guided alone by the laws, to join forces fraternally with the other subject nations, black and white, and driven by the impetus of liberty to assault tyranny, break the yoke of despotism, and establish justice and freedom throughout the land that extended from Bosnia and Montenegro through Roumeli and Mani to Crete and Asia Minor, to Syria and Egypt.[67]

The "Thourios" put the principles and aspirations of Rhigas's political theory into a language that could touch the emotions of the popular masses. In this, too, Rhigas followed the practically oriented political calculus that had guided his projects from their original inception. According to available evidence, the "Thourios" had indeed great appeal among those whom intellectual Enlightenment could not reach, but who nevertheless shared the disaffection that emerged out of the disintegration of the Ottoman Empire.[68] Rhigas's achievement of the unity of theory and practice in revolutionary politics proved of relevance on all levels to the gropings of a society yearning for change and liberty.

CHAPTER EIGHT

The Enlightenment as Social Criticism

THE WILL TO criticism was the defining characteristic of the Enlightenment. The conscious pursuit of criticism can be seen as the underlying mental attitude that reconciled the diverse outlooks that made up the Enlightenment. Criticism and doubt toward established beliefs and accepted authority represented the most daring manifestations of the early Enlightenment in a period of "crisis for the European conscience."[1] Later on, social criticism and the vision of social reconstruction that activated it was what made Rousseau, and his opponents among the philosophes, representatives of the same intellectual movement.[2]

The sharpest edge of Enlightenment criticism was directed against conventional Christianity, the Church, and the censorship imposed by it. Christianity constituted the rival set of beliefs that fostered uncritical faith and by extension, in the eyes of the Enlightenment, superstition. It symbolized, that is, everything that the Enlightenment was fighting against. In this ideological confrontation, the Church and the various mechanisms of censorship formed the formidable structure of organized power that stood in the way of the progress of the Enlightenment, by taking advantage, according to its opponents, of prejudices that were hypnotizing the human spirit. For this reason, the Church strove to strangle the movement that was threatening to rend the veil of ignorance and had, ever since the period of the Renaissance in European culture, persecuted those who labored in the interests of the progress of knowledge. The struggle between the Enlightenment and the Church can thus be seen as the fundamental ideological fissure in European society during the eighteenth century. As the most prominent exponent of the crusade against obscurantism and intolerance, which the "enlightened" conscience associated with the Church, Voltaire, for all his recantations and philosophical ambiguities, remained the most representative figure of the Enlightenment, a shining beacon to his supporters and a scapegoat for his opponents.[3]

With regard to the Greek experience, the disposition to criticism has already been noted in the examination of other dimensions of the process of intellectual change in earlier sections of this study. The theory of cultural regeneration and political change expressed in *Novel Geography* constitutes a characteristic manifestation of this intellectual and moral position. The emergence of a critical attitude was the surest sign that the Enlightenment had become a reality in the consciousness of at least a section of Greek society. This was no small achievement for a culture whose intellectual boundaries had only a few decades previously been defined by Orthodox Christianity. The extent and complexity of the critical spirit in the Neohellenic Enlightenment may be grasped by tracing its evolution at three successive stages: beginning at the level of cultural criticism, in a typical trajectory of expanding Enlightenment claims, the spirit of dissent moved on to the criticism of existing social structures and finally focused on a condemnation of the Church and traditional religion, which the champions of the Enlightenment viewed as their main rival. The different aspects of cultural criticism have been described in previous chapters. The present chapter is devoted to an analysis of the arguments advanced in a body of writing that illustrates the radical turn of Greek thought as reflected in social criticism.

THE STRUCTURE OF SOCIETY: FETTERS TO NATIONAL REVIVAL

The radical turn in Greek thought was reflected in the emergence of a critical literature that took the form either of popular satire or of theoretical analysis. The latter was directly associated with the revived tradition of radical civic humanism in the ranks of the Enlightenment. In either case, the criticism of existing social structures was now explicitly interwoven with the problem of national liberation. In this sense, the social criticism of the Neohellenic Enlightenment represented a continuation of Rhigas's republican political thought. In this regard too, the transition from cultural to social criticism signalized the evolution of Greek thought in the period that was inaugurated with Moisiodax's *Apology* and culminated in its remarkable diversification in the years following the French Revolution.

The resentment and moral contempt inspired by entrenched structures of power in certain strata of Greek society were registered in a popular satire in verse composed around the turn of the eighteenth and nineteenth centuries under the title *Rossoanglogallos* (Russo-Anglo-Frenchman), the *terminus ante quem* being 1805. Surviving evidence suggests that the satire, which took the form of a dialogue, was quite well known and frequently recited in certain circles of Greek society at the time. The militancy of its social protest, however, and the clearly subversive character of its reflections on the problem of Greek freedom from Ottoman tyranny, caused it to remain unpublished and its author to stay anonymous. Its pointed ideological content indicates that its author belonged to the politically progressive social groups of the time and was probably associated with the circles of Rhigas and Psalidas. It was these groups that championed the most radical programs of social change and were seriously preoccupied with projects of national liberation. The historical evidence for the identity of the author of the satire, however, is so meager that no conjecture can be made with any degree of certainty. All that can be inferred from the text is that the author had some connection with contemporary Italian radicalism, if, at least, the similarity of title with the corresponding work *Il Misogallo* by Vittorio Alfieri can be regarded as acceptable evidence. The text has an empirical interest in itself because it delineates a picture of the Greek social structure at the time, drawing a profile of dominant social and economic groups and their political orientations as well as their interplay with foreign political forces at work in the Eastern Mediterranean during the period of Ottoman decline at the close of the eighteenth century.[4]

The author of *Rossoanglogallos* was convinced that the national revival of Greece was absolutely impossible, and all hopes in that direction remained empty talk, so long as the existing social structure survived. Those in positions of spiritual, political, and economic leadership, who were expected to

care most about the nation's predicament and to concern themselves with
the problems and possibilities of its revival, had chosen to submit unconditionally to the double tyranny of alien despotism and corruption. The
Orthodox hierarchy was given to shameless exploitation of popular superstition, and their only preoccupation was with the amassment of wealth
and the pleasures of the flesh. "As to Hellas, they cared little if she was tyrannized," in the words of the bishop, one of the characters in the dialogue
used by the author of the *Rosoanglogallos* to satirize the indifference of the
higher echelons of the clergy to the common interest. The church hierarchy
counseled the pious in confessional to remain loyal to the Sultan and taught
the Phanariot potentates who surrounded them how to make the most of
Ottoman despotism at the expense of their compatriots. In their loyalty to
tyranny, the urban aristocracy of the Phanariots were rivaled only by the
landed primates who oppressed the peasantry. No one, even among the
faithful of Mahomet, was as loyal as the landed primates to the Ottoman
government. They tyrannized and pillaged the poor peasants in order to pay
off their beloved Turks, who shielded them from the wrath of the oppressed
and exploited.

The attack on these groups of social notables, especially the Phanariots,
was an important sign of the changing social psychology of the Greeks.
It was an integral part of the liberation of Greek consciousness from the
inherited identification with the prevailing Ottoman system, within which
the Phanariots had been integrated and had risen to prominence. The questioning of the Phanariots' moral authority, obvious in this criticism, was a
clear indication of the repudiation of their leadership by those over whom
it was exercised.

If these social groups that thrived under tyranny felt no scruples about
justice and freedom, what of the bourgeois merchants who ought to be the
natural enemies of tyranny and the champions of freedom and Enlightenment? The author sorrowfully and resentfully notes that the actual attitude
of the Greek mercantile classes dispelled any illusions that freedom might
come through their initiative. Despite Greece's tyrannical yoke, their only
concern was with business. They spent their wealth on buying favors from
the Turks in order to ruin their business rivals. Furthermore, they thought
that those few among them who spent their wealth on the education and
awakening of the nation were ill advised and simply wasting their time.
For the "prudent" majority of the merchant class, the Turkish yoke was an

insignificant nuisance in comparison with the satisfaction and consolation offered to them by their wealth.

This bleak profile of the political predispositions of those segments of Greek society that commanded wealth and influence left no room for hope that they could ever rally to the cause of freedom. In the appraisal of the satire, they seemed to have too much at stake in the structures sustained by tyranny, and they had obviously been morally debased to the point that no courage or sacrifice could be reasonably expected of them. Some Greeks, however, even though they had given up hope on the leadership of their own society, still harbored some expectations in the much-vaunted philanthropy and pretentious admiration of classical Greek glories evinced by certain foreign nations. The militant realism of the satire, however, did not spare this last illusion, which had been fostered for years by the propaganda of foreign powers with imperial designs on the Ottoman inheritance, according to the anonymous author.

Accordingly, the author of the *Rossoanglogallos* closed by directing his fire in turn against each of the three foreign powers featured in the satire's title. The Russians were taken to task for cruelly abandoning the Greeks after stirring their hopes in three successive Russo-Turkish wars. The Russians and the English together were accused of undermining and obstructing the French attempts to liberate Greece. Finally, the French themselves were blamed for the intensification of the sufferings of the Greek nation after their abortive adventures in the East. Such was the supposed philanthropy of those nations that would still be captives of ignorance had it not been for the lights of Hellenic wisdom.[5]

The satire was eloquent in its bitter realism. No hope could be expected from either a leadership that had compromised with alien despotism or from self-appointed foreign protectors. For those freedom-loving Greeks, who were ready to "seize the arms of vengeance and despair," the Greek problem had been redefined by social criticism as a clear choice between resignation and revolution. Such was the message of another patriot as well who sought the protection of anonymity for his revolutionary call. The bare outline of explicit radical social criticism, initiated in *Rossoanglogallos,* was a faint prelude to the moral and social theory of revolution spelled out by Anonymous the Hellene in *Hellenic Nomarchy Being a Discourse on Freedom,* which appeared in 1806.[6]

The title coined a new word, *nomarchy*, which signified the rule of law (*nomos* and *arche*) and constituted a clever linguistic play on the word monarchy, of which it was meant to denote the exact opposite. The long subtitle on the title page explained the contents of the treatise: "Hellenic Nomarchy, or a Discourse on Freedom proving how superior Nomarchic Government is to all the rest; that only in such a state is human Freedom secure; what Freedom is and of how many achievements it is the cause; that Hellas must as soon as possible break her chains; for what causes she has remained captive until now and what causes will make her free."[7] The motto of the work was "reflect—that is enough," which was reminiscent of Rhigas's apothegm: "Whoever thinks freely, thinks correctly." The work was dedicated to the memory of that great patriot, the precursor of freedom who sacrificed his life for the love of the Hellenic motherland. The recognition of Rhigas's pivotal position in Greek liberation efforts is a clear indication that the author of *Hellenic Nomarchy* felt himself to belong to the tradition of Balkan radicalism inaugurated by the patriot from Velestino. The prospective reader was warned not to waste his time reading the book if he belonged to the worshippers of scholastic grammar who could not utter the name of Hellas without sighing.[8] The *Hellenic Nomarchy* placed the Greek problem within a fully fledged framework of republican theory and analyzed it as a question of radical moral reform and social revolution. The Anonymous Hellene combined a lively awareness of the problems of Greek society with a profound acquaintance with the social thought of the Enlightenment. Throughout his treatise he alluded to the great tradition of European literature, from the ancient Greek historians and moralists to his contemporary dramatists and political philosophers. The result was the most significant monument of political thought in the Neohellenic Enlightenment, offering an incisive interpretation of the predicament and prospects of the Greek nation in terms of the political theory of Montesquieu and Rousseau, Alfieri and Beccaria, with Aristotle and Xenophon, and Polybius and Plutarch constantly in the background.

The foundation of political argument was a theory of human nature premised on the foremost aspirations of the Enlightenment: truth and happiness. The journey toward truth and certain knowledge of the nature of things was the essence of the experiences of an enlightened mind. The point of departure was universal doubt that encompassed one's own beliefs as well as the teachings of others. Certainty could be reached if the various propositions about truth were subjected to careful examination, if conflict-ing views on a subject were impartially scrutinized, if finally the probable was chosen over the impossible and the arduous over the ambiguous. Only this method could satisfy the profound human craving for truth. Thus the labyrinth of superficiality and irrelevance in which current opinions wan-dered, eventually breeding skepticism and agnosticism about the possibility of happiness, could be transcended.

Human beings, according to the anonymous author, are endowed by nature with reason that guides them in the pursuit of happiness. In an original state of nature, self-sufficiency and the preservation of life was the primary human preoccupation. So long as natural self-sufficiency lasted, complete human happiness was a fact of nature. However, when the first man made the fatal move and called another to his assistance, the state of nature came to an end. Self-sufficiency was replaced by mutual dependence, and the original carefree happiness was replaced by the strains of society. In a world of incompatible human wills, happiness was transformed into an eminently social problem. It became the task of government to reconsider the conflicting desires and wills of men in order to make happiness possible. This could be achieved if the happiness of the greatest number of the citi-zens was secured. The best government was that which achieved the greatest happiness for the greatest number.[9] This echo of the principle of utility in the text of the Anonymous Hellene most likely derived from its original for-mulation in the work of Beccaria, on whom Bentham, who made it famous in the history of political thought, also drew.

This happy state, however, was only a vision of the future. The reality of the present was reflected in the anarchy of human needs and desires unleashed by the destruction of natural self-sufficiency. The anarchy of needs and the inevitable conflicts and injustices that followed culminated in the rise of tyranny. Monarchy was established as an illusory refuge amid human adversity. This made possible the rise of inequality among men and the transformation of monarchy into tyranny. It is not difficult to detect in the theoretical background of this argumentation the genealogy of social corruption presented by Rousseau in his discourse on the origins of inequal-ity. Amid the ensuing depravity, humanity awoke to a yearning of redemp-tion in a different political order that would enable them to recover their lost original happiness. This is how the expectation of nomarchy came to stir the hearts of men.[10]

Nomarchy as a principle of government was the exact opposite of the principles of monarchy and of its extreme version, tyranny. In fact, nomarchy can be understood as a systematic antithesis to monarchy. It is a regime of general liberty, while in monarchy only one is free, and tyranny wipes out the liberty of the rest entirely. Nomarchy is a regime of equality as against monarchy, which thrives only on inequality. Nomarchy is a regime of social harmony and concord, while in monarchy discord and dissension simmer beneath the seemingly monolithic surface. Tyranny is civil war in disguise. Finally, nomarchy is a regime of virtue, which is stifled by monarchy. Tyranny is but a hive of vices. Institutionally, nomarchy can be expressed in either an aristocratic or a democratic regime. The basic difference between these two types of government is to be found in the forms into which they tend to degenerate—oligarchy and anarchy respectively. In their uncorrupted form, however, both aristocracy and democracy preserve freedom and the spirit of nomarchy. Thus choice between the two depends on their respective compatibility with other dimensions of the polity, such as the number of inhabitants or the nature of the climate. Clearly, the Anonymous Hellene derived his problematic of forms of government from Montesquieu. Nomarchy was the principle that shaped the spirits of aristocratic or democratic republics.[11]

The dedication to republican ideals was cultivated by the system of laws, and education provided the basis of the ethical quality of life in a nomarchy. Ethical life was actualized in the unity of the individual with the community in the pursuit of a common purpose of public happiness. The felicity and virtue of the citizens in a polity of freedom sustained a noble emulation in working for the good of the community. Friendship was the most beautiful flower of the virtue of free souls united in their strivings for common purposes. The Aristotelian ideal of friendship and the example of the great men of the past who were honored as the heroes of the community were the greatest source of inspiration of public commitment.[12] The Anonymous Hellene passionately urged his beloved compatriots to live up to this moral example. The vision of nomarchic polity was an invitation to a recovery of Hellenic patriotism. No human act could be more meaningful and inspiring than self-sacrifice in a just war in defense of the freedom of the motherland. Such was the ethical power of nomarchy: it actualized the moral splendor of freedom that transformed human beings into heroes.[13]

In disclosing this vision to his compatriots, the anonymous patriot hoped to inspire them to strive for its achievement by breaking the fetters of their homeland's captivity. If, for the ancient Hellenes, nomarchy was a way of life, for their modern descendants it was just a yearning, a hope of redemption from their enslavement. They had reached that low state as a result of the workings of a relentless law of decay and corruption that shaped the history of humanity. Nomarchy, a human creation, could not escape the universal logic of social change. Although it was the best form of government, the only one conducive to human happiness, nomarchy suffered from the inevitable imperfections of its human provenance. It was subject to the law of development from infancy to youth and from mature adulthood to aging and death. The end of nomarchy could come in conquest by its neighbors or in subjugation by a tyrant.

The classical theory of the corruption of regimes, elaborated by Plato and Aristotle and systematically expounded by Polybius in his concept of cyclical change, returned to the thought of the modern Greeks through their contact with modern radical republicanism. Although the Anonymous Hellene quoted ancient moralists like Xenophon and Plutarch, the classicism of his political ideas was that of the Enlightenment and modern civic humanism. In his account of historical corruption, he followed Machiavelli rather than Aristotle. The controversial Florentine was naturally never mentioned by the Anonymous Hellene, who absorbed the Machiavellian influence indirectly from the eighteenth-century Italian heirs of Machiavelli, among whom he lived and whose traces are obvious in his thought.[14] The account of the moral and social disintegration of the best regime in *Hellenic Nomarchy* is directly reminiscent of Machiavelli's anatomy of social corruption in the *Discourses on Livy* and more concretely in the *Florentine Histories*.[15]

Humanity's bleak destiny could be appreciated if one took into account the fact that nine-tenths of the globe were ruled by various types of despotic government. Tyranny was the living experience of mankind, and very little theoretical explanation was necessary to make its nature plain to them. The Greeks in particular, who sighed under Ottoman despotism, did not need any instruction concerning the depravity of tyranny and its mortifying effects. The anonymous patriot, however, felt it relevant to his discourse on freedom to dispel the mythology about those tyrants whom modern illusions marveled to be virtuous and enlightened. These monarchs simply disguised their viciousness behind religion and the laws. The supposed enlightened despots refrained from no tyrannical wrong-doing at the expense of their subjects—injustice, extortion, plunder, and death—but they conveniently ascribed all their actions to the laws that they contrived and enacted by themselves and that they alone violated. Only one moral certainty emerged out of the analysis of tyranny: unfettered authority corrupted even the most virtuous man. The moral degradation wrought by tyranny was reflected in the pitiful resignation of modern nations to the reality of their subjugation. They had been so completely accustomed to the moral predicament of slavery that they no longer resisted the unlimited power of their tyrants, but simply rejoiced and praised them when they did not practice all the evil that lay within their grip. If there were any just and virtuous monarchs left, the anonymous patriot pointed out, they should immediately descend and abandon their thrones. None could be found, however, because thrones perverted the nature of those who sat on them and made them incapable of ethical conduct.[16]

The repudiation of despotism in all its guises, including its "enlightened" version, which had dominated Greek political thought just a few decades earlier, was still another indication of the ideological liberation experienced by Greek consciousness. In republicanism, the Enlightenment had presented a political alternative to the disappointed expectations from absolutism. The bitterness of the denunciation of enlightened despotism was partly the psychological product of this disenchantment. Its real political significance, however, lay in the decisive break with the past that the repudiation of absolutism involved. Enlightened absolutism was essentially an attempt to integrate the past in a new order and to save it by correcting its abuses. By discounting this ideology, radical republicanism not only transcended the moderation and hesitations of earlier phases of the Enlightenment, but more fundamentally it appeared to sever its bonds with the past, to repudiate any attachment to it, and to look instead to a different future in terms of institutions, social structure, and moral culture.

The anonymous patriot's repeatedly expressed pessimism was only a dramatic reminder to his compatriots. The spectacle of captivity and the experience of corruption were intimately familiar to them. The historical destiny of their nation had simply been a concrete application of the theory of corruption. A consideration of the fall of Greece provided the conceptual link between the political theory of republican liberty and the radical criticism of contemporary society, which was the anonymous patriot's main target. Contemplation of the theory of nomarchy and of the awesome effects of the cycle of its corruption set the context for reflection on the historical and social logic of the Greek problem. Such reflection was a necessary prerequisite to any attempt at reconstruction. Theoretical reflection was a necessary precondition to practically oriented action.

In order to identify the obstacles, the Anonymous Hellene turned to a brief survey of Greek history, focusing on the process of corruption of ancient republican institutions and the rise of superstition and despotism.[17] The anonymous patriot reconstructed this process in a state of obvious psychic agitation. His rage was indeed that of a child of the Enlightenment. His passionate concern for the destiny of his homeland brought back to life the philosophic reflections of Voltaire and Montesquieu on the grim decline of Greece. In both its logic and eloquence, his historical analysis of the fall of Greece, with all its brevity, has an epic quality that resounds like the immortal pages on the same subject written by that other great admirer of Montesquieu, Edward Gibbon.

The tyranny of superstition was not the last of the gradations of corruption. The cycle of decay kept unfolding until it reached the most terrifying and dehumanized extreme, which was marked by the subjugation of Greece to Ottoman despotism. Superstition and ignorance had for centuries prepared the triumph of the barbarians whose wild tide could not be stemmed any longer by the enfeebled Greeks. The contemporary predicament of Greece, which so much agitated the anonymous author of *Hellenic Nomarchy,* was the eventual bitter product of three successive cycles of tyranny: the tyranny of the Romans, the tyranny of the Priests, and finally the most barbaric and detestable of all—the tyranny of the Ottomans.[18]

The rule of the Ottomans was, for the Anonymous Hellene, the paradigm of despotism. Their government was based on a few imperfect and cruel laws among which the foremost was the word and the desires of the tyrant. Although their religion was monotheistic, they were totally gripped by superstition. Their mores were savage, their character arrogant, and their ignorance complete and general. The tyrant himself was completely lawless and lived in idleness and corruption. He knew nothing of the sciences and foreign languages, and of his own language he knew just a few words, which sufficed for his commands of injustice and death. Such was the statue of folly that commanded the system of tyranny. Despotic government was exercised by a swarm of slaves who transmitted the dictates of tyranny through a hierarchy of despotic command. The system was cemented by the decrees of superstition and ignorance which represented the only legislative output. The law of tyranny was adjudicated through a system of extortion, torture, and death at the expense of the oppressed subjects. The hierarchy of despotism extended into the provinces and made its oppressive weight felt in the daily lives of the subject races through the distribution of local governorships to still another circle of slaves. These regional satraps in turn discharged their authority by relying on the dregs of society, local informers, and criminals. They used them to force heavy exactions out of their Christian subjects in order to make up for the debts they had incurred in vying for the illicit fruits of the venality of despotism.[19]

Such was the nature of the Ottoman regime. Its despicable effects were revealed in the moral debasement of the leading classes of the subject peoples, which had compromised with tyranny. In his analysis of the sociology of captivity, the Anonymous Hellene had repeatedly alluded to these stewards of tyranny. They included the landed primates and local notables who acted as the intermediaries between the Ottoman tyrants and the oppressed peasantry and were indistinguishable from the former in rapacity and cruelty. Corrupted by the habits of tyranny and unrestrained by its total lawlessness, they were driven by an unharnessed greed in the manipulation of the levies, whose collection they farmed from their Ottoman masters. They knew neither shame before men nor fear before God and remained unmoved by the supplications of widows and orphans and indifferent to the sufferings of their fellow Christians. They were not simply the faithful servants of the tyranny under which they thrived, but were the worst enemies of their own enslaved and suffering nation.

Beyond the barbaric local notables, there were those vile pseudo-aristocrats of Constantinople, the Phanariots, whose proximity to the throne of the tyrant made them the willing valets and apologists of despotism. Without a trace of virtue, comfortable in their voluntary servility, shielded behind their empty arrogance and pretentiousness, they chose to remain blind to the vision of freedom and tried to obfuscate reflection on its possibilities. They tried to sow doubt as to the possibility of freedom by suggesting that the formidable monarchy of the Ottomans could never be vanquished and by insinuating that the Greeks were incapable of governing themselves. Freedom was not only meaningless, but its price in blood was much too high to deserve the risk of savage Ottoman retaliation. Such were the arguments of the stewards of despotism. Tyranny, like liberty, could not survive without zealous defenders.[20]

The abject misery of the lower orders of society constituted the other face of the Janus of corruption. Reduced under the despotic yoke, the Greeks had descended to the utmost of misery. The moral sociology of tyranny now shifted its vantage point from the top, from where it surveyed the spectacle of despotism as a form of government, to a consideration of the predicament of the victims of despotism at the bottom of the captive society. The author of *Hellenic Nomarchy* grieved at the sight of his beloved compatriots. The horrors of captivity afflicted with greatest intensity the most useful and productive orders of society. This was the measure of the injustice of despotism. It was evident in the indescribable suffering of the farmers, the worthiest class in all societies. These unfortunate producers of the common sustenance could barely subsist on the fruit of their own labor because of the rapacity of the Ottoman masters and their collaborators, the landlords and the monks. The deprivations that resulted were further aggravated by the losses caused by forced labor and corvée in the service of monstrous local tyrants. All this kept the peasantry in a condition of extreme misery, perpetually on the verge of starvation.

The plight of urban artisans and traders was no less horrid. Unfair and burdensome levies, extortions of merchandise, conscripted labor, and the forced idleness of innumerable religious holidays not only made profit impossible, but rendered survival problematical. Not only was the practice of their crafts obstructed by the oppression of Ottoman tyrants and of Christian notables who acted as the foremen of tyranny, but the useful artisans and traders, amid the lawlessness of despotism, lacked even the basic safety of their life, honor, and property. The paralyzing misery of the countryside was supplemented by the grim consternation of life in the captive cities and towns of Greece. Sighs and tears greeted the visitor who ventured into a Greek city where the experience of life consisted just of sorrow, fear, captivity, and death. A murmur of melancholy and a silence of despair prevailed in the hearts of the children of Greece.

The foremost enemies of liberty and collaborators of tyranny were to be found among the monks and the hierarchy of the Church. The authors of *Novel Geography*, a source that the anonymous patriot had undoubtedly read,[21] had complained a few years earlier that the ecclesiastical prelates had turned the Church into a marketplace of sacraments. That was a relatively mild complaint in comparison with the vehement eloquence with which the author of *Hellenic Nomarchy* denounced the higher clergy as the primary enemy of liberty. With tears in his eyes, he begged all those wise and virtuous men, who undoubtedly existed among the hierarchy, to forgive the daring of his denunciations against all those ignorant monks who were unworthy of their holy orders.

According to the author of the *Hellenic Nomarchy,* nothing of the moral attributes of authentic evangelical Christianity had survived among the clergy of the Greek Orthodox Church after the long centuries of Roman and Ottoman captivity. No piety, no philanthropy, no compassion, no mutual charity, and no concord were to be found in the bosom of the hierarchy. The holy synod of prelates resembled a fold of wolves devouring the innocent sheep of the Orthodox flock. The darkness of ignorance prevailing among the modern Greeks allowed this intolerable state of affairs to be perpetuated in the ranks of the Church, but the light of learning and the sun of truth would soon reveal to all the real depravity of the clergy. Such was the task of enlightenment that the anonymous patriot set himself. His attack on the kingdom of darkness took the form of an analysis of the role of the clergy in Greek society.

The Anonymous Hellene's description showed the clergy of the Orthodox Church to be organized in a power structure that paralleled the administrative structure of Ottoman despotism. At the center in Constantinople, in the shadow of the throne of the sultan, sat the head of the Church, the Ecumenical Patriarch, surrounded by the synod of senior hierarchs. The patriarch and the synod presided over a system of hieratic control which, through the provincial archbishops and local bishops, extended its tentacles throughout the empire. At the bottom of the system were the ubiquitous monks who roamed the provinces and the cities, rekindling superstitious beliefs and blind fears. It was the combined weight of alien despotism and hierocratic obscurantism and exploitation that crushed and debased the popular masses and carried the effects of corruption to the utmost.

The monks practiced none of the apostolic and evangelical precepts. They observed no fast and practiced no charity; they hated virtue wherever they found it in laymen and clergymen alike. They used the confessions that the pious made to them, seeking spiritual comfort and consolation, in order to betray them to their enemies and tyrants, and with the example they set

by their conduct, they preached the exact opposite of the apostolic teachings of concord, brotherhood, equality, and freedom. Such was the greatest
plague of Greek society—one hundred thousand of them. Their hundreds
of monasteries and shrines were like bleeding wounds on the body of the
motherland. One could only imagine what the Word of Wisdom, sweetest Jesus, would say to these presumed servants of His who were primarily
responsible for delaying the liberation of Greece.

Indeed, the cause of freedom was for them the worst mortal sin. They
never preached in their sermons any of those evangelical precepts that
might inspire zeal for social reconstruction. They never spoke of concord
and mutual love, nor did they ever urge the faithful to dedicate themselves
and strive for the causes of faith and homeland. They remained completely
silent on the subject of the Greeks' national descent and on the great moral
examples of the ancients. They said nothing of the best form of government and of the nature of virtue. In his earnestness, the enlightened patriot
expected the Orthodox clergy to become preachers of republican values.
Although this was not a direct logical corollary of his moral critique of
the social role of the clergy, it revealed eloquently the purposes and aspirations of his anatomy of Greek society. His outrage, however, was entirely
understandable in view of the attitude of the official Church. Tyranny for it
was the rightful divine punishment of the sins of the people. Such was the
consolation with which the hierarchy tried to keep the faithful in the fold at
that time of ideological conflict and rising doubt. The Anonymous Hellene
was sure that this was Judas's inspiration.

The anonymous patriot, agitated and driven by his zeal for freedom, concluded his fierce attack on hieratic bankruptcy by inviting the hierarchs and
all the Greek clergy to embrace his own version of virtue. By joining in the
far-ranging project of moral reform that was required for the reconstruction
of Greek society, they would free themselves from the onus of treachery
and spiritual deception and recover the evangelical dignity of the Church,
which was urged upon them by all patriots, and especially by the new Hippocrates, the virtuous Greek philosopher of Paris, Adamantios Korais.[22]

The moral bankruptcy of the clergy was only one of two causes delaying the liberation of the nation. The other, equally decisive factor was the
absence of worthy persons able to work for national reconstruction. The
flight of these persons from their native land to the communities of the diaspora deprived the subjugated nation of the invaluable services they could

render to the cause of social and moral regeneration. Both the product and the cause of prolonged captivity, their absence was nonetheless also symptomatic of some moral failures of their own. Some were forced away by the intolerable burden of tyranny. Others went away pressed by the necessity of making a living for themselves and their families. Most of the youth in the diaspora were driven by the desire to pursue higher studies and seek out the lights of European learning. However, once their fortune was amassed and an adequate education, or, as in many cases, a good name and honorable reputation were acquired, what was it that still kept these expatriates from their native land? Some argued that they discharged their obligations and benefited their homeland more by the gifts and generous donations they could make from the accumulation of wealth made possible by their profitable enterprises abroad. The scholars claimed that the more they learned, and the more books they wrote by staying abroad, amounted to that much more useful service to their compatriots.

His patriotic zeal and knowledge of the actual needs of Greek society, however, contributed to the Anonymous Hellene's judgment that the presence of these experienced men of affairs, who had acquired the useful habits of modern civil society, as well as the learning and enlightenment of the young scholars who attended the universities and academies of Europe, were urgently required for the tasks of reconstruction of Greek society. If they failed to perceive this pressing need of their community, they were guilty of callous insensitivity and even of willful indifference to the problems and pleas of their homeland. The moral defects could not be disguised by the pretensions of a hypocritical zeal. The merchants who refused to return did so out of greed, the relentless pursuit of private profit. The occasional gifts they made to their homeland were enough to soften the pangs of conscience. As to the students who haunted for years the academies of Europe, the content of their studies was the best indication of their motivation. Most of them were indifferent to the study of politics, law, and military science, precisely the branches of learning most relevant to the needs of their society's reconstruction. They chose instead to study profit-making medicine which, after all, cured only the diseases of the body, not the social ills of Greece. What was worse, others wasted their years on the idleness of mythology and poetry, which kept them remote from pressing contemporary problems. Such were the moral failures of men detached from social purposes.[23] Ironically, the anonymous patriot himself could be held accountable for the same moral failures, since he lived in Italy and directed his tirades against tyranny and corruption from abroad. He might reply, of course, in self-defense that in his absence he wrote about politics and not about idle subjects, and that he was in continual communication with his homeland, as was made amply clear by his detailed information and acute awareness of her social problems.

In view of this general picture, no one could pretend or be so blind as to seriously believe that in the face of Greek passivity and indifference, freedom could be visited upon Greece through the intervention of a foreign despot. A legacy of bitter disappointments inspired the unequivocal determination of the anonymous patriot's argument at this point. The Russian expectation, that empty mirage that, in the author's judgment, had viciously deluded many generations, was not even mentioned. But the transient hopes stirred by the exploits of the French Revolution and Napoleon were cited as a case of misguided expectations from self-seeking tyrants. The sorry experience of Italy was evoked in order to dramatize what liberation by foreigners might bring. Liberation could be achieved only through the common strivings and united efforts of all patriotic Greeks.[24]

The sociology of captivity was thus concluded by a return to the problematic of freedom. The *Hellenic Nomarchy* closed with a consideration of the prospects of national liberation. The recovery of freedom was not based on the feverish wishes of patriotism but on the logic of history. The inescapable cycle of social corruption, which had subverted the original nomarchic polities of ancient Greece, had now caught in its throes the formidable despotism of the Ottomans. The law of decay had reduced to paralysis the savage power that had once spelled awe and sent tremors of mortal fear throughout Europe. The signs of disintegration were unmistakable in the rebelliousness of local satraps who defied the authority of the sultan, in the incessant intrigues and relentless pressures of foreign powers, in the awesome lawlessness that pervaded the empire. The decay of despotism was the major negative cause of hope in the calculus of freedom. There were many positive causes as well to brighten the prospects of redemption.

The most eloquent indication that the spiral of Greek history had taken an upward trend was the progress of the Enlightenment. The safest sign of the progress of cultural and moral reconstruction at work in Greek society came in a generally observable change in attitude toward the intellectuals. Although these educated men did not yet enjoy all the respect and honor that they deserved, still they were no longer subject to persecution, contempt, and ridicule.[25] The bitter experiences that had poisoned the efforts of successive generations of enlightened men, from Anthrakitis to Moisiodax, seemed to have run their course. Even some among the primates and notables, a group that previously used to do everything in their power to shield their children from the effects of learning, now went out of their way to secure the lights of modern education for their sons.[26]

The most salutary effect of the change in intellectual climate was an increased awareness of the lamentable predicament to which tyranny had reduced Greece. The students who read Xenophon and Plutarch and the other historians and philosophers of their ancestral heritage could not help but resent the effects of despotism and long for the recovery of freedom. They no longer hesitated to utter the name of freedom lest the hierarchs or primates hear them and accuse them of atheism. With a courage that was impossible in servile souls, the enlightened youth of Greece proclaimed openly their yearning for freedom and instructed in word and deed all those around them of their patriotic duties and obligations. The vicissitudes of tyranny had not, after all, entirely stamped out virtue and patriotism from Greek society. The temple of virtue had not been completely ravaged in captive Greece, and its faithful were ready to heed its voice and fulfill their duties to the motherland.[27]

Hope could be inspired not only by the progress of Enlightenment and by the revival of patriotic virtues, but also by the valiant spirit of resistance that motivated the heroic defiance of tyranny by the *klephts*, the ardent warriors of the Greek mountains. Their unbending resistance and their consistent heroic victories made plain the irresistible decline of Ottoman power and pointed at the facility with which Greek freedom could be conquered. The valor of these mountain warriors was all the more heartening in that it indicated that the national character of the Greek people remained essentially uncontaminated by the corrupting effects of tyranny. Following Rousseau, the Anonymous Hellene observes that their great physical vigor, the product of a simple and healthy diet and a natural way of life, fostered their bravery and natural inclination to the martial arts. Their spirit was inventive and upright. Their sincerity, rectitude, and courage were exemplary. Hospitality was a natural virtue for them, and in their respect for the elderly they resembled the ancient Spartans. The sublimity of their souls was evident in their contempt for their tyrants, in their constancy amid the hardships of their condition, in their unwavering dedication to the cause of freedom. In all these social virtues, the modern Greeks were the true descendants of the ancient Hellenes. It seemed, therefore, that despite the anonymous patriot's grim pessimism over the mortifying effects of tyranny on the popular masses, a section of the Greek community had, according to his account, escaped the contamination of despotism and became the repository of his hopes.

This was the conclusion of the author's reflections on the distinctive social and moral qualities of nations. These qualities constituted what was known as national character, which in turn was shaped by three factors: first, by the geographical location of a country or province on the globe. This was the cause of racial differences. The second factor in human differentiation had to do with the climate of different regions, which determined the moral temper of men and the nature of political regimes. The third factor was partly the combined product of the two others and had to do with the special social circumstances and cultural conventions of each region, which forged the character of its inhabitants. Such conventions and social accidents as form of government, religion, social mores, and number of inhabitants were the decisive influences that molded the national character of a people. The author of *Hellenic Nomarchy* appeared to be a quite sophisticated reader of Montesquieu. Far from succumbing to a crude geographical determinism or more specifically to the facile climatological reductionism in the explanation of political and national differences, which the superficial misreading of Montesquieu had popularized in the later thought of the Enlightenment and its epigones, the Anonymous Hellene had successfully grasped Montesquieu's primary emphasis on immanent human causes and social history as the determinants of political sociology.[28]

Reflecting on the problems posed by Greek national character in these terms, the anonymous patriot could draw a heartening comparison between Ancients and Moderns. Although the original Hellenic purity did not remain uncontaminated during the long centuries of Roman yoke, the barbaric tyranny of the Ottomans did not amount to an irreparable adulteration of the Greek character for two reasons: first, because the religious difference kept the two races apart; second, because the total exclusion of the masses of the Greek people from the workings of government spared them the corruption of despotism, although they had to sustain all the mortifying hardships of its oppressive burden. Besides these sociological causes, the Greek character was saved from the corruption of despotism as a consequence of an act of determined human will: it was the uncompromising resentment and hatred of the Greeks for their alien tyrants that kept them apart and saved them from the contamination of despotism. Living in the same natural environment as the ancient Hellenes, the modern Greeks managed, through the interplay of these social causes, to preserve their original spirit. The most heartening manifestation of this was the occasional resistance to tyranny that gave to the actions of the Moderns an ethical quality worthy of the heroism of the ancient Spartans. The recovery of Spartan virtues was the most hopeful omen for the Greek future. The spirit of nomarchy was once again alive. It only remained to reclaim its institutional and structural forms.[29]

The vision of freedom embodied in a return to nomarchy was the appropriate conclusion of the author's discourse on republican theory. The recovery of freedom, however, remained just a yearning for the future that only revolutionary practice could achieve. The signs of the times and the consideration of the possibilities of liberty left no doubt in the anonymous patriot's mind. The example of a fellow Balkan people, the Serbs, clearly pointed the way that the Greeks should follow. The revival of Spartan valor among the Souliots and Maniots was not simply a source of hope and pride, but also a reminder of the moral obligations incumbent on every patriot. The ground of the struggle had already been broken by Rhigas, the great hero who first realized the necessary unity of the theory of enlightenment and the practice of revolution in the pursuit of freedom.[30] The vision of a Neohellenic nomarchy that should guide the strivings of the modern Greeks was a genuine response to his inspiring invitation and a monument to his martyrdom.

The ideological lineage that the Anonymous Hellene traced between his position and that of Rhigas derived from a conscious self-definition. The *Hellenic Nomarchy* belonged to the tradition of Greek radical republicanism that sprang from the reception of French revolutionary ideas into Greek thought. Rhigas had been the most heroic representative of that tradition of Greek revolutionary enlightenment, while the Anonymous Hellene provided it with its most comprehensive theoretical expression. The radicalism of the *Hellenic Nomarchy* can be fully grasped if it is borne in mind that this treatise of republican political theory was written in 1806, well after the French Revolution had consumed its radical momentum domestically and the hopes of many European liberals and partisans of the Enlightenment

had been belied by the experience of the Terror and the rise of the Napoleonic dictatorship. Yet no mention of the Terror is made in the pages of
Hellenic Nomarchy, and in talking about the construction of a republican
polity its author remained silent about the problems and dangers contingent
on such attempts and dramatized by the Jacobin phase of the French Revolution. Thus, despite the tribute that the Anonymous Hellene paid to Korais
as a protagonist of the Greek intellectual revival, he remained distant from
the latter's theoretical position and moderate republican sympathies, which
were tempered by a liberal appraisal of revolutionary France.

THE "KINGDOM OF DARKNESS"

The sharpness of the attack of *Hellenic Nomarchy* on the Church as the foremost collaborator of tyranny indicated the point at which the lines of ideological conflict were drawn in Greek society. Social criticism had found its
major target. The assault was increasingly focused on the role of the clergy
as the major obstacle to the fulfillment of patriotic strivings in the cause of
freedom. Therefore, in its essence the conflict over the Church was political,
not religious. This was obvious in the great lengths to which the exponents
of the Enlightenment went in order to prove their orthodoxy. They repeatedly stressed that their quarrel with the Church had to do exclusively with
the corruption of a segment of the clergy, mainly in its higher echelons, and
its compromises with tyranny. The men of the Enlightenment argued that
their criticism substantively aspired to restore the Church to its original and
becoming dignity through a recovery of the genuine meaning and practice
of evangelical Christianity.

In only two isolated cases was this limit transcended and the basic tenets
of religion subjected to questioning. Both cases occurred during the years
of ferment provoked by the French Revolution in the 1790s. Although both
instances were quite atypical of the mainstream of the social thought of the
Greek Enlightenment, they constituted, nevertheless, characteristic hints
at the extent of ideological gropings provoked by the Enlightenment. The
first of these cases of religious doubt came with the satire that has been
tentatively established—on rather tenuous and entirely internal and conjec-
tural evidence—as the work of the "Anonymous of 1787," which has more
recently been associated with models drawn from the work of Diderot. This

was a satirical work connected with the social climate of the Danubian principalities. Written in quite shocking libertine language, it combined a damning parody of the corruption and sexual perversity of the clergy (particularly of the monastic orders) with an irreverent subjection of even the transcendental and metaphysical beliefs and sacraments of the faith to the ridicule of satire.[31]

The other case came in the reaction of Christodoulos Efstathiou Pamplekis (1733–1793) to the persecution he was subjected to by some members of the clergy for his philosophical views. Christodoulos belonged to the same age cohort as Moisiodax and had studied at the Athonite Academy under Voulgaris. It seems that, while on Mount Athos, he was involved in the factional quarrels with the enemies of modern learning who tried, and finally succeeded, to disrupt the work of Voulgaris at the Athonite Academy. He went on to Europe and published two books in Venice and Vienna before settling as teacher of philosophy in Leipzig after more brawls with the local Greek clergy in Vienna. The first book attributed to him, *True Politics* (1781), was a dreary exposition of the conventional maxims of political rectitude designed, by the author's own admission, to instruct those destined by birthright to lead society in their duties and to combat the audacity of those who wanted to subvert the authority of princes. Following the dictates of right reason, correct judgment, and religion, Pamplekis hoped to stem the tide of infected opinions rising in his century and the hateful principles first enunciated by Machiavelli.[32] The aspirations of this early work were therefore quite in line with the acceptable moral and political standards prevailing in conservative Greek thought at the time. Coming after Moisiodax's *Apology*, Christodoulos's *True Politics* was an entirely conventional and colorless work.

A second book followed, based on the selection, translation, and exegesis of articles from the *Encyclopédie* of D'Alembert and Diderot, entitled *Of Philosopher, Philosophy, Physics, Metaphysics, Spiritual, and Divine Principles*. Although Christodoulos adopted and argued the basic theoretical tenets of the Enlightenment, setting up philosophy against superstition and pointing at the disastrous effects of blind respect for the Ancients, he remained circumscribed in his philosophical explorations.[33] The treatise concluded with a discourse on the existence of God, which was posited as an incontrovertible truth, not only on the authority of ancient philosophers but also on the basis of the arguments of all modern philosophers who deserved admiration and respect: Bacon, Descartes, Locke, Leibniz, Newton, Clarke, and Wolff.[34] The pantheon of the Enlightenment was invoked once again, but this time it was used not in support of cultural change, but in arguing the existence of a deity. In discussing the moral, physical, and metaphysical proofs of the existence of God, Christodoulos tried to develop a philosophical position not only against atheism but against deism and the theory of natural religion as well. He specifically dissociated his position from the philosophy of Spinoza. To this end he relied on the arguments advanced by Samuel Clarke against deism.[35] This enabled him to conclude with a theory of a personal God whose knowledge was the greatest blessing of mankind and whose existence was the source of men's duties and hopes.[36]

The publication of this book gave Christodoulos's enemies the pretext they had been seeking to settle old accounts with him. The personal vindictiveness felt toward him was such that, seven years after the publication of the work, amid the hysteria created in conservative circles by the regicide in France in the fateful year 1793, Dionysios, the bishop of Platamon, Pamplekis's former fellow pupil at the Athonite Academy, published, probably in Trieste, a violent attack on Christodoulos's views entitled *Akolouthia of the One-eyed Antichrist Christodoulos.* The violence and *ad hominem* invective of this text drove Pamplekis, whose philosophical and social views appeared to have evolved significantly since the publication of his book, to retaliate in kind. In a tract he composed in response to the polemics against him, entitled, characteristically, *Of Theocracy,*[37] he began with a militant defense of the Enlightenment, extolling the wisdom of Voltaire and Rousseau and pointing out that their enemies had not even seen their writings, let alone read them, and attacked them just out of ignorance. As to the calumnies against him, which described him as another Voltaire or Rousseau, he stated unequivocally that he would consider it an honor to be as enlightened as those wise men had been. He went on to castigate the corruption, perversion, and obscurantism of the clergy and especially of the monks, whom he had met on Mount Athos and elsewhere, because, as he saw it, they cultivated and exploited popular superstition and were thus responsible for the nation's captivity. The illicit and disgusting exploits of the clergy were common knowledge and the object of general resentment, so Pamplekis wondered why he alone was singled out as an accuser of the monks.[38]

The damning indictment of clerical practices formed the basis of an intrinsic critique of religious doctrines. Drawing a contrast between

Enlightenment, reflected in virtue and philosophy, and darkness, expressed in ignorance and vice, Christodoulos elevated right reason as the exclusive standard of his judgment. He could, therefore, indict asceticism as the mark of savage beasts rather than of sainthood, celibacy as an offense to nature and to the divine will, and the wisdom of the Scriptures as plagiarism of ancient secular philosophy. He rejected the veneration of prophets and saints, whom he did not recognize as anything but mere men. Denouncing most of the transcendental beliefs of the faith and rejecting the paraphernalia of ecclesiastical traditions and the sacred creed of the Church as inventions through which the monks kept in subjection the minds of men, he concluded with the statement of a principle concerning the existence of a divine essence derived from a simplified view of pantheistic deism.[39]

There is clear evidence in Pamplekis's text that he had read the parody of the clergy and religion by "Anonymous of 1789": he used precisely the same satirical characterization as the earlier source in describing the bishops of the Church.[40] The two texts stand together as the only cases in which the Enlightenment, caught in the tension of sharp ideological polemics, went beyond anticlericalism and the prudent and circumscribed deism implicit in pleas, such as those of Moisiodax, for a purified and rationalized religion to an explicit denial of the truth of Orthodox religious faith. Christodoulos died a few days before the hasty publication of his tract. The controversy around his person, however, did not end with his passing. In November 1793, both Christodoulos and his text were anathematized by the Church. His enemies remained busy in vilifying him and very often misrepresenting his views in their polemics.[41] The anathema by the Church was never rescinded. His Greek students at Leipzig, however, erected a monument in his memory in a local public garden as a tribute to a man who had "dedicated his life to philosophical study and to the consideration of the nature of things," according to the inscription of his disciples.[42] It was a symbolically eloquent gesture: it made plain that the Enlightenment could not be exorcised by ecclesiastical anathemas, persecution, and personal libels. None of these could curb the commitment and courage of the partisans of the new philosophy and the force of their convictions, which drove them to such dramatic acts of public defiance of traditional authority.

With the crystallization of ideological conflict between the proponents and opponents of the Enlightenment, the Church, as the self-conscious defender of traditional order and values, assumed a militant position that provoked the outraged criticism of the enlightened intelligentsia. The espousal of the cause of Counterenlightenment by the Church as an official policy, combined with the widespread incidence of corruption in the ranks of the hierarchy and of the monastic orders, provided all the arguments that the partisans of philosophy and liberty needed in their ideological crusade. During the first two decades of the nineteenth century, while the Enlightenment seemed to be reaching maturity and self-confidence, anticlericalism provided the essential content of the claims advanced on behalf of cultural renewal and national revival. This was clearly expressed in concrete cases of ideological conflict, which were usually precipitated by the ongoing struggle over the content of education. Both sides knew that control over the educational system and over the socialization of the younger generations was going to be the decisive determinant of the outcome of the conflict. In the absence of formal structures of organized political life, the educational system and the contest over the nature of its institutions and curriculum became the primary battleground on which the conflict was fought out.

The major centers of education and culture in the Greek world witnessed acute ideological polarization and conflict produced by attempts at educational innovation. One of the sharpest confrontations unfolded in Smyrna, where a venerable and deeply entrenched tradition of religious and grammatical learning was faced with the sudden challenge of a highly successful project in enlightened education. The ideological battle that ensued was registered in a remarkable text that placed the efforts of the Church to suppress the attempt at cultural innovation in the broader context of clerical corruption and poignantly analyzed the motives behind the struggle. The vehemence and the quite libertine language of the attack were probably the major factors that caused the text to remain unpublished, as well as the anonymity of its author. This source ranks with Christodoulos Pamplekis's *Of Theocracy* and the *Hellenic Nomarchy* as the most eloquent indictment of the attitude of the Church to the Enlightenment.[43]

The anonymous author, having by way of preface proclaimed his firm devotion to the truths of Orthodoxy, went on to express his sorrow at the decay and corruption to be found in the ranks of the ecclesiastical hierarchy. The behavior of the bishops toward the flock that had been entrusted to their spiritual care by the Church was not, according to the author, fitting to the successors of the Apostles. Each chapter of the work describes a particular phase of this unbefitting episcopal behavior. The process began with the appointment of the bishop, usually as a result of simony and the obsequious flattery of powerful secular officials among the unbelievers who ruled over the Christian people. The newly appointed prelate then proceeded to resort to all kinds of artifice and coercion in order to exploit his flock as effectively as possible. To this end, according to the author, the bishop exploited to the extreme the hypnotic effect of religion on the minds of ordinary people. The entire process culminated in the prelate abandoning his see to the looting of greedy *locum-tenentes* and exarchs, and returning to Constantinople, he established himself in a mansion overlooking the Bosporus, where he delivered himself wholeheartedly to a life of voluptuous pleasure. This description leads to the conclusion set out in the following chapter, in which "the prelates are censured as enemies of the people."[44]

In his indictment of the clergy, the anonymous patriot inveighs against clerics for collaborating with the Ottoman tyrant,[45] comments on their ignorance and their hostility to learning and education, and insists that their complete indifference to their pastoral duties is responsible not only for the spread of superstition, but also for the success of Roman Catholic propaganda among Orthodox Christians.

The details of his account demonstrate the author's familiarity with social conditions in Western Asia Minor, which, at the time of writing of his text, had evolved into one of the most important centers of the Greek Enlightenment. In order to document his criticism, the author refers to the persecution by fanatical traditionalists of distinguished intellectual figures at centers of education such as the new Patriarchal Academy at Xirokini [Kureçesme] in Constantinople, the Academy at Kydonies, and the Philological Gymnasium in Smyrna; he is presumably alluding here to the experiences of two enlightened scholars, Dorotheos Proios and Benjamin of Lesbos, and he explicitly names the director of the Gymnasium in Smyrna, Constantinos Koumas.[46]

The ideological conflicts in Smyrna that erupted on the founding of the Philological Gymnasium in 1809–1810 form the main episode and culmination of the narrative. The author records several details that make his work an important historical source and allow the reader to infer that his testimony was the result of personal involvement in the events.[47] He maintains that the higher ranks of the clergy in Smyrna incited the rabble of the city against the scholars of the Enlightenment, out of a fear that their teaching might open the eyes of the ordinary people. The text is particularly eloquent on this point:

> The prelates hate the light of philosophy as those suffering from ophthalmia hate the sun or as thieves the lamp. Prelates would have the Greek youth unlearned and uneducated, so that they will bend their necks like unreasoning animals to the yoke of deception. They would have Christians uneducated, so that they will take as articles of faith the inventions of superstition, which the Church of Christ dismisses as heresies. The Priests of our people hate enlightenment because it is a threat to their illegal incomes and unjust rights. They hate the enlightenment of the people because it is a double-edged knife, which will one day cut off the heads of the many-headed Hydra, by which I mean superstition . . . .
>
> The Saints [are embarrassed] when they see scientific and philological works issuing into the light of day. . . . teach us, I say to thee father, not how to [reject] the world, but how to live well in the world, not the misanthropy of Timon, but the philanthropy of Socrates, not hallucinations but morals . . . not things that are above and beyond men, but things that are beneficial to men, and the duties of civil society.[48]

It is obvious, on the basis of this textual evidence, that the author's attitude to religion presupposes a critique more fundamental than the mere condemnation of corruption and superstition in the bosom of the Church. The very nature of religion as a social institution is called into question. This becomes evident from his comments on the influence exercised by religious sentiments and ritual on the minds of ordinary people, made in the context of the enthronement of a new bishop: "the simple people listen with mouths wide open, and as they turn their eyes on this gold-bedecked statue, they imagine they are looking at god himself."[49]

The momentum and intensity of the ideological conflict raging at the time can explain both the vehemence of the language and the occasional excesses of the arguments of this text. A historical criticism of the text would naturally point to the existence of a significant tradition of sacred and classical learning that flourished in the Orthodox Church as well as to the leading role of the hierarchy in the educational endeavors in the subjugated Orthodox community. The text, despite all the counterarguments that could be advanced in criticism of the position of its author, was a quite important register of a certain ideological climate and of a state of consciousness at a critical point of social and cultural change in Greek society. As such, it dramatically recorded the militancy that was expressed mainly in the form of opposition to the Church, as the social and intellectual structure that was perceived as the major rival of the new system of values.[50]

One important theoretical issue should be briefly considered, however, in connection with the religious criticism, which represented the sharpest expression of the Enlightenment's critical temper. The basic question that has to be resolved is the following: was the anticlericalism of the Enlightenment simply an attack on clerical corruption, a critique, however vehement, of the moral failures of ecclesiastical leadership, motivated by genuine belief in the spiritual and ethical requirements of the faith as most of the religious critics insisted, or did the attack on the Church in fact involve the espousal of an essentially deist attitude on the part of the critics and even lead them to a critique of the fundamentals of the faith itself? The answers to these questions are complex, especially in view of the obvious tension between the professed intentions and protestations of religious orthodoxy on the part of certain authors and the basically antireligious import of their arguments.

This is the case with the *Hellenic Nomarchy* and the *Indictment of Prelates*. The authors' protestations of genuine belief in evangelical truth and Orthodoxy cannot disguise their basically deist religious preferences, reflected in their taste for a simplified and rationalized religion. In this regard it would be fair to suggest that the protestations of Orthodoxy were primarily dictated by tactical considerations concerning the credibility and appeal of the overall argument, which addressed itself to an audience that had not yet been emancipated from religious belief. Recalling earlier analyses of religious criticism, one might say that the anticlericalism of *Novel Geography* and the antagonism that Moisiodax spelled out between educational progress and the requirements of religion were early manifestations of this intellectual position. Korais's religious position could be largely understood in similar terms, as we shall see in the following chapter. In all of these cases, anticlericalism was an integral part of the theoretical attitude that was shaped by the recovery of civic humanism in Greek thought. Criticism of the moral and civic failures of the Christian Church was the concrete expression of the interpretation of the problems of Greek society in the light of the social theory of European radicalism.

In more extreme cases like those of Pamplekis and the "Anonymous of 1789," things are more clear-cut: their religious criticism went well beyond deism to a questioning, refutation, and even subjection to ridicule of basic dogmas and mysteries of the faith—a position that amounted essentially to a rejection of religious belief. Some turns of the argument in the *Indictment of Prelates,* especially the suggestion about the hypnotizing power of religion on the masses—which almost hints at the simile of the "opium of the people"—can be taken as an indication that this text as well belonged to the current of anticlericalism that developed into a critique of the faith itself.

These, however, were marginal cases that represented exceptionally radical and atypical religious views. On the whole, the Greek Enlightenment was not in principle anti-Christian. Anticlericalism was the inevitable product of corruption in the ranks of the Church, but an intrinsic critique of the faith remained beyond the purpose of the great majority of the representatives of the Greek Enlightenment. If the criticism and denunciation of clerical corruption essentially undermined the faith by putting to question the integrity of religion as an organic system of belief and behavior, this was a largely unanticipated consequence of religious criticism. This, however, has been a universal characteristic of the process and experience of secularization. In its general religious attitude, the Greek Enlightenment, like the German Enlightenment and similar movements in the European periphery, called for a purification of the faith and the rectification of the morals of its ministers whose services it wanted to enlist in the general effort of social reconstruction.

The issue of religious criticism in the Greek Enlightenment, therefore, can be clarified in terms of a basic typology of diverse theoretical attitudes. Besides the traditional Christian criticism of bad priests, which was by no means peculiar to the Enlightenment, the new philosophy gave rise to two approaches to the problem of the Church. One was that associated with the anticlericalism of civic humanism, which in most cases attempted to retain the basic elements of Christian doctrine and stressed that all it called for was a purification of the Church and a recovery of genuine evangelical faith. This, of course, amounted to a Protestant attitude, despite the professions of strict Orthodoxy by its exponents, some of whom, like Moisiodax and the authors of *Novel Geography,* were ordained clergymen. The second approach was that represented by the more outspoken critics of

religion whose original attitude was informed by the basic tenets of European deism. Under the pressure of ideological confrontation, however, they
moved toward an intrinsic critique and rejection of the fundamentals of
religious faith—something that the representatives of civic anticlericalism,
conscious of the exigencies of political strategy and maybe theoretically
uncertain about religion in their own minds, were careful to avoid.

CHAPTER NINE

The Republican Synthesis

A Matrix for Nationalism

SOCIAL CRITICISM PREPARED the ground for positive theoretical reflection. The old society was shown to be corrupt beyond repair and existing morality to have utterly decayed. Radical social criticism invited constructive political theory to take over. The Enlightenment's response to this challenge involved the creative interplay of criticism and utopia. Once again that eloquent critic of the pretensions of the Enlightenment, Jean Jacques Rousseau, offers the most profound commentary on the problem. His yearning for Sparta and for the Age of Gold[1] was not an escape from society but an indictment of its corruption. The elaboration of the utopian vision provided the standard of judgment and criticism of actual conditions and projected the models of how things might be. The classicist republicanism of the Enlightenment, which enshrined civic virtue and the public ethos, was a comment not only on the fierce egotism of masterless men but mainly on the corruption and depravity of despotism, the suffocating political reality of the age.

The republican solution was inspired by the reading of the classics in the context of the political requirements of the age. Faced with the devastating effects of despotic corruption, Montesquieu found in Machiavelli's republican project an inspiration for his own study of the sociological and moral conditions of a re-created political community. The Enlightenment's political alternative was thus inspired by the critical diagnosis of the problems and needs of a changing society, rather than from a supposed example of the decaying Italian republics.[2]

The republican vision was feasible in those parts of the world of the Enlightenment where social conditions had made the party of humanity a serious contestant in the ideological battle that dominated the politics of the age. In the areas on the periphery of the Enlightenment to the south and east of Europe, where traditional structures and mentalities remained formidable and appeared unshakable to prudent minds, the weight of actual conditions pointed toward a more down-to-earth approach. Where the espousal of the cause of the Enlightenment seemed like an eccentricity of foreign inspiration, a careful reading of the nature of things tempered the utopian vision into a reform program. This was the social meaning of the Enlightenment in Italy and in Spain.[3] Although the ideological premises of the Italian and Spanish exponents of the Enlightenment were identical with those of the party of humanity to the north and across the Atlantic, their critical reflections on the state of their societies directed the main thrust of their intellectual energies to the conception of programs of socioeconomic, administrative, and legal reform rather than to republican projects that remained a distant source of inspiration. Such was the shape taken by the yearning of radical reconstruction inspired by social criticism in the periphery of the world of the Enlightenment.

In the Greek case, the challenge of delineating the guidelines of political and moral reconstruction was taken by Adamantios Korais (1748–1833). His achievement consisted of the elaboration of a maturely thought-out republican synthesis as a resolution of the Greek problem, worked through in the successive phases of his political thought. His political vision was inspired by the ideals of republican classicism, but in his reflections he never lost sight of the exigencies of actual conditions, and he never failed to contemplate realistically the possibilities and relevance of social and cultural reform. A medical doctor by training, educated at the famous medical school of Montpellier, he was an accomplished scholar in a wide range of disciplines and left a monumental corpus of writings on medicine, theology, classical philology, linguistics, history, and political theory.[4]

Although in intellectual temper Korais was a liberal republican, in his practical politics he was a reformer with a shrewd sense of tactics and a realistic perception of concrete social needs. He often contemplated the philosophical problems of republican politics, but he never lapsed into rigid utopian projects that might compromise or endanger the concrete social and cultural reforms he proposed on the basis of a well-reasoned appreciation of the needs of Greek society. The dualism between his moderate theoretical republicanism and his practically minded reformism, which he considered as the safest path to political change, was reflected in his political writings.

Korais's republicanism was an instrument of moral and social reform, not a path to utopia. He had reached political maturity by observing the French Revolution unfold before his eyes in the 1790s in Paris, as we have seen in detail above. His espousal of the revolutionary cause and his liberal critique of what he saw as a new tyranny in the advent of the Terror, combined with his systematic study of the classics, formed the intellectual basis of his political thought. The Jacobins had discredited political classicism and had proved that ancient republicanism was not only irrelevant to modern problems, but also dangerous. Korais's liberal critique of Jacobin tyranny was a clear indication of his view concerning the futility of the attempt to revive ancient institutions. In his commentaries on the French Revolution in the 1790s, he anticipated many of Benjamin Constant's liberal arguments.[5]

The moral dilemmas that this might create for an adorer of Hellenic classicism like Korais were solved by his reading of Montesquieu, whose wisdom he never put to doubt. Montesquieu, combining the insights of Aristotle and Locke, had taught that a modern republican civic order, tempered by liberalism, could flourish if it embraced the principle of moderation. It was precisely this virtue that Korais made the basis of his republican synthesis. Since he entertained no illusions concerning the possibility of a revival of ancient institutions or practices, he simply put his hopes in a recovery of an attitude of civic rectitude, necessary to achieve social and political reform, through classical education and the pursuit of the golden mean in ethics. Republicanism was the instrument of this moral education. The objective was an accession to the politics of modern liberty that until then had been stifled by despotism.

Montesquieu was joined in Korais's admiration by Condorcet.[6] The intellectual affinity he felt with the last of the philosophes had a sentimental source in the impression made upon Korais's sense of fairness by the courage Condorcet had shown in criticizing the excesses of the Revolution. Beyond this emotional attachment, Korais's connection with Condorcet's philosophical legacy acquired substantive content through his ties with Condorcet's intellectual successors, the *Idéologues*. This ideological pressure group was influential in French intellectual circles under the Directoire and around the turn of the eighteenth and nineteenth centuries. The *Idéologues* had inherited their epistemology from Condillac and a conception of the human sciences and the theory of progress from Condorcet. In a very substantive sense, they were the last genuine epigones of the Enlightenment before the movement was transcended in nineteenth-century currents of thought.[7] Korais's social thought was shaped by the views of the *Idéologues* who dominated the social and intellectual milieu in which he moved during his long residence in Paris. Through his ties in *Idéologue* circles, Korais became involved with the *Societé des Observateurs de l'Homme,* the influential anthropological association of the first years of Napoleon's rule.[8] This scientific connection directed Korais's reflections to the problems of culture, language, and civilization as historical phenomena related to the evolution of human society. The contemplation of these issues provided the foundation of his social theory.

THE LOGIC OF THE ENLIGHTENMENT

Korais grounded his social theory on a consideration of the logic of Enlightenment. The theoretical questions to which he had to frame an answer, before considering the concrete political and social problems that preoccupied him, could be stated thus: how is the Enlightenment possible? What are the sociological conditions of an enlightened, ethically regenerated community? These issues were raised and explored by Korais in his *Mémoire sur l'état actuel de la civilisation dans la Grèce,* which he read at a meeting of the *Societé des Observateurs de l'Homme* on 6 January 1803.[9] The *Mémoire* was Korais's "Esquisse on the Progress of the Greek Mind." It represented, nevertheless, a much more realistic and sociologically oriented analysis of the prospects of Enlightenment than Condorcet's essay, which had inspired it. If Condorcet, in drawing his panorama of the strides of reason in human history, had occasionally lapsed into a schematized caricature of the Enlightenment,[10] Korais's reflections on the possibilities of enlightenment in a concrete social context derived from a realistic theory of cultural change and moral reform.

The first historical relation that Korais discussed was the struggle of civilization and barbarism in the evolution of humanity. This relation, however, was not posed in terms of an empty abstraction, but it was derived by showing the historical origins of barbarism. For this purpose, the republican theory of history was evoked in order to trace and illuminate the degeneration and corruption of the Greek people from the cultural splendor of classical Greece to the depravity of modern times. The misery, oppression, and slavery that composed the condition of the modern Greeks before the beginnings of the Enlightenment in the mid-eighteenth century were thus shown to be the products of the revolutions of history, not a predicament intrinsic to the character of the people as some foreign slanderers had insinuated.[11] Furthermore, Korais was careful to demonstrate that barbarism worked through specific social structures: its nefarious effects became felt through the conduct of an ignorant clergy, of social notables who acted as the valets of alien despotism, and a superstitious people sighing under the most horrid exploitation and oppression.[12] Such were the social conditions of barbarism against which the battle of Enlightenment had to be waged. It was against this background that Korais reconstructed the social dynamics of civilization.

In Korais's judgment, the first factor conducive to social and cultural change in Greece was, of course, the influences emanating from the European Enlightenment, especially from that mainspring of civilization, France. Thus, the signs of cultural revival in Southeastern Europe were presented not as isolated phenomena but as the local manifestations of a truly transnational tide of civilization rising throughout Europe. The decisive local dynamic, however, was offered by the economic forces at work in the basis of society. It was economic exchange and commerce more than anything else that provided the infrastructure of social change. The transition from the subsistence economic activities of traditional society to commercial exchange proved the decisive factor that set the train of change in motion. A new commercial class was added to the fabric of society and provided the initiative and leadership for new pursuits. Commercial success and the exigencies of business transactions opened the eyes of the new class to the social benefit of modern education, to the necessity of studying the national vernacular and foreign languages, and of becoming familiar with the ways and learning of the civilized nations. These new orientations helped in gradually opening up the closed traditional society and became so many channels for the transmission of new ideas. Thus Korais managed to reconstruct step by step all the links in the causal chain through which economic change affected cultural life. His sense of the social dynamics of civilization was not in the least mechanistic, but viewed society as an integral universe.[13]

Commercial development had one important consequence, which was to prove of critical significance for the future of Greek culture and freedom. This was the expansion of navigation through the construction of a merchant marine. Technological innovation in the means of economic activity was thus included by Korais in his theory of social change. In addition, he pointed to another dimension of expanded navigation: It spread the network of contacts and communication with enlightened cultures. Navigation offered still another concrete infrastructure to Enlightenment. Besides this cultural effect of navigation, the presence of a merchant marine, composed of numerous ships armored against piracy and manned by experienced crews, provided the enslaved Greeks with their first weapon in a future struggle for freedom. These remarks proved quite prescient in view of the fact that the Greek merchant marine carried later on a major burden in fighting the war of Greek independence. Korais added a sardonic comment here, emphasizing the blindness and self-destructiveness of despotism: the Ottoman Porte might have sunk the Greek merchant marine rather than tolerate it for reasons of short-run economic gain, if it could calculate its real significance.[14]

The progress of commerce and navigation brought a veritable renaissance to the islands of the Greek Archipelago. Among them Korais singled out in particular Hydra and Chios. The rocky and barren island of Hydra had become the basis of the most important Greek commercial fleet. This development brought wealth, social prosperity, and cultural progress to the formerly poor island, whose great achievements in navigation were in fact a harbinger of Greek freedom. Chios, the island off the coast of Asia Minor where Korais's own family originated, had witnessed a veritable miracle of cultural achievements emerge out of the commercial progress of her inhabitants. Korais proudly announced that Chios had become the hearth of Greek culture and a model of republican self-government. The public spirit of her inhabitants allowed them to fend off the intrusions of despotism and enjoy the benefits of social harmony and prosperity amid a flourishing culture.[15] In his analysis of this process of social change, Korais offered an empirical application of Montesquieu's theory of the relation of commerce to liberty and showed concretely how economic change in the guise of commercial expansion can undermine the foundations of despotism and prepare the advent of a modern liberal republic.[16]

Two cardinal historical events proved the decisive immediate causes that heightened the pace of these processes and stirred the ferment that agitated Greek society and Greek minds at the close of the eighteenth century. The first of these events was the Russian victory over the Ottomans in the war of 1768–1774. It dramatized the weakness of the formerly formidable empire of the Ottomans that had overawed the powers of Europe in the past. The Russian interventions in the East demonstrated to the Greeks that their savage masters could be vanquished and thus made them aware of the possibility of freedom. The other dramatic event that intensified the tremors of change in the East was the French Revolution. The great victories of the French nation, in conquering their political freedom domestically and spreading the principles of their Revolution throughout the rest of Europe, showed the necessity of Enlightenment for any people striving for similar goals.[17]

It was under the pressure of such events and processes that a ferment of enlightenment had been precipitated in Greek society. What Korais perceived unfolding was indeed a moral revolution. Enlightenment began at the moment the nation took consciousness of the depravity of its predicament—a consciousness that stimulated the search for remedies. Korais sought to account for this phenomenon in terms of his medical training, declaring that love of learning became an epidemic that infected everyone. The signs of a recovery of civilization in the Greek lands were multiple— the foundation of new schools, the cultivation of the Greek language, the publication of useful secular books, the translation of major philosophic and scientific texts of the Enlightenment, and the massive migration of students to European institutions of higher learning. The most heartening sign of all, however, was the return of educated scholars from Europe to the bosom of their homeland where they sought to put their lights to the common advantage. Even among the apostles of darkness and superstition, the clergy, one could find some enlightened men who showed receptivity to the requirements and aspirations of the new moral revolution.[18] Civilization had reappeared in its ancient abode, and Korais, deeply moved and

proud, attempted to explain in terms of the social thought of the Enlightenment the miracle that was about to replace the misery and darkness of
a few decades earlier with the signs of hope and progress. The moral and
political product of this recovery of civilization was clearly stated by Korais:
the enslaved and oppressed people were preparing to become a nation.[19]
The destitute collectivity that sustained the effects of despotic oppression
was on its way to becoming an ethical community of autonomous citizens.
This was the deeper meaning of the moral revolution described by Korais.
It was the yearning for this ethical community that had stirred the agitation experienced by Greek minds. The omens of the times were good: the
heroic resistance of the Souliots against despotism suggested that the moral
community of the nation was being re-created through a recovery of the
patriotic ethic of the Ancients.[20] Freed from the fatalism and deception bred
by the expectation of foreign assistance, the modern Greeks relied primarily
on their own strivings in their effort for civilization and liberty. They thus
proved by their own deeds that they were the true descendants and successors of the heroes of classical Hellas. Korais could conclude his report on the
condition of civilization in Greece with a feeling that he had been faithful
both to truth and to the honor of his homeland.[21]

In the *Mémoire* Korais showed himself to be an accomplished *Idéologue.*
The philosophy that underlay his essay combined the very successful application of their analytical method to a case study in cultural anthropology with the early aspirations of the new science of comparative ethnology.
Korais's competence in medical, philological, and historical studies represented the unity of learning required by the philosophy of Ideology: all
branches of knowledge followed the same analytical method and therefore
shared an identical basic logic.[22] Korais's espousal of the analytical method
of Ideology transpired both in the linguistic preoccupations of his philology (analyzing texts by studying words, their constitutive element) and in
his approach to history typified by the *Mémoire:* although his focus was on
the totality of a set of human phenomena that he described with the term
civilization, he attempted to present his subject by analyzing the dynamics
of the more partial phenomena that formed its constitutive parts.[23] The
Ideology had clearly inherited the Enlightenment's view of historiography
as history of culture and attempted to put it to practice by applying the
analytical method, which demonstrated the workings and interaction of the
components of a civilization.

By analyzing the processes through which civilization was reconstructed in Greece, Korais responded to still another theoretical requirement of Ideology: he made his contribution to the effort to retrace a genealogy of human knowledge through the insights of the comparative method. The description of the rise of the modern Greeks from barbarism and backwardness to civilization could illuminate some of the central theoretical concerns of the genetic study of civilization by the anthropology of the *Idéologues*. It was a comparative case history that presented important evidence on such topics as the origin and generation of social ideas, the formation and progress of language, the development of culture, and the interdependence between the material and moral components in the life of a people.[24] Korais's paper so successfully applied the theory of Ideology to his Greek case study that his presentation had a noteworthy impact on the research orientations of the *Societé des Observateurs de l'Homme* which, under the impression of Korais's account of the strivings of the Greek nation, was attracted to the philhellenic movement of the time.[25]

THE DIALECTIC OF CULTURE AND FREEDOM

Korais's investigation of the reemergence of civilization in modern Greece was in fact motivated by his desire to survey the origins of an incipient movement of national liberation. Political emancipation, however, could not be seriously contemplated before an infrastructure of freedom had been created by cultural reconstruction. Korais knew that very well. The philosophy of civilization provided the basis of a theory of the interaction between culture and freedom that formed the essence of Korais's view of the Greek problem. Despotism was the primary and overwhelming enemy, and political liberty and national independence were the deeply cherished goals, but the road to freedom had to pass first through the conquest of ignorance and the destruction of the kingdom of darkness. In Korais's fully politicized thought, the conception of the Greek problem as an issue of cultural renewal entertained by earlier exponents of the Enlightenment, such as Voulgaris and Moisiodax, was explicitly endowed with its appropriate political meaning. Cultural renewal was a goal valid in itself, but only an intermediate one. Its deeper significance derived from the fact that it was an absolutely necessary condition to political freedom. In assuming this theoretical posture, Korais showed that he was fully conscious of the political meaning of the Enlightenment. Cultural renewal and enlightenment were conceived as parts of a long-term political strategy that comprised political freedom and national sovereignty as its ultimate if distant goals.

Before explicitly political and hence subversive goals could be realistically contemplated and pursued, Korais insisted, the nation should attain maturity through appropriate cultural preparation. In this view also, he did not diverge from the tenets of the *Idéologues*, who held that the cultural and political condition of a society ran in close parallelism and had to conform with each other.[26] Education should spread as widely as possible among the modern Greeks, who should by this means familiarize themselves thoroughly with the culture of the Enlightenment and with the classics of their ancient heritage. Korais felt it as one of his primary obligations to the cause of Greek regeneration to provide his compatriots with editions of the Greek classics that would help revive among the Moderns the wisdom and virtue of the Ancients.

He himself had come to the study of the classics and to systematic philological research through his studies on the history of Greek medicine. That initial pursuit, in which he became involved during his years in the medical school of the University of Montpellier, was the combined product of a modern Greek's sensitivity to the intellectual heritage of the ancient ancestors of his nation and of the Hippocratic revival in late eighteenth-century medicine that was an integral part of the intellectual universe of the Enlightenment, and of the *Ideology* in particular.[27] Out of this research emerged Korais's monumental edition of Hippocrates, *Of Airs, Waters, Places,* which established the modern Greek editor's reputation as a classical scholar.[28] Contemplating the needs of his nation in terms of his theory of the dialectic of culture and freedom, Korais decided to put his expertise as a classicist and a philologist to the production of a series of editions of classical texts that would fill the needs of modern Greek education and culture in classical scholarship and in edifying political and ethical instruction. It was in this spirit that he initiated with the economic assistance of the wealthy Greek merchants the six Zosima brothers, a series of classical texts that were to compose a *Hellenic Library.*

Korais's *Hellenic Library* was initiated in Paris in 1805 with the publication of a volume entitled *Precursor to the Hellenic Library,* which comprised texts in ancient history by Claudius Aelian and other minor historians and was introduced by a prefatory essay that outlined the objectives of the project and the editor's cultural theories. Subsequently, sixteen volumes of classical authors were published between 1807 and 1826; these included Isocrates in two volumes, Plutarch in six volumes, Strabo in four, Aristotle in two, Xenophon's *Memorabilia* and Plato's *Gorgias* in one, and the orator Lycurgus in one. In addition, nine volumes, entitled *Parerga of the Hellenic Library*, were published between 1809 and 1827; these included Polyaenus, Aesop, Marcus Aurelius, Onesandrus and Tyrtaeus, Plutarch, Epictetus, and Arrian. Besides the classical authors he included in the *Hellenic Library* and the *Parerga*, Korais edited independently texts by Hippocrates, Theophrastus, Heliodorus, and Hierocles, as well as Homer's *Iliad*.[29] This monumental corpus of work established Korais as one of the major classicists of his time. In the extensive prolegomena he included in each of these volumes, especially those in the *Hellenic Library*, Korais argued repeatedly the necessary relation between culture and freedom—an outlook that turned the concern for education into a national crusade.

In these essays, which he entitled "Improvised Reflections on Greek Culture and Language," notably in the prolegomena in the six volumes of Plutarch's *Parallel Lives* published between 1809–1814, Korais expounded his theory of the dialectic of culture and freedom. His arguments resumed the earlier themes put forward by the exponents of the Enlightenment against scholastic education and dry grammatical learning. Korais added to these battle cries of the Enlightenment the credibility of serious scholarship and the persuasiveness of moderation, which was dictated by his shrewd political sense. He pleaded for a decisive transition from sterile grammatical drilling to substantive education that would combine the ethical message of the classics with modern philosophy and science. The Renaissance of Europe had been achieved in this manner, he insisted, and the regeneration of Greece could be accomplished only by following the same method.[30] "Those are most useful to the nation today who burn rather than compose grammatical treatises,"[31] he exclaimed at a moment of exacerbation.

A central issue in his theory of cultural reconstruction was the language question, which became his major philological preoccupation. This emphasis derived both from the practical importance of language as the medium of education and enlightenment and from the theoretical attention paid to the issue of language in the epistemology of the Enlightenment and in the theory of Ideology. In this direction too, Korais managed to work out an integral synthesis that enabled the philosophic principles of his thought to bear on the practical problems that preoccupied his nation. Language reform was an integral part of the general effort at cultural regeneration of the nation. The archaic language of scholastic learning, as well as the artificial Attic Greek advocated by the patriarch of the Greek Enlightenment Evgenios Voulgaris, by making access to learning more difficult rather than easier, had sealed off the lights from the vast majority of potential Greek students and had fettered the progress of education. The language of education and learning, therefore, had to be simplified in order to be made accessible to all native speakers of modern Greek. At the same time a serious effort ought to be made through education and literature to purify the spoken language from the vulgarities of barbarisms and solecisms in order to demonstrate the linguistic continuity between ancient and modern Greek. The reestablishment of the linguistic purity of modern Greek would enable its speakers to approach ancient texts much more naturally and read them with greater facility as integral components of their intellectual patrimony. Thus language reform, far from being an issue of external forms and grammatical typicalities, touched on the very substance of the issue of moral education as a condition of national revival.[32]

Korais's solution to the language problem provoked strong reactions from many different directions. His plea for a simplification of the language, with its implication of a democratized enlightenment, precipitated strong reactions on the part of the archaists and the champions of the traditional order. The attacks on Korais by these two groups occasionally overlapped, though their ideological positions did not coincide. Archaists like Neophytos Doukas and Athanasios Stageiritis distanced themselves from the course followed by the Enlightenment largely because of their disagreement with Korais on the language question. In the first two decades of the nineteenth century the diverging views of the language question became the major focus of ideological conflict in pre-independence Greek politics. Korais's conservative enemies attacked him for adulterating the genuine traditions of the Greek language and culture and subjected to ridicule his linguistic usages and style. The real stake in the quarrel, however, became unmistakable when Korais was described by his major ideological critic, Panayiotis Kodrikas, as a Jacobin subverter of inherited tradition and of the established order and an enemy of true religion. Korais's theories were denounced as a peril for the nation. The quarrel over the language, Kodrikas insisted, was essentially about the fundamental traditions and customs of the nation, not about a few vulgar words of modern Greek.[33]

Korais came under attack for his linguistic views from the direction of what could be considered the ideological "Left" of the time as well. His attempt to purify the language and to reform the spoken vernacular, so as to make its affinities with ancient Greek apparent, displeased the radicals in Psalidas's circle in Ioannina.[34] During his lifetime, however, Korais had primarily to contend with the attacks of conservatives and traditionalists who had been scared by the French Revolution into an all-out attack on the Enlightenment. The misguided maltreatment of Korais by the Greek ideological Left, and especially by the proponents of the spoken demotic language in subsequent language quarrels in Greece, had to await the transformations of Greek political culture that followed the dissipation of the legacy of the Enlightenment in the nineteenth century. Such criticisms of Korais's linguistic views took his arguments out of their historical and political context and, therefore, distorted both the purpose and significance of his ideas on cultural change.

The energy and persistence with which Korais and his followers fought the battles of the language question were indicative of the importance they attributed to cultural reform as a condition of political change. If the substantive stakes had not been so high, the philological issues of the language question in themselves could not have generated the force with which the conflict was fought. Language acquired an inordinate importance as the medium of culture and education through which a new social morality was expected to be attained as the precondition of political change. Beyond the reform of language and education, Korais discussed repeatedly and at length the other practical components of the project of cultural change: the full utilization of the great advantages of printing, which, following Condorcet, he considered a major agent in the progress of the Enlightenment;[35] the establishment of new schools, libraries, and museums; the award of scholarships to deserving young men to study in Europe; the introduction of new curricula and teaching methods; the publication of useful secular books.[36] What this project of cultural reconstruction called for was a decisive break with tradition. Korais preferred to state his views in positive rather than negative terms. He outlined the projects of reconstruction and analyzed their requirements in practical and theoretical terms instead of attacking existing structures and potential obstacles. He had passed from criticism to synthesis.

He did not hesitate, however, when he deemed it necessary to take up the arms of criticism and to aim them at the usual targets of the Enlightenment, the obscurantism and corruption of a segment of the higher clergy, the darkness of Byzantinism in the past and of its survivals in the present, the sterility of traditional education.[37] His crusade against customary mythologies was directed also against the vestiges of the traditional political belief in the Russian expectation. He employed the arguments of logic and history in order to dispel any ill-conceived ideas that might still survive in Greek minds concerning the possibility of Russian aid to the Greek cause.[38]

By thus projecting the models of a new culture and a new society, Korais expected to contribute in laying the foundations of a process of change that would certainly be long term, but which would surely lead eventually to the maturity of the social and moral presuppositions that would make a decisive break with the past inevitable. In the *Mémoire* he had spoken of a moral revolution fermenting the minds of the modern Greeks. The distant product of that revolution would be a political one that would elevate the nation from the predicament of slavery to the moral community of freedom and independence.

THE ETHIC OF REVIVAL

Economic development in the form of commercial expansion, and its consequences in opening up the closed universe of traditional society, as well as cultural reform and its effects upon collective mentalities and modes of behavior, set the necessary structural and intellectual conditions for the radical transformation of society. But the actual task of social and political change that would generate the ethical community of an enlightened nation could only be the work of appropriately motivated moral personalities. The theory of civilization examined the context of ethical practice. Politics, however, involved a transition from contemplation to action. Korais's next priority was to spell out the ethical content of this transition and to articulate a social ethic pertinent to the needs of national revival. The republican ethos of the Enlightenment and its original source of inspiration in classical public morality provided the ingredients of his response.

The purpose of education in the classics that Korais advocated was to cultivate the republican ethos of public spirit, civic virtue, and dedication to the common good—an ethos that would inspire the descendants of the ancient Hellenes to strive for the liberation of their motherland. Characteristically, Korais first expounded his theory of the ethic of revival in the prolegomena he wrote for his Greek translation of Beccaria's treatise *Of Crimes and Punishments*. The celebrated text, which sought to humanize criminal procedure, was presented by Korais to educated Greek youth as an initiation to a future role that the motherland was bound to ask of them to perform: the task of legislation in a free society. Beccaria's discourse, which in the mainstream of the Enlightenment represented a manifesto of the theory of personal freedoms, was put by Korais to interesting new uses in order to promote collective civic purposes. Korais was clearly looking to the future, to a community of justice and virtue, a community that would educate its members in the duties of upright citizenship, obedience to the laws, and submission to the rule of reason.[39]

In developing this moral theory, Korais began from the typical republican problematic of history. He noted the evils that had accompanied the degeneration of the republics of ancient Hellas and the extremities that marked the recent political transformation of France. Enlightenment, the combined product of the wisdom of the Greeks' ancient ancestors and of the sciences of modern Europe, could alone rectify and avert such sorry situations.[40] The duty of the youth of Greece was to strive for the return of civilization to their homeland. The guiding example of their zeal ought to be the wisdom and glory of their ancestors. Classical virtues should unite the youth of the nation in a noble emulation in the service of civic causes and the common good. Their reward would be the public admiration and recognition of their strivings. Korais explained to his compatriots the nature of the moral choices that confronted them by reminding them of the dilemma that faced Heracles at the start of his career—as recounted by Prodicus in Xenophon's *Memorabilia*.[41] Korais felt that no less an arduous and self-abnegating choice was required of the sons of modern Greece in order to relieve her of the evils of despotism, darkness, and corruption.

Self-abnegation, a noble poverty, uprooting of individual passions, dedication to the cause of national enlightenment and moral regeneration, social harmony and concord in pursuit of shared goals, a burning concern for the common welfare—such ought to be the moral sentiments of worthy Greek souls. The classics were full of such ethical examples that ought to inspire the moral strivings of the modern Greeks. Korais searched the classical texts and projected before the conscience of his compatriots these moral models that he urged them to emulate—if they desired to recover the glory that was Greece. There could be no other way that might lead to freedom, short of a sincere espousal of the republican civic ethos by all those who cherished these goals. Korais had reached this position through the study of Rousseau's political philosophy, and he accordingly announced his intention at this time of translating the *Social Contract,* in which the Genevan philosopher examines the birth of political society.[42]

The turn to Rousseau gave his moral concerns a distinct political character. The moral reconstruction of human personalities and the concomitant ethical commitment led inevitably to a social revolution. The Greek problem had finally been recast in unequivocal political terms. The original conception that saw it as an issue of cultural renewal had been broadened to comprise the perspectives of ethical commitment and political activism as the preconditions of national revival.

Korais's synthesis represented the culmination of the intellectual process that led to a definition of Neohellenic consciousness in terms of a modern Greek historical connection with ancient Hellenism. The gradual consolidation of that link through several decades of historical writing had provided the intellectual basis to a novel self-definition of the modern Greeks. Korais's classicism broadened the historical knowledge of the Hellenic past in the direction of an in-depth acquaintance with the civilization and moral culture of the Ancients. This expanded awareness of the substance of the Hellenic heritage infused the newly articulated Neohellenic historical consciousness with a clearly political content. The civilization of ancient Hellas provided explicit paradigms of political life and community that could be, and were seen by modern Greek neoclassicism, as the models of how things might become in the case of the Ancients' modern progeny as well. Korais of course knew that the political epilogue of modern republicanism, the revolutionary radicalism of the Jacobins, had ended in tyranny rather than in freedom. His historical sense made him aware that classical republicanism could not be resurrected in modern times as an integral system of symbols and institutions. Classical republicanism was of relevance to the political needs of modern nations only as a guide for the public ethics of their citizens. Such was the use reserved for political classicism in the Greek revival by Adamantios Korais.[43]

Even in this ostensibly limited role, the Greek classics possessed a profoundly revolutionary potentiality. They set the symbolic framework of a collective self-conception that was new and decisively different from the traditional consciousness shared among Christian peoples regardless of ethnic identity. Self-conception in terms of the classical heritage meant that the modern Greeks became conscious of their distinct historical personality. Such consciousness provided the foundation of a modern national identity. Furthermore, the very republican symbolism that constituted the content of this national consciousness pointed at the institutional and structural context that might be most pertinent to the historical personality of the new nation. This context could not be specified otherwise except on the model of the Enlightenment's system of republican institutions. It did not necessarily have to conform to Rousseau's Sparta or to the Roman republic of virtue of the Jacobins, but it could certainly not be much different from the republican nations that would constitute Kant's international system of perpetual peace.[44] This was the only political order that the moral culture of republicanism could be expected to animate. Certainly this political vision was much different from the actual order of things in Greek society during the decay of Ottoman despotism. It was in the contrast between this alternative vision and the repulsiveness of actual conditions, which were becoming increasingly unacceptable to enlightened minds, that a revolutionary dynamic could be felt to be at work in the evolution of Greek thought.

THE SHAPE OF THE BODY POLITIC

Although Korais had reflected extensively on the social and moral preconditions of the recovery of Greek freedom, the precise shape that a liberated Greek polity should take became the object of his thinking only once the Greek War of Independence had broken out and posed the problem of institutional forms with great urgency. He had argued all along that although the overthrow of the yoke of Ottoman despotism ought to be the overriding aim that should inform and inspire more partial short-term objectives, the actual act of revolt had to wait until the necessary presuppositions for its success had been achieved. To his mind, the eventual Greek Revolution was not so much a question of military preparedness. In the *Mémoire* he had shown that the inner structure of despotism had decayed and that its force had been sapped by corruption. So according to his calculus of revival, the growing Greek navy and the valiant formations of Greek resistance could easily cope with the Ottoman military threat. What really preoccupied his mind was the outcome of the internal struggle that was to be waged among rival segments of the Greek society itself over the control of the liberated land.

On the eve of the Greek uprising, the split between the proponents and opponents of the Enlightenment as the guiding philosophy of Greek revival had developed into an irreconcilable ideological battle, and Korais knew that the victory of the former could only be assured if the social and cultural conditions of a liberal society, like those of the world of the enlightened West, had reached maturity in Greece as well. His apprenticeship in the philosophy of Ideology transpired at this point too. He viewed the universe of human phenomena as an integral totality in which forms of culture like language and the shape of political institutions were interdependent on each other and on the character of the social structure and the natural environment. It was essential to achieve the pertinent maturity in social and cultural conditions in order to secure the consolidation of a certain shape of political institutions. It was imperative for the Greeks to postpone their rising until the emergence of such conditions in Greece would secure with complete certainty the transition from despotism to the system of liberal republicanism visualized by the last generation of the Neohellenic Enlightenment. Inspired by Condorcet's theory of progress, Korais did not doubt that such a felicitous juncture of historical circumstances would come after a period of social change and cultural renewal. He estimated that several decades were required for the social conditions of a free republic to mature in Greece.[45] For precisely this reason, he had thrown all his energy into the effort of cultural revival and moral reconstruction that ought to precede the conquest of freedom. This tactic had been the main thrust of his social thought to the exclusion of explicitly political themes except on topical issues in the twenty years or so between the composition of the *Mémoire* and the outbreak of the Greek Revolution.

The tactical message that emerged from Korais's conception of the Greek problem was one of prudence and determination to await the auspicious moment for seizing the time. Things in Greece worked out otherwise. The Revolution was not started by the intelligentsia of the Enlightenment, but by peasants in Epirus and the Peloponnese driven to despair by the ravages of Ottoman troops. When the news reached Paris, however, the aging theoretician of the Greek revival, despite his earlier philosophical reservations about the advisability of an immediate revolution, felt his soul shaken by a great quake. Amid the convulsions of his soul and the tears of his emotion upon observing his compatriots seize the arms of vengeance and despair, Korais regretted that his advanced age and failing health did not allow him to rush to join the ranks of those fighting the tyrants.[46] In typical intellectual fashion instead, he conceived as his own vocation to prepare the fighting heroes for the new political condition of which the struggle for freedom was the historic prelude. The way to go about this new task led once again to the classics. Korais chose to present his views on the shape of the new polity by editing and commenting on Aristotle's *Politics* and *Nichomachean Ethics.* In his prolegomena to these editions, which came out in the first two years of the Greek struggle for freedom, he outlined in full his republican political theory.

The philosophical presuppositions of this political position had been explicitly elaborated by Korais in his ideological controversies with Panayiotis Kodrikas, the major critic of his cultural theories a few years earlier. In an anonymously published pamphlet entitled *Improvised Diatribe on the Notorious Doctrine of the Skeptics and Sophists Defining Good and Evil by Convention* (1819), Korais had attacked his ideological enemies for depriving moral notions and values of independent validity and reducing them to conventional practices. His conservative opponents had clearly put forward this argument to counter the criticism leveled against established social structures and moral codes by the new social theory of the Enlightenment, which relied on the authority of the absolute truths of natural philosophy. Korais turned his enemies' arguments against them, demonstrating that they were not only contrary to enlightened moral philosophy but also impious and destructive of the national community.[47]

Before turning to Korais's substantive arguments, it is important to notice one issue that surfaced in the debate and which clarifies his own conception of his philosophical position. His enemies had used his identification with the philosophy of Ideology as an occasion to apply to him the term *idéologue* as an abusive epithet denoting demagoguery and subversiveness. Ideology itself was identified by them with the philosophy of Spinoza. Korais defended the *Ideology* against these misrepresentations and pointed out that those who had first attacked it as a nebulous system of thought had been the flatterers of Napoleonic despotism. That first enemy of the *Ideology* himself might have avoided his own fall from the peak of power and glory to the depths of misfortune, had he tried to derive some lessons of legitimate government from it instead of calumniating against it. The adversaries of Ideology were simply obscurantists and enemies of the lights of progress.[48]

Following these preliminaries, Korais proceeded to a refutation of the doctrine that convention alone defines good and evil, right and wrong. Against this view he insisted that justice derives from the nature of things, from the natural order of the cosmos. In support of his arguments, he marshaled the testimony of classical wisdom and evangelical truth.[49] The major thrust of his reasoning was an argument for natural law, which was extended to form the basis of a republican theory. The starting point was the ancient Aristotelian conception of man as by nature a political animal. It followed that justice was that system of rules that was conducive to the existence of well-ordered, virtuous, and prosperous communities. Such was the intention of the law of nature. In concrete political terms this meant the foundation of human communities on equality, which alone could provide the social basis for the rule of law.[50] With this point adequately emphasized and supported by the authority of the Ancients and the Scriptures, Korais could feel that he had proven his case. In unfolding his argument against the reduction of justice to convention, he did not omit to reveal the sources of his inspiration in Montesquieu's wisdom.[51] The reading of the classics in the light of the social thought of the Enlightenment had provided the intellectual matrix of his political theory.

The philosophical position that Korais reached amid the ideological controversies of the immediate prerevolutionary years formed the intellectual background of his conception of a Neohellenic republic. In composing the prolegomena to Aristotle's *Politics,* Korais declared that the time had arrived to come to grips with the greatest of issues, the freedom of Greece. Original Greek freedom, which had flourished in the republics of classical Hellas, had been lost amid the dissension and strife between rich and poor vying for political power. This was the lesson of Aristotle. Social conflict was at the root of the cycle of corruption that destroyed classical republican liberty and led to the enslavement of Greece by a succession of tyrannical regimes, the last and most odious of which was Ottoman despotism. The end point of this cycle of corruption was marked by the Greeks' heroic struggle to regain their liberty. Korais's purpose was to teach to them the principles of political knowledge that would enable them to avoid the disasters brought upon them in earlier ages by ignorance and insufficient understanding of the nature of politics.[52]

The Greek problem had entered a definitely new phase. The immediate priority was no longer the preparation for and conquest of liberty. That had been achieved in the outburst of heroism that had thrown the Ottoman yoke off the Greek lands. The issue of greatest urgency had therefore become not the conquest but the safeguard and consolidation of liberty. This task was much more difficult because if the recovery of liberty required only valor and heroism, its preservation presupposed justice, prudence, and virtue.[53] Korais therefore felt that what the Greeks needed as their preparation for citizenship was a clear and precise knowledge of the meaning and content of the principles of enlightened politics. This political education was necessary in order to avoid conflicting interpretations and irreconcilable concepts—which could be easily bred by the moral relativism he combated in his *Diatribe against Skeptics.* By removing such occasions of ideological controversies, an important source of civil strife in the new republic would be neutralized.

Korais warned his compatriots that personal happiness in a political community could not be divorced from a consideration of the happiness of others. It followed that virtue was nothing else but care and concern for the public interest. The law, the commonly accepted system of public conventions of the city, was defined following Rousseau as the expression of the general will. In this context, freedom meant the individual's power to do everything that was allowed by the laws.[54] Freedom found its most positive and noble actualization in the respect of the laws and of the freedom of one's fellow citizens. This moral behavior gave substance to the reality of the community of free citizens. Not only theoretical knowledge of these principles, but also systematic civic education in their practice was requisite for the achievement of the community of free citizens. The republican citizen's life had to be a regimen of consistent training in the practice of moral freedom from childhood to old age. The moral upbringing of children in the virtues of citizenship was an essential precondition for the creation of a political community founded on justice and equality. Its citizens could be considered genuine lovers of freedom only if they strove for the freedom and prosperity of the motherland.[55]

The sociological nature of the regime that would make possible the operation of these moral principles would be akin to that of Aristotle's republican polity. It would be a political regime based on the middle classes of citizens, those virtuous and industrious classes that constituted the pillars of society and motherland. The legislators of the community should be selected from these classes, and the social objective of their legislation ought to be the achievement of a rough equality of properties among the citizens. This would provide the sociological basis to social harmony and communal solidarity. To avoid disruptions of the harmony of the community, special care ought to be taken to discourage and prevent the accumulation of great wealth in the hands of a few citizens. A mode of production based on an agricultural economy would provide the best inducement to civic virtue and the most effective safeguard to public liberty.[56]

It is interesting to contrast the premium put by Korais on agriculture as the safest economic basis of a republic with his earlier emphasis on commerce as an agent of social change, civilization, and liberty in the *Mémoire*. The tension that this contrast implies in his social thought could be interpreted in terms of a shift in the focus of his reflections generated by the changing political context of his theory. His preoccupation with the conditions and dynamics of social changes, which would bring about the collapse of despotism, in the earlier phase of his thought, gave way to concern for the sound foundation and stability of the new republic under the revolutionary circumstances of the Greek war of independence. This can explain his transition from a dynamic to a static political problematic, reflected in the contrast between commerce and agriculture as alternative economic bases for the republic.

In addition to the basic sociological conditions of a republican polity, Korais was aware that certain political measures were necessary for its smooth operation: the selection of public officials distinguished for their virtue and dedication to the public interest; universal military service that would train all citizens for service in a citizen militia to replace the plague of mercenary armies; finally, universal public education that would establish the foundations of an enlightened culture and cultivate a republican civic ethos.[57]

With these prescriptions for the new body politic, Korais entered the most radical phase of his political thought. To a considerable extent and, as it might appear, despite his earlier liberal critique of the excesses of the French Revolution, his vision of the new Greece was informed by the model of the republic of virtue. Radical republicanism became dominant in his thought once actual conditions moved forward to the point that gradual reform was no longer a relevant option, and the task of state building in its awesome entirety became the most immediate and pressing priority. Korais's rereading of the classics, in the light of the social thought of the Enlightenment, had made it possible to use Aristotle, the philosopher of the Scholastics, for revolutionary purposes. The language of Aristotle and the republican inspiration provided Korais with the armory for his program of social transformation. The new Greece that was to emerge from this transformation was to be a republic born of the Enlightenment, but at the same time it could claim direct ancestry from Hellas. The identity of modern Greece ought to be composed by these two main dimensions of past and present.

Korais was aware of the serious obstacles that the realization of his vision had to surmount. The serious consideration he paid to these obstacles, his awareness of the great historical and structural difficulties awaiting his program, saved his thought from utopianism and kept it within the domain of realistic social reflection. His preoccupation with concrete social problems came forward in his insistence on the need to regulate the role of the clergy in independent Greece. This preoccupation indicates not only the predispositions instilled in him by his radical republicanism, but also his fears as to who the enemies of the republican reconstruction of Greek society were going to be. He therefore insisted that particular care should be exercised in the selection of the clergy, in their education, and in the regulation of their activities in the context of the new independent state. Korais was the first to suggest that the Church of free Greece should be emancipated from the administrative control of the Patriarchate of Constantinople so long as the latter remained under the yoke of tyranny.[58] What Korais essentially suggested in his eight articles on the regulation of the Church was a civil constitution of the Church, turning it into an arm of the secular state, on the Protestant model.

Korais's commentary on the role of the Church in the new republic followed logically from his view of religion in an enlightened society. His enlightenment was not anti-Christian, and like Rousseau, he abhorred atheism as the agent of moral laxity. His criticism had earlier been directed at the deviations of certain members of the higher clergy from evangelical morality. Such moral deviations had allowed corruption to creep into the bosom of the Church and had turned it into an upholder of tyranny. Korais called for a recovery of the genuine spiritual mission of the clergy and a resurrection of the pure faith of the ancient Church as part of the wider program of the moral regeneration of the nation. Although he mercilessly attacked superstition, he never questioned the truth of Orthodox doctrine, and he was quite aware of both the power of religion and the influence of the Church as a source of consolation and hope and as an agent of moral authority and spiritual education among the masses of his people. It was entirely reasonable, therefore, to try to enlist the support of the Church in the crusade of Enlightenment. To this end, Korais never failed to distinguish between virtuous and corrupt prelates and to praise any enlightening initiatives he found among the higher clergy. His views on religion and the Church were expounded in a whole body of theological writings that sought to purify Orthodox faith from the increments of superstitious traditions and to remold religion in a way that would integrate it effectively into the set of cultural preconditions of political reform.[59]

Korais's insistence on the construction of the relevant social context of republican institutions reflected his apprehensions about modern politics. In his reflections on the subject, he lamented the loss of public man and the civic ethos, dramatized, as he felt it, in the divorce of politics from ethics in modern times. Public life in classical Hellas was marked by the unity of politics and ethics, which provided the foundation of freedom. The philosophy of Socrates, Plato, and Aristotle pointed to the model of the ethical community of free men who were united in their shared civic ethos and in their common purpose of rendering their services for the public good. Such behavior was freedom actualized. The ethos of free citizenship was cultivated through one's involvement in public service and the moral recognition that followed on the part of the community, not in the form of honorific distinctions but in the trust demonstrated in the assignment of public duties and responsibilities to the virtuous citizen through the vote of his fellow citizens. The loss of unity between public and private morality gave rise to tyranny that destroyed republican liberty in ancient Hellas. Unjust wars of aggression externally and the total war of all against all within society were the products of the total separation of ethics from politics.[60]

In the political sociology of modern Europe, the major obstacles to the reunification of morals and politics and the re-creation of the ethical community of republican liberty were posed by two disruptive and recalcitrant factions: the monks and the aristocrats. Both of these social formations enjoyed unfair material advantages and social privileges, which they stood to lose if they submitted to the requirements of an enlightened political community. Korais, who was quite familiar with the historical experience of both modern Europe and Greece, had every reason to feel apprehensive over the disruptions that might be caused by the two self-seeking, vain, and disorderly factions in their opposition to social reform.[61] As an *Idéologue* and intellectual scion of the Enlightenment, however, he did not despair. His faith in the theory of progress and his intellectual debt to Condorcet came forth in his hope that a future recovery of the unity of politics and morals was possible as a part of the triumph of reason over the passions—a triumph that would create the preconditions of a just society.[62] Korais quoted Condorcet's philosophic prophecy as a harbinger of hope, but in his usual practical good sense he also looked for a concrete method that might help in achieving the desirable goals. He discovered a political approach to the moral reform of society in the *Idéologues'* suggestion that through systematic education a people could be inculcated with virtue.[63]

It is clear from these reflections as to how political change might be achieved that Korais's republicanism did not have atavistic purposes. He was unequivocal on this point: in constituting their own new polity, the Greeks should look at the example of contemporary states founded on the principles of justice.[64] The inspiration of his thought might have been Periclean Athens, but the paradigm he projected before his compatriots was the greatest modern republic that had put the ideals of the Enlightenment into practice to the infinite fascination of all progressive minds at the beginning of the nineteenth century. The United States of America presented the most heartening evidence that a republic of free citizens, born of the Enlightenment, was a realistic project, a tangible hope. Korais therefore urged his compatriots to follow in everything the political system of the "Anglo-Americans"—a system, he insisted, that both the judgment of political philosophers and the even more convincing proof of experience had shown to be the most perfect and best ordered among all existing societies. In this appraisal too, Korais remained true to Condorcet's inspiration.[65] This faith can explain Korais's great interest in American politics and thought and the inclusion of the most distinguished among the Founding Fathers in the pantheon of wise men who should serve as points of reference in determining the course of Greek political affairs.[66] His admiration for the United States found an even more concrete expression in 1823, in his correspondence with Thomas Jefferson. The two men had met in Paris and, despite their limited contact, were connected by a web of intellectual ties through their shared interest in the classics and adherence to the philosophy of Ideology and Jefferson's active philhellenism.[67] In this famous correspondence, Korais sought Jefferson's assistance in promoting the Greek cause in the United States, but the occasion was used to exchange some views as to how to shape the institutions of the new Hellenic republic.[68]

Korais's appeal to Jefferson, besides its significance as an indication of the nature of his political thought, is an important pointer to the practical political activities in which the dean of the Greek Enlightenment was involved throughout his life. Promotion of the Greek cause in international philhellenic circles had been a central concern in Korais's life. To this end, he had made very effective use of his scholarly connections and the respect he enjoyed as an accomplished classicist in nurturing interest in the Greek revival and soliciting support for the Greek strivings for freedom. In addition to the projection of Greek rights and claims internationally, Korais tried actively to influence developments within Greek society as well. In the two decades before the Greek Revolution, his major practical effort was directed toward the encouragement of cultural reconstruction through the tangible support of schools and libraries, the printing and dissemination of relevant books (notably his series of editions of classical authors in the *Hellenic Library*), and the encouragement of the young to pursue the study of enlightened subjects. In support of this effort, Korais managed to mobilize a segment of the Greek commercial magnates of the diaspora on whose material assistance he depended for his most important cultural projects. Through his wide-ranging correspondence, which kept him in uninterrupted contact with developments in his homeland, Korais tendered his expert advice on a wide range of issues pertaining to the Greek revival and attempted to contribute substantively to the imperative of the edification of public ethics, which he saw as a prerequisite to the revival of the nation.

With the outbreak of the Revolution, Korais's involvement in practical politics continued with a unique energy for his advanced age. He full-heartedly championed the republican cause, and he used his enormous moral authority and experience in order to sustain the attempts of the revolutionaries to establish a system of republican institutions in the liberated lands. As it happened, with the gradual unfolding of his political thought that culminated in his republican theory, the cause of republican Greece was Korais's last practical commitment, which dominated the final decade of his life. His concern for the shape of the new body politic found expression in his *Notes on the Provisional Constitution of Greece,* a text in which he commented on a number of issues arising out of the republican charter voted by the first National Assembly of revolutionary Greece in January 1822.

Korais's constitutional commentary was a much less radical text in comparison with Rhigas's charter for a Hellenic republic. Korais, whose republican inspiration was combined with a liberal temper even at that most radical phase of his thought, concentrated on practical issues and attempted to indicate ways in which existing conditions could be remolded to approximate the shape of a liberal republic.[69] With his usual mature political sense, his perceptiveness, and his ability to identify the real issues, Korais discussed the concrete political problems that he felt might emerge in the process of an effort to construct a republic. He tried to anticipate the practical problems in legislation and institution-building that were bound to arise in such a monumental undertaking, and he made precise suggestions as to how to confront the historic challenge.

The major political preoccupation emerging out of the *Notes on the Provisional Constitution of Greece* is clearly the creation of an institutional context conducive to equality, as the necessary basis of the republic. Korais also voiced his opposition to that complete denial of republicanism, a monarchical form of government that, he soberly warned, was too expensive for war-torn Greece to maintain.[70] These major political concerns were carried over in the new prolegomena opening Korais's second edition of Beccaria, which he reissued to serve as the basis of the penal code of the new republic. In this essay Korais reiterated many of the themes of his republican theory, and he returned with ever-greater zeal to his caveats against what he described as the "leprosy of a hereditary aristocracy" and the adoption of monarchical institutions.[71] Montesquieu's indictment of court politics and their corrupting influence on society was quoted at length to strengthen Korais's argument.[72] The fears that gripped Korais's mind as the Greek Revolution wore on after the initial victories and early enthusiasm are obvious in these turns of his thinking. He knew that the fate of the Enlightenment was to be decided amid the turmoil of interlocking political currents, conflicting forces, and civil strife that punctuated the Greek Revolution. There could be no higher stake.

The dean of the Greek Enlightenment, however, might have felt some comfort when the Third National Assembly of revolutionary Greece, meeting at Troizen in April 1827, expressed in a special message of acknowledgments the respect and appreciation of the fighting nation for Korais's strivings on behalf of the enlightenment of his compatriots. The message stated that the nation, assembled in convention to deliberate about its highest interests, embraced the old sage's golden words and wise counsels, conversed with his books, and absorbed the enlightenment of his virtuous opinions.[73] It was the Enlightenment's finest hour. A nation fighting for its freedom reached self-consciousness by making the aspirations of the Enlightenment the matrix of its fate.

A necessary postscript should be added to this consideration of the assimilation and adaptation of the ideas of the Enlightenment by Korais in the context of the requirements of the Greek revival. His thought was stamped throughout by an obvious eclecticism, which selected, from the diverse strands and traditions of the philosophical universe of the Enlightenment and its epigones, those elements that could most effectively strengthen his arguments on the different aspects of the Greek problem. The foregoing pages illustrated the uses to which he put arguments drawn from classical Greek thought reinterpreted in terms of French eighteenth-century neoclassicism, from a rationalized Christianity that at times bordered on deism and was certainly closer to Protestantism than to Orthodoxy, and from the republican and liberal traditions of the Enlightenment. To all these, his occasional appeals to Benthamite liberal utilitarianism could be added.[74] A critique of his thought as philosophically incoherent would be unfair, however. Among the diverse influences on his thought, the tradition that ran from Montesquieu through Condorcet to the *Idéologues* was the dominant one, and it can account best for his political preference for liberal republicanism. The other theoretical threads in his thought were basically incorporated in the overall context set by this mainstream tradition. To the extent that he managed to weave all these intellectual threads together into a coherent system, one could talk of a theoretical synthesis in which the Greek Enlightenment culminated. Although certain philosophical tensions remained, the synthesis was meaningfully expressed in Korais's systematically thought-out conception and resolution of the Greek problem.

Politically, his synthesis involved a modification of the radical republicanism of the revolutionary strand of the Greek Enlightenment represented by Rhigas and the author of *Hellenic Nomarchy*. Korais's modified republicanism was still radically different from all versions of political paternalism visualized by the earlier theory of enlightened absolutism. Korais's ambition for the new Greece involved the achievement of a liberal polity endowed with civic virtue. The difficulties inherent both in the theory and practice of this model can best explain the strains in his thought—but, it might be added, they were difficulties worthy of a serious political theorist who wanted both to understand and change the world.

The solemn acclamation of Korais's ideas by the delegates of the Greek nation was a gesture of great symbolic significance. It dramatized the distance traveled by Greek collective consciousness in the century that had witnessed the unfolding of the Enlightenment. The leadership of revolutionary Greece appeared to assume a political and ideological position that involved a complete transcendence of the political theory that a century earlier represented the crystallization of the political consciousness of the first Phanariots. Under the impact of the new ideas that came from enlightened Europe, the modern Greeks came to conceive of themselves as a distinct nation whose self-definition was based primarily on a historical connection with ancient Hellenism. The cultural collectivity delineated by this historical identity was in the process of becoming an ethical community of free and equal citizens: that is, a modern nation.

The awakening of national consciousness had come as the result of the growth of a movement of Enlightenment. This intellectual process was essentially an itinerary toward a new mode of collective consciousness, a modern sense of national identity. The new identity found expression in the yearnings for cultural change, in the hatred of despotism, in the criticism of existing social structures and belief systems, and finally in the vision of freedom that projected a different society in which the novel self-conception could flourish. The determination of those Greeks who shared the new sense of identity to assert it dynamically was demonstrated by their participation in the Revolution and by the role of protagonists they assumed in one particular aspect of the whole endeavor: the creation of the new political institutions of the nation rising to statehood and freedom from that supreme struggle.

The conception of the nation that inspired their efforts was that galvanized by the French Revolution, which had set it up as an alternative source of legitimacy against the legitimacy of traditional kingship. The ideology of the nation as the community of free and equal citizens thus dispelled traditional mythologies of dynastic rights and enshrined in their place the inalienable rights of the individual. It is hardly necessary to belabor the point of the revolutionary impact of such new conceptions in the context of corporate social structures sanctioned by traditional mentalities. Nationalism emerged as a new cultural system capable of arresting the psychic strain and symbolic confusion created by the disintegration of the old ideology. In the face of this, nationalism could render otherwise incomprehensible social situations meaningful and make it possible to act purposefully within them. In short, it could provide those "maps of problematic social reality and matrices for the creation of collective conscience"[75] that were urgently needed by a changing society groping for a new order of things.

Korais's republican theory responded to precisely such needs. His political theory marked the culmination of the process of ideological change that channeled the ideas of the Enlightenment into Greek culture. Indeed, it represented the final denial and transcendence of an earlier conceptual synthesis that has been identified as the political theory against which the process of ideological change had evolved. A distinctly Hellenic national conscience had thus dislocated the shared consciousness of the Christian people that the Romans of the East had inherited from Byzantium. A republican conception of the political community was projected against the hierarchical paternalism of Christian monarchy. A modern secular culture, based on a recovery of classical humanism, was projected as a substitute for traditional religion in the definition of social morality and as the conceptual framework of self-awareness.

The new democratic nationalism, born of the cosmopolitanism of the Enlightenment that Korais so much cherished, thus became the intellectual matrix for the evaluation of the past, the criticism of the present, and the conception of the future of the resurrected Greek nation. Korais had helped give final political expression to the gropings of a century of social change and cultural innovation. In a very real sense he was the founding father of the new nation.

His political theory had not simply transcended conventional ideology, but it also effectively connected Greek thought with the most forward-looking orientations of European social thought that had sprung from the dialectic of the Enlightenment. Such was felt to be Korais's legacy by the most progressive of his followers. One of them, Frangiskos Pylarinos, in a funeral oration on Korais's graveside on 8 April 1833, characterized his contribution in these terms:

> As a profound critic and erudite classicist you attempted with all available literary means to spread in the bosom of your homeland the philosophical mission of the nineteenth century, that is the promotion of FREEDOM, EQUALITY and SOCIALISM . . . You spoke and wrote the language of Washington, Jefferson and Lafayette, who are the genuine representatives of human perfection . . . As far as Greece was concerned you have been a revolutionary in religion, philosophy and politics . . . You strove to uproot the powerful supports of tyranny . . . You attempted to introduce in the motherland the blessings for which humanity has struggled in the last three centuries: the liberty of conscience, the independence of thinking, the freedom of the general will in the government of society . . . living in the most democratic of centuries, you had to proclaim the fecund and most ethical principle, the principle of NATIONAL SOVEREIGNTY, the democratic system of our time, genuine national representation which is nothing else but justice expressed as political equality . . . You introduced, in short, in our common homeland all the progressive seeds of true politics and you proved the superiority and morality of the political principles of Washington's land . . . You proved that all free nations are obliged to promote liberty . . . these sentiments express love of COSMOPOLITANISM, that is of Humanity . . .[76]

There could be no more faithful blueprint of the purposes of Korais's political thought.

CHAPTER TEN

The Fate of the Enlightenment

THE VISION OF radical transformation of Greek society involved in the message of the Enlightenment did not naturally remain unchallenged. The articulation of a political alternative, based on systematic social and cultural criticism that demythologized and rejected existing structures of social relations and accepted codes of moral values, was bound to provoke the reaction of all those with a stake in the *status quo*.

THE SCENE OF IDEOLOGICAL CONFLICT

The counterattack began with the reaction of conservative circles against the French Revolution in the 1790s.[1] The polemic culminated in a campaign against the ideas of Rhigas, whose theory and practice represented the most radical expression of the revolutionary dynamic in Greek politics at the time. Rhigas was officially condemned by the Church during the brief first patriarchate of Gregory V (1797–1798). In a stern letter to the metropolitan of Smyrna, the patriarch expressed his grave concern over the alleged appearance in that diocese of a pamphlet entitled "New Political Constitution of the Inhabitants of Roumeli" and ordered the metropolitan to make every effort to capture all copies of the pamphlet that might be in circulation and send them forthwith to Constantinople. That pamphlet was "full of rottenness," the patriarch warned, "and with its turbid ideas it ran counter to the doctrines of Orthodox faith."[2]

Rhigas's ideas were not simply disowned by the highest spiritual authority in Greek society, but his politics and system of values became the object of vilification by conservative critics who rejected vehemently everything that he stood for. Among his enemies was the idiosyncratic but prolific critic of the Enlightenment, Michael Perdikaris, who composed a long tract under the title "Rhigas or Against Pseudophilhellenes," in which he indicted Rhigas's ideas and political initiative. Neither liberation from the Ottomans nor Enlightenment but rectification of morals and of Christian faith was what the Greek nation needed, in Perdikaris's judgment. The real danger to the nation came from the impious pollution of French philosophy. Perdikaris therefore came to the following interesting political conclusion: "I do not pray for freedom, nor do I judge it to be in the interests of this Nation, and indeed I pray to God to increase and consolidate the high state of this most clement Monarchy, so that the Nation, having been enlightened and adorned, shall be subject not to the authority of another Nation, but to the nation of our fellows, the upright Ottomans, with whom it has always ruled in common, rather than been subjected."[3] At about the same time, the monk Cyril Lavriotis, known for his connections with the oracular tradition and his involvement with various movements of the Counter-enlightenment, rejoiced at Rhigas's undoing as a deserving punishment to a disturbed mind.[4]

The attack against the Enlightenment proceeded from such specific targets as the French regicide, the French invasion of Egypt, and the revolutionary impact of Rhigas's politics to a widening cycle of polemics directed at the entire philosophic outlook of which these dramatic political events were perceived as mere symptoms. This rival intellectual and political outlook was readily identified as "French philosophy," and those who could be considered as its major exponents in the eyes of its conservative enemies were singled out as the targets of the polemic. The major villains were felt to be Voltaire, Rousseau, and d'Holbach. The influence of their libertine ideas was detected at the root of a loosening of moral standards among

Greek youth, whose taste for the European Enlightenment alarmed the conservative Phanariot critic Alexander Kalphoglou, who expressed his fears in a "Moral Versification" satirizing the prevailing Francophilia.[5] The same fears were expressed in another satire composed roughly in the decade 1793–1803, *The Lantern of Diogenes,* attributed to Agapios Chapipis, an archimandrite of the Holy Sepulchre. The composer's concern with moral laxness and the distortion of moral values in modern society led him to an indictment of such ideas as liberty and equality and to a critique of the principles and social consequences of the French Revolution. He went on to a denunciation of that self-professed critic of religion and inspirer of the Revolution, Voltaire, who was charged with primary responsibility for the moral decay that infected modern society.[6]

Similar concerns preoccupied Perdikaris, as well, who resumed his attack on the Enlightenment by widening its scope. In his *Preamble to Hermelos,* he denounced the corruption that stemmed from the teaching of immoral French philosophers "who pretended to liberate men from the darkness of superstition and threw them instead in the chaos of impiety." Perdikaris was no less severe in his strictures against Greek youth who fled to Europe in pursuit of higher studies, became infected with dangerous modern ideas and aped the corrupt manners of the West. Although he ridiculed all the pretensions of the enlightened intelligentsia, Perdikaris did not spare the moral failures of the established leadership of Greek society. His criticism was directed with unmitigated severity toward all orders of society. Not only were the modernizing philosophers and their European models, "Collins, Hobbes, Rousseau" denounced, but also the ecclesiastical hierarchy, the monastic orders, the old aristocracy, and the rising new professional and commercial classes.[7]

Out of Perdikaris's compulsive animadversions emerged a sociological profile of the Greek political scene that was remarkably similar in its components to the sociological surveys delineated by contemporary radical critics as well. What is absent from Perdikaris's criticism of the social structure is any sense of the position of the largest segment of Greek society, the peasant class. His strictures, however, with their anti-intellectual, antimodern, and antiestablishment thrust, may be taken as the articulation in the Greek context of a reactionary viewpoint with a basis in a version of populist Catonism, which is a typical response to situations of social change and ideological radicalization.[8] The fact that Perdikaris opened his campaign against the Enlightenment by denouncing the most radical manifestation of revolutionary politics in the case of Rhigas may be helpful in locating his own ideological position in the politics of the time. His eventual theoretical thesis expanded his censure of the modernizing threat of the Enlightenment to a reprobation of a traditional leadership that did not possess the competence and moral authority to arrest the strides of the new philosophy.

The indictment of the philosophy of the Enlightenment as the destroyer of the moral fabric of society was combined with a sustained effort to vindicate the truth of revealed religion and Orthodox doctrine against the skepticism and doubt bred by the new ideas. This dimension, as well, of the conservative campaign against the Enlightenment can be traced in the momentous decade of the 1790s. A *Trophy of Orthodox Faith,* published in 1791 by Antonios Manouel in Vienna, opened this revived tradition of Christian apologetics. Ironically, this trophy of Orthodoxy was a translation of a Roman Catholic work, Geminiano Gaeto's *Giovine Istruito,* but it performed its function adequately: it marshaled philosophical and scriptural arguments against "the alleged sages and sharp wits" of the modern age, such as Spinoza, Hobbes, Bayle, Voltaire, d'Argens, and other such insolent, verbose, and atheist Freemasons.[9] Against these critics of religion, who invited the faithful to shake off the burden of the faith, live freely in civil society, enjoy the pleasures of life, and lose their souls, the *Trophy* proclaimed the fundamental doctrines of Christian faith and insisted that religion was not against but above reason.[10]

One year later, in 1792, the *Censure of the Atheists and the Impious* followed.[11] Its two volumes proved, respectively, the existence of God and the immortality of the soul and were dedicated significantly to Anthimos, Patriarch of the sacred city of Jerusalem. The Enlightenment and its modern exponents were not specifically singled out as targets of attack, but the more general theme of atheism was selected for refutation. The dedication to Anthimos of Jerusalem, however, a known enemy of modern philosophy with whose name the tract *Paternal Instruction* was to be associated a few years later, was indicative of the political objectives of the work. Of similar purposes was another *Admonitory Discourse Against Voltaire and His Followers* composed for his students by Makarios Kavadias.[12] Voltaire's name had by then become a symbolic term characterizing collectively all enemies of religion. Scriptural authority was invoked in support of the Christian position, without, however, any serious attempt at a refutation of what was implied in Voltaire's or the Enlightenment's philosophic arguments on religion, which in fact were ignored by most of these polemicists. The names of the representatives of the Enlightenment were appended to these texts of counterenlightenment in a sloganizing manner, with no serious attempt to refute their views.

The armory of Christian apologetics was much strengthened when two of the most respected representatives of Greek learning, who had earlier made decisive contributions in breaking the ground for the advent of the Enlightenment itself, Nikiphoros Theotokis and Evgenios Voulgaris, enlisted their authority to the campaign to stem the tide that their own earlier efforts had initiated. Theotokis's contribution consisted of a translation of the anti-Voltairean work *L'authenticité des livres tant de Nouveau que de l'Ancien Testament demontrée et leur veracité défendue ou refutation de La Bible enfin expliquée de Voltaire* by Joseph Guillaume Clémence. Other than Voulgaris's writings earlier on, this was the only serious attempt made in Greek thought to come to terms with Voltaire's religious criticism. The tone of seriousness was set in Theotokis's own prolegomena, which opened the work. Voltaire was taken to task for his work *La Bible enfin expliquée,* which was characterized as the "summit of his infidelity and depravity." The censure, however, did not proceed in the usual way by heaping abuse and vilification on the refuted enemy of religion, the familiar technique of the opponents of the Enlightenment. Theotokis instead put forward methodological objections and drew philosophical distinctions in order to indicate what he considered the hollowness of Voltaire's position.[13] The seriousness with which Theotokis attempted to approach the problem was not emulated by those, like Makarios Kavadias, who used his book as the source of their own anti-Voltairean arguments.

Voulgaris made his own contribution to Christian apologetics by translating Soame Jenyns's essay on the *Internal Clarity of Christianity,* which was published independently and was also included in a collection of essays vindicating basic Christian beliefs under the title *Spartion Entriton.*[14] Voulgaris's willingness to contribute to the crusade against the secularizing effects of the Enlightenment encouraged the most fanatical enemies of the movement to claim him as one of their kind[15]—an ironic turn in the career of the man who had not been allowed to pursue an undisrupted teaching vocation in his native country by the intellectual progenitors of his latest acclaimants.

With the realignment of such illustrious names of the Enlightenment as Voulgaris and Theotokis, the attempt to check the development of the movement of ideological change lost its earlier spasmodic character and acquired a programmatic thrust. This was reflected in a third dimension of the intellectual campaign against the Enlightenment, which involved an attempt to refute the intellectual presuppositions of liberal thought. Two manifestations of this attempt indicate how the conservative outlook perceptively connected the process of intellectual innovation with the multiplying claims of emancipation from traditional authority and the rise of new politics that put to question the social *status quo.*

The first attack on the intellectual presuppositions of liberal thought came in the guise of a *Trophy from the Helladic Panoply Against the Followers of Copernicus.*[16] It was the work of Sergios Makraios, a Church official and professor at the Patriarchal Academy in Constantinople. Drawing on ancient Greek astronomical erudition, he attempted to demolish the Copernican theory of the heliocentric system in three dialogues composed in ancient Greek. The work was meant to be a response to Kodrikas's translation of Fontenelle's *Entretiens sur la pluralité des mondes* and was characteristically dedicated to the patriarch Anthimos of Jerusalem. Not even the author of the *Trophy of Orthodox Faith* a few years earlier attempted to refute the Copernican theory,[17] but Makraios's own *Trophy* eloquently suggested how much modern science was still suspected and feared by the innermost circles of the conservative power structure and its ideologists. The most eloquent comment on this attitude was made by Ioannis Pezaros, another priest and teacher in Tyrnavo in Thessaly, upon hearing of Makraios's refutation of Copernicus: "Alas! We are still infantile and timorous."[18]

The refutation of modern science was joined by an attack on the new history, represented by a translation of Bossuet's *Discours sur l'histoire universelle* printed at the Patriarchal press in Constantinople. It is interesting to note in this connection that Voulgaris had attempted a translation of Bossuet's *Politique tirée des propres paroles de l'écriture sainte,* which, however, remained unpublished,[19] probably in view of the development of Greek historical and political thought in the eighteenth century precisely in the opposite direction from that to which Bossuet's work pointed. The patriarchate, however, apparently wanted to resurrect the providential logic of human history for which Bossuet had argued. The brief prefatory note stressed that the meaning discernible in the rise and fall of great nations and empires not only confirmed the clear traces of divine providence, but also pointed to the fact that in human affairs prudence always triumphed.[20] The political and social lesson that the work sought to transmit was clear. The perspective on historical wisdom affirmed by the top ecclesiastical circles through the Greek edition of Bossuet represented a belated attempt to undo the political effects of the redefinition of Greek historical identity in terms of the rediscovery of ancient Hellas in the historiography of the Enlightenment. Subversive classicism no less than modern science and deism were unmistakably perceived as among the enemies of the faith and of the traditional *status quo* it sanctioned.

The developing conservative argument set the context for the elaboration of a militant theory of Counterenlightenment. Its most articulate exponent was Athanasios Parios, hieromonach and advocate of the spirit of Orthodoxy and director of the School of Chios from 1786. In his youth he had been a disciple of Ierotheos Dendrinos, the conservative teacher of Smyrna, who had prevented the young Moisiodax from going to Europe to study, asserting that the way to European education was the way to atheism.[21] Parios inherited his master's zeal, and he first took sides in the ideological debates of the end of the eighteenth century when he circulated copies of a letter he had addressed in 1791 to Korais in which he censured the latter's views on fasting.[22] Parios soon joined the polemics against the French Revolution and the Enlightenment. He began by attempting to refute Korais's *Fraternal Instruction* with a conservative text, *New Rapsakis*, which, however, remained unpublished.[23] In 1798 he composed the first polemical tract to be published by the new patriarchal press in Constantinople, entitled *Christian Apology.* The polemics against revolutionary France that set the tone of the first edition[24] were expanded in the two subsequent editions of the work into a full-scale denunciation of the Enlightenment and a determined affirmation of Orthodox principles.

Against the Enlightenment's and the Revolution's claims to liberty, Parios argued that men are neither born nor can they be free in society, and he dismissed the aspiration for equality as an unreal illusion. Against the claims of the *illuminati,* as he called them, on behalf of the Enlightenment, he emphasized that the only real light comes from above as against human enlightenment, which amounts to vanity and spiritual darkness. He warned the faithful that atheism was a necessary condition of secular liberty. He regretted that the "law of grace" did not permit any longer the imposition of capital punishment on those who disseminated such ideas, but he satisfied himself that it was still possible to apply a similar punishment to their polluted books, which ought to be "censured, stigmatized, and burnt." Parios was quite perceptive in identifying the social texture of the enemy movement: besides the self-styled philosophers and other libertines, the new ideas were readily received by merchants and artisans—men who did not understand anything about them and were thus deceived by godless propagandists.[25]

The attack on the Enlightenment was carried over in Parios's *Response to the Irrational Zeal of those Philosophers Who Return from Europe* (1802). This was an indictment of secular learning and modern culture as the foremost sources of moral danger to a Christian soul. Parios argued that those who sought philosophy in Europe suffered from a terrible misconception: they forgot that true philosophy was taught only by the Scriptures and its purpose was the salvation of the soul. Only the light of this philosophy that was given from heaven could assure true human felicity. So Parios warned, it was pathetic on the part of the new philosophers to despise the wisdom of the fathers of the Church and to want to revive the Ancients or to adopt the theories of impious European thinkers who ridiculed the Christian saints, including Descartes, Rousseau, and Voltaire in France, and Collins, Newton, and Toland in England, as "the wonders of nature." Parios went on to argue that secular knowledge that undermined the faith was harmful to human felicity. Two major moral dangers lurked for those who went to Europe: besides exposure to Latin heresy, they took a grave risk of losing their ethical sobriety amid the ferment of immorality and atheism spreading from revolutionary France. "Enlightened Europe," which for the partisans of the Enlightenment had been paradise transposed on earth, appeared to Parios as the threshold of Hades. Hence he concluded with a feverish exhortation to parents to avoid sending their sons to Europe. It appeared indeed terrible to Parios that the Greek mercantile classes risked the salvation of the soul of their own offspring by exposing them to the moral dangers and atheism of Europe for the sake of vain profit-making, which motivated their commercial missions to the West.[26]

Parios expressed, albeit in rather extreme terms, the general attitude of the Orthodox Church on the problems posed by cultural and social change in Greek society. Although occasionally his arguments, in their pessimism and consternation, show a noteworthy affinity with those connected with the intransigent counterrevolutionary Catholicism of Joseph de Maistre, whose image of the executioner as the pillar of the social order Parios repeatedly approximated, his inspiration derived primarily from the Orthodox fundamentalism centered on Mount Athos at the turn of the eighteenth and nineteenth centuries. The revival of Orthodox spirituality in this period was represented by Makarios Notaras, Archbishop of Corinth, and by Nikodimos Hagiorite, both of whom were later canonized by the Orthodox Church. The new saints, both of them leading figures and inspirers of the movement of spiritual renewal known as the Kollyvades, on account of their views as to the day on which memorial services for the dead should be held, emphasized the most mystical aspects of the Orthodox tradition, what is known as "neptic" theology. They advocated a revival of the fourteenth-century spiritual movement known as Hesychasm, which stressed inner action and the continual invocation of the name of Jesus for the deification of the faithful, and expounded a traditional system of morality as the only appropriate road to salvation amid the temptations of society.[27] Parios had been a disciple and correspondent of both of these saints. It was ironic, however, that Nikodimos Hagiorite, who was in many ways his inspiration, directly borrowed many of his arguments, with a tolerance that comes as a surprise to the modern scholar, from Roman Catholic mystical theology, especially from earlier translations of works that belonged to the intellectual climate of Ignatius Loyola.[28] The religious apologetics, with which the Roman Catholic Church in the West had fought an earlier defiance, that of the Protestant Reformation, were proving useful in combating, two centuries later, the new ideological challenges facing the Orthodox Church in the East as well. These borrowings from Western religious thought, however, were subsidiary and incidental to the Orthodox spiritual revival, whose main inspiration came from the collection of writings by Eastern Christian authors from the early desert fathers to the Hesychasts of the fourteenth century, compiled by Saints Makarios Notaras and Nikodimos Hagiorite and published in Venice in 1782 under the evocative title *Philokalia* (Love of beauty).

The mystical movement of Makarios of Corinth and Nikodimos Hagiorite obviously represented a *Weltanschauung* entirely different and diametrically opposed to secular philosophic Enlightenment. Indeed, it expressed an alternative conception of what Enlightenment might be: in its advocacy of moral rectitude based on the mortification of the flesh and self abnegation inspired by the divine light of faith and mystical communion with God, the religious system of late eighteenth-century Greek Orthodox mysticism could and did claim that it represented the only possible variety of genuine enlightenment as against the deceptive illusions of secular philosophy. The inspiration of Parios's political position by these spiritual premises, therefore, can be seen as a veritable form of Counterenlightenment.

Although Parios's Counterenlightenment was the most significant indication of the degree of ideological polarization in Greek society, the battle against the Enlightenment was not fought in its entirety in the extreme terms in which he cast his position. Other equally determined opponents of the implications of modern ideas realized, perhaps due to a better tactical sense, that certain concessions to some of the claims of cultural renovation had to be made. If Parios, with his inspiration from Orthodox fundamentalism, expressed the uncompromising insistence on the traditional values that marked the eventual attitude of the Church toward the Enlightenment, Panayiotis Kodrikas gradually became the representative of the modified outlook of the Phanariot establishment toward the European ideas that had been originally introduced and promoted in Greek society primarily by this social group.

From the early eighteenth century through the 1780s, the Phanariots had championed the ideas of cultural change and intellectual modernization and maintained a political posture inspired by the ideas of enlightened absolutism, expressed in its most mature form by Dimitrios Katartzis. After the outbreak of the French Revolution, however, and especially after Catherine II modified her attitude toward the Enlightenment and entered into an alliance with Turkey against revolutionary France, the Phanariot position was rigidified in the advocacy of controlled enlightenment from above without any concessions to the further implications and claims of the movement. Katartzis's eventual silence indicated this hardening of the Phanariot ideological position. The Phanariots, however, did not relapse into a purely reactionary attitude, nor did they espouse the tenets of Counterenlightenment. In this their attitude was similar to that of the aging Voulgaris. In both cases, there was an entrenchment in earlier theoretical positions against the logical consequences immanent in those original attitudes.

Kodrikas, who had made a career in the Phanariot courts in the principalities where he had been a disciple of Katartzis before joining the first
Ottoman diplomatic mission to Paris, was a man of liberal sympathies. He
attempted a translation of Pope's *Essay on Man,* and his translation and
updating of Fontenelle's *Entretiens sur la pluralité des mondes,* probably at
the urging of Moisiodax, had precipitated the publication of Makraios's
Trophy Against the Followers of Copernicus, and, according to a testimony,
it was condemned by the Church.[29] Clearly, Kodrikas was not a man of
the Counterenlightenment, but still he fought fiercely against the more
radical ideological position represented by Korais and his followers in the
two decades prior to the Greek Revolution. The formal issue in the controversy that raged between 1816 and 1821 was the language question. Against
Korais's arguments for the simplification and purification of modern Greek,
Kodrikas insisted that the linguistic medium of the nation ought to be
the official language cultivated and used by the patriarchal and Phanariot
courts. Kodrikas was of course aware that the conflict was not essentially
between two linguistic theories, but between two rival political visions concerning the future of the nation. Kodrikas did not propose to undo the
Enlightenment, but only to arrest its subversive implications, which he saw
as destructive of the social order and of the genuine traditions of Orthodox
Hellenism. In his view, Korais was not simply an editor of classical authors
and a language reformer, but "a self-declared legislator, and a disrupter of
common customs," and his theory was nothing less than "a systematic heresy, which has the drastic aim not only of the general overthrow of both the
shape and form and the entire organic construct of our National Dialect,
but also of the complete overturning and disruption of the morals and general customs of the Nation." Koraism thus aimed at "the general disruption
of established order," and its legislator was in practice a "Demagogue"; in
the disputes relating to the language question, what in fact was at issue was
the "most important customs of our Nation, not merely two or three Gre-
co-barbarian words."[30]

The controversy was fought with great intensity in an ardent exchange
of polemical pamphlets between Korais and his followers on the one side
and Kodrikas and his friends on the other.[31] The Greek periodical press of
the time, notably the journals *Learned Mercury,* which in 1816 had passed
under the control of Korais's disciples, and *Kalliope,* which expressed the

views of the opposite side, became the vehicles of the philological battle. Korais enjoyed the support of the greater part of the younger generation of the Enlightenment, who enthusiastically defended his theories. Kodrikas, however, although with few disciples, enjoyed powerful support among the ruling groups in Greek society, especially in the bosom of the Church and in Phanariot circles. His major work against Korais's linguistic theory was dedicated to the Czar of Russia—an eloquent indication of imperial favor—while the Patriarchate of Constantinople went all out in Kodrikas's support, as suggested by the letter of congratulation addressed to him by the reigning and a former patriarch on the occasion of the publication of his book.[32]

The controversy between Korais and Kodrikas dominated the politics of the Greek diaspora in Western Europe, especially in Paris, Vienna, and the cities of Northern Italy. The battle of the pamphlets that punctuated the controversy indicated the vitality of Greek politics and underlined the liberal temper of the age that witnessed the culmination of the Greek Enlightenment. Like the pamphleteering controversies of the American Revolution, and the assault on the ancien régime and on the enemies of the philosophes by the partisans of the new ideas in France,[33] the Greek battle of the pamphlets indicated how the development of rival cultural outlooks and the consequent intellectual controversies might be translated, with the development of their relevant social bases, into political conflict.

Ideological controversy was not limited to the intelligentsia of the diaspora. The centers of the Enlightenment within the Greek world were no less lively scenes of ideological confrontations. The Enlightenment had from the outset proceeded amid disputation and strife, and its maturity in the first two decades of the nineteenth century provoked only an intensification of the opposition of its rivals. The older geography of the Enlightenment had, by the end of the eighteenth century, been transformed into a geography of ideological conflict.

At Ioannina, Athanasios Psalidas and his followers, whose bastion was the Kaplaneios School, were involved in a continual battle with the enemies of modern learning, led by the Balanos family, who controlled a rival traditional school in that city.[34] The Danubian principalities, where the Enlightenment enjoyed greater liberty to develop and make itself felt, also witnessed the emergence of strong opposition. Actually, the most determined opposition to the Enlightenment's claims first surfaced in the principalities in

the form of the persecution that broke Moisiodax's efforts. Opposition
to the Enlightenment continued in Moldavia and Wallachia: some of the
strongest polemics against the French Revolution came out of the Phanariot courts. The two princely academies, which counted on their faculties
some of the most articulate and radical exponents of the Enlightenment as
well as some of its most determined opponents, experienced in the first two
decades of the nineteenth century the ferment of acute ideological controversy. In the second decade of the new century, the Academy of Jassy passed
finally under conservative control with the forced resignation of its progressive director and professor of experimental science and mathematics, Stephanos Doungas, who was accused of heresy. In the Academy of Bucharest at
the same time, the director Neophytos Doukas came under attack by the
conservatives led by Samuel of Andros, an associate of Parios and preacher
of the patriarchate. Doukas's work *The Dialogues of Aeschines,* published in
1814, provoked considerable reactions in religious environments.[35]

Ideological conflict between the partisans and rivals of the Enlightenment stirred as well the new area that was added to the geography of the
Enlightenment at the close of the eighteenth century, the triangle of Chi-
os-Smyrna-Kydonies in the Northeastern Aegean. The establishment of
schools following modern secular curricula and the appearance of a progressive intelligentsia in Western Asia Minor and in the nearby island of
Chios, an area with direct access and close ties of administrative and ecclesiastical control with neighboring Constantinople, indicated how decisively
social change in that area of intense commercial activity influenced cultural differentiation. Smyrna was the most cosmopolitan city of the Levant,
and although its educational system was dominated by the conservative
Evangelical School, in which intellectual traditionalism was entrenched, the
establishment, by modernizing segments of the community of a rival school
emphasizing science education, the Philological Gymnasium, precipitated
a monumental ideological controversy, which has been noted in an earlier
chapter.[36] At Kydonies, the local academy had developed in the first two
decades of the nineteenth century into one of the most dynamic centers
of Enlightenment learning. Modern science, mathematics, and philosophy
were taught by Benjamin Lesvios, possibly the most creative representative
of Neohellenic philosophical thought. He had studied in Pisa and Paris
and, like Korais, espoused the theories of the *Idéologues.* Besides the teaching of the sciences, the academy had become an active center of patriotic

classicism, which was displayed in performances of ancient tragedies such as Euripides's *Hecuba* in the original language, to the amazement of foreign visitors like the French scholar Ambroise Firmin-Didot, who comments on the performance. On such occasions the doors and windows were kept closed to avoid provoking the suspicions of the local Turkish garrison over the patriotic emotion stimulated by the presentation of ancient Greek glories.[37] Finally, in Chios, Korais's own home island whose school system had been dominated by Parios's sullen conservatism for decades (1786–1811), the direction of the local school of higher learning passed in 1811 to Korais's most trusted younger associate, Neophytos Vamvas. Thus Parios's influence on local culture was neutralized, and with Vamvas's efforts and Korais's support, Chios could boast a model modern college.[38]

Chios, however, was the only case in which the Enlightenment survived in the educational system until the last few months before the outbreak of the Greek War of Independence, despite the systematic polemics of its opponents. In Kydonies, Lesvios was forced to resign in 1812, after years of intellectual feuds with the conservatives and under sustained attack by a senior official of the patriarchate, Dorotheos Voulismas.[39] In Smyrna, as well, the Philological Gymnasium closed down in 1819 after years of subversive attacks by the conservatives, who stirred up the uneducated masses and guilds of the town against its headmaster Constantinos Koumas and his associates, the Oikonomos brothers. An attempt to renovate higher education in Constantinople during the patriarchate of Cyril VI, who summoned Koumas to head the new school at Xirokrini (Kuruçesme) in 1813, came to an abrupt end when Koumas, faced with plots and obstruction, found the task impossible and returned to Smyrna.[40] Finally, in the winter of 1821, the Church also succeeded, through the activities of Plato, the metropolitan bishop of Chios, in closing down the Chios high school, just a few weeks before the outbreak of the Greek uprising, thus finally managing to neutralize the Enlightenment in the East.

These localized conflicts and attacks on the Enlightenment appeared to converge in a coordinated campaign when Gregory V returned to the throne for his third patriarchate in 1818–1821. Gregory V, himself a disciple of Ierotheos Dendrinos during his student days at Smyrna, had initiated the campaign against revolutionary enlightenment during his first patriarchate in 1797–1798, when he anathematized the French Revolution and Rhigas. After a short period as patriarch in 1806–1808, he returned to the throne at a time when Greek society was practically on the verge of revolution and resumed his earlier campaign with a heightened determination to wipe out the effects of the Enlightenment. The patriarch's initiatives in those years came as the culmination of a resolute effort by the Church to suppress ideological dissent and to reaffirm traditional values. Already, in 1816, Stephanos Doungas was forced to submit the manuscript of his *Physics* to the censorship of the patriarchal synod; accepting the judgment of his censors, he renounced it as heretical and signed a confession of faith in Orthodoxy and Aristotelianism.[41] In 1817, a fierce attack on Korais was issued by one of the patriarchate's clergy in the West, Ignatios Skalioras, the chaplain of the Greek church in Leipzig. His *Epistle Stigmatizing the New Philosophy* was the most vicious personal libel—and there had been several of them—aimed at Korais, who was stigmatized not only as atheist and subversive, but also as a common thief and insolvent merchant (recalling the failure of Korais's youthful mercantile venture in Amsterdam in 1771–1777), who had turned in desperation to philosophy. Being incompetent in this new pursuit also, Korais, according to Skalioras, appropriated Moisiodax's ideas and those of many other European writers and presented them as his own.[42] This pointer at an intellectual parentage between Moisiodax and Korais was probably the only accurate, though fortuitous, observation in that libel.

With Gregory's return to the patriarchal throne, the indictment of the Enlightenment took a much more solemn, almost apocalyptic tone. In a series of official pastoral gestures, the patriarch and his synod sternly cautioned the faithful and condemned the most intolerable manifestations of the rising tide of impiety and godlessness. In 1819, the patriarch and the synod issued an encyclical to the hierarchy, the clergy, and the pious flock warning against the abandonment of traditional grammatical learning in favor of modern science and mathematics, which were held to be detrimental to the true faith and the salvation of the soul. The encyclical concluded by admonishing against the innovation of naming children at baptism with pagan Greek names, thus abandoning the names sanctified by the martyrs and saints of the Church.[43] Later in the same year in an official letter, the patriarch congratulated Kodrikas for his linguistic treatise against Korais.

As anticlericalism became the primary content of the movement for cultural renewal, the Church responded in kind. A few years after the composition of "Indictment of Prelates," another tract, entitled *Crito's Reflections,* censured in remarkably milder language the construction of a luxurious mansion as residence of the archbishop of Adrianople and suggested that the pertinent expenditures could be put to much more socially beneficial uses by endowing a school of modern learning. The text repeated the familiar moral arguments and appealed to the values of civic humanism, urging public-mindedness, moral uprightness, and dedication to collective causes. Yet the simple insinuation of the moral failures implied in the hierarchy's tendency to spend funds collected from public donations on projects designed to enhance the external splendor of the Church or the personal comfort of its bishops provoked the rage of the patriarchate, and *Crito's Reflections* was burnt publicly in Constantinople as a blasphemous text.[44] The suggestion for the burning of this appeal on behalf of educational progress came from Hilarion of Sinai, the chief censor and director of the press of the patriarchate who, in the years immediately before 1821, acquired great notoriety in the eyes of the partisans of the Enlightenment for his determined persecution of their views.

The real stakes in the conflict became unmistakable when the chief censor issued an appeal to all scholars and learned men of the nation to submit their writings for publication to the patriarchal press—a gesture that would mean that they both acknowledged the authority of the Church and willingly accepted the directives of official censorship. In his proclamation, the chief censor extolled the benefits that could be derived from printing for the edification of the nation, but he warned that the key to the printing press had to stay in the firm hands of the rulers, who would make sure to keep its effects under control, lest what was supposed to be the abode of the Muses become Pandora's box.[45]

The Church finally realized that since it could not stop the Enlightenment, it had to try to co-opt its partisans. This was the real purpose of the new initiative. Its motives became crystal clear in the chief censor's hurrahs for the reigning sultan of the Ottoman Empire. The embodiment of despotism, the crown of tyranny, was hailed by a high ecclesiastical dignitary responsible for the cultural policies of the Ecumenical Patriarchate in these terms:

> Long live our Most Serene and Mighty Sovereign, the Crown of the great kings, his predecessors, the most magnanimous and heroic Sultan Mahmud II. May his Empire live throughout the centuries, vanquishing all enemies.

His sacred Majesty, following upon the unrivalled, farsighted and wisest providence with which, to the admiring amazement of all political observers, wonderfully governs His God-guarded realm, persecuting all sorts of vice, and striving to preserve order everywhere and to secure the true happiness of His subjects, royally awards to the various nationalities which find succour under His mighty wings, the liberty to establish and cultivate all those projects which contribute to their moral order, the improvement of each nation and the progress of human learning. Besides the other royal benefices which His Majesty has magnificently bestowed upon our Nation, He has entrusted to us the keys of a public National Press, curtailing first unreasonable liberty and imperially decreeing the enjoyment of all the benefits of printing, but avoiding everything that might obscure the splendor of our sincere submission—especially through the publication of subversive books.[46]

The position originally enunciated in *Paternal Instruction* was now fully rationalized. The exaltation of despotism was rounded up in the encomia that followed the praise of the ecumenical patriarch Gregory V, "the shining distributor of spiritual gifts," the Phanariot princes and grand dragomans of the Sublime Porte, and summarily all those prominent in the ecclesiastical and secular establishment.[47] In a way, the worldview of the *Hellenic Nomarchy* was reflected in reverse in the pages of Hilarion.

The encomium of tyranny, by presenting the obverse outlook of the same picture that so much grieved the men of the Enlightenment, vindicated the most damning charges leveled by social critics against the social establishment that thrived under the aegis of despotism. Once the chief ideologist of what to the mind of the Enlightenment appeared as the kingdom of darkness put forward arguments like these, the social critics were left with nothing more to expose. Their task was completed. Indeed, the proclamation of the chief censor was widely distributed and printed even in the pages of the very last issue of *Melissa* (Bee), the most socially and ideologically radical journal published in Paris by the republican intellectuals of the diaspora. Hilarion's text was reproduced integrally without any other commentary except several exclamation marks in parenthesis following the encomia of the sultan and the Greek power structure.

The same issue of *Melissa* contained a direct response denouncing the treachery of the censor's proclamation and warning against the sinister designs behind the establishment of a central press controlled by the patriarchate. The real response, however, was given in some other items contained in the journal. Several reports announced the burning of *Crito's Reflections,* ascribing responsibility for it to Hilarion. One went on to recapitulate the argument of the pamphlet, and another commented that what the "sacred tyrants" had in mind was a reestablishment in Greece of the Inquisition that once flourished in Spain.

Other reports gave details about the relentless persecution of the enlightened faculty of the philological gymnasium of Smyrna, thus indicating that the tensions that inspired the "Indictment of Prelates" remained unabated. Finally, some communications from Constantinople reported new incidents of corruption and obscurantism among the "Sardanapali of the Bosporus," the reverend prelates of the patriarchate.[48]

The final act in the drama of the persecution of the Enlightenment by the Church was played out in the climate of panic created by Turkish reprisals in Constantinople after the outbreak of the Greek War of Independence in the Peloponnese. In March 1821, a synod was urgently summoned at the ecumenical patriarchate, which was attended not only by the prelates who were its canonical members but also by lay dignitaries. The purpose of this synod was to mollify Ottoman wrath through the "forbidding of lessons in philosophy," the specific targets being Korais, Koumas, and Benjamin of Lesbos, who were regarded as fomenters of revolution.[49]

The colliding ideological positions and the political stakes of each side in the conflict were thrown into clear relief in that last issue of *Melissa.* The argument was no longer over the respective philosophical and practical merits of the Enlightenment and the ideologies it sought to displace. The stand of the Enlightenment was recognized by both its proponents and its enemies as a call for radical social change and political revolution. Against this cause stood the guardians of the traditional order who wanted to preserve both the values they held sacred, but also the privileges and social and material advantages that these values justified and made possible. Pressed by the drive of the Enlightenment for social change and revolution, the partisans of the traditional order dropped all pretensions and openly embraced the cause of alien despotism as their last line of defense. This last position might be best understood as a gesture of desperation, but in unmasking the real political concerns behind the elaborate theological arguments, historical claims, and appeals to practical reason of the enemies of the Enlightenment, this final expression of panic and despair vindicated all the charges against the "kingdom of darkness." The Enlightenment, as expressed in social criticism, had come full circle.

The issue of *Melissa* in which this epilogue to the ideological controversies of the Enlightenment was written appeared in the spring of 1821. It was the last issue of the journal. Publication was suspended, as the attention and energies of the republican ideologues who wrote and edited the periodical were captivated by something else incomparably bigger and more soul-shaking than the war against the "kingdom of darkness." News coming from Greece spoke of another war, a real war of liberation that had broken out in the mother country. Although the news that reached Paris from the Greek East in the spring of 1821 was confused and contradictory, it seemed that finally the moment of truth had come. The republican social critics could hope that the time was ripe to put the Enlightenment into practice. Although they had not started the war of liberation themselves, they had every reason to believe that the omens were auspicious.

The repressive measures aimed at stifling the Enlightenment came at a time when Greek society was experiencing the tremors of revolutionary fervor. The second decade of the nineteenth century had witnessed a new Russo-Turkish war and a Russian invasion of the principalities (1808–1812). The high drama of the Napoleonic empire came to an end in 1814–1815 but not without a new, if partial, French occupation of the Ionian Islands in 1807–1814 following the Treaty of Tilsit. With the Treaty of Vienna in 1815, the seven islands, reconstituted as a semiautonomous state, became a British protectorate and continued to exercise a sharp fascination on Greek minds as the only Greek territory under liberal and civilized rule.

Meanwhile, within the Ottoman Empire, the Serbs were up in arms fighting for their liberation between 1804 and 1813; two local satraps, Pasvanoglou in northern Bulgaria and Ali Pasha Tepelenli in Epirus, were carving practically independent principalities for themselves out of the territories of the empire in defiance of the authority of the sultan. Ali Pasha had further entered into diplomatic dealings with both the British and Napoleon and had encouraged the Greeks to think that he might cooperate with them in overthrowing the Ottoman yoke. All these events of the wider international and Balkan environment intensified the revolutionary restlessness that was stirred by social change and the spreading Enlightenment among the Greeks. In 1808, the rising of Efthymios Vlachavas in central Greece added one more to the list of abortive, peasant-based revolts that had punctuated the centuries of Ottoman rule. The social banditry of the *klephts,* who defied and harassed the Ottoman authorities and the Greek notables alike, continued rampant in the Greek mountains. From a form of primitive social protest, Greek social banditry was increasingly becoming invested, thanks to the romantic interpretations of philhellenes such as Byron, with the glamour of a formation of resistance against oppression. Some of the popularized national notions that had been introduced in Greek consciousness by the intelligentsia of the Enlightenment had found their way into the system of social communication of these formations of resistance. The appearance of some vague sense of nationality both in the revolt of 1808 and among the *klephts* was significant of the climate of the times.[50]

The restlessness abetted by social and political change acquired a revolutionary dynamic when, upon the conclusion of the Napoleonic Wars and the termination of the continental blockade that had greatly benefited the Greek merchant marine and Greek mercantile activities, the Greek economy entered into a phase of serious recession. The causes of the recession were multiple and had to do both with the structure and the transnational nature of the Greek economy, which made it extremely vulnerable to international developments.[51] The recession came at a time of heightened and rising expectations within Greek society. Those who were hardest hit were the small and medium Greek merchants of the diaspora and the commercial cities of the Ottoman Empire. It was from the ranks of this social group that there emerged in 1814 the organizers of a revolutionary secret society aiming at the preparation of a national rising for the liberation of Greece. This *Philiki Etaireia* (Society of Friends), as the organization was named, was largely a coalition of men engaged in commercial and mercantile occupations and intellectuals, men engaged in the professions or in education. According to a detailed study of the *Etaireia's* membership, the two largest categories of its initiates were merchants (53.7 percent) and professionals, that is, educated men (13.1 percent).[52] A significant proportion of the intelligentsia of the Enlightenment and especially their younger disciples enrolled. To attract conservative support and to shed the damaging reputation of Jacobinism or Carbonarism, the leaders of the Society encouraged the impression that they had some connection with the Russian court. They also attempted to attract some senior clergymen to the organization. Some clergymen did enroll, including fifteen bishops (9.5 percent of the Society's members were clergymen). When the patriarch Gregory V, however, was approached while in exile on Mount Athos between his second and third patriarchates, he refused to join, arguing that he was bound by oath to respect the authority of the sultan. Therefore, when he returned to the patriarchal throne in 1818, he was well aware of these subversive activities and intentions. The foreign minister of the Czar, Count Ioannis Capodistrias, to whom the Society offered its leadership, also refused to join. These setbacks did not diminish the Society's revolutionary zeal. Its agents roamed widely in the Greek world and, appealing alike to venerable millenarian hopes or to new national sentiments, cultivated the climate of revolutionary expectancy that agitated Greek society.[53] This was the political context of the wave of persecution against the Enlightenment and its subversive implications led by Gregory V on the eve of the Greek Revolution.

Despite the persecutions and the defeats inflicted by the determined attack of the organized power structure against its exponents and its bases, the movement of the Enlightenment during these same years appeared to be possessed by self-confidence and optimism for the future. Amid the prevailing climate of rising expectations, it was perhaps difficult to read clearly the alarming signs reflected in the gradual decay of some of the Enlightenment's traditional strongholds like Ioannina, as well as the determination and gains of its enemies in such major centers as Constantinople, Smyrna, and the principalities. All this foreshadowed the Enlightenment's future ebb and eventual surrender, but it was not yet clearly discernible. None of this could be sensed among the multiplying militant young followers of Korais in the diaspora who propagated the principles of republicanism and exposed clerical corruption in their radical journal, *Melissa,* in Paris.

These epigones of the Enlightenment composed a remarkable group of committed intellectuals. One of the least radical of them, Neophytos Vamvas, in his treatise *Elements of Moral Philosophy,* had practically developed the vocabulary of modern liberal politics in the Greek language, thus giving fairly authentic expression to the spirit of Korais. He began with a definition of natural law as the knowledge of mankind's inalienable natural rights: "Natural law is said to be knowledge of what is naturally lawful. And what is naturally lawful is any idea or obligation accepted by all, solely with the aid of reason." He went on, however, to insist on the desirability of change and innovation in legal systems according to the evolving needs of society.

"Right reason often requires that human laws be modified, and this modification has its cause in natural law, since modifications need to be made to human laws according to different circumstances, places and people." The treatise introduced and explained the notions of the state of nature and the original equality and natural liberty of all human beings; the transition to civil society and the conclusion of the social contract in pursuit of the common good; civil liberty and political obligation, forms of government, the meaning of the nation, and a theory of democracy.[54] In short, the treatise on moral philosophy provided an education in free citizenship and was written with the prospect of the impending change in the political status of the Greeks. Consequently, the meaning of political liberty formed the primary content of the new moral education:

> Political freedom is nothing other than natural liberty, deprived only of the power of abuse; whence it becomes apparent that political liberty is fully in accord with right reason and can therefore justly be called the perfected natural state of man.[55]

Some of the more radical of Korais's followers finally brought out the first Greek translations of Rousseau's *Discourse on the Origin of Inequality* and *The Social Contract*,[56] more than two decades after the first translations of Montesquieu in the 1790s. Montesquieu was read to gain understanding of the historical predicament of the nation, while Rousseau was perceived as a critic of corrupt society, an apostle of humanity, and an enemy of tyranny.[57] The transition from Montesquieu to Rousseau was characteristic of the curve followed by liberal Greek political thought in a time of profound soul-searching and consciousness-raising amid acute ideological conflict.

The translation of the *Discourse on the Origin of Inequality* was warmly welcomed in a review in the journal *Logios Ermis*. The reviewer urged his compatriots to immerse themselves in philosophical readings, beginning with books on experimental psychology, politics, and morals, in order to broaden and deepen their familiarity with these subjects that were eminently relevant to the most pressing needs of their society. It was pointed out that besides the contribution of the Greek classics, the study of politics and ethics had been greatly advanced in the writings of celebrated modern European philosophers, especially British, such as Locke, Berkeley, Hume, Reid, Adam Smith, and others, as well as French, such as

Bayle, Voltaire, Montesquieu, Rousseau, Helvetius, D'Alembert, Diderot, Mably, and Condorcet.

The translator, Spyridon Valetas, who hid behind the pseudonym Dimitrios Aristomenous, was accorded public praise because "guided by sound judgement, he has translated and made known to us Greeks, too, the excellent treatise of J. J. Rousseau, one of the most famous philosophers of France." In the analysis of the book, the accusations of Rousseau's enemies are refuted, and reference is made to the "eternal war declared by the author on tyranny."[58] This is an example of the way in which Greek translations of texts of the Enlightenment promoted ideological ends: they served as an exhortation for education in free citizenship and cultivated the anticipation of imminent changes in the political predicament of Hellenism.

The journal, in whose pages this syllabus of revolution was published, was the Greek Enlightenment's foremost vehicle in those years. *Logios Ermis* (Learned Mercury), published in Vienna since 1811, had passed after some editorial troubles in 1814–1815 into the control of Korais's local disciples in 1816. Its pages after that date radiated the confident and optimistic psychology of the younger followers of the Enlightenment, those who were preparing to receive the mantle from its aging third generation that had brought the movement to full maturity. Published twice a month, *Logios Ermis* continued consistently the campaign for the promotion of cultural change; it published translations and original contributions indicating the interests and attainments of the Greek enlightened intelligentsia, waged resolutely the battle against the enemies of the radical wing of the Enlightenment, and reported its gains everywhere. The achievements of intellectual progress within Greek society and in the diaspora were proudly reviewed to substantiate an optimistic sense of an expanding horizon of enlightenment: even in distant Cyprus at the southeastern and most backward extremity of the subjugated Hellenic world, *Logios Ermis* reported that a school of modern learning, modeled on the Philological Gymnasium of Smyrna, was in operation in 1819.[59]

What emerged most significantly from the pages of *Logios Ermis* was a firm and heartening impression that a Greek liberal culture had finally, after a century of struggles, come into its own. Assertive and self-confident, this liberal culture, born of the Enlightenment, appeared to have overcome the feeling of inferiority toward European civilization that had tormented Greek consciousness for centuries. Instead, it felt perfectly integrated in the cosmopolitan progressive culture of civilized humanity.[60] The final attainment of the cherished identification with enlightened Europe, to which all previous generations of the Greek Enlightenment had aspired, infused Greek liberalism with a sense of security and fortitude that was best reflected in its confident attitude toward its formidable enemies. This attitude was indicative of the social psychology that nineteenth-century liberalism derived from the theory of progress that promised its eventual triumph.

The sense of optimism and confidence that prevailed in Greek progressive thought at the close of the second decade of the nineteenth century was not confined to the intelligentsia of the diaspora. It was also shared by the intellectuals who were fighting the good battle of the Enlightenment within the enslaved society. No one expressed this outlook better than the brilliant mathematician and philosopher Benjamin Lesvios, one of the most distinguished and respected progressive scholars in the early nineteenth century. Lesvios may be regarded as the most important philosophical thinker of the Neohellenic Enlightenment. Lacking the amazing complexity of Voulgaris, but more consistent in his philosophical thought, he too was a follower of the philosophy of the *Idéologues*, like Korais. Indeed, it was he who coined the word *idealogia* to convey in the Greek language the name of the philosophical current that he felt gave expression to the most advanced form of philosophical speculation of his time. Lesvios's political thought is condensed in his treatise *Elements of Ethics,* a work that remained unpublished in his lifetime. Benjamin began this essay with two chapters "concerning the natural rights of man" and "concerning natural obligations," in which he expounded the fundamental principles of radical liberalism, inspired by the theory of progress. The moral basis of his political thought may be discerned in the following characteristic phrases: "in the theatre of the world [. . .] each retains his own natural rights," and "the greatest tyranny in the world would be if one were to dominate the minds of reasonable men, so as to take away from them their independence and self-sufficiency." On the horizon of Lesvios's thought the scholar discerns the robust liberalism of the great century of the "liberation of nations." His concerns about domination of the minds of reasonable beings foreshadows some of the quests of nineteenth-century political thought, which culminated in the theoretical analyses of Alexis de Tocqueville and J. S. Mill.

Despite the persecutions to which he had been subjected at Kydonies and later in Wallachia, he not only refused to capitulate and compromise his philosophical views, but enthusiastically joined the *Philiki Etaireia* and subscribed to revolutionary politics. Writing on the eve of the Greek Revolution, at precisely the time of the great wave of persecution by the Church, Lesvios celebrated the strides of the Enlightenment and the achievements of Greek liberal culture. Abandoning his elegiac mood of a couple of years earlier when he lamented the cultural desolation of his homeland in an address to the Bavarian philhellene scholar Friedrich Thiersch, Lesvios brought himself to rejoice in the reality of a Greek renaissance at just about the time Greece was on the verge of the war of independence.

The darkness and ignorance inherited from Byzantium, where "minds are given over entirely to religious debate," had finally been dissipated, declared Lesvios, and the Muses were back in their ancient abode. With the dawn of the new century, the Greek Parnassus was revisited by the Muses and the new Enlightenment spread widely and revitalized the movements of life that lay dormant until then beneath the yoke of tyranny.[61] With this confident sense of the achievements of the present and an optimistic vision of future prospects, the Greek Enlightenment enlisted its forces in the war of independence that broke out in 1821.

BEYOND THE ENLIGHTENMENT

The outbreak of the Greek War of Independence in the spring of 1821 was an invitation to the intelligentsia of the Enlightenment to pass from theory to practice. They did not start the Revolution themselves, although many of them had contributed to the creation of the climate of revolutionary expectancy that prepared its outbreak through their participation in the *Philiki Etaireia* and mostly by means of their crusade for cultural change. Indeed, many of the most distinguished living exponents of the Greek Enlightenment rushed to the Greek heartlands, where the revolutionary struggle was fought, to enlist their services in the supreme effort of the nation. Others, like Korais and Psalidas, attempted to make their contribution from a distance through political counsel and active involvement in the projects of European philhellenism. Most notable was the enthusiasm of Greek students in European universities and the younger intelligentsia of the diaspora, who rushed to Greece to fight and help in the construction of a new state in the liberated territories.[62]

The Revolution itself was largely a peasant war fought amid intense social cleavages, which escalated in two civil wars in 1823–1824. In this context, the group of Western-minded intellectuals were a small minority and, on account of their ideas, a quite unpopular one. Their presence, nevertheless, was strongly felt in the politics of the Greek Revolution because of the advantages they enjoyed in terms of education, political experience, and knowledge of international affairs. In two particular aspects of the revolutionary struggle their contribution was decisive: they articulated the ideological aspirations of the Greek War of Independence in terms of their own political liberalism, and they managed to frame the institutions of the new state following Western models of state building, often against the resolute opposition of entrenched interests and power groups that wanted to preserve the traditional semifeudal nature of Greek society and just replace the Ottomans in exercising control over it.[63]

An analysis of these complicated political and social struggles is beyond the scope of this work. The articulation of the liberal aspiration during the Greek Revolution, however, should be briefly noted as the fitting conclusion of this attempt to reconstruct the reception and embattled development of the Enlightenment in Greek political thought. The most representative sources, in which the expression and gradual retreat of liberal aspirations could be traced, are offered by the constitutional documents voted by the five national assemblies that convened during the decade of revolution, when efforts were being made to lay the foundations of the free Greek state (1822–1832). The *Provisional Constitution of Greece,* approved by the First National Assembly at Epidauros on 1 January 1822, and the Greek Declaration of Independence that accompanied it, were clearly informed by the aspirations of the Enlightenment for liberal political institutions and a republican system of government. As a constitutional program, the text aroused the interest of major contemporary political thinkers among both Greek intellectuals and the wider European intelligentsia. Its publication provided the occasion for the critical commentaries by Adamantios Korais and Jeremy Bentham. Their comments were designed to reinforce the liberal-democratic character of the constitution stressing the need to ensure complete control of the legislative authority over the executive organs.[64] The overall principles of liberal constitutionalism were reaffirmed in the resolutions and the constitutional charter voted by the Second National Assembly at Astros in mid-April 1823.[65] By 1827, however, when the Third

National Assembly convened in Troizen, the domestic political climate and international pressures were such that the institutional expression of Greek political aspirations had to be significantly reshaped. The *Political Constitution of Greece,* which was voted in May 1827, essentially abandoned the aspiration for a system of liberal institutions. Although the principles of constitutionalism were reaffirmed, the context was set for the establishment of personal rule by Ioannis Capodistrias, who had been elected as the first governor of free Greece. The democratic thrust of the earlier constitutions was stamped out and replaced by faith in the beneficence of a strong executive.[66] Furthermore, to enable Capodistrias to exercise his difficult duties unencumbered, the constitution was provisionally suspended and he was allowed dictatorial powers.

The Fourth National Assembly, which convened at Argos in July-August 1829, voted no new constitutional measures but limited itself to the passage of several resolutions confirming the actions of Governor Capodistrias. In addition, it delegated to him full authority to handle all critical national issues urgently pressing upon the nascent Greek state.[67] By making the head of state plenipotentiary in every important national issue, the National Assembly essentially removed its own *raison d'être.* It thus paved the way for the eventual establishment of monarchical government. This was done by the new *Political Constitution of Greece,* voted by the Fifth National Assembly that convened at Argos and Nafplion from December 1831 to March 1832. The new charter established a Greek monarchy modeled on the French restoration. Thus, within a decade, the original political aspiration of the Enlightenment for a liberal republic was relinquished. The constitutional charter of 1832 provided for an indirectly elected lower chamber of deputies, which was in turn effectively neutralized by the prerogatives of a senate appointed by the king. The crown was hereditary, nonresponsible, and enjoyed wide prerogatives, including the selection and appointment of a cabinet of ministers.[68]

If they failed to achieve the liberal republic dreamt by the Enlightenment, however, the Greek Westernizers did manage to shape the administrative institutions of the new state on the model of the prototypes they knew and admired in Europe. The arduous task of state building produced at the close of the War of Independence a constitutional state, endowed with the legal, bureaucratic, and judicial machinery that distinguished contemporary European states. Furthermore, the new state had turned the local Orthodox

Church into one of its arms by severing any administrative ties between the local hierarchy and the Ecumenical Patriarchate in Constantinople, which remained subject to the Ottoman Empire. Greece became a secular state by shedding the traditions that the Orthodox Church had inherited from Byzantium and by turning the local branch of the Orthodox Church into a state church in the fashion of Protestant European states. But there was one aspect of modern state building in which the Greek Westernizers failed to complete their task, and that had to do with the creation of a regular army. This required the suppression of the primitive armed bands and personal armies of the chieftains who had fought in the revolutionary war against the Ottomans and against each other, and the imposition of military discipline within the context of a unified regular army under the control of the central authority. Since the Westernizers did not possess an army of their own to impose their will, they left this task to Capodistrias and the Bavarian dynasty that succeeded him.[69]

Beyond the constitutional expectations and the attempts at state building on the Western model, the liberal aspirations that animated the political culture of revolutionary Greece were eloquently expressed in the press of the period and in an outpouring of political pamphlets and leaflets.[70] This literature belonged integrally to the political tradition of the Enlightenment and represented its legacy in the politics of the Greek Revolution. The inarticulate hopes of the oppressed Greek peasantry, whose main motivation was to appropriate the lands left behind by the Turkish landlords, and the traditional outlook of the diverse power groups, who wanted to consolidate their own authority and preserve existing hierarchies in the new state, were manifested in the social cleavages and civil conflicts of the revolutionary decade. These largely inchoate strivings and the recurrence of millenarian outbursts and acts of individual heroism and sacrifice, motivated by traditional notions of honor and shame typical of Mediterranean society, largely set the social temper of the Greek Revolution but cannot be qualified as its ideological expression. To the extent that it is possible to talk of an articulate ideology of the Greek War of Independence, this ideology could be sought in the ideas and values imprinted in the political literature and press of the revolutionary decade.

The political philosophy that emerged clearly from these sources was the democratic nationalism of the Enlightenment, of which Korais had been the most articulate exponent. The names and ideas of Rousseau, Mably, and

Mirabeau continued to be firmly imprinted on the political consciousness.[71] Vattel's law of nations provided the conceptual context for the understanding of the new condition of the revolutionary and belligerent Greeks;[72] and Volney's philosophy of natural law or natural principles of ethics, introduced with the axiom that equality and justice are one and the same thing, was translated and printed at the national press.[73] Amid the social conflicts of the Revolution, a distant echo of the criticism of *Hellenic Nomarchy* resounded in the pages of a series of dialogues attacking sharply the landed primates, the Phanariots, and other social groups posing obstacles on the way to a consolidation of a Greek liberal polity. This political claim was made clear in the final dialogue, in which it was noted that the press "is still in chains" in liberated Greece and patriots are called upon to defend the rights of all their fellow citizens.[74]

Upon realizing that Capodistrias did not intend to create the republican system for which the Enlightenment had clamored, Korais plunged with an energy uncommon in one of his age into the final political struggle of his life. He began his anti-Capodistrian campaign by composing a series of dialogues that admonished the Greeks how to avoid a new subjugation to "Christian Turks," as he put it.[75] Throughout the struggle, the moral temper of Greek politics was set by a ubiquitous and passionate appeal to selflessness and patriotism, which was expected to transform mere mortals into heroes and represented the full flowering of the philosophy of civic virtue inherited from the Enlightenment.

Yet the political culture of the new state that acceded to independence in 1832, upon the conclusion of an agreement among the three great powers (Great Britain, France, and Russia) that had assumed the role of Greece's "protectors," was shaped by values and cultural forces quite different from those expressed in the Greek Revolution. The coming of independence marked the formal abandonment of the aspirations of the liberal nationalism of the Enlightenment, with the imposition by the protecting powers and the acceptance—albeit reluctant on the part of many segments of Greek public opinion—of an absolute monarchy to rule over the new state. The monarchical option was expected to secure Great Power support for the Greek cause, but as it eventually turned out, even the last vestiges of the restricted constitutionalism of the last revolutionary National Assembly had to be given up in order to secure that support. This turn of events was to a considerable degree an effect of the international political climate prevailing in Restoration Europe. The legitimacy of liberal constitutionalism, however, had already been effectively undermined by domestic factionalism and fratricidal strife that had reduced Greece to chaos and anarchy following the assassination of Capodistrias in September 1831. The monarchial option was accepted with the hope that it would bring order and rescue the country from the prevailing chaos.[76]

The Enlightenment's dream of a liberal republic was thus lost, and the new body politic took the shape of a kingdom. The eventual political outcome of the Greek War of Independence was very different from the visions harbored by the men of the Enlightenment and from the aspirations of the revolutionary leaders who drew up the original Greek constitutional charters. Furthermore, the consolidation of the domestic social order under the Greek kingdom produced a sequence of bitter disappointments for the lower social orders—and especially the peasantry who had fought in the Revolution hoping to improve their economic condition through the expropriation of former Turkish lands. Some of these lands were finally sold to eligible buyers in 1835, to the great disappointment of the landless peasantry. This was only one of many indications of a general conservative trend in the consolidation of the postrevolutionary *status quo* under the aegis of the Bavarian dynasty. The new regime preserved the administrative institutions of the secular state, but its centralized policy was in practice inimical to all vestiges of the liberal heritage of the Enlightenment.[77] In contradistinction with the ideas of this legacy, it encouraged a political culture of state paternalism that would strengthen the loyalty of the people to the crown. Some aspects of traditional popular culture were not averse to the idea of monarchy, and the political purposes of the new nationalism that was in the making in the postrevolutionary period formed the common denominator for the necessary ideological amalgam.

The politics of the Enlightenment was clearly on the wane, although in certain respects the new regime proved receptive to a part of its ideological legacy. This was most pronounced in the question of the Greek Church, whose separation from Constantinople was maintained during the first two decades of the Bavarian monarchy. Significantly, the ecclesiastical exponent of this policy of autocephaly for the Church of Greece was Theoklitos Pharmakidis, a follower of Korais and editor of *Logios Ermis* in the last and most militant phase of the journal.[78] Another area in which the new regime seemed to defer to the symbolic legacy of the Enlightenment was its encouragement of a neoclassicist revival in Greek culture, of which the most important manifestation was the establishment of the University of Athens in 1837—the first modern university in the entire area of the Balkans and the Near East. The new university was expected to radiate hellenic culture in those regions, besides, of course, meeting the needs of the new state in trained personnel. This, however, was a classicism inspired by European romantic hellenism, which was particularly pronounced in Bavaria under Ludwig I, father of Greece's King Otho. The romantic neoclassicism of the Greek kingdom had little to do with the political classicism of the Enlightenment and its republican implications.

The most dramatic indication of the gradual dissipation of the legacy of the Enlightenment can be traced on a personal level by following the later stages in the careers of those of its original adherents who survived the Greek Revolution. The most striking *volte face* was that of Constantinos Oikonomos, who in the 1810s was in the vanguard of the struggle for progressive education in Smyrna; when he settled in Greece in 1834, however, after a long and distinguished sojourn in Russia, he became the most illustrious of the adversaries of the Enlightenment.

The opposite fate befell Grigorios Constantas, the most distinguished surviving member of the mature generation of the Enlightenment, who was effectively dismissed from his position of director of the Aegina orphanage and retired in 1835 to his village in Thessaly, still under Ottoman rule, where he died ignored and forgotten in 1844. The revolutionary decade witnessed the passing of the most influential exponents of the Enlightenment: Lesvios died in 1824 while a senator of the fledgling new republic; Psalidas died ignored in exile on Corfu in 1829; Korais died embittered in 1833, having seen his writings burnt publicly in Nafplion by the supporters of Capodistrias; in Constantinople the patriarchate intervened and canceled a memorial service planned by Korais's local followers, on account of the views he expressed in one of his last religious writings, *Ieratikos Synekdimos*. In free Greece, Theoklitos Pharmakidis, as the architect of the independence of the Greek Church, and Neophytos Vamvas, who continued to insist on the translation of the Scriptures into modern Greek, provoked widespread reaction and severe personal attacks by the conservatives led by Constantinos Oikonomos, unequivocally the strongest voice of Orthodoxy in the Greek state down to his death in 1857. Theophilos Kairis, a progressive teacher at the Academy of Kydonies before the Revolution who remained faithful to his religious nonconformism, was subjected to persecution, hauled before the courts for his religious convictions, and finally died in jail. Though there were strong voices among the epigones of the Enlightenment, such as N. I. Saripolos and Georgios Athanasiou, who defended Kairis and the principle of freedom of conscience and succeeded in vindicating him posthumously before the Areopagus, the supreme court of the new state, Kairis's fate was indicative of the weakness of Greek liberalism in the mid-nineteenth century.[79]

REORIENTATIONS

While the Enlightenment was on the wane in postrevolutionary Greek politics, the signs of an ideological reorientation of Greek political culture toward a new type of nationalism were unmistakable. The cultural and intellectual climate within which this new nationalism was shaped was very different from the climate that produced the liberal nationalism of the Enlightenment. A period of religious revival began in Greece in the 1830s with the formation, under secret Russian sponsorship, of the "Philorthodox Society," which combined as its goals the safeguard of an allegedly threatened Orthodoxy and the liberation of unredeemed Greek provinces in European Turkey.[80] In the same years, a strong conservative reaction against the educational activities of Protestant missionaries in Greece triggered a controversy over the issue of religious toleration, in the course of which the liberals came under severe attack as willing to tolerate an adulteration of the Orthodox faith. This process of conservative religious realignment in Greek society, abetted by encouragement from Constantinople, culminated in a surge of Orthodox fundamentalism and millenarianism in the 1850s. On a certain level, this could be interpreted as a process of desecularization that undermined whatever impact the Enlightenment's ideas might have had among the wider strata of Greek society.

The signs of a resurgence of religious conservatism were multiple, and what was more significant, they were detectable on all levels of Greek society: official state policy, intellectual life, and popular culture. In 1850, the severed relations between the Church of Greece and the Ecumenical Patriarchate were restored in a compromise that recognized the primacy of Constantinople and affirmed the dedication of the Church of Greece to

Orthodox tradition and canon law. The ecclesiastical settlement was hailed as a healing of a wound in the body of the Church and a contribution to the unity of Orthodoxy; the state soon officially recognized the Church in a bill of 1852, proclaiming the synod of the Church of Greece as the guardian of spiritual and national unity.

Persecution of religious dissent was stepped up in the 1850s. Not only was the Protestant missionary Jonas King tried and condemned for prose-lytism, but distinguished men of letters who were well known as critics of conventional religion were subjected to persecution. As we have seen, in 1853, Theophilos Kairis died in jail; in 1856, the satirist and social critic Andreas Laskaratos was excommunicated and anathematized; in 1859, the poet Panayiotis Synodinos was tried and found guilty of offending religion. In popular culture, the 1850s witnessed an outburst of religious funda-mentalism stimulated by the preaching of Christophoros Papoulakos, while Kosmas Flamiatos gave warning of the threat of Protestantism; millenari-anism resounded throughout the decade with the prophecies of Ioannis P. Seriphios in 1852, followed by the resurrection of the tradition of Agath-angelos, whose roots went back to the 1750s, and which was revived on the occasion of the Crimean War (1854–1856); the folk hero of the Greek War of Independence, General Ioannis Makriyannis, embittered by his treat-ment at the hands of the new state, sought refuge in visions of God and dreams that he recorded in a cryptic text.[81] The cumulative effect of the surge of religious sentiment might be interpreted as a reaction against the dangers seen by the religious conscience as menacing the "Greek tradition," as a consequence of the modernization and secularization symbolized by the Enlightenment and the founding of a Westernized state.

The preoccupation with the safeguarding of the unity, integrity, and gen-uineness of Orthodoxy was just the most ideologically charged expression of a persisting cultural conflict in Greek society between Western influences and modes of modern thought on the one hand, and the entrenched pat-terns of traditional mentalities characteristic of the Greek East on the other. The fact that the conservative campaign found its battle cry in the notion of unity essentially signaled that the whole movement was a protest against the cultural schism that was perceived as the result of the intrusion of foreign ideas into the bosom of Greek society.

In this context, the argument for unity was transmitted from the contro-versy over the ecclesiastical question to political rhetoric and to philosophical discourse. In politics, the value of unity was extolled against the discredited partisanship of rival political factions whose incessant conflicts had repeatedly led the nation to the verge of disaster during the Revolution, and thereafter threatened constantly to disrupt the smooth functioning of the state. The argument against political divisiveness served quite effectively the purposes of the absolutist state, whose main concern was the consolidation of centralized authority against liberal pressures for constitutionalism and the centrifugal tendencies of entrenched sectional interests, which found in constitutionalism a convenient and legitimate cover for their own oligarchic aspirations.[82] The ideological attacks of the supporters of the crown against the political parties as perpetrators of civil strife, combined with a widespread antipathy toward political alignments and groupings in general inherited from the sobering and bitter experiences of the Revolution, cultivated a normative climate that denied legitimacy to political parties in Greek political culture. Parties came to be thought of simply as agents of strife, motivated by the pursuit of personal gain on the part of ambitious and uninhibited leaders and self-seeking followers.

This dismal view of the role of political parties had, to be sure, considerable historical substance to it, as even a casual perusal of Greek political history will make plain. The net effect, however, was that political parties were perceived in a totally negative light in Greek political culture. Their essential role in representative government, which derived from their character as aggregating structures mediating between the state and the citizens, remained unrecognized. The crucial advantages of party spirit in creating an atmosphere of mutual tolerance and making possible the conduct of government by free discussion, on which classical European liberalism had insisted, were also lost on Greek political thought.[83] Thus, despite the tenacity and resilience of partisan divisions in Greek political life, which reflected the interplay between the domestic fragmentation of Greek society and the conflicting foreign influences on Greek politics, in the normative sphere, partisan alignments came to be perceived as an illegitimate and morally unacceptable aberration that undermined the most sacred priority, national unity, a goal deemed indispensable to the survival and greatness of the nation. Very few liberal voices took exception to this view, which has since prevailed with an unusual persistence in Greek political culture, providing priceless rhetorical ammunition to conservative and authoritarian shades of opinion during the following decades.

The notion of unity, triumphant in political rhetoric, was on its way to becoming the central idea defining the cultural *Zeitgeist* in mid-nineteenth century Greece. This was effectively achieved once the idea of unity was received and rationalized in philosophical discourse and thus became part of the unquestioned premises and philosophical presuppositions of collective consciousness.

The theme of unity dominated the last theoretical treatment of ancient Greek history that was still influenced by the Enlightenment's republican philosophy of history, Georgios G. Kozakis-Typaldos's *Philosophical Essay on the Progress and Fall of Ancient Greece* (1839). The essay explained the achievements of ancient Hellenism in terms of the interplay of civic virtue and liberty that sustained all well-ordered republics. It was precisely the slackening of rigid republican morality, the loss of personal rectitude and public-spiritedness that undermined social solidarity in the ancient republics, which led to the loss of Greek freedom. Up to this point the republican theory held its ground. The consideration of the problem of Greece's subjugation to the Romans led to the identification of three causes of her downfall: the pursuit of extreme independence by the Greek republics; civil strife within and between them; and political revolutions caused by mob pressures on ancient republican institutions. This diagnosis formed the basis of an appeal on behalf of political virtue and social solidarity, but it was also read as a pointer to a higher political truth: this was the "lofty notion of moral unity which is the ultimate and most necessary of all social notions since it primarily molds and shapes the nationality."[84] Incomplete national unity was the Ancients' greatest political and moral failure, from which their modern progeny had to derive sober lessons in charting their own political course.

This last restatement of the republican theory of history essentially constituted an epitaph to the Enlightenment. Within two years of its appearance, the basic principles of the Enlightenment came under severe attack by a new philosophy of history. The new philosophical outlook began from a fundamental criticism and refutation of the basic tenets of eighteenth-century liberal individualism. This task was accomplished in the pages of an *Essay on the Philosophy of History* published by Markos Renieris in 1841.

Writing under the influence of the rediscovery of Vico in the age of romanticism, the Italian-educated Renieris stressed that the liberal individualism of eighteenth-century philosophy was only a very partial truth, inferior to the wisdom of social collectivities such as the people, the *Volk*, who are the repository of true values and genuine knowledge. The full negation of the philosophy of the Enlightenment came with the affirmation of the final truth of Christian religion. In the doctrine of the Trinity, the antagonism between ego and nonego was resolved, and true unity, the fundamental spiritual requirement of the age following the collapse of individualism, was achieved. The triumph of the new philosophy had special implications for Greece: once she had discovered the meaning of the true philosophy and had solved her own philosophical problems, Greece was destined to solve the philosophical problem of the East—and with the philosophical, the even-sharper political problem of the East as well.[85] So the new philosophical outlook taking root in Greece at mid-nineteenth century came full circle to connect the negation of the Enlightenment with the political aspirations of Greece in the Near East. The prominent position occupied in Greek nineteenth century society by the author of these views, and the leading role played by him in promoting Greek irredentism, could be taken as indications of the social action associated with the new philosophical climate.

By following the vicissitudes of Neohellenic thought, we are approaching directly the final formulation of the ideology of Greek irredentism in the crucial decade of the 1840s. A final dimension of the intellectual climate, directly bearing on the elaboration of this ideology, is found in the historiography of the period. Stimulated by the reaction to Fallmerayer's theories, Greek historical scholarship was rallying its forces in order to refute his racist claims concerning the descent of modern Greeks from the Slavic and Albanian tribes that penetrated the Byzantine Empire from the seventh century onward.[86] In response to this provocation, Greek scholars elaborated the historical doctrine of the ethnological and cultural continuity of the Greek nation and Greek civilization. This doctrine found its most mature formulation in the monumental five-volume *History of the Greek Nation* published by Constantinos Paparrigopoulos between 1861 and 1874. He began his researches with a monograph published in 1844 under the title *The Last Year of Greek Freedom,* which dealt with ancient Greece's fall to the Romans in 146 BC. In trying to capture the meaning of Greek history, Paparrigopoulos noted, one has to follow the processes leading from discord and division to unity. The climax of division at the end of the ancient era had brought about the loss of freedom and the subjugation to the Romans. Since then, however, several processes of unification had set in, reaching their maturity in the author's time:

> Polytheism has been replaced by the unity of Christianity; the variety of dialects by the unity of language, the different tribes by the unity of the nation. Fortified in this three-dimensional panoply the Greek people is struggling to recover its political unity.[87]

Modern Greek historical scholarship was thus set on its theoretical course. Paparrigopoulos did not complete his historical synthesis until several decades later, but the new theory of Greek history found its pioneering formulation in the researches of Spyridon Zambelios at midcentury. He turned to the study of Greek folk poetry in order to demonstrate the continuity of the Greek nation as reflected in the unity of its culture. This unity was found in the striking affinities of modern folk poetry with ancient Greek literary traditions. If, therefore, the historical continuity between ancient and modern Hellenism could be substantiated on the basis of the genuine traditions of popular culture that were transmitted unadulterated through the Byzantine Middle Ages, the origins of the modern Greek nation could be traced precisely in the Byzantine centuries according to Zambelios.[88] This was a decisive moment in Greek intellectual history. Byzantium, which was still seen by Greek neoclassicism as an age of superstitious folly and barbarism, was for the first time perceived in a different light; instead of being a disastrous rupture in the evolution of Greek civilization, an abominable interruption in Greek history, as suggested by the Enlightenment, the Byzantine Empire was perceived as the context that preserved Greek nationality and culture and assured its survival amid the vicissitudes of the Roman conquest and the barbaric invasions. It was precisely this theory of Greek history that Paparrigopoulos enshrined as the cornerstone of modern Greek national consciousness. To the Enlightenment's discovery of the historical bonds between ancient Hellas and the modern Greeks, nineteenth-century historicism added a rehabilitation of Byzantium, thus fostering a three-dimensional sense of historical identity in terms of which the new nation came to conceive of itself. Subsequent researches in linguistics and folklore consolidated this sense of national continuity, and the rehabilitation of Byzantium proceeded apace with the waning of the Enlightenment.

One may wonder as to what was the position reserved for the heritage of classical Greece in the new outlook. Markos Renieris interpreted classical Greek civilization as a struggle between the ego and the collectivity, culminating in the triumph of the ego, which he saw achieved in Platonic thought.[89] Despite this eventual triumph of the ego, he did not discount classical civilization, which provided Greece's major claim to glory and was therefore necessary in creating the symbolism of Greek identity and sense of dignity. Precisely for the same reason, the major preoccupation of Greek historicism was to connect the modern Greeks ethnologically and culturally directly to the Ancients (in this, romantic historicism shared one of the basic tenets of the Greek Enlightenment). Even the revived Orthodox consciousness did not go all the way to reject wholesale pagan classicism: the concept of a "Grecochristian" civilization, appropriately enough first coined by Zambelios,[90] was adopted instead by its spokesmen. They tried to integrate a moralistic understanding of classical philosophy into a framework of Christian thought by pointing at the classical learning of the major Church Fathers as a precedent. What changed fundamentally was the understanding, the meaning, accorded to the classics. The republican reading of the classics, as conceived by Korais, was abandoned and replaced by a purely rhetorical celebration of ancient Greek greatness. The significance of the change lay in the fact that the potentialities of social criticism inherent in the classicism of the Enlightenment (of which Korais's synthesis was typical) was displaced by the ideology of ancestral worship that merely sustained the modern Greek claim to glory. One consequence of this was that social criticism as a form of consciousness was almost excluded from the modern Greek intellectual universe and was replaced by an intolerant sense of self-sufficiency and self-confidence, based on the argument of continuity between the classical past and Neohellenic present.

Thus the theme of unity, on which all intellectual strands of the period seem to converge, emerged as a product of the philosophical critique of liberalism and as the battle cry of religious militancy that combined their forces in an attack on the legacy of the Enlightenment. With the scholarly researches of Greek national historicism it was given a "scientific" basis to sustain its claims. The cultural climate was thus ripe for a translation of these converging intellectual orientations into a political program. This political articulation came in the form of the ideology of the Great Idea that was to inspire Greek irredentism from then onward. In the same year that saw the publication of Paparrigopoulos's first monograph, Ioannis Kolettis, one of the leaders who rose to prominence in the politics of the Greek War of Independence, in an address to the National Assembly drafting the Greek Constitution that King Otho was forced to grant by the military pronunciamento of 3 September 1843, voiced the new political aspirations and described his vision of Greece's mission in the world:

> By her geographical location, Greece is the center of Europe; with the East on her right and the West on her left, she has been destined through her downfall to enlighten the West and through her regeneration to enlighten the East. The first task has been fulfilled by our ancestors; the second is assigned to us. In the spirit of our oath and of this great idea, I have seen the delegates of the nation assembling to deliberate not simply on the fate of Greece, but for the entire Greek race. [. . .] we have been led astray and away from that great idea of the fatherland which was first expressed in the song of Rhigas. At that time all of us who bore the Greek name, united in one spirit, we realized a part of the whole goal[. . . .]
>
> Each of us has in himself a sense of his splendid Greek origin. Each of us is aware that this Assembly is convening in Athens, whose splendor, grandeur and inimitable achievements have been admired throughout the centuries. Athens, and the rest of Greece divided in the past in particular states, fell and through her downfall she has enlightened the world. Contemporary Greece, united as she is in one state, one purpose, one religion, should therefore inspire great expectations to the world.[91]

Greece's unity of power and purpose and her civilizing mission in the East were, of course, to be accomplished at the expense of the traditional rival, the Ottoman Empire. The rise of the great empire of the Ottoman Turks since the fourteenth century had been associated with the decline and retreat of Hellenism in the East: Asia Minor; the Balkans; Constantinople, the cherished queen of all cities; the Greek heartlands finally fell one after another to the Turkish onslaught. This created a long tradition of anguish and resentment reflected in folk poetry and late Byzantine and post-Byzantine political thought.[92] Along with it went a millenarian faith in the eventual resurrection of the empire and the rebirth of Hellenism and Greek glory. This belief shaped most of Greek political thinking during the *Tourkokratia*. The anti-Turkish tone of the millennarian tradition was strengthened in the eighteenth century under the impact of the Enlightenment view of the barbarian and decadent Turk who brought destruction to civilization wherever he encountered it.[93] This outlook was espoused wholeheartedly by the Greek exponents of the Enlightenment in whose thought the revival of classical Greek ideals and learning, in the context of modern Greek civilization, became contingent on the overthrow and disappearance of the presence of the Turks. This conception of the Greek problem became the most powerful strand in Neohellenic nationalist thinking; it lived through the Enlightenment and the Revolution and became the centerpiece of the Great Idea. It was probably the only one of the themes of Enlightenment thought that was not questioned by the exponents of the Great Idea.[94]

In the new framework, traditional anti-Turkish symbolism, reinforced by the experiences of fighting an all-out War of Independence against the Turks, was linked with a political program that visualized the replacement of the Ottoman Empire by a Greek state in the East led by the Greek crown. The small kingdom was to lead the struggle for the liberation of unredeemed Greeks and the recovery of historic Greek territories in pursuit of Panhellenic unity. All resources and energy of the Greek kingdom were to be mobilized to this end and all diplomatic opportunities to be seized to promote it.[95] Also, the unredeemed Greeks of the periphery were to be converted to the values of the Great Idea through education and the creation of a network of political and cultural ties with free Greece. In an age of romanticism, when the mystique of nationalism was swaying the whole of Europe, the appeal of this political program grew so powerful that over the decades, dissent or criticism came to be regarded simply as a betrayal of the most sacred values and cherished aspirations of the nation.

The new nationalist ideology, born of a fundamental reorientation of Greek thought, contributed decisively to the ascendancy of conservative forces in Greek society. Basically it fulfilled a social function that tended to consolidate their control. By making external preoccupations the major priority of Greek politics, it distracted attention from domestic problems and provided an emotional outlet for the defusing of social pressures on the structures of Greek society.[96] By pointing to a common national goal beyond the narrow frontiers of the Greek kingdom, the ideology of the Great Idea deprived domestic social conflicts of legitimacy and left the *status quo* unquestioned.

Several qualifications, distinctions, and caveats should be added here. First of all, it has to be noted that irredentism was by no means the only channel through which domestic social pressures were defused. Other mechanisms as well served the same purpose in the course of the nineteenth century: social mobility through patronage or through education or the widespread phenomenon of brigandage offered alternative ways of alleviating the destitution of the lower, especially rural, social strata. Emigration to Southern Russia, Egypt, and Asia Minor throughout the nineteenth century, and to America toward the end of the century, provided the classic mechanism sustaining the *status quo* by removing the demographic surpluses that could furnish the potential social bases of protest movements.[97]

It must be noted secondly that, although acceptance of the Great Idea as an ultimate goal was general and remained an unquestioned precondition of political legitimacy, disagreements over specific objectives and tactics and over the precise territorial content of irredentism remained always points of controversy and contention in Greek political thought.[98] All this tied in inextricably with other issues agitating Greek politics, such as constitutionalism and the role of the "protecting" powers, which constantly preoccupied the political class. This tug-of-war between conflicting interests formed the context to which the currents of liberal ideas that represented the ideological heritage of the Enlightenment had to adjust.

Third, it is essential to keep in mind that, whatever the stakes in and uses of irredentism in internal party struggles, the aspirations of the Great Idea possessed independent appeal to the masses, especially to the demoralized lower social strata of the cities. The political culture of disappointed expectations that took root in the Greek kingdom as the promises of the Revolution proved to be vain hopes found an outlet in the political romanticism of irredentism.[99] At the same time, irredentism became the last resort of a new hope: the great national effort that was to lead to the liberation of the unredeemed might also foretell the amelioration of the lot of those living within the frontiers of independent Greece. The vision of national redemption for the unliberated brethren carried with it an inchoate promise of civil liberties and social progress for the formally free but disappointed Greek citizens.

Seen in this perspective, the politics of the Great Idea will be understood to spring from deep and pressing needs of Greek society. The most tangible of these needs, of which everyone was acutely aware at the time, had to do with the fact that the long-term economic and demographic viability of the Greek state was contingent upon substantial territorial changes that would make self-sustaining socioeconomic development possible. A final

distinction should, therefore, be kept in mind when thinking of Greek irredentism. Although the Great Idea dominated Greek domestic politics and
foreign policy throughout the period in which classical European imperialism reached its heyday, it should never be confused with it. Greece simply
did not meet the historical presuppositions of imperialist expansion. Greek
irredentism, therefore, despite all its inherent contradictions, never ceased
being a liberation movement. This will become adequately clear after an
examination of the nature and meaning of Greek nationalism in the unredeemed areas themselves.

The meaning of Greek irredentism was not identical inside and outside
Greece. For a nation that felt its greatest part under alien rule after the
achievement of independence by a small fraction of its historic territories,
irredentism was an almost inevitable preoccupation. Furthermore, if within
Greece irredentist nationalism served conservative social functions, for the
unredeemed Greek populations in Thessaly and Epirus, Macedonia and
Thrace, Asia Minor and Pontos, the Ionian and Aegean Islands, Crete and
Cyprus, it possessed a different meaning. For them, the dream of the Great
Idea did not involve mere national aggrandizement but carried the promise
of their redemption from arbitrary and autocratic rule; far from representing the fantasies of political romanticism, nationalism for the unredeemed
Greeks of the Ottoman Empire was a concrete aspiration for political order
and material progress under the aegis of a national entity with which they
could identify symbolically and culturally.

This broader meaning provided the moral and psychological momentum
of Greek irredentism. It was this dimension of the ideology of the Great
Idea that made it possible for Greek irredentism to penetrate so widely
within a few decades and to take such an effective hold among the populations of the unredeemed Greek periphery. And it was precisely when the
prospect of social progress, civil liberties, and orderly government emerged
for the subjects of the Ottoman Empire, in the era of reforms initiated in
1839 with the *Tanzimat* and culminating in the *Hatti-Humayun* of 1856,
that the meaning of irredentism became immensely complicated for the
unredeemed Greeks themselves as well. It was under these changed circumstances that serious modifications appeared in the political aspirations
of the Greek bourgeoisie of the unredeemed regions, thus intensifying the
contradictions in the politics of the Great Idea.[100] It is interesting to note, in
conclusion, that in this context a neo-Phanariot ideology reemerged toward

the close of the nineteenth century among the Greek lay and ecclesiastical leadership in the Ottoman Empire, who toyed with the idea of taking over the empire from within and turning it into the "Ottoman Empire of the Greek Nation." For these latter-day "Phanariots," this pathetic mirage was all the more lamentable in that it was conjured up not before but after the century of nationalism, and at a time that Turkish nationalism was about to disrupt definitively the schemes of multiethnic coexistence conceived by the cosmopolitan Young Ottoman liberal intellectuals and the last Ottoman Sultans who patronized them.[101] These developments, however, which belonged to a belated "Ottoman Enlightenment," heralded the beginning of the end of the Great Idea and are related to the story of the Greek Enlightenment only in the sense of representing its dialectical antithesis.

The foregoing brief reconstruction of the ideological evolution of Greek politics in the decades following the War of Independence has established adequately, I hope, the failure of the Enlightenment to take root and provide the ideological basis of a liberal political culture, on the pattern exemplified in the political and cultural history of Western Europe. The dissipation of the legacy of the Enlightenment in Greek culture was not, of course, completed overnight. Although the political culture of irredentist nationalism that prevailed in Greece at mid-century had little affinity with the substantive heritage of the Enlightenment, the latter's survival in Greek politics and in Greek thought remained discernible throughout the period of ideological transformation. In Greek culture, the most striking survival of the Enlightenment was a recurring critique and denunciation of Byzantium as an age of darkness and barbarism that was repeatedly voiced by major representatives of Greek letters and Greek scholarship down to the 1870s, when they were finally silenced by the prevalence of Paparrigopoulos's theory of Greek history.[102] In Greek politics, the heritage of the Enlightenment passed on to the liberal students of the University of Athens, who clamored for democratic liberties and constitutionalism against Othonian absolutism and in 1848 made the wave of revolution sweeping the rest of Europe felt in Greece as well.[103]

The political legacy of the Enlightenment lingered on in a tradition of Greek liberalism in the nineteenth century, represented in the reform-minded and Western-oriented politics of Alexandros Mavrokordatos and Epaminondas Deliyiorgis, and experienced its finest hour in the discussions of the National Assembly of 1862–1864, which elaborated the liberal Greek

Constitution of 1864. In the hybrid political culture of the new state, however, the liberal legacy of the Enlightenment remained weak and indecisive
in the face of the prevailing nationalism. The endemic weakness of Greek
socialism, which emerged toward the end of the nineteenth century,[104] was
directly connected with the weakness of Greek liberalism and ultimately
resulted from the same structural causes.

The decline of the Enlightenment was the undisputed ideological reality
in Greek political culture by the middle of the nineteenth century. Irredentist nationalism was thus left as the dominant ideological force in the politics of the new state. The ideological influences that were decisive in shaping
this new nationalism were quite different from the liberal nationalism of
the Enlightenment and the French Revolution. The nature of these influences has been hinted at by the foregoing consideration of the philosophical and historiographical doctrines that created the cultural context for the
articulation of Greek irredentism. The tide of European romanticism and
the impact of German historical theories as they had been elaborated by
Fichte and Schelling constituted the paramount intellectual influences in
the redefinition of the content and values of nationalism. This phenomenon
was naturally by no means unique to Greek political thought. Similar ideological transformations, which were in the making elsewhere in Europe, set
the broader environment that provided important stimuli to developments
in Greek thought.[105]

The intolerant and exclusive irredentism, which dislocated the legacy of
the Enlightenment, was the product of the interplay of Greek traditions
with the new cultural influences emanating from Europe. The final ideological configuration had its distant origins in Herder's cultural nationalism,
which had been one of the inspirations of Greek historicism in the period
of Enlightenment. The heritage of Herder's ideas, however, was cast in a
new guise upon its reception in Eastern European culture. Reinterpreted by
Herder's own heirs in Germany, his ideas developed into aggressive nationalism, based on an organicist conception of the national collectivity, which
demanded a total identification of the individual with the interests of the
culture and the race. This obviously involved a fundamental rejection of the
central philosophical and political principles of the Enlightenment—universality, rationalism, and liberal individualism.[106]

In no other regard was the powerful impact of irredentism on Greek
political thought and the concomitant decline of the Enlightenment more

evident than in the evolution in the content and meaning of the idea of liberty. A brief consideration of this problem might be the most fitting conclusion of this survey of the Enlightenment's fate in Greek thought. The Greek idea of freedom in the nineteenth century evolved from the conception of civil liberty and participation in the community of free citizens visualized by the Enlightenment, to an exclusivist conception of independence for the national collectivity, often at the expense of the personal liberty and moral freedom of the individual members of that collectivity. The humanist and liberal aspirations of the Enlightenment were lost in the theory of national independence, which depreciated the individual, whom it considered an expendable quantity, for the sake of national greatness. As this conception of national greatness came to be increasingly identified with the political aspirations of a crown that attempted to appropriate the symbolism of a Byzantine ideology, Greek nationalism shed the final vestiges of the legacy of the Enlightenment.

Epilogue

The Conditions of Liberal Politics

THE CONSIDERATION OF Greek intellectual and political history in the eighteenth and the early nineteenth centuries in this book has made possible the reconstruction of an integral ideological curve from the initial pains of rationalism to its culmination in a conscious and articulate political liberalism. Along this trajectory, nevertheless, the Enlightenment often precipitated reactions from the representatives of conventional culture and ideology, notably the Orthodox Church, which, during the centuries of Ottoman rule, had assumed the political leadership of the subject Christian peoples of the Balkans and had become the unquestionable exponent of authoritative opinion and values. The transmission of the Enlightenment, mostly through Italian and secondarily through Central European channels, from its major centers in Northwestern Europe to the Greek East, was the first instance of the process of universalization of Western European thought and culture that has been one of the central features of modern history in the last two centuries.[1] This historical characteristic of the intellectual process described in this book adds to it an intrinsic theoretical interest that broadens the significance of the particular substantive problems examined in the foregoing pages.

The reception and development of the Enlightenment in Southeastern Europe turned out to be an embattled process. Despite the full intellectual unfolding of the local Enlightenment from its philosophical premises to the articulation of its social and political implications, the legacy of the movement at the level of secular political thought was eventually dissipated and replaced in the nineteenth century by an illiberal irredentist nationalism. This sealed the historical failure of the Enlightenment to provide the basis of a liberal political culture, in contrast to what happened in the Atlantic world. The phenomena investigated in this project, therefore, might be construed to entail a theoretical paradox in the divergence between a fully developed ideology informed by the principles of the Enlightenment and the structural constraints of its social basis that prevented it from becoming a predominant political tradition.

The identification of this paradox obviously raises some very interesting theoretical issues concerning the interrelationship between ideas and their structural milieu and the role of ideas in social and political change. These are among the most important—and hopeless—theoretical issues in social science, and have continuously preoccupied and agitated social theory ever since it became fully conscious of them in the nineteenth century. This book does not, of course, pretend to tackle directly any of these issues, but in its modest way it does discuss a body of evidence bearing on some concrete aspects of these broader problems. It has illustrated how cultural change and transformations in political ideology register the deeper mutations in the structures of society and how, in turn, systems of thought and ideological options might provide the cognitive means for comprehending these changes and articulating programs of social action and political alternatives that might shape and give direction to the effects of change.

It was precisely in such terms that the social ideology of the Enlightenment, as represented by a group of Westernized Greek intellectuals and supported by an economically modernized social stratum, expressed and explained the strains, tensions, and possibilities immanent in the social changes in Balkan society in the age of the "democratic revolution" or of the "democratic Enlightenment." The exponents of this ideology projected an option for the future before the collective consciousness of their compatriots.

In their argument for cultural transformation and political change on the paradigm of Western European nations, the followers of the Enlightenment suggested a potential direction in the development of Greek consciousness and society that represented a radical break with existing social realities and ideological traditions.

In articulating this alternative, they remained largely unconscious of the inner tension between the full intellectual development and the anemic social basis of their theoretical position. This tension was connected with the position of the followers of the Enlightenment in Greek society: they formed a very small fraction of the population concentrated in the commercial cities of the Balkans and Asia Minor and in the communities of the Greek diaspora, and by the nature of things they were generally isolated from the main mass of a traditional, religiously oriented, and largely non-literate peasant society. Isolated for the most part from the mass of society they wanted to guide and transform, the men (and very few women in later phases) of the Enlightenment fought their battle with the representatives of conventional ideology. These conflicts, however, were fought mainly in the sphere of formal culture and were felt in the society at large only to a very limited degree, if at all.

The greatest social achievement of the Greek Enlightenment, however, was that it broke through these structural constraints and managed to make itself felt within Greek society. The Greek intelligentsia did not remain isolated in the diaspora, but managed to create a number of major educational centers informed by the Enlightenment in several of the bigger Greek cities and penetrated even beyond into certain regions in the countryside wherever conditions were propitious. Furthermore, in the three decades between the French and the Greek Revolutions, cultural innovation and the propagation of the new liberal and radical ideas contributed decisively to the creation of the climate of expectancy that prepared Greek society psychologically for the War of Independence.

Against this background, the intellectuals of the Enlightenment could attempt to appeal to and speak for Greek collective consciousness. Although the Enlightenment's aspiration was to become the integral content of a totally redefined Greek collective consciousness, it remained only an option, a possibility of reorientation that was only partially realized. What the Enlightenment did achieve was its own full unfolding into an alternative social theory. It appears, therefore, that rather than being a determinate product of a certain structural environment, intellectual development progressed to a large degree autonomously as a critical theoretical response to that structural milieu and was moved by a dynamic of its own, derived from the vitality of its exponents and the strength of its original sources in the mainstream of European thought and culture. The interplay of these factors makes the study of ideological change in eighteenth- and nineteenth-century Greek culture a quite pertinent context for the elaboration of a social history of ideas, with a broader theoretical interest.

Beyond these wider theoretical implications, the issues explored in this study point at some fundamental and enduring problems in the Greek political experience, which in turn raise a central question in political theory concerning the conditions and nature of liberal politics. The development of the Enlightenment, and the cleavages it precipitated in Greek society, produced four theoretical responses to the fundamental problems of Greek politics. As illustrated in the foregoing pages, these four responses comprised a negative position of an integral Counterenlightenment, eventually espoused by the Church; a position of conservative realism that wanted to tame the Enlightenment and arrest its practical implications, but shrewdly refrained from advocating a completely reactionary stand; a liberal republicanism that espoused the Enlightenment's politics wholeheartedly—and therefore was in its essence profoundly subversive in the Greek context— but remained conscious of the tactical imperative to avoid a total break with Greek social realities and an open confrontation with the Church; finally, a revolutionary strand that espoused radical republicanism and visualized a total transformation of Greek society.

Considered in their specific social and historical context, the theoretical options offered by the Enlightenment invite a critical reflection. The political aspirations of the Enlightenment were originally rather painlessly introduced into Greek thought by means of a redefinition of the traditional theory of Christian monarchy. This redefinition produced a theory of enlightened absolutism as the agent of cultural reform and benevolent government—a vision that was sustained by its powerful association with the Greek hopes in Russian help in overthrowing the Ottoman yoke. The Russian connection that sustained the theory of enlightened absolutism eventually discredited it, once Russian promises proved just a mirage of political expediency.

The radicalization of Greek political thought that ensued, reinforced by the influences of the French Revolution, gave birth to a theory of democratic republicanism, which, though tangential to the problems of Greek society as a practical solution, was nevertheless inspired by a profound analysis of the social predicament of Neohellenism. The republican program, which sought through civic virtue to reconstitute a national community by setting such a formidable task to itself, appeared conscious of the enormity of the project of political change and moral reconstruction required by the Enlightenment. The Greek republican democrats obviously thought that the obstacles to political change in Greek society were so redoubtable that only a total effort at radical transformation of existing conditions could cope with them.

The final synthesis in the political theory of the Greek Enlightenment, attained by Adamantios Korais, involved a modification of radical republicanism by an appeal to political moderation and a recognition of the virtues of liberalism. This theoretical position should be appraised, not on the basis of pure criteria of philosophical consistency obvious to the contemporary student of political theory, but not necessarily relevant to the purposes of the committed intellectuals of the Enlightenment, who arrived at it eclectically, taking into account the constraints of their environment and with specific goals in mind. It is precisely against these social goals that the relevance of the political theory of the Greek Enlightenment should be evaluated. In this perspective, Korais's preference for a liberal republic might appear irrelevant because the bases of social moderation that could sustain such a political system were absent in Ottoman Greece, which was a far cry from modern liberal England. His awareness of this obvious fact can explain Korais's argument for evolutionary change and postponement of the revolutionary outburst until the preconditions for such a republic could reach maturity. Otherwise, he feared that the battle might be lost for the Enlightenment—as actually happened. The Enlightenment, therefore, remained a vision of possibilities and alternatives and a framework of social and cultural criticism in Greek history, rather than a workable blueprint of actual developments.

As against the options immanent in the ideas of the Enlightenment, the theoretical positions of its enemies aspired to an obstruction of the changes that made the Enlightenment a possible alternative. The Counterenlightenment called for a regression into a theocratic community of

Christian believers and mystics that would preserve Greece as a latter-day Byzantine cultural survival, constituting a picturesque detail on the map of a changing Europe. So long as the spiritual and cultural purposes of the scheme were assured, the Counterenlightenment remained indifferent to the political context, and under the circumstances of the turn of the eighteenth and nineteenth centuries, it was perfectly content to submit and sustain the infidel absolutism of the Ottomans. Although differing in its cultural preferences, conservative realism, which had inherited the theory of enlightened despotism, was equally prepared to compromise with the Ottomans in order to arrest the subversive dangers posed by the Enlightenment. This theoretical position involved a realization that controlled and guided innovation was essential in order to assure the achievement of the overriding political goal, which sought the preservation of the social *status quo*. Change could be geared to the needs of existing power structures, and some lessons from the West could be relevant in strengthening the prevailing order of things, so long as the legitimacy of traditional values and symbols remained untarnished.

The transmission of the Enlightenment into Greek culture was made possible by the emergence of new groups of socially and geographically mobile merchants and intellectuals—joined by disenchanted elements in the traditional leadership groups—who broke with tradition and received custom. Most of them originated in geographically remote and isolated mountainous highlands or agriculturally barren islands and, denied the opportunities and privileges they craved in the Ottoman social context, they turned by necessity to the West, where they traveled in order to buy and sell or to be educated and pursue fortune. In this process, they learned the habits, virtues, and vices of the West, and they absorbed the mental patterns, science, and culture of "enlightened" Europe. It was these social groups who projected the Enlightenment as an option before Greek collective consciousness and analyzed the Greek problem in terms of cultural innovation and political change on the model of Western liberalism.

These groups stood for novel, indeed revolutionary, social aspirations in the Balkan context: they cultivated acquisitive values, pleaded for a government of law, and espoused the idea of a free nation as a way of political existence. In these strata, the Enlightenment found its social basis. Comparatively speaking, the power of the Western Enlightenment was not due to a more extensive social basis. The crucial distinction seems to have been in the diversity characterizing the public of the Enlightenment in the West—a diversity that was lacking in the East.[2] The new ideas and the liberal temper were confined among the new merchants and intellectuals who had been in touch with the West. Enlightenment and liberalism encountered active opposition, suspicion, and resentment in practically all other social milieux in the Greek East.

At the time that the effects of the age of the democratic revolution were felt in Southeastern Europe, political leadership appeared to pass into the hands of the new social groups. While the traditional leadership identified its fortunes with alien despotism, it seemed that the new social groups would manage to shape the future of the nation according to their own political and cultural aspirations. The very success of the new political class, however, eventually undermined its liberal aspirations. Not only were the most progressive and radical elements politically isolated, but the wealthier merchants, who gradually developed serious stakes in social order, joined forces with the older oligarchic elements and modified their liberal pretensions. Thus, when the War of Independence appeared imminent, the Greek political class felt that it had much to lose if the Revolution took a decidedly radical turn. This gave a conservative edge to the Greek Revolution, which was reinforced by the climate of political and social reaction prevailing in Restoration Europe. Thus, the differentiations in the attitudes and power of Westernized mercantile elements in Greek society deprived the intelligentsia of the Enlightenment of its natural social allies. As a consequence, in the politics of the Greek Revolution, political liberalism and its radical extensions found themselves in a social vacuum. This explains the gradual erosion and eventual loss of the social bases of the Enlightenment, which were in any case meager. This sealed the political fate of liberalism. The republican Hellas of the Enlightenment, with its radical implications, was depoliticized and replaced by the "classical reaction" of romantic hellenism.[3]

These were the circumstances of the birth of the new Greece. Of the four ideological programs that aspired to shape the future of the new nation, the one that eventually appeared victorious from the struggles of the periods of the Enlightenment and the Greek Revolution was the conservatism first enunciated in its essentials by Panayiotis Kodrikas. Although, in the immediate pre-independence political struggles, Korais and his followers seemed to be winning the battle, in the longer run Kodrikas's ideas were victorious: both his linguistic theory and his conception of the Greek national community preserved by the Church and held together by the values of its traditional heritage eventually prevailed in nineteenth-century Greek culture.[4]

In politics, liberalism became entangled in a strange paradox. The system of modern administrative institutions created by state building during the Greek Revolution and under the Bavarian dynasty, to which a complete set of liberal parliamentary institutions was gradually added as a result of the constitutional risings of 1843 and 1862, was superimposed upon and was inevitably distorted in its workings by a nonliberal society which originally resisted this process of modern institution building. As a matter of fact, the superimposition of modern liberal institutions on the traditional, fragmented, and semifeudal society that emerged from Ottoman captivity into the Greek kingdom increased the distance between the state and society and preserved the feeling that the state was an alien and external body that threatened and held society in some sort of bondage. The pattern of authority relations, stamped by distrust and suspicion of the state, was thus bequeathed by the Ottoman dominion—the version of absolutist old regime in the Greek historical experience—to the liberal political system. Eventually, the liberal institutions and all the trappings of parliamentary politics—universal suffrage, elections, partisan alignments, regular transfers of power after electoral contests—instead of transforming and liberalizing the society upon which they were grafted, were distorted by it and became mechanisms through which traditional practices—patron-client relations, patterns of traditional obligation and dependence, and the overall fragmentation of society—were preserved. The modern liberal state, rather than becoming the impartial umpire of social conflict and the agent of political and cultural unification of the society, became the object of an enormous spoils system that perpetuated the premodern and nonliberal traits of the society. This was the paradox of Greek liberalism. It was in the context of this failure of the modern state to unify the society that irredentist nationalism became the only psychological and cultural force that could provide superordinate national goals that might bridge conflicting sectional interests and mitigate the effects of social fragmentation.[5] The measure of liberalism's failure can be best appreciated in view of the fact that constitutional government and significant political change in Greece were achieved not as a consequence of liberal politics but by military interventions in politics in 1843, 1862, and 1909—a feature of the Greek political system that inaugurated an ominous tradition in twentieth-century politics.[6]

These weaknesses of Greek liberalism invite a final word of explanation, which might be attempted by resuming the consideration of the structural dimensions of the Enlightenment identified in the opening chapter of this study. A comparison between the initial geography of the Enlightenment in the eighteenth century and the geopolitical location of the Greek kingdom in the Hellenic world in the middle decades of the nineteenth century reveals that the areas that witnessed the growth and flowering of the Enlightenment, the commercial cities of Northern Greece and Western Asia Minor, remained outside the original boundaries of independent Greece. The geographical shape of the Greek kingdom deprived it as well of the sociological dimension of the Enlightenment, the emergence of professional, mercantile, and vocational groups whose engagement in new modes of economic activity and experience of social change made them receptive to new ideas and political liberalism. It was precisely these social groups that were left out of the Greek kingdom that was created in the regions of the classical Greek heartlands, to the neoclassicist's delight, but which were the most conservative and virtually unaffected by change areas of Greece. Furthermore, the sociological and demographic evolution of the kingdom itself, at the time that the fate of the Enlightenment was at stake, was marked by an absolute and proportional increase in agricultural population[7]—a development quite in line with the aspiration of the Bavarian dynasty to create a nation of small peasant proprietors whose loyalty to paternalist monarchy would be assured.[8] The bulk of free Greeks in the middle of the nineteenth century would have comfortably fit into Karl Marx's sack of potatoes.[9]

Thus, the sociological character of the Greek kingdom left the political and intellectual liberals, who gravitated to free Greece, in a vacuum. The exigencies of the War of Independence had forced them into precarious and frequently broken alliances with their conservative rivals. Despite the compromises required by these alliances and the weight of international circumstances, the intelligentsia of the Enlightenment managed to mediate the new modes of collective self-conception that inspired the Revolution and largely shaped the new nation's sense of identity. In the independent kingdom, however, the liberals, lacking political allies, were forced to be integrated into the *status quo* at the expense of their principles. The sacrifice of liberal principles was made smoother by reference to the broader climate of romanticism and nationalism prevailing in Europe, which sanctioned the new political and cultural choices.

The original alliance between the liberal intellectuals and the rising mercantile bourgeoisie was dictated by the pressing need felt by the new professional and commercial classes for a national state ruled by the laws as the framework of their economic activities, whose continuation and orderly transaction was jeopardized by the arbitrary and unpredictable whims of Ottoman absolutism. Once the national state was achieved, the revolutionary liberalism of the pre-independence period lost much of its practical relevance so far as the new professional and commercial classes were concerned. Furthermore, as noted a moment ago, the economically advanced social groups that were likely to support a liberal political system remained, for the most part, outside the confines of the new state in which the fate of liberalism was decided. The middle class that did emerge in the new nation found its interests best served by its incorporation into the ruling coalition of conservative interests that enjoyed all the advantages that could be derived from the state spoils system. This left the liberal intellectuals alone in their vision of a community of free citizens under the rule of law. The danger of complete isolation obliged those who believed in liberal ideas to become absorbed almost without protest in the social and political realities of the new state, which they had failed to shape in accordance with their original dreams. In this way, the political and intellectual leaders, who had aspired to shape society on the liberal model, were finally absorbed into the social oligarchy that distorted the substance of liberal institutions and introduced a system of party political interests and patron-client relations that was an obstacle in the path of long-tern political and social reform.

The final outcome gave dramatic expression to the negative relationship between the Greek Enlightenment and the main body of Greek society. Greek liberalism was dominated by individuals isolated from the social forces, to whose desires they occasionally gave direction. With the exception of a few cases, the weakness of the very social strata that might have supported the claims of political liberalism never allowed the occasional alignments to develop into articulate social movements capable of confronting other social formations in the struggle for political power. This weakness was not unconnected, although not entirely determined, by the comprador character of the Greek economy.[10] An examination of this dimension of the social history of Greek liberalism clearly lies beyond the scope of the present analysis. This hint, however, might well account for the social isolation and ultimate failure of Greek liberalism as a system of political principles and moral values.

This brief set of hints at the structural reasons for the weakness of Greek liberalism constitute an attempt to suggest a historical sociology of Greek political thought. From what might be called the phenomenology of political life as reflected in prevalent modes of political behavior and political culture, the analysis moved on to the structural dimensions of the political system and the conflicts and alliances of political forces, and finally hinted at the transnational and international factors emanating from the broader systemic environment of particular national societies. This concluding analysis has revealed, I hope, the absence of the basic social preconditions of liberal politics in the Greek experience. The Greek middle class that might aspire to a liberal political system lacked the dynamism and determination contingent on autonomous development and thus both failed to achieve a revolutionary break with the past and eventually was absorbed into a conservative coalition inimical to social change and democratic politics.[11]

As a consequence of these structural preconditions, a "natural liberalism," which might have formed the basis of a politically unified nation and an integrated cultural pattern, remained alien to the Greek political experience. Indeed, if modern Greek historical realities are measured against the ideal type of a liberal society,[12] the nature of Greek politics will appear to approximate a counterpoint of political liberalism. Instead of shared frames of mind and an integrated cultural pattern, profound cultural cleavages and conflicting ideological traditions harbor mutually exclusive social visions. Political ethics, therefore, has never been taken for granted, and unanimity, in stark contrast to liberal politics, has never been a problem. Instead of the battle between Whig and democrat, there has been a many-sided political conflict arising from the cleavages of a fragmented society—a society that has not been effectively transformed and integrated by the processes of the liberal democratic experience.[13] The absence of a unified political community intensifies antagonisms and nurtures extremism. Democracy therefore, instead of becoming a basic method of politics and a procedure of political contests, long remained one of the stakes in social conflict.[14] The liberal democratic transformation of Greek society could be considered complete only if democracy were politically and psychologically transformed from a stake into a method of public life. To the extent that the prevailing configuration of structural conditions did not make this possible, one could reasonably talk of a failure of liberalism in Greek politics, at least until 1974.

This has been the basic meaning of Greek political history in the nineteenth and twentieth centuries. From the vantage point of the failure of liberalism, the tragedies of the modern Greek historical experience could be put in perspective. Looking into the past, one is confronted by the paradox of a brave movement of Enlightenment, whose promise remained unfulfilled—an antinomy underlined by the optimism and the great human potential of that historical moment. Turning to the future, one is confronted with the tragedies of twentieth-century Greek history that constituted the distant consequences of liberal failure. The drama of the Enlightenment consisted in unfulfilled promises and disappointed hopes, but the tragedies of the twentieth century involved enormous human costs for large masses of people, who had to shoulder the consequences of failures of statesmanship produced by an authoritarian political tradition.

Abbreviations

Argyropoulou, *Neoellinikos stochasmos*

Roxane Argyropoulou, *Neoellinikos ithikos kai politikos stochasmos* (Thessaloniki, 2003)

Camariano, *Académies princières*

Ariadna Camariano-Cioran, *Les académies princières de Bucarest et de Jassy et leurs professeurs* (Thessaloniki, 1974)

DIEEE

Deltion tis Istorikis kai Ethnologikis Etaireias tis Ellados

Diimero Korai

Diimero Korai 29 kai 30 Apriliou 1983. Proseggiseis sti glossiki theoria, ti skepsi kai to ergo tou Korai (Athens, 1984)

Dimaras, *Neoellinikos Diaphotismos*

C. Th. Dimaras, *Neoellinikos Diaphotismos.* Fourth ed. (Athens, 1985)

Dimaras, *Istorika Phrontismata*

C. Th. Dimaras, *Istorika Phrontismata,* ed. by P. Polemi (Athens, 1992)

Dimaras, *Neoelliniki logotechnia*

C. Th. Dimaras, *Istoria tis neoellinikis logotechnias.* Ninth ed. (Athens, 2000)

Époque phanariote	*Symposium. L'époque phanariote* (Thessaloniki, 1974)
Gay, *Rise of Modern Paganism*	Peter Gay, *The Enlightenment. An Interpretation.* I: *The Rise of Modern Paganism* (New York, 1966)
Gay, *Science of Freedom*	Peter Gay, *The Enlightenment. An Interpretation.* II: *The Science of Freedom* (New York, 1969)
Gedeon, *Pnevmatiki Kinisis*	Manuel Gedeon, *I pnevmatiki kinisis tou genous kata ton XVIII kai XIX aiona,* ed. by A. Angelou—Ph. Iliou (Athens, 1976)
Henderson, *Revival*	G. P. Henderson, *The Revival of Greek Thought 1620–1830* (Albany, NY, 1970)
HR/RH	*The Historical Review/La Revue Historique* (Institute for Neohellenic Research)
Israel, *Radical Enlightenment*	Jonathan I. Israel, *Radical Enlightenment. Philosophy and the Making of Modernity 1650– 1750* (Oxford, 2001)
Israel, *Enlightenment Contested*	Jonathan I. Israel, *Enlightenment Contested. Philosophy, Modernity, and the Emancipation of Man 1650–1752* (Oxford, 2006)
Israel, *Democratic Enlightenment*	Jonathan I. Israel, *Democratic Enlightenment. Philosophy, Revolution and Human Rights 1750–1790* (Oxford, 2011)
Kitromilides, *Enlightenment, Nationalism, Orthodoxy*	P. M. Kitromilides, *Enlightenment, Nationalism, Orthodoxy. Studies in the Culture and Political Thought of Southeastern Europe* (Aldershot, 1994)
Kitromilides, *Orthodox Commonwealth*	P. M. Kitromilides, *An Orthodox Commonwealth. Symbolic Legacies and Cultural Encounters in Southeastern Europe* (Aldershot, 2007)
Kitromilides, ed., *Korais and the European Enlightenment*	P. M. Kitromilides, ed., *Adamantios Korais and the European Enlightenment* (=*SVEC,* Oxford, 2010:10)
Korais, *Allilographia*	Adamantios Korais, *Allilographia,* ed. C. Th. Dimaras, Alkis Angelou, Aik. Koumarianou, E. N. Franghiscos I: *1774–1798* (Athens, 1964) II: *1799–1809* (Athens, 1966) III: *1810–1816* (Athens, 1979)

IV: *1817–1822* (Athens, 1982)
V: *1823–1826* (Athens, 1983)
VI: *1827–1833* (Athens, 1984)

Ladas—Hadjidimos, *E.V.*   G. G. Ladas—A. D. Hadjidimos, *Elliniki*
1791–1795   *Vivliographia 1791–1795* (Athens, 1970)

Ladas—Hadjidimos, *E.V.*   G. G. Ladas—A. D. Hadjidimos, *Elliniki*
1796–1799   *Vivliographia 1796–1799* (Athens, 1973)

Legrand, *B. H. XVIIIe siècle*   Émile Legrand, *Bibliographie Hellénique. XVIIIe siècle,* ed. by Louis Petit—Hubert Pernot (Paris, 1928), I–II

Petropulos, *Politics and*   J. A. Petropulos, *Politics and Statecraft in the*
   Statecraft   *Kingdom of Greece 1833–1843* (Princeton, 1968)

RESEE   *Revue des Études Sud-Est européennes*

Rhigas, *Apanta ta sozomena*   Rhigas Velestinlis, *Apanta ta sozomena,* general editor P. M. Kitromilides (Athens: Greek Parliament, 2000–2002)
I: *Scholeion ton delikaton eraston,* ed. by P. S. Pistas (2000)
II: *Physikis apanthisma,* ed. by C. Th. Petsios (2002)
III: *Ithikos tripous,* ed. by Ines Di Salvo (2000)
IV: *Neos Anacharsis,* ed. by Anna Tabaki (2000)
V: *Nea politiki dioikisis ton katoikon tis Roumelis, tis Mikras Asias, ton Mesogeion Nison kai tis Vlachobogdanias,* ed. by P. M. Kitromilides (2000)

SVEC   *Studies on Voltaire and the Eighteenth Century*

Voulgaris, *Logiki*   Evgenios Voulgaris, *I logiki ek palaion kai neoteron syneranistheisa* (Leipzig, 1766)

Notes

INTRODUCTION TO THE AMERICAN EDITION

1. P. M. Kitromilides, "The Debt of a Student of Nationalism," *Elie Kedourie, 1926–1992: History, Philosophy, Politics,* ed. Sylvia Kedourie (London, 1998), 92–98.

2. Published by the Cultural Foundation of the National Bank of Greece.

3. Published by Editura Omonia, Bucharest, and Aletheia Publishing House, St. Petersburg, respectively.

4. Raphael Demos, "The Neo-Hellenic Enlightenment (1750–1821): A General Survey," *Journal of the History of Ideas* 19 (1958): 523–541, and "True Happiness, or the Basis of all Religion: By Athanasios Psalidas," trans. Raphael Demos, *Journal of the History of Ideas* 21 (1960): 481–496; Loukis Theocharides, *The Greek National Revival and the French Enlightenment* (PhD diss., University of Pittsburgh, 1971); Richard Clogg, ed., *The Movement for Greek Independence, 1770–1821: A Collection of Documents* (London, 1976).

5. Rogers M. Smith, "Beyond Tocqueville, Myrdal, and Hartz: The Multiple Traditions in America," *American Political Science Review* 87 (1993): 549–566.

6. See P. M. Kitromilides, "The Enlightenment and the Greek Cultural Tradition," *History of European Ideas* 36 (2010): 39–46.

7. "Orthodoxy and the West: Reformation to Enlightenment," *The Cambridge History of Christianity*, vol. 5: *Eastern Christianity*, ed. Michael Angold (Cambridge, 2006), 187–209.

8. *The Enlightenment in National Context*, ed. Roy Potter and M. Teich (Cambridge, 1981). The omission of the Greek case from the collection is curious considering that important work on the subject by the initiator of the study of the Greek Enlightenment, C. Th. Dimaras, had been available in French since at least 1969. See the comments in *From Republican Polity to National Community*, ed. P. M. Kitromilides (Oxford, 2003), 12–14.

9. *Cultural Transfers: France and Britain in the Long Eighteenth Century*, ed. Ann Thomson, Simon Burrows, and Edmond Dziembowski (Oxford, 2010).

10. See Anna Tabaki, *Peri Neoellinikou Diaphotismou* (Athens, 2004), 77–179.

11. *Peripheries of the Enlightenment*, ed. Richard Butterwick, Simon Davies, and Gabriel Sanchez Espinosa (Oxford, 2008).

12. On the idea of "Adriatic Enlightenment" see Larry Wolff, *Venice and the Slavs* (Stanford, 2001), 319–324, 328–331.

13. For Russia as a periphery of the Enlightenment see Simon Dixon, "Prosveshcenie: Enlightenment in Eighteenth-century Russia," *Peripheries of the Enlightenment*, 229–249.

14. John Pocock, *Barbarism and Religion* (Cambridge, 1999), 1:13.

15. John Robertson, *The Case for the Enlightenment: Scotland and Naples, 1680–1760* (Cambridge, 2005). See also P. M. Kitromilides, "Varieties of Enlightenment," *In the Footsteps of Herodotus: Toward European Political Thought*, ed. Janet Coleman and P. M. Kitromilides (Florence, 2012), 109–116.

16. Israel, *Democratic Enlightenment*, 5–8.

17. Israel, *Enlightenment Contested*, 663–696.

18. The subject is treated at greater length in P. M. Kitromilides, "Paradigm Nation: The Study of Nationalism and the 'Canonization' of Greece," *The Making of Modern Greece*, ed. Roderick Beaton and David Ricks (London, 2009), 21–31.

PROLOGUE

1. This view of the Enlightenment is completely contrary to that presented by Carl L. Becker, *The Heavenly City of Eighteenth-Century Philosophers* (New Haven and London, 1932). See Peter Gay's critique, "Carl Becker's Heavenly City," in *The Party of Humanity* (New York, 1971), 188–210.

2. Ernst Cassirer, *The Philosophy of the Enlightenment* (Princeton, 1951), 234–253.

3. Sven Stelling-Michaud, "Lumières et politique," *SVEC* 27 (1963): 1519–1543. Also Alfred Cobban, *In Search of Humanity* (New York, 1960), 161–179, and Gay, *Science of Freedom*, 398–496.

4. Gay, *The Party of Humanity*, 262–290.

5. Lucien Goldmann, *The Philosophy of the Enlightenment* (Cambridge, MA, 1973), 34–39.

6. Louis Hartz, *The Founding of New Societies* (New York, 1964), 1–122. The works by Bernard Bailyn, *The Ideological Origins of the American Revolution* (Cambridge, MA, 1967), 22–54, and Louis Hartz, *The Liberal Tradition in America* (New York, 1955) are germane to an understanding of these issues. My own thoughts on the transformation of the Enlightenment into a liberal political tradition are greatly indebted to Professor Hartz's works.

7. See P. M. Kitromilides, "The Enlightenment East and West: A Comparative Perspective on the Ideological Origins of the Balkan Political Traditions," *Canadian Review of Studies in Nationalism* 10 (1983): 51–70 [reprinted: *Enlightenment, Nationalism, Orthodoxy*, Study No. I].

8. Fernand Braudel, *The Mediterranean and the Mediterranean World in the Age of Philip II* (New York, 1972), 1:276–352. Braudel's thesis that Mediterranean society formed a single entity in the sixteenth century could, I believe, also be argued for the following centuries, at least down to the time of the French Revolution.

9. For the cultural content of this process, which remained generally alien to the experience of the outlying parts of Europe, cf. John U. Nef, *The Cultural Foundations of Industrial Civilization* (Cambridge, 1958).

10. For a case in point, illustrating in comparative perspective the depth and extent of the reception of the Enlightenment in Mediterranean Europe, but also its deeper unity, see John Robertson, *The Case for the Enlightenment: Scotland and Naples, 1680–1760* (Cambridge, 2005).

I. THE LONG ROAD TO ENLIGHTENMENT

1. The method employed here attempts to follow that delineated in Arthur O. Lovejoy, *The Great Chain of Being* (Cambridge, MA, 1936), 3–23, and the more recent methodological principles arising out of Quentin Skinner's writings in the history of political thought. The relevant contributions to the debate are assembled in *Meaning and Context: Quentin Skinner and his Critics,* ed. James Tully (Princeton, 1990).

2. Cf. Sheldon Wolin, *Politics and Vision* (Boston, 1960), 1–27.

3. See Philip Sherrard, *The Greek East and the Latin West* (London, 1959), 117–120, 122, 166–167. See also Basile Tatakis, *La philosophie byzantine* (Paris, 1959), 137–140, 228.

4. Ernest Barker, *Social and Political Thought in Byzantium,* (Oxford, 1957), 130; Tatakis, *La philosophie byzantine,* 161–222. Paul Lemerle, *Le premier humanisme byzantin* (Paris, 1971), 210–220, disputes Psellos's contribution to the criticism of Aristotle but confirms the predominance of Aristotelianism in Byzantine philosophy.

Compare the appraisal by R. R. Bolgar, *The Classical Heritage and its Beneficiaries* (Cambridge, 1954), 76–78, and the reappraisals in *Byzantium and the Classical Tradition*, ed. Margaret Mullett and Roger Scott (Birmingham, 1981) and finally the new perspectives introduced by Anthony Kaldellis, *Hellenism in Byzantium. The Transformations of Greek Identity and the Reception of the Classical Tradition* (Cambridge, 2007).

5. See especially Plethon's memorials on political reform, translated in Barker, *Social and Political Thought,* 198–212. Also Plethon, *Traité des lois,* ed. C. Alexandre (Paris, 1858), especially on his theory of a civil religion, and François Masai, *Plethon et le Platonisme de Mistra* (Paris, 1956), 66–101, and compare R. R. Bolgar, *The Classical Heritage,* 86–87. For the historical context, see D. Zakythinos, *La Despotat grec de Morée,* vol. 2: *vie et institutions,* 2nd ed. (London, 1975), 365–376. For Pletho's impact on the Renaissance, James Hankins, *Plato in the Italian Renaissance* (Leiden, 1991), 193–217. The article by N. Patrick Peritore, "The Political Thought of Gemistos Plethon: A Renaissance Byzantine Reformer," *Polity* 10 (1977): 168–191, is a useful survey from the standpoint of political science.

6. See Steven Runciman, "Byzantine and Hellene in the Fourteenth Century," *Tomos Constantinou Armenopoulou* (Thessaloniki, 1952), 27–31; D. M. Nicol, "The Byzantine Church and Hellenic Learning in the Fourteenth Century," in his *Byzantium: Its Ecclesiastical History and Relations with the Western World* (London, 1972), Study XII; Angeliki Laiou, "From Roman to Hellene," *The Byzantine Fellowship Lectures,* no. 1, ed. N. M. Vaporis (Brookline, MA, 1974), 13–28. For the ideological context, see Hélène Ahrweiler, *L'idéologie politique de l'empire byzantin* (Paris, 1975), 75–128. For an assessment of the interpretative controversies on these phenomena, see Michael Angold, "Byzantine 'Nationalism' and the Nicean Empire," *Byzantine and Modern Greek Studies* 1 (1975): 49–79.

7. Barker, *Social and Political Thought in Byzantium,* 198.

8. Cf. S. G. Xydis, "The Medieval Origins of Modern Greek Nationalism," *Balkan Studies* 9 (1968): 1–20.

9. See Gennadios Scholarios, *Oeuvres Complètes,* ed. Louis Petit et al. (Paris, 1930), 3:1–204, for his anti-Latin polemic, esp. 171–174, repudiating any idea of Western help as detrimental to the true interests of the Orthodox East, and ibid. (Paris, 1935), 4:1–189, for his polemic against Plethon: note 180–181 on the burning of Plethon's *Laws* as the befitting punishment for a work advocating pagan polytheism. On this subject see John Monfasani, *George of Trebizond* (Leiden, 1976), 207. On the general background of these ideological controversies on the eve of the fall of the Byzantine Empire, see briefly Steven Runciman, *The Fall of Constantinople: 1453* (Cambridge, 1965), 1–21, 68–72, and D. A. Zakythinos, "Ideologikai syngrouseis eis tin poliorkoumenin Constantinoupolin," *Nea Estia* 37 (1950): 794–799.

10. The question of the privileges enjoyed by the Orthodox Church under the Ottoman Empire is a contentious historical problem that is frequently clouded by

the ideological manipulation of history and misunderstanding of the sources. For
general surveys, see N. Eleftheriadis, *Anatolikai Meletai: Ta pronomia tou Oikoume-
nikou Patriarcheiou* (Smyrna, 1909), and K. Amantos, "Oi pronomiakoi orismoi
tou mousoulmanismou yper ton Christianon," *Ellinika* 9 (1936): 103–106. Of the
many references by M. I. Gedeon to the question of privileges, see especially *Vracheia
semeiosis peri ton Ekklisiastikon imon dikaion* (Constantinople, 1909), and *Ai phaseis
tou par'imin ekklisiastikou zitimatos* (Constantinople, 1910). On the position of
the Church under the Ottomans more generally, two classic accounts are N. Iorga,
Byzance après Byzance (Bucharest, 1935), 80–112, and Steven Runciman, *The Great
Church in Captivity* (Cambridge, 1968), 165–207. On the relations between the
Church and the subject people, Manuel Gedeon's "Chronographou symperasmata,"
O en Constantinoupolei Ellinikos Philologikos Syllogos 11 (1887–1888/1888–1889):
72–78 is very revealing.

11. On the ways in which the Church adapted ideologically to the realities of
captivity, see Chr. G. Patrinelis, *O Theodoros Agallianos taftizomenos pros ton Theoph-
anin Mideias kai oi anekdotoi logoi tou* (Athens, 1966), 68–85. On the ideological
structure that set the framework of the relations of the Patriarchate of Constantinople with the Ottoman state and more specifically on the contribution of the first
patriarch after the Fall, Gennadios Scholarios (1454–1456, 1463, 1464–1465), to
the ideological adjustment of the Church, see Speros Vryonis, Jr., "The Byzantine
Patriarchate and Turkish Islam," *Byzantinoslavica* 57 (1996): 69–111. The adaptation
at the level of the ideological function of political institutions is thrown into relief
by a careful comparison of representative writings dealing with the ideology of the
Christian Empire, such as the *Epagoge* of 880, by Basil I, and the text of the "Tomos
zitimaton tinon anangaion, on ai lyseis egenonto para ton agiotaton kai makariota-
ton tessaron Patriarchon kai exedothisan dokimastheisai kata tous orous kai kanonas
tis Katholikis kai Apostolikis anatolikis Ekklisias" of 1663, which codifies the
political views of the Church as crystallized under the rule of the Muslim Ottoman
state. See Kallinikos Delikanis, *Patriarchikon Engraphon tomos tritos* (Constantinople, 1905), 93–118, and D. G. Apostolopoulos, *To Mega Nomimon* (Athens, 1978),
39–58. On these questions, see also P. Konortas, *Les rapports juridiques et politiques
entre le patriarcat orthodoxe de Constantinople et l'administration ottomane de 1453 à
1600* (PhD diss., University of Paris I, 1985), 250–269, 318–339.

12. On the integration of the Orthodox Church into the Ottoman institutional structure, see H. A. R. Gibb and Harold Bowen, *Islamic Society and the West*
(London, 1957), vol. 1, part 2, pp. 208–216, 224–225, 233–239, 249–251. More
recent authoritative contributions, which draw on Ottoman *berats,* imperial edicts
regulating the accession of the Orthodox hierarchy, include Elizabeth Zachariadou,
Deka tourkika eggrapha gia tin Megali Ekklisia (1483–1567) (Athens, 1996) and P.
Konortas, *Othomanikes theoriseis gia to Oikoumeniko Patriarcheio* (Athens, 1998). The
prehistory of these institutional arrangements in Ottoman society unfolded during

the centuries of Byzantine decline and the rise of Muslim power in Asia Minor. See Speros Vryonis, Jr., *The Decline of Medieval Hellenism in Asia Minor and the Process of Islamization from the Eleventh through the Fifteenth Century* (Berkeley, 1971), 223–244. For the fiscal aspects of the functioning of the Orthodox Church as an institution of the Ottoman Empire, see J. Kabrda, *Le système fiscal de l'église orthodoxe dans l'Empire Ottoman* (Brno, 1969).

13. Cf. Scholarios, *Oeuvres Complètes,* 4:211–231, his pastoral encyclical on the Fall of Constantinople.

14. On this problem, see generally the comprehensive study of Deno J. Geanakoplos, *Greek Scholars in Venice* (Cambridge, MA, 1962), and more recently Jonathan Harris, *Greek Emigrés in the West, 1400–1520* (London, 1995), 21–38, 119–149. This migration, however, led to an important tradition of cultivation of Greek literature in the West by successive generations of scholars of Greek descent. This tradition was also linked with the manifestations of a current of "civic humanism" among the circles of Greek scholars in the West during the sixteenth and seventeenth centuries; an important ideological expression of this was the preservation of knowledge of classical antiquity among the intellectuals of the Greek diaspora. It was from these circles of later humanists that emerged the first visionaries of the future freedom of the Greeks. For this political aspect of the history of the Greek intellectual diaspora, see M. I. Manousakas, "Ekkliseis ton Ellinon logion pros tous igemones tis Europis gia tin apeleftherosin tis Ellados," *Praktika tis Akadimias Athinon* 59 (1984): 196–249, esp. 199–229.

15. Cléobule Tsourkas, *Les débuts de l'enseignement philosophique et de la libre pensée dans les Balkans: La vie et l'oeuvre de Theophile Corydalée* (Thessaloniki, 1967), 27.

16. Sherrard, *The Greek East and the Latin West,* 172–175. On philosophical currents in Padua in the sixteenth and seventeenth centuries, see Tsourkas, *Les débuts de l'enseignement philosophique,* 180–195, and for the general intellectual background see John Leofric Stocks, *Aristotelianism* (Boston, 1925), 131–135, and especially John Herman Randall, "The Development of Scientific Method in the School of Padua," *Journal of the History of Ideas* 1 (1940): 177–206, idem, *The School of Padua and the Emergence of Modern Science* (Padua, 1961), and finally, idem, "Paduan Aristotelianism Reconsidered," *Renaissance Essays in Honor of P. P. Kristeller* (New York, 1976), 278–282; these works and the ensuing debate have effectively revived the study of Paduan Aristotelianism, and they would greatly enhance the appreciation of Corydaleus's contribution, were they noted by Greek specialists.

17. Tsourkas, *Les débuts,* 195.

18. Ibid., 33–80, on the life of Corydaleus. The study by C. B. Schmidt, *Cesare Cremonini, un aristotelico al tempo di Galilei* (Venice, 1980), is important for an understanding of the philosophy of Corydaleus's teacher; for his ideological disputes, note the comments by W. J. Bouwsma, *Venice and the Defense of Republican Liberty* (Berkeley, 1968), 254 and 501.

19. On the career and policies of Patriarch Cyril I Loukaris, see Runciman, *The Great Church in Captivity,* 259–288, with a survey of sources on p. 259, but especially Gunnar Hering, *Ökumenisches Patriarchat und europäische Politik 1620–1638* (Wiesbaden, 1968).

20. Tsourkas, *Les débuts,* 207.

21. Ibid., 211–212. For a detailed analysis of Corydaleus's philosophy, see 219–352, but see also the detailed critique by Linos Benakis, *Ellinika* 13 (1970): 399–404. See also Henderson, *Revival,* 12–19, and C. Noica (Nicasius), "Theophile Corydallée, philosophe byzantin et dernier grand commentateur d'Aristote," *Archives de Philosophie* 32 (1969): 476–484. An important contribution to setting Corydaleus's philosophy in the context of the post-Byzantine philosophical tradition is the collection of texts in *I Elliniki Philosophia apo to 1453 os to 1821,* vol. 1: *I kyriarchia tou Aristotelismou: Prokorydaliki kai korydaliki periodos,* ed. N. K. Psimmenos (Athens, 1988), esp. 173–186 and the texts that follow.

22. Of the extensive bibliography, see the assessment by Cyril Mango, "The Phanariots and the Byzantine Tradition," in his *Byzantium and its Image* (London, 1984), Study XVIII, which provides a critical survey of the bibliography on the subject. What Mango has to say is illuminating, but I believe his assessment of Rhigas Velestinlis as a bearer of the Phanariot tradition is debatable. The most important collective contribution is the *Symposium: L'époque phanariote* (Thessaloniki, 1974). The older work by N. Iorga, *Byzance après Byzance,* esp. 220–241, still retains its interest. Important for the Phanariot mentality is M. I. Gedeon, "Peri tis Phanariotikis koinonias mechri ton archon tis enestosis ekatontaetiridos," *O en Constantinoupolei Ellinikos Philologikos Syllogos* 11 (1887–1888/1888–1889): 55–71.

23. The bibliography on Alexandros Mavrokordatos is voluminous. The oldest biographical sketch occurs in J. A. Fabricius, *Bibliotheca Graeca* 11 (Hamburg, 1722), 774–776. Alexandre C. Stourdza, *L'Europe orientale et le rôle historique des Mavrocordato 1660–1830* (Paris, 1913), 30–64, is still a substantial contribution. C. Amantos, "Alexandros Mavrokordatos o ex Aporriton," *Ellinika* 5 (1932): 335–350, covers the earlier bibliography. Among more recent studies, see Nestor Camariano, *Alexandre Mavrocordato le Grand Dragoman: Son activité diplomatique 1673–1709* (Thessaloniki, 1970); Henderson, *Revival,* 20–27; and for the biographical problems, Z. Tsirpanlis, "Alexandros Mavrokordatos o ex Aporriton: Nea stoicheia kai nees apopseis," *Dodoni* 4 (1975): 273–291.

24. See *Pneumaticum instrumentum circulandi sanguinis sive de motu & usu pulmonum dissertatio philsophico-medica authore Alexandro Maurocordato Constaninopolitano* (Bolonia, 1664). Further editions appeared in Frankfurt, 1665, Leipzig, 1870, and again Leipzig, 1870, ed. Marinos Vretos, and Florence, 1965, ed. L. Guerrieri. For Alexandros Mavrokordatos's medical training see also C. S. Bartsocas, "Alexander Mavrocordatos (1641–1709): Physician and Statesman," *Journal of the History of Medicine* 28 (1973): 392–395.

25. For Alexandros Mavrokordatos's teaching of the elements of "modern physiology" in Constantinople, see D. G. Apostolopoulos, "Gia tin proistoria tou Neoellinikou Diaphotismou: Stoicheia Physiologias ton dekato ebdomo aiona stin Constantinoupoli," *O Eranistis* 11 (1974): 296–310.

26. Alexandros Mavrokordatos, *Istoria iera itoi ta Iudaika* (Bucharest, 1716), i.

27. Ibid., prefatory text on "The Purpose of the Work," n.p.

28. Alexandros Mavrokordatos, *Phrontismata* (Vienna, 1805).

29. Alexandros Mavrokordatos, *Epistolai C,* ed. Th. Livadas, (Trieste, 1879), xlix.

30. Mavrokordatos, *Phrontismata,* 64–65.

31. C. Th. Dimaras, "Alexandre Mavrocordato, Machiavel et La Rochefoucauld," in *La Grèce au temps des Lumières* (Geneva, 1969), 19–25.

32. Mavrokordatos, *Phrontismata,* 202.

33. Idem, *Epistolai,* 93.

34. See Fabricius, *Bibliotheca Graeca,* 793–795. For details on his political career, see Stourdza, *Le rôle historique des Mavrocordato,* 92–129, and on his philosophical views, Alkis Angelou, *Platonos Tychai* (Athens, 1963), 63–81, to be read in conjunction with the comments by P. Kondylis, *O Neoellinikos Diaphotismos: Oi philosophikes idees* (Athens, 1988), 234–235.

35. Nikolaos Mavrokordatos, "Nouthesiai pros ton yion aftou Constantinon" (1726), and "Encheiridion en o Gnomai kai Phrontismata peri ithi kai politeian," Eudoxiu de Hurmuzaki, *Documente privitoare la istoria Romanilor,* vol. 13, ed. A. Papadopoulos-Kerameus (Bucharest, 1909), 461–504.

36. Nikolaos Mavrokordatos, *Peri kathikonton Vivlos: Liber de Officiis* (Leipzig, 1722), 32–45. For Mavrokordatos's debts to Cicero in the composition of the *De officiis,* see P. Noutsos, "Nicolas Mavrocordatos et Cicéron," *Dodoni* 11 (1982): 217–225.

37. Mavrokordatos, *Liber de Officiis,* chapters 3–9, 14–15. Note especially 16–17, stressing the need to show particular care for the externalities of religion: embellishment of churches and protection of the Church with every means available.

38. Ambrosius Marlianus, *Theatron Politikon,* trans. N. Mavrokordatos, ed. Seraphim Pisidios (Leipzig, 1758). The original by Ambrogio Marliani (1589–1659) under the title *Theatrum politicum: in quo quid agendum sit a principe* [. . .] was published in Rome, 1631. The authenticity of the attribution of the translation to N. Mavrokordatos was disputed by A. Camariano in *Revista Istorica Romana* 11–12 (1941–1942): 259–260. This, however, does not make it less representative of the political ideas prevailing in the Phanariot milieu, since the alleged real translator, Ioannis Avramios, was a high official in Nicholas's court.

39. *Theatron Politikon,* passim.

40. For the distant Mediterranean and Hellenistic sources of this political tradition and its Christian reworking in the Byzantine period, see Francis Dvornik, *Early Christian and Byzantine Political Philosophy,* 2 vols. (Washington, DC, 1966), esp. chapters 5, 7, 10–12.

41. Nikolaos Alexandrou Mavrokordatos, *Philotheou Parerga,* ed. Grigorios Constantas (Vienna, 1800), 24–25, 35–38, 123. New edition, accompanied by French translation, by Jacques Bouchard, *Les loisirs de Philothée* (Athens and Montreal, 1989). On the importance of this work as the starting point of the "Phanariot century," see Dimaras, *Neoellinikos Diaphotismos,* 262–282. Nicolaos's identification with Ottoman authority is clear from *De Officiis,* 110.

42. See Jacques Bouchard, "Les relations épistolaires de Nicolas Mavrocordatos avec Jean Le Clerc et William Wake," *O Eranistis* 11 (1974): 67–92. The reference to Locke is on p. 77.

43. *Les loisoirs de Philothée,* 126.

44. Ibid., 86.

45. Ibid., 120.

46. Ibid., 118, 184–186: references to Plato's dialogues *Phaido, Phaidros, The Republic, The Laws,* and *Timaeus.*

47. *Les loisirs de Philothée,* 178. During Nikolaos's rule in Wallachia, Plato's *Crito* and *Phaido* were taught in the Academy of Bucharest in 1726-1727 by Nikolaos's friend and appointee Georgios Chrysogonis of Trebizond. Dimitrios Prokopiou, "Epitetmimenl eparithmisis ton kata ton parelthonta aiona logion Graikon, kai peri tinon en to nyn aioni anthounton," in J. A. Fabricius, *Bibliotheca Graeca,* 793, notes that "Nikolaos, son of Alexandros Mavrokordatos" was "indeed a lover of Plato, and also an investigator and praiser of the moderns." It should be pointed out that Mavrokordatos's interest in Plato might have been connected with the anti-Aristotelian tendencies in the thought of D. Cantemir, who flourished in the principalities as a thinker and statesman at the beginning of the eighteenth century, just before the arrival of N. Mavrokordatos. See Vlad Georgescu, *Political Ideas and the Enlightenment in the Romanian Principalities* (Boulder, 1971), 75.

48. On the tradition of "religious humanism" in Greek culture, especially in the seventeenth century, see briefly Dimaras, *Neolleniki Logotechnia,* 56- 62, 73–81, 131–137.

49. Methodios Anthrakitis, *Theoriai Christianikai* (Venice, 1699), 7.

50. Ibid., 210–211, 216, 224.

51. Ibid., 231–232.

52. The passage cited in ibid., 215. The text of Damaskinos Studitis is published from MS 764 of Iviron Monastery, Mount Athos, by Eleni Kakoulidi, "Damaskinou Stouditi Dialogos," *Dodoni* 3 (1974): 443–458.

53. Gedeon, *Pnevmatiki kinisis,* 99.

54. Methodios Anthrakitis, *Odos Mathematikis . . . ,* trans. from the Latin, ed. Balanos Vasilopoulos (Venice, 1749), vols. 1–3.

55. See Paul Hazard, *The European Mind* (New York, 1963), 133–138.

56. Besides Gedeon's comments, other sources on the Anthrakitis case include G. Zaviras, *Nea Ellas,* ed. T. Gritsopoulos (Athens, 1972), 418–421; G. P. Kournoutos,

"Scholeia tis Tourkokratoumenis Kastorias," *Geras Antoniou Keramopoulou* (Athens, 1953), 445–448, 458–463; Alkis Angelou, "I diki tou Methodiou Anthrakiti," *Aphieroma eis tin Ipeiron,* ed. L. Vranousis (Athens, 1956), 168–182; V. Bobou-Stamati, *Istorikis erevnas apotelesmata* (Athens, 2002), 305–321 with source material on the content of his teaching.

57. The text of Anthrakitis's confession was published by D. Chatzis in *Ellinika* 17 (1962): 296–306.

58. The text of the excommunication issued by the Synod in August 1723 was published in *Ekklisiastiki Alitheia* 2 (1881–1882): 495–500. See also Gedeon, *Pnevmatiki kinisis,* 52–53, 99–101.

59. See Angelou, "I diki tou Methodiou Anthrakiti," 172.

60. Ibid., 173.

61. Gedeon, *Pnevmatiki kinisis,* 100–101. On the defense of Anthrakitis by the municipal notables of Ioannina in a letter to a senior member of the Synod, see P. Aravantinos, *Chronographia tis Ipirou* (Athens, 1857), 2:277–278n and on the support he found in his earlier struggles with the Peripatetics from the urban notables of Kastoria, Kournoutos, "Scholeia Kastorias," 461.

62. The manuscript of Anthrakitis's *Logic,* preserved in the library of the Modern Greek department of the University of Budapest, is examined in Henderson, *Revival,* 34–36. The edict which lifted Anthrakitis's excommunication and ordered him to teach nothing else but Peripatetic philosophy following Corydaleus was published by Phil. Vapheidis in *Ekklisiastiki Alitheia* 20 (1900): 125.

63. Gedeon, *Pnevmatiki kinisis,* 52. Gedeon is the only source on the case of Pachomios. See ibid., 50–53. For Pachomios's rival, Iannakos, a teacher in Thessaloniki, see Nafkratios Tsoulkanakis, "Ioannis o tou Ioannou, didaskalos tis en Thessalonikis scholis," *Klironomia* 7 (1975): 353–386.

64. Gedeon, *Pnevmatiki kinisis,* 50.

65. Alexander Drummond, *Travels through Different Cities of Germany, Italy, Greece and Several Parts of Asia* (London, 1754), 96. On the cultural background see P. M. Kitromilides, "Septinsular Enlightenment," VII Panionian Congress, *Praktika* (Athens, 2004), 1:241–257.

66. Evgenios Voulgaris, *Logiki* (Leipzig, 1766), 43. For a brief account of Katiphoros, see Ath. Karathanasis, *I Phlangineios Scholi tis Venetias* (Thessaloniki, 1986), 119–122. In connection with this important, though enigmatic, pioneer of modern philosophical ideas in Greek culture and education, many points, particularly of a biographical nature, remain unclear. The work of his contemporary Ioannis Kontonis, "Logos eis ton Aidesimotaton kai Logiotaton Antonion Katiphoron," *Philologika analekta Zakynthou,* ed. N. Katramis (Zakynthos, 1880), 395–409, is enlightening, but still leaves some confusion, as does P. Chiotis, *Mneia peri Antoniou tou Katiphorou* (Zakynthos, 1858). For his encounter with Frederick II, see Sp. D. Viazis, "Antonios Katiphoros," *Ekklisiastiki Alitheia* 10 (1890): 108–111, 114–117.

67. Antonios Katiphoros, *Grammatiki Elliniki akrivestati* (Venice, 1734), dedicatory epistle, n.p. A concrete example of Katiphoros's linguistic preferences is furnished by his translation *Istoria tis Palaias kai Neas Diathikis* (Venice, 1737), "in order to rectify the morals of every Christian person."

68. Katiphoros, *Grammatiki,* "To the Wise Professors of Greek Youth . . . ," n.p.

69. Vikentios Damodos, *Epitomos Logiki kat' Aristotelin* (Venice, 1759), 11. For biographical profiles, see Elias Tsitselis, *Kephalliniaka Symmikta* (Athens, 1904), 1:109–118, and the account by C. Th. Dimaras, "Chronologika Vikentiou Damodou," *Istorika Phrontismata,* 71–77, 270–271. The whole subject has been significantly renewed by Vassiliki Bobou-Stamati, *O Vikentios Damodos: Viographia-ergographia. 1700–1752* (Athens, 1998).

70. Damodos, *Epitomos Logiki,* 8.

71. See Vassiliki Bobou-Stamati, "I Syntomos Idea tis Logikis kata tin Methodon ton Neoteron, tou Vikentiou Damodou," *Defkalion* 21 (March 1978): 64–85.

72. V. Damodos, *Techni Ritoriki* (Venice, 1759), 3. Compare idem, *Epitomos Logiki,* 7.

73. Vikentios Damodos, *Synopsis Ithikis Philosophias,* ed. T. Zisis and L. Depountis (Athens, 1940), 90.

74. See Stamati, *Damodos,* 96–217, listing a total of 150 manuscripts.

75. Voulgaris, *Logiki,* 41–44.

76. *Syllogi anekdoton syngrammaton tou aoidimou Eugeniou tou Voulgareos,* ed. G. Ainian (Athens, 1838), 1:xii–xiii.

77. For an appraisal of the evidence, see Bobou-Stamati, *Damodos,* 54, 56–58.

78. Biographical sketches of Voulgaris are offered by A. Papadopoulos Vretos, *Biographie de l'Archevêque Evgenios Voulgaris* (Athens, 1868), and C. Sathas, *Neoelliniki Philologia* (Athens, 1868), 566–571. See also K. D. Kolokotsas, "Evgenios o Voulgaris kai to ergon autou," *Athina* 30 (1949): 177–208. The most important recent contribution is Stephen Batalden, *Catherine II's Greek Prelate: Eugenios Voulgaris in Russia, 1771–1806* (Boulder, 1982), though the section on Voulgaris's early life and activity in Greece (pp. 1–12) merely repeats older information. Henderson, *Revival,* 41–75, is a useful introduction to Voulgaris's philosophy. A perceptive recent reappraisal is Iannis Carras, "'Topos' and Utopia in Evgenios Voulgaris' Life and Work (1716–1806)," *HR/RH* 1 (2004): 127–156. The latest major contribution to the subject is the bicentennial symposium *Evgenios Voulgaris,* ed. Helen Angelomatis (Athens, 2009). Voulgaris's own testimony on his intellectual experience at Ioannina has survived in letters roughly contemporary with the events. See National Library of Greece, MS Codex 2390, fols 476–478, and MS Codex 3053, fol. 280, April 18, 1752.

79. For Voulgaris's own account, see his letter of January 29, 1762, to patriarch Cyril V, in Ainian, *Syllogi anekdoton syngrammaton,* 1:54–64. See also P. M. Kitromilides, "Athos and the Enlightenment," *Orthodox Commonwealth,* Study VII.

80. See below, chapter 4.

81. Voulgaris, *Logiki,* 139–140, footnote.

82. The letter is quoted in P. Kalligas, *Meletai kai Logoi* (Athens, 1899), 2:209. For further accounts of Voulgaris's intellectual activities and state of mind while in Leipzig, see his surviving manuscript letters in National Library of Greece MS Codex 2390, fols 716–747. On the Enlightenment environment at Leipzig, which must have certainly influenced Voulgaris's evolving outlook, see Martin Mulsow, *Freigeister im Gottsched-Kreis: Wolffianismus, studentische Aktivitäten und Religionskritik in Leipzig 1740–174* (Göttingen, 2007), esp. 11–14, 28–29, 38–40, 81–82, 112–114.

83. Voulgaris, *Logiki,* 44.

84. Ibid., 45.

85. Ibid., 58.

86. Ibid., 59.

87. See Christian Wolff, *Preliminary Discourse on Philosophy in General* (Indianapolis, 1963), chapter 6, paragraphs 151–171.

88. Voulgaris, *Logiki,* 60–61.

89. Ibid., 61.

90. Ibid., 63–68.

91. "Memoir for Enlightened Persons of Good Intention," *The Political Writings of Leibniz,* ed. Patrick Riley (Cambridge, 1972), 103–110.

92. On the philosophical issues surrounding the use of Locke in Voulgaris's work, compare Henderson, *Revival,* 56–62.

93. Voulgaris, *Logiki,* 139n2.

94. Alexandros Mavrokordatos, *Epistolai,* No. 14, p. 20. See also, No. 15, p. 22, No. 18, pp. 23–26, and No. 20, pp. 27–28.

95. For characteristic passages indicative of both his style and his social and political views, see Ilias Miniatis, *Didachai eis tin Agian kai Megalin Tessarakostin* (Venice, 1738), 101, 360–363, 364–372, 382–394.

96. Voulgaris, *Logiki,* 49. On Voulgaris's views on language see Peter Mackridge, *Language and National Identity in Greece, 1766–1976* (Oxford, 2009), 83–87.

97. Wolff, *Preliminary Discourse,* 84.

98. Ibid., 87.

99. For an appreciation of Voulgaris's philosophical accomplishment by a contemporary Scottish philosopher, see James Burnet, Lord Monboddo, *Of the Origin and Progress of Language,* 2nd ed. (Edinburgh, 1774), 1:45, and idem, *Ancient Metaphysics or the Science of Universals* (Edinburgh, 1779), vol. 1, part 2, p. 479n.

100. Antonio Genovesi, *Stoicheia tis Metaphysikis* (Vienna, 1806); W. J. S. Gravesande, *Eisagogi eis tin Philosophian* (Moscow, 1805); J. A. von Segner, *Ton mathematikon stoicheion ai pragmateiai ai archoeidestatai* (Leipzig, 1767); A. Tacquet, *Stoicheia geometrias* (Vienna, 1805).

101. The unpublished and unfinished translation, under the title "Ypotyposis i ypomnima philosophikon peri tou kata anthropon nou ek tou Anglou Lokiou," is

preserved in MS Codex 1333 in the National Library of Greece. See I. and A. Sakkelion, *Katalogos ton cheirographon tis Ethnikis Vivliothikis tis Ellados* (Athens, 1892), 242, MS No. 1333. Understanding of the connection between Voulgaris and Locke's philosophy has for long relied on A. Angelou, "Comment la pensée néohellénique a fait la connaissance de l'Essai de John Locke," *L'Hellénisme contemporain* 9 (1955): 230–249. Although this article was important at the time it was written as a record of available evidence, it is now in need of considerable revision regarding both the dates of the intellectual contacts and the channels through which Greek culture, and Voulgaris in particular, came to know Locke's thought. Curiously enough, until quite recently, scholars of Neohellenic philosophy, e.g., N. K. Psimmenos, *I Elliniki philosophia apo to 1453 os to 1821,* and P. Kondylis, *O Neollenikos Diaphotismos,* accepted Angelou's hypotheses without weighing their historical validity. The whole question is reexamined in my study, "John Locke and the Greek Intellectual Tradition," *Locke's Philosophy: Content and Context,* ed. G. A. J. Rogers (Oxford, 1994), 217–235. Compare Israel, *Radical Enlightenment*, 522–527, on the broader background of Locke's reception in the continental Enlightenment.

102. Voulgaris, *Logiki*, 311n.

103. Voulgaris's Greek version of *Memnon* was appended in the translation of Momars, *Bosporomachia,* ed. E. Voulgaris (Leipzig, 1766), 136–148. See also C. Th. Dimaras, "La fortune de Voltaire en Grèce," in *La Grèce au temps des Lumières,* 61–94, and Anna Tabaki, "La reception du théâtre de Voltaire dans le Sud-Est de l'Europe," *Voltaire et ses combats*, ed. Ulla Kölving and Christiane Mervaud (Oxford, 1997), vol. 2, 1539–1549.

104. *Peri ton Dichonoion ton en tais Ekklisiais tis Polonias Dokimion Istorikon kai Kritikon* [. . .] *kai Schediasma peri tis Anexithriskeias* (Leipzig, 1768), 180–185, 187–192.

105. Ibid., "To the Reader." *Schediasma peri tis Anexithriskeias* appears on 217–284. The two texts are reprinted in *Ek ton syngrammaton Evgeniou tou Voulgareos,* vol. 2, ed. G. Ainian (Athens, 1838).

106. *Schediasma,* 217. On this subject, see also Martin Knapp, *Evjenios Vulgaris im Einfluss der Aufklärung: Der Begriff der Toleranz bei Vulgaris und Voltaire* (Amsterdam, 1984), esp. 98–116, while on 117–119 an attempt is made at a systematic comparison of the attitudes of Locke, Voltaire, and Voulgaris in their writings on toleration. This comparative textual analysis establishes precisely the content of the affinity of Voulgaris's argumentation with the concerns of European literature on religious toleration.

107. For biographical details see Camariano, *Académies princières,* 560 568; Zoi Mourouti-Genakou, *O Nikiphoros Theotokis 1731–1800 kai i symvoli aftou eis tin paideian tou genous* (Athens, 1979); and Gregory L. Bruess, *Religion, Identity, and Empire: A Greek Archbishop in the Russia of Catherine the Great* (Boulder, 1997).

108. Nikiphoros Theotokis, *Stoicheia Physikis,* vol. 1 (Leipzig, 1766), address "To the Reader." See also introductory chapter, 1–4.

109. Ibid., "To the Reader."

110. See Eugenios Voulgaris, *Peri systimatos tou pantos epitomos ekthesis* (Vienna, 1805), 35–38.

111. Theotokis, *Stoicheia Physikis,* vol. 4, fol. *6ʳ.

112. Ibid., 43–47, 47–46, 64–87.

113. The observation is due to Iosipos Moisiodax in his prolegomena to *Moral Philosophy* in 1761. See P. M. Kitromilides, *Iosipos Moisiodax,* 2nd ed. (Athens, 2004), 326.

114. Linos Benakis, *Metavyzantini Philosophia* (Athens, 2001), 33–72. Zerzoulis's *Physics* was discovered in 1993 in a manuscript in the University Library of Jassy. See ibid., 101–113.

115. See Nikiphoros Theotokis, *Stoicheion mathematikon* [. . .] vols. 1–3 (Moscow, 1798–1799), and *Stoicheia Geographias,* ed. Anthimos Gazis (Vienna, 1804).

116. On the Greek presses of Venice see G. Ploumidis, *To venetikon typographeion tou Dimitriou kai tou Panou Theodosiou, 1755–1824* (Athens, 1969), and G. Veloudis, *To Elliniko typographeio ton Glykydon sti Venetia, 1670–1754: Symvoli sti meleti tou Ellinikou vivliou kata tin epochi tis Tourkokratias* (Athens, 1987). From the extensive literature on the Greek community of Venice we may single out two authoritative general accounts separated by a century: Ioannis Veloudos, *Ellinon Orthodoxon apoikia en Venetia: Istorikon ypomnima* (Venice, 1893), and M. I. Manousakas, "Episkopisi tis istorias tis Ellinikis Orthodoxis Adelphotitos tis Venetias, 1498–1953," *Ta Istorika* 11 (1980): 243–264. M. I. Manousakas has also compiled two comprehensive bibliographies on the Greeks in Venice. See *Thisavrismata* 10 (1973): 7–87, and ibid., 17 (1980): 7–21.

117. Although the movement of intellectual change in eighteenth-century Southeastern Europe can be followed reliably on the basis of rich textual evidence, the deeper sociological nature of pertinent phenomena in the same period has not been adequately examined. The reciprocities between developments in the intellectual and social spheres have received even less precise attention. A number of works, however, are suggestive in this direction, and to their evidence the interpretations attempted in this essay are indebted. Among them none is more comprehensive and suggestive than Traian Stoianovich, "The Conquering Balkan Orthodox Merchant," *The Journal of Economic History* 20 (1960): 234–313 [reprinted in his *Between East and West: The Balkan and Mediterranean Worlds* (New Rochelle, NY, 1992), 2:1–77]. See also N. Svoronos, *Le commerce de Salonique au XVIIIe siècle* (Paris, 1956), 347–367, and N. Todorov, "Sur quelques aspects du passage du féodalisme au capitalisme dans les territoires Balkaniques de l'Empire Ottoman," *RESEE* 1 (1963): 103–136 [reprinted in his *La ville balkanique sous les Ottomans* (London, 1977), Study IV]. Finally, a classic study focusing on the social and economic background of political and cultural change in a particularly important region in the long eighteenth century is M. B. Sakellariou, *I Peloponnisos kata tin Defteran Tourkokratian (1715–1821),* 2nd revised ed. (Athens, 2012), (originally published in 1939).

118. The social bases of the Enlightenment can be best understood through a study of book circulation. In this connection, the contributions of Philippe Iliou are quite suggestive: "Pour une étude quantitative du public des lecteurs grecs à l'époque des Lumières et de la Révolution, 1749–1832," *Actes du premier congrès international des études balkaniques* (Sofia, 1969), 4:475–480; idem, "Vivlia me syndromites: Ta chronia tou Diaphotismou, 1749–1821," *O Eranistis* 12 (1975): 101–179. Iliou's studies are now collected in the volume *Istories tou Ellinikou Vivliou,* ed. Anna Matthaiou et al. (Irakleio, 2005). See also Leandros Vranousis, "Post-Byzantine Hellenism and Europe: Manuscripts, Books and Printing Presses," *Modern Greek Studies Yearbook* 2 (1986): 1–71.

119. Gay, *Rise of Modern Paganism,* 2–19. For the possibilities of studying the Enlightenment in terms of a chronological ordering in intellectual generations, see Louis Gottschalk, "Three Generations: A Plausible Interpretation of the French Philosophes?" *Studies in Eighteenth Century Culture* 2 (1972): 3–12. For a suggestion concerning the Greek Enlightenment see Anna Tabaki, "Les Lumières néohelleniques. Un essai de définition et de périodisation," *The Enlightenment in Europe,* ed. Werner Schneiders (Berlin, 2003), 45–56.

120. In Jonathan Israel's sense.

2. THE FORMATION OF MODERN GREEK HISTORICAL CONSCIOUSNESS

1. See Ernst Cassirer, *The Philosophy of the Enlightenment* (Princeton, 1951), 197–233; Paul Hazard, *The European Mind* (New York, 1963), 29–52; Norman Hampson, *A Cultural History of the Enlightenment* (New York, 1968), 232–250. The first cultural historian to note the historiographical significance of eighteenth-century thought was Wilhelm Dilthey, "Das achtzehnte Jahrhundert und die geschichtliche Welt," *Gesammelte Schriften* (Stuttgart, 1959), 3:209–268.

2. Georges Gusdorf, *De l'histoire des sciences à l'histoire de la pensée* (Paris, 1966), 43–92, and idem, *L'avènement des sciences humaines au siècle des lumières* (Paris, 1973), 373–495. See also Hugh Trevor-Roper, "The Historical Philosophy of the Enlightenment," *SVEC* 27 (1963): 1667–1687.

3. On Giannone, see Trevor-Roper, "Historical Philosophy," 1672, 1682–1683; Gay, *Rise of Modern Paganism,* 372–373; and Gusdorf, *L'avènement des sciences humaines,* 494–495. See also *Opere di Pietro Giannone,* ed. Sergio Bertelli and G. Ricuperati, *Illuministi Italiani* (Milan and Naples, 1971), 1:xi–xxvi, and Giuseppe Ricuperati, *La città terrena di Pietro Giannone* (Florence, 2001), on his purposeful secularization of historical knowledge and the reactions it elicited. On Spain, see Richard Herr, *The Eighteenth-Century Revolution in Spain* (Princeton, 1958), 337–347.

4. See Constantinos M. Koumas, *Istoriai ton anthropinon praxeon* (Vienna, 1831), 6:xxxvii–xlix. The passage cited is on p. xxxix. See the appraisal by Maria A.

Stasinopoulou, *Weltgeschichte im Denken eines Griechsischen Aufklärers: Konstantinos M. Koumas als Historiograph* (Frankfurt-am-Main, 1992), 250–252. See also D. A. Zakythinos, "Metavyzantini kai neotera Elliniki istoriographia," *Metavyzantina kai Nea Ellinika* (Athens, 1978), 23–66. This is a more complete survey of eighteenth-century sources than Peter Topping, "Greek Historical Writing on the Period 1453–1914," *Journal of Modern History* 33 (1961): 157–173.

5. Dorotheos of Monemvasia, *Vivlion Istorikon,* first published in Venice in 1631, ed. Apostolos Tzigaras. On this work, see Sp. Lambros, "Dorotheou Vivlion Istorikon," *Neos Ellinomnimon* 16 (1922): 137–190. On its sources, manuscripts, and editions, see G. Moravcsik, *Byzantinoturcica* (Berlin, 1958), 1:412–414, and Elisabeth Zachariadou, "Mia italiki pigi tou Pseudo-Dorotheou gia tin istoria ton Othomanon," *Peloponnisiaka* 5 (1961): 46–59. At least twenty-three editions of the book have been identified, all printed in Venice: 1631, 1637, 1654, 1673, 1676, 1681, 1684, 1686, 1691, 1740, 1743, 1750, 1752, 1761, 1763, 1767, 1778, 1781, 1786, 1792, 1798, 1805, 1818. For bibliographical details, see Th. Papadopoulos, *Elliniki Vivliographia, 1466–1800* (Athens, 1984), 154–155, and Ladas and Chatzidimos, *EV 1791–1795,* 116–117. Another chronographical source with close affinity to the *Vivlion Istorikon* was the *Nea Synopsis Diaphoron Istorion* by Mathaios Kigalas (Venice, 1637). Both sources had easily identifiable connections with the millenarian traditions current during the period of Ottoman rule. See Cyril Mango, "The Legend of Leo the Wise," *Byzantium and its Image* (London, 1984), Study XVI, especially 75 and 78.

6. *Vivlion Istorikon* (Venice, 1743), preface.

7. Ibid., 111–116. On the Byzantine chronographical tradition, which is carried on by the *Vivlion Istorikon,* see Cyril Mango, *Byzantium: The Empire of New Rome* (London, 1980), 139–200.

8. Nektarios, patriarch of Jerusalem, *Epitomi tis Ierokosmikis Istorias,* ed. Amvrosios Gradenigos (Venice, 1677). The following editions are known: 1677, 1729, 1758, 1770, 1783, 1805. For a useful analysis, see M. I. Manousakas, "I Epitomi tis Ierokosmikis Istorias tou Nektariou Ierosolymon kai ai pigai aftis," *Kritika Chronika* 1 (1947): 291–332. This study is reprinted as an introduction to the most recent edition of the work (Athens, 1980), sponsored by the Monastery of Sinai, to the brotherhood of which Patriarch Nektarios belonged.

9. *Epitomi tis Ierokosmikis Istorias* (Venice, 1770), 1–2, 3, 251–254.

10. Ibid., 256–257.

11. Kaisarios Dapontes, *Phanari Gynaikon,* preface, ed. E. Souloyiannis, *Texts and Studies of Modern Greek Literature* 65 (Athens, 1970). The text is extracted from a manuscript deposited in the monastery of Xeropotamou, Mount Athos, Xeropotamou MS 253, fols. 1–4.

12. Kaisarios Dapontes, *Kathreptis Gynaikon* (Leipzig, 1766).

13. Ibid., preface, n.p.

14. Ibid., 2:59–60, 63, 65–68, 169, and 1:259–260, 294–298, 311.

15. Ibid., 2:400–401. See also Dimaras, *Neoelliniki Logotechnia,* 160. On eighteenth-century millenarian currents, see below, chapter 4.

16. Dapontes, *Ephimerides Dakikai,* ed. Émile Legrand (Paris, 1880), vols. 1–3. The text is a chronicle of the war of the combined Russian and German forces against the Ottoman Empire from 1736 to 1739. See also his *Geographiki Istoria,* ibid., 3:65–71, where the lament for Greece reveals his affinities with millenarianism. See also the sketch of a biography of Constantine Mavrokordatos, ibid., 1:332–352, for Dapontes's ideas on enlightened absolutism. For his view of America, see *Kathreptis Gynaikon,* 2:45–46. For a profile, see R. M. Dawkins, *The Monks of Athos* (London, 1936), 65–73, and on his place in eighteenth-century Balkan culture, P. M. Kitromilides, "Balkan Mentality: History, Legend, Imagination," *Orthodoxy Commonwealth,* Study I.

17. Georg Veloudis, *Der neugrichische Alexander: Tradition in Bewahrung und Wandel* (Munich, 1968), 167–226. For the tradition and the uses of the Alexander legend in medieval literature, which forms the prehistory of its modern Greek uses, see George Cary, *The Medieval Alexander* (Cambridge, 1956). See especially 248–259, 266–272, for the moral models associated with the image of Alexander in European literature.

18. Athanasios Skiadas, *Genos, Ithos, Kindynoi kai Katorthomata Petrou tou Protou* (Venice, 1737), preface, n.p. Text reprinted in Legrand, *B.H., XVIIIe Siècle,* 1:256–259.

19. François de Salignac, *Tychai Tilemachou,* trans. A. Skiadas (Venice, 1743), vols. 1–2. Later editions in a Greek translation by D. P. Govdelas appeared in Budapest, 1801, and Venice, 1803. On the significance of the work as a channel for political criticism, acutely noted by Voltaire, *The Age of Louis XIV* (New York, 1961), 361–362, see Paul Hazard, *The European Mind,* 280–283. For its reception in the Greek context, see Camariano, *Académies princières,* 312–314. For the contribution made by the translator, Athanasios Skiadas, to the intellectual and cultural reorientation of Hellenism in the early eighteenth century, see C. Th. Dimaras, *Istorika Phrontismata* (Athens, 1992), 1:124.

20. Charles Rollin, *Palaia Istoria,* trans. Alexandros Kangellarios (Venice, 1750), vols. 1–16. For the content of each volume, see Legrand, *B.H. XVIIIe Siècle,* 1:380–384. The translator, A. Kangellarios, had edited the 1729 edition of *Epitomi tis Ierokosmikis Istorias.* His transition to the new project was significant of the intellectual gropings of the age.

21. See Rollin, *Palaia Istoria,* vol. 1, opening address "To knowledge- and history-lovers among the Greek nation," n.p., *B.H. XVIIIe siècle,* 1:386–387.

22. See Paul Hazard, *European Thought in the Eighteenth Century* (New York, 1963), 189–192, and Gusdorf, *L'avènement des sciences humaines,* 434–437, and much more thoroughly, Chantal Grell, *Le Dix-huitième siècle et l' antiquité en*

France, 1680–1789 (Oxford, 1995), esp. 7–16, 34–35, 39–41, 877–881. On the uses of Rollin in the promotion of enlightenment in Italy, especially by Giannone, see the introduction to *Discorsi sopra gli annali di Tito Livio, Opere di Pietro Giannone,* 734, 739–740. It was through Italy that Greek culture usually made its contact with the Enlightenment, and some common problems facing the two cultures account for the similarities in the reception of enlightened thought in each context. Rollin's pedagogical views are stated in *Parangelmata dia tin kalin anatrophin ton paidon,* ed. Alexandros Kangellarios (Venice, 1752). This text was originally included in vol. 16 of *Palaia Istoria* (Venice, 1750) and was reprinted as a separate item for being "very beneficial to the Youth, particularly since there is nothing like it in the simple Romaic speech." On the significance of this pamphlet, see Anna Tabaki, "Oi pedagogikes antilipseis stin elliniki metaphrasi ton Parangel-maton [. . .] tou Charles Rollin," *Ellinika* 45 (1995): 75–84, and for a general appraisal of Rollin's pedagogical views, see P. Mesnard, "Rollin forge l'esprit de l'en-seignement secondaire (1661–1741)," *Les grandes pédagogues,* ed. J. Chateau (Paris, 1956), 146–167.

23. Montesquieu, "Pensées Diverses," in *Oeuvres Complètes de Montesquieu* (Paris, 1846), 624. For the place of Rollin in eighteenth-century French learning, see Augustin Sicard, *Les études classiques avant la Révolution* (Paris, 1887), 38–43, 169–183, and passim.

24. Rollin, *Palaia Istoria,* 1:1–50: "Pretheories on the Usefulness Derived from Secular History in Reference to the Faith." See esp. 1–5, 26–31, 40–43.

25. Gay, *Rise of Modern Paganism,* 75. Note Rollin's acknowledgment of his sources in *Palaia Istoria,* 1:40–41.

26. Camariano, *Académies princières,* 235–244, esp. 237–239. See also Koumas, *Istoriai ton anthropinon praxeon* (Vienna, 1831), 16:xliii–xliv for a critical assessment of the translation of Rollin and its place in Greek culture. The supposed reprint of the work in 1773 cannot be documented by any surviving copies and the hypothesis must be discarded.

27. Georgios Sakellarios, *Archaiologia Synoptiki ton Ellinon* (Vienna, 1796): "Pros tous philellinas anagnostas," n.p. This work, according to G. Zaviras, *Nea Ellas* (Athens, 1872), 243, was a translation of the section on the Greeks in J. H. Daniel Moldenhauer, *Einleitung in die Altertümer der Egyptier, Jüden, Griechen und Römer* (Königsberg and Leipzig, 1754). For details, see L. Vranousis, *Ephimeris 1797: Prole-gomena* (Athens, 1995), 645–649.

28. Sakellarios, *Archaiologia synoptiki,* 96

29. Manuel Tenedios, *Diatrivi eis Thoukydidin* (Vienna, 1799), 9–12. On p. 10n4 appears the following quotation from Mably's essay "Sur les Grecs": "C'est un ouvrage que tous les Princes et leurs Ministres devraient lire tous les ans ou plutôt savoir par coeur." Compare Thomas Hobbes, *Eight Books of the Peloponnesian Wars Written by Thucydides* (London, 1634). Two complete editions of the text of

Thucydides's histories appeared in the following years, one in Venice, ed. Sp. Vlantis (1802), and another in Vienna, ed. Neophytos Doukas (1805).

30. Abbé Millot, *Stoicheia tis genikis istorias palaias kai neoteras,* trans. Gr. Constantas and Zisis Kavras (Venice, 1806), 1:ix.

31. Ibid.

32. Ibid., xiv, xix, xxi, xxiv, 1–12. See also 167–207, where an attempt is made to compare the political institutions of Sparta and Athens. Vol. 2, 171–352, is devoted to the history of ancient Rome. On Millot's work, see also the comments of Constantinos Koumas, *Istoriai ton anthropinon praxeon,* 16:xliv–xlvi.

33. V. Papaefthemiou, *Istoria Synoptiki tis Ellados* (Vienna, 1807), xix.

34. On the relevant cultural background of the European Enlightenment, see Gay, *Rise of Modern Paganism,* 31–126, and Israel, *Enlightenment Contested,* 436–470. For an argument on the European sources of modern Greek classicism, see Cyril Mango, "Byzantinism and Romantic Hellenism," *Byzantium and its Image* (London, 1984), Study I. Although Mango's arguments tend rather to overstate the case, they do cast the problem in clear relief.

35. Anthimos Gazis, *Vivliothikis Ellinikis Vivlia Dyo* (Venice, 1807), 2:308.

36. Ibid., 309–323. See also Georgios Zaviras, *Nea Ellas i Ellinikon Theatron,* essentially the first exhaustive treatise on modern Greek literature and intellectual history in the Ottoman period, composed at about the same time as Gazis's work by the learned Greek merchant of Buda. The work was published in Athens, 1872, edited by G. P. Kremos, and reprinted with an introduction by T. Gritsopoulos (Athens, 1972). For a survey of Greek attitudes toward Byzantium in this period, see Anna Tabaki, "Byzance à travers les lumières néo-helléniques," *Europe: Revue litteraire mensuelle* 822 (October 1997): 147–161.

37. *Vivlos Chroniki periechousa tin Istorian tis Vyzantidos,* ed. Agapios Loverdos (Venice, 1767). See the editor's proemium. On the work and its translator, Ioannis Stanos, see Nikos Svoronos, "Ioannis Stanos," *Athina* 49 (1939): 232–242. On the beginnings of Byzantine studies in the seventeenth century and the pertinent outlook of eighteenth-century historiography, see George Ostrogorsky, *History of the Byzantine State* (New Brunswick, 1969), 2–6. Both Montesquieu and Gibbon extensively utilized Byzantine sources in their works, and their respective accounts of the decline of the Christian Roman Empire indicate how the Enlightenment's historical criticism could sustain the teleology of reason.

38. See below, chapter 10.

39. *Apologia Istorikokritiki,* attributed to "Anastasios Oikonomos of Ambelakia," but probably composed by Sotiris Louizis (Trieste, 1814). The book's objective was to refute the slanders against the modern Greeks in the work of Jacob Ludwig Salomo Bartholdy, *Bruchstücke zur näheren Kenntniss des heutigen Griechenlands, gesammelt auf einer Reise im Jahre 1803–1804* (Berlin, 1805). A French translation appeared in Paris 1807, 2 vols. When the French translation appeared, Panayiotis Kodrikas published,

over the initials N. K., a rebuttal of Bartholdy's views in the *Magasin Encylcopédique,* 1808. The appearance of the work provoked an outrage among Greek intellectuals in Europe. On the debate that ensued, see K. Simopoulos, *Xenoi Taxidiotes stin Ellada, 1800–1810* (Athens, 1975), 180–225. On the background to the composition of *Apologia Istorikokritiki* and its author, see E. C. Protopsaltis, *I epanastatiki kinisis ton Ellinon kata ton defteron epi Aikaterinis B′ Rossotourkikon polemon* (Athens, 1959), 106–109. The author of the *Apologia* was aware of the earlier attack on the Greeks by the Abbate Compagnioni, *Saggio su gli Ebrei e su i Greci,* which was published in 1792 and saw a second edition in Milan, 1802. Compagnioni was answered by Ioanis Donas Paschalis (1761–1839), in his *Lettera in apologia* (1793), which appeared in a Greek edition under the title *Epistoli apologitiki enos Markionos Frangiskou Albergatou Kapakellou kata tis epistolis tou Kyr Abba Kompagnonou anastrephomenis peri tin omoiotita, neosti par'ekeinou anakalyphtheisan, anameson Evraion kai Ellinon* (Venice, 1802). The arguments of the two most notorious "slanderers of the nation" are set forth by Emmanuel N. Frangiskos, "Dyo 'Kategoroi tou Genous': C. D. Pauw, 1788 kai J. S. Bartholdy, 1805," *Periigiseis ston Elliniko choro* (Athens, 1968), 49–66. See also P. M. Kitromilides, "Kritiki kai Politiki: I ideologiki simasia tis epikrisis tou ellinismou apo ton J. L. S. Bartholdy," *DIEEE* 24 (1981): 377–410.

40. *Apologia Istorikokritiki,* vii, 53, survey of ancient Greek achievements; 5–74, 191–224, profiles of modern Greek scholars, especially 208–209 in praise of Korais.

41. Gregorios Paliouritis, *Epitomi Istorias tis Ellados* (Venice, 1815), 1:x–xvii, from the dedicatory epistle to the Greek Brotherhood of Leghorn. The passage cited is on p. xi.

42. Ibid., xviii–xix.

43. Ibid., xviii–xix.

44. Ibid., xix, xxi, xxiii–xxiv.

45. Gregorios Paliouritis, *Archaiologia Elliniki* (Venice, 1815), v–viii, 237–251. On this important representative of Greek civic humanism, see Polykarpos Synodinos, "Gregorios Paliouritis," *Ipirotika Chronika* 2 (1927): 173–181, and Steph. Betis, "Symvoli sti meleti tou Ipirotikou Diaphotismou. Gregorios Paliouritis," *Ipirotiki Estia* 19 (1970): 419–430, 540–554.

46. Vilaras's lyric poetry links him with Italian radicalism, which nurtured the Italian revolutionary movements. See L. Vranousis, "'I Anoixi' tou Vilara kai to italiko tis protypo: Apo tin Italiki 'Arkadia' tou Metastasio kai tou Parini stin Ipiro tou Vilara kai sta Eptanisa tou Matesi," *O Eranistis* 11 (1974): 627–648.

47. See *Apanta Ioannou Vilara,* ed. S. Raphtanis (Zakynthos, 1871), 33–49 (Crito), and 51–58 (Funeral Oration). For Vilaras's radical philosophical views that formed the background to his literary choices, see Henry Holland, *Travels in the Ionian Isles, Albania, Thessaly, Macedonia, etc., during the Years 1812 and 1813* (London, 1815), 256–257, 273–276. According to Holland, his discussions with Vilaras had revealed him to be an adherent of materialism and determinism.

48. This program was most characteristically presented in Ioannis Patousas, *Enkyklopaideia Philologiki* (Venice, 1710), vols. 1–4. The work went through several subsequent editions, 1741, 1744, 1758, 1778, 1780, 1795, 1802, 1804, 1817, and 1819 and was used by successive generations of students as a textbook of Greek literature.

49. See Skiadas, *Genos, Ethos* [. . .], preface. Another popular biography of Peter the Great by the Greek priest and scholar Antonios Katiphoros, *Vita di Pietro il Grande,* was reprinted in Venice six times between 1736 and 1792. See Philippos Iliou, *Prosthikes stin Elliniki Vivliographia* (Athens, 1973), 236. Katiphoros's work was the original of Skiadas's Greek version. On the Russian connection in Greek political thought, see below, chapter 4.

50. Georgios Konstantinou, *Pangosmios Istoria tis Oikoumenis,* vol. 1: *To Vaslieion tis megalis Rossias* (Venice, 1759), ix.

51. Ibid., x–xii, 2–3, 10–11. A second volume in the series dealing with China appeared next: Georgios Constantinou, *Istoria tou Vasileiou tis Kinas* (Venice, 1763). On p. 248 of this work a projected third volume on the kingdoms of India was announced, but was never published.

52. See Gay, *Science of Freedom,* 391

53. The original appeared as *Storia della guerra presente tra Russia e la Porta Ottomana* (Venice, 1770). For further clarification, see P. M. Kitromilides, "Ideologikes epiloges kai istoriographiki praxi: Spyridon Papadopoulos kai Domenico Caminer," *Thisavrismata* 20 (1990): 500–517.

54. Spyridon Papadopoulos, *Istoria tou parontos polemou anametaxy tis Rousias kai tis Othomanikis Portas* (Venice, 1770), 1:6–7. This was a history of the second Russo-Turkish war of the eighteenth century and was completed in six volumes published in Venice between 1770 and 1773. On the lively interest, participation, and consequences of this war for the Greeks, see A. Camariano-Cioran, "La guerre russo-turque de 1768–1774 et les Grecs," *RESEE* 3 (1965): 513 547.

55. Agapios Loverdos, *Istoria ton Dyo Eton 1787–1788* (Venice, 1791), vi.

56. The passage cited is from *Istoria ton Dyo Eton,* vii–viii. On the author, see K. Tsitselis, *Kephalliniaka Symmikta* (Athens, 1904), 1:315–317, and the more recent details added by Ath. Karathanasis, *I Phlangineios Scholi tis Venetias* (Thessaloniki, 1986), 128–132. On the work and its sources, see P. M. Kitromilides, "The Identity of a Book: European Power Politics and Ideological Motivations in Agapios Loverdos's *Istoria ton dyo eton* (Venice 1791)," *Thisavrismata* 28 (1998): 433–449. On the outbreak of the Russo-Turkish war, see the pamphlet, *Aitiologia tou Parontos Polemou metaxy Rossias kai Tourkias 1787* (Venice, 1791).

57. P. Lambanitziotis, *Istoria tis Tavrikis Chersonisou* (Vienna, 1792), preface, n.p.

58. Archimandrite Kyprianos, *Istoria Chronologiki tis Nisou Kyprou* (Venice, 1788), 300–332, on the *Tourkokratia* in Cyprus. For an English version of this section of the work, see C. D. Cobham, *Excerpta Cypria* (Cambridge, 1908), 344–368.

59. Kyprianos has not yet received the attention he deserves as a representative of eighteenth century historiography. For biographical and bibliographical details, see P. M. Kitromilides, *Kypriaki logiosyni 1571–1878* (Nicosia, 2002), 174–177. See also G. Kolias, "Oi phileleftheres idees tou Archimandriti Kyprianou," *Imerologion tis Megalis Ellados* (Athens, 1935), 229–238, and Th. Papadopoullos's introduction in the 1971 reprint of *Istoria Chronologiki tis Nisou Kyprou* (Nicosia, 1971), 1–5.

60. Kyprianos, *Istoria Chronologiki,* 3, footnote reference to the Venice edition of Buffon's works. See also 11, 13, 15, 268, and 301 for the use of Vincenzo Coronelli's cartographic work.

61. Kyprianos, *Istoria Chronologiki,* viii. His critique was directed at Steffano Lusignano, *Corograffia e breve historia universale dell'isola di Cipro* (Bologna, 1573), which nevertheless, remained his major source.

62. Kyprianos, *Istoria chronologiki,* ix.

63. Ibid., 74.

64. Ibid., 114, 139, 204.

65. Ibid., 153.

66. Ibid., 153, 202–204, 281, 294.

67. Ibid., 110–312. Also 396–397: "On Memorable Catastrophes."

68. Ibid., v–ix, 333–362.

69. Ibid., 312, 316.

70. Ibid., 308.

71. Ibid., 325, 329.

72. Ibid., 53n and 294. See also 306 for the religious reasons behind the Cypriot preference for Ottoman rule.

73. Ibid., vii.

74. Ibid., 363–369: analysis of the material possibilities of life in Cyprus, based on a survey of economic activities and production.

75. Ibid., 264.

76. The importance of local history in Enlightenment historiography is stressed by Constantinos Koumas in his review of modern Greek historical literature, *Istoriai ton anthropinon praxeon* (Vienna, 1831), 6:xlvi–xlviii, in which, however, there is no mention of the earliest and fullest example, the *Istoria chronologiki tis Nisou Kyprou* by archimandrite Kyprianos, though two other representative texts are cited: the *Istoria Souliou kai Pargas* by Christophoros Peraivos (Paris, 1803) and the second, fuller edition (Venice, 1815), and Korais's historical sketch of ancient Chios, which was included in *Atakta* (Paris, 1830), 3:1–278, under the title "Chiaki archaiologia." According to Koumas, this work by Korais formed "an example for other learned men, to encourage them, also, each to write the history of his birthplace, from which the entire history of the Greeks will emerge." The deeper political aspirations of local history, however, are evident in Koumas's comment on Peraivos: "This little history shows that Greece will once again produce a Thucydides, if her children perform deeds with weapons that are worthy of historical record."

3. THE GEOGRAPHY OF CIVILIZATION

1. Rousseau, *Émile, Oeuvres complètes* (Paris, 1969), 4:771, 831–832.

2. Cf. René Pomeau, "Voyage et lumières dans la littérature française du XVIIIe siècle," *SVEC* 57 (1967): 1269–1289. See also Geoffrey Atkinson, *Les relations de voyages du XVIIe siècle et l'évolution des idées: Contribution à l'étude de la formation de l'esprit du XVIIIème siècle,* new ed. (Geneva, 1972), and George B. Parks, "Travel as Education," in R. F. Jones et al., *The Seventeenth Century: Studies in the History of English Thought and Literature from Bacon to Pope* (Stanford, 1951), 264–290. On the formation of geographical knowledge in connection with the secularization of the concept of space and the findings of the new "scientific" travels at the period of the Enlightenment, see David N. Livingstone, *The Geographical Tradition* (Oxford, 1992), 102–138.

3. Such sources included descriptions of the Holy Land and the Sacred City of Jerusalem printed in 1690 (Venice), 1728 (Venice), 1749 (Vienna), 1780, bilingual edition in Greek and Turkish printed in Greek characters *(karamanli)* for Turkish-speaking Orthodox in Asia Minor (Leipzig), 1787 (Vienna), 1799 (Vienna). Descriptions of Mount Athos and the Great Lavra, the senior monastery on the Holy Mountain, were printed in 1701 (Wallachia, Snagov Monastery), 1745 (Venice), 1772 (Venice), 1780 (Venice). Descriptions of the Sacred and God-trodden Mount of Sinai were printed in 1768 (Venice), two in 1773 (both in Venice), 1778 (Venice), 1784 (bilingual *karamanli* ed., Venice). There were also descriptions of another major shrine of Orthodox pilgrimage, the monastery of the Blessed Virgin of Kykkos in Cyprus, printed in 1751 and 1782 (both in Venice). All of these texts continued to be reprinted into the nineteenth century.

4. The conception of the universe prevalent in pre-Enlightenment Greek learning was based on the Neoaristotelianism of Corydaleus that dominated Greek educational institutions. Teaching manuals of geography following the Ptolemaic system and its updating by Corydaleus were in wide use in the eighteenth century. See Camariano, *Académies princières,* 246. On Corydaleus's geographical views, see Tsourkas, *Les débuts de l'enseignement philosophique et de la libre pensée dans les Balkans* (Thessaloniki, 1967), 194–195, 303–305, 384.

5. Chrysanthos Notaras, *Eisagogi eis ta geographika kai sphairika* (Paris, 1716, reprinted Venice, 1718). The author later became Patriarch of Jerusalem and composed a historical description of the Holy Land (Venice, 1728). Methodios Anthrakitis adopted Chrysanthos's geographical theory in his *Odou mathematikis tomos tritos* (Venice, 1749), 221. On Chrysanthos's training and cartographical projects, see Germain Aujac, "Cartes géographiques en grec modern imprimées à Padoue en 1700," *Geographia Antiqua* 6 (1997): 165–181.

6. Meletios Mitrou, *Geographia palaia kai nea,* 2nd ed., ed. Anthimos Gazis (Venice, 1807). References are to this edition. The title chosen by Meletios for his work was obviously inspired by the corresponding titles used by Phillipe Briet (Brietus),

Parallela geographiae veteris et novae (Paris, 1648), and Philippe Cluver (Cluverius), *Introductioni in universum geographiam tam veterem quam novam* (Elzevir, 1624), which were also his main sources. For a biographical profile of the author, see 1:xiv–xvi, and for his sources, 26–29. See also C. V. Kyriakopoulos, *Meletios (Mitrou) Athinon o Geographos, 1661–1714* (Athens, 1990), vols. 1–2.

7. Meletios, *Geographia*, 1–4. One of the earliest recordings of the word "cosmopolite" in a modern Greek source was in the four-language dictionary compiled by Gerasimos Vlachos: *Thisavros Tetraglossos* (Venice, 1659, reprinted 1723, 1784). The meaning of the word was defined as "that who observes the things of the world," and its foreign language equivalents were given as *mundanus* in Latin and *secolare* in Italian.

8. Meletios, *Geographia*, 1:3.

9. Ibid., 100, 125, 231–232, 312, 322, 245–247. Compare Paul Hazard, *European Thought in the Eighteenth Century* (Gloucester, MA, 1973), 440, 444–445 on the image of Paris as the heart of European civilization in the eighteenth century.

10. Meletios, *Geographia*, 2:247–250, 356–361, 415–416. Spyridon Lambros, "O Meletios Athinon os archaiodiphis kai stylokopas," *Neos Ellinomnimon* 3 (1906): 59–105, is a classic study of Meletios's method in his description of Greece and a pioneering contribution to the study of his work.

11. Montesquieu, *Lettres Persanes*, No. XIX.

12. Georgios Phatzeas, *Grammatiki Geographiki* (Venice, 1760), vols. 1–3. This was a Greek rendering of the Italian translation of Patrick Gordon's *Geography Anatomized or a Compleat Geographical Grammar,* which between its first appearance in London in 1693 and 1754 went through twenty editions. On this work and its place in geographical literature, see Margarita Bowen, *Empiricism and Geographical Thought: From Francis Bacon to Alexander von Humboldt* (Cambridge, 1981), 147–148. The enlarged twentieth edition of 1754 was possibly the source of the Italian translation, entitled *Grammatica Geografica* (Venice, 1760), which formed the basis of the Greek edition of the same year. Both books were printed at the same printing house, Antonio Zatta. For Phatzeas's own account of his motivation in bringing this work to light, see *Grammatiki Geographiki*, 1:vi, xix–xx, xxviii, xxxi–xxxii. For biographical details, see G. Ploumidis, "O Archiepiskopos Philadelpheias Gregorios Phatzeas, 1762–1768," *Thisavrismata* 4 (1967), 85–113, esp. 102–106 on the composition of the geography.

13. *Grammatiki Geographiki*, 1:178–195.

14. Ibid., 219–240, especially 222, 239–240.

15. Ibid., 2:203–207, 212–214, 219, 221–223, 225–226.

16. Ibid., 132–147.

17. Ibid., 179.

18. Ibid., 177.

19. Ibid., 171.

20. Ibid., 142–145, 369–370, 231.

21. Ibid., 135–138.

22. Ibid., 142–144. In addition to Constantinople and Mount Athos, Phatzeas also mentions advanced Greek schools in Thessaloniki, Ioannina, two in Athens, Tripolitza, Veria, Livadeia, Larisa, Trikki in Thessaly, Trikala in the Peloponnese, Siatista, Argyrokastro, and Patras.

23. Such geography textbooks explicitly produced for school use were Nikiphoros Theotokis, *Stoicheia Geographias,* written in 1774, obviously as a manual of his courses at Jassy but published only in 1804 by Anthimos Gazis in Vienna, and Iosipos Moisiodax, *Theoria tis Geographias,* composed in 1767 in Bucharest as a teaching aid to his lectures, which is preserved in Codex 749 of Saint Panteleimon Monastery on Mount Athos. On the composition of the *Geography* of Nikiphoros Theotokis, see Z. Mourouti-Gekakou, *O Nikiphoros Theotokis kai i symvoli autou eis tin paideian tou genous* (Athens, 1979), 148–152, and for the teaching of geography in the princely academies, see Camariano, *Académies princières,* 244–251, 560–569, 595–597. An interesting eighteenth-century geographical text is the *Geographiki Istoria* by Caisarios Daponte, which points to the popularization of secular geographical knowledge among a broad public. Daponte's work is a verse account of several European countries, which in fact he had never visited, extolling "truly wonderful and curious things." Extracts from it were published by Émile Legrand, *Bibliothèque grecque vulgaire* (Paris, 1881), 3:247–279. The text is preserved in Codex 193, fols. 1–201ʳ in the General State Archives of Greece, Athens.

24. Theotokis, *Stoicheia Geographias,* ed. A. Gazis (Vienna 1804), 66–67.

25. Compare Montesquieu, *De l'esprit des Lois,* book III and especially book XIX, chapters 1–5.

26. Theotokis, *Stoicheia Geographias,* 80–81, 104–105, 122, 89, 127, 140–143, 154–155, 177–179, 187, 193.

27. Ibid., 201–207.

28. Iosipos Moisiodax, *Theoria tis Geographias* (Vienna, 1781), 52–62, 106–132. Note 162–163, footnote, for his praise of the progress of the English in scientific knowledge, civilization, and philhellenism.

29. Daniel Philippidis and Gregorios Constantas, *Geographia Neoteriki* (Vienna, 1791). A new edition of the text by Aik. Koumarianou was published in Athens in 1988. The introduction to this edition (pp. 9*–79*) is useful for biographical and bibliographical details. See Barbié du Bocage's review of the original edition in *Magasin Encyclopédique* 6 (1797): 76–90, where the sources of the work are cited as the geographical treatises by Nicole de la Croix, *Géographie Moderne* (Paris, 1748), and the sections "Géographie Ancienne," "Histoire Ancienne," and "Géographie" of the *Encyclopédie Méthodique* of Charles Joseph Panckouke. The authors of these sections, on the ideas of which Philippidis and Constantas based themselves faithfully, were E. Mentelle, F. Robert, and N. Masson de Morvilliers. For insights into the intellectual outlook that formed the background to this work, see the correspondence among D.

Philippidis, Barbié du Bocage, A. Gazis, *Allilographia, 1794–1819,* ed. Aik. Kouma-rianou (Athens, 1966); and on Gregorios Constantas, see R. N. Kamilaris, *Gregoriou Constanta biographia-logoi-epistolai* (Athens, 1897), and Dimaras, *Istorika Phrontis-mata,* 87–96. On Daniel Philippidis as a philosopher, see Gregorios Karaphylis, *I philosophiki provlimatiki tou Dimitriou-Daniel Philippidi* (Thessaloniki, 1993).

    30. *Geographia Neoteriki* (Vienna, 1791), 1–90.

    31. Ibid., 106–107.

    32. Ibid., 76–83.

    33. Ibid., 95–97.

    34. Ibid., 91. This was a common theme in eighteenth-century treatises on politi-cal geography. See Hazard, *European Thought in the Eighteenth Century,* 437.

    35. Montesquieu, *Lettres persanes,* Nos. XXXVI, XLVIII, LVIII, LXVIII. Com-pare Paul Hazard, *The European Mind, 1680–1715* (New York, 1963), 3–28. On the tradition of this genre in European literature, see G. L. van Roosbroeck, *Persian Letters before Montesquieu* (New York, 1932).

    36. *Geographia Neoteriki,* 358–359.

    37. Ibid., 359, 366–367, 372, 457, 473, 368.

    38. Ibid., 371–372, 413–417. The reference to Machiavelli on 413.

    39. Ibid., 363–364.

    40. Ibid., 411. Also 359, 439.

    41. Ibid., 393–394.

    42. Ibid., 453–454.

    43. Ibid., 481–483, 488–490, 497, 534–544.

    44. Ibid., 370. Compare 554, 564–565.

    45. Ibid., 558. Also Hazard, *European Thought in the Eighteenth Century,* 442–445. See also Louis Réau, *L'Europe française au siècle des lumières* (Paris, 1938).

    46. *Geographia Neoteriki,* 561, 577–580.

    47. Ibid., 564.

    48. Ibid., 564–566. These views of the dialectical relationship between reform and social change and the precipitation of the Revolution call to the reader's mind Alexis de Tocqueville, *L'ancien régime et la Révolution* (Paris, 1856), especially part 3.

    49. *Geographia Neoteriki,* 108–123. The source of the review is the *Encyclopédie Méthodique/Géographie Ancienne* (Paris, 1789), 2:29–34: "Précis chonologique et historique des révolutions de la Grèce," text by Mentelle.

    50. *Geographia Neoteriki,* 113.

    51. Ibid., 121.

    52. On the theory of the influence of the climate and its limits, see Montesquieu, *De l'esprit des Lois,* books 14–27. Also Livingstone, *Geographical Tradition,* 121–123.

    53. *Geographia Neoteriki,* 136.

    54. Ibid., 128.

    55. Ibid., 139–140.

56. Ibid., 136.

57. Ibid., 149, 262.

58. Ibid., 135–136.

59. Ibid., 177–183. The following paragraphs are based on this passage. For the linguistic views of Philippidis and Constantas, see Dimaras, *Istorika phrontismata,* 78–86. For a critique of the linguistic practice of the *Geographia Neoteriki,* see C. Sathas, *Istoria tou zitimatos tis Neoellinikis glossis* (Athens, 1870), 178–185. This echoes the earlier critique by P. Kodrikas, *Meleti tis koinis Ellinikis dialektou* (Paris, 1818), xxxiii. See also P. Mackridge, *Language and National Identity in Greece* (Oxford, 2009), 98–101.

60. *Geographia Neoteriki,* 183.

61. Ibid., 255–260.

62. Compare Montesquieu, *Considérations sur les causes de la grandeur et de la décadence des Romains,* chapters 21–23.

63. *Geographia Neoteriki,* 178.

64. Ibid., 164–190.

65. Ibid,. 176.

66. Ibid., 245, 262.

67. Ibid., 284.

68. Ibid., 231.

69. Ibid., 242.

70. Ibid., 141.

71. Ibid., 210–243. This detailed description was meant as an empirical model of applied research on social geography. Note the methodological observations, 213–214. The eventual composition was an impressive piece of empirical sociological analysis.

72. Ibid., 215–216.

73. Ibid., 218.

74. Ibid., compare Montesquieu, *De l'esprit des Lois,* book XVII, chapter 2. Benjamin R. Barber, *The Death of Communal Liberty* (Princeton, 1974), provides suggestive evidence on the moral and political possibilities of communal life, drawn from the actual historical experience of another mountainous region of Europe which practiced republican self-government and communal liberty for many centuries.

75. Compare J. J. Rousseau, "Projet de constitution pour la Corse," *Oeuvres complètes* (Paris, 1964), 3:901–939.

76. *Geographia Neoteriki,* 229–231, for the forceful exhortation to the Meliotes, the authors' fellow countrymen.

77. Ibid., 231.

78. For a characterization of the utopian outlook, see Judith N. Shklar, "The Political Theory of Utopia: From Melancholy to Nostalgia," in her *Political Thought and Political Thinkers,* ed. Stanley Hoffmann (Chicago, 1998), 161–174.

79. For the interplay of these choices in the political thought of the Enlightenment, see Franco Venturi, *Utopia and Reform in the Enlightenment* (Cambridge,
1971).

80. Montesquieu, *Lettres persanes,* Nos. II, VIII. Also Shklar, "Politics and the
Intellect," *Political Thought and Political Thinkers,* 94–104.

81. The geographical literature of the Modern Greek Enlightenment is not
exhausted with the works discussed in detail in this chapter, nor does it come to
an end with the *Geographia Neoteriki* in 1791. On the contrary, the production
of texts on geography intensified, particularly during the first two decades of the
nineteenth century. Interest in geography was very much alive in this period when
the Enlightenment reached its climax, judging from the wide range of geographical
publications, consisting of atlases, maps, and geographical dictionaries, as well as
more general surveys and teaching handbooks. The circulation of special geographic
monographs on particular regions may be considered of paramount importance in
the development of geographical knowledge, the outstanding example being the *Geo-
graphikon tis Roumounias* by Daniel Philippidis (Vienna, 1816). The same broad line
was followed by texts on Albania and Epiros, by Kosmas Thesprotos and Athanasios
Psalidas, which were preserved in a manuscript by Thesprotos but have only been
published relatively recently. See Kosmas Thesprotos and Athanasios Psalidas, *Geographia Alvanias kai Ipirou,* ed. Ath. Ch. Papacharisis (Ioannina, 1964). The *Ipirotika*
of Athanasios Stageiritis (Vienna, 1819), is inferior to Philippidis's empiricism. Of
the comprehensive geographical treatises of the early nineteenth century, noteworthy are the *Geographia Methodiki apasis tis oikoumenis,* by Dionysios Pyrros (Venice,
1818), and the "Emporogeographikon Lexikon" by Nikolaos Papadopoulos, *Ermis o
Kerdoos,* vols. 3–4 (Venice, 1816–1817, reprinted Athens, 1988). This last work is of
particular interest in that it links economic or "commercial" geography, as it is called,
with the beginnings of the discipline of political economy in Greek culture. A good,
though incomplete, guide is offered by Antonios Miliarakis, *Neoelliniki Geographiki
philologia itoi katalogos ton apo tou 1800–1889 geographithenton ypo ton Ellinon* (Athens, 1889, reprinted 1981). See also V. A. Mystakidis, *Kriseis, Diorthoseis, Prosthikai*
(Constantinople, 1890) and the critique of this work by G. Hirschfeld, "Zur Geschichte der Geographie bei den Neugriechen," *Berliner Philologische Wochenschrift,*
fasc. 9–10 (1 and 8 March 1890). The two texts can be found in a modern reprint by
Cultura publishing house (Athens, n.d.)

4. ENLIGHTENED ABSOLUTISM AS A PATH TO CHANGE

1. Fritz Hartung, *Enlightened Despotism* (London, 1957); and Gay, *Science of
Freedom,* 483–496 and 682–689. For a survey of older scholarship on the subject,
see Michel Lhéritier, "Le despotisme éclairé de Frédéric II à la Révolution française,"
Bulletin of the International Committee of Historical Sciences 9, no. 35 (June 1937):

181–225. For historical assessments of individual manifestations of the phenomenon, see *Enlightened Absolutism,* ed. H. M. Scott (London, 1990).

2. Cf. Richard Koebner, "Despot and Despotism: Vicissitudes of a Political Term," *Journal of the Warburg and Courtauld Institutes* 14 (1951): 275–302.

3. Paul Hazard, *European Thought in the Eighteenth Century* (Cleveland, 1963), 329, and Alfred Cobban, *In Search of Humanity* (New York, 1961), 161–179.

4. See, e.g., R. R. Palmer, *The Age of the Democratic Revolution,* vol. 1: *The Challenge* (Princeton, 1959), 373–407, and more generally, M. Anderson, *Europe in the Eighteenth Century, 1713–1783* (London, 1961), 121–129.

5. Montesquieu, *De l'esprit des Lois,* book III, chapters 9–10; book V, chapters 14–18; and J. J. Rousseau, *Du contrat social,* book III, chapter 6.

6. Voltaire, *Histoire de l'Empire de Russie sous Pierre le Grand* (Paris, 1828), vols. 1–2. See esp. vol. 1, chapters 6, 7, 10; vol. 2, chapters 9, 11–14. Compare J. H. Brumfitt, *Voltaire Historian* (Oxford, 1958), 12, 74–75, and esp. Larry Wolff, *Inventing Eastern Europe* (Stanford, 1994), 195–234.

7. Peter Gay, *Voltaire's Politics: The Poet as Realist* (Princeton, 1959), 144–184.

8. Denis Diderot, "Pages Contre un Tyran," *Oeuvres Politiques,* ed. Paul Vernière (Paris, 1963), 135–148.

9. On Diderot's relations with Catherine II, see *Oeuvres Politiques,* 213–327, and Arthur Wilson, "Diderot in Russia, 1773–1774," *The Eighteenth Century in Russia,* ed. J. G. Garrard, (Oxford, 1973), 166–197.

10. See Leonard Krieger, *An Essay on the Theory of Enlightened Despotism* (Chicago, 1975), 20–22.

11. Compare Machiavelli, *The Prince,* chapters 15–16, 19, 21. Frederick II's *Anti-Machiavel,* 1740, was the most prominent among the treatises with which enlightened monarchs attempted to proclaim their good intentions by disassociating themselves from Machiavelli's moral theory.

12. See Claude Fauriel, *Chants populaires de la Grèce moderne* (Paris, 1825), 2:340; and Émile Legrand, *Recueil de chansons populaires grecques* (Paris, 1874), 76, 108–114. On the emergence of this millenarian tradition in Greek folklore and its impact on late Byzantine political thought during the centuries of the disintegration of the Eastern Roman Empire, see Speros Vryonis, Jr., *The Decline of Medieval Hellenism in Asia Minor and the Process of Islamization from the Eleventh through the Fifteenth Centuries* (Berkeley and London, 1971), 408–438.

13. This was a dominant theme in Greek political thought during the first centuries of Ottoman captivity. See Cyril Mango, "Byzantinism and Romantic Hellenism," *Byzantium and its Image* (London, 1984), Study I, esp. 32–36, and N. G. Politis, "Demodeis doxasiai peri apokatastaseos tou Ellinikou ethnous," *Laographika Symmikta* (Athens, 1920), 1:14–27, for a survey of the themes dominating popular expectations of national redemption. The most important of the older studies on the chresmological tradition is that by Nikos Veis, "Peri tou istorimenou chrismologiou

tis Kratikis Vivliothikis tou Verolinou kai tou thrylou tou 'marmaromenou vasilia,' *Byzantinisch-Neugriechischer Jahrbücher* 13 (1936–1937): 203–244, B. Knös, "Les Oracles de Léon le Sage," *Aphieroma sti mnimi tou Manoli Triantaphyllidi* (Athens, 1960), 155–188, and Cyril Mango, "The Legend of Leo the Wise," *Byzantium and its Image,* Study XVI, 59–93. Asterios Argyriou, *Les éxégèses grecques de l'Apocalypse à l'époque turque, 1453–1821: Esquisse d'une histoire des courants idéologiques au sein du peuple grec asservi* (Thessaloniki, 1982), provides a systematic analysis that marks a considerable advance in the study of the subject.

14. Eric J. Hobsbawm, *Social Bandits and Primitive Rebels* (Glencoe, IL, 1959), 57–65, 105–107, and idem, *Bandits* (London, 1969), 23; and Norman Cohn, *The Pursuit of the Millenium* (London, 1957), esp. 21–32, 307–314.

15. Compare Fernand Braudel, *The Mediterranean and the Mediterranean World in the Age of Philip II* (New York, 1972), 769–770. For the historical and cultural background to these early international orientations of Greek political thought, see esp. E. Eickoff, *Venedig, Wien und die Osmanen, 1645–1700* (Munich, 1970), and the earlier works by A. Bernardy, *Venezia e il Turco nella seconda metà del secolo XVII* (Florence, 1902), and *L'ultima guerra turco-veneziana, 1714–1718* (Florence, 1902). Also Paolo Preto, *Venezia e i Turchi* (Florence, 1975).

16. On the historical origins of these Russian claims, see briefly George Ostrogorsky, *History of the Byzantine State* (New Brunswick, 1969), 553–572, and Dimitri Obolensky, *The Byzantine Commonwealth* (London, 1971), 363–367. For a broader analysis of the subject, see Obolensky, "Russia's Byzantine Heritage," *Oxford Slavonic Papers* 1 (1950): 37–63. On the eighteenth-century background, B. H. Sumner, *Peter the Great and the Ottoman Empire* (Oxford, 1949), 26–36. On the powerful symbolism of the "Third Rome," see D. Stremooukhoff, "Moscow the Third Rome: Sources of the Doctrine," *Speculum* 28 (1953): 84–101, Cyril Toumanoff, "Moscow the Third Rome: Genesis and Significance of a Politico-Religious Idea," *The Catholic Historical Review* 49 (1954–1955): 411–447; and Ihor Sevcenko, "Byzantine Cultural Influences," in *Rewriting Russian History: Soviet Interpretations of Russia's Past,* ed. C. E. Black (New York, 1956), 143–197, esp. 150.The subject is reappraised quite convincingly by Donald Ostrowski, "'Moscow the Third Rome' as a Historical Ghost," *Byzantium: Faith and Power (1261–1557). Perspectives on Late Byzantine Art and Culture,* ed. Sarah T. Brooks (New York, New Haven, and London, 2007), 170–179.

17. See, characteristically, C. Dapontes, "Katalogos Istorikos," *Mesainoniki Vivliothiki,* ed. C. Sathas (Venice, 1872), 3:141–142. On the various exponents of the Russian expectation, see P. M. Kontoyiannis, *Oi Ellines kata ton proton epi Aikaterinis B´ Rossotourkikon polemon 1768–1774* (Athens, 1903), 10–11, 12–17, 20–22, 90–92; and Evlogios Kourilas, "Theoklitos Polyeidis kai to Lefkoma aftou en Germania," *Thrakika* 5 (1934): 85–100. The evidence is not equally clear or convincing in all cases. In the case of Gordius, matters have been clarified by Argyriou, *Les éxégèses grecques,* 304–354.

18. The idea belongs to Evlogios Kourilas, *Thrakika* 5 (1934), 80. It is contested by N. Veis, "Peri tou istorimenou chrismologiou," 244xxxiii n3.

19. Kourilas, *Thrakika* 4 (1933): 153–156; and ibid. 5 (1934): 69–84, 132–140, 153–160. On Polyeidis's travels, see also N. G. Svoronos, "I Elliniki paroikia tis Minorkas," *Mélanges Merlier* (Athens, 1956), 2:323–349, esp. 331–333. An important source for the broader diplomatic picture, the dynamic of which in European international relations of the time was determined by the Russo-Prussian rapprochement, is the work by C. Dapontes, *Ephimerides Dakikai,* ed. E. Legrand, 3 vols. (Paris, 1880–1888), which covers the events of the Russo-Turkish war of 1736–1739 with a diplomatic vision of truly impressive breadth.

20. Theoklitos Polyeidis, *Sacra Tuba Fidei* (Stockholm, 1736), 5.

21. On the impact of imperial decline on Byzantine political thought, see briefly D. M. Nicol in *The Cambridge History of Medieval Political Thought,* ed. J. M. Burns (Cambridge, 1988), 74–79, and Ihor Sevcenko, "The Decline of Byzantium Seen Through the Eyes of Its Intellectuals," *Dumbarton Oaks Papers* 15 (1961): 169–186.

22. In addition to the studies by Cyril Mango and Nikos Veis cited in note 13 above see the bibliography referred to by Mango in *Byzantium and its Image,* Addenda et Corrigenda, Study XVI, 3–4.

23. Compare Veis, "Peri tou istorimenou chrismologiou," 244xxx–244xxxii, and Argyriou, *Les éxégèses grecques,* 110.

24. Kourilas in *Thrakika* 5 (1934), 156–158. For an analysis and appraisal of the content, purpose, and impact of Polyeidis oracles, see N. G. Politis, "Agathangelos," *Estia* 27 (January–June 1889): 38–40.

25. The evidence comes from Voulgaris's student Theophilos, bishop of Campania. See S. Efstratiadis, "O Kampanias Theophilos," *Ipirotika Chronika* 2 (1927): 67–70. For relations between Voulgaris and Polyeidis on Mount Athos, see also E. Voulgaris, *Peri ton meta to schisma agion tis Orthodoxou Anatolikis Ekklisias kai ton ginomenon en afti thavmaton. Epistoli pros Petron ton Klairkion* (Athens, 1844), 54–55.

26. See Paul Hazard, *The European Mind* (New York, 1963), 77, 362.

27. See generally Dimitri S. von Mohrenschildt, *Russia in the Intellectual Life of Eighteenth-Century France* (New York, 1936), and Albert Lortholary, *Le mirage russe en France au XVIIIe siècle* (Paris, 1951), and more recently Martin Malia, *Russia under Western Eyes* (Cambridge, MA, 1999), 15–84.

28. For the bibliographical details, see chapter 2, footnotes 18 and 50, and Dimaras, *Neoelliniki Logotechnia,* 144–145, particularly on the language in which these works are written. For the historical background, see Ap. Vakalopoulos, "O Megas Petros kai oi Ellines kata ta teli tou 17ou kai tis arches tou 18ou aiona," *Epistimoniki Epetiris Philosophikis Scholis Panepistimiou Thessalonikis* 11 (1971): 247–259, and for a Balkan perspective, see Paul Cernovodeanu, "Pierre le Grand dans l'historiographie roumaine et balkanique du XVIIIe siècle," *RESEE* 13 (1975): 77–95.

29. Russian propaganda in the Balkans is a complex historical theme, which is only hinted at here. See generally Robert Lee Wolff, *The Balkans in Our Time* (Cambridge, MA, 1974), 69–71. For more details in connection with the Greeks, see P. M. Kontoyiannis, *Oi Ellines*, 5–35, 64–99, and C. Sathas, *Tourkokratoumeni Hellas* (Athens, 1869), 448–465, and for the strategy of the Church in this context, P. M. Kitromilides, "Initiatives of the Great Church in the Mid-Eighteenth Century," *Orthodox Commonwealth*, Study V.

30. Voulgaris's career in Russia has been effectively explored by Stephen K. Batalden, *Catherine II's Greek Prelate: Eugenios Voulgaris in Russia, 1771–1806* (Boulder, 1982). On 93–98, his connection with the "Eastern policy of Russia" is weighed, along with the general rationale of the program that we have called the "Russian expectation" in these pages.

31. Evgenios Voulgaris, trans., *Eisigisis tis Aftokratorikis Megaleiotitos Aikaterinas B′* (Moscow, 1770). Voulgaris referred to his work on the translation in a letter of 1771 to Neophytos Kafsokalyvitis. See National Library of Greece, MS Codex 2390, fols 727–728. Also National Library of Greece MS Codex 2952, fols 291–292. There was a Greek edition of the Nakaz that preceded the one by Voulgaris: *Ermineia tis krataiotatis kai sevastis Aikaterinis II Autokratorissis pason ton Rosion pros to soma ton epistaton dia tin Ekthesin enos neou kodikos nomon* (Venice, 1770). See Ines di Salvo, *Beccaria nella cultura neogreca antecedente a Korais* (Palermo, 1982), 9–11, and P. I. Zepos, "Nomothetikai prospatheiai Aikaterinis tis Megalis kai synchronoi pothoi Ellinikoi," *Epetiris Etaireias Vyzantinon Spoudon* 23 (1953): 593–603. Also Isabel de Madariaga, *Russia in the Age of Catherine the Great* (London, 1981), 139–163.

32. Voulgaris, *Eisigisis*, 3. On Catherine's use of Montesquieu's work, see W. Gareth Jones, "The Spirit of the Nakaz. Catherine II's Literary Debt to Montesquieu," *The Slavonic and East European Review* 74 (1998): 658–671.

33. Voulgaris, *Eisigisis*, chapters 3–10, 18–19, 22.

34. Ibid., chapters 12–14.

35. Ibid., chapters 15–16.

36. Ibid., 3–7.

37. See Denis Diderot, "Observations sur le Nakaz," in *Oeuvres Politiques*, 343–458, and Arthur M. Wilson, *Diderot* (New York, 1972), 650–652. For a survey of historiographical and ideological controversies over Catherine's modernizing policies, especially as represented by the *Instruction*, see Basil Dmytryshyn, ed., *Modernization of Russia under Peter I and Catherine II* (New York, 1974), 87–157.

38. Voulgaris, *Eisigisis*, viii–xvii (from the separately paginated opening addresses by Voulgaris).

39. Ibid., xxvi–xxxiii.

40. On the designs of Catherine II on the Balkans, see briefly L. S. Stavrianos, *The Balkans since 1453* (New York, 1958), 187–197; de Madariaga, *Russia in the Age of Catherine the Great*, 205–236, 377–412, and Edgar Hösch, "Das sogenannte

griechische Projekt Katharinas II," *Jahrbücher für Geschichte Osteuropas,* N.S., 12 (1964): 168–206. For a historical reappraisal, see Hugh Radsdale, "Evaluating the Traditions of Russian Aggression: Catherine II and the Greek Project," *The Slavonic and East European Review* 66 (1988): 91–117.

41. Voulgaris, *Eisigisis,* "Eisitirios Prodioikisis," 18.

42. Ibid., 17–18, and more generally, 17–24, on Greek hopes in Catherine's policies.

43. Evgenios Voulgaris, *Stochasmoi eis tous parontas krisimous kairous tou Otho-manikou kratous* (Kerkyra, 1854). Batalden, *Eugenios Voulgaris in Russia,* 66–69, 239, dates the first publication of this important essay in St. Petersburg, 1772. See also P. M. Kitromilides, "I politiki skepsi tou Evgeniou Voulgari," *Praktika tou E΄ Diethnous Panioniou Synedriou* (Argostoli, 1991), 4:601–604.

44. *Stochasmoi eis tous parontas krisimous kairous tou Othomanikou kratous,* 8–9, 18–22.

45. Ibid., 42–43.

46. Ibid., 43.

47. For a general survey, see A. Camariano-Cioran, "La guerre russo-turque de 1768–1774 et les Grecs," *RESEE* 3 (1965): 513–547. Also Israel, *Democratic Enlightenment,* 609–618.

Of the earlier sources, the most important are P. M. Kontoyiannis, *Oi Ellines,* and M. B. Sakellariou, *I Peloponnisos kata tin defteran Tourkokratian, 1715–1821,* 2nd ed. (Athens, 2012), 219-270.

48. According to Stephen Batalden, *Catherine II's Greek Prelate,* 161–162, the text was a translation of an Italian original attributed to Antonio Ghika. See Evgenios Voulgaris, *Iketiria tou genous ton Graikon pros pasan tin christianikin Evropin* (possibly St. Petersburg, 1771). The text is reproduced in Ph. Iliou, *Prosthikes stin Elliniki Vivliographia* (Athens, 1793), 290–300.

49. See Evgenios Voulgaris, *Epi ti panendoxo eirini in i aeisevastos, eftychis, efsevis, pason ton Rossion autokrator Aikaterina B΄ meta pollas te kai megalas as dia te gis kai thalassis irato nikas, tois Othomanois echarisato* (St. Petersburg, 3 August 1774).

50. Evgenios Voulgaris, trans., *Ouoltairou Epistoli pros tin Autokratorissan ton Rosson* (St. Petersburg, 1771). The text is reproduced in Iliou, *Prosthikes,* 303–307.

51. *Vosporos en Vorysthenei* (Moscow, 1810), 358 (letter dated 3 January 1790).

52. Athanasios Psalidas, *Vera felicitas sive fundamentum omnis religionis* (Vienna, 1791), unnumbered dedication page.

53. Athanasios Psalidas, *Aikaterina i B΄* (Vienna, 1792), 3–5.

54. See Sathas, *Tourkokratoumeni Hellas,* 538–564; G. T. Kolias, *Oi Ellines kata ton Rossotourkikon polemon, 1787–1792* (Athens, 1940), and E. G. Protopsaltis, *I epanastatiki kinisis ton Ellinon kata ton defteron epi Aikaterinis B΄ Rosotourkikon polemon, 1787–1792* (Athens, 1959). The most recent and comprehensive scholarly treatment of the war of 1787–1792 and its effects on the Ottoman Empire is

Stanford J. Shaw, *Between Old and New: The Ottoman Empire under Sultan Selim III, 1789–1807* (Cambridge, MA, 1971), 21–68.

55. The quotation is from Athanasios Komninos Ypsilantis, *Ta meta tin Alosin* (Constantinople, 1870), 534. On Dapontes's disappointment, see Kontoyiannis, *Oi Ellines,* 375–377.

56. A. Psalidas, *Kalokinimata itoi Encheiridion kata phthonou kai kata tis Logikis tou Evgeniou* (Vienna, 1795).

57. Psalidas, *Vera felicitas,* conclusion of address to the reader, n.p.

58. Psalidas, *Kalokinimata,* 25.

59. Ibid., 26–27.

60. Psalidas, *Aikaterina B΄,* 12. Praise of Voulgaris was combined with Russian-inspired millenarian hopes, ibid., 12–21.

61. *Kalokinimata,* 6. Psalidas's insistence on this program is also clear in a letter written by him on 25 October 1799, in which he seeks the assistance of "Greek lovers of the Muses everywhere" for the publication of a five-volume work on which he had embarked, covering the entire spectrum of modern knowledge, including the "Categories of the famous German Kant, the Natural Theology of Leibniz, that outstanding philosopher, practical Philosophy, of which the parts are Natural Right, Ethics, Politics and Economics [. . .] and finally Experimental Physics [. . .] according to the glorious Lavoisier." See C. Ath. Diamantis, "O Athanasios Psalidas kai to archeion tou," *DIEEE* 16 (1962), 306. Manuscripts preserving the texts survive in several libraries. Particularly worth mentioning is a manuscript entitled "Praktikis philosophias eisagogi, to Dikaion tis physeos tin Ithikin kai Politikin periechousa" (Ioannina, 1799), which is preserved in St. Petersburg. See L. Vranousis, "O Chr. Christovasilis sti Rossia," *Ipirotiko Imerologio* 5 (1983): 307. Political works by Psalidas are also transmitted by MS No. 32 in the Dimitsana Public Library.

62. See L. I. Vranousis, *Athanasios Psalidas* (Ioannina, 1952), 24–73.

63. Evgenios Voulgaris, *Epistoli* (Trieste, 1797), 13, 18, 34–41. Psalidas's criticisms were refuted by the author of "Elenchos tou pseudotalanismou tis Ellados," who wrote under the pseudonym Apostolis o Philadelpheus, even before Voulgaris himself answered them in his *Epistoli* of 1797 to Pangratios. Athanasios Parios is probably the writer hiding behind the pseudonym. The text, which is preserved in four manuscripts, remained unpublished. A critical edition was produced by Ath. Photopoulos, "Elenchos tou pseudotalanismou tis Hellados: Orthodoxi apantisi sti dytiki proklisi peri ta teli tou IH΄ aiona," *Mnimosyni* 11 (1988–1990): 302–364. The refutation of Psalidas's charges occurs in chapter 3 of the text, 344–351: "That the sycophancies against Kyr Evgenios are transparent, and nothing else. Proven."

64. Iosipos Moisiodax, *Transformation de l'Oraison d'Isocrate sur l'art de regner pour Nicoclès ou Chapitres Politiques* (Venice, 1779), 4. For a general analysis, see Katerina Kinini, "Le discours à Nicoclès par Moisiodax," *Ellinika* 29 (1976): 61–115, and P. M. Kitromilides, *The Enlightenment as Social Criticism. Iosipos*

Moisiodax and Greek Culture in the Eighteenth Century (Princeton, 1992), 169–171. On the intellectual background of Moisiodax's early political ideas, see Alexandru Duțu, "Le miroirs des princes dans la culture roumaine," *RESEE* 6 (1968): 439–479.

65. Moisiodax, *Chapitres politiques,* 5–6.

66. Ibid., 9–10.

67. Ibid., 13.

68. Ibid., 17–18, 21–22.

69. Ibid., 25–26.

70. Ibid., 29–30, 37–39, 41–42, 45–46.

71. Ibid., 53, 33–34, 57–58.

72. On Katartzis's life, work, and theory, the major authority remains Dimaras, *Neoellinikos Diaphotismos,* 177–243.

73. D. Katartzis, *Ta Evriskomena,* ed. C. Th. Dimaras (Athens 1970), 29–35.

74. Katartzis, *Ta Evriskomena,* 7.

75. Ibid., 94. The original formulation belonged to Gassendi, but the idea was made famous in Locke's *Essay Concerning Human Understanding.* See Richard L. Aaron, *John Locke* (Oxford, 1955), 31–35, esp. 31n4, for the Gassendi locus.

76. Katartzis, *Ta Evriskomena,* 26–29. The passage quoted is on 27.

77. *Système complet d'éducation publique, physique et morale* [. . .] *dans les différents établissements ordonnés par sa majesté impériale Catherine II* par M. Betzky, traduit en français par M. Clerc (Neuchatel, 1777). See Dimaras, *Neoellinikos Diaphotismos,* 230, on sources of Katartzis's pedagogical ideas.

78. Katartzis, *Ta Evriskomena,* 10–24, especially 18–20: an outline of grammatical rules of the Romaic language. See ibid., 217–261: Katartzis's "Grammar of the Romaic Language" and P. Mackridge, *Language and National Identity in Greece* (Oxford, 2009), 92–97.

79. Katartzis, *Ta Evriskomena,* 22.

80. Ibid., 9, 313–328, on method of translations presented as preface to Katartzis's own translation of Réal de Curban, *Science du Gouvernement.*

81. Katartzis, *Ta Evriskomena,* 63, 65, 70.

82. Ibid., 56–58, 66–68.

83. Ibid., 51.

84. Ibid., 54.

85. Ibid., 55, 81, 61. On the connections of Katartzis's thought with the philosophy of the Enlightenment, see Dimaras, *Neoellinikos Diaphotismos,* 199–200, 236–237, and idem, "D. Catargi, 'philosophe' grec," *SVEC* 25 (1963): 509–518.

86. Katartzis, *Ta Evriskomena,* 36–37.

87. Ibid., 192–193.

88. Ibid., 94–203.

89. Ibid., 195, 127, 138. The "Systematic Diagram" of knowledge, explicitly derived from that of D'Alembert, appears in facsimile facing p. 144. Compare

D'Alembert, *Discours Préliminaire de l'Encyclopédie,* ed. F. Picavet (Paris, 1895), 164–175, and 176–181 for an analysis of D'Alembert's "Système des connaissances humaines" in comparison to Bacon's division of the sciences.

90. Katartzis, *Ta Evriskomena,* 145–167: survey of Greek bibliography and 168–203: commentary on the needs of Greek culture.

91. Katartzis, *Ta Evriskomena,* 60, 115–116, 169.

92. Ibid., 68. Compare Aristotle, *Politics,* I, 1253a.

93. Katartzis, *Ta Evriskomena,* 44–45, 202, and compare Aristotle, *Politics,* III, 1274b–1278b.

94. Katartzis, *Ta Evriskomena,* 104–105.

95. Ibid., 45, 90.

96. Ibid., 87.

97. Ibid., 91–92.

98. Ibid., 312.

99. Ibid., 55, 65, 70.

100. Katartzis, *Ta Evriskomena,* 78. See Dimaras, *Neoellinikos Diaphotismos,* 236–238, on Katartzis's appropriation of the symbolism of the Byzantine tradition of mirrors of princes.

101. Katartzis, *Ta Evriskomena,* 417–426: contents of the translation of Réal de Curban's *Science du Gouvernement.* See Kitromilides, *The Enlightenment as Social Criticism,* 177–178, on the significance of the acquaintance with Réal's work in the principalities.

102. Katartzis, *Ta Evriskomena,* 328.

103. See R. R. Palmer, *The Age of the Democratic Revolution,* vol. 1: *The Challenge* (Princeton, 1959), 61–62.

104. Another author who belonged to the intellectual milieu of the principalities and wrote extensively on the theory of enlightened absolutism was Athanasios Christopoulos. See his "Politika parallila" and "Politika sophismata," in *Apanta,* ed. G. Valetas (Athens, 1969), 341–477. For this important author and his literary oeuvre, see Nestor Camariano, *Athanasios Christopoulos: Sa vie, son oeuvre littéraire et ses rapports avec la culture roumaine* (Thessaloniki, 1981). The sequel to the study announced by the author, p. 14, which was to deal with Christopoulos's political works, unfortunately never appeared.

105. Serfdom was abolished by Prince Constantine Mavrokordatos in 1741. His reforms were noted in the *Mercure de France* in 1742.

106. The reform programs of Phanariot princes were codified in the official charters of the principalities promulgated by some of them. Among the most notable such documents were the *Codex Constantinou Mavrokordatou* (Bucharest, 1741) and the *Codex Politikos* of the Principality of Moldavia, issued by Prince Skarlaros Kalliamachis (Jassy, 1816–1817), parts 1–2. Phanariot rule in the principalities has been the subject of a lively and controversial historiography. On the relevant debates,

see Trajan Ionescu-Niscov, "L'Époque phanariote dans l'historiographie roumaine et étrangère," *Époque phanariote,* 145–157; and Vlad Georgescu, *Political Ideas and the Enlightenment in the Roumanian Principalities* (Boulder, 1971), 7–12. For an overview by Romania's greatest historian, see Nicolae Iorga, "Le despotisme éclairé dans les pays roumains au XVIIIe siècle," *Bulletin of the International Committee of Historical Sciences* 9, no. 34 (March 1937): 101–115. See also Joseph Gottwald, "Phanariotische Studien," *Leipziger Vierteljahresschrift für Südosteuropa* 4 (1941): 1–58, and see Robert Lee Wolff, *The Balkans in Our Time,* 61–66. For particular aspects of Phanariot policy, especially regarding the peasant question, see the contributions by S. Papacostea and Florin Constantiniu, *Époque phanariote,* 365–384; and Fl. Constantiniu, "Quelques aspects de la politique agraire des Phanariotes," *Revue Roumaine d'Histoire* 4 (1965): 667–680. On Phanariot cultural policies, see the contributions by A. Camariano-Cioran, St. Barsanescu, Al. Duţu, Dan Simonescu, *Époque phanariote,* 49–60, 77–84, 127–134.

107. Iosipos Moisiodax, *Apologia* (Vienna, 1780), 83–85, and P. M. Kitromilides, *The Enlightenemnt as Social Criticism,* 90–93.

5. ANCIENTS AND MODERNS

1. For a general review, see Gilbert Highet, *The Classical Tradition* (New York and London, 1949), 261–288, and more recently Lawrence Lipking, "Ancient and Moderns," *The Classical Tradition,* ed. Anthony Grafton, Glenn W. Most, and Salvatore Setlis (Cambridge, MA, 2010), 44–46. The most important specialist treatment remains that of Richard Foster Jones, *Ancients and Moderns* (Gloucester, MA, 1961). See also idem, *The Seventeenth Century* (Stanford, 1951), 21–40. Both these works by Jones focus on England. For France, see Hubert Gillot, *La Querelle des Anciens et des Modernes en France* (Nancy, 1914)and more recently Terence Cave, "Ancients and Moderns: France," *The Cambridge History of Literary Criticism,* ed. Glyn P. Norton (Cambridge, 1999), 3:417-425. On the origins of the dispute, see C. Vasoli, "La Première Querelle des 'Ancients' et des 'Modernes' aux origines de la Renaissance," *Classical Influences on European Culture, AD 1500–1700,* R. R. Bolgar, ed. (Cambridge, 1976), 67–80.

2. On the role of ancient culture in the formation of the Enlightenment, see Gay, *Rise of Modern Paganism,* 279–308, and Israel, *Enlightenment Contested,* 436–470.

3. Compare Stanley Rosen, *G. W. F. Hegel* (New Haven and London, 1974), 3–16.

4. For biographical profiles of Moisiodax, see Camariano, *Académies princières,* 569–598; and Alkis Angelou's long introduction in his edition of Iosipos Moisiodax, *Apologia* (Athens, 1976), xiii–lxxxvi, which attempts a psychographic profile but fails to transcend the limitations of just a literary approach. See also P. M. Kitromilides, *The Enlightenment as Social Criticism: Iosipos Moisiodax and Greek Culture in the*

Eighteenth Century (Princeton, 1992). On the significance of Muratori's contribution to intellectual change in Italian culture, see Franco Venturi, *Settecento Riformatore: Da Muratori a Beccaria* (Turin, 1969), 138–142, 153–160, 162–186.

5. Iosipos Moisiodax, *Ithiki Philosophia* (Venice, 1761), 1, prolegomena, xiv–xiv. The text of the prolegomena is republished in P. M. Kitromilides, *Iosipos Moisiodax: Oi syntetagemenes tis Valkanikis skepsis ton 18o aiona* (Athens, 2004), 323–344.

6. *Ithiki Philosophia,* xi–xiv.

7. Ibid., xvi–xxi.

8. Ibid., xxii–xxx.

9. Ibid., xxxiii.

10. Iosipos Moisiodax, *Pragmateia peri paidon agogis i Paidagogia* (Venice, 1779), proemium, 4–9. Henceforth cited as *Paidagogia.*

11. Ibid., 15–17, 19–26, 34, 42–52, 54, 71–72. The close reliance of the *Paidagogia* on Locke's *Some Thoughts Concerning Education,* which Moisiodax must have known in Pierre Coste's French translation, has been effectively demonstrated by Emmanuel Kriaras, "I Paidagogia tou Moisiodakos kai i schesi tis me to paidagogiko syngramma tou Locke," *Byzantinisch-Neugriechische Jahrbücher* 18 (1943): 135–153.

12. Moisiodax, *Paidagogia,* 58–59, 78, 108–110.

13. Ibid., 81–86, 91–95.

14. Ibid., 110–138, 144–147, 157–158, 160–165.

15. Ibid., 100–106. Compare Rhigas Velestinlis, *Physikis Apanthisma* (Vienna, 1790), 106.

16. Moisiodax, *Paidagogia,* p. 11. On the relevance of the metaphor of the ship as an indicator of the emergence of a modern conception of politics, see Michael Walzer, *The Revolution of the Saints* (Cambridge, MA, 1965), 179–183.

17. Moisiodax, *Paidagogia,* 33.

18. Ibid., 73–74.

19. Ibid., 5–6, 27–28, 31, 42–52, 94–95.

20. Ibid., 63.

21. Iosipos Moisiodax, *Apologia* (Vienna, 1780), 1–42, 87–94, 95–131.

22. For Moisiodax's attitude toward Aristotle and Aristotelianism, see *Apologia* v–vi, 9–13, 115–117n, 120, 137–138n, 160–164.

23. See Montesquieu, "Des Anciens" and "Des Modernes," in *Pensées Diverses, Oeuvres Complètes* (Paris, 1846), 622–624; and compare Fontenelle, "Digression sur les anciens et les modernes," in *Entretiens sur la pluralité des mondes—Digression sur les anciens et les modernes,* ed. R. Shackleton (Oxford, 1955), 161–176.

24. Moisiodax, *Apologia,* 10–15, 152–160, and compare D'Alembert, *Discours préliminaire de l'Encyclopédie,* ed. F. Picavet (Paris, 1894), 92–113 for a graphic presentation of the philosophic pantheon of the Enlightenment.

25. Moisiodax, *Apologia,* 13–18, 21–23, 28–33, 97–100, 122–126. The passage cited is on p. 122.

26. Ibid., 98 and 33 respectively.

27. Ibid., 182n.

28. Ibid., 38–40, 83–85.

29. With the specific content ascribed to the term *anomie* by Émile Durkheim.

30. Moisiodax opened his *Apology* by referring to these charges of his enemies. See iii–iv. Many years after Moisiodax's death, a former follower, turned severe critic of the Enlightenment, repeated the charge that Moisiodax supported the use of the simple language because as a nonnative speaker he did not have an adequate grasp of the intricacies of Greek grammar. See Panayiotis Kodrikas, *Meleti tis koinis Ellinikis Dialektou* (Paris, 1818), xxiv–xxvi.

31. Moisiodax, *Apologia,* 35–36 (and note), 170–171.

32. Ibid., 128. For Voulgaris's own account of the dissolution of the Athonite Academy, see his letter to the Patriarch Kyrillos V, *Syllogi Anekdoton Syngrammaton tou aoidimou Eugeniou tou Voulgareos,* ed. G. Ainian (Athens, 1838), 1:54–64. The two testimonies form a good reflection of the points of convergence and divergence in the characters of the two men.

6 THE REVOLUTION IN FRANCE

1. G. W. F. Hegel, *The Phenomenology of the Mind,* trans. J. B. Baillie (New York, 1967), 559–598.

2. Karl Marx, *The Communist Manifesto,* in Marx and Engels, *Selected Works* (New York, 1969), 56.

3. The most eloquent expression of these conflicting reactions to the French Revolution was the debate between Edmund Burke and Tom Paine, whose most famous products were Burke's *Reflexions on the Revolution in France* (London, 1790) and Paine's response, *The Rights of Man* (London, 1791).

4. On the impact of the French Revolution on Southeastern Europe, see generally the classic, if now somewhat dated, account by L. S. Stavrianos, *The Balkans since 1453* (New York, 1958), 198–213, and N. Iorga, *La Révolution française et le Sud-Est de l'Europe* (Bucharest, 1934). Traian Stoianovich's *A Study in Balkan Civilization* (New York, 1967), 144–154, is insightful, like everything else he has written on Balkan society. See also idem, "The Social Foundations of Balkan Politics, 1750–1941," in *The Balkans in Transition,* ed. Charles and Barbara Jelavich (Berkeley and Los Angeles, 1963), esp. 305–312 on the social context of the reception of French revolutionary influences in Southeastern Europe, and his latest contribution in *Balkan Worlds: The First and Last Europe* (Armonk, NY, 1994), 168–176. For an interpretation from the perspective of the history of ideas, see P. M. Kitromilides, *I Galliki Epanastasi kai i Notioanatoliki Evropi,* 2nd ed. (Athens, 2000).

5. See C. Th. Dimaras, "Dix années de culture grecque dans leur perspective historique, 1791–1800," in *La Grèce au temps des Lumières* (Geneva, 1969), 37–60.

6. G. Constantas and D. Philippidis, *Geographia Neoteriki* (Vienna, 1791), 565.

7. Korais, *Allilographia,* 1:91.

8. Ibid., 91, 99.

9. Ibid., 100–101.

10. Ibid., 101–102 and 345. Korais was arguing against the spiteful criticisms leveled against the Greek nation by Cornelis de Pauw, *Recherches philosophiques sur les Grecs* (Berlin, 1788).

11. Korais, *Allilographia* 1:108–110.

12. Ibid., 118.

13. Ibid., 112, 115.

14. Ibid., 112–119, letter of 8 September 1789, describing the outbreak of the Revolution. Korais's letters on the French Revolution were collected in a French edition: *Lettres de Coray au protopsalte de Smyrne Dimitrios Lotos sur les évènements de la Révolution française, 1782–1793,* trans. and ed. le Marquis de Queux de Saint Hilaire (Paris, 1880). For the importance of Korais's testimony as a source on the French Revolution, see Hippolyte Taine, *Les origines de la France contémporaine* (Paris, 1881), 2:138 and 192.

15. Korais, *Allilographia,* 1:127–128. Writing on 15 August 1790, Korais gives advice to his compatriots in Smyrna on how to contain the malpractices and bring clerical corruption under control: ibid., 124–126.

16. Ibid., 118–119. The passage from Saint Paul occurs in *Epistle to the Galatians,* Gal. 5:13.

17. Ibid., 139–145, letter of 31 January 1791. See also 199.

18. Ibid., 228.

19. Ibid., 154–156, 159–160.

20. Ibid., 196–199, letter of 15 November 1791. The passage quoted is on p. 199. Korais's description of "Voltaire's triumph" is one of the fullest eyewitness accounts of the event. On this, compare the evidence gleaned by G. Desnoiresterres, *Voltaire et la société au XVIIIe siècle* (Paris, 1876), 8:491–501.

21. Korais, *Allilographia,* 1:284.

22. Ibid., 225.

23. Ibid., 192–196.

24. Ibid., 228, 195, 244.

25. Ibid., 222.

26. Ibid., 247, 234–235, 237, 242.

27. Ibid., 117.

28. Ibid., letter of 8 September 1792, 264–271, 273–275; letter of 21 January 1793, 293–301; letter of 25 January 1793, 305–307. See also Michael Walzer, *Regicide and Revolution* (Cambridge, 1974), 47–89.

29. Korais, *Allilographia,* 1:306.

30. Ibid., 301.

31. Ibid., 299, 306.

32. Ibid., 306. See Pierre Crosclaude, *Malesherbes témoin et interprète de son temps* (Paris, 1961), 703–716.

33. Korais, *Allilographia*, 1:274, 283.

34. Ibid., 278–281.

35. Ibid., 279–280. See Hippocrates, *Of Airs, Waters, Places*, XII–XVI. On the influence of this Hippocratic text on Montesquieu, see R. Shackleton, *Montesquieu: A Critical Biography* (Oxford, 1961), 307.

36. Korais, *Allilographia*, 1:281, 294.

37. Ibid., 104–105, 358.

38. Ibid., 307.

39. Ibid., 228.

40. Ibid., 307.

41. Ibid., 412–413, 501.

42. Ibid., 307.

43. Ibid., 376.

44. Ibid., 306, 412, 247.

45. Kirykos Chaïretis, *Istoria peri tou thanatou tou vasileos tis Gallias Louigki XVI* (Venice, 1793). The passages quoted are on pp. 5, 8–9, 20.

46. *Ta kata tin athemiton apotomin Loudobikou dekatou ektou vasileos tis Gallias* (Vienna, 1793). See Ladas-Chatzidimos, *EV 1791–1795,* 264. Authorship is attributed to Polyzois Kontos by A. K. Dimitrakopoulos, *Prosthikai kai Diorthoseis eis tin Neoellinikin Philologian C. Satha* (Leipzig, 1871), 112.

47. Gedeon, *Pnevmatiki kinisis,* 57, 82.

48. Albert Camus, *L'homme revolté* (Paris, 1951), 140–163, esp. 149–150.

49. On Pamplekis see below, chapter 7.

50. Polyzois Kontos, *Nekrikoi Dialogoi* (Vienna, 1793).

51. Kelestinos Rodios, *I athliotis ton dokesisophon* (Trieste, 1793).

52. G. G. Papadopoulos and G. P. Angelopoulos, eds., *Ta kata ton aoidimon* [. . .] *Patriarchin Constantinoupoleos Gregorion V,* vol. 1 (Athens, 1865), 201–204, and vol. 2 (1866), 504–506; M. Gedeon, ed., *Kanonikai Diataxeis* (Constantinople, 1888), 1:304–305; P. G. Zerlentis, "Patriarchon Grammata Diataktika pros tous nisiotas peri doulikis ypotagis eis tous kratountas," *DIEEE* 9 (1926): 97–116; Evmenios Phanourakis, ed., "Anekdota Ekklisiastika Engrapha ton chronon tis Tourkokratias," *Kritika Chronika* 1 (1947): 498–500.

53. On Ottoman reactions to French pressures, see Bernard Lewis, *The Emergence of Modern Turkey* (London, 1968), 64–73, and "The Impact of the French Revolution on Turkey," in *The New Asia: Readings in the History of Mankind,* ed. G. S. Métraux and F. Crouzet (New York, 1965), 31–59; and S. J. Shaw, *Between Old and New: The Ottoman Empire under Sultan Selim III, 1789–1807* (Cambridge, MA, 1971), 191–199, 247–251.

54. On the willing compliance of the Church with Ottoman dictates, see Gedeon, *Pnevmatiki kinisis,* 86, and J. Kabrda, *Quelques firmans concernant les relations franco-turques lors de l'expédition de Bonaparte en Egypte, 1798–1799* (Paris, 1947), 20–25.

55. *Didaskalia Patriki syntetheisa para tou Makariotatou Patriarchou tis Ayias Poleos Ierousalim kyr Anthimou eis opheleian ton Orthodoxon Christianon* (Constantinople, 1798). For an English version and thorough investigation of the background, see Richard Clogg, "The *Dhidhaskalia Patriki,* 1798: An Orthodox Reaction to French Revolutionary Propaganda," *Middle Eastern Studies* 5 (1969): 87–115 [reprinted: *Anatolica: Studies on the Greek East in the 18th and 19th Centuries* (Aldershot, 1996), Study IV].

56. D. Thereianos, *Adamantios Korais* (Trieste, 1889), 1:312.

57. A. Korais, *Adelphiki Didaskalia pros tous evriskomenous kata pasan tin Othomanikin epikrateian Graikous* (Rome, 1798), 25–26, 29, 53–54. The pamphlet was in fact printed in Paris and was the subject of a review written by Korais's friend Chardon de la Rochette, in the periodical *La Décade Philosophique* 4 (1799): 218–225, who was unaware of the identity of the author. Authorship was acknowledged by Korais only in a private document, the will he drew up in 1809. See A. Korais, *Epistolai,* ed. N. Damalas (Athens, 1885), 2:26. The pamphlet was attributed to Korais by Zacharias Mathas, *Katalogos Istorikos ton proton episkopon kai ton ephexis Patriarchon tis en Constantinoupolei Ayias kai Megalis tou Christou Ekklisias* (Nauplio, 1837), 267n. The text is reproduced in *Politika phylladia tou Adamantiou Korai,* Centre for Neohellenic Research/ National Hellenic Research Foundation (Athens, 1983).

58. See Thereianos, *Adamantios Korais,* 313–318.

59. *Asma polemistirion* (1800) and *Salpisma polemistirion* (1801) were both printed in Paris but give places of publication as Egypt and Alexandria respectively. The *Salpisma polemistirion* was reprinted in 1821. The two texts are reproduced in *Politika phylladia.* The first indication that *Asma polemistirion* was the work of the author who had composed *Adelphiki Didaskalia* as well was given in Fabricius, *Bibliotheca Graeca,* ed. Gottlieb Christopher Harles (Hamburg, 1808), 11:562–565. For the *Asma polemistirion,* see also the special study under the same title by Ph. Iliou (Athens, 1982), which contains much interesting evidence as to the dissemination of the work.

60. Korais, *Allilographia,* 1:282.

61. Ibid., 96–99, 102–103, 160–162, 362–367.

62. Ibid., 282.

63. Ibid., 345–346.

64. See *supra,* chapter 4.

65. Aik. Koumarianou, "Energeies tou Constantinou Stamati gia tin apeleftherosi tis Ellados, 1798–1799," *Praktika tou Tritou Panioniou Synedriou* (Athens, 1967), 1:154–174. On his ties with Katartzis, see Dimaras, *Neoellinikos Diaphotismos,* 181, 185.

For his observations on the French Revolution, see Émile Legrand, ed., *Lettres de Constantin Stamaty à Panagiotis Kodrikas sur la Révolution française* (Paris, 1872), 25–79, new ed. by P. Michailaris (Athens, 2002). On the revolutionary pamphlet *Pros tous Romaious tis Ellados,* published in 1798 to arouse the Greeks in support of the French, see L. Vranousis, "Agnosta patriotika phylladia kai anekdota keimena tis epochis tou Riga kai tou Korai," *Epetiris tou Mesaionikou Archeiou* 15/16 (1965–1966): 125–329, esp. 127–130, 140–167. The text is on 210–222. On the French occupation of the Ionian Islands and its political and social consequences, see E. Rodocanachi, *Bonaparte et les îles Ioniennes* (Paris, 1899), 1–173. On the ideological effects of the French presence in the Ionian Islands, see A. Camariano Cioran, "Les îles Ioniennes de 1797 à 1807 et l'essor du courant philofrançais parmi les Grecs," *Praktika tou Tritou Panioniou Synedriou,* 1:83–114.

66. The percentages have been derived from quantitative indicators in Dimaras, *La Grèce au temps des Lumières,* 104–105.

67. *Encheiridion Metaphysiko-Dialektikon i Epitomi Akribestati tou Deigmatos tou Kyriou Lockiou perivoitou Philosophou peri tis Anthropinis Dianoias* (Venice, 1796). This was a Greek version of Dr. Winne's abridgment of Locke's *Essay,* translated into Italian by Francesco Soave: *Saggio Filosofico di Gio: Locke su l'umano intelletto* (Venice, 1785). The Greek translator was Ioannis Litinos, a priest from Zakynthos and former student of Katiphoros. See Ladas-Chatzidimos, *E.V. 1795–1799,* 22.

68. Fontenelle, *Omiliai peri plithyos kosmon,* trans. Panayiotakis Kodrikas (Vienna, 1794).

69. See Fontenelle, *Entretiens sur la pluralité des mondes—Digression sur les anciens et les modernes,* ed. Robert Shackleton (Oxford, 1955), 2–6, 11–28. The tendency on the part of French astronomers to cling to the Cartesian theory "out of an excess of national pride" was also noted by Iosipos Moisiodax, *Theoria tis Geographias* (Vienna, 1781), 131n1.

70. Fontenelle, *Omiliai peri plithyos kosmon,* trans. Kodrikas, proemium and 76 77, 298, 307, 310–311. On these questions Kodrikas echoes views already expressed by Moisiodax, *Theoria tis Geographias,* 62n1, and 110–111.

71. Montesquieu, *Erevna peri proodou kai ptoseos ton Romaion* (Leipzig, 1795). The translator remained unidentified, but it was suggested that he was G. Emmanuel from Constantinople, on the basis of the testimony of G. Zaviras, *Nea Ellas,* ed. G. Kremos (Athens, 1870), 24. The second translation of the *Considérations,* comprising only chapters 1–6 of the work, was published as Part Two of the book, *Vivlion Diirimenon eis meri dyo* (Venice, 1796), 77–154, by an unidentified translator. On the ideological significance of the Greek translations of Montesquieu, see P. M. Kitromilides, "Politikos oumanismos kai Diaphotismos: Symvoli sti dierevnisi tis ideologikis leitourgias tis politikis theorias tou Montesquieu," *Philosophia kai Politiki* (Athens, 1982), 291–304, esp. 298–300, and Roxane D. Argyropoulos, "Présence de Montesquieu en Grèce de la Révolution française à l'independance grecque," in *Montesquieu du Nord au Sud: Cahiers Montesquieu* 6 (2001): 89–96.

72. Montesquieu, *Erevna,* proemium.

73. *Katichisis Eleftherou Anthropou* (Venice, 1797). The text is reproduced in its entirety in Ph. Iliou, *Prosthikes stin Elliniki Vivliographia* (Athens, 1973), 257–264. On the significance of "republican catechisms" compare Emmet Kennedy, "The French Revolutionary Catechisms," *SVEC* 199 (1981): 353–362.

74. The debate on the ideological effects of the French Revolution on the rest of Europe and the pertinent literature are endless and have been enriched even further by publications motivated by the bicentennial anniversary of 1789. For an appraisal of the ideological consequences of the French Revolution from the vantage point of the smaller European nations, see Simon Schama, *Patriots and Liberators: Revolution in the Netherlands, 1780–1813* (New York, 1977), 2–15. For the Greek world, *La Révolution française et l'hellénisme moderne* (Athens, 1989), and the contributions by Loukia Droulia and P. M. Kitromilides in *L'image de la Révolution française,* ed. M. Vovelle (Paris and Oxford, 1989), 2:1437–1445 and 1460–1469, respectively.

7. THE ENLIGHTENMENT'S POLITICAL ALTERNATIVE

1. Cf. Barrington Moore, Jr., *Social Origins of Dictatorship and Democracy* (Boston, 1966), 486–505.

2. Given Rhigas's central place in the symbolism of Greek nationalism, the bibliography on his life and thought is quite voluminous, but most of it is of very little use to a serious study of his thought. Two older collections of documents on Rhigas's political activities are of seminal importance: Émile Legrand, ed., *Documents inédits concernant Rhigas Velestinlis et ses compagnons de martyre, tirés des archives de Vienne en Autriche* (Paris, 1892), and Constantinos Amantos, *Anekdota Engrapha peri Rhiga Velestinli* (Athens, 1930). The study of Ap. Daskalakis, *Rhigas Velestinlis, La Révolution française et les préludes de l'indépendence hellénique* (Paris, 1937), 205–226, contains a useful survey of sources, and has long been the established authority for students of Rhigas who do not have access to Greek sources. See, however, the critiques by Nestor Camariano, "Contribution à la bibliographie des Oeuvres de Rigas Velestinlis," *Balcania* 1 (1938): 211–229, and by C. Amantos in *Athina* 48 (1938): 246–249. Daskalakis's study, nevertheless, constitutes the source of Rhigas's treatment by R. R. Palmer, *The Age of the Democratic Revolution,* vol. 2: *The Struggle* (Princeton, 1964), 173–174, 334–335, and by Hans Kohn, *The Idea of Nationalism* (New York, 1944), 537–539. The study of the subject has been placed on a new basis by the researches of L. I. Vranousis, whose *Rigas* (Athens, 1953), although now dated, was for decades an indispensable source. The study of the subject has been further advanced by the updated Romanian edition of the work *Rigas: Un patriot grec din Principate* (Bucharest, 1980). The more recent contribution by Camariano, *Académies princières,* 209–210, 447–449, is also very useful in its investigation of the Romanian sources. The older biography in English by Elizabeth M. Edmonds, *Rhigas Pheraios: The Protomartyr of Greek Independence*

(London, 1890), is interesting as a document of Rhigas's reception. A modern, reliable biography in English, synthesizing earlier but not producing new research, is C. M. Woodhouse, *Rhigas Velestinlis. The Protomartyr of the Greek Revolution* (Limni, Evia, 1995). Very useful are the critical reviews of Cornelia Papacostea-Danielopolu, "Rigas Velestinlis et les recherches contemporaines," *RESEE* 11 (1973): 563–567, and Nestor Camariano, "Rigas Velestinlis: Compléments et corrections concernant sa vie et son activités," *REESE* 18 (1980): 687–719 and 19 (1981): 41–69, with many points of clarification of mainly biographical interest. The bibliographical survey is continued by Ath. Karathanasis in *Ypereia* 1 (1990): 449–456.

3. Rhigas Velestinlis, *Physikis Apanthisma dia tous anchinous kai philomatheis Ellinas* (Vienna, 1790), 45.

4. Ibid., vi–ix, address to the reader. The two sentences quoted from *Émile* are the following: "L'écolier écoute en classe le verbiage de son maître, comme il écoutoit au maillot le babil de sa nourrice. Il me semble que ce seroit l'instruire fort utilement, que de l'élever à n' y rien comprendre" (p. vii) and "Les pédagogues étalent en grand appareil les instructions qu'ils donnent à leurs disciples, et qu'elles sont des mots, encore des mots, et toujours des mots [. . .]" (p. viii). Comparison with Rousseau's text reveals that Rigas abbreviated the second passage. See J. J. Rousseau, *Oeuvres complètes* (Paris, 1969), 4:293 and 346.

5. Rhigas, *Physikis Apanthisma,* 64. For criticisms of Aristotelian natural history and Ptolemaic cosmology, see 23, 129.

6. Ibid., 106n.

7. Ibid., 58–59.

8. Ibid., 23–24. Rhigas's narrative betrays some confusion on the chronology of Galileo's and Copernicus's works.

9. Rhigas Velestinlis, *Scholeion ton delikaton eraston* (Vienna, 1790), address to the reader, iii.

10. See Jacques Barzun's introduction in Nicolas-Edme Restif de la Bretonne, *Les Nuits de Paris,* trans. L. Asher and E. Fertig (New York, 1964), v–xvii. On the place of Restif in the politics of the Enlightenment, see Sven Stelling-Michaud, "Lumières et politique," *SVEC* 27 (1963): 1527–1528. Mark Poster, *The Utopian Thought of Restif de la Bretonne* (New York, 1971), stresses Restif's debt to Rousseau and interprets his literary work as an indication of the deeper subversive currents in French society at the time of the Revolution. The study of Restif has been set on a new footing by the recent book by David Coward, *The Philosophy of Restif de la Bretonne* (Oxford, 1991) (= *SVEC,* vol. 283).

11. Rhigas, *Scholeion ton delikaton eraston,* 63, 68, and *passim.* My analysis is greatly indebted to the excellent introduction by P. S. Pistas in his edition of the work (Athens, 1971), xv–lxxvi, and subsequently in *Apanta ta sozomena* 1:19–67.

12. *Erotos Apotelesmata* (Vienna, 1792). The work was anonymously published and reprinted in 1798 (Constantinople), 1809 and 1816 (Vienna), and 1836

(Venice) and has been attributed to both Rhigas and Psalidas. See, for instance, Vranousis, *Rhigas,* 201–217. For problems of authorship and pertinent bibliography, see Ladas-Chatzidimos, *E. V. 1791–1795,* 128–136. The work has now been definitively attributed to Ioannis Karatzas by Hans Eideneier, "O syngrapheas tou 'Erotos Apotelesmata'," *Thisavrismata* 24 (1994): 282–285.

13. On the period 1790–1796 in Rhigas's life, see Vranousis, *Rhigas,* 35–48.

14. Rhigas Velestinlis, *Ithikos Tripous* (Vienna, 1797), which comprises the following works: Metastasio's "Olympiade" (7–116), and Marmontel's "La Bergère des Alpes," (119–188). An important contribution to the study of the subject is made by L. Vranousis, "Rigas kai Marmontel," *Ellinogallika: Aphieroma ston Roger Milliex* (Athens, 1990), 121–157. S. Gesner's "Der erste Schiffer," translated by Rhigas's associate A. Koronios, completed the *Ithikos Tripous,* 193–238. On the composition of the work see the important introduction by Anna Tabaki in *Apanta ta sozomena* 3:9-46.

15. Michelle Buchanan, "Marmontel: un auteur à succès du XVIIIe siècle," *SVEC* 55 (1967) : 321–331. On the general cultural background of the new ideas and sentiments, the monumental study by Robert Mauzi, *L'idée du bonheur au XVIIIe siècle* (Paris, 1960), especially 458–484, retains always its interest.

16. Rhigas, *Ithikos Tripous,* 118.

17. Ibid., 3–4, introductory explanatory notes on the Olympic games.

18. See Gay, *Rise of Modern Paganism,* 84. For more details on the importance of the work, see Émile Egger, *L'héllénisme en France* (Paris, 1869), 2:294–300; Maurice Badolle, *L'Abbé Jean-Jacques Barthélemy, 1716–1795 et l'héllénisme en France dans la seconde moitié de XVIIIe siècle* (Paris, n.d.), 227–331, and Chantal Grell, *Le Dix-huitième siècle et l'antiquité en France* (Oxford, 1995), 302–304, 716–717, 1149–1154.

19. See G. Laios, *O Ellinikos typos tis Viennis apo tou 1784 mechri tou* 1821 (Athens, 1961), 26–71, with useful bibliographical indications, and idem, "Adelphoi Pouliou," *DIEEE* 12 (1957–1958), 202–270. The surviving issues of the *Ephimeris* for the years 1791, 1792, 1793, 1794, and 1797 have now been collected in a five-volume reprint, edited with introductory essays and commentary by L. I. Vranousis (Athens, 1995).

20. Georgios K. Sakellarios, *Archaiologia Synoptiki ton Ellinon* (Vienna, 1796).

21. Abbé Barthélemy, *Periigisis tou neou Anarcharsidos eis tin Ellada,* trans. G. Sakellarios (Vienna, 1797), vol. 1, translator's preface, vii–xii.

22. *Neos Anacharsis,* vol. 4 (Vienna, 1797), trans. G. Ventotis and Rhigas Velestinlis, chapters 35–39, pp. 99–348. Essential on the context of the project is the introduction by Anna Tabaki in *Apanta ta sozomena* 4:11–87.

23. Rhigas, *Physikis Apanthisma,* 106. Quite revealing are Rhigas's handwritten marginal notes in his personal copy of N. Darvaris, *Alithis Odos Eudaimonias* (Vienna, 1796), 214: next to the name Admetos in the index, Rhigas wrote, "Admetos was one of the Argonauts and King of Velestino; it is said by Apollonius Rhodius

in the Argonautica." This indicates Rhigas's interest in the ancient Greek past of his native village. The book now belongs to the collection of rare books and manuscripts of the Library of the Greek Parliament, no. XIV 4, NLL 311.

24. *Neos Anacharsis,* 4:148, 213–214.

25. Ibid., 125–216.

26. Ibid., 133.

27. Ibid., 197, 347. Also 84, 97–98, and 181 in the first section of the book translated by George Ventotis.

28. Ibid., 246–247.

29. Rhigas's maps are reproduced in detail in the edition of his complete works, *Apanta Neoellinon Klassikon: Rhigas Velestinlis—Pheraios,* ed. L. Vranousis (Athens, n.d.), 2:569–664. Besides the "Map of Greece," Rhigas published maps of the principalities of Wallachia and Moldavia, all in Vienna 1797. For details, see G. Laios, "Oi chartes tou Rhiga," *DIEEE* 14 (1960): 231–312. For the map of Wallachia in particular, see the studies by Anna Avramea, "I Nea Charta tis Vlachias tou Riga" kai i aftographos epexergasia tis: Scholion D. Zakythinou," *Praktika tis Akadimias Athinon* 53 (1978): 375–407, and idem, "Ta toponymia tis Vlachias ston cheirographo charti tou Riga," *O Eranistis* 19 (1981): 100–119. The older study by A. Ubicini, "La grande carte de la Grèce par Rhigas," *Revue de Géographie* 8 (April 1881): 241–259, and 9 (July–December 1881): 9–25, despite its title, is just a general biographical sketch of Rhigas, rather than a serious cartographical examination of his maps. The impressions made by the cartographic activities of "Rhigas the Thessalian" among his contemporaries is clear from the testimony of Johann Christian von Engel, *Geschichte des Ungarischen Reiches und seiner Nebenländer* (Halle, 1797), 1:473. The latest research is summarized by G. Tolias, *Mapping Greece, 1420–1800: A History* (Athens, 2011), 383–386.

30. *Charta tis Ellados* (Vienna, 1797), fol. 4 (frontispiece). See Vranousis, ed., *Ta erga tou Rhiga,* 2:572–573, 592.

31. *Charta tis Ellados,* fol. 1, and Vranousis, *Ta erga tou Rhiga,* (Athens, n.d.), 2:576–577, 581, 584–585.

32. *Charta tis Ellados,* fols 7–8, 11. On Rhigas's relations with Pasvanoglou, see Woodhouse, *Rhigas Velestinlis,* 21–23, 47–48, 90–91, 146–147.

33. *Charta tis Ellados,* fol. 12.

34. Ibid., fol. 4. The explanatory memoir on fol. 3, in Vranousis, ed., *Ta erga tou Rhiga,* 2:573–575.

35. Alexander's portrait is reprodced in detail in Vranousis, ed., *Ta erga tou Rhiga,* 2:667–670. On this subject, see also the study by Olga Gratsiou, "To monophyllo tou Riga tou 1797: Paratiriseis sti Neoelliniki eikonographia tou Megalou Alexandrou," *Mnimon* 8 (1980): 130–149.

36. See Alexis Politis, "I prosgraphomeni ston Rhiga proti ekdosi tou Agathangelou," *O Eranistis* 8 (1969): 573–592.

37. On the problem of Rhigas's organization, see C. Amantos, *Anekdota Engrapha*, xii–xv; Vranousis, *Rhigas,* 67–71, and Woodhouse, *Rhigas Velestinlis,* 81–97. The effectiveness of any such attempt by Rhigas was already questioned by I. K. Philimon, *Dokimion Istorikon peri tis Philikis Etaireias* (Nauplion, 1834), 95–98. No direct links between Rhigas's initiative and the Philiki Etaireia are discernible in the historical record.

38. The legend surrounding Rhigas was started by Chr. Perraivos, *Syntomos viographia Rhiga Pheraiou* (Athens, 1860). Perraivos's claims were critically refuted by Amantos, *Anekdota Engrapha,* xii–xv. For the claims of the Greek left on Rhigas, see G. Kordatos, *Rhigas Pheraios kai i Valkaniki omospondia* (Athens, 1945). In an earlier work, however, Kordatos had described Rhigas as "a forerunner of Greek imperialism." See Kordatos, *O Rhigas Pheraios kai i epochi tou* (Athens, 1931), 82. For another leftist treatment of Rhigas, see T. Vournas, *O politis Rhigas Velestinlis* (Athens, 1956).

39. See Émile Legrand, ed., *Documents inédits* and C. Amantos, *Anekdota Engrapha.* The documents collected by Legrand formed the basis of the most precise account of Rhigas's martyrdom by Sp. Lambros, *Apokalypseis peri tou martyriou tou Rhiga* (Athens, 1892). The more recent researches by P. K. Enepekidis, *Rhigas—Ypsilantis—Kapodistrias* (Athens, 1965), 11–96, have added some interesting details, but have not resolved any longstanding problems. See also Olga Katsiardi, "Rhigas Pheraios: Nea stoicheia apo ta archeia tis Tergestis," *Mnimon* 7 (1979): 150–174. After the interrogation, the Austrian authorities handed the Greek patriots to the Ottomans, who executed them in Belgrade on 24 June 1798.

40. See C. Amantos, "Rhigas Velestinlis," *Ellinika* 5 (1932): 48–50, and idem, *Anekdota Engrapha,* xi.

41. Legrand, *Documents inédits,* 65; and Amantos, *Anekdota Engrapha,* xiv–xv, 122–128; and more generally Vranousis, *Rhigas,* 61–67, 74–79, and Woodhouse, *Rhigas Velestinlis,* 98–109. Also Olga Katsiardi, "Ellinika diavimata ston Bonaparti," *O Eranistis* 14 (1977): 36–68.

42. Legrand, *Documents inédits,* 11–13, 23–25. On the broader political background in the Habsburg domains that influenced the interrogation, see Ernst Wangermann, *From Joseph II to the Jacobin Trials* (Oxford, 1969), 137–191.

43. Legrand, *Documents inédits,* 59–75, esp. 61, 65, 69.

44. Ibid., 91.

45. Ibid., 83.

46. Ibid.

47. Rhigas, *Nea politiki dioikisis ton katoikon tis Roumelis, tis Mikras Asias, ton Mesogeion nison kai tis Vlachobogdanias.* First published in Vienna by the Pouliou brothers in 1797. All exemplars of the original edition disappeared following Rhigas's arrest and the confiscation of his revolutionary pamphlet. The text was discovered in a manuscript copy on the island of Zakynthos by P. Chiotis, who published it in the Athenian journal *Parthenon* in 1871: 507–512, 545–556. It was reprinted in

a separate edition by Th. P. Volidis, ed., *To politevma tou Rhiga* (Athens, 1924). A different version of the text has been transmitted by a manuscript that has been more recently discovered in a family archive on the island of Kythera. It has been published by Emm. Stathis, *To Syntagma kai o Thourios tou Rhiga* (Athens, 1996). This text appears to transmit Rhigas's authentic text, which apparently was subjected to some editorial correction to make the language conform to the grammar and diction of the learned Greek of the time by its first editor, Panayiotis Chiotis, in his 1871 edition. Accordingly, to recover Rhigas's original style in *Apanta ta sozomena,* the text of the Kythera manuscript was used. For the text see *Apanta ta sozomena,* 5:31–71, and for its history, ibid., 21–29.

48. Rhigas, *Physikis Apanthisma,* 176: "Announcement: If some patriot desires to labor for the benefit of the Nation by translating a book, let him not attempt the *Esprit des Lois par monsieur Montesquieu,* because this one is almost translated by myself and upon its completion it will be printed." The manuscript has been lost. For the theoretical significance of the project, see P. M. Kitromilides, *I Galliki Epanastasi kai i Notioanatoliki Evropi,* 2nd ed. (Athens, 2000), 142–145.

49. See *Apanta ta sozomena,* 5:35–45.

50. For Condorcet's constitutional texts, see *Oeuvres de Condorcet,* ed. A. Condorcet O'Connor and M. F. Arago (Paris, 1847), 12:335–415, 417–422, 423–501.

51. See Jacques Godechot, ed., *Les Constitutions de la France depuis 1789* (Paris, 1970), 69–77, and 79–92: text of the Constitution of 1793. For the background, see Georges Lefebvre, *The French Revolution,* vol. 2: *From 1793 to 1799* (New York, 1964), 39–136, esp. 54–64, and Godechot, *Les institutions de la France sous la Révolution et l'Empire* (Paris, 1968), 273–289. On the attitude of Babeuf and Buonarroti, see Maurice Dommanget, "Les Égaux et la Constitution de 1793," *Babeuf et les problémes du Babouvisme,* ed. Albert Soboul (Paris, 1963), 73–105.

52. See *Apanta ta sozomena* 5:45–70. The most complete political analysis is by A. J. Manessis, "L'activité et les projets politiques d'un patriote grec dans les Balkans vers la fin du XVIIIe siècle," *Balkan Studies* 3 (1962): 75–118. See also A. Svolos, "Ta prota Ellinika politevmata kai i epidrasis tis Gallikis Epanastaseos," *Ephimeris ton Ellinon nomikon* 2 (1935): 737–739. More recently P. M. Kitromilides, "An Enlightenment Perspective on Balkan Cultural Pluralism: The Republican Vision of Rhigas Velestinlis," *History of Political Thought* 24 (2003): 465–479.

53. Rhigas, "Ta dikaia tou anthropou," articles 1–15. See also Argyropoulou, *Neoellinikos stochasmos,* 82–90.

54. Rhigas, "Ta dikaia tou anthropou," articles 16–34.

55. [*Constitution*], article 123.

56. "Ta dikaia tou anthropou," article 35.

57. Montesquieu, *De l'esprit des lois,* Book IX, chapters 2–3; and J. J. Rousseau, *Du Contrat Social,* Book III, chapter 11. Montesquieu's discussion of England as a republic disguised under the institutions of a monarchy and Rousseau's project

for Poland indicate that neither excluded the possibility of an extensive republican system. On the problem, see generally Stanley Hoffmann, "The Areal Division of Powers in the Writings of French Political Thinkers," *Area and Power,* ed. Arthur Maass (Glencoe, IL, 1959), 113–144.

58. Cf. Jürgen Habermas, *Theory and Practice* (Boston, 1973), 106.

59. Rhigas, "Ta dikaia tou anthropou," articles 3, 7, and esp. 34, and [*Constitution*], articles 2, 4, 7, 122.

60. Rhigas, [*Constitution*], article 7.

61. L. S. Stavrianos, *Balkan Federation* (Northampton, MA, 1944), 34–36, 44. See also, N. Botzaris, *Visions Valkaniques dans la préparation de la Révolution grecque 1789–1821* (Geneva, 1962), 17–33, 179. For other interpretations of Rhigas's social and political thought, see N. I. Pantazopoulos, *Rhigas Velestinlis: I politiki ideologia tou Ellinismou proangelos tis Epanastaseos* (Thessaloniki, 1964); and D. A. Zakythinos, *The Making of Modern Greece: From Byzantium to Independence* (Oxford, 1976), 157–167.

62. N. Iorga, *Histoire des relations entre la France et les Roumains* (Paris, 1918), 120–135. On the Greek cultural infrastructure of the Balkans, see Peter F. Sugar, *Southeastern Europe under Ottoman Rule, 1354–1804* (Seattle and London, 1977), 251–258, and for the Romanian lands in particular, D. Popovici, *La littérature roumaine à l' époque des Lumières* (Sibiu, 1945), 59–77.

63. Although Vlad Georgescu, *Political Ideas and the Enlightenment in the Romanian Principalities,* (Boulder, 1971), 77, 169, denies that Rhigas's ideas had a serious impact on Romanian political thought, Iorga, *Histoire des relations entre la France et les Roumains,* 75–80, 86–88, 141, acknowledges that it was through Greek cultural channels that the influence of progressive European ideas was transmitted into Romanian thought.

64. L. S. Stavrianos, "Antecedents to Balkan Revolutions," *Journal of Modern History* 29 (1957): 335–348, Jacques Godechot, *La Grande Nation: l'expansion révolutionnaire de la France dans le monde, 1789–1799* (Paris, 1956), 1:197–200, and P. M. Kitromilides, *I Galliki Epanastasi kai i Notioanatoliki Evropi,* 69–71, 133–173.

65. A. Korais, *Adelphiki Didaskalia* (Rome[=Paris], 1798), iv–v; *Elliniki Nomarchia* (Athens, 1957), 52, 82–86. The earliest published biographical sketch of Rhigas was composed by Korais's associate C. Nikolopoulos, in *Biographie universelle, ancienne et moderne* (Paris, 1824): 37:477–479. In this essay, Rhigas's politics was explicitly linked with the outlook expressed by the authors of *Adelphiki Didaskalia* and *Elliniki Nomarchia.*

66. Rhigas, [*Constitution*], article 123.

67. The text of "Thourios" was published by Claude Fauriel, *Chants populaires de la Grèce moderne* (Paris, 1825), 2:20–28. Its inclusion in a collection of folk poetry is indicative of its wide dissemination and integral reception into Greek popular

culture. Note Fauriel's comments, ibid., 18–19, and the authoritative comments by Ioannis G. Gennadios, *Kriseis kai skepseis peri ton epistolon tou aoidimou Korai* (Trieste, 1903), 40–41n36. See also *Apanta ta sozomena* 5:73–77, 105–115.

68. L. Koutsonikas, *Geniki Istoria tis Ellinikis Epanastaseos* (Athens, 1863), 1:145–146, and Anargyros Chatzianargyrou, *Ta Spetsiotika* (Athens, 1861), 1:46. See also Jacovaky Rizo Neroulos, *Cours de littérature grecque moderne* (Geneva, 1828), 48–49; and A. R. Rangabé, *Précis d'une histoire de la littérature néohellénique* (Berlin, 1877), 114. It is interesting that pictures of Rhigas formed part of popular iconography. This cultural phenomenon, however, is attested by late nineteenth- and twentieth-century evidence, which is to be interpreted historically with reference rather to the formation of the national community centered on the Greek state, which had incorporated Rhigas into its national pantheon, than as genuine evidence of the reverberations of Rhigas's ideas among the popular masses.

8. THE ENLIGHTENMENT AS SOCIAL CRITICISM

1. See Paul Hazard, *The European Mind* (New York, 1963), 119–154. This predisposition gave rise to what has been described as "radical Enlightenment." See Israel, *Radical Enlightenment.*

2. Gay, *Rise of Modern Paganism,* 3–19. See also Lucien Goldmann, *The Philosophy of the Enlightenment* (Cambridge MA, 1973), 5–15, 41–49.

3. For the complexity of Enlightenment religious thought and the place occupied by criticism of the Church and of organized religion in this context, see Ernst Cassirer, *The Philosophy of the Enlightenment* (Princeton, 1951), 134–196, and Israel, *Radical Enlightenment,* 208–212, 218–229, 375–405, 447–476. On the "crisis of religious authority" see Israel, *Enlightenment Contested,* part 2. On the attitude of Voltaire in particular, see Peter Gay, *The Party of Humanity* (Princeton, 1959), 48–54. The confrontation with the Church, as a central axis of the development of the Enlightenment, has been the focus of the synthesis by Franco Venturi, *Settecento riformatore,* vol. 2: *La chiesa e la repubblica dentro I loro limiti, 1758–1774* (Turin, 1976).

4. C. Th. Dimaras, ed., "To keimeno tou Rossoanglogallou," *Ellinika* 17 (1962): 188–201, henceforth cited as *Rossoanglogallos.* The text was first recorded by William Martin Leake, *Researches in Greece* (London, 1814), 140–154, who heard it recited during his travels in Greece. This is an indication of how widespread the satire was, at least among those segments of Greek society that were likely to come into contact with a European visitor. See C. Th. Dimaras, "Me pente Anglous stin Ellada, 1811–1814," *Angloelliniki Epitheoresi* 3, no. 10 (May–June 1948): 293–300. All related documents are now assembled in C. Th. Dimaras, *O Rossoanglogallos* (Athens, 1990).

5. *Rossoanglogallos,* verses 78–121 (hierarchy), 130–201 (Phanariots), 50–81 (landed notables), 210–245 (merchants), 358–398 (foreigners).

6. The authorship of the work remains an open and controversial question in modern Greek studies. For a survey of earlier conflicting views, see Christos P. Frangos, "I symvoli tou Athanasiou Psalida sti demiourgia epanastatikou pnevmatos stin Ipiro: O Athanasios Psalidas kai i *Elliniki Nomarchia*," *Dodoni* 1 (1972), 97 and 98–103, which attributes the work to Athanasios Psalidas. Although this view is not established on firm external evidence and therefore cannot be accepted, it points to a likely intellectual milieu from which the work could have emerged. A more recent view attributing the work to Adamantios Korais cannot be taken seriously, especially in view of the fact that it rests entirely on a misinterpretation of internal evidence. The case was presented to the Academy of Athens on 20 April 1978—see *Praktika tis Akadimias Athinon* 53 (1978): 248–253—but was convincingly refuted by N. B. Tomadakis, "Einai syngrapheas tis *Ellinikis Nomarchias*, Anonymou tou Ellinos o Adamantios Korais?" *Neoellinikon Archeion* 2 (1985): 13–63. The question of the authorship of the *Hellenic Nomarchy* has been reconsidered by Costas A. Papachristou, *Poios egrapse tin Elliniki Nomarchia* (Athens, 1987), who reassesses and rejects earlier attributions of the work to named authors, and suggests that it was written by Georgios Kalaras from Corinth (+1825). In this case too, however, despite the thoroughgoing research, the decisive evidence that would make it convincing is lacking. The problem of authorship cannot be settled without the discovery of some firm external evidence linking the work to a particular author. My hunch would be that the only likely source of such evidence might be the security records and intelligence reports kept by the Austrian police on the activities of Greek patriots who moved between the Greek communities in the northern Italian cities and the Hapsburg domains. An investigation in the relevant archival records in Vienna might be the only way of obtaining acceptable evidence bearing on this problem. I may add here that in my opinion Greek radical circles in Livorno are perhaps the likeliest place in which to search for traces of the author.

7. Anonymou tou Ellinos, *Elliniki Nomarchia itoi Logos peri Eleftherias* (first published, Italy, 1806), ed. G. Valetas (Athens, 1957), 49, henceforth cited *Elliniki Nomarchia*. A modern critical edition was also published by N. B. Tomadakis (Athens, 1948), and a photographic reprint was published in 1976 by the Historical and Ethnological Society of Greece. References in the following notes are to the 1957 edition. On the coinage "nomarchia" see also Stephanos Koumanoudis, *Synagogi neon lexeon* (Athens, 1900), 700, and on the ideological significance of the work, see P. M. Kitromilides, *I Galliki Epanastasi kai i Notioanatoliki Evropi* (Athens, 2000), 138–139, 154–156. See also P. I. Zeppos, "Elliniki Nomarchia: Dokimion Scheseos dikaiou kai eleftherias," *Praktika tis Akadimias Athinon* 50 (1975): 83*–94,*, P. Chr. Noutsos, *Elliniki Nomarchia, Symvoli stin erevna ton pigon tis* (Athens-Ioannina, 1982) and more recently P. M. Kitromilides, "From Republican Patriotism to National Sentiment. A Reading of Hellenic Nomarchy," *European Journal of Political Theory* 5 (2006): 50–60.

8. *Elliniki Nomarchia,* 50–52. Compare Rhigas, *Physikis Apanthisma* (Vienna, 1790), 24.

9. *Elliniki Nomarchia,* 55–56. See also Georges Gusdorf, *La conscience révolutionnaire: Les Idéologues* (Paris, 1978), 252–260, for the redefinition of the concept of happiness during the revolutionary era, which might be regarded as the wider background of Anonymous's views on this subject.

10. *Elliniki Nomarchia,* 56–57.

11. Ibid., 58–60, 67–71. Cf. Montesquieu, *de l'esprit des lois,* books III and VIII.

12. *Elliniki Nomarchia,* 69–70, 202–103.

13. Ibid., 72–75, 86–107.

14. For the relevant background, see Elizabeth Rawson, *The Spartan Tradition in European Thought* (Oxford, 1969), 301–305. The author of *Hellenic Nomarchy* was directly influenced by Alfieri, whose *Della Tyrannide* he quoted in his treatise. See *Elliniki Nomarchia,* 157.

15. *Elliniki Nomarchia,* 108–109. Cf. Machiavelli, *The Discourses,* book 1, chapters 16–18. The theme of corruption runs through the *Florentine Histories* and recurs in the opening chapters of most of the books that compose it; e.g., book 2, chapters 5, 8, book 3, chapter 1; book 4, chapter 1; book 5, chapter 1; book 7, chapter 5. Compare J. G. A. Pocock, *The Machiavellian Moment* (Princeton, 1975), 204–211.

16. *Elliniki Nomarchia,* 110–113. The passage quoted is on p. 111.

17. Ibid., 119–123.

18. Ibid., 124–126. This was the typical view of Greek history held by the historiography of the Enlightenment. See Montesquieu, *Considérations sur les causes de la grandeur des Romains et de leur décadence,* chapters 21–23; Voltaire, *Essai sur les moeurs,* chapters 87, 89, 91, and 93.

19. *Elliniki Nomarchia,* 127–135. This analysis of despotism in the East was a graphic supplement to Montesquieu's indictment of absolutism in the West. Compare Mark Hulliung, *Montesquieu and the Old Regime* (Berkeley and London, 1976), 27–53.

20. *Elliniki Nomarchia,* 137–143, 202–204. Compare Marc-Philippe Zallony, *Essai sur les Phanariotes* (Marseille, 1824), for another damning indictment of the moral bankruptcy of the political leadership of Greek society, written in a spirit similar to that of *Hellenic Nomarchy.*

21. *Elliniki Nomarchia,* 135–136, on the author's familiarity with sources on geography.

22. Ibid., 150–154, 163–182. About the same period, the learned archimandrite Neophytos Doukas criticized the Orthodox clergy, and especially monasticism, in his *Epistoli pros ton Panagiotaton Patriarchin kyrion Kyrillon peri Ekklisiastikis eftaxias* (Vienna, 1815). Although more restrained in their expression, his views, particularly with regard to the monks, do not differ substantively from those of *Hellenic Nomarchy.* See esp. 54–55. N. B. Tomadakis attempts to censure the views of Anonymous on the Church and the clergy in his edition of the *Elliniki Nomarchia,* xiv–xvi.

23. Ibid., 183–194. Also compare 154–162 on the social consequences of the use of money. Anonymous's views here are obviously inspired by Rousseau.

24. Ibid., 195–200.

25. Ibid., 205–208.

26. Ibid., 209. Note a characteristic example cited in Dimaras, *Neoellinikos Diaphotismos,* 41.

27. *Elliniki Nomarchia,* 209–210, 144–149.

28. Montesquieu, *De l'esprit des lois,* book XIX; and especially *Considérations,* chapter 18.

29. *Elliniki Nomarchia,* 210–215.

30. Ibid., 216–223. Compare 82–86.

31. Text of "Anonymous of 1789" and commentary in Dimaras, *Neoellinikos Diaphotismos,* 412–428. See also C. Papacostea-Danielopolu, *Literatura in limba Grecă din principatele române, 1774–1830* (Bucharest, 1982), 164–166, and A. Pippidi, "L'aceuil de la philosophie française du XVIIIe siècle," in idem, *Byzantins, Ottomans, Roumains* (Paris, 2006), 289–338.

32. *Alithis Politiki* (Venice, 1781), published anonymously but attributed to Christodoulos Pamplekis. See G. Zaviras, *Nea Ellas* (Athens, 1872), 553. The passages quoted are from pp. 4–8. The source of Pamplekis's work is *La véritable politique des personnes de qualité* (1st ed., Paris, 1692), probably via the French-Italian edition of 1752. The model of Pamplekis's work was circulated anonymously and is attributed to Nicolas Remond des Cours.

33. Christodoulos from Acarnania, *Peri philosophou, philosophias, physikon, metaphysikon, pnevmatikon kai theion archon* (Vienna, 1786), 32, 67. For a detailed identification of the entries translated from the *Encyclopédie,* see P. Chr. Noutsos, *Neoelliniki Philosophia* (Athens, 1982), 56–57.

34. *Peri philosophou,* 378–380.

35. Ibid., 404. Compare Hazard, *The European Mind,* 254–255, Cassirer, *The Philosophy of the Enlightenment,* 177–178, and Israel, *Enlightenment Contested,* 211–213, 766.

36. Christodoulos, *Peri philosophou,* 409–412.

37. [Christodoulos Pamplekis], *Apantisis Anonymou pros tous autou aphronas katigorous, eponomastheisa peri theokratias.* In view of Christodoulos's familiarily with the contents of the *Encyclopédie,* documented by the evidence of his earlier book, *Peri Philosophou,* it can be reasonably assumed that the term theocracy in the title of his last book and the usages of the term in the text are based on the entry "Théocratie," *Encyclopédie ou Dictionnaire raisonné des sciences, des arts et métiers* (2nd ed., Neuchâtel, 1771), 16:210–212. The text is preserved jointly with that of the aggressive satire published by bishop Dionysios of Platamon in the form of a religious service under the title *Akolouthia tou eterophthalmou kai antichristou Christodoulou tou ex Akarnanias* [originally printed Trieste, 1793] (Leipzig, 1793), 55–168. Only two

known copies of this pamphlet have survived. References that follow are to this edition. For excerpts see Ladas-Chatzidimos, *EV, 1791–1795*, 208–227. New edition, ed. by P. M. Kitromilides (Athens, 2013).

38. *Apantisis Anonymou*, 59, 72, 138. The attacks on the clergy and the monks, especially those of Mount Athos, are on 77–79, 129–140.

39. Ibid., 105–115, 124–129, and esp. 148–151 for the critique of the Creed. The definition of God is on 154–155.

40. Ibid., 162, for the satirical expression "of all Xerokampia," which also occurs about the same period in the text by "Anonymous of 1789."

41. D. Govdelas, *O exostrakismos tou asevous Christodoulou* (Buda, 1800). The text of the excommunication issued by the Patriarch of Constantinople, Neophytos VII, and the Synod in November 1793, is reprinted from Govdelas's pamphlet by M. I. Gedeon, *Kanonikai diataxeis ton agiotaton patriarchon Constantinoupoleos* (Constantinople, 1888), 279–290. On the reception of Pamplekis in Greek ideology, see the important study by Ph. Iliou, "I siopi yia ton Christodoulo Pampleki," *Ta Istorika*, no. 4 (December 1985): 387–404.

42. See Georgios Zaviras, *Nea Ellas*, 553.

43. The existence of the manuscript has been publicly known since at least the publication of Spyridon P. Lambros, *Catalogue of the Greek Manuscripts on Mount Athos* (Cambridge, 1900), 2:427, MS 6262, 7, fols 89a–125. Lambros omitted the original title, *Livellos kata ton Archiereon* [Indictment of Prelates], and described the content of this part of the codex as a "Sketch of a composition on the clergy as enemy of education." In a subsequent source, the text was dismissed as "worthless." See Tryphon Evangelidis, *I paideia epi Tourkokratias* (Athens, 1936), 2:248. The manuscript is deposited in the library of the Monastery of Saint Panteleimon on Mount Athos, Codex 755, and is henceforth cited as *Livellos*. The text in fact runs from fol. 89 to fol. 126. The title is given in the table of contents of the miscellany codex, fol. 133. On this subject, see P. M. Kitromilides, "Ideologikis synepeies tis koinonikis diamachis sti Smyrni, 1809–1810," *Deltio Kentrou Mikrasiatikon Spoudon* 3 (1982): 9–39, where extensive passages from the text are cited and set in context.

44. See *Livellos*, chapters entitled "Provivasmos," "Apodimia," "Epistrophi eis Constantinoupolin," "I sklirotera mastix tou genous eisin oi archiereis," "Oi archiereis apelenchontai echthroi tou genous."

45. Ibid., 105.

46. Ibid., 117. For Koumas's own account, see *Istoriai ton anthropinon praxeon* (Vienna, 1832), 12:582–595.

47. For an eyewitness account, Stephanos Oikonomos, "Peri ton kata to en Smyrni Philologikon Scholeion symvanton," in C. Oikonomos, *Ta sozomena philologika syngrammata*, ed. Sophoklis Oikonomos (Athens, 1871), 1:456–474. See also Nikos A. Veis, "Symvoli eis ta scholika pragmata tis Smyrnis," *Mikrasiatika Chronika* 1 (1938), 193–237, and Ph. Iliou, *Koinonikoi agones kai Diaphotismos: I*

periptosi tis Smyrnis (1819) (Athens, 1986). The bibliography is set out in Kitromilides, "Ideologikes synepeies."

48. *Livellos,* 119–122.

49. Ibid., 101.

50. For a general survey, see Richard Clogg, "Anticlericalism in Preindependence Greece, 1750–1821," *The Orthodox Churches and the West,* ed. Derek Baker (Oxford, 1976), 257–276, reprinted in idem, *Anatolica* (Aldershof, 1996), Study VII, and more recently, Anna Tabaki, "Lumières et critiques des Églises au XVIIIe siecle: le cas grec," *Les Lumières et leur combat. La critique de la religion et des Églises à l'époque des Lumières,* ed. Jean Mondot (Berlin, 2004), 245–258.

9. THE REPUBLICAN SYNTHESIS

1. See Judith Shklar, *Men and Citizens: A Study of Rousseau's Social Theory* (Cambridge, 1969), 1–32.

2. The argument for the inspiration of Enlightenment republicanism by the example of eighteenth-century Italian republics is put forward by Franco Venturi, *Utopia and Reform in the Enlightenment* (Cambridge, 1971), 18–46. An excellent analysis of Montesquieu's views on republicanism is the little-known article by Bernard Groethuysen, "Le libéralisme de Montesquieu et la liberté telle que l'entendent les républicains," *Europe: Revue mensuelle,* 27, no. 37 (January, 1949): 2–16.

3. On the orientations of the Enlightenment toward reform in Italy and in Spain, see Franco Venturi, *Italy and the Enlightenment* (New York, 1972), 63; Richard Herr, *The Eighteenth Century Revolution in Spain* (Princeton, 1958), 48–57, 84–85, 358–359; and Iris M. Zavala, "Dreams of Reality: Enlightened Hopes for an Unattainable Spain," *Studies in Eighteenth Century Culture,* ed. R. C. Rosbottom 6 (1977): 459–470. Franco Venturi, *Settecento Riformatore,* vol. 1 (Turin, 1969) and vol. 2 (Turin, 1977), offers a monumental analysis of the Italian Enlightenment from the perspective of reform efforts. The subject has been enhanced by Jonathan Israel, *Radical Enlightenment,* 528–540, 664–683; *Enlightenment Contested,* 513–542, and *Democratic Enlightenment,* 349–410.

4. Dionysios Thereianos's *Adamantios Korais,* 3 vols. (Trieste, 1889–1890) is a monumental biography that is still indispensable, despite progress made in this area since it first appeared. The study by Ioannis Gennadios, *Kriseis kai skepseis peri ton epistolon tou aoidimou A. Korai* (Trieste, 1903), is an important contribution to the foundation of scholarship relating to Korais. C. Amantos, "Adamantios Korais," *Ellinika* 6 (1933): 7–36, and idem, "To ergon tou Adamantiou Korai," *I ekatontaetiris tou Adamantiou Korai* (Athens, 1935), 1–18, both bear the imprint of one of Greece's best modern historians, who has been responsible for the revival of interest in Korais in the twentieth century. The chapter on Korais in Dimaras, *Neoelliniki Logotechnia,* 251–281, 556–562, is an authoritative account by the foremost literary

historian of the Greek Enlightenment. Dimaras's older study, *O Korais kai i epochi tou* (Athens, 1953), is a study of Korais's time accompanied by texts by Korais and his contemporaries. An informative, though not entirely reliable and now dated, introduction in English is Stephen Chaconas's *Adamantios Korais: A Study in Greek Nationalism* (New York, 1942). The more recent book by E. G. Vallianatos, *From Graikos to Hellene: Adamantios Korais and the Greek Revolution* (Athens, 1987), is a synthesis of earlier sources but is not conversant with the latest research. See also most recently *Adamantios Korais and the European Enlightenment,* ed. P. M. Kitromilides, with an extensive bibliography.

5. See above, chapter 6, for an analysis of Korais's early writings during the 1790s and his impressions of the French Revolution. Compare Benjamin Constant, *Oeuvres politiques,* ed. Charles Louandre (Paris, 1874), 1–16, 258–285, 337–360. Note the pertinent remarks by Judith N. Shklar, *Freedom and Independence: A Study of the Political Ideas of Hegel's Phenomenology of Mind* (Cambridge, 1976), 88–89.

6. Alexandre Koyré, "Condorcet," *Journal of the History of Ideas* 9 (1948): 131–152, offers a lucid analysis that identifies all the elements in Condorcet's thought that might have been thought to have influenced Korais.

7. François Picavet's *Les Idéologues* (Paris, 1891) remains the monumental study of this last generation of the Enlightenment, although the subject has more recently been exhaustively reexamined by Sergio Moravia, *Il tramonto dell' illuminismo: Filosofia e politica nella società francese, 1770–1810* (Bari, 1968) and idem, *Il pensiero degli Idéologues: Scienza e filosofia in Francia 1780–1815* (Florence, 1974). Georges Gusdorf's *Introduction aux sciences humaines* (Paris, 1960), 271–331, is a very useful analysis, as too is the longer treatment by the same author, *La conscience révolutionnaire: Les Idéologues* (Paris, 1978). On the relation of the *Idéologues* to Condorcet's thought, see Moravia, *Il tramonto dell' illuminismo,* 123–135, 216–221, and Keith M. Baker, *Condorcet: From Natural Philosophy to Social Mathematics* (Chicago, 1975), 112, 392–395.

8. On the *Société des Observateurs de l'Homme,* see George W. Stocking, "French Anthropology in 1800," *Isis* 55 (1964): 134–150, reprinted in his *Race, Culture, and Evolution* (New York, 1968), 13–41, with many bibliographical indications, and more recently, Benjamin Kilborne, "Anthropological Thought in the Wake of the French Revolution: La société des observateurs de l'homme," *Archives européennes de sociologie* 23 (1982): 73–91. On some anthropological and geographical projects of the society, see Sergio Moravia, "Philosophie et géographie à la fin du XVIIIe siècle," *SVEC* 57 (1967): 937–1011. On Korais's participation in the Société des observateurs de l'homme in particular, see Aikaterini Koumarianou, "O Korais kai i Société des observateurs de l'homme," *Diimero Korai,* 113–142, and Jean-Luc Chappey, *La Société des observateurs de l'homme (1799–1804): Des anthropologues au temps de Bonaparte* (Paris, 2002), 24–25, 376–377.

9. *Mémoire sur l'état actuel de la civilisation dans la Grèce lu à la Société des observateurs de l'homme,* le 16 nivose an XI, 6 Janvier 1803 par Coray, docteur en médecine

et membre de la dite Société (Paris, 1803), 66pp. Henceforth cited as *Mémoire*. A Greek translation by A. Constantinidis appeared in Athens in 1853. A Greek translation is also included in D. Thereianos, *Adamantios Korais* (Trieste, 1890), 3:xlvi–xcii. The French text was reprinted *in Lettres inédites de Coray à Chardon de la Rochette, 1790–1796*, ed. E. Egger and De Queux de Saint-Hilaire (Paris, 1877), 451–490. References below are to this edition. An excellent English translation by Elie Kedourie was included in his *Nationalism in Asia and Africa* (New York, 1970), 153–189. Note Kedourie's comments, ibid., 37–48. Korais's own account of the meeting of the Society and of the reception of his paper was given in a letter to his collaborator Alexandros Vassiliou, dated 13 January 1803. See Korais, *Allilographia*, 2:61–65, esp. 63–64. Korais's participation in the "Société des observateurs de l'homme" and his reading of the *Mémoire* returned to the forefront of ideological conflict in the ranks of Greek men of learning in Paris some time later. See *Melissa, i Ephimeris Elliniki* 2 (1820): 179–198.

10. Gay, *Science of Freedom,* 122.

11. Korais, *Mémoire,* 451–454. The work that most upset Korais was that by Cornelis de Pauw, *Recherches philosophiques sur les Grecs,* 2 vols. (Berlin, 1787), to which he explicitly refers in the *Mémoire,* 459. The issue had agitated his mind for years, as it is evident in his correspondence. See *Allilographia* 1:102. For his response to de Pauw, see A. Korais, ed., *Traité d'Hippocrate des Airs, des Eaux et des Lieux* (Paris, 1800), Discours préliminaire, cxx–cxxii, n1, and Thereianos, *Adamantios Korais,* 1:290–291.

12. *Mémoire,* 454–455.

13. Ibid., 457–462.

14. Ibid., 464–465.

15. Ibid., 465–470, 471–474. Korais's observations on the advanced society of Chios could be appraised against the evidence of other sources, such as A. M. Vlastos, *Chiaka itoi istoria tis nisou Chiou* (Ermoupolis, 1840), 2:127–144, in order to establish the empirical basis for the picture of Greek culture presented in the *Mémoire,* and the social abstractions made by Korais.

16. Montesquieu, *De l'esprit des lois,* books 20–21. Compare Louis Althusser, *Politics and History* (London, 1972), 53–55.

17. *Mémoire,* 462–464, 476, 481–482, and his "Dialogue between Two Greek Inhabitants of Venice upon Hearing of the Illustrious Victories of Emperor Napoleon" (1805), which juxtaposes the possibilities offered to the Greeks by French and Russian policy respectively.

18. *Mémoire,* 475, 482–485. In a later work in 1814, Korais notes the example of the metropolitan bishops of Ephesos, Meletios Petrokokkinos, and Dionysios Kalliarchis, and extols their contribution to the advancement of Greek education and culture. See *Syllogi Prolegomenon,* vol. 1, ed. Ph. Phournarakis (Paris, 1833), 555–556.

19. *Mémoire,* 476.

20. Ibid., 477–481. The idealization of the Souliotes in Korais's *Mémoire* is not an isolated phenomenon. A similar picture dominates the contemporary work by Christophoros Perraivos, *Istoria syntomos tou Souliou kai Pargas* (Paris, 1803). Perraivos, who was in constant communication with Korais from 1801 on, was probably his main source of information. Korais's and Perraivos's writings about the Souliotes are good examples of the ideological treatment that often informs historical narratives.

21. *Mémoire*, 485–489.

22. Gusdorf, *Introduction aux sciences humaines*, 271–280, and idem, *La conscience révolutionnaire : Les Idéologues*, 369–383, 492–517. See also Roxane D. Argyropoulos, "Adamance Coray et sa réflexion philosophique: vers une anthropologie médicale et culturelle," *Korais and the European Enlightenment*, 187–212.

23. See Lucien Febvre, et al., *Civilisation: le mot et l'idée* (Paris, 1930), 1–45, for the meaning of the term *civilization* in the thought of the Enlightenment and in Korais's time. See also Fernand Braudel, *Écrits sur l'histoire* (Paris, 1969), 258–266. Korais was the first Greek author to use the concept of civilization, which he rendered in Greek with the word *politismos*. See *Allilographia*, vol. 2, *1799–1809*, 153–155, in a letter to Alexandros Vasileiou relating to the Greek translation of the text of the *Mémoire*. Interestingly, the term civilization-*politismos* is also used in the contemporary bilingual work by Antonios Melikis, *Essai sur l'état de la civilisation des Phéaciens/Dokimion peri politismou ton Phaiakon* (Corfu, 1811). Although the French title immediately calls Korais's work to mind, the *Mémoire* is not mentioned by Melikis. Page 31 offers the following definition: "Civilization means essentially a witty and affable attitude, opposing rusticity." Melikis's French text was translated into Greek by Nikolaos Mavrommatis, whose name, together with that of Korais, could be associated with the coining of the term *politismos* in modern Greek.

24. See Gusdorf, *Introduction*, 321–331. The latest treatment of Korais's contribution is V. Mourdoukoutas, "Korais and the Idea of Progress: From Theory to Action," *Korais and the European Enlightenment*, 225–244.

25. See Paul Broca, "Histoire des progrès des études anthropologiques depuis la fondation de la Société en 1859," *Mémoires: Société d'Anthropologie de Paris* 3 (1869): cvii–cviii; and Sergio Moravia, *Il pensiero degli Idéologues*, 669. Out of the philhellenic turn of the interests of the *Société des Observateurs de l'Homme* emerged, two decades later, Claude Fauriel's monumental edition of Greek folk poetry: *Chants populaires de la Grèce moderne*, 2 vols. (Paris, 1824–1825). Although Korais, as a true child of the Enlightenment, remained generally indifferent to the reorientation of European culture toward romanticism reflected in the newly discovered interest in folk poetry, it seems that he had at least some limited contacts with Fauriel. See Miodrag Ibrovac, *Claude Fauriel et la fortune Européenne des poésies populaires grecque et serbe* (Paris, 1966), 114–118. On Fauriel's research, see Charles Rearick, *Beyond the Enlightenment: Historians and Folklore in Nineteenth Century France* (Bloomington and London, 1974), 62–81. Korais's indifference to Fauriel's initiation of

the systematic study of Greek folklore is illuminated by Alexis Politis, "Korais kai Fauriel," *O Eranistis* 11 (1974), 264–295.

26. See Gusdorf, *Introduction,* 274.

27. On the Neohippocratic revival in eighteenth-century French medicine, see E. LeRoy Ladurie, J. Meyer, et al., *Médecins, climat et epidémies à la fin du XVIIIe siècle* (Paris and The Hague, 1972), 9–20; and Robert Darnton, *Mesmerism and the End of the Enlightenment in France* (Cambridge MA, 1968), 116; and, most importantly, Martin S. Staum, *Cabanis: Enlightenment and Medical Philosophy in the French Revolution* (Princeton, 1980), 49–58, 95–97, 220–223.

28. Hippocrates, *Peri aeron, ydaton, topon: Traité d'Hippocrate des airs, des eaux et des lieux.* Traduction nouvelle avec le texte grec . . . par Coray (Paris, 1800), vols. 1–2. For an analysis of the text and its historical fortunes, see Geneviève Miller, "'Airs, Waters, and Places' in History," *Journal of the History of Medicine and Allied Sciences* 17 (1962): 129–140, esp. 137–138 for an appraisal of Korais's edition. For the edition and Korais's aspirations, see Nikos Nikolaou, "I ippokratiki philologia kai o Korais," *Diimero Korai,* 85–101.

29. For Korais's statement of the objectives of the project, see *Prodromos Ellinikis Vivliothikis* (Paris, 1805), i–ix. For precise bibliographical citations of the various editions in the series, see G. G. Ladas, *Vivliographikai Erevnai anapheromenai eis ta erga tou Adamantiou Korai* (Athens, 1934), 41–42. On the broader significance of the project see Ioannis D. Evrigenis, "Enlightenment, Emancipation, and National Identity: Korais and the Ancients," *Korais and the European Enlightenment,* 91–108.

30. Adamantios Korais, *Syllogi ton eis tin Ellinikin Vivliothikin kai ta Parerga Prolegomenon,* ed. Ph. Phournarakis (Paris, 1833), 1:249–251.

31. Ibid., 67.

32. On Korais's views on language, see briefly ibid., 136–142. For a complete survey of the sources, see Vincenzo Rotolo, *A. Korais e la Questione della lingua in Grecia* (Palermo, 1965). See also the contributions by C. Th. Dimaras and V. Rotolo in *Diimero Korai,* 9–28 and 45–58, respectively, and more recently Peter Mackridge, "Korais and the Greek Language Question," *Korais and the European Enlightenment,* 127–149, and idem, *Language and National Identity in Greece, 1776–1976* (Oxford, 2009), 102–125.

33. Panayiotis Kodrikas, *Meleti tis koinis Ellinikis dialektou* (Paris, 1818), lii, and more generally, xlv–lxvii. For the background and issues of the conflict and a complete collection of the relevant primary sources, see Ap. B. Daskalakis, *Korais kai Kodrikas* (Athens, 1966). Also Mackridge, *Language and National Identity,* 133–142.

34. See L. Vranousis, *Athanasios Psalidas* (Ioannina, 1952), 101–103, 112. Korais's linguistic views are parodied from the point of view of Phanariot demoticism in the principalities in the satirical play *Korakistika,* which was published probably in Constantinople in 1813 by Iakovakis Rizos Neroulos. For the more general ramifications of the question, see Em. I. Moschonas, *I dimotikistiki antithesi stin Koraiki "mesi odo"* (Athens, 1981).

35. Korais put a great emphasis on printing as a technical agent for the promotion of the Enlightenment. See his prolegomena to Aristotle, *Ithika Nikomacheia* (Paris, 1822), xxvii–xxix. Compare Condorcet, *Esquisse d'un tableau historique des progrès de l'esprit humain*, ed. O. H. Prior (Paris, 1933), 116–120.

36. See *Syllogi prolegomenon*, 1:66–67, 117–118, 136–140, 158–161, 165–175, 178–193, 256–262, 351–353, 544–547.

37. Korais's most articulate critique of the abuses of the higher clergy is *Symvouli trion episkopon*, which purports to have been published in London though it was in fact printed in Paris in 1820. The main body of this book consists of a translation of a text supposedly written in 1553 by Vicentius de Durantibus, bishop of Termoli, and published by the Catholic clergyman Juan Antonio Llorente (1756–1823) in his *Monuments historiques concernant les deux pragmatiques-sanctions de France* (Paris, 1818), 169–190. Korais prefaces his translation with an introduction and appends extensive notes, in which he justifies his views on the need for the reformation of the Church and the purification of its doctrines and practices from many traditional abuses. Although the concern of both the main text and the notes is the reformation of the Catholic Church, Korais's message that the Orthodox Church had similar needs was quite clear. For further evidence of Korais's critique of traditional religious culture and its exponents, see *Syllogi prolegomenon*, pp. 70–73, 140–142, 154–158, 181–187, 253–256, 320–324, 346–347.

38. Notably in the 1805 Dialogue: *Ti prepei na kamosin oi Graikoi eis tas parousas peristaseis* (Paris, 1805).

39. Cesare Beccaria, *Peri amartimaton kai poinon politikos theoroumenon*, trans. Diamantis Korais (Paris, 1802), prolegomena, xv–xvi. For this publication, see Ines di Salvo, "L'opera 'Dei delitti e delle pene' di C. Beccaria nella traduzione di A. Korais," in idem, *Percorsi Neogreci* (Palermo, 2008), 29–49.

40. *Peri amartimaton kai poinon*, v–ix.

41. Ibid., xiii. See Xenophon, *Memorabilia*, book 2, chapter 1, paragraphs 21–34.

42. See commentary on Beccaria, in *Peri amartimaton kai poinon*, 210.

43. For an evaluation of Korais's contribution to the development of Greek nationalism, see Hans Kohn, *The Idea of Nationalism* (New York, 1944), 534–543.

44. Immanuel Kant, "Perpetual Peace," *Kant's Political Writings*, ed. Hans Reiss (Cambridge, 1970), 93–130, esp. 99–102. On the character of Korais's republicanism, see Nicholas Kaltchas, *Introduction to the Constitutional History of Modern Greece* (New York, 1940), 9–18.

45. In his *Autobiography*, written in 1829 and published for the first time in *Syllogi prolegomenon* (1833), vii–xxxix, esp. p. xxix, Korais argued that the Greek Revolution ought to be timed toward the middle of the nineteenth century. By coming thirty years ahead of time, the Revolution had preempted the emergence of a mature and enlightened leadership that might have conducted the fortunes of the nation with greater wisdom.

46. *Aristotelous Politikon ta sozomena,* ed. A. Korais (Paris, 1821), prolegomena, cxlii. For the testimony of an eyewitness see John Bowring, *Autobiographical Recollections* (London, 1877), 323.

47. *Diatrivi aftoschedios peri tou perivoitou dogmatos ton Skeptikon philosophon kai sophiston "Nomo Kalon, Nomo Kakon,"* published pseudonymously in Leipzig under the name of Stephanos Pantazes but written by Korais (Vienna, 1819), 2–3.

48. Ibid., 31–32, 89. On the conflict between Napoleon and the *Idéologues,* Georges Lefebvre, *Napoleon* (New York, 1969), 1:4, 9–20, 60–68, 141–159; and Sergio Moravia, *Il tramonto dell' illuminismo,* 298–313, and idem, *Ii pensiero degli Idéologues,* 753.

49. *Diatrivi aftoschedios,* 35–64.

50. Ibid., 59–60, 63.

51. Ibid., 95n29. Montesquieu was quoted from *Esprit des Lois,* book I, chapter 1 and book XXVI, chapter 3.

52. *Aristotelous Politikon ta sozomena,* ed. A. Korais, prolegomena, pp. i–cxlii. The text of the prolegomena under the title "Political Exhortations to the Greeks" *(Politikai peraineseis pros tous Ellinas)* was reissued by Em. Pantelakis (Athens, 1923) as part of the ideological prelude of the declaration of the Hellenic Republic, 1924–1935, and has been frequently reprinted since then. A German translation by a Swiss admirer of Korais was brought out as *Politische Ermahnungen an die Hellenen,* trans. Johan Kaspar von Orelli (Zurich, 1823). Interestingly, Korais is compared to Fichte by the translator, who describes the two thinkers as "literary architects" of their nations. See also Argyropoulou, *Neoellinikos stochasmos,* 116–122.

53. *Aristotelous Politikon ta sozomena,* ed. A. Korais, lii–liii, lxxxvi–lxxxviii.

54. Ibid., lxxxviii–cii.

55. Ibid., lxi, lxxxviii–xci, cxiv–cxviii.

56. Ibid., cii–cxiv, cxxxviii–cxlix.

57. Ibid., cix–cxi, cxxxv–cxxxvii.

58. Ibid., cxx–cxxiv: Korais's eight articles for the regulation of the Church in the new republic. The eight articles are translated in P. M. Kitromilides, "The Orthodox Church in Modern State Formation in South-East Europe," *Ottomans into Europeans,* ed. Alina Mungiu-Pippidi and Wim Van Meurs (London, 2010), 31–50, esp. 43–44.

59. Korais left a significant corpus of religious writings, of which the most important are: *Orthodoxos didaskalia,* translation of the work of Platon [Levshin], Metropolitan of Moscow (Leipzig, 1782); *Synopsis tis ieras istorias kai tis katichiseos* (Venice, 1783); *Synekdimos ieratikos* (Paris, 1831). All of these works went through several editions. It is significant to note that Korais made his appearance in Greek letters with the first two of these theological writings. The *Orthodoxos Didaskalia* of Platon of Moscow has been described by a modern student of Russian theology as a work redolent of the spirit of the Enlightenment rather than of Orthodoxy. See George Florovsky, "The Ways of Russian Theology," *Collected Works,* vol. 5 (Belmont

MA, 1974), 142–146. It was perhaps this feature that attracted Korais to the work and supplied the stimulus for its translation. Florovsky notes, characteristically, that Joseph II, the Austrian emperor, described Platon as "plus philosophe que prêtre," ibid., 143. On the religious ideas of Korais, see the survey by D. S. Balanos, *Ai thriskeftikai ideai tou Adamantiou Korai* (Athens, 1920). It should be noted that the publication of the *Ieratikos synekdimos* in 1831 provoked a strong reaction in ecclesiastical circles because of the severe criticism of the clergy in the prologue and Korais's views on the ranks of the priesthood and the titles of clergymen. The ecclesiastical circles of the patriarchate in Constantinople were so annoyed that they prevented the holding of a memorial service for Korais in Constantinople three months after his death, in 1833. See M. I. Gedeon, *Aposimeiomata chronographou* (Athens, 1932), 303, and, for greater detail, Kyriaki Mamoni, "To Oikoumeniko Patriarcheio kai o Koraismos," *Korais kai Chios,* vol. 2 (Athens, 1985), 185–197. It is indicative that Korais's prologue was omitted from the second edition of the *Ieratikos synekdimos* (Athens, 1883). Korais's religious views were criticized by his former supporter Constantinos Oikonomos in his *Peri ton trion ieratikon tis Ekklisias vathmon epistolimaia diatrivi* (Nafplio, 1835), 299–300, and *Epikrisis eis tin peri Neoellinikis Ekklisias syntomon apantisin tou Neophytou Vamva* (Athens, 1839), 117–118, 127, 309–310. Oikonomos's polemic inaugurated a long tradition of criticism of Korais from the standpoint of Orthodox thought, which has revived at the end of the twentieth century, frequently showing ignorance of the sources and with historically inaccurate deductions and generalizations. For a reasoned discussion see Al. Papaderos, *Metakenosis: Griechenlands kulturelle Herausforderung durch die Aufklärung in der sicht des Korais und des Oikonomos* (Meisenheim am Glan, 1970).

60. *Aristotelous Ethika Nikomacheia,* ed. A. Korais (Paris, 1822), prolegomena, x–xxvii.

61. Ibid., xli–l.

62. Ibid., xliii–xliv, quoting Condorcet, *Esquisse d'un tableau historique des progrès de l'esprit humain,* p.440 of the 1822 edition.

63. *Aristotelous Ithika Nikomacheia,* ed. A. Korais, lxxiv, referring to Destutt de Tracy, *Quels sont les moyens de fonder la morale d'un peuple* (Paris, 1819). Compare Picavet, *Les Idéologues,* 391–398.

64. A. Korais, *Simeioseis eis to prosorinon politevma tis Ellados tou 1822 etous,* ed. Th. P. Volidis (Athens, 1933), 20. Henceforth cited as *Simeioseis.* For Korais's views on constitutional questions, see also Theodosios G. Kokkaliadis and Georgios P. Mouraphis, *O Adamantios Korais peri politeias kai dikaiou* (Chios, 1935).

65. Korais, *Simeioseis,* 39. See also 20, 38, 45, 70, 73, 135, for the use of examples from the American constitutional system. Korais's lively interest in the application of the Enlightenment, which he perceived practiced in the United States, is reflected in the notes he kept on his readings, which have survived in his manuscripts. See St. D. Kavvadas, *I en Chio Vivliothiki Korai* (Athens, 1933), 130, MS

No. 332; 132, MS No. 357; 133, MS No. 366; 154, MS Nos. 537, 539; 155, MS
No. 542; 157, MS No. 563. Regarding the intellectual climate that shaped Korais's
views of America, compare Condorcet, "De l'influence de la révolution d'Amerique
sur l'Europe," in *Oeuvres* (Paris, 1847), 8:3–113. On the fascination exercised by the
American model on the European mind, see Durand Echeveria, *Mirage in the West: A
History of the French Image of American Society to 1815* (Princeton, 1957), esp. 3–78,
116–74; and more specifically on the impact of the American Revolution on Europe,
see R. R. Palmer, *The Age of the Democratic Revolution*, vol. 1: *The Challenge* (Princeton, 1954), 239–282.

66. See *Lykourgou Logos kata Leokratous*, ed. A. Korais (Paris, 1826), prolegomena
in the form of a political dialogue, ix–xcvi. The American personalities appearing in
the dialogue were Washington and Franklin, who were joined by Lafayette.

67. On Jefferson's ties with the *Idéologues,* see Gilbert Chinard, *Jefferson et les
Idéologues* (Baltimore, 1925). On the background of American philhellenism and Jefferson's interest in modern Greece, see James A. Field, *America and the Mediterranean
World, 1776–1882* (Princeton, 1969), 58–67, 121–33; and Stephen A. Larrabee,
Hellas Observed: The American Experience of Greece 1775–1865 (New York, 1957),
esp. 3–92. Jefferson's correspondence offers very interesting primary evidence on
the interrelations between the liberalism and classicism of the Enlightenment with
philhellenism. See *The Writings of Thomas Jefferson,* ed. Albert E. Bergh (Washington,
DC: The Thomas Jefferson Memorial Association, 1907), 5:39, 89; 6:299; 10:146,
and esp. 15:333, 336, 480–490. For appraisals of Jefferson's classicism, see Gilbert
Chinard, "Thomas Jefferson as a Classical Scholar," *The American Scholar* 1 (1932):
133–143; and Louis B. Wright, "Thomas Jefferson and the Classics," *Proceedings of
the American Philosophical Society* 87 (1943): 223–233, and more recently Carl J.
Richard, *The Founders and the Classics: Greece, Rome, and American Enlightenment*
(Cambridge MA, 1994) for the broader background.

68. See "The Jefferson-Korais Correspondence," ed. Stephen Chaconas, *The Journal of Modern History* 14 (1942): 64–70, 593–596, for Korais's letters to Jefferson
from Paris dated 10 July 1823, 28 December 1823, and 30 January 1825. For Jefferson's response, dated 31 October 1823 from Monticello, see *The Writings of Thomas
Jefferson,* 10:480–490. For the most recent edition see Athanasios Moulakis, "I
Allilographia Korai-Jefferson," *Korais kai Chios* (Athens, 1984), 1:269–283, and for
perceptive commentary Ioannis D. Evrigenis, "A Founder on Founding: Jefferson's
Advice to Koraes," *HR/RH* 1 (2004): 157–181. On another American connection of
Korais, see George Soulis, "Adamantios Korais and Edward Everett," *Mélanges offerts
à Octave et Melpo Merlier* (Athens, 1956), 2:397–407.

69. The liberal aspiration that dominated this phase of Korais's political thought
can be seen from his involvement from 1823–1825 in the question of the translation
into Greek of Pierre François Daunou's *Essai sur les garanties individuelles,* which ultimately appeared in a Greek edition entitled *Dokimion peri ton prosopikon asphaleion,*

translated by Korais's friend Philippos Phournarakis (Paris, 1825). Se Ph. Iliou, "Stin trochia ton Ideologon: Korais—Daunou—Phournarakis," *Chiaka Chronika* 10 (1978): 36–68. On Korais's commitment to the morality of liberalism versus the claims of nationalism see P. M. Kitromilides, "Adamantios Korais and the dilemmas of liberal nationalism," *Korais and the European Enlightenment,* 213–223.

70. *Simeioseis,* 85, and *Politikon ta sozomena,* ed. A. Korais, prolegomena, cvi.

71. Beccaria, *Peri amartimaton kai poinon,* trans. A. Korais, 2nd ed. (Paris, 1823), xlvi.

72. Ibid., lxx–lxxi. See also Montesquieu, *De l'esprit des lois,* book 3, chapter 5.

73. A. Z. Mamoukas, *Ta kata tin anagennisin tis Ellados* (Athens, 1840), 8:61.

74. For the points of contact between Korais's thought and the ideas of Bentham, see P. M. Kitromilides, "Jeremy Bentham and Adamantios Korais," *Enlightenment, Nationalism, Orthodoxy,* Study VIII. Korais's interest in political economy, based on the testimony of his relevant readings, is noted by Ph. Iliou in his introduction to Stamatis Petrou, *Grammata apo to Amsterdam* (Athens, 1976), lx–lxi.

75. Clifford Geertz, "Ideology as a Cultural System," in David Apter, ed., *Ideology and Discontent* (New York, 1964), 64.

76. Frangiskos Pylarinos, "Logos epitaphios [. . .] eis tin thanin tou D. Korai . . .," *Le Polyglotte,* Année 1833, Seconde Livraison, Paris Imprimérie d'Auffray, 1833: 4–8. The quotations translated here appear on pp. 5, 6, 7; emphasis is in the original. This is the first source in which the Greek equivalent *(koinonismos)* of the term socialism is coined. Pylarinos's text was first drawn to the attention of scholars by Philippos Iliou, ed., *Grammata apo to Amsterdam,* lxxi–lxxii.

10. THE FATE OF THE ENLIGHTENMENT

1. See chapter 6.

2. G. Papadopoulos and A. Angelopoulos, *Ta kata ton [. . .] Patriarchin Gregorion E´* (Athens, 1866), 2:498–499.

3. Michael Perdikaris, "Rhigas i kata pseudophilhellinon," ed. L. Vranousis, *Epetiris tou Mesaionikou Archeiou* 11 (1961): 17–191. The passages cited are on pp. 21–22 and 33.

4. For Kyrillos Lavriotis's criticism of Rhigas, see Asterios Argyriou, *Les éxégèses grecques de l'Apocalpyse à l'époque turque, 1453–1828* (Thessaloniki, 1982), 626–631.

5. Alexandros Kalphoglou, *"Ithiki Stichourgia," Epistolai G.P. Kremou kai Ithiki Stichourgia A.K. Byzantiou,* ed. G. P. Kremos (Leipzig, 1870), 50–75. The name J. B. de Mirabaud refers to the baron D'Holbach, an emblematic figure of materialism and atheism for the enemies of the Enlightenment to whom the former's atheistic treatise *Système de la Nature* (1770) was attributed in the eighteenth century. On the author, see Nestor Camariano, "Nouvelles données sur Alexandre Calfoglou de Byzance et ses *Vers Moraux,*" in *Époque phanariote,* 93–125.

6. *Epanodos itoi Phanari tou Diogenous* (Ermoupolis, 1839). On the authorship of the satire, see Dimaras, *Istorika Phrontismata,* 103–112.

7. Michael Perdikaris, *Prodioikisis eis ton Ermilon* (Vienna, 1817), 1–112.

8. Barrington Moore Jr., *Social Origins of Dictatorship and Democracy* (Boston, 1966), 490–496.

9. Antonios Manouel, *Tropaion Orthodoxou Pisteos* (Vienna, 1791), xix.

10. Ibid., xii, 103, 150, 276.

11. Prokopiou Peloponnisiou, *Vivlion kaloumenon elenchos kata atheon kai dyssevon,* ed. the Monk Parthenios Agiotaphitis (Venice, 1792), vols. 1–2.

12. Makarios Kavadias, *Logos parainetikos pros tous idious mathitas, i kata Ouoltairou kai ton opadon* (Venice, 1802). On the author, see Spyros Asdrachas, "Makarios Kavadias," *O Eranistis* 2 (1964), 225–246.

13. Nikiphoros Theotokis, *Apodeixis tou kyrous ton tis Neas kai Palaias Diathikis Vivlion* (Vienna, 1794), translator's prolegomena, vi–xvii.

14. Evgenios Voulgaris, *Spartion Entriton* (Leipzig, 1804). The first part of the book, pp. 3–100, is taken up by Jenyns's essay, which was also published separately under the title *Exetasis peri tis esoterikis saphineias tou Christianismou* (Leipzig, 1804).

15. See Athanasios Parios's manuscript proemium dated 30 November 1802, to *Theologiki Pragmateia,* attributed to Voulgaris, Gennadeion Library, MS K11, folios 1–4, extolling Voulgaris as a staunch champion of the faith and commending his effort to fill the gaps in Orthodox theological literature, which did not possess, according to Parios, a complete corpus of scholastic theology comparable to Roman Catholic Thomism.

16. Sergios Makraios, *Tropaion ek tis Elladikis panoplias kata ton opadon tou Kopernikou* (Vienna, 1797).

17. Antonios Manouel, *Tropaion Orthodoxou Pisteos,* 12–13.

18. C. Koumas, *Istoriai ton anthropinon praxeon* (Vienna, 1837), 12:571. For the dispute over the heliocentric system see P. Kondylis, *O Neollenikos Diaphotismos: Oi philosophikes idees* (Athens, 1989), 109–128, and V. N. Makridis, *Die religiöse kritik am Kopernikanischen Weltbild in Griechenland zwischen 1794 und 1821* (Frankfurt, 1995).

19. Stephen Batalden, *Catherine II's Greek Prelate: Eugenios Voulgaris in Russia, 1771–1806* (Boulder, 1982), 84–85, 159–160.

20. Bossuetou, *Logos eis tin Genikin Istorian* (Constantinople, 1817), vols. 1–2.

21. Moisiodax, *Apologia* (Vienna, 1780), 166n2.

22. See Korais, *Allilographia,* 1:150–153.

23. Athanasios Parios, *Neos Rapsakis,* Gennadeion Library, MS 265, fols 1–23. For extracts see Aik. Koumarianou, "O Neos Rapsakis," *O Eranistis* 6 (1968): 1–18. The complete text was published by L. Vranousis in *Epetiris Mesaionikou Archeiou* 15/16 (1965–1966): 305–329.

24. *Christianiki Apologia* (Constantinople, 1798), 24–34.

25. *Christianiki Apologia* (Leipzig, 1805), 14–29, 29–33, 34–43, 116, 139.

26. Nathanael Neokaissareus, *Antiphonisis pros ton paralogon zilon ton apo tis Europis erchomenon philosophon* (Trieste, 1802), 36, 17–25, 38, 59–72.

27. The revival of Orthodox spirituality in the eighteenth century is a major historiographical issue that it is impossible to survey with any bibliographical completeness here. For a comprehensive study see Kallistos Ware, "The Spirituality of the Philokalia," *Sobornost* 13 (1991): 6–24, and the survey by G. Podskalsky, *Griechische Theologie in der Zeit der Türkenherrschaft, 1453–1821* (Munich, 1988), 377–382, with earlier bibliography.

28. These affinities are noted by Louis Bouyer, *La spiritualité orthodoxe et la spiritualité protestante et anglicane* (Aubier, 1965), 59–66. See also K. Papoulidis, "I syngeneia tou vivliou 'Aoratos Polemos' tou Nikodimou Agioreiti me to 'Combattimento Spirituale' tou Lorenzo Scupoli," *Makedonika* 10 (1970): 23–33, and idem, "I syngeneia tou vivliou 'Gymnasmata Pnevmatika' tou Ayiou Nikodimou tou Agioreiti me to 'Exercicios Spirituales' tou Ayiou Ignatiou de Loyala," *Makedonika* 11 (1971): 167–172. The question of Nikodimos Hagiorite's "borrowings" from Catholic spirituality is dealt with, on the basis of new manuscript discoveries, by F. N. Frangiskos, "'Aoratos Polemos', (1796) 'Gymnasmata Pnevmatika' (1800): I patrotita ton 'metaphraseon' tou Nikodimou Ayioreiti," *O Eranistis* 19 (1993): 102–135.

29. J. C. Hobhouse, *A Journey Through Albania and Other Provinces of Turkey in Europe and Asia* (London, 1813), 2:573. For Kodrikas's participation in the embassy to the Directorate of the French Republic, see M. Herbette, *Une ambassade Turque sous le Directoire* (Paris, 1902), 9–16.

30. P. Kodrikas, *Meleti tis koinis Ellinikis dialektou* (Paris, 1818), xvi–xxiv, xxxviii–xlv, l–liii, 145–76. The passages cited are on pp. l–lii. For an intellectual profile of Kodrikas, see C. Th. Dimaras, *Phrontismata* (Athens, 1962), 67–88.

31. Some of these texts were collected and edited in the volume *Eranos eis Adamantion Korain* (Athens, 1965). See especially the contributions by A. Angelou, Aik. Koumarianou, E. Chatzidaki, and V. Skouvaras, 157–208, 228–358.

32. The dedication to Czar Alexander I appears in Kodrikas, *Meleti,* preceding the main text (n.p.). The two congratulatory letters from the reigning patriarch Gregory V and ex-patriarch Cyril VI to Kodrikas were published in *Kalliopi* 2 (1820): 186–188.

33. See Bernard Bailyn, *The Ideological Origins of the American Revolution* (Cambridge, MA, 1967), 1–21; and Daniel Mornet, *Les origines intellectuelles de la Révolution Française, 1715–1787,* 5th ed. (Paris, 1954), 97–144, 205–318, esp. 431–451. Mornet's work is a classic analysis of the role of ideas in political change, and his method has much to teach the study of similar processes in other societies. For an appraisal, see Robert Darnton, "In Search of the Enlightenment: Recent Attempts to Create a Social History of Ideas," *The Journal of Modern History* 43 (1971): 113–132. On the subject of pamphlets and pamphleteering see also Robert Darnton, *The*

Literary Underground of the Old Regions (Cambridge, MA, 1982), 29–36, 144–146, 199–208.

34. L. Vranousis, *Athanasios Psalidas* (Ioannina, 1952), 38–45.

35. See Camariano, *Académies princières,* 494–511, 653–659; and C. Th. Dimaras, "Enas dioktis tou Neophytou Douka: Samouil o Andrios," *Aphieroma eis tin Ipiron* (Athens, 1956), 137–148. The intellectual connection between Samuel and Parios is also attested by the circumstance that the "Teacher Samuel from Andros" edited the posthumous edition of Athanasios's work *Alexikakon pharmakon* (Leipzig, 1818), to which he prefaced his own anti-Voltairean prologue. Reactions against Doukas were recorded in the anonymous pamphlet *Antirrisis eis tous en to Vivliario tou Aischinou proskollithentas dialogous tou Didaskalou Neophytou Douka* ([Vienna], 1817).

36. See chapter 8.

37. See A. Firmin Didot, *Notes d'un voyage fait dans le Levant en 1818 et 1817* (Paris, 1826), 383–387. Also, Richard Clogg, "Two Accounts of the Academy of Ayvalik (Kydonies) in 1818–1819," *RESEE* 10 (1972): 633–667.

38. See C. Amantos, *Ta grammata eis tin Chion kata tin Tourkokratian 1566–1822,* 2nd ed. (Athens, 1976), 18–37.

39. See A. Angelou, "Pros tin akmi tou Neoellinikou Diaphotismou," *Mikrasiatika Chronika* 7 (1957): 1–81; and M. Stephanidis, *Ai physikai epistimai en Elladi pro tis Epanastaseos* (Athens, 1926), 28–34, 49–54. See also Roxane D. Argyropoulou, *O Beniamin Lesvios kai i evrpoaiki skepsi tou dekatou ogdoou aiona* (Athens, 2003), 65–82.

40. C. Koumas, *Istoriai,* 12:587–595.

41. Camariano, *Académies princières,* 654–655, and Manuel Gedeon, *Chronika tis Patriarchikis Akadimias* (Constantinople, 1883), 183–185.

42. Ignatios Skalioras, *Epistoli tis neas philosophias steliteftiki* (Leipzig, 1817), 3–4, 18–19, 23–24.

43. The text of the encyclical is published in C. Th. Dimaras, *O Korais kai i epochi tou* (Athens, 1953), 299–304. On the political motivation of these initiatives, see Ioannis Philimon, *Dokimion istorikon peri tis Ellinikis Epanastaseos* (Athens, 1859), 1:97.

44. *Stochasmoi tou Kritonos* (Paris, 1819). The text is reprinted with a commentary by D. Ginis in *Eranos eis Adamantion Korain* (Athens, 1965), 140–156. On the chief protagonist, see B. Sphyroeras, "Ilarion Sinaitis o Kris, 1765–1838," *Epistimoniki Epetiris Philosophikis Scholis Panepistimiou Athinon* (1969–1970): 225–310. On his later career, N. M. Vaporis, "The Translation of the Scriptures and the Ecumenical Patriarchate: The Translation Efforts of Hilarion of Tirnovo," *Byzantine and Modern Greek Studies* 1 (1975): 141–173.

45. The text was published in *Melissa* (1821): 250–262. The complete set of the three issues of *Melissa* is available in a reprint by ELIA, with an introduction by Aik. Koumarianou (Athens, 1984).

46. Ibid., 252–256.

47. Ibid,. 256–257.

48. Ibid., 263–275, 301–306, 312–315.

49. On the 1821 synod see Costas Lappas "Patriarchiki Synodos 'Peri kathaireseos ton philosophikon mathimaton' ton Martio tou 1821: Mia martyria tou Constantinou Oikonomou," *Mnimon* 11 (1987): 123–153.

50. C. Sathas, *Tourkokratoumeni Ellas* (Athens, 1869), 564–609, conveys the climate of revolutionary expectancy in pre-independence Greece through a survey of the sources. For a more recent survey, see Douglas Dakin, *The Greek Struggle for Independence* (Berkeley, 1973), 26–69. On Ali Pasha and the social role of the *klephts* in the outbreak of the Revolution, see Denis N. Skiotis, *The Lion and the Phoenix: Ali Pasha and the Greek Revolution* (PhD diss., Harvard University, 1971); and idem, "Mountain Warriors and the Greek Revolution," in *War, Technology and Society in the Middle East,* ed. V. J. Parry and M. E. Yapp (Oxford, 1975), 308–329. The recent study by K. E. Fleming, *The Muslim Bonaparte: Diplomacy and Orientalism in Ali Pasha's Greece* (Princeton, 1999), draws on these earlier studies and raises interesting theoretical questions. A major new source has been made available with the appearance of *Archeio Ali Pasa,* ed. V. Panayiotopoulos et al., vols. 1–4 (Athens, 2009).

51. George B. Leon, "The Greek Merchant Marine, 1453–1850," *The Greek Merchant Marine,* ed. S. A. Papadoupoulos (Athens, 1972), 32–42.

52. George D. Frangos, "The Philike Etaireia: A Premature National Coalition," *The Struggle for Greek Independence,* ed. Richard Clogg (London, 1971), 87–103.

53. See I. Philimon, *Dokimion istorikon peri tis Philikis Etaireias* (Nafplion, 1834), 212–219.

54. Neophytos Vamvas, *Stoicheia tis Philosophikis Ithikis* (Venice, 1818), 4–5, 39–73, 207–246.

55. Ibid., 214.

56. *J. J. Rousseau tou ek Genevis Logos peri archis kai vaseos tis anisotitos ton anthropon pros allilous,* trans. Spyridon Valetas (Paris, 1818); and *J. J. Rousseau Peri tis Koinonikis Synthikis i Archai tou Politikou Dikaiomatos,* trans. Gregorios Zalykis, posthumously published by C. Nikolopoulos (Paris, 1828). For a detailed review, see Argyropoulou, *Neoellinikos stochasmos,* 91–115. On the significance of the translations of Rousseau in the broader Balkan context, see P. M. Kitromilides, *I Galliki Epanastasi kai i Notioanatoliki Evropi* (Athens, 2000), 145–153.

57. Spyridon Valetas, trans., *Logos peri anisotitos,* translator's address to the reader, vii–viii.

58. *Ermis o Logios* 9, no. 6 (15 March 1819): 213–218. The review was signed with the initials P. Th.

59. *Ermis o Logios* 10, no. 17 (1 September 1820): 519–521.

60. See Catherine Coumarianou, "Cosmopolitisme et Héllénisme dans le 'Mercure Savant,' première revue grecque, 1811–1821," *Proceedings of the IVth*

Congress of the International Comparative Literature Association 1964 (The Hague and Paris, 1966): 601–608. See also A. Camariano Cioran, "Le rôle de la revue 'Loghios Hermés' de Vienne sans les relations culturelles internationale au XIXe siècle," *RESEE* 13 (1975) : 549–558. On the history of this periodical, see also G. Laios, *O ellinikos typos tis Viennis apo tou 1784 mechri tou 1821* (Athens, 1961), 92–118. Useful assistance to researchers is provided by E. N. Frangiskos's index, *Ta ellinika proepanastatika periodika*, vol. 2: *"Ermis o Logios" 1811–1821* (Athens, 1976). For a more general appraisal of the Greek press in this period see Anna Tabaki, "La presse prérevolutionaire grecque: reflet de nouvelles conceptions esthétiques et culturelles dans le Sud-Est européen," *RESEE* 34 (1996): 133–140.

61. Lesvios's address to Thiersch is included in his *Stoicheia Arithmitikis*, Gennadeion Library MS 48, pp. iii–viii, but is omitted from the published version (Vienna, 1818). A more optimistic turn in his thought is reflected in *Geometrias Eukleidou Stoicheia* (Vienna, 1820), from which the passages cited are drawn, 17–20. See also his *Stoicheia Metaphysikis* (Vienna, 1820), iii–vi, xii–xiii. The term *idealogia* is on p. x. A full critical edition of B. Lesvios's *Stoicheia Ithikis* has been published by Roxani Argyropoulou (Athens, 1994). See pp. 52 and 54 for the passages cited. See also idem, *O Veniamin Lesvios,* 200–215, on Benjamin's political thought. The importance of the concept of freedom in Benjamin's ethics is also stressed by Th. Papadopoulos, *Oi philosophikes kai koinoniko-politikes antilipseis tou Veniamin Lesviou* (Athens, 1982), 75–84, and by Myrto Dragona-Monachou, "Veniamin o Lesvios: eleftheria, i dynamis tis ekplirosis tou aftexousiou," *Defkalion* 21 (1978): 96–130. For Benjamin's activities at the princely Academy of Bucharest, see Camariano, *Académies princières,* 525–541, and Roxane D. Argryopoulos, "Le discours de Benjamin de Lesbos à l'Académie princière de Bucarest, 1918," *Époque phanariote,* 167–174.

62. On the participation and effectiveness of the "noble breed of the learned" in the liberation struggle, see Nikolaos Dragoumis, *Istorikai Anamniseis,* 2nd ed. (Athens, 1879), 1:4–7. Benjamin of Lesbos and Gregorios Constantas were elected members of the Second National Assembly at Astros. See A. Z. Mamoukas, *Ta kata tin anagennesin tis Ellados* (Piraeus 1839), 2:65. See also Alkis Angelou, *Oi Logioi kai o Agonas* (Athens, 1971), and on the advent of the "educated" in revolutionary Greece, P. M. Kitromilides, "Jeremy Bentham and Adamantios Korais," *The Bentham Newsletter* (June 1985): 34–48. Reprinted in *Enlightenment, Nationalism, Orthodoxy,* Study VIII.

63. On these cleavages, see Petropulos, *Politics and Statecraft,* 19–106. This is a monumental work, and my analysis of nineteenth-century political history is greatly indebted to it. See also P. N. Diamandouros, *Political Modernization, Social Conflict and Cultural Cleavage in the Formation of the Modern Greek State: 1821–1828* (PhD diss., Columbia University, 1972).

64. For the pertinent texts, see *Archeia tis Ellinikis Palingenesias 1821–1832* (Athens, 1971), 3:25–35, 40–41, 47–50. On Korais's commentary, see chapter 9, this book. On Bentham's views see *Securities against Misrule and Other Constitutional*

Writings for Tripoli and Greece, ed. Philip Schofield (Oxford, 1990), 216–256, and F. Rosen, *Bentham, Byron and Greece: Constitutionalism, Nationalism, and Early Liberal Political Thought* (Oxford, 1992), 77–102.

65. *Archeia tis Ellinikis Palingenesias,* 3:89–98.

66. Ibid., 651–662.

67. Ibid. (Athens, 1973), 4:155–199.

68. Ibid. (Athens, 1974), 5:271–304. For the political context of the process of constitution making during the Greek Revolution and its immediate aftermath, see N. Kaltchas, *Introduction to the Constitutional History of Modern Greece* (New York, 1940), 34–95.

69. Petropulos, *Politics and Statecraft,* 165–172.

70. Aik. Koumarianou, ed., *O typos ston Agona,* 3 vols. (Athens, 1971). For a listing of political pamphlets and leaflets, see I. K. Mazarakis-Ainian, *Ta Ellinika Typographeia tou Agonos 1821–1827* (Athens, 1973), 64–95; and idem, *Monophylla tou Agonos 1821–1827* (Athens, 1973), 27–48.

71. See Aik. Koumarianou, ed., *O typos ston Agona,* 1:79, 217, 276; 2:11–12, 29; 3:177, 180, 303: references to Bentham, Beccaria, Jefferson, Mably, Mirabeau, Montesquieu, Newton, Rousseau. Note especially the pamphlet on the liberty of the press based on Mirabeau: *Peri Typou ek tou Mirabeau* [. . .] (Nafplion, 1831).

72. *Apospasmata ek ton tou Kyriou Vattelou peri Dikaiou ton Ethnon* (Nafplion, 1826).

73. Volney, *Physikos Nomos i Physikai Archai tis Ithikis,* trans. C. Pentedekas (Aigina, 1828).

74. S. B., *Epta Pligai tis Ellados* (Aigina, 1827). The pamphlet was the work of Spyridon Valetas, who had translated Rousseau's *Discourse on the Origins of Inequality* in 1818. On the author and his subsequent translation projects, see Tr. E. Sklavenitis, "O Spyridon Valetas kai i metaphrasi tis Politikis Oikonomias tou J. B. Say," *I Epanastasi tou 1821: Meletes sti mnimi tis Despoinas Themeli-Katiphori* (Athens, 1994), 107–156.

75. Korais's anti-Capodistrian dialogues are reprinted in the series *Politika Phylladia tou Adamantiou Korai* (Athens, 1983), nos. 9 and 10. For his campaign against Capodistrias, see Chr. Loukos, *I antipolitefsi kata tou Kyverniti Ioanni Capodistria 1828–1831* (Athens, 1988), 263–274.

76. Petropulos, *Politics and Statecraft,* 107–150.

77. For an understanding of the logic of the Regency's policies, the testimony of one of the major protagonists is of fundamental importance. See Georg Maurer, *Das griechische Volk in öffentlicher, kirchlicher und privatrechtlicher Beziehung vor und nach dem Freiheitskampfe is zum 31 Juli 1835,* 3 vols. (Heidelberg, 1835). Petropulos's *Politics and Statecraft,* 153–192, is germane to these issues. On the question of land distribution, see William W. McGrew, *Land and Revolution in Modern Greece, 1800–1881* (Kent, OH, 1985), esp. 95–110, 161–175.

78. See Charles A. Frazee, *The Orthodox Church and Independent Greece,
1821–1852* (Cambridge, 1969), and P. M. Kitromilides, "The Legacy of the French
Revolution: Orthodoxy and Nationalism," *The Cambridge History of Christianity,*
vol. 5: *Eastern Christianity,* ed. Michael Angold (Cambridge, 2006), 229–249,
esp. 229–237.

79. The Kairis case has given rise to an extensive bibliography. For the views of
one of the protagonists, see G. Athanasiou, *Ta kata Kairin, itoi to kirygma tis alitheias*
(Athens, 1840). N. I. Saripolos's speeches at Kairis's trial appear in *Ta meta thanaton*
(Athens, 1890), 347–380. What was really at stake in the Kairis case was perceived
by several contemporary foreign observers who were sensitive to questions of freedom of conscience. See, by way of example, Henri Carle, "Un nouveau Socrate chez
les Grecs modernes: Theophile Cairis," *Almanach de la libre conscience pour l'année
1870* (Paris), 27–35. D. Paschalis, *Theophilos Kairis, istoriki kai philosophiki meleti*
(Athens, 1928), is still of seminal importance. On the climate of the period, see Aik.
Koumarianou, "I eleftherophrosyni tou Theophilou Kairi," *Epoches* 46 (February
1967): 184–200. A useful bibliography is presented by I. P. Zographos, "Vivliographia Theophilou kai Euanthias Kairi," *Nea Estia* 54 (1953): 1152–1132, and D. I.
Polemis, 'Epilogi Kairikis Vivliographias,' *Petalon* 4 (Andros, 1984): 182–201.

80. See Petropulos, *Politics and Statecraft,* 329–343, 519–533; and Barbara Jelavich, "The Philorthodox Conspiracy of 1839," *Balkan Studies* 7 (1966): 89–102.

81. See Dimaras, *Neoellinikos Diaphotismos,* 403–404, and idem, *Ellinikos
romantismos* (Athens, 1983), 374–382, 388–390. For the conflict between liberals
and conservatives over religious issues, see also Nomikos M. Vaporis, *The Controversy
of the Translation of the Scriptures into Modern Greek and its Effects, 1818–1843* (PhD
diss., Columbia University, 1970), which brings out effectively the broader political implications of these cleavages. For the religious settlement that terminated the
schism between the Ecumenical Patriarchate and the Church of Greece, see G. D.
Metallinos, *Elladikou aftokephalou paraleipomena,* 2nd ed. (Athens, 1989), 123–277.

82. Dimitrios Vernardakis, *Capodistrias kai Othon* (Trieste, 1875; reprinted Athens, 1962).

83. Elie Halévy, *The Growth of Philosophic Radicalism* (London, 1972), 146; and
Guido de Ruggiero, *The History of European Liberalism* (Boston, 1959), 359–362.
On the Greek background, Petropulos, *Politics and Statecraft,* 149–150, 158–161,
and esp. 192–201, where he notes the deliberate antiparty policy and rhetoric. Also
Gunnar Hering, *Die politischen Parteien in Griechenland 1821–1936* (Munich,
1992), 1:174–224. An indication of the indictment of political parties in the political thought of the period is given by the pamphlet *I exantlisis ton kommaton itoi ta
ithika gegonota tis koinonias mas,* published anonymously by Pavlos Kalligas (Athens,
1842).

84. Georgios G. Kozakis Typaldos, *Philosophikon Dokimion peri tis proodou kai
tis ptoseos tis Palaias Ellados* (Athens, 1839), iii–iv, 505–511. Quotation on national

unity on p. 505. See the analysis of the work by Roxani Argyropoulou, *Neoellinikos stochasmos,* 197–209.

85. Markos Renieris, *Philosophia tis istorias: Dokimion* (Athens, 1841), 38–92, 159–67, xii–xiii. On the general intellectual background, see C. Th. Dimaras, "L'heure de Vico pour la Grèce," *La Grèce au temps des Lumières* (Geneva, 1969), 133–152. Also P. Chr. Noutsos, *Neoelliniki Philosophia* (Athens, 1981), 131–137, and Argyropoulou, *Neoellinikos stochasmos,* 248–260.

86. See Jakob Philipp Fallmerayer, *Geschichte der halbinsel Morea während des Mittelalters* (Stuttgart, 1830–1836). On the debate that ensued, see Georg Veloudis, "Jakob Philipp Fallmerayer und die Enstehung des neugriechischen Historismus," *Südest-Forschungen* 29 (1970): 43–90. See also the collection *Jakob Philipp Fallmerayer,* ed. E. Thurnher (Innsbruck, 1993), esp. 47–74: Armin Hohlweg, "Jakob Philipp Fallmerayer und seine geistige Umwelt."

87. Constantinos Paparrigopoulos, *To teleftaion etos tis Ellinikis eleftherias* (Athens, 1844), 3–4. The first complete edition of *Istoria tou Ellinikou Ethnous,* vols. 1–5, appeared in Athens 1860–1874. On the whole question, see C. Th. Dimaras, *Constantinos Paparrigopoulos* (Athens, 1986), and D. Kontos, *Konstantinos Paparrigopoulos and the Emergence of the Idea of a Greek Nation* (PhD diss., University of Cincinnati, 1986).

88. Spyridon Zambelios, *Asmata Dimotika tis Ellados* (Athens, 1852), prolegomena; and idem, *Byzantinai meletai peri pigon tis Neoellinikis ethnotitos* (Athens, 1857). See also D. A. Zakythinos, "Spyridon Zambelios: O theoretikos tis istorionomias; O istorikos tou Byzantinou ellenismou," *Metavyzantina kai Nea Ellinika* (Athens, 1978), 529–553; Anna Tabaki, "I metavasi apo ton Dipahotismo ston romantismo. I periptosi tou Ioanni kai tou Spyridona Zambeliou," *Praktika tou V Diethnous Panioniou Synedriou* (Argostoli, 1991), 4:199–211, esp. 208–211, and Ioannis Koubourlis, *La formation de l'histoire nationale grecque. L'apport de Spyridon Zambélios (1815–1881)* (Athens, 2005).

89. Renieris, *Dokimion philosophias tis istorias,* 112–158.

90. Zambelios, *Asmata Dimotika tis Ellados,* 464. Other early uses of the neologism 'ellinochristianikos' are collected in the *Synagogi neon lexeon* by Stephanos Koumanoudis (Athens, 1900), 358.

91. For the full text of the speech, delivered on 14 January 1844, see *I tis tritis Septemvriou en Athinais Ethniki Synelefsis: Praktika* (Athens, 1844), 190–191, and for commentary, Dimaras, *Ellinikos romantismos,* 359–369, 404–418.

92. On these distant historical origins, see Anthony Bryer, "The Great Idea," *History Today* 15/3 (March 1965): 159–168.

93. See, for instance, Montesquieu, *Lettres persanes,* No. XIX and for the broader cultural background Larry Wolff, *Inventing Eastern Europe* (Stanford, 1994), 171–183.

94. J. C. Voyatzidis, "La Grande Idée," *Le cinq-centième anniversaire de la prise de Constantinople,* special issue of the journal *L'Héllénisme Contemporain* (Athens,

29 May 1953): 279–287; and D. A. Zakythinos, *The Making of Modern Greece from Byzantium to Independence* (Oxford, 1976), 191–198.

95. See E. Driault and M. Lhéritier, *Histoire Diplomatique de la Grèce de 1821 à nos jours,* vol. 2: *Le Règne d'Othon; La Grande Idée 1830–1862* (Paris, 1925), for a survey of the politics of the Great Idea.

96. See Nikolaos Dragoumis, *Istorikai anamniseis,* 2:162–172. Also L. S. Stavrianos, *The Balkans since 1453* (New York, 1958), 468, and A. A. Pepelasis, "The Image of the Past and Economic Backwardness," *Human Organization* 17, no. 4 (Winter 1958–1959): 19–27.

97. On brigandage, see Petropulos, *Politics and Statecraft,* 323–325. See also Romilly Jenkins, *The Dilessi Murders* (London, 1961), which despite its biases, does provide several insights. Above all, see John Kolliopoulos, *Brigands with a Cause. Brigandage and Irredentism in Modern Greece, 1821–1912* (Oxford, 1987), a work of importance to the understanding of brigandage as a phenomenon of general impact on Greek political life and the formation of the institutions of the Greek state. For an understanding of the structure of Greek society in the nineteenth century, Constantinos Tsoukalas, *Exartisi kai Anaparagogi* (Athens, 1977) is pivotal. See pp. 147–160 for the social function of emigration.

98. See Dragoumis, *Istorikai anamniseis,* 2:183. For a critique of Kolettis's irredentist program, see Al. Mavrokordatos, "Ypomnima tou 1848," ibid., 165–183, and compare Georgios N. Philaretos, *Xenokratia kai Vasileia en Elladi, 1821–1897* (Athens, 1897), 93–96, 100, 169. On the dilemmas of Greek nationalism see also G. Augustinos, *Consciousness and History: Nationalist Critics of Greek Society* (Boulder, 1977), 7–39, 117–143.

99. The most representative instance of the disappointed expectations that shaped Greek political culture in the nineteenth century was registered in General Makriyannis's bitterness at the postrevolutionary political and social realities in the Greek kingdom. A folk hero of the War of Independence, Makriyannis later became involved in irredentist projects. See Ioannis Makriyannis, *Apomnimonevmata,* ed. Sp. Asdrachas (Athens, n.d.), 5–7, 14, 85, 335, 340–344, 359, 416–419, 463–464, 480–484, 525.

100. Cf. Tsoukalas, *Exartisi kai Anaparagogi,* 362–371.

101. See the excellent study by Şerif Mardin, *The Genesis of Young Ottoman Thought* (Princeton, 1962).

102. See Dimaras, *Neoellinikos Diaphotismos,* 394–400, and the contributions by Alexis Politis and P. M. Kitromilides in *Byzantium and the Modern Greek Identity,* ed. P. Magdalino and D. Ricks (Aldershot, 1998), 1–14 and 25–33, respectively.

103. Epaminondas Deliyiorgis, *Politika Imerologia-Politikai Simeioseis* (Athens, 1896), 8–9.

104. On the genesis of Greek socialism, see Moskov, *I ethniki kai koinoniki syneidisi stin Ellada* (Thessaloniki, 1972), 173–213; George B. Leon, *The Greek*

Socialist Movement and the First World War: The Road to Unity (Boulder, 1976), 1–18, and especially P. Chr. Noutsos, ed., *I sosialistiki skepsi stin Ellada,* vol. 1, *1875–1907* (Athens, 1990).

105. Compare Leonard Krieger, *The German Idea of Freedom* (Boston, 1957), 176–196.

106. Hans Kohn, *The Idea of Nationalism* (New York, 1944), 427–451, and Isaiah Berlin, "The Counter-Enlightenment," *Against the Current* (Oxford, 1981), 1–24. Isaiah Berlin, *Vico and Herder* (New York, 1976) is essential for an understanding of these intellectual developments.

EPILOGUE

1. L. S. Stavrianos, "The Influence of the West on the Balkans," in *The Balkans in Transition*, ed. Charles and Barbara Jelavich (Berkeley, 1963), 184–226, and Elie Kedourie, *Nationalism in Asia and Africa* (New York, 1970), 42–48.

2. See G. Bollème et al., *Livre et société dans la France du XVIIIe siècle* (Paris and The Hague, 1965); and M. T. Boussy, et al., *Livre et société dans la France du XVIIIe siècle*, vol. 2 (Paris and The Hague, 1970), as well as the following the studies by Robert Darnton, "Reading, Writing and Publishing in Eighteenth Century France: A Case Study in the Sociology of Literature," *Daedalus* (Winter 1971): 214–256; and "The *Encyclopédie* Wars in Prerevolutionary France," *The American Historical Review* 78 (1973): 1331–1352; and the related studies in his collection *The Literary Underground of the Old Regime* (Cambridge, MA, 1982).

3. Traian Stoianovich, "Social Foundations of Balkan Politics, 1750–1941," *The Balkans in Transition,* 308–312. The term 'classical reaction' is on p. 312. Reprinted in the author's *Between East and West*, vol. 3 (New Rochelle, NY, 1995), 111–138.

4. This was quite perceptively noted by C. Sathas, *Neoellinikis Philologias Parartima: Istoria tou Zitimatos tis Neoellinikis Glossis* (Athens, 1870), 211. Sathas's own strictures against the most progressive manifestations of the thought of the Enlightenment were indicative of the new attitude toward the movement. See ibid., 147–154, 191, and 208 for censures of Moisiodax and Katartzis, Philippidis, and Vilaras.

5. A similar social function was fulfilled by irredentist nationalism in post-unification Italy. A comparison between Greece and Italy might be revealing on the role of nationalism in political systems characterized by a high degree of social fragmentation.

6. A comparable case is offered by the role of the military in Spanish politics, equally generated by the weakness of Spanish liberalism to achieve sustained political change. For a reasoned appraisal of the historical significance of civil-military relations in Greece, see Thanos Veremis, *The Military in Greek Politics: From Independence to Democracy* (London, 1997).

7. V. Panayiotopoulos, "La révolution industrielle et la Grèce," in *La Révolution Industrielle dans le Sud-Est Européen-XIX siècle* (Sofia, 1977), 227–242 and G. Dertilis, *Istoria tou ellinikou kratous 1830–1920* (Athens, 2004), 2 : 595–609.

8. Petropulos, *Politics and Statecraft,* 236. On the complexity of state-building problems "from zero" see Dertilis, *Istoria*, 1: 107–115, 141–164 for a much broader perspective than can be attempted here.

9. Karl Marx, "The Eighteenth Brumaire of Louis Bonaparte," in *Selected Works, Marx and Engels* (New York, 1969), 171–175. On the Greek socio-economic background see Dertilis, *Istoria*, 1: 195–251.

10. On these issues, see C. Tsoukalas, *Exartisi kai Anaparagogi* (Athens, 1977), part 1.

11. Barrington Moore Jr., *Social Origins of Dictatorship and Democracy* (Boston, 1966), 430–431.

12. Louis Hartz, *The Liberal Tradition in America* (New York, 1955), 3–32.

13. Samuel H. Beer, *British Politics in the Collectivist Age* (New York, 1967), 3–68.

14. This view of liberal democracy is due to Joseph A. Schumpeter, *Capitalism, Socialism and Democracy* (New York, 1962), 269–283.

Acknowledgments

This book has had a long history and correspondingly the list of my debts is also long. It is impossible to record here all the debts I have incurred over the years I have been working on the subject and on the book in its successive incarnations in various languages. I will have to limit myself to what I can remember and to obligations I have incurred in connection with the preparation of this edition.

My most profound and enduring debts to the great scholars who taught me and supervised my work at the Harvard Graduate School of Arts and Sciences have been recorded in the introduction to the American edition. I only need to add that I will never forget what I owe to them intellectually and morally. To my three Harvard teachers, Michael Walzer, Judith Shklar, and Stanley Hoffmann, I would like to add my recollection of the debt I have to the late Professor Robert Lee Wolff and to Dennis Skiotis, both of whom taught me Byzantine, Ottoman, Balkan, Greek, and Turkish history at Harvard and encouraged me in many ways in my work on the Enlightenment.

Over the years my thinking and research on the Enlightenment and on the history of political thought has greatly benefited from a continuing dialogue with a small group of friends and colleagues in Greece and abroad to whom I feel I owe all those intellectual and moral blessings that derive from the social virtue of friendship as understood in the great European tradition from Aristotle to Montaigne. They include Roxane Argyropoulou, Anna Tabaki, Vassiliki Stamati, Pericles Vallianos, Jeffrey Abramson, Larry Wolff, Ioannis Evrigenis, George Varouxakis, Lea Campos Boralevi, Terence Cave, John Robertson, Simon Dixon, Michel Delon, Andrei Pippidi, Fred Rosen, and John Dunn. I cannot forget Susan Okin, a true friend and a great source of intellectual and moral inspiration, who left us so early. I am grateful to each of them for all they have taught me and for our shared faith in the power of ideas. Besides them, Tony Molho has always been an unfailing source of inspiration and support.

As an educator I have been fortunate throughout my career to be surrounded by young people, many of them now colleagues, who have been responsive to my wish for dialogue with the younger generations, a dialogue which unfailingly renewed my own ideas. To name them all would require a long list, but I would like to single out Ioannis Evrigenis, Stavros Anestides, Nikos Panou, and Nicolaos Pissis for their responsiveness to my requests for help in connection with the preparation of this book.

In preparing the English-language version of this work I was fortunate to have a reliable collaborator in the person of a close friend, Dr. David Hardy, a classical scholar with an extraordinary command of Greek in all phases of its evolution. He helped me translate parts of the Greek text and assisted me in polishing the English-language version of this work. His untimely death deprived me of a true friend and of the pleasure of sharing with him the joy of the eventual publication to which he was looking forward.

My greatest debt is owed to Michael Sandel. I am grateful to him for a friendship that extends over more than thirty years now, for our shared concerns in political and moral theory and for his support and encouragement in my work.

Michael Aronson and Kathleen Drummy at Harvard University Press have been very supportive and patient with me through the long and at times trying process of the gestation of this book. I owe them a great deal. I should also like to record my gratitude to the three anonymous referees at HUP for their excellent advice and enthusiasm.

Sections of two chapters of this book appeared in journals a number of years ago: parts of chapter 7 were incorporated in an article under the title "An Enlightenment Perspective on Balkan Cultural Pluralism: The Republican Vision of Rhigas Velestinlis," *History of Political Thought* 24, no. 3 (Autumn 2003): 465–479, and sections of chapter 10 were published as parts of a longer article entitled "The Dialectic of Intolerance: Ideological Dimensions of Ethnic Conflicts," *Journal of the Hellenic Diaspora* 6, no. 4 (1979): 5–30. I am grateful to the publishers of the two journals, Imprint Academic, Exeter, UK, and Pella Publishing House, New York, for permission to reprint.

The map of the geography of the Enlightenment in Southeastern Europe was expertly produced by Elpida Daniil at the National Cartographic Center in Thessaloniki. I am very grateful to her and to the National Cartographic Center, of whose excellent professional work I feel very proud.

The final manuscript was electronically produced by Kalliopi Angeli, to whom I have entrusted all my books for over ten years now, without ever being disappointed. I am most grateful to her for being such a good collaborator.

My wife, Maria Constantoudaki, and our son Michael Emmanuel, by their presence in my life, have made it all meaningful.

Index

Provisional Constitution of Greece (1822), 316
Prussia, Prussians, 44, 98, 122, 124, 129
Psalidas, Athanasios, 60, 134–139, 195,
   232, 272, 302, 315, 321, 380n81, 386n61,
   386n63, 398n12, 404n6; *Kalokinimata*,
   135, 137; *Vera Felicitas,* 133
Psellos, Michael, 22, 355n4
Ptolemy, Claudius, Ptolemaic system, 52,
   90, 98, 198, 203, 375n4
Pylarinos, Frangiskos, 290, 417n76
Pyrrhonism, 63, 124
Pyrros, Dionysios, *Geographia Methodiki*,
   380n81

radicalism, 23, 139, 201, 291, 312, 340,
   342; Balkan, 235; Greek, 404n6;
   European, 224, 257; intellectual, 228;
   Italian, 232, 372n46; republican, 17, 224;
   revolutionary, 275; social, 218
Ramus, Peter, 45
rationalism, 56, 157, 336; Cartesian, 41;
   German, 44–45,47
Rawls, John, *Theory of Justice*, 3
Raynal, abbé Guillaume, *Histoire
   philosophique de deux Indes*, 119
Réal de Curban, Gaspard de, 148; *La science
   de gouvernement*, 153
regicide, 184–185, 187, 190, 252, 292
Reid, Thomas Mayne, 312
relativism: moral, 280
religion, 107, 182, 250–259, 282–283, 294,
   322–323; civil, 11, 102, 356n5; natural,
   252; "religion of humanity", 182, 186
religious communities (*millets*), 24
Renaissance, 6, 16, 24, 26, 35, 55, 156, 224,
   231, 270, 356n5; humanism, 23
Renieris, Markos, 328; *Essay on the Philosophy of History*, 325
Republic of Saint Mark, 54. *See also* Venice
republic: aristocratic, 237; Athenian, 111;
   French, 419n29; Hellenic, 23, 214, 217–
   225, 285, 286; monastic, 109; republic of
   virtue, 276; Venetian, 26

republicanism, 62, 80–81, 101–102, 105,
   107, 111, 113–114, 128, 171–172, 186–
   187, 189, 196, 198–199, 200–201, 202,
   210, 214, 215–216, 221–224, 226–227,
   232, 235, 237–238, 239, 249–250,
   260–262, 273–276, 280–284, 285–286,
   288, 289, 309, 311, 316, 325, 402n57,
   408n2, 413n44; classicist, 260; democratic, 340; liberal, 262, 339; modern,
   275; political, 81; radical, 17, 223, 249,
   282; utopian, 114
Restif de la Bretonne, N.-E., 204–205,
   397n10; *Contemporaines mêlées*, 204
revolution, 103–104, 178, 205, 213,
   215–217, 222–223, 234, 308; American,
   302, 416n65; French, 11, 178–189, 191,
   192, 195–196, 197, 199, 207, 214, 219,
   227, 232, 246, 250, 262, 266, 272, 297,
   300, 355n8, 378n48, 391n3, 392n14,
   395n65, 396n74, 397n10; Greek, 11, 216,
   276, 277, 285, 286, 301, 311, 315, 316,
   318, 319, 321, 338, 342–343, 413n45,
   423n68
Rhigas Velestinlis, 12, 57, 142, 173, 200–
   229, 232, 235, 249, 286, 288, 291, 292,
   294, 304, 329, 359n22, 396n2, 397n2,
   397n4, 397n8, 398nn12–13, 398n23,
   399n23, 399n29, 399n32, 400nn37–39,
   400n47, 401n47, 402n61, 402n63,
   402n65, 403n68, 417n4; and Perdikaris,
   292; *Apanta ta sozomena*, 401n47; *A
   School for Delicate Lovers*, 204, 206, 207,
   213; *Chart*, 211; *Ethical Tripod*, 207, 215;
   Florilegy of Physics, 167, 202–204, 209,
   213; *New Political Constitution*, 217;
   Thourios, 228, 229, 402n67
Rila, monastery, 211
Robert, F., 377n29
Robertson, John, 10
Robespierre, Maximilien de, 188, 219
Rollin, Charles, 72, 73, 75, 79, 370n22,
   370n26; *Histoire ancienne*, 71–73
Romaioi, 135

Wallachia, 31, 54, 69, 143, 153, 173,
196, 201, 202, 218, 303, 314, 361n47,
399n29
Walzer, Michael, 3
war: civil, 181, 182; Peloponnesian, 74;
Persian, 210; Russo-Turkish, 125; Rus-
so-Turkish (1736–1739), 122, 383n19,
(1768–1774), 57, 83, 130, 131, (1787–
1792), 84, 134, 200, 385n54
War of Independence, Greek, 276, 281, 304,
308, 315–318, 320, 323, 426n99
Washington George, 290, 416n66
Weltanschauung, 33, 299
West, 2, 18, 22, 24–26, 56, 73, 85, 95,
358n14, 405n19; Latin, 22, 23
Westernization, 337, 341, 342
Wolff, Christian, 45–48, 50, 127, 252
Wynne, John, 197

Xenophon, 166, 235, 238, 247, 274; *Memo-
rabilia*, 270, 274
Xeropotamou Monastery (Athos), 368n11
Xirokrini, Patriarchal School at, 255, 304

Young Ottomans, 333
Ypsilantis, Alexandros, Hospodar of
Wallachia, 153, 173

Zagora, 226
Zakynthos (Zante), 39, 395n67, 400n47
Zambelios, Spyridon, 327, 328
Zaviras, Georgios, 317n36
Zeitgeist, 325
Zerzoulis, Nikolaos, 52, 53, 57; *Physics*,
366n114
Zeus, 133
Zosima Brothers, 269